PICTURESQUE

INDIA

PICTURESQUE INDIA

A HANDBOOK FOR EUROPEAN TRAVELLERS

W.S.CAINE

GYAN

Published by

Gyan Publishing House
5, Ansari Road
Daryaganj, New Delhi-110002
Phone: 011-47034999, 9811692060
E-mail: books@gyanbooks.com

Distribution Network
gyanbooks.com
India, USA, Canada, UK, Australia, France

ISBN : 978-81-212-9763-9 (PB)
First Published, 1890

2nd Impression 2023

Printed at: Gyan Press, Delhi.

PICTURESQUE INDIA
Author: W.S.CAINE

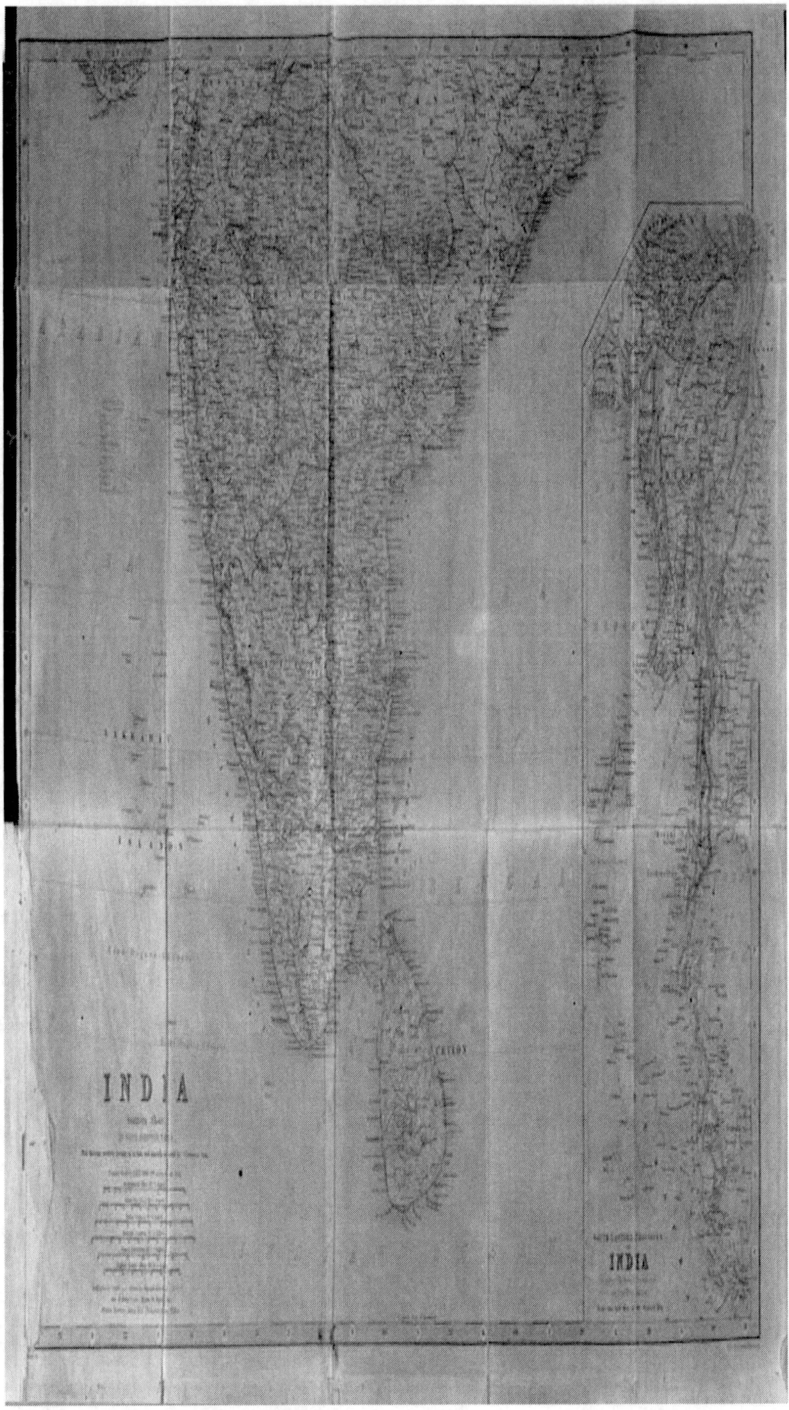
INDIA
CEYLON
INDIA

P. & O. STEAMER "ARCADIA" PASSING THROUGH SUEZ CANAL.

[*Frontispiece.*

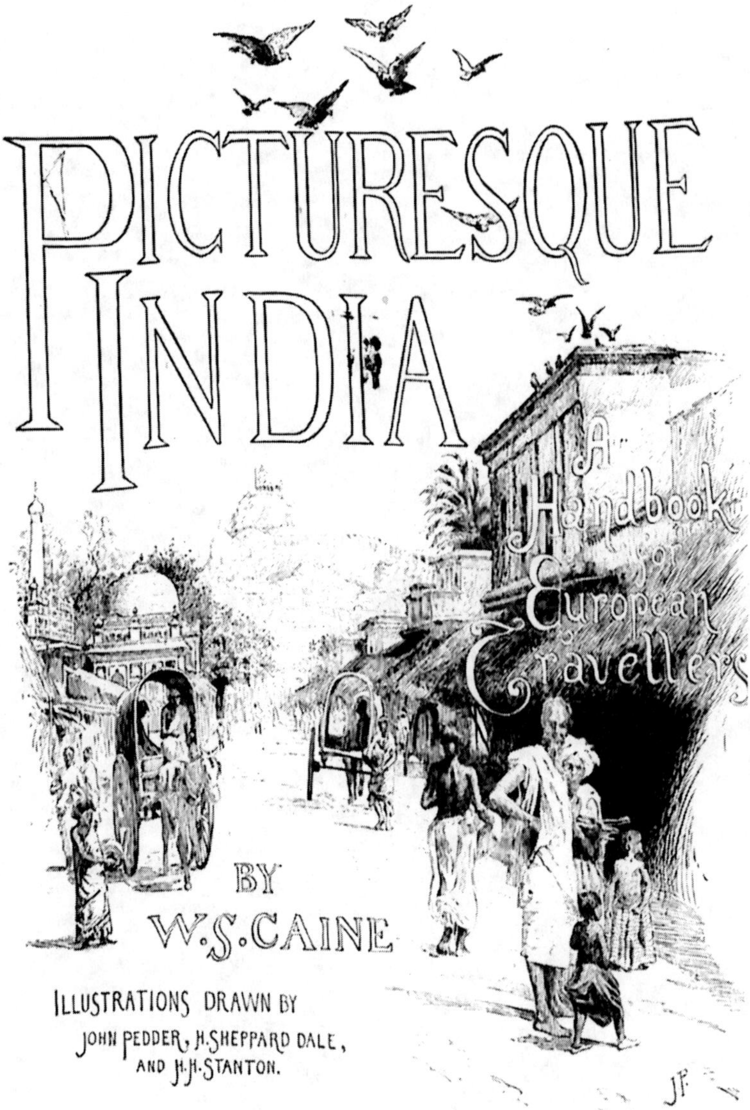
PICTURESQUE
INDIA
A
Handbook
for
European
Travellers
BY
W. S. CAINE
ILLUSTRATIONS DRAWN BY
JOHN PEDDER, H. SHEPPARD DALE,
AND H. H. STANTON.
J.P.

1890.

I Dedicate

THIS BOOK

TO MY OLD FRIEND

WILLIAM DIGBY, C.I.E.,

Secretary of the Indian Political Agency,

WHO FIRST INSPIRED ME WITH A WISH TO SEE INDIA,

AND KNOW HER PEOPLE.

PREFACE.

QUEEN VICTORIA is Empress of India; the object of this book has been to try to interest holiday people in our greatest dependency and its two hundred millions of our fellow subjects. During the two winters I have spent in India I have been much affected by the many social, political and religious problems awaiting solution by its people and their Government, but I do not discuss them in these pages, which contain no controversial matter, either political or religious. I only try to rouse superficial interest, by a plain statement of what may be seen by an ordinary traveller, in the most accessible portions of British India. My longest excursion does not leave the Railroad more than fifty miles, and none of the places described are inaccessible to a British tourist in good health.

I have supplemented my verbal descriptions with illustrations of buildings, scenery, types of nationality and incidents of the bazar which will, I believe, be found very helpful to my readers; one good picture is worth many pages of written description, and I can vouch for their truth and accuracy. Messrs. Pedder, Dale and Stanton have been much aided in their work by photographs published by Messrs. Bourne and Shepherd, of Calcutta; Messrs. Frith & Co. of Reigate; Mr. Lala Deen Dyal, of Indore; and Messrs. Nicholas & Co. of Madras, whom I desire to thank, and whose pictures I warmly commend to my readers. The two maps of Northern and Southern India have been specially prepared for this book by Messrs. W. and A. K. Johnston, with the railways completed to January, 1890. It is the best Map of India of its size, now extant.

I desire to acknowledge gratefully the permission I have received to make extracts from the writings of Sir W. W. Hunter, Sir George Birdwood, and Sir Edwin Arnold, and the valuable help which a careful study of Mr. James Fergusson's History of Indian and Eastern Architecture has given me in the preparation of this book.

W. S. CAINE.

CLAPHAM COMMON, LONDON,
September, 1890.

CONTENTS.

CHAPTER IV.

AHMADABAD.

CHAPTER V.

ABU.

CHAPTER VI.

AJMIR—JODHPUR—UDAIPUR.

CHAPTER VII.

JAIPUR.

CHAPTER VIII.

ULWAR.

CHAPTER IX.

DELHI.

CHAPTER X.

SAHARANPUR—SIMLA—AMRITSAR.

CHAPTER XI.

LAHORE.

CHAPTER XII.

RAWAL PINDI—SEALKOT—ATTOCK—THE INDUS—PESHAWAR.

CHAPTER XIII.

MULTAN AND SIND.

CHAPTER XIV.

AGRA.

CHAPTER XV.

FATEHPUR SIKRI

CHAPTER XVI.

GWALIOR.

CHAPTER XVII.

MUTTRA—BINDRABAN—GOVERDHAN—BHARTPUR—ALIGARH.

CHAPTER XVIII.

CAWNPUR.

CHAPTER XIX.

LUCKNOW—JAUNPUR—AJODHYA.

CHAPTER XX.

BENARES.

CHAPTER XXI.

PATNA.

CHAPTER XXII.

CALCUTTA.

CHAPTER XXIII.

DARJILING.

CHAPTER XXIV.

ALLAHABAD.

CHAPTER XXV.

JABALPUR.

CHAPTER XXVI.

BHOPAL—INDORE.

CHAPTER XXVII.

ELLORA—DAULATABAD—AURANGABAD—AJUNTA.

CHAPTER XXVIII.

NASIK.

CHAPTER XXIX.

BOMBAY TO PUNA.

CHAPTER XXX.

PUNA TO GOA.

CHAPTER XXXI.

BIJAPUR.

CHAPTER XXXII.

THE NIZAM'S STATE.

CHAPTER XXXIII.

HAIDARABAD TO MADRAS.

CHAPTER XXXIV.

MADRAS.

CHAPTER XXXV.

MYSORE STATE.

CHAPTER XXXVI.

MADRAS TO TANJORE.

CHAPTER XXXVII.

TRICHINOPOLI AND MADURA.

CHAPTER XXXVIII.

TINNEVELLI.

CHAPTER XXXIX.

CEYLON.

CHAPTER XL.

THE NORTH-WEST FRONTIER OF INDIA.

(*Written specially for this book by the Hon. George N. Curzon, M.P.*)

LIST OF ILLUSTRATIONS.

31

INTRODUCTION.

It has been a difficult task to compress into a single volume even the superficial information necessary to enable a would-be traveller to a vast country like India, to decide where he will go, what he would like to see, or how much he can accomplish in a given time, and my success can at best be only partial and comparative. I have not crowded my pages with a single sentence which I thought unnecessary. It will be found that I endeavour, by constant references, to embrace some very valuable standard books on special subjects, which every intelligent traveller in India will do well to have always with him, notably those written by Mr. Fergusson on Indian Architecture and by Sir George Birdwood on Indian Art. The best popular handbooks on Indian History, Ethnology, Sociology and Politics, which the traveller can take with him, are "India, Past and Present," by Mr. James Samuelson, Sir W. W. Hunter's "Indian Empire," the "Statistical Abstract," and "Moral and Material Progress of India," published annually by the India Office; "India," by Sir John Strachey, and "The Annual Report of the Indian National Congress," which may be obtained at 25 Craven Street, London, from the Indian Political Agency. The following is a brief list of useful standard works on India, which may be obtained through any bookseller :—

GENERAL.

The Imperial Gazetteer of India. 14 volumes. By Sir W. W. Hunter, K.C.S.I.

The Indian Empire ; its history, people and products ; a condensation into one volume of the Statistical survey of India. Sir W. W. Hunter, K.C.S.I.

History of India. Hindu and Muhammedan periods. Mount Stuart Elphinstone.

India Revisited. Sir E. Arnold, K.C.I.E.

Modern India. Sir George Campbell.
Geography of British India. G. Smith.
India. Sir John Strachey.
A brief history of the Indian People. Sir W. W. Hunter, K.C.S.I.
England's Work in India. Sir W. W. Hunter, K.C.S.I.
History of the Indian Mutiny. Col. G. B. Malleson.
New India. H. S. Cotton.
India; past and present. J. Samuelson.
Industrial Arts of India. Sir George Birdwood.
India for the Indians—and England. Wm. Digby, C.I.E.

ARCHÆOLOGY.

History of Indian and Eastern Architecture. J. Fergusson.
Essays on Indian Antiquities. Jas. Prinsep.

RELIGION.

India, what it can teach us. Max Müller.
The Religions of India. A. Barth.
The faith and progress of the Brahmo-Somaj. P. C. Mozoomdar.
Religious thought and life in India. Sir Monier Williams.
Sketch of the Religious Sects of the Hindus. H. H. Wilson.
Indian Caste. Dr. J. Wilson.
The Light of Asia. Sir Edwin Arnold.
Buddhism. T. W. Rhys Davids.
The Indian Musaalmans. Sir W. W. Hunter, K.C.S.I.
The Parsis, their history and religion. Framji Dhosabhai.
Missionary Conference Reports—published in Calcutta at intervals.
History of Protestant Missions in India. Sherring.

Barth's "Religions of India," Fergusson's "Indian Architecture," Sir George Birdwood's "Industrial Arts of India," and Sir W. W. Hunter's "Indian Empire," are, in my judgment, the four most valuable books the ordinary tourist can read before he goes, and take with him as trusty companions on his journey. Messrs. Thacker & Co. of Bombay, Calcutta, and Newgate Street, London, and Newman & Co. Lim. of Calcutta, keep in stock every standard book on India, and travellers will be able to select from their shelves many guides and handbooks, local and general, as well as works on Fauna and Flora, the customs and religions of the peoples of India, its history, geography, &c. &c.

Very few travellers will care to visit India during the hot or rainy seasons, and the climate is so equable during what is called the "cold season," (from the end of October to the middle of March), that very little information on the subject of outfit is needful. The traveller who intends to confine himself to the north of a line drawn from Bombay to Calcutta, will find ordinary summer clothing, as worn in England, all that is necessary, with a light and heavy overcoat. It is best to wear flannel underclothing, and, indeed, I wear nothing but flannel all over India. My own outfit is always a very simple one, and as I am going again to India for the third time this winter, I will give a list of what I shall put in my portmanteau:—

Shoes . . .	2 pair of brown canvas shoes.
	1 " light walking boots.
	1 " dress shoes.
	1 " slippers.
	1 " thin brown canvas leggings for riding.
Socks. . .	12 pair new merino.
Shirts . . .	6 white dress shirts.
	4 thin flannel with collars attached.
	4 thick " " " "
Collars . .	1 dozen white linen.
Drawers. . .	6 very thin, all wool.
	4 medium " "
Sleeping dress .	6 pairs flannel pyjamas.

12 woven cholera belts.
2 suits of dark grey flannel, carefully made by a good tailor. Coats made *to* wear without waistcoat if desired.
1 suit of warm tweed, for the voyage and Northern India.
1 morning coat and waistcoat of thin black cloth.
1 pair thin grey tweed trousers.
1 dress suit of light cloth.
1 grey alpaca dust coat, without lining.
1 light overcoat.
1 medium ulster.
1 good felt wide-awake hat.
2 light silk caps for railway and ship.
6 towels.
6 pillow-slips.
Handkerchiefs and small sundries to suit my own tastes and habits.
A white umbrella.

With this outfit, any gentleman can go with comfort to any place written about in this book. Of course, if the traveller intends to hunt, fish and shoot, or do anything exceptional, he must fit himself out for it without my help.

Washing can be done at short notice everywhere in India, so that there is no need to overburden oneself with underclothing. A necessary part of every traveller's baggage is a bedding kit, for use in railway carriages, and at Dâk bungalows and even at some hotels, which only provide bedsteads. This kit is best obtained in Bombay, but two pairs of really good blankets and a woollen travelling rug will be found of service, and should be brought from England.

The sun-hats, which are the universal wear in India, are best purchased in Bombay.

Umbrellas should be white, as it never rains in the cold season, and the sun is often fierce during the day.

The tradesmen in the large cities of India are quite as good as they are at home, and no difficulty will be experienced in supplementing my list. If any time is to be spent in Southern India, half-a-dozen suits of white cotton will be desirable, but these can be got better and cheaper in India than at home.

A lady, who has spent a winter travelling in India, writes to me as follows:—

"It is unnecessary for ladies travelling in India to burden themselves with a large quantity of luggage. It is desirable to take a variety of morning and evening dresses, such as would be worn at home in spring or summer weather. On the voyage, and in the Northern parts of India, warm dresses, jackets, and wraps are needed. A plentiful supply of underclothing, both warm and cool, will be required, especially on the voyage, when it is impossible to get any washing done. Elaborate trimmings on underclothing will fare badly in India, where the washermen treat such things with ruinous roughness.

"Dust cloaks and gauze veils are indispensable for the hot and dusty provinces in India, and a thin riding-habit will often be found useful. The dresses for wearing on ship-board should be good and well made. These should include a comfortable serge or stuff gown, and one of thin silk or foulard. Thin beige, serge or cotton skirts, with silk or cotton blouses, make good wear both for the voyages and for India.

"No one 'dresses for dinner' on board ship, though a little change is generally made from the attire of the morning.

"Hats or caps are always worn on deck, generally of the deer-stalker order, and a comfortable warm hood for wear on deck in the evening will be found very welcome. A good rug, ulster, warm jacket and Shetland wrap will be required, both for the voyage, and for the cold evenings and mornings in the North-West Provinces and the Punjab.

"There is a 'baggage day,' once or twice a week during the voyage, when portmanteaus in the luggage room may be got at and opened, so that warm garments worn in the Bay of Biscay and the Mediterranean may be exchanged for thinner clothing for the Red Sea, and *vice versâ* on the way home; the cabins, therefore, need not be unreasonably crowded with trunks.

"A large hanging pocket with several divisions will be found useful in the state-room.

"Ladies will of course make up their list of toilet necessaries and other travelling comforts to suit their own requirements, but I recommend as articles that will often be found very useful, either on the voyage or in India:—A Rubber hot-water bottle, and folding bath, Rimmel's vinegar, Pears' soap, a travelling Etna or small 'afternoon tea' basket, Keating's powder, some towels, sheets and pillow-cases, and a pair of good Jaeger blankets.

"Silk or 'Anglo-Indian' underclothing is very safe and pleasant for use in India, and to avoid risk of chills, it is a wise precaution to wear one of those woven belts of wool, known to the outfitters by the unnecessarily alarming name of 'Cholera belts.'

"Hospitality in India is boundless and universal, and it is well to have one or two good evening dresses of some material that will suffer least from package. Of course travellers are not expected to be as smart as other folk.

"Pith or other sun-hats should be bought in Bombay after arrival;

the double awnings of the steamer. render them quite unnecessary on the voyage.

"In addition to any parasol or sunshade, a strong, double-lined, white umbrella will be found useful as a protection from the sun, which is always fierce in the middle of the day, as well as two pair of blue or tinted spectacles.

"White canvas shoes will be pleasant both for deck use and travel in the country, and a pair of thick, woollen socks will be useful, to pull over the shoes when visiting mosques, and other holy places, where the shoes must be either removed, or covered by an appearance of removal."

To most travellers, the first thought in deciding on a journey is:—What will it cost? This question will be completely answered by a shilling hand-book published by Messrs Thos. Cook & Sons, Ludgate Circus, London, the well-known excursion agents, who have branch offices in Bombay and Calcutta, and who are giving very close attention to the development of Indian business. In this little volume, sixteen different tours in India are quoted, which will give a general idea of the cost of Railway journeys. It also contains the fullest information with regard to every detail of Indian travel.

The fares of the various steamship companies to India and back are as follows:—

Peninsular & Oriental Co., to Bombay, Karachi or Madras, or Calcutta, or Ceylon, and BACK to London:—

For three months:—1st Class £90; 2nd Class £55.
For six months:—1st Class £100; 2nd Class £60.
Extra viâ Brindisi:—1st Class £12; 2nd Class £6.

"Clan" line, or "Hall" line, Liverpool to Bombay and back, available for six months:—

1st Class only, £85 10*s*. £5 extra to Calcutta.

British India Co., London to Calcutta and back:—

1st Class, £94 10*s*; 2nd Class, £57 12*s*.

I advise all travellers to go by the P. & O. Co.'s steamers. The other lines are very comfortable and well-managed, but the slight extra cost by P. & O. is fully compensated for by speed and general comfort. I write with the experience of nine voyages.

The following round tour will be found to include the greater part of India, and is quite as much as ought to be undertaken by the most energetic traveller in the most extended tour possible during the cold season.

From Bombay to Jabalpur, Allahabad, Mirzapur, Patna, Calcutta, Darjiling and back to Calcutta, Benares, Lucknow, Cawnpur, Agra, Aligarh, Delhi, Umballa, Amritsar, Lahore, Peshawar, Multan, Rewari, Ulwar, Jaipur, Ajmir, Mt. Abu, Ahmedabad, Baroda, and back to Bombay. Bombay to Puna, Bijapur, Haidarabad, Raichur, Madras, Bangalore, Mysore, Utakamand, Trichinopoli, Madura, Tinnivelli, Tanjore, Madras, and back to Bombay. The first-class railway fares for the whole of this tour amount to about 720 Rupees; second class, 380 Rupees; third class, 100 Rupees.

It is necessary to engage a travelling servant, for it is not the custom in many Indian hotels, or in any of the Dâk bungalows, to provide service. A first-rate servant may be had for 30 Rupees per month, and a good, useful fellow as low as 15 Rupees. An allowance of 30 Rupees more will suffice for their food. So that 50 to 60 Rupees per month will be an ample estimate for the cost of a personal attendant. He will pay porters, stamps for letters, telegrams, tips, cabs and such like, which will amount to 20 Rupees a month, will take railway tickets, and look after luggage arrangements. Thos. Cook & Sons, Bombay, will provide this servant, if written to beforehand.

It will thus be seen that about 350 Rupees will suffice for wages, food and third class fare for a personal attendant on a four months' tour in India.

The usual charge for hotels is 5 to 7 Rupees each day, for four meals and a bed-room. Carriages, except in large cities, may be hired for 3 or 4 Rupees a day. I find it easy to travel with comfort in India for 12 Rupees a day, outside railway fares.

It will be seen by these figures, that the actual cost of a tour in India of four months, with the passage out and home by P. & O.

steamer, need not, with a little economy, exceed £380, and may be done luxuriously for £500.

Return ticket London to Bombay, First Class, £100.

Railway Fares for self, say	720 rupees.		
„ for servant	110 „		
Wages and food of servant	250 „		
Hotel expenses for four months	750 „	2800 Rupees.	
Carriages	470 „		
Petty expenses	500 „		

2800 rupees at 10 to £1 = say £280.

Railway travelling in India is very comfortable. All first and second class carriages are convertible at night into sleeping berths, and have good lavatories. There are excellent meals to be obtained at regular intervals at the various refreshment rooms. At most junctions, and at many minor stations even, there are waiting-rooms, with bedsteads for the use of travellers. Although all the railway companies lag sadly behind European and American enterprise, they do a great deal for the comfort of long-journey passengers. It is impossible to speak too highly of the universal civility and kindness of Indian station-masters. Adventurous travellers, alighting at road-side stations for remote places of interest, who have written a day or two beforehand to the station-master, will find whatever resources the place possesses ready for his use. It may be that he wants a shake-down for the night in the station, a country cart to visit some out-of-the-way antiquity, or at some more important place, a bed at the Dâk Bungalow, and some conveyance to take him there from the station; whatever it may be, let him write beforehand to the station-master, and if it is to be had at all, it will be duly provided.

In case of illness, however slight, an English doctor should be consulted. There is no place in India, likely to be visited by the ordinary tourist, from which an English doctor is far distant. If travellers are subject to any infirmity, they should not depend upon the drugs available in India, but take out medicine from England, made up specially under the prescription of their own medical man. The compressed drugs of Messrs. Burroughs, Welcome & Co., Snow Hill

Buildings, London, E.C., are thoroughly reliable. I showed some of them, that I had taken with me round the world, and afterwards to India and back, to a distinguished physician, who, after careful examination, pronounced them as good as ever. They were then three years old. A whole medicine-chest of these compressed drugs can be packed into a small cigar-box.

The best railway guide for India is "Newman's Indian Bradshaw," which may be purchased from Thos. Cook & Son, or Stanford's, 55, Charing Cross.

A little care is necessary with regard to diet. An experienced medical officer in India, whom I once had occasion to consult, summed up the question of diet in these words: "Never eat twice cooked food, butter your own toast, and avoid alcohol." The exhortation about toast will be understood in a moment by any one who has seen a native cook do it with a greasy old rag. Drinking water is not always good, but soda-water is cheap and universal, and excellent tea may be had at every important railway station. It is not wise to purchase fruit indiscriminately at small roadside stations, except oranges, bananas, and such other fruit as have an outside rind to be removed.

There are of course districts in India full of intense interest to the traveller, such as Kashmir, Burma, Nepal, Orissa, Travancore and Assam, which I have hardly referred to in this book, for the excellent reason that I have had no experience of them, or knowledge beyond that which I have acquired from books. This volume, as I have already said, is only intended as a help to travellers in visiting the more beaten tracks of this vast country. Trübners, of Ludgate Hill, or Thacker & Co., Newgate Street, London, have upon their shelves a great variety of books, a selection from which will enable anyone to inform himself fully with regard to Remoter India.

It will be observed that I have given much information, necessarily condensed, with regard to Christian Missions in India; I have generally selected those stations to be found in cities where the traveller is likely to remain a few days. Most missionaries welcome with cordiality any traveller who is really interested in missionary enterprise, and they are always delighted to show their schools and other institutions, or give every possible information on the social customs and native institutions of the communities among whom they labour. These gentlemen are generally men of culture, thoroughly in earnest in their efforts to improve and elevate their people, and are charming companions to those travellers who can appreciate their work. I think any book professing to be a guide or help to the traveller in India would not be complete without, at any rate, indicating those mission stations worthy of his attention. My information on this subject may be relied upon, as it has in every case been supplied to me by missionaries on the spot. The best work is no doubt being done in remote places in rural Bengal, Orissa, Travancore, or among the wild hill tribes and Aborigines. My book does not reach these districts. Every ten years there is published in Calcutta "Baddeley's Directory of Missionaries," which gives a complete statistical return of every mission in British and Native India.

The politician will find India a country of vast unsolved problems which are now being discussed with much acuteness by educated Indians.

The Indian National Congress of representative men from all over India, called into existence six years ago, meets every year between Christmas and New Year's day, at some capital of a province or other central place, for the discussion of such constitutional reforms as they think ripe and urgent. Their chief demand is for some scheme of representation which shall at any rate admit educated Indians to a due and reasonable share in the legislation and administration of their own country.

The Congress for the year 1890 will be held in Calcutta. European visitors are always made very welcome, and seats in the best portion of the auditorium are reserved for them. Apart from its political interest, the spectacle is impressive and remarkable, being an assemblage of three or four thousand persons gathered together from every part of India, all attired in the characteristic dress of their districts. The report of every year's Congress has been printed in a volume of 150 or 200 pages, which may be obtained, with other kindred literature, from the offices of the Indian Political Agency, 25, Craven Street, London, W.C.

The aspirations of the Congress are strongly opposed by many Anglo-Indians and an influential section of Indian Society, of whom Sir Syed Ahmed of Aligarh is the chosen leader and mouthpiece. They have not any agency in England, like the Congress party, but their views have been expressed in numerous pamphlets, which can be got through any of the Indian booksellers in London already mentioned.

It will greatly increase the interest which an English traveller must feel in his Indian fellow subjects, to have some surface knowledge at any rate of those social and political problems which are exciting them from time to time. Those who pass through India visiting only Anglo-Indians, can learn but little of the inner life and aspirations of the Native Indian. I shall myself be glad to give letters of introduction to native gentlemen, to any English traveller who really wishes to get below the surface.

It will also give me much pleasure at any time, to answer enquiries, within reasonable limits, from any traveller who intends visiting India.

I have, wherever I have felt enough confidence to do so, named the best hotels. None of the Indian hotels are first-rate. They are as a rule furnished as a speculation by some wealthy native, and leased to a caterer. Their management continually changes, and it is better, before going up country from Bombay, to call at Thos. Cook & Son's offices, and get a list of the best managed hotels from them. By constant enquiry from travellers and from other sources of information they manage to keep up a list, which is really the only safe hotel guide in India. Newman's Indian Bradshaw also contains a fairly trustworthy list of hotels and clubs. G. F. Kellner & Co., who are the "Spiers and Pond" of Northern India, have a good many hotels at the railway stations, which are all clean and well managed. It is always well in the case of both hotels and Dâk bungalows, to order rooms beforehand, stating hour of arrival, and ordering conveyance from the station.

One of the many small annoyances of travel, is the general unwieldiness of guide-books. My own custom for many years has been to take my guide-book to a binder, and have it cut up in thin volumes of about 50 or 100 pages, bound in limp cloth or Morocco. I advise my readers to treat this book in the same fashion, of course ordering a fresh copy at once for their own library shelves.

I have not thought it convenient to allocate the towns to their respective provinces. It will be found that I have arranged them along the respective trunk lines and their branches. The contents of each chapter, and a very full index will enable the reader to turn at once to any point of attraction. I have also provided an index to the full and comprehensive maps prepared for this book by Messrs. W. & A. K. Johnston, so far as all the places mentioned in this volume are concerned. It will be found that in many cases the spelling of this map and of railway guides in India as well as other books, differs slightly from that used by me. I have adopted Sir Wm. Hunter's spelling throughout my book, as it is now the recognized standard.

PICTURESQUE INDIA.

CHAPTER I.

BOMBAY.

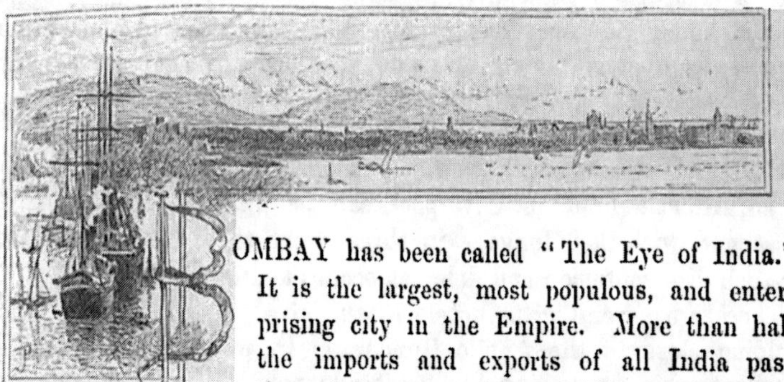

BOMBAY has been called "The Eye of India." It is the largest, most populous, and enterprising city in the Empire. More than half the imports and exports of all India pass through its custom house. Nine-tenths of the persons entering or leaving the country do so at Bombay; it is without exception the finest modern city in Asia, and the noblest monument of British enterprise in the world. The traveller, eager for the wonders of Agra, Delhi, or Benares, is too often satisfied with a couple of days spent in driving through its spacious streets, neglectful of the wonderful life of this great city and seaport, seeing nothing of its institutions, its arts and manufactures, or the interesting peoples who make up its population of 800,000 souls. A month may be spent in Bombay, and at the end many things still be unseen that ought to have been seen. As the steamer rounds Colába point, and proceeds slowly to her moorings, the panorama of Bombay city, with the noble public buildings towering above the masts in her docks, the low coast line beyond sweeping round the vast bay dotted with palm-clad islands, backed by the lofty blue mountains of

Matheran and Mahableshwar, fully justify the name given by the old Portuguese navigators in the 16th century—Bom Bahia, the beautiful bay.

As the vessel drops anchor a swarm of boats cluster round her, and in a moment the deck is crowded with native boatmen, hotel cadgers, friends of passengers, and such like, producing immediate pandemonium. The Steamship Companies, so far as my experience goes, do not provide any transport from ship to shore, and the confusion and inconvenience to passengers is very great. It is impossible to get any luggage off, and the best course to pursue is to leave everything packed up in the cabin, and go ashore in a boat as best one may, with a hand-bag for the night, getting the heavy baggage from the custom house the next day, where it is landed from the ship in hopeless confusion, taking hours to sort out and get passed. The whole business of getting ashore at Bombay is worse than any port I have ever landed at; I am told that the P. and O. Co. intend to get a good steam-tender, and the sooner they do so the better. If an Atlantic liner in Liverpool can be cleared of six hundred passengers with their luggage in three hours, there is no justification for such dire confusion and delay as occurs at Bombay.

There are several good hotels in the city. The Apollo is a new building close to the Apollo Bunder, clean, well-managed, with an excellent table, possessing the great advantage of isolation, one side overlooking the harbour, and the other commanding a fine view across Back Bay to Malabar Hill. Watson's Hotel is a very large one in the centre of the city, surrounded by the principal public offices; the Great Western and the Victoria are well-placed, good hotels, and in the suburbs are the Adelphi Hotel, at Byculla, and the Family Hotel, at Cumballa Hill, all of which are well-managed establishments.

A gentleman, travelling alone, will, if he can manage it, get a bedroom at the Byculla or Bombay Club, both of which are excellent, and have sleeping rooms or tents for forty or fifty members each. Almost every member of the civil and military services, the leading merchants, bankers, and lawyers, are members of one or other club, and, if intending travellers have acquaintance in Bombay, they can, without much difficulty, get themselves elected as honorary members, by writing a month or two beforehand; a longer notice, however, is necessary to secure bedrooms. The Yacht Club is the most pleasant resort in

STREET SCENE IN BOMBAY.

Bombay, commanding a splendid view of the harbour. It has an excellent restaurant and newsroom, with vast verandahs overhanging the water. There are no bedrooms, but anyone remaining more than a day or two in Bombay should become an honorary member. Its committee are hospitable, and no difficulty is made about any well accredited traveller. Ladies are admitted as guests to any meal.

Having settled himself in club or hotel, the traveller will be eager to have a look at Bombay. Carriages are plentiful and good, and though dearer than anywhere else in India, except Calcutta, appear very cheap to the European. Victorias with one horse, can be got for five rupees a day, and a phaeton, with a pair, for ten. Starting from the Apollo Hotel, the fine building just opposite on the right is the Sailors' Home, and on the left the Young Men's Christian Association. Driving along the Mayo Road we pass the front of that magnificent series of public buildings of which Bombay people are so justly proud; first, the Elphinstone College, then the Secretariat, the University, the High Court, the Public Works Office, the Post Office, and the Telegraph Office. Opposite to this, at the junction of Esplanade and Hornby Roads, is the beautiful statue of the Empress of India.

Turning down Esplanade Road, at the angle formed by Hornby Row, is the Cathedral High School, a fine Gothic building; the stately mansion just beyond is the new residence of a Parsi merchant prince and philanthropist, Mr. Jamsetji N. Tata. At the end of this road is the Mechanics' Institute, the gift of the Sassoons. Turning to the right, and following Esplanade Cross Road, the building on the right is the Francis Xavier College, beyond which, opposite the Free Church, is the National General Hospital; this road ends at the Crawford Market, where a halt may be made to purchase fruit. Returning by Market Road, the School of Art stands on the right, the Salvation Army Headquarters on the left, and presently the gorgeous terminus of the Great India Peninsula Railway is reached, in front of which is the well-managed European Hospital. Hornby Row reaches back to the statue of the Empress, and a turn to the left, along Church Gate Street, opens out into Elphinstone Circle, the heart of the business quarter, in which are placed the Town Hall, the Cathedral, and most of the leading banks. This round will occupy the morning. After tiffin a drive may be taken along Queen's Road to Malabar Hill and Cumballa, returning by Grant Road and the native bazaars. By this time the traveller will have a good surface knowledge of the city, and may address himself to detail.

Travellers who intend spending more than a day or two in this city should purchase "Maclean's Guide to Bombay" for 5 rupees. It is a complete *vade mecum*, full of information and detail, besides being a most readable book.

The various government buildings, though handsome in elevation,

ON THE ROAD TO MALABAR HILL.

have no details of interest, containing merely a succession of offices for the use of the clerks connected with the different departments. The finest of these is the *Secretariat*, built at a cost of £130,000, from a design of Col. Wilkins, R.E. The whole elevation presents a clear, unbroken frontage to Back Bay of 450 feet, and looks very imposing when viewed from the Esplanade; the style is Venetian Gothic. Here are located all the financial departments of the government of Bombay. Next to the Secretariat are the University Senate Hall, and the University Library and Clock Tower. These buildings are from designs by Sir Gilbert Scott, in 13th century French architecture.

The Hall is 104 feet in length, 44 feet in breadth, with a height of 63 feet, presenting an unbroken line of roofing from end to end. There are some fine stained-glass windows, seen to best effect in the forenoon. A carillon in the clock tower plays by machinery every hour. The view of the city and harbour, looking over both bays, well repays the climb of 250 feet to the summit of the tower.

The High Court is a huge building 560 feet long, in the early English Gothic style, erected at a cost of £164,000; the smaller building next to it, in Venetian Gothic, is the Public Works Office.

The Post and Telegraph Offices should be viewed from Back Bay. Opposite to the post-office is the superb white marble statue of Her Majesty, by Noble, R.A., one of the finest modern monuments in the world, the gift to Bombay of Khanderao, the Gaekwar of Baroda. The statue itself is of colossal size, measuring 8 feet; the pedestal and canopy, 42 feet in total height, are designed in pure Gothic. Khanderao also presented the town of Bombay with the beautiful Sailors' Home on the Apollo Bunder, so that this magnificent range of public buildings, fully worthy of any European capital, begin and end with the generous gifts of the chief native prince within the presidency.

The finest building in all Bombay is the new railway station and offices of the Great India Peninsula Railway, completed in 1888. Its great dome, surmounted by a huge figure of Progress, dominates the whole city, and is conspicuous from every open space; this building is also in the Italian Gothic style, and the architect, Mr. F. W. Stevens, has certainly succeeded in distancing all Indian rivals. The waiting and refreshment rooms are spacious and lofty, and are, with the grand central staircase, and the palatial booking-offices, one mass of beautiful and artistic decoration, in which coloured marbles, fine carving in stone and wood, encaustic tiles, and ornamented railings, are the chief features, having a special interest from being the handiwork of the students of the Bombay School of Art. This railway station is replete with every accommodation and comfort for passengers, and is a striking contrast to the dark and dirty sheds which do duty for stations at Calcutta. It has cost this railway company about £300,000, and is a fitting monument to an unbroken prosperity, that has nearly doubled the value of its shareholders' property in twenty-five years.

The School of Art is situated in a pleasant garden not far from the Great India Peninsula Railway terminus. It is a plain, solid building, admirably fitted for its purpose, the gift of Sir Jamsetji Jijibhai. This school has had considerable influence on the arts and manufactures of the city, of which I write further on. Sound practical teaching is given in drawing, designing, modelling, wood engraving, ceramics, decorative painting, and sculpture in wood and stone. The beautiful pottery for which this school is famous is shown in a separate building about 150 yards off, where a large and varied stock is kept for sale. This pottery is, perhaps, the cheapest, and, for the price, the most decorative ware in existence; the manager packs it carefully. I have had some elaborate pieces sent to England without the slightest damage. This school of pottery is due to the energy of Mr. Geo. Terry, who is the director and superintendent. He introduced some of the best workmen from Sind, and the work Mr. Terry's pupils turn out in glazed ware is almost equal in quality to the celebrated products of that province. The Bombay ware may be known by its greater finish. Mr. Terry has developed original varieties, adapted from the Ajanta Cave paintings, and the popular mythological paintings of modern Hinduism. He has to endure competition from imitators, of whom beware; it is better to buy only direct from the school itself.

The Goculdas Tejpal Hospital lies just behind the School of Art, in Esplanade Cross Road; this was built mainly at the cost of Mr. Tejpal, and Mr. R. J. Jijibhai, each of whom gave £15,000, the Government finding the site and £10,000. It is rather mixed in its styles, but one should not look a gift-horse in the mouth. The patients are all Indians.

The Elphinstone High School is in the same road; the length of this palatial academy is 452 feet, and it contains no less than twenty-eight class-rooms, 30 by 25 feet, with a great central hall 70 feet long and a library nearly as large. £15,000 of the cost was contributed by Sir Albert Sassoon, the head of that notable family of Persian Jews.

The Pestonji Cama Hospital for Women and Children is a handsome mediæval Gothic building in Cruickshank Road, and was built at the cost of the Parsi gentleman whose name it bears. It is one of the best designed hospitals in India, and deserves the attention of every traveller who is interested in the new movement for supplying medical aid to the women of India, associated with the honoured name of Lady Dufferin. The only other hospitals worth notice are the European, the Jamsetji Jijibhai, the General, and the Cowasji Jehangir Ophthalmic Hospitals.

WATER CARRIER—CRAWFORD MARKET.

The Victoria Museum and Gardens, are about half a mile beyond the Byculla Railway Station, and make a pleasant excursion in the early morning, when a delightful hour may be spent strolling about the gardens, fragrant with tropical flowers and shrubs, many of which are familiar to the Englishman in his own hot-houses, or at Kew, but which here flourish with a tenfold luxuriance. In the evening, from four to six, the gardens are crowded with thousands of gaily dressed Indians, especially when the band plays. There is a rather mouldy collection of wild beasts in the menagerie. The contents of the museum itself are trivial, and badly arranged. There is, however, a fine statue of the late Prince Consort, by Noble. A thoroughly well-arranged collection of Indian Art, on the lines of South Kensington, would be a great addition to this handsome and capacious museum.

The series of public buildings thus enumerated have been almost entirely erected during the last thirty years at a cost of about a million sterling, of which one quarter has been given by Parsis and other wealthy Indians.

The markets of Bombay, like those of every Asiatic city, are full of picturesque interest to a European visitor.

The one most worthy of attention is the Crawford Market, at the north-east corner of the Esplanade, standing on 72,000 yards of land of which about 6,000 is under cover. The fruit and flower stalls are in the main building, which presents a very handsome elevation to the street; behind is a great iron shed, 350 feet by 100, devoted to vegetables, cereals, and spices. The beef market, being abhorred by Hindus, is in a separate building at the back of all; mutton and goat's flesh, with fish, being under another roof, and sadly overcrowded.

The poultry dealers throng the open spaces, their stock of fowls, ducks, turkeys and other birds being all alive in wicker cages. Parrots, mynas, love-birds, cockatoos and singing-birds of all sorts, as well as fighting-quails, are also offered for sale.

The best time to visit the market is in the early morning, about seven o'clock, when the flower and fruit stalls are at their best, and the fresh fish is being brought in from the bay.

The Government Dockyard is one of the oldest institutions in Bombay, having been in existence since 1736. It consists of a series of moderate sized graving-docks, with the necessary workshops, and contains no special feature of interest. It was here that the East India Company built their war-ships, and from time to time a good many battle ships in the days of the wooden walls of old England were turned out for the British Admiralty. Nothing bigger than gunboats and barges are now built here, and it exists mainly for repair work. It is in contemplation to build a superb graving-dock, capable of taking in a first-class modern ironclad, at the joint cost of Great Britain and India.

Behind the Town Hall, a homely building of fifty years ago, is the Castle and Arsenal. An order must be obtained from the Inspector-General of Ordnance, the general officer commanding, or if the visitor be a foreigner, from the Secretariat; it is readily granted. Here are stored every kind of warlike material and ordnance, sufficient to furnish an army of 10,000 men at a day's notice. The workshops employ nearly a thousand artizans, making tents, harness, saddlery, accoutrements, and other equipments, or cleaning and repairing small arms.

In the Compound the European stranger will probably see his first banyan trees, one of which is 300 years old, whose shade is utilized as a sort of museum of ancient and curious guns. Three of these were captured in the last Burmese war; one was made at Ostend in 1601; another, very highly decorated, bears an inscription "Jan Verbruggen me fecit, 1757," and one long piece of twenty-one feet, ten tons in weight, was made at Poona in 1771, and captured at Ahmednagar by the Duke of Wellington in 1803. A collection of quaint old weapons of native manufacture is exhibited in the armoury of the old Council Hall.

A BOMBAY SAILING-BOAT.

An interesting boat excursion may be made from the Apollo Bunder to visit the various docks and basins along the harbour frontage, starting from Colaba Point and rowing up to the Mazagon Bunder. The old lighthouse on Colaba Point has not been used since 1874, when its lofty successor on the Prongs Reef, seen one and a half mile seaward, was completed.

The next important building is the Observatory, then the Pilot Bunder, after which a landing should be made to visit the Sassoon Dock, the oldest in the port, in which large ships can load and discharge. Continuing up the harbour, the Apollo Bunder, the Yacht Club, the Dockyard, Custom House and Arsenal are successively passed. The long stretch of vacant ground which follows is the Mody Bay reclamation land, taken in from the foreshore by the Government at a cost of £300,000. It is being gradually taken up for various purposes, the two large buildings already erected being ice manufactories. The Prince's Dock lies just beyond, called after the Prince of Wales, who laid the foundation-stone during his visit in 1875. This magnificent dock is 1,460 feet by 1,000, 30 acres in area, accommodating about 30 ocean steamers and sailing-ships. Passing three busy basins, Mazagon Bunder is reached, near which is a new fish market.

Returning to Apollo Bunder, a visit may be paid to some of the port defences, such as Cross Island, Middle Ground and Oyster Rock Batteries, and the two coast defence ironclads, the *Abyssinia* and *Magdala*, orders for which may be obtained when writing for a permit to visit the Arsenal.

Bombay, after New Orleans, is the greatest cotton port in the world, and a visit should be paid to the Cotton Green about noon, at which time "high change" sets in at a yard opposite to the Colaba terminus of the tramway. Any open market in India is sure to be a

A CORNER OF THE COTTON GREEN.

striking picture of native life, brightened with an endless variety of costume and kaleidoscopic colour. The cotton market of Bombay is no exception. Four million cwts. are exported from Bombay in the year, and over two millions more are consumed in the 82 mills in the Bombay presidency, the bulk of which are in tho city; the value of all this cotton is about £12,000,000.

The spinning and weaving of cotton by machinery has had a great impulse during the last 20 years, the number of mills having increased from 14 in 1870 to 82 in 1888. These mills are not content with a market in India, but are rapidly driving out Manchester from the eastern markets in all coarse yarns. The exports of yarn and other cotton manufactures from India in 1870 were of the total value of £170,000; in 1888 they had increased to £1,150,000. This singularly successful industry is mainly in the hands of Parsis, and some of the mills, notably those of which Messrs. Tata & Sons, the Alliance Cotton Mill Co., Limited, Messrs. Maneckji Petit & Sons, Messrs. J. N. Petit & Co., and Messrs. David Sassoon & Co. are the managing agents, are among the finest and most modern in the world, having been erected regardless of cost by such well-known English firms as Asa Lees & Sons, and Platt Bros., of Oldham. A note sent to any of these firms will procure permission to visit their mills; it is interesting to observe the difference between the workmanship of the Indian and Lancashire hands. There are, roughly speaking, two and a half persons employed in every Indian mill to one in Lancashire. A well condensed history of this cotton industry will be found in "Maclean's Guide."

The Hindu temples of Bombay are lacking in interest, and as the traveller will certainly visit such sacred Hindu cities as Benares and Muttra, it would be a pity to take up much time in visiting those of Bombay. But when a drive is being taken to Malabar Hill some morning or evening, it will be well worth while to see the Walkeshwar Temple and Tank. There has been a temple in this very holy place from time immorial, but the series of handsome shrines of the ordinary Hindu type which now surround the tank are none of them more than 150 years old. The various buildings interspersed with the temples are the houses of the resident Brahman priests, and Dharmsalas, lodging places for pilgrims, owned by rich and pious Hindus, who grant the free use of them on application for a limited period. Many of the wealthy merchants have small houses here, to which they repair on festival days with their friends and families. There is a cleft rock on the beach, just behind the tank, through which pilgrims squeeze themselves as an act of piety, signifying regeneration.

Walkeshwar is a strange and interesting sight to the foreigner just landed in India, and here he will probably see for the first time those fakirs, or holy ascetics, who play so large a part in Hindu society. If an intelligent and experienced missionary can be secured as guide, or an English-speaking Brahman, it will greatly increase the interest of the visit. There is a group of temples at Breach Candy also well worth seeing, one of which, built by Mr. Dhakji, a late prime minister of Baroda, is among the best specimens of modern Hindu architecture in India.

A FAKIR.

The Muhammadans possess nearly 100 mosques, scattered all over the town and island. The oldest and most interesting is the Jama Masjid, near the Crawford Market. The best time to visit it is on Friday at noon, when its courtyards are crowded with thousands of pious Musalmans. It is open to visitors, but the shoes must be removed before entering.

The Parsi Fire temples are all severely plain buildings, inside and out. None but Parsis are admitted.

The human life of Bombay differs from that of every other Indian city by the dominating element of the Parsis, who, by their wonderful energy, enterprise and education, have become the most important and powerful influence in the Bombay Presidency. These people are the descendants of ancient Persians, who fled from their native land before the Muhammadan conquerors of Persia, and who settled at Surat 1,100 or 1,200 years ago. They now number in all about 70,000, the great majority of whom reside in Bombay. They speak English fluently, and it is carefully taught in their schools. The founder of their religion was

Zoroaster, whom tradition says was a disciple of the Hebrew prophet Daniel. He teaches a pure and lofty morality, summed up in three precepts of two words each, viz., good thoughts, good words, good deeds, of which the Parsi continually reminds himself by the triple coil of his white cotton girdle, which never leaves him

The Parsis are often spoken of as "Fire Worshippers," a term which they rightly repudiate with indignation. They are Theists. God, according to the Parsi faith, is the emblem of glory, refulgence, and spiritual life; and therefore the Parsi, when praying, either faces the sun, or stands before fire, as the most fitting symbol of the Deity. The interior of their temples is entirely empty, except for the sacred fire in a small recess, which is never allowed to expire. The walls are bare, without the slightest decoration. There is no pleasanter sight in Bombay than the groups of pious Zoroastrians praying at sunset along the shores of Back Bay.

The "good deeds" of the Parsis are in evidence all over Bombay, and are by no means confined to their own people. The charities of Sir Jamsetji Jijibhai, his sons and grandsons, would need a volume to describe. Hospitals, schools, dispensaries, colleges, and other valuable institutions are scattered over town and province with a lavish hand. One of his sons is known to have thus given away a quarter of a million sterling.

The Elphinstone College building, the University Hall, two of the three Bombay hospitals, and seven dispensaries, testify to the benevolence of this remarkable people towards the public generally. It is impossible to describe what they have done for their co-religionists. No community in the history of the world has, in proportion to its numbers and wealth, such a charitable record to produce; it puts modern Christianity to the blush. No more profitable day can be spent in Bombay, than by visiting, in company with some intelligent Parsi, their educational and benevolent institutions. The cultured young men of the best families are always delighted to undertake so pleasant a duty.

A fitting illustration of the princely generosity of these Parsi merchants may be found in the list of gifts to the public from the wealth of one man, Sir Cowasji Jehangir Readymoney, C.S.I., the descendent of a long line of Parsi Bankers, who deservedly earned the pseudonym of "Readymoney" as much by their scrupulous integrity as by their success in trade. In 1857, he built, at a cost of

66,000 rupees, the noble civil hospital at Surat. In 1863, he erected the Ophthalmic hospital at Byculla, Bombay, spending 97,000 rupees. The beautiful Civil Engineering College at Poona, and the European Strangers' Home at Bombay would never have been called into exist-

A PARSI MERCHANT.

ence but for his munificence, contributing 50,000 rupees to the former, and 72,000 to the latter. The superb University Hall and Elphinstone College were practically founded by Sir Cowasji, who gave 100,000 rupees to the hall, and 200,000 to the college; he also gave 10,000 towards the furnishing of University Hall. In 1868, he called into existence the fine lunatic asylum at Haiderabad, Sind, by a contribution of 50,000 rupees. He has erected drinking fountains throughout Bombay at a cost of 50,000 rupees, some of them, such as the one in front of the cathedral, being very artistic structures.

His charity began at home, but did not stop there. His money flowed out to the Lancashire relief fund, the War Victims' fund of the Franco-Prussian War, Jesuit and Presbyterian schools, famine-stricken districts in remote India, and in a hundred other channels, all over the world. His public benefactions reach a sum of at least 1,300,000 rupees, and his private charities were discovered after his death to have been 400,000, all spent without respect to race or creed. When Sir Cowasji sent £200 to London for charities, as a thank-offering for the recovery of the Prince of Wales, *Punch*, commenting thereon, said: "Is Mr. Readymoney a Parsi? at anyrate he is not *parsimonious*."

One of the leading peculiarities of the Parsi religion is the method pursued for the disposal of the bodies of their dead. No one should pass through Bombay without paying a visit to the Dakhmas, or Towers of Silence. These strange towers, about 90 feet in diameter and 15 feet high, are built in the midst of a beautiful garden on the top of Malabar Hill, looking across the wide ocean towards the setting sun, and surrounded by the villas and bungalows of the wealthy merchants of Bombay.

The garden is approached by a long private road, to which all access is barred, except to Parsis, and those who have received permission from the Secretary of the Parsi Society. This leads to a flight of steps, at the top of which is the house of prayer, where the sacred fire is kept burning with incense and sandal wood, and never allowed to die down. It is not permitted to enter, but from its terrace is obtained on the one side a glorious view of the whole city of Bombay, the harbour beyond, and the magnificent ranges of the Ghats in the distance. On the other side is a lovely garden sloping down to the ocean, glorious in parterres, flowering shrubs and palms, with five low circular structures of solid granite rising solemnly out of the foliage. Ranged round the summit of these towers, crowded closely together, are rows of loathsome vultures, which, black against the sunset sky, dominate the whole scene and seem to crowd out of view all their beautiful surroundings. These birds are still and silent; but when the gate is unlocked for a funeral,

A TOWER OF SILENCE

they begin to stir and show signs of excitement, which increases as the procession winds slowly up the hill, followed by the mourners reciting funeral prayers. After the mourners comes a man leading a white dog, the emblem of faithfulness, followed by a crowd of priests in pure white robes, with relations and friends of the dead man, holding a handkerchief between them, in token of sympathy and fellow feeling. On reaching the House of Prayer, the mourners enter, and chant prayers while the corpse bearers enter the Tower of Silence with the dead body, which they expose naked on the platform which is erected inside, invisible to all outsiders.

A BOMBAY BRAHMAN.

The moment they withdraw, the rows of expectant vultures drop silently down into the tower, and in ten minutes have stripped every particle of flesh off the corpse, reducing it to a bare skeleton before the mourners have finished their prayers. The skeleton remains three or four weeks exposed to the tropical sun, when the bleached bones are reverently placed in a centre well within the tower, where Parsis of high and low degree are left to turn into dust without distinction.

Hindu charities are large and generous, but usually confined to their own people. Their benevolent endowments generally feed the hungry, clothe the naked, or erect and maintain temples. Of late years, however, the more educated Hindu, more or less permeated with Western notions, has established schools and colleges; the University Library owing its foundation to the generous contribution of £20,000 from Mr. Premchand Roychand, who also gave the same sum to Calcutta University for a travelling scholarship.

The most curious and interesting of the Hindu charities is the Hospital for Aged and Infirm Animals, at Pinjrapole, which is a unique institution. Here, in cages and inclosures, are hundreds of decrepit cows, mangy dogs and cats, parrots, pigeons, and other domestic pets, fed and cared for tenderly in their old age. It is open to the public at any time of the day, and should certainly be seen by every traveller.

The population of Bombay city is officially classified thus:—

Europeans . . .	10,451
Eurasians . . .	1,168
Native Christians and Goanese . . .	30,708
Hindus of all castes, and out-castes . .	503,851
Jains	17,218
Muhammadans . .	158,024
Parsis	48,597
Jews	3,321
Negroes	689
Chinese	169
All races and castes .	773,196

A BRAHMAN WOMAN.

These alone would make a motley crowd in the streets of the city; but added to them are numbers of strangers from every part of Asia and India, Arabs from Muscat and Zanzibar, Afghans, Beluchis, Malagasis, Malays, Rajputs, Sikhs, Moormen from Ceylon, Madrasis, Tamils, and a host of others, all wearing distinctive clothing and turbans.

All these mixed nationalities are, of course, seen to best advantage in the native town, which lies right and left of Sheik Abdul Rahman Street, a continuation of Esplanade Market Road, beyond the Crawford Markets. The traveller will find a never-ending amusement and interest in the crowds of gaily dressed Indians swarming in and out of the shops, the quaintly frescoed houses, or the mosques and temples.

Everything is done in the open air. The shops are frontless, and the bargains driven on the parapet in front, while each handicraft is pursued under the eyes of every passer-by. In India everything is hand-wrought, and is therefore a work of art.

At busy times of the day, the narrow cross streets, in which the various trades and crafts group themselves, are blocked with a noisy, good-humoured crowd of men and women, innumerable ox-carts, fakirs, pedlars, beggars, water-carriers, dogs, crows, kites, pigeons, and parrots.

A MUHAMMADAN WOMAN.

The Nul Bazar, between Parel and Duncan Road, is where the natives get most of their food supply, and is always densely crowded in the forenoon. Here also congregate the women who sell the cakes of dried cow dung, the universal fuel of India.

The cloth market, where all the dealers in piece goods congregate, is in Sheik Memon Street, close to the Jama Musjid. Here may be seen fine lofty houses, with carved wooden pillars and balconies, the residences of wealthy Hindu merchants, and temples studded all over with little black and red images of gods and goddesses.

The handloom weavers congregate in the streets and alleys near Babual Tank, on the road to Mazagon.

The workers in brass and copper, a most picturesque trade, are to be found in the copper bazar, opposite the Mombadevy Tank, where are manufactured with deafening clang the endless utensils of the Hindu, such as lotas, dishes, bowls, candlesticks, gods, bells, spoons, and other domestic and sacred objects.

There are more than six thousand goldsmiths, jewellers, and dealers in precious stones scattered all over Bombay. Every Indian has a love of jewellery, and a wealthy Hindu often has £20,000 or £30,000 worth in his safe for the decoration of himself and the ladies of his zenana, while the poor choose this form of investment in preference to any other. It is a common thing to see some woman sweeping the streets or carrying a load of cow dung, with gold and silver bangles, and armlets of considerable value, or wearing a handsome hemi-spherical gold ornament, peculiar to the women of Bombay.

One of the distinctive art manufactures of Bombay is wood carving. Sir Geo. Birdwood says:—

"In Bombay, the wealthy native gentlemen have their reception rooms furnished in European style. It is always the same furniture that is to be seen in these Bombay houses, made of the *shisham* or blackwood trees, and elaborately carved in a style obviously derived from the Dutch. . . . . . The carving is very skilful, but in a style of decoration utterly inapplicable to chairs, couches, and tables, and looks absolutely hideous when 'French polished,' an 'improvement' introduced during the last twenty years to suit European taste. When, however, this wood is used for the reproduction of the inlaid wooden doors of old Hindu temples, the effect is always good. . . . . . I once saw in a Parsi house in Bombay some stately blackwood couches, which had been designed in the Assyrian style from Rawlinson's Ancient Monarchies. The common jackwood furniture of Bombay, rectangular in its forms, and simply fluted and beaded for its ornamentation, is far superior in taste to the blackwood furniture, for which the place is celebrated."

A FUEL SELLER.

If the traveller wishes to take home some specimens of this manufacture, he may buy screens, tea-poys, desks, inkstands, and other small objects of purely native shapes, which are thoroughly artistic work. The process of wood carving, and large stocks of everything produced, may be seen at the East India Art Manufactory at Gowalla Tank, Messrs. John Roberts & Co., Marine Street, or at Mr. Jamsitji Nowrowji's workshops.

Besides this carved furniture, many beautiful articles are produced in the well-known "Bombay inlaid work," which is to be found in every fancy shop in London in the shape of work-boxes, glove-boxes, card-cases, and what not. This pretty trade has dribbled down through Sind and Gujarat from Persia. The inlay is made up of tin wire, sandal-wood, ebony, ivory, sappan-wood, stag-horn, and other materials. Boxes are also produced in sandal-wood, without inlay, chiefly in low relief floriated patterns.

Ivory and tortoiseshell are worked up into ornaments for women, combs, bracelets, elephants, tigers, cows, peacocks, with hunting, social, and mythological subjects, and fans. It is well worth while for the bric-a-brac collectors to hunt the native bazars for specimens, especially of combs and bracelets, some of which are exceedingly fine work.

PARSI WOMEN.

Almost every art manufacture of the Bombay presidency may be purchased in the native quarter, and those who wish to make collections will do well to seek the guidance and counsel of some intelligent native familiar with the bazars and able to speak English, paying him a small commission; he will, of course, get another from the sellers, but it is better to make him feel that he is your broker, not theirs. There are, of course, plenty of art dealers in the English quarter who have large and varied stocks, but most of them ask about 20 per cent. more than the Regent Street shops in London. The Bombay bazar is as good and cheap a market as any in India in which to buy silk and cotton saris, the beautiful gold, silver, or embroidered-bordered garments of the women, and the figured silk saris worn by Parsi ladies, many of which are worth as much as £100, are mostly woven in China for this special demand, and embroidered by themselves. Any Parsi gentleman will inform the traveller where these splendid garments may be purchased.

Anyone interested in municipal institutions should pay a visit to the weekly meeting of the City Council. It consists of 72 members, 16 of whom are nominated by Government, 16 by the justices of the peace resident in Bombay, 2 by the University, 2 by the Chamber of Commerce, and 36 by popular election from the wards in the city. The members are paid 30 rupees for every meeting of the council they attend. Their debates are conducted in English, with great ability and intelligence.

There is an excellent salt-water swimming-bath at Back Bay, near the band-stand, and another on the shore of the Warden Road at Breach Candy. Ladies may use the latter at certain times of the day.

The proper time of the day for making calls in European society in Bombay, and indeed all over India, is from 11 to 1.30, or, in the case of personal friends only, from 4 to 5 o'clock in the evening. Letters of introduction to native gentlemen should be sent by a servant or posted, with addressed cards. The visitors' books of the Governor and his wife lie upon the hall table of Government House, Malabar Point, from 11 A.M. to 1.30. Letters of introduction should be left personally, with cards, and the book signed. Persons who have been presented at Court, or are otherwise possessed of recognised social status, may, without letters of introduction, inscribe their names and addresses in the Governor's book, who usually invites them to any general festivity, such as a garden party or an "at home," if one occurs during their stay in Bombay.

Society "takes the air" after 5 o'clock in the evening, when the esplanade is gay with carriages and riders, their *rendezvous* being the band-stand, when there is music.

Good shooting may be had in the country all round Bombay. There are many districts easily accessible by an ordinary Bunder boat, where nice bags of snipe may be made, and later in the season, in January and February, the large grey quail is abundant over the same ground. In the muddy flats inland from the sea, and in the creeks and shallows of the bay, duck, teal, widgeon, snipe, redshanks, golden plover, and other birds are plentiful enough. The sportsman who wishes to spend much of his time in shooting should engage a regular *shikari*. They are easily obtained for five to ten rupees a week, know all the best and most accessible spots, and will engage boats and boatmen.

THE CAVES OF ELEPHANTA are visited as a matter of course by every stranger who comes to Bombay. Apart from the interest attaching to the caves themselves, it is a most delightful and pleasant excursion, and is usually made the opportunity for some little festivity or picnic. Elephanta is a small green island, six miles distant from the Bunder across the bay. It may be reached by a sailing-boat, if the wind be fair, but it is always uncertain when a sailing-boat will

THE GREAT CAVE AT ELEPHANTA.

get back. Messrs. Thos. Cook & Son keep a nice steam-launch, which may be hired for a reasonable sum, and it is usual for parties in the same hotel who have become friendly to club together and hire it. On certain days of the week it is run early in the morning as an omnibus, and single fares, including breakfast on board, are charged. The best time for private parties is after tiffin. An hour is enough for the passage, an hour and a half to view the caves, with a pleasant sail home in the cool of the evening. The beautiful prospect of Bombay city, standing out against the crimson sunset, may be enhanced by afternoon tea and some of the famous cakes made by Peliti, the Italian confectioner in Meadow Street.

The pretty island opposite to Elephanta is Butcher's Island, where the quarantine hospitals are placed. Elephanta is a hill about 600 feet high, covered with dense jungle, its beaches being mangrove swamps, which may be observed on each side of the slippery concrete blocks on which passengers are landed. The island is sacred to Siva, the destroyer god of the Hindus, and, as is fit, is the home of malaria and poisonous cobras, rock, and carpet snakes. The island swarms with curious insects and brilliant beetles, which are caught, and offered for sale by children at the landing-place. Here also are coolies with chairs fixed on poles, in which, for a few annas, they will carry visitors up the flight of steps which lead to the caves, at the top of which is the quaint bungalow of the keeper, a retired non-commissioned officer, who is a most intelligent guide.

There is no necessity for filling pages with a lengthy description of these interesting Hindu monuments, dating from about the 10th century. The principal temple is 130 feet square, the roof of the cave being sustained by 26 massive fluted pillars, and 16 pilasters. Round the walls are groups of massive figures, from 12 to 20 feet high, carved out of the solid rock. It is a Siva-Linga temple, and the object of its arrangements is to represent Siva in the all-productiveness of Nature.

The authorities have compiled a careful and accurate description of the temples and all their details, copies of which have been pasted on thin boards, one of which is given to each visitor as he enters, enabling him easily and intelligibly to understand the significance of the decorations, and the various groups of gods and goddesses.

The caves have been terribly knocked about by Portuguese iconoclasts, but at their best they must have been greatly inferior to the cave temples at Ellora or Ajanta. If the traveller does not intend to visit either of these greater groups of rock temples, he ought to give a day to those at KENHERI, excavated in one of the high hills of Salsette Island.

It is a somewhat fatiguing excursion. The train at 6.0 a.m. from Victoria Station to Thana arrives at 7.12. The drive to the foot of the hill is about six miles, three or four of which can be done in a bullock gharry, and the rest must be walked, the caves being reached about 10 a.m. It is better, therefore, to go to Thana the night before, sleep at the Travellers' Bungalow, and start for the caves before daybreak, so as to arrive before the heat of the day sets in. The station-master, or the messman of the bungalow will, if written to beforehand, order the bullock-cart. The whole trip may be arranged at Cook's Excursion Offices.

The caves are 109 in number. The largest of these, dating from the 5th century, is a noble temple, 90 feet long, 40 feet broad, with a vaulted nave 40 feet high, resting on 34 pillars, flanked by side aisles. At the upper end is a domed dagoba of solid rock, 19 feet high and 49 feet in circumference. The total length of temple, portico, and area is 142 feet. From this flights of steps lead to a series of Viharas (monasteries), consisting of two rooms each, with an entrance portico, and stone water-cisterns.

The Durbar Cave is about 100 feet long by 40 wide, but only 9 feet high. It is plain and simple in its decoration, merely surrounded by columns, with a stone bench in front.

If any of my readers wish to know more details about these marvellous excavations I must refer them to that excellent book, which will be in their portmanteaux, if they have taken the advice offered in my preface, "Fergusson's History of Indian Architecture."

The Vehar Lake, an artificial reservoir formed to provide Bombay with pure water, may be visited the afternoon of the day set apart for Kenheri. It may be reached by carriage from Thana, after tiffin at the Travellers' Bungalow, returning to Bombay from Bhandup Station, close to the lake, in time for dinner. The lake is very pretty, covering an area of about 1,500 acres. The fine waterworks connected with Vehar cost the city nearly £800,000, and the corporation have sanctioned further expenditure of about as much again. When completed, the water supply of Bombay will be about 100 million gallons daily. They are under the skilful management of Mr. S. Tomlinson, the deputy-engineer, who possesses a very wide knowledge of water engineering, having visited most of the important waterworks of Europe, America, and the Colonies, in a recent tour round the world taken for the purpose. Travellers who take more than a passing interest in such matters will find every courtesy and attention from this gentleman, whose office is in the Municipal Buildings, in Rampart Row.

BASSEIN.—This ancient Portuguese city, now a desolate ruin, is about forty miles from Bombay. The 6.30 train from Colaba Station reaches Bassein Road at 8.47, returning at 6.55, arriving at Bombay at 9.20 P.M. A note beforehand to the Mamlatdar at Bassein, or the station-master at Bassein Road (consult Cook) will secure a conveyance to the ruins, which are some three miles distant.

The first object of interest is the massive double Sea-gate. The walls and ramparts of the Fort are well preserved, and are about thirty feet high. The Cathedral of St. Joseph is roofless, but the walls and tower are still standing. To the left of the Sea-gate is the

THE CATHEDRAL, BASSEIN.

gateway of the Castle, with the date 1606; behind it are some ruined palaces. At the end of the main road leading from the Sea-gate is the church and convent of the Augustines; the next building is the factory, and in the garden of one of the ruined palaces stands all that is left of the church and beautiful cloister of the Misericordia, cheek by jowl with a temple to Siva. None of these buildings have any great architectural interest. The Church of the Jesuits, founded in 1548 by Francis Xavier, has a fine arch still standing with fluted columns. Near the Town Bungalow is the Church of San Antonio, the oldest and largest of all; the arched ceiling of the principal chapel is still in good condition.

There is a melancholy pathos of departed greatness about old Bassein. For more than two centuries it was, after Goa, the chief

European settlement in the East Indies, and during this time it rose to great prosperity and influence; its hidalgos, or nobles, who alone were allowed to live within the walls, were proverbial for their wealth and magnificence, dwelling in stately buildings two stories high, graced with covered balconies and large windows. The Marathas subdued the Portuguese in 1739, after a siege of three months, and from that time Bassein has been the dwelling-place of bats and jackals.

I have heard of delightful moonlight trips to Bassein in steam-launches, up the bay to Thana, and on by the Ghodbandar river to Bassein, a distance of some fifty miles, winding in and out of wooded islands, and by palm groves. I have no doubt that Cook and Son could arrange such a trip, on timely notice, at no very serious cost to a party of a dozen. An interesting trip may be made to the ancient Hindu Temple of Amaranth, leaving Bombay by the 7.30 train for Kalyan Junction, returning the same afternoon.

In this chapter I have only touched the fringe of all the interesting sights of Bombay and its neighbourhood, but I have indicated the principal, and for the rest, are they not written in Maclean's guide?

Missions.—Just four per cent. of the Indian population of Bombay are Christian, and this includes Portuguese and Eurasians. The Church Missionary Society established a station in Bombay in 1820. They have a community of 185 Christians, of whom 64 are communicants, with 533 children in their schools. The Indian Female Normal School Society has two ladies working in co-operation with the C. M. S. They have two girls' schools, with a total attendance of about 220, and a staff of about 24 European and Indian ladies acting under their superintendence as school teachers and Bible women. There are four ordained missionaries: Rev. H. C. Squires, secretary; Rev. J. M. Macdonald, in charge of the church in Girgaum; Rev. J. A. Harris, in charge of the Robert Money School with 280 pupils, mostly Hindus; and the Rev. W. T. S. Tisdall, who specially devotes himself to Musalmans. Mr. Squires lives near the church in Girgaum. English as well as vernacular services are held in the mission church.

The S. P. G. station centres in their handsome church in Kamatipura, where services are held in English, Maratha, and Tamil, by one or other of the four missionaries in charge. There are

334 Christians, old and young, connected with the mission, of whom 179 are communicants. 171 children are in three schools. The Rev. G. Ledgard, who is in charge, resides at the Adelphi Hotel, Clare Road, Byculla. He is a missionary of wide experience, spread over a period of thirty years.

The work of the Free Church of Scotland may be said to date from the close of the year 1829, when Dr. John Wilson first settled in Bombay, after a residence of nearly a year in the Konkan districts, the first seat of the Scottish Mission in Western India. In addition to the work of preaching and publishing in the vernacular, from the outset of his Bombay career, Dr. Wilson directed his attention to the subject of Christian education, and in 1831 he laid the foundation of the educational work which has now grown to be one of extent and importance. With the aid of the ladies' society of the Free Church of Scotland for Female Education in India and Africa, schools for native girls, Christian and heathen, have been maintained for upwards of fifty years. These have, along with similar agencies in other missions, done much to advance the cause of education among the women of India which is so striking a feature of the Indian missions of our time.

The educational work of the mission may be described in connection with the buildings in which it is carried on. The highest development of this branch of the work is the Wilson College, which, since 1861, has been affiliated to the University of Bombay. Until June 1889 the work of the College was carried on in the same building with the school, but was transferred to its new premises on Back Bay in 1889. The new building is near the foot of Malabar Hill on the Back Bay Reclamation. This site was presented to the College by the Government of Bombay, which also gave a grant in aid of the building amounting to nearly half the total cost. When the Principal's residence and the home for students will have been completed, the total cost of the buildings erected on the site will reach the sum of about Rs200,000. The college has a staff of six missionary professors, and the number of undergraduates in attendance is 220. These go through the full university course for the degrees in Arts. Religious instruction is daily imparted to each class during the first college hour. This is the distinguishing feature of the college as a Missionary Institution, and it does not seem to interfere with its academical success, as it stands high among the affiliated colleges, and attracts numbers of the ablest students. In addition to the daily Bible classes, special Sunday classes, attendance at which is optional, are from time to time held in the college. Courses of lectures on religious subjects have also been organised. The college has thus been for many years a centre of Christian influence and effort amongst the educated natives of Bombay.

The High School conducted by the Mission is in the thickly populated district of Khetwadi, close to the Girgaum police court. In this building there are four hundred boys, of all classes and races, who are going through a course of English education, from the lowest to the highest stages. Religious instruction, in the lower classes conducted in the vernacular, and in the higher classes in English, is the work of the first school hour. These classes are taught by the missionaries—one of the ladies taking part, the native pastor and native Christian teachers. Amongst the pupils are Hindus, Parsis, Musalmans, Bom Israel and Christians. The school is now comfortably accommodated in the building which it used to share with the college; it continues to be popular, and the attendance has been growing from year to year. It receives an annual grant from Government, which, together with the fees paid by the pupils, yields a local income of about Rs.10,000. The college is also aided liberally by Government, and has a large income from fees. More than half of the total cost of college and school is thus provided independently of the contributions of the home church.

Immediately opposite the Girgaum police court is the Ambroli native church, in which the native congregation connected with the mission worships. Opposite the church still stands the old Ambroli mission-house in which Dr. Wilson spent the best years of his missionary activity. This is, therefore, the district with which the mission is most closely associated. The native church is under its own Indian pastor, nearly the half of whose salary is provided by the members of the congregation, who meet, also, all the other expenses connected with the maintenance of the church services. Two services are held every Sunday in the church; an English service at 7.30 a.m., conducted by the missionaries, and a Marathi service at 4. p.m., conducted by the native pastor. At 8.30 a.m. a large Sunday school, under the superintendence of the native pastor, assembles in the adjoining building of the Ambroli girls' school; it is a pretty sight.

An interesting work is carried on amongst Musalmans by one of the agents of the mission, himself a convert from Muhammadanism.

In the same compound as Dr. Mackichan's house at Gowalia is the girls' boarding school, in which about forty girls reside. These receive a thorough education in Marathi, and also in English. Some of them are being trained as teachers, and during the past years this school has furnished a number of Christian teachers for the Hindu girls' schools of the mission.

The Hindu girls' schools are the Ambroli school and the Girgaum school. The Ambroli school is situated in the compound of the native church. It has generally an attendance of 180 girls, many of them from the higher castes. The Girgaum school is in a hired house on the Girgaum road. The school has been carried on for a number of years. It contains about 100 pupils, and is, in all respects, similar to the Ambroli school.

Zenana mission work is carried on amongst Marathi and Gujarati speaking families by three ladies of the mission. They have access to a large number of houses, chiefly Hindu, but including also some Parsi families. Some of these Zenana pupils were formerly in the day-schools of the mission, and thus the Christian influence brought to bear upon them in their earlier days is continued after they are married into their own homes.

In connection with the Free Church of Scotland there is also a congregation of European residents which worships in the Free Church, Esplanade. There are services at 11 a.m. and 6 p.m. The manse is in Marine lines.

The American Marathi Mission at Byculla has the following missionaries:—Rev. E. S. Hume, Mrs. E. S. Hume, Rev. J. E. Abbott, Miss Abbott, Miss Lyman, Miss Millard. The church is at Bhendi Bazar, with services (Marathi) on Sunday 9 a.m. and 4 p.m. There is a Christian congregation of about 250, of whom 105 are communicants who support their pastor, besides paying the church sexton, and carrying on mission work at Lalitpur, N. W. P., where there is an organised church and a school. This excellent mission has twelve Sunday schools in the city, attended by about 600 men, women and children. Of these one is held in a chapel, one in a Government school-house, three in private houses, and the rest in rooms belonging to, or hired by the mission. Thirty Christians attached to the congregation teach in these Sabbath schools. There are three Christian Endeavour societies connected with the congregation, containing in the aggregate more than 125 members. One of these, which is for adults only, is responsible for all the evangelistic work done in the city in connection with the mission, which employs no paid preachers. In this way, preaching, Sunday-school work and tract distribution, are managed here by the native church, not by the mission. There is a school for native Christian children. It includes primary, intermediate and high school departments, and is attended by 130 girls and boys in nearly equal proportions.

In connection with this day-school there is a boarding department containing forty-two girls, and a similar one in which are thirty-six boys. There are seven vernacular schools for native children. The aggregate number attending these schools is about 225. Three are for girls only, and one more is for girls and boys. There are two papers published by the mission, one of which is a weekly paper in English and Marathi, and now in its forty-ninth year. The other is an illustrated young people's monthly magazine, in Marathi, of sixteen pages. It is now in its eighteenth year. The work in connection with Bible-women is at present under the charge of Miss Abbott.

The Established Church of Scotland has a mission under the charge of Rev. A. B. Wann, B.D., who lives in the Carnac Road. Mr. W. F. Milvin is the principal of a high school of 220 pupils, in which he has the assistance of twelve non-Christian teachers. This mission was established in 1835. There is a small church of eighteen communicants.

The Salvation Army have their headquarters in Esplanade Market Road. Their work is as yet in its infancy; but their methods are full of interest to the student of Christian missions, and ought not to be passed by without careful attention. They are doing good work among sailors and other Europeans, besides rescue work and prison visitation. They are held in high esteem by many of the leading Parsis and Hindus, who subsidise the army for temperance work among the cotton-mill hands.

CHAPTER II.

SURAT.

SURAT is a large town on the banks of the river Tapti, and is well worth a visit. There is no hotel, but there are bedrooms at the railway refreshment-rooms, and a town bungalow. The city is densely populated, and has often been ravaged by fire; the main thoroughfares are lined with handsome houses, the residences of wealthy Parsis and Brahmans, whose façades, decorated with rich and elaborate wood-carving, are extremely quaint. Surat was founded in 1540, by a Turkish general, in the service of the Gujarat kings, who built the castle and the two walls; it has been a notable military fortress from that time till 1862, when the troops were withdrawn. The city is surrounded by a brick wall, about six miles in circumference, flanked by small bastions, now in a very tumbledown condition. It has twelve gates. There is a smaller inner wall, protecting the castle.

The castle, a place of great historic interest, stands in a commanding position on the bank of the river, about the centre of the city. It is a mass of irregular fortifications, flanked at each corner by round towers, from which fine views of the city, park, and river may be obtained. The castle itself is a very picturesque building; the walls are eight feet thick, covering about an acre, and the main tower is 80 feet high. It is garrisoned by half-a-dozen native soldiers, whose main occupation, when I visited it early one morning in 1889, appeared to be the amusement of sundry offenders imprisoned in a sort of Wombwell's menagerie cage, with a barred front, and whose crime was that of having drunk too much fermented toddy the night before. Near the castle is a pretty garden of eight acres, in which are specimens of the trees and shrubs indigenous to Surat, beyond which, across a small creek, is a brick dam with six sluices, to prevent the Tapti, in the

HOUSE OF CARVED TEAK, SURAT.

rainy season, flooding the town. Within a few yards of this dam are some tolerably well-preserved portions of the old city wall.

From the promenade of the public gardens a good view is obtained of one of the finest railway bridges in India, constructed by 17 spans of lattice girders, carried upon cast-iron columns, which are sunk through 43 feet of sand and mud, the accumulation of ages of rainy seasons; the cost of this bridge was £70,000. From the castle a fine road runs through the station to a lofty clock-tower, 100 feet high, which can be ascended, by eighty-five steep steps, for the view. A little further on is the Town Hall, a handsome quadrangle, built 250 years ago as a travellers' bungalow, when Surat was in its splendour.

The English, Dutch, and Portuguese factories, massive buildings, strong and solid, interesting relics of the last century, are now used as private dwellings. The mosques and temples of the city are quaint and picturesque, but without any special antiquarian or architectural interest.

The hospitals for sick animals are well worth visiting; there are three or four in Surat, and about 1000 head of cattle can be accommodated by them. The sick are physicked, the feeble taken tenderly into the suburbs to graze on green pastures, and the chance calves nursed into maturity and used as servants to the hospital patients. There are cages of deteriorated street dogs—a gruesome sight—fowls with hopeless pip, attenuated sheep and goats, ragged old cage-birds; and at Ovington hospital, even insects are cared for, for in a separate chamber bugs, fleas, and other vermin are fondly cherished.

The most interesting sights of Surat are the old cemeteries, in which lie buried governors, soldiers, and merchants who died in the palmy days of the city. The English cemetery is at the end of a long dirty lane; a wooden doorway opens into an expanse of weeds, long grass, and brushwood, scattered with huge Oriental-looking tombs, and backed by fine trees. Some of the mausoleums are forty or fifty feet high, the quaint inscriptions dating from 1630 to 1820. We are told that a president of the Honourable Company of English Merchants "went unmarried to the heavenly nuptials in the year of Christ 1649," and that Mistress Mary Price, a governor's wife, "through the spotted veil of small-pox, rendered a pure and unspotted soul to God."

The Dutch cemetery is more neglected and wild than the English. There are a good many fruit trees scattered about the ground, the fruit of which is offered for sale by the guardian, who lives in the ruinous little lodge at the gate. The principal monument is that of Baron Van Reede.

Leading out of the Dutch cemetery is the Armenian, a small enclosure with graves at one end; the slabs have epitaphs in Armenian characters, each ornamented with carvings of two cherubs and a candlestick.

At the time when these cemeteries were in use, Surat was a very different place from to-day. Then it was the most thriving city in India, with a population close upon a million, and with the main trade of India centering on its wharves. The trade of the district to-day is a mere ghost of its former magnitude, Bombay having entirely superseded Surat. The exports are now small, being only about £450,000 for the seven ports of Surat district. Grain, cotton, timber, bamboos, cocoa-nuts, and mahua flowers for distilling native spirit, are the main articles of commerce. Surat is said to be the most drunken city in India.

The spinning and weaving of cotton cloth employs the great bulk of the population, and there are some fine mills. Silk brocade and embroidery are also largely manufactured by hand-looms. An afternoon may be pleasantly spent in a ramble through the bazars.

The present population of Surat is 107,000, of whom 74 per cent. are Hindu, 20 per cent. Muhammadan, and 6 per cent. Parsis. There are about 350 Christians in the city.

There are some excellent conjurers and snake-charmers at Surat, and if the traveller finds time hang heavily, he may take the opportunity of sending for some of these wonderful people, and have an exhibition of their powers.

The first Christian Missionaries to occupy Surat were the Capuchin Friars, who in the middle of the 17th century established a monastery near the buildings now occupied by the Irish Presbyterian Mission. The Capuchins exercised considerable influence in Surat from 1660 till 1670, and were able to induce so cruel a tyrant as Sivaji to spare their own lives and those of others who took refuge with them.

A Protestant Mission was first established in Surat in 1812. It was in connection with the Baptist Mission in Bengal, and was conducted by C. C. Aratoon, a Baptist convert. Messrs. Fyvie and Skinner, agents of the London Missionary Society, arrived in Surat in 1815. The present Mission Press, from which millions of Christian books and Scriptures in Gujarati have been issued, was started by Mr. Skinner in 1820, and the whole of the New Testament was printed in it before the end of 1821. This may fairly be considered the first edition of the Scriptures in Gujarati, as the edition in that language printed and published at Serampore in 1820 and handed over to the London Mission at Surat, is not intelligible.

In 1846, the London Mission concentrating their forces in other parts of their extensive field, retired from Surat. Just then the Rev. Robert Montgomery of the Irish Presbyterian Mission, on account of

TRAVELLING SNAKE CHARMERS AND JUGGLERS.

the conversion of a well-known Muhammadan Munshi A. Rahman, was compelled by the Rana to withdraw from Porbandar in Kathiawar; and arrangements having been made for the transference of Surat from the London Mission to the Irish Presbyterian Church, Mr. Montgomery was appointed to Surat, where he remained till his retirement in 1877.

The Irish Presbyterian Mission, except the Salvation Army, which in 1888 and 1889 commenced operations in Gujarat, is the only aggressive organization for the spread of Christianity in Surat. There are English Episcopal and Roman Catholic churches in the city, one for each communion, but for the sole benefit of the Christians attached to these denominations. The Episcopal Protestant Church was consecrated by Bishop Heber in 1827, and a service is held in it in English, every Sunday, if a chaplain is sent from Bombay for the purpose, or a layman can be got to read the prayers. The small Roman Catholic population, chiefly composed of Goanese servants, is under the spiritual care of a Goanese priest.

The Irish Presbyterian Mission Church, which is primarily for the use of the native Christian congregation, but sometimes used for English services when a European congregation can be got together, was built in 1835. There are two Gujarati services, the first at 8 a.m. and the second at 5 p.m., held in it on Sundays. A short service for the benefit of the Christians residing in the immediate neighbourhood, is held in it at 9 a.m. on Mondays, Tuesdays, Thursdays and Saturdays.

The Irish Presbyterian Mission at the present date—December, 1889—has a working staff of the following agents at Surat:—

Missionary, Rev. William Beatty, B.A.; Principal of the English School, Mr. Alfred S. Jervis, assisted by seven Native Christian Agents.

The agencies at work are:—

I. A Mission Press, from which there is a continuous flow of Christian books. It has also a type-founding establishment. Nearly 8,000,000 pages, of which upwards of 5¼ million were of purely religious literature, issued from the Mission Press, Surat, in 1888, and 110,835 books were bound in it.

II. One High School, and one Branch English School, with a staff of twenty-two teachers, and 520 pupils.

III. Five Vernacular Boys' Schools, with a staff of twenty teachers in all. All the boys of the schools in Surat are brought together on Wednesday mornings for examination on religious subjects by the Missionary and Catechists.

IV. An Evangelistic or Preaching Staff, which consists of:—

1. The Missionary.
2. The Catechists and four Bible Teachers.
3. The Colporteur.

V. An Orphanage for Girls, which is under the care of Miss Beatty, the daughter of the Missionary, as a voluntary worker without salary. There are 23 inmates cared for and educated in it. Already 366 girls have enjoyed its fostering care, and many of those who were brought up in it are now in positions of usefulness, and even of trust and affluence.

VI. Sunday Schools. There are five Sunday schools connected with the station, three for Christians and enquirers, and two for purely Hindu children.

VII. There are three lady missionaries in charge of the Zenana department. One of them, Mrs. Philip Jacob, daughter of the Rev. R. Montgomery, who lived so long at this station, works at her own expense, under the direction of the Zenana Mission. The other workers are Miss McKee and Miss Stavely. The former has charge of the Anglo-Vernacular and High School for Girls, the Female Normal Class, and the six vernacular schools and two Sunday schools. Mrs. Jacob has the superintendence of two Bible-women, who are supported by the British and Foreign Bible Society.

The Anglo-Vernacular School for Girls is in a very prosperous state, owing to the unremitting attention and hard work of Miss McKee. The grant-in-aid earned this year nearly trebled the amount gained at the previous examination, and exceeded the amount allowed to be drawn according to Government rule by Rs. 120. It has attained this year the status of a High School.

The Training Class for teachers, also under Miss McKee, consists of twelve girls. They are all qualifying for Mission work as Christian teachers for Vernacular schools or Bible-women. Miss McKee is assisted by a teacher trained in the Ahmedabad Training College.

VIII. Christian community. The total number of baptized persons connected with this mission station at the end of 1888 was 190, and the community numbered 224.

The town of Broach, which is midway between Surat and Baroda, has no attractions to the traveller, except for a few days in November, when the great religious fair is held at Sakaltirth, 10 miles above

Broach, on the banks of the sacred Narbada. At Sakaltirth, on an island, is a very famous banian tree, said to form cover for 10,000 men, which tradition says grew from the toothpick of Kabir.

Broach is a great cotton market, with a population of 40,000. It presents a picturesque appearance from the river, from the edge of which a massive stone wall runs for about a mile, with the town standing on rising ground behind it. It is an ancient place, and was settled in the 1st century by a Hindu sage called Bhragu, whence the name, and quickly became an important trading centre. The English had a factory there in the 17th century. The magnificent bridge over the Narbada has 25 spans of 180 feet. The supporting columns are sunk in the bed of the river to a depth of 125 feet below the level of the road.

The Rev. T. McAulis and seven assistants carry on a vigorous mission in connection with the Irish Presbyterian Church.

CHAPTER III.

BARODA.

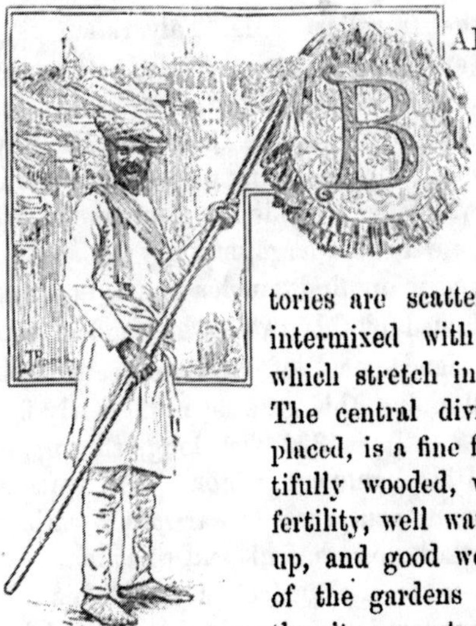

BARODA is a non-tributary independent Native State of the first rank, in direct political relation with the Government of India. Its ruler is called "the Gaekwar," which signifies "a cowherd." His territories are scattered patches of various sizes, intermixed with British Territory, some of which stretch into the peninsula of Kathiawar. The central division, in which the capital is placed, is a fine fertile plain, perfectly flat, beautifully wooded, with rich alluvial soil of great fertility, well watered by streams that never dry up, and good wells and reservoirs. It is one of the gardens of India, and the suburbs of the city are extremely beautiful. The total area of the Gaekwar's territory is 4,400 square miles, with a population of 2,185,000. Of these 90 per cent. are Hindus, 2 per cent. Jains, 8½ per cent. Musalmans. There are about 8,000 Parsis, and less than 200 Christians. (The Parsis are almost all settled at Navasari, a thriving little town on the Bombay and Baroda line, where the sacred fire of this wonderful people has been burning for 500 years. They are mainly engaged in weaving the fine cotton for which the central State of Baroda is famous.) There are two ancient hill forts, Songarh and Saler, within easy reach of Navasari.

Travellers who are studying Indian arts and manufactures will find much to interest them in the State of Baroda. At Vohora

Kathor, a famous deep-red dye is manufactured from the roots of the moringa tree; Sojitia is famous for knives and edge-tools; Daboi, within an easy railway journey of Baroda city, is noted for turbans, saris and other loom work of fine quality; Patan, for a fine quality of pottery, light and strong, very tastefully decorated. Mr. Dinshaw A. Talyarkhan, the municipal commissioner of Baroda city, has a most interesting collection of the arts and manufactures of the whole state, which I had the advantage of studying. He takes much pleasure in assisting English visitors to see the various towns and villages whence these products come, and a letter written to him will secure every facility to the traveller. Mr. Talyarkhan is a cultured Parsi gentleman, who speaks English perfectly, with a very wide knowledge of many important native states.

Daboi is within an easy journey of Baroda by the Gaekwar's Railway. It is an old town surrounded by a quadrangular rampart, two miles in circumference, built of large hewn stones; inside the rampart there is a beautiful colonnade; within the walls is a large masonry tank with a noble flight of steps round it, and many fine temples on the embankment. The ramparts are surrounded by fifty-two towers, and in each face is a double gate. The handsomest of these is called the "Diamond Gate." A temple adjoining this gate is a singularly fine specimen of Hindu architecture. It is 320 feet long, the upper story being supported by rows of elephants cut in stone. All parts of the temple are covered with elaborate sculptures of warriors in various combats, lions, camels, birds, snakes, flowers, fruit and what-not.

Fifteen miles from Bahadarpur is the ancient city and historic fortress of Champaner, situated on an isolated rock of great height. The upper fort is almost impregnable, though it was captured by the Emperor Humayun in 1535, who climbed in with a few chosen followers by iron spikes driven in the face of the rock. The old city, deserted entirely a hundred years ago, is now a jungle, strewn with the ruins of wells, mosques and palaces, ghosts of the vanished splendour of Sultan Mahmud Begara. There is no accommodation there, and it is not healthy, but it makes a pleasant day's excursion on horseback from Bahadarpur, a thriving little place with a good timber trade. Arrangements for the journey should be made beforehand, by writing to the Bahadarpur station-master.

The military force maintained by the Baroda State is five batteries of artillery, a small cavalry force of 120 officers and men, and six

STATE ELEPHANT OF THE GAEKWAR.

regiments of infantry. There is also a large irregular force of about 13,000 men. This army, more ornamental than useful, costs the Gaekwar nearly £400,000 a year.

Luxuriant crops are grown of grain, cotton, tobacco, opium, sugar-cane, and oil-seeds, and Baroda is famous for a breed of white cattle of great size and strength, of which splendid specimens may be seen in the royal stables.

The population of Baroda city is about 110,000, of which 84,000 are Hindus, and 20,000 Musalmans. There is a good Bungalow a mile and a half from the station, and some very indifferent sleeping accommodation in the railway refreshment rooms. The three or four main streets of the city are singularly picturesque, lined with fine houses belonging to merchants, bankers and nobles, many of the façades being finely-carved teak-wood. The rest of the town consists of a labyrinth of mean and overcrowded alleys. Near the water-gate are some interesting aviaries and menageries, and the Filkhana, or elephant stables, where there are some fine specimens of these noble animals. Khande Rao kept up a stud of about a hundred, perhaps the finest in India, but there are less than half that number now.

The college and high school is a fine building with a remarkably handsome central-domed hall, and a large number of students, many of whom graduate at Bombay University.

There are a great many Hindu temples in Baroda, some of which will repay a visit. The most notable are those of Vithal Mandir, Swami Naryan Mandir, and the temple of Khandoba, the tutelary god of the Gaekwars.

The Maharaja is always glad to see European travellers, and there is no difficulty about procuring an interview. He spends most of his time at his country palace, about seven miles from the town. He sees visitors without any ceremony, in his reception room, a large apartment with windows at both ends, handsomely furnished in European fashion, with a few good pictures, by well-known English and French artists, on the walls, a view of Windsor Castle, painted by his order, to commemorate his visit to the Queen, being in the place of honour. He speaks English perfectly.

This fine young prince succeeded to the throne after the deposition of Malhar Rao for attempting to poison Colonel Phayre, the British Resident, with a cup of pomelo juice in which ground diamonds had been mixed. He had previously tried the same trick on his brother

PART OF THE GAEKWAR'S NEW PALACE.

and predecessor, Khande Rao, and was a bad lot all round—an Eastern tyrant of the worst description. After his deposition the widow of Khande Rao was allowed to exercise the right of adoption, and her choice fell upon the present Gaekwar, then a lad of eleven, the descendant of a distant and obscure branch of the family. He had the best tutors possible, and showed himself possessed of rare qualities of mind and earnestness of purpose. Five years ago he was formally installed on the throne, and invested with full sovereign powers. He applied himself with such energy to his new responsibilities that his health soon broke down under the strain, compelling him to spend a year in England and some of the European capitals. His entire administration is Indian. He has surrounded himself with the best advisers he could get, many of whom have been transferred to his service from the British Government. Great reforms have been effected in the management of the State finances. The lavish expenditure of his immediate predecessors has disappeared, and their most vexatious taxes have been abolished. Regular courts of justice, a fine police force, good sanitation, waterworks, markets, hospitals, dispensaries, schools and colleges have taken the place and absorbed the cost of wild beast fights and other barbaric splendours. It is less than twenty years since his predecessor lavished a million rupees on the festivals incident to the marriage of a favourite pigeon to one belonging to the Prime Minister.

The Gaekwar has just completed a superb modern palace, estimated to cost £300,000. It is the most elaborate specimen of Indo-Saracenic style in all India, and its internal decorations are wonderful in detail and variety.

A visit must be paid to the old Nazar Bagh Palace in the heart of the city to see the treasure-room. Huge cheetahs, carefully muzzled, used for hunting bucks, are usually to be seen on the palace steps. The Regalia of Baroda is valued at £3,000,000 sterling. The jewels worn by the Maharaja on state occasions are those shown to strangers. These consist of a gorgeous collar of 500 diamonds, some of them as big as walnuts, arranged in five rows, surrounded by a top and bottom row of emeralds the same size; the pendant is a famous diamond called "The Star of the Deccan." An aigrette to match is worn in the turban. The rest of the jewels consist of strings of pearls of perfect roundness, graduated from the size of a pea to a large marble; wondrous rings, necklaces, clusters of sapphires and rubies as big as grapes; and, greatest marvel of all, a carpet, about ten feet by six, woven entirely of strings of pure and coloured pearls, with great central and corner circles of diamonds. This carpet took three years to make, and cost £200,000. It was one of Khande Rao's mad freaks, and was intended to be sent to Mecca to please a Muhammadan lady who had fascinated him, but the scandal of such a thing being done by a Hindu prince, was too serious, and it never left Baroda. Behind the Nazar Bagh is situated the great walled arena where former Gaekwars held wild beast fights and other shows for the amusement of their court and the populace of the city.

At a little distance from the palace are two guns, weighing 280 pounds each, of solid gold, with two companions of silver, the ammunition waggons, bullock harness, and ramrods being all silver. These were made at the order of Malhar Rao as a piece of extravagance intended to take the shine out of Khande Rao's carpet. I suspect the present Maharaja would like nothing better than to coin them down into good money, and build that Technical School, which it is one of his dearest hopes to possess.

A public park, just outside the city, has been established for the use and pleasure of the people. The river meanders through, and its banks are dotted with pretty summer-houses and pavilions tenanted by lions, tigers, and other interesting beasts. Deer and antelope are tethered on the lawn, while every tree swarms with the beautiful birds that are one of India's greatest charms. Bulbuls, pheasants, mynas, green parrots with a flight as beautiful as the pigeons in their company, hoopoes, shrikes, kites, sun-birds, and peacocks, with many others, forming a vast aviary, rendered doubly attractive by the tame freedom of its inhabitants.

There are some remarkable Baulis in the neighbourhood of Baroda that ought not to be overlooked. They are nearly 500 years old. Some of them are circular wells, with galleried apartments round them, below the surface, while others are surrounded with open pavilions, of Hindu architecture, with pyramidal roofs. They contain excellent water. The finest of these is the Nine Lakh Well, which cost 900,000 rupees.

Baroda is not an easy country to travel through, as there are not more than 80 miles of good road in the whole principality; but the best and most cultivated land is round the capital, and readily accessible.

The total revenue of the State in 1881, was £1,120,000, which is made up of the following items :—

Land revenue, £850,000; customs, £94,000; taxes on castes and trades, £31,000; abkari (liquor and opium), £42,000; forests, £7,000; tributary states, £64,000; justice, £26,000.

The administration consists of the Diwan, or Prime Minister, who exercises supervision over the whole. Under him are four cabinet ministers: (1) political and military; (2) judicial and educational; (3) police, jail, municipality, health, and public works; (4) treasury and mint.

Their salaries are about £1,500 a-year each.

Baroda has the right of coinage, which is hand-made at present; but shortly machinery will be introduced into the Mint. The coins are curious and worth collecting.

The only place of interest between Baroda and Ahmadabad, is Mehmadabad, a town of 8,000 inhabitants. It was built by Mahmud Begara, King of Gujarat, from whom it takes its name, in 1479; the gateways of the old walls, a step-well in the town, the Dhundia reservoir, and two beautiful tombs built by Mahmud in 1484, are worth seeing.

At Anand Junction, a small branch railway leads to Godhra, the little capital of the Panch Mahal country, long famous for the sport afforded by its wild tracts of jungle, and for the excellent fishing in the Mhye River. At Dakor, 20 miles along the line from Anand, is the celebrated temple where the holy image of Krishna, brought from Dwarka, is now enshrined. The idol's throne is a masterpiece of wood-carving, overlaid with silver and gold, presented by the Gaekwar at a cost of £12,000. During the full moons of October and November, from 50 to 100,000 pilgrims repair to the temple at Dakor.

Cambay, 18 miles from Anand Junction, is a seaport town of 35,000 inhabitants. It was mentioned by Marco Polo (A.D. 1300) as a place of great trade, but the harbour has silted up. It is a picturesque city, with a fine old mosque built by Muhammad Shah in 1325 A.D. It is celebrated for the manufacture of agate, carnelian and onyx ornaments, the stones being found in the neighbourhood.

CHAPTER IV.

AHMADABAD.

AHMADABAD is the chief city in the district of the same name, in the province of Gujarat, with an area of nearly 4,000 square miles, and a population of 900,000. The city has a population of 130,000, of which 68 per cent. are Hindus and 22 per cent. Musalmans, the balance being mostly Jains, who are very strong and influential; and a large sprinkling of Parsis.

Ahmadabad is one of the most beautiful and picturesque cities in all India, and no traveller should pass it by. It stands on the left bank of the Sabarmati River, the Fort and its dependencies occupying the whole of the river frontage; the walls, which are bastioned every 50 yards, are in good preservation, stretching east and west about a mile, enclosing an area of about two square miles. The fourteen fine gateways, whose great teak doors are studded with spikes as a defence against battering elephants, are worthy of notice. The river is about 600 yards wide, but during the winter months, the stream is shallow, and not more than 100 yards across. The surrounding country is fertile, well wooded, with good cultivation, rendered additionally interesting by the remains of old suburbs, with their mosques, temples, and Musalman tombs. The walls and fort were built by

Ahmad Shah (1413—43), the second Musalman King of Gujarat, after whom the city is named, but they have been altered and repaired since, till not much of the original fabric is left. Ahmadabad has a great history, and in the height of its prosperity contained a population of nearly a million.

There are three or four nicely furnished bed-rooms at the railway-station, and travellers who don't mind a little noise, will find themselves very comfortable. The Town Bungalow is a well-ordered place, nearer the centre of things. The water supply is bad all through the city, the municipality being at present engaged upon new waterworks of some magnitude. Strangers had better keep to soda-water or tea.

The chief attractions of Ahmadabad, are the superb buildings of ancient Musalman architecture, which, more than in any other city in India, illustrate the results of the contact of Saracenic and Hindu forms. Here, the vigorous aggressiveness of Musalman art, which has all its own way at Agra and Delhi, has been forced to submit itself to the influence of Hindu or Jain architects, the Jain predominating. Even the mosques are, in all their detail and decoration, entirely Hindu.

The mosques of Ahmadabad are among the finest in the East, though the most beautiful are not remarkable for size. It is best to devote a day to the mosques and tombs alone, if the traveller is not pressed for time. The mosques best worth seeing are: the Jama Masjid, the Queen's, the Rani Sipri, Muhafiz Khan's; Sidi Sayyid's, Sayyid Alam's, and Shujat Khan's. There are of course a score of others worthy of the notice of an archæologist, but these are the finest, and contain within themselves illustrations of every architectural detail peculiar to their class.

The Jama Masjid is in the Manik Chauk, in the very centre of the city; the entrance is poor and mean, but opens out into a great quadrangle 382 feet by 258, at one end of which is the mosque, with its 260 pillars and 15 domes, the three central ones being much larger than the rest. The minarets are gone, having fallen during an earthquake some fifty years ago, and have never been rebuilt. This mosque was built by Ahmad Shah, whose splendid tomb is within an enclosure on the east side. It is a building about 36 feet square, paved with parti-coloured marbles. The central sarcophagus is that of the great king himself, the other two being those of his son and grandson; they are of white marble, richly carved with floral designs. A short

THE SABARMATI RIVER, AHMADABAD.

distance off, down a narrow dirty lane, are the tombs of the queens of Ahmad Shah, choked up with mean buildings. They are placed in a rectangular court, with a colonnade running round it. Some of the sarcophagi are finely carved.

The Queen's Mosque is close to the Town Bungalow. There are three domes, each crowning compartments entered by lofty archways. On either side of the centre arch are minarets, which are only carried up as high as the top of the façade. It is not known whether they were ever finished, or if they were, like those of the Jama, destroyed by some earthquake. The mosque is a little over 100 feet long, by 44 feet deep; it is beautifully proportioned, and with the exception of the minarets, is not elaborately sculptured. Near the mosque is a fine mausoleum, the tomb of a princess named Rupavati, about 40 feet square, in excellent preservation, having been recently restored. This tomb is ornamented with the chain and censer, a favourite Hindu device.

The mosque and tomb of Rani Sipri, or Isni, are two of the most exquisitely beautiful buildings in all India; Mr. Sheppard Dale's illustrations will give a better idea of the charming and infinite detail of their architecture than pages of description. They are small buildings, the mosque being 54 feet long by 19 feet wide, and the tomb 36 feet square. Rani Sipri was a daughter-in-law of Ahmad Shah, and her mosque and mausoleum were built by herself and completed in the year 1431. Both are in red sandstone, and the mosque windows are perfect specimens of fine carving, one of which is drawn on page 54; their designs are various, and will repay the most careful study. There are six double pillars in front of the mosque, and six single ones behind, all of which are about ten feet high. The two minarets are about fifty feet high, with four stories tapering up to the top. The whole building, from the base of the pillars to the topmost stone of the minaret, is one continuous triumph of the sculptor's art. The tomb contains two sarcophagi, and its windows are beautiful pierced work.

The mosque of Muháfiz Khan is about 300 yards walk from the Town Bungalow. It was built in 1465 by a governor of the city whose name it bears. It is in almost perfect preservation, and is a beautiful little building, 51 feet by 36, with two minarets 50 feet high. Its details are nearly equal in merit to those of Rani Sipri, which they closely resemble.

THE JAMA MASJID, AHMADABAD.

Sidi Sayyid's Mosque is situated within the walls of the fort; it is now desecrated, and is an office connected with the local administra-

A CORNER OF RANI SIPRI'S MOSQUE.

tion. The interior is without interest, but on going round to the back of the building, five arched windows are seen; one of these has been destroyed, but the remaining four form the finest examples of pierced marble lattice-work in existence, and are alone worth coming

RANI SIPRI'S TOMB.

to Ahmadabad to see. These windows will be familiar to all who have visited the Indian Museum at South Kensington, where there are good copies of the two best. I give an illustration of one, which

WINDOW IN SIDI SAYYID'S MOSQUE.

is a conventional treatment of a tree. Another window is a design of palms, and the others are panelled in various patterns. The greatest possible skill is displayed both in the artistic treatment of the designs, and in the perfection of the carving itself. Beautiful as are the windows of the Taj Mahal at Agra, they are distinctly inferior in both design and workmanship to those of Sidi Sayyid's Mosque at Ahmadabad.

Shah Alam's Mosque is reached by a drive of about half-an-hour beyond the city walls; it was built about 1420, and with its adjacent tombs forms a very fine and richly decorated group of buildings. On the west side of a great court is the mosque, with handsome minarets nearly 100 feet high, the stories being surrounded by galleries supported with brackets. The tomb is one of the most notable in Gujarat, and in its pristine splendour was adorned with gold and precious stones, the beautiful hammered and perforated brass gates fully illustrating the ancient skill of the natives of Gujarat in metal-work. The drive may be continued a mile or two further, to Butwa, to see the mosque and tomb of Kutb-ul-Alam, returning by way of the enchanting Kankariya Tank.

These are but a few of the many beautiful and interesting mosques with which Ahmadabad abounds. Those who wish to thoroughly master their details should study Chapter V. of the "Indian Saracenic

STREET SCENE, AHMADABAD.

Architecture" section of *Fergusson's* volume, or the more expanded criticism contained in "Architecture of Ahmadabad," by Messrs. Hope and Fergusson. The general character of all of them is alike: a mosque proper, with minarets, containing spaces for worshippers, and a mimbar from which the Koran is read. This is placed at one end of a colonnaded courtyard, in the centre of which is a large tank for ablutions. Leading out of this yard is the Rozah, a garden or open space, in the centre of which is the mausoleum covering the tombs of the founder of the mosque and his family. These Rozahs should never be passed by, as they all contain beautiful little buildings, generally of marble, with exquisite pierced windows and sculptured columns. These are grouped in picturesque confusion round the larger mausoleum of the founder, and are tombs of his family, his favourite ministers, or some holy man who was his spiritual adviser and guide. The Rozah of Shah Alam's Mosque is the most charming of them all, every nook and corner presenting a picture of sculptured column and lace-like screen or window that would make Alma Tadema's mouth water. In the flush of Ahmadabad's glory, towards the end of the 16th century, there were not less than a thousand mosques, tombs and cenotaphs in city and suburbs, all surrounded by carefully kept gardens. They are beautiful enough in their ruin and decay to give some idea of what they must have been when those who built them, or whose fathers were buried in them, loved and tended them.

The Hindu temples of the city are hardly worth notice, but a visit should be made to the magnificent shrine of Hathi Sing, a rich Jain merchant, who built it, some thirty years ago, with the adjacent mansion and rest-house for pilgrims, at a cost of £100,000. This temple is just outside the Delhi Gate, and is dedicated to Dharmanath, one of the Jain Tirthankars, whose image crowned with diamonds is in the inner temple.

The temple stands in a quadrangle of about 50 pagoda domes, and is 150 feet long by 100 wide; there is a fine corridor surrounding the inner courtyard. All round the corridor are rooms, or chapels, in which are placed figures of the Jain Tirthankars, or saints, of whom Dharmanath stands in the front rank.

The whole building is a mass of elaborate carving, tesselated marble pavements, and richly coloured decorations, and is probably the noblest modern sacred building in all India.

In and round Ahmadabad are several Baulis, or wells, round which, deep down beneath the surface of the soil, are pillared galleries of great extent and beauty, built as cool refuges from the fierce heat of summer. The finest of these is that known as Dada Hari's, at the end of a sandy line just outside the Daryapur Gate. Steps lead down from portico to portico, all as elaborately carved as the Mosque and

Rozah above, until at last a circular well, surrounded by pillars, is reached, 30 feet below the surface; the length of the whole series is more than 150 feet. There is an older well, about 100 yards further, called *Mata Bhawani*, in the final portico of which is a small temple to Bhawani. These wells are very curious and interesting, and should not be left unvisited.

The *Tin Darwaza*, or Triple Gateway, is a richly carved building crossing the main street, built by Ahmad I.; it appears in the initial illustration of this chapter. Opposite the middle arch is an ancient fountain called the Karanj.

The large Pinjrapol, or Hospital for Sick Animals, is an inclosure of about 3 acres, surrounded by sheds and cages, in which about 1,000 aged and diseased domestic animals have their declining years made easy. To such a degree is this care for animal life carried, that a room is reserved for the vermin which trouble the bodies of the ultra-Faithful, who will not even kill an attacking flea, which, when captured, is reverently conveyed to Pinjrapol. These interesting prisoners are fed on the bodies of men poor enough, for a small consideration, to pass the night on a bed in their private apartment.

A few yards from the entrance to Pinjrapol are some curious old tombs, more ancient than any other building in the city, called the Nau Gaz Piri (the nine yard saints). They are nine in number, and about 18 feet long.

The Bhadr, or citadel, is in the centre of the town. Azim Khan's palace is the only important building within its area, except Sidi Sayyid's mosque, already described. The palace, which was built in 1636 by the viceroy whose name it bears, was originally a serai, or hotel, for the use of country nobles. In the Peshwa's time it was used as an arsenal, and is now the city jail. There is an imposing tower, about 60 feet high. Behind the jail, and across the compound, is the handsome residence and offices of the collector.

No one should quit Ahmadabad without driving out to the ruined and deserted city of Sarkhej. This beautiful place was one of those splendid freaks of extravagance which makes it possible to believe any of the wildest stories of the "Arabian Nights." In the middle of the 15th century, Sultan Mahmud Begara thought he would like a country villa. He proceeded to dig out a large lake of 18 acres in extent, with 30 feet of water in it. This he surrounded with splendid flights of steps, above which rise a succession of palaces and pavilions. Here is the resplendent tomb of a favourite vizier, that would cost £50,000 to reproduce; here also he buried his queen in like magnificence, and provided a similar mausoleum for himself when his time came. Behind this rozah, in a cloistered square of over an acre, he built a mosque, only second in pretensions to the famous Moti Masjid at Agra. All this ruined grandeur now stands solitary and forgotten, the home of storks, crows, parrots, monkeys, jackals, and alligators, with trees and brushwood choking its stately courtyards, visited only two or three times in the year by some tourist who has the good sense to give more than twenty-four hours to Ahmadabad, as he scrambles on for Delhi and Agra.

The drive to Sarkhej is across the Sabarmati River, fordable for carriages throughout the winter. Hundreds of gaily-dressed men and women are washing themselves or their clothing, or baling water into great earthenware pots on bullock-carts; in those picturesque groups which can only be seen in this land of supple grace and flowing garments (see pages 51 and 65). Then for six miles along a sandy, dusty road, through fields and past ancient tombs. The massive brick tomb, about two miles from Ahmadabad, is that of Azam, the Persian architect of Sarkhej. The mosque and rozah of Sarkhej are entered by a raised terrace and covered gateway. The first building on the left, is the tomb of Mahmud Begara and his two sons. Beyond is a delightful portico, leading to a terrace and steps, overlooking the tank. Passing a pretty well and fountain, a covered pavilion, also overlooking the tank, leads into the tomb of Bibi Rajbaie, Mahmud's queen. Across the courtyard is a noble pavilion, raised on a stepped platform, the richly-decorated roof crowned with domes, and supported by sixteen pillars. Opposite this is the gorgeous tomb of Gunj Baksh, begun by Mahmud Shah in 1445 and completed by Begara in 1451. Gunj Baksh was the vizier and spiritual guide of Sultan Ahmad, who retired to Sarkhej at the death of his great master, living himself to the venerable age of 111 years. The whole structure is about 150 feet by 165; it is crowned by a great central cupola, surrounded by fifty-two smaller ones. The shrine is octagonal, surrounded by finely-worked lattice windows of brass, the floor being coloured marbles, and the roof heavily gilt. A small door leads from the yard of the tomb to that of the mosque, perhaps the loveliest of

SARKHEJ.

all the Ahmadabad group. On leaving the mosque the carriage may be sent to the other end of the tank, and joined after visiting the supply-sluice of the tank, which, like all other tank supply-sluices, is beautifully decorated, and a stroll through the deserted palaces and pavilions along the margin.

The art manufactures of Ahmadabad are famous all over India. An old proverb of the place says, "Ahmadabad hangs on three threads—gold, silk, and cotton," and the proverb still holds good, as these three threads still support a large portion of the population. The trades of Ahmadabad, like those of most other large Indian cities, are vested in guilds, composed of all the freemen of the trade caste, governed by two hereditary *seths*, or chiefs of the guild, and some elected colleagues called *mahajans*. Membership is also hereditary; but outsiders may be admitted, on proof of capacity, by payment of an entrance fee, varying from £2 to £50. Every boy born into one of these trade castes learns his father's handicraft as a matter of course, entering the guild as a full member when he has mastered it. The *Nagar-seth*, or city lord of Ahmadabad, is the titular head of all the guilds, and is the highest personage in the city. The smallest infringement of the rigid rules of these guilds is punished by heavy fines, which form their chief source of income. Under this ancient system the beautiful art manufactures of India, which for centuries have been encouraged by the great native chiefs, and sought for by European wealth, were founded and fostered.

Ahmadabad has always been famous for its brass and copper work. The lovely gates and screens of Shah Alam's tomb give evidence of the power of its brass-workers nearly 500 years ago. The braziers of to-day still produce graceful and delicately-cut brass screens, beautiful boxes covered with intricate tracery, rings, lamps, chains, idols, jewel-caskets, and inkstands, besides a great variety of domestic utensils, some of which are even more perfect, as works of art, than the purely ornamental.

The leather-workers are a large community; they make boots and shoes, slippers and saddlery, handsomely-painted leather shields, which look well on the wall of an English hall, and finely-embroidered leather mats.

The jewellers are numerous, their special work being the chopped-gold form of jewellery worn throughout India, the art of which is carried to the highest perfection at Ahmadabad, and which is in great request among the people of Gujarat. "It is made of chopped pieces, like jujubes, of the purest gold, flat, or in cubes, or by the removal of the angles made octahedrous, strung on red silk. It is the finest archaic jewellery in India. The nail-head earrings are identical with those represented on Assyrian sculptures. It is generally in solid gold, for people in India hoard their money in the shape of jewellery, but it is also made hollow to perfection at Surat, the pieces being filled with lac."—*Birdwood.*

The exquisite stone carving, which decorates alike the ancient mosques and Hathi Sing's new temple, finds its match in the craft of wood-carvers. The city is full of specimens of this beautiful art, on the door-frames, balconies, windows, and wooden pillars of the houses in every bazar and side street; some of the mansions of the richer merchants are more picturesque than any in Nuremburg, being one mass of carving, figures, animals, trees, and flowers, from roadway to roof, often gaily painted.

There is also a considerable trade carried on in the Blackwood furniture and other decorative objects, already referred to at page 21. Lacquered wooden bracelets, toys, and other turnery are also largely produced at Ahmadabad.

In spite of the rapid growth of cotton mills in India, the hand-weaving of cotton cloth still thrives in the city. Large quantities of English yarns are used, and worked up into *saris, dhotis* or loin-cloths, *chalotas* or waist-cloths, and quilts, which find their way to every village bazar in the Bombay Presidency. Calico printing is also a craft of some consequence, and its products are very well worth the attention of the connoisseur in such art fabrics. At one time cotton hand-weaving was the most important industry of Ahmadabad, but it appears doomed to eventual extinction by the mechanical productions of Manchester and Bombay. A strong effort, however, is being made by the wealthier merchants, led by Mr. Ranchorelal Chotalal, C.I.E., to secure its permanence in Ahmadabad, even though it must be transferred from hand to machine. There are now four or five factories at work in the city, representing a capital of between £300,000 and £400,000, employing about 3,000 hands at good wages.

While the cotton "thread" of the proverb still holds, the "gold thread" is stronger than ever, for the drawing of gold and silver wire and thread, the making of gold and silver lace therefrom, with foils and tinsel, is one of the most thriving industries of the bazars. Nothing is prettier than the drawing out by hand of gold and silver wire. You may give a rupee to one of these clever craftsmen, and he will presently return it to you a coil of 800 yards of silver wire. The lace which is made from these fine gold and silver threads, and the thin foils and spangles, are used for trimming shoes and caps, for the edging of *saris* and jackets, turbans and petticoats, for stamping muslins and chintzes, embroidering shawls and other woollen fabrics, the manufacture of gold and silver cloths of state, and especially for the manufacture of the *kincobs* or brocades for which Ahmadabad and Benares are so famous.

"Silk thread" successfully defies machinery, and is as flourishing as of old. All the processes of silk manufacture are carried on in this city. The raw silk comes from different parts of India, from China, Persia, and even Bokhara, the yearly import being about 200,000 pounds, valued at £150,000. It is reeled, sorted, spun, warped, dyed, dressed, woven and brocaded. The most beautiful silk fabrics in the world are made here.

Kincobs are highly ornamented gold and silver-wrought silk brocades, some of which are literally stiff with the precious metals. Those produced at Ahmadabad are more highly prized than any other. Sir George Birdwood maintains that the *kincobs* of India were worn by Ulysses, Helen of Troy, Solomon, Queen Esther, and Herod. These beautiful fabrics are of course costly, but small pieces are manufactured, suitable for cushion-covers or table-mats, which may be purchased as specimens. A "piece" of *kincob* large enough for a robe costs anything from £40 to £1,000. Some lovely tablecloths can be had, in white, black, or cream-coloured silk, with *kincob* borders, from £3 to £10 each. To weave these brocades, or *kincobs*, a more complicated loom is necessary than for ordinary silk weaving. A kind of inverted heddles, called the *naksh* (design), are hung above the warp immediately behind the heddles, the other end of the cords being fastened to a horizontal band running below the warp. Like the cords of a heddle, the *naksh* strings when they cross the warp have loops, through which certain of the warp threads are passed. But instead of getting an up-and-down motion from treddles pressed by the weaver's foot, the *naksh* is worked from above by a child seated on a bench over his father's head. The little fellow holds a bar of wood, and by giving it a twist, draws up the cords attached to the threads of the warp, which, according to the *naksh*, or pattern, are at any time to appear in the surface of the web. The weaver at the head of the loom adds variety to his design by working silks of divers colours into the woof, along with threads of silver and gold; and thus the vision grows in the sight of the young child seated aloft.

The spread amongst wealthy natives of the European fashion of plain dressing, is seriously affecting the piece trade in Kincobs, which are now only worn as State robes. A pure "cloth of gold" is also

WATER-CARTS IN THE SABARMATI RIVER.

made at Ahmadabad, called "Soneri," and of silver, called "Ruperi." Silk muslins and nets are made here, which are also brocaded, or stamped with gold leaf, and of course, an infinite variety of dyed silk piece goods, turbans, and cummerbunds.

The common pottery of Ahmadabad is very artistic and decorative, superior to most other earthenware manufactures of India; the natural colour of the clay is brightened with ochres and mica; no glaze is used, but the surface of the pottery is polished by bamboo sticks and agates. The potter's wheel is primitive, being a horizontal fly-wheel, two or three feet wide, loaded round the rim to make it spin truly and steadily. The great jars, four or five feet high, ranged round the potter's shop, are used by the natives for storing their grain or pulse, or for bringing water from the river. The rest of his products are water-pots, bottles, tiles, bricks, idols, and toys. The consumption of pottery is enormous in India, as cups and basins are seldom drunk out of twice, and never by two persons. The native liquor shop, where *mowra* and other spirit is retailed, may be easily found by the *débris* of broken potsherds scattered about the pavement.

Ahmadabad is a great paper-making place, though the manufacture is suffering sadly from foreign competition. Its trade in hand-made paper is mainly with native states, and native merchants whose methods of business require a good tough article. It is made principally from jute rags. The paper-makers here turn out large quantities of those mock ornaments for idols which are so common in every Hindu temple. They are cut out of thick paper, in various shapes, and stuck over with bits of many-coloured tinfoil, peacock's feathers, &c. The great occasion for the use of these ornaments is the birthday of Krishna. A rich Hindu will often spend two or three hundred rupees in decking a single image of his god with this paper rubbish.

All these great staple trades, combined with the endless variety of the ordinary handicrafts of the country, carried on in houses and shops that are themselves marvels of glyptic art, place the bazars of Ahmadabad among the most delightful and amusing in India.

The cantonments of Ahmadabad are about two miles out of the city, at the end of a well-made road, lined with fine trees. Very few troops are stationed here, being only a half battery of artillery, a company of European infantry, and a battalion of Native infantry.

Of the modern buildings in Ahmadabad, one that will attract the notice of a visitor is the large English High School built by the Irish Presbyterian Mission in 1874, at a cost exceeding 30,000 rupees. It stands facing the Oliphant Road, and almost touching the Government Training College for Teachers. The Mission school has at present an attendance of about 200 boys, whom it prepares for the entrance examination of the Bombay University. Scripture instruction forms a part of the daily lessons in each class. The same mission has in the city three Vernacular Schools for boys, and two for girls, with a very large attendance of scholars. A Mission Dispensary for women and children was opened in 1886, and has been from the first under the charge of a fully-qualified lady doctor. Divine service in Gujarati is conducted in the hall of the Mission High School every Sunday morning and afternoon, and daily prayers are held in the same building each evening.

One of the chief features of the mission work at the Ahmadabad station is the Christian colony established in 1860 at the village of Ranipur, about four miles from the city. There some 300 native Christians live together, supporting themselves solely by farming, their land being rented by themselves direct from the Government. This village has its church, built from subscriptions raised entirely in India, and largely from the native Christian community; its school for boys and girls, its mission bungalow, and its resident native evangelist. The colony would seem to have thriven, for it can show many fairly comfortable houses; its buffaloes and bullocks are fat and strong; both well and tank supply the village with water for man and beast, and its irrigated fields are tilled by English ploughs. In connection with the different mission stations in Gujarat of the Irish Presbyterian Church, no less than four other similar Christian colonies have been founded—Wallacepur, Bhalaj, Brookhill, and Carrypur—each one of which forms a distinct nucleus for manifold Christian agencies, while at the same time attaining a prosperity beyond the average of most villages in the district.

A little to the north-east of the Queen's Mosque at Mirzapur is the Episcopal church, at which divine service in English is held every Sunday. This building can seat 140 persons, and was erected in 1848 at a cost of 12,000 rupees. The chaplain resides in the cantonment, three miles distant, where very recently a second and larger English church has been built.

A few yards south-east of the same mosque stands the Roman Catholic church. The resident priest occupies a building in the same compound, and a small English school is conducted on the premises.

In the neighbourhood of the railway station the Salvation Army has its headquarters for Gujarat, a district where this organisation is exceptionally busy.

In 1573 Ahmadabad was, with the rest of Gujarat, subjugated by Akbar. During the 16th and 17th centuries Ahmadabad was one of the most splendid cities of Western India. There were, according to Ferishta, 360 different wards, each surrounded by a wall. The decay

F 2

of the Mughal Empire, and the rise of the Maratha power, led to disastrous changes. Early in the 18th century the authority of the Court of Delhi in Gujarat had become merely nominal, and various leaders, Musalman and Maratha, contended for the possession of Ahmadabad. In the year 1738 the city fell into the hands of two of these combatants, Damaji Gaekwar and Momin Khan, who, though of different creeds, had united their armies for the promotion of their personal interests, and now exercised an equal share of authority, and divided the revenues between them. The Maratha chief, Damaji Gaekwar, having subsequently been imprisoned by the Peshwa, the agent of his Mughal partner took advantage of his absence to usurp the whole power of the city, but permitted Damaji's collector to realize his master's pecuniary claims. Damaji, on obtaining his liberty, united his forces with those of Ragunath Rao, who was engaged in an expedition for establishing the Peshwa's claims in Gujarat. In the troubles that followed, combined Maratha armies gained possession of Ahmadabad in 1753. The city was subsequently recaptured by Momin Khan in 1755-56, and finally acquired by the Marathas in 1757. In 1780 it was stormed and captured by a British force under General Goddard. The British, however, did not then retain it. The place was restored to the Marathas, with whom it remained till 1818, when, on the overthrow of the Peshwa's power, it reverted to the British Government.

In the days of its prosperity the city is said to have contained a population of about 900,000 souls; and so great was its wealth, that some of the traders and merchants were believed to have fortunes of not less than one million sterling. During the disorders of the latter part of the 18th century Ahmadabad suffered severely, and in 1818, when it came under British rule, was greatly depopulated and became a melancholy wreck.

KATHIAWAR.—The traveller with ample time on his hands may find it worth while to spend a few days in seeing this very interesting peninsula, which has within the last year or two been opened up by railway. Kathiawar is a political agency under the government of Bombay, having under its control the 187 separate states, which make a map of the district more like a tesselated pavement than anything else. Of these, 13 pay no tribute, 97 pay tribute to the British Government, 78 to the Gaekwar of Baroda, 134 also paying tribute to the Nawab of Junagarh. These states are divided into seven classes.

Chiefs of the 1st and 2nd classes exercise plenary jurisdiction; the judicial powers of the remaining classes are graded in a diminishing scale, the residuary jurisdiction being vested in British political officers, the Political Agent superintending the whole, as may be expected. Society is not too well ordered in this district, and there are bands of outlaws and dacoits who give the government a great deal of trouble. The Nawab of Bhavnagar has done very much to improve his principality by the inauguration of municipal institutions and other reforms, and the State of Porbander, which formerly gave much cause for anxiety, has been brought into a condition of much prosperity by Mr. F. S. Lely, one of the ablest civil servants in the Bombay Presidency.

BHIL WOMEN OF KATHIAWAR.

The towns of importance opened up by the railway are Bhavnagar, Junagarh, and Somnath. The train leaving Ahmadabad at 8 A.M. reaches Bhavnagar at 5 P.M., and Junagarh at 9.30 P.M. the same day. Verawal, the station for Somnath, is about four hours journey from Junagarh. These remote and primitive cities have much to interest the traveller. The town bungalows of all the leading towns in Kathiawar are clean and well built. Bhavnagar is one of the largest states, with a population of 400,000, mainly Hindus. The capital is a great centre for the cotton trade, and exports to Bombay about £1,500,000 worth of raw cotton yearly. It has a good safe harbour. There are no buildings of importance, and it is hardly worth a visit from the ordinary tourist. The politician, if well introduced to the Maharaja, would find much interest in the various improvements of recent years

—waterworks, a college and high school, an hospital and dispensary. He has also built a lovely pavilion of white marble on the pearl lake to the memory of his wife. His country was dry-nursed for him during a long minority by British administrators, and the Thakur, being an enlightened young prince, has raised upon the foundation thus laid a model native state.

Junagarh is the capital of the state of the same name, next in importance to Bhavnagar. It is one of the most picturesque cities in India, surrounded by high hills, and full of historical and antiquarian interest. The tombs of the Nawabs, new buildings of the present century, are, of their kind, very beautiful. The Lip-arkot or citadel is a very old building, parts of it dating back to the time of Asoka, B.C. 270. The walls of this ancient fortress are 60 or 70 feet high, with three massive gateways. The citadel contains some interesting Buddhist caves, and the moat, which is cut out of the solid rock, is honeycombed with curious caves; a Hindu temple converted into a mosque, a very ancient underground Hindu temple, some fine tombs, old cannons, and deep wells, the bottoms of which are reached by long flights of steps.

Near Junagarh is the sacred mountain of Girnar, 3,700 feet high, on the road to which is the finest of Asoka's stone columns, carefully preserved under a shed. Girnar is one of the holy places of Jainism. A rock at the foot of the mountain is covered with a set of Asoka's inscriptions, and there are other inscriptions 200 or 300 years older still. The temples of Girnar are clustered on a ledge 600 feet from the summit, and were probably erected in the 10th, 11th and 12th centuries. A full description of these will be found in Fergusson's "History of Indian Architecture," page 228. The view from the summit of Girnar is superb.

Somnath is an ancient city, whose grandeur is lost in the obscurity of history, and only suggested by the vast area of ruined temples, mosques, and tombs which surround it. Between the railway terminus at Verawal and Somnath is a very large temple and tank, sacred to Sri Krishna, who died here. There is a large Gujarat fortress, entrenched with a rock-cut moat. The Junagarh gate is triple, of Hindu architecture, and probably dating from the 7th or 8th century. The bazar is narrow, full of quaintly-carved old houses. The old temple, from which the famous "gates of Somnath," now in the fort at Agra, were taken by Mahmud of Ghazni in 1026 A.D., had a fabulous reputation in old times for its wealth and splendour: though now almost a ruin, it furnishes enough to show that it must have been a place of great magnitude and importance.

The town of Verawal is a flourishing seaport and commercial centre, from which Somnath is distant two or three miles. There is probably a town bungalow of some sort at Verawal, but as the train leaves Junagarh at 8 A.M., arriving at Verawal about noon, returning at 2.30 the same day, it will be better to persuade the Junagarh station-master to allow a 1st class compartment to remain at Verawal over-night till next day, sleeping in it, and taking cooked provisions. This will give thirteen or fourteen hours of daylight available for visiting Somnath.

Fifteen miles from Songad station are the marvellous Jain temples of Palitana, of which a full description will be found in Fergusson's "Indian Architecture," p. 226. These temples and shrines are scattered by hundreds over the summits of the two peaks, about 2,000 feet high, of Satrunjaya Hill, the holiest of all the fine Jain sacred mountains, viz., Satrunjaya, Girnar, Abu, Parasnath, and Gwalior. Conveyance from Songad to Palitana may be obtained by writing to the deputy political agent at Songad.

At Siddhpur, sixty-four miles north of Ahmadabad, are the gigantic fragments of a famous Shiva temple of great holiness, to which many thousands of Hindu pilgrims resort. Palanpur is the capital of a small native State, with nothing of great interest about it.

TWO MINARS, AHMADABAD.

CHAPTER V.

ABU.

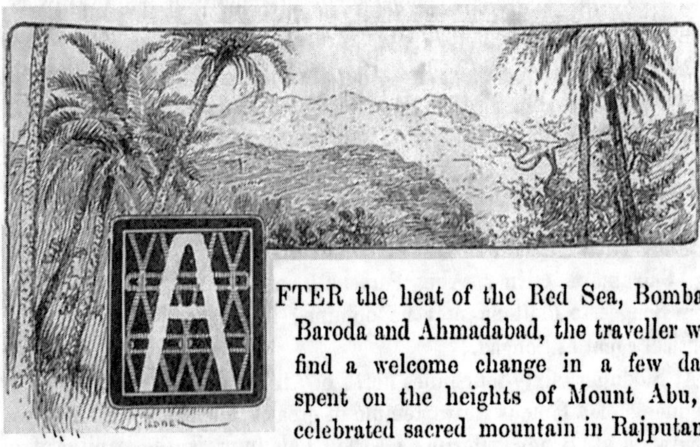

AFTER the heat of the Red Sea, Bombay, Baroda and Ahmadabad, the traveller will find a welcome change in a few days spent on the heights of Mount Abu, a celebrated sacred mountain in Rajputana.

The journey from Ahmadabad had better be taken at night, reaching Abu Road about 7 A.M. There is a refreshment-room at the station; but it is best to write the day before to the messman at the travellers' bungalow, which is about half a mile from the station on the way to the mountain, ordering a breakfast to be ready on arrival. A small party can have sleeping accommodation here if required. The distance from the station to Abu is sixteen miles, which can be done in about four hours on ponies, or in six hours on Jhampans, chairs carried by coolies. These conveyances, whichever may be preferred, should be ordered a day or two previously. A line to the station-master will suffice. The road is bad, and winds along the edge of precipices. It is hardly safe to travel by night on ponies, and the journey should be taken by daylight, both for this reason, and that the exquisite scenery may not be missed.

There is a good hotel at Abu, but rather small, and a travellers' bungalow of two rooms. During the cold season accommodation is always to be had, but it is better to write beforehand.

Mount Abu is a striking object in the landscape for about thirty miles of the Rajputana Railway. It stands out of the great plain, a huge island of granite, finely wooded to the summit, which is an undulating plateau, the topmost point being 5,650 feet above the sea. In

A JHAMPAN, MOUNT ABU.

the midst of this plateau, cut up by granite rocks of fantastic shapes, is Abu, a picturesque village on the margin of a pretty lake, dotted with green islands, whose banks are bright with bungalow and garden. Here is the summer residence of the British agent for Rajputana, an English church, a military sanitarium, the Lawrence school, the hotel, and many private bungalows. The lake is surrounded by a path, from different points of which pleasant views are obtained. The air is rare and refreshing, and the temperature at night quite cold. Good sport may be had in the dense jungles, which clothe the flanks of Mount Abu, and the native Bhils are famous hunters. Bears may be shot, and by good chance a panther or tiger may be found, but they have to be looked for.

The great sights of Mount Abu are the famous Jain temples, the finest in India, and these alone, without the scenery, fully repay the journey. These temples, called the Delwara, are about a mile from the hotel, and an order to view them must be obtained from the

THE DELWARA TEMPLES.

resident magistrate. Ask the hotel-keeper to get them when writing for rooms. They date from the 11th century, and are in perfect preservation. They are built entirely of white marble, and, as no quarries of that material exist nearer than 300 miles, the labour in transporting it across the plains, and dragging it up to the top of this steep mountain, must have been an undertaking worthy of ancient Egypt.

The older of the two was built A.D. 1032 by a merchant named Vimala Sah, and is simpler and bolder than the other, which was built by two brothers, Tejpala and Vastupala, about A.D. 1200. These brothers had previously built almost as fine a temple at Girnar, a sacred mountain of the Jains in Kathiawar, near Junagarh.

The Vimala Sah temple is enclosed in a courtyard about 140 × 90 feet, surrounded by a double colonnade of pillars, which form porticoes to a range of 55 cells. Each cell is occupied by a cross-

INTERIOR OF THE VIMALA SAH TEMPLE.

legged image of Parswanatha, the Jain saint to whom the temple is dedicated. Over the door of each cell, and on the jambs, are sculptured scenes from his life, elaborate devices of human figures interspersed with foliage.

It is an important point in the Jain religion, that the patron saint of the temple should be honoured by a great number of his images, and that each should enjoy a separate shrine.

Within this marvellous courtyard is a still more marvellous temple, which, as in other Jain temples, is a cell, lighted only from the door, containing brazen images of Parswanatha. This cell is covered with the pyramidal roof, called a Sikra, which is common alike to Jain and Hindu temples all over India. The portico of the cell consists of forty-eight elaborately carved pillars, which, rising to a certain height, branch off into curious angular struts of white marble, between which, springing from the capitals of the thicker columns, are dwarf pillars. These forty-eight columns form an octagon, on which rests a dome that in richness of ornament and delicacy of detail is probably unsurpassed in the world. Above two rows of ornament are sixteen pedestals, on each of which is mounted a finely-carved image, and in the centre is a marvellous pendant of rare beauty. Facing the entrance to the temple is a square building containing nine white marble elephants, on each of which is a male figure, though some have been broken away. This represents Vimala Sah and his family going in procession to the temple. Vimala Sah is represented by the clay figure on horseback, the original statue having been destroyed by some Moslem iconoclast.

The picturesqueness of the situation and surroundings of these splendid temples adds greatly to their charm. There are five in all, but the Delwara are incomparably the finest. They are reputed to have cost eighteen millions sterling, and to have occupied fourteen years in building. They are all, however, worth careful inspection, the temple of Rishabhanath, the first of the twenty-four Tirthankars, or deified men whom the Jains worship, being larger than either of the Delwara. The shrine here has four doors, and the image of the saint inside is fourfold, facing each door; the two others are known as the Dailak and Gorakhalanchau.

Three days should be given to Mount Abu for the full enjoyment of its invigorating air, beautiful scenery, and wonderful temples; but it is quite possible, by arriving at Abu Road in the early morning, to spend twenty-four hours on the summit, and catch the mail train for Ajmere or Jodhpur at four o'clock the next day.

CHAPTER VI.

AJMIR—JODHPUR—UDAIPUR.

AJMIR is the administrative headquarters of the important British province of Ajmir-Merwara, an isolated area of 2,700 square miles, with a population of 460,000, entirely surrounded by independent Rajput states. It is placed on the crest of the great Rajputana watershed, the fort of Taragarh, which dominates the city, being 2,855 feet above sea level. It is an ancient, beautiful city, full of interest, both historical and architectural; its gay busy bazars, and its old houses with carved fronts, some of which are among the finest in India, giving an added attraction to its superb situation. It is a town of 49,000 inhabitants, of which about 30,000 are Hindu, and 18,000 Musalman. A well-built stone wall, with five gateways, surrounds the city. There is an excellent town bungalow, and one of the nicest hotels in India, the "Rajputana."

The finest specimen of early Indian Mahommedan architecture is to

THE ARHAI-DIN-KA-JHONPRA MOSQUE.

be found at Ajmir. The "Arhai-din-Ka-Jhonpra" Mosque, which literally translated is "the house of two and a half days," is beautifully situated on the lower slope of the hill opposite the Fort of Taragarh. It was originally a very fine Jain temple, dating from about the tenth century, but in the year 1236, Altamsh, having conquered the city and slain its Raja, converted it into a Musalman mosque in two days and a half; hence its name. Only the west side of the Jain temple was left standing, in front of which Altamsh erected a screen of seven arches, similar to, but much more beautiful than, the mosque of the Kutab-Minar at Delhi. The central arch is twenty-two feet wide, the two right and left thirteen and a half feet, and the outer ones ten and a half feet. The height of the screen over the great central arch is fifty-six feet. This arch is flanked by two minarets, which seem to have crumbled away to mere stumps, ornamented with convex flutes alternately semi-circular and rectangular, like the decoration of the Kutab-Minar at Delhi. The decoration of the whole façade of this wonderful screen is of unique beauty.

Fergusson expresses the opinion that no mosque in Cairo or Persia is so exquisite in detail, and that nothing in Spain or Syria can approach these mosques of Altamsh at Ajmir and Delhi for beauty of surface decoration. Nothing can exceed the taste with which the Cufic and Togra inscriptions are interwoven with the more purely architectural decorations, or the manner in which they give life and variety to the whole, without ever interfering with the constructive lines of the design. The buildings, when I visited them in 1888, were in a shameful condition of neglect and decay, but I was informed that the Government had at last determined to take some steps towards repairing and restoring this supremely interesting and historical mosque.

THE DARGAH, situated on the southern side of the city, is a strange group of buildings clustering round the burial-place of a famous saint, one Kwaja Sahib, who died at Ajmir, A.D. 1235. His memory is revered, and tomb held sacred, by both Hindus and Musalmans, and his eldest lineal descendant holds to-day the lucrative appointment of curator of his shrine. It is imperative that the shoes be removed before entering the enclosure. Many of the courtyards never see the sun, and the pavements are as cold as ice, so it is best to come wearing two or three pairs of thick socks, or with a large pair pulled over the shoes. The magnificent gateway is called the *Dilkusha*, or "heart expanding," opening out into a wide courtyard, containing

THE DARGAH, AJMIR.

two vast iron pots, in which messes of rice, oil, sugar, raisins and almonds are cooked and distributed to the pilgrims who come from a distance to the great annual festival of the holy Kwaja. Some 10,000 lbs. of ingredients are cooked in the larger, and nearly

6,000 lbs. in the smaller. The cost of filling the large pot is over £100; they are called the great and little *Deg*. When the pudding is ready, a supply is ladled out for the pilgrims, and then the men of the suburb of Indrakot and the servants of the Dargah have the hereditary right to scramble for what is left. Swathing themselves in cloths to the eyes, to save themselves from being burnt, the strongest of them finally tumble into the caldron, and scrape it clean. The courtyard is crowded with thousands of spectators, for this is one of the great annual feasts of Ajmir; but the traveller need not time his visit to see this gruesome spectacle.

The tomb of the Kwaja is a square domed building with two doorways, one of which has a silver archway. The mosque, which was built by Akbar, has fallen into decay. Further on is a beautiful mosque of white marble, built by Shah Jahan, the builder of the Taj Mahal. It has eleven arches, and a Persian inscription runs the whole length of the building under the eaves. This building will charm the traveller who has not yet reached Delhi and Agra. In the centre of the inclosure is a deep well or tank cut in the solid rock, round which are grouped many fine tombs. This well is reached by a succession of wide steps, up and down which a stream of worshippers are continually passing. This great tank, all in warm shadow, surrounded by white marble tombs, intermingled with the deep green foliage, topped with the lofty hills which surround Ajmir, ablaze with sunlight, forms a picture not easily forgotten.

When visitors return to the entrance-gate, and have made their expected gift of a couple of rupees to the shrine, they are subjected to the pretty custom so prevalent throughout India: garlands of sweet-smelling flowers are hung round their necks, which politeness requires should not be taken off till home is reached.

Just outside the entrance of the Dargah, are two small venerable-looking pavilions, with carved pillars. These are probably Hindu temples, though they are not now used as such.

The old fortress of Taragarh is seen from every part of the city, perched on the summit of a lofty and steep hill, 1,000 feet above the streets. It is a stiff walk, and most visitors go up in jhampans, or litters, carried by eight coolies. The fort covers an area of 80 acres, and was an impregnable place in its day. There is nothing of architectural interest in its buildings, but the view is superb, especially in the early morning.

The Ana Sagar, one of the loveliest tanks in India, is about three miles out of the North gate. This is a lake of many hundreds of acres in area. It is best viewed from the beautiful marble pavilion built by Shah Jahan, in the Daulat Bagh, or garden of splendour, a beautiful park full of fine old trees, in the midst of which is the residence of the Chief Commissioner. The water of this lake is conveyed by two underground aqueducts to Ajmir, for the supply of its inhabitants. Going or returning, the strongly-fortified old palace of Akbar, now used as public offices, should be observed, and a visit paid to the Mayo College, conspicuously placed in the centre of a fine

THE DAULAT BAGH, AJMIR.

park, represented in the initial illustration to this chapter. This college, whose object is to provide an education in accordance with European ideas for the sons of Rajput nobles, was established by the Earl of Mayo in 1870. It is supported by endowments given by Rajput princes, by the contributions of the pupils, and by Government grants. This valuable institution has already borne excellent fruit in the growing enlightenment of the Rajput populations.

Seven miles from Ajmir is the lake and village of Pushkar. The road passes through a deep defile on the far side of the range of mountains seen from the pavilion at Ana Sagar. The shore of the lake, in front of the village, is lined with a succession of temples and bathing ghats, which during October and November are crowded with pilgrims, over 100,000 repairing to the sacred Melas held during those months. At these Melas, like all others in India, a regular fair is held, and a large trade done in sheep, cattle, horses, camels, and merchandise of all sorts. The temples are all modern, without interest, except that one is the only temple in India dedicated to Brahma, who here performed a sacrifice so holy, that paradise is gained by bathing in the lake on a certain day in the year.

The Bazars of Ajmir present the same interesting features as other Indian towns—the only artistic product special to the place being carved animals in white marble and reddish sandstone, excellent in workmanship and moderate in price.

The cantonment of Nasirabad is 14 miles from Ajmir, with lines for about 2,000 troops, native and English.

A mission of the United Presbyterian Church of Scotland was established at Ajmir in 1862. The present Missionaries are: Rev. James Gray and Rev. Dr. Husband. Zenana Missionaries:—Mrs. Dignan and Miss Dr. Grant. The work carried on consists of one Anglo-Vernacular and seven Vernacular village schools, two hospitals and dispensaries, in which 50,000 patients were treated during the last year, three girls' schools, Zenana visiting, eight Sunday schools, a mission printing press, in which about thirty men are employed, and a Christian settlement eight miles from Ajmir. There is a Christian community of 226, while the native church numbers 108 members, only a few of whom are in any way supported by the Mission. Bazar and village preaching is regularly carried on by the Missionaries and their helpers. Two English services are kept up by the Missionaries: one in the Railway Institute on Sunday evening, the other in the Mission Church on Tuesday night.

The Church of England Mission is under the care of Rev. B. H. Skelton. Services are held in All Saints', near the Law Courts, every Sunday morning; in St. Mary's, a new church, morning and evening on Sunday, and on stated days during the week.

The Society for the Propagation of the Gospel established a mission in 1882. It is managed by a native pastor—Rev. Jara Chand; the membership is 123; there is one school with sixty pupils on the roll. Public preaching is carried on by Mr. Chand and two Catechists in the town and villages around.

The Methodist Episcopal Church Mission is conducted by Rev. A. Gilruth. English and vernacular work is carried on. Two

THE ANA SAGAR, AJMIR.

English services in the church on the Beawar road, each Sunday, morning and evening.

The Roman Catholic Church has a large congregation, composed mainly of Portuguese and Eurasians; the chapel is near Government College.

JODHPUR, or, as it is sometimes called, Marwar, is the largest of the Rajputana States; its greatest length is about 300 miles, and its greatest width 130 miles. It contains an area of 37,000 square miles. The population of the state is about 3,000,000, 86 per cent. Hindus, 10 per cent. Jains, with 4 per cent. of Muhammadans. The Rajput caste predominates.

The aspect of the country, viewed from the short line of sixty-four miles from Marwar Junction to the capital, is that of a sandy plain, from which rise here and there picturesque conical hills, from 600 to 1,000 feet in height. Some of these are crowned with temples, and on the summit of one, the Nadolai Hill, has been placed a colossal stone elephant.

The soil is poor and sterile, except in the valley of the Loni River, where are excellent crops of cereals. This river is crossed about half-way between Marwar and Jodhpur.

The villages are groups of beehive-shaped huts, the larger houses seen in some of them being the residences of the *Thakurs*, to whom concessions of land have been made, and who owe feudal or military service to the Maharaja, paying a money share of the produce as well.

The city of Jodhpur was founded by the Maharaja Jodha in 1550, and has been the seat of the capital ever since. Jodhpur is one of the most picturesque towns in India, standing on the edge of a rocky ridge of sandstone, 400 feet above the plain, with a splendid citadel dominating it, perched on an isolated rock 800 feet high. The palace covers nearly half of the area of the citadel, which is, roughly, 500 yards by 200. The Diwan, or Hall of 1,000 Pillars, is a large and handsome building, and the view from the upper fort is very extensive.

The main streets of the city are lined with fine houses, palaces of the Maharaja, and the town residences of the nobles and thakurs, many of whom are very wealthy. A strong wall, six miles in circumference, with seven gates, encircles the city. There are many beautiful tanks of strong masonry, with steps descending to the water, surrounded by glittering temples, and handsome wells.

The suburb of Maha Mandir, a quarter of a mile outside the city walls, has a fine pagoda, visible from a great distance, with a richly-decorated interior. There are two palaces near this temple, in one of which the Maharaja's confidential priest lives in considerable state. The ghost of his predecessor lives in the other, with a golden canopy over his bed; no living person is allowed to sleep in this building.

A pleasant drive of three miles leads to another suburb, where are the ruins of Mandor, the site of the ancient capital of Marwar,

KHOWASIN STHAMBA, CHITOR.

previous to its conquest by the Rajputs. The mound on which these ruins are built is called Jodhagir, or the Warrior's Hill. Here are scattered the tombs of the princes and nobles of the country, and there are many curious stone effigies of these chieftains.

A little further out into the country are some fine gardens, surrounding a clear deep lake, and three miles further on is the *Bal Samundar*, another sheet of water half-a-mile in length, with crags of red sandstone and fine palm-trees fringing the shores.

The deserted palace of Ajit Singh is worth a visit, though it is dirty, and full of bats and other vermin. It is interesting from the gigantic figures of divinities and other heroes with which it is decorated.

Udaipur.—In my introduction to this book, I have urged all travellers in India to see something of country life in districts remote

TOWER OF VICTORY, CHITOR.

from railways and Europeans. A visit to the beautiful city of Udaipur, in Rajputana, makes an excellent opportunity.

Leaving Ajmir at 1.40 P.M. the train arrives at Chitor Station at

11 P.M., close to which is a good Dak bungalow. From Chitor a new road has recently been constructed to Udaipur, along which a mail-tonga runs daily; the distance is seventy miles; the fare is fifteen rupees. A special tonga may be engaged by writing to the mail-agent, or the station-master at Chitor, who will take care that the order is placed in the right hands. It is better to write a week or ten days beforehand, and thus make sure by written confirmation that your instructions are clearly understood.

There are four Dak bungalows on the road—Banin, 14 miles; Mungerwar, 30 miles; Minar, 43 miles; Daboke, 59 miles, from Chitor, and if it is intended to break the long tonga journey, it will be best to leave it to the mail-agent to decide which shall be chosen, though Minar is the best, containing two good rooms. There is a good bungalow at Udaipur, where accommodation may be had. I advise travellers to write to the Resident, making full inquiries about it beforehand. Probably Messrs. Thos. Cook & Son, Bombay, would arrange the whole trip from Ajmir and back, with timely notice.

Chitor is an ancient city, crowned by a famous fortress, called Chitorgarh. The town is surrounded by a wall, connecting with the fort. Chitor was the capital of the surrounding country as far back as A.D. 700, but it has been deserted since its capture by the Emperor Akbar. The fort is 200 to 300 feet above the town, on the summit of a long precipitous rock, covered with dense jungle. It is worth visiting for the sake of a venerable Jain monument, called the Khowasin Sthamba, a remarkable square pillar, 75 feet high, 30 feet thick at the base, and 15 feet at the top, covered with sculptured Jain figures, and inscribed with the date A.D. 896. The whole of the interior of the fortress is covered with ruined temples, tanks, and palaces, the remains of the ancient city. Among these is a notable column, erected in 1450 to commemorate a great victory, 122 feet high, 35 feet broad at the base, tapering in nine storeys to a diameter of 18 feet under the cupola. It stands on a terrace 42 feet square, and is covered with sculpture representing mythological subjects.

In A.D. 1290 Chitor was taken by storm by Ala-ud-din. On this occasion the women of the city, rather than fall into the hands of the Musalmans, performed the awful sacrifice of "Johur." Several thousands of them, including the queen, were suffocated in the vaults of the fort; the men all dying in battle.

The palace of Bhim, of the 13th century, and that of Khumbo

Rana, early 15th century, are well preserved, and the beauty of detail is considerable. The Ram Pol is the finest of the gateways, and Mira Baie's temple (A.D. 1450) is a very magnificent ruin. A pleasant and profitable day may be spent at Chitor, wandering among these interesting and historical remains of the ancient Rajput capital, whose brightest days were a thousand years ago.

Udaipur is the capital of a native state in Rajputana of the same name, with a total population of 1,500,000, mainly Hindus; the

THE PALACE, UDAIPUR.

population of the city itself being about 40,000. The scenery throughout the state is very beautiful, and that of the Aravalli mountains, above the capital, is said to equal Kashmir. The state is well provided with lakes and tanks, some of which are very large. The Dhebar tank, 20 miles from Udaipur city, is 9 miles long, 5 broad, and covers an area of 21 square miles. The masonry dam is 1,200 feet long, by 95 feet high, 50 feet thick at the base, and 15 at the top. There are three distinct tribes of aborigines in the hills of Udaipur—the Nehairs, Minas, and Bhils.

The city of Udaipur, with its noble palace overlooking a romantic lake, surrounded by wooded hills, its great temple of Jagannath, the mansions of its Rajput nobles, its cenotaphs, flower-gardens, fountains, orange and lemon groves, is one of the most beautiful and picturesque in the world.

The Royal Palace has been thus described: "It is a most imposing pile, of a regular form, built of granite and marble, rising at least 100 feet from the ground, and flanked with octagonal towers, crowned with cupolas. Although built at various periods, uniformity of design has been very well preserved; nor is there in the East a more striking and majestic structure. It stands upon the very crest of a ridge running parallel to, but considerably elevated above, the margin of the lake; the terrace, which is at the east and chief front of the palace, extends throughout its length, and is supported by a triple row of arches from the declivity of the ridge. The height of this arcaded wall is full 50 feet; and although all is hollow beneath, yet it is so admirably constructed that an entire range of stables is built on the extreme verge of the terrace, on which the whole personal force of the Rana, elephants, horse, and foot, are often assembled. From this terrace the city and valley lie before the spectator, whose vision is bounded only by the hills shutting out the plains; while from the summit of the palace nothing obstructs its range over lake and mountain."—*Tod's Annals of Rajasthan.*

Many other beautiful palaces and mansions surround the lake, and occupy the wooded islands dotted over its surface. The only boats permitted are those belonging to the Maharana; but, like all India princes, he is politeness itself, and a request for the use of a boat, made through the Resident, will be certain to be met with a favourable reply. Every island is a grove or garden, with noble palaces or pavilions, and each forms a subject for a fresh picture. The most interesting is the Jagmandir, noted as the asylum of Shah Jahan, when in revolt against his father, Jahangir; this splendid palace was built for him during his residence at Udaipur.

A chain of fortresses, surrounding the city wall, commanding every road leading thereto, adds greatly to the charm of the scenery. Two miles from the capital is the lovely burning ground where the Maharanas, their wives and families, have been cremated since Udaipur became the capital in 1580. Here, in a beautiful garden full of trees and flowers, are scattered hundreds of tombs, great and small, but the smallest and meanest a work of art worthy of notice. The finest is the cenotaph of Singram Sinh, a famous king of Udaipur,

THE JAGMANDIR, UDAIPUR.

who was burned here with twenty-one of his wives, A.D. 1733. The variety of style and architecture is infinite. It is a fifty-six pillared portico, with an octagonal dome in the centre, supported on eight pillars with carved brackets. There is a chapter on cenotaphs in Fergusson, page 470, which give details and illustrations of some of these beautiful monuments, which, with their lovely sylvan surroundings, form the most charming cemetery imaginable.

The fortified hill, south of the city which it commands, is called Eklingarh. At the foot of the hill is an interesting building called the Gobardan Belas, a country residence and farm-house of the royal family.

Twelve miles north of Udaipur, at Eklingji, in a narrow defile, is an interesting shrine and temple sacred to Mahadeo, the tutelary divinity of the Mewar Rajputs. The shrine is of white marble, under an open vaulted temple, with a colonnade. The Maharana, as vice-regent of Siva, performs the ceremonies instead of the priests, on the occasion of his visit to the shrine. There is a beautiful lake here, surrounded by hills, the embankment of which is studded with temples and shrines of various kinds. At the further end of the Eklingji gorge a gateway is built across the mouth, with a wall crowning the heights on either side.

The Maharana of Udaipur is a "sacred man" of the Hindu pantheon, and is an object of worship. He is the representative of the Solar Race. According to his genealogy, he is the lineal descendant of a triple royal line. He is the living representative of the legendary hero of the Ramayana, descending in direct line from Rama, from the Sassanian kings of Persia, and from the Caesars of Rome. He is always portrayed with an aureole round the head.

The Maharana has fifty-one feudatory nobles, who enjoy rights and privileges which do not exist in other parts of Rajputana. They maintain much pomp and state in their own localities. When a feudatory noble enters the Maharana's presence the whole court rises. The reputed income of these nobles is about two millions of rupees, and that of the Maharana about three and a half millions. The military force of the state is about 26,000 men of all arms.

Much of the lac so largely used all over the north and west of India for the manufacture of native jewellery, is collected in the neighbouring forest by the Bhils.

Twenty-four miles from Udaipur is Nathdwara, where is one of the most sacred shrines in India, dedicated to Vishnu. The idol was brought from Muttra during the persecutions of Aurangzeb. There is a splendid road from Udaipur, made by Mr. G. T. Williams, the Raj engineer, during the Residency of Dr. Stratton; Mr. Williams also completed the Dak road from Chitor. The road to Nathdwara passes through Eklingji, the scenery is very picturesque all the way, and on the Eklingji Ghat magnificent.

Eight miles beyond Nathdwara is the superb tank of Raj Samund, the bund of which is some two miles long, all of white marble. In the centre of the bund is the town of Kankroli, with a temple sacred to Vishnu, almost as old as Nathdwara.

The United Presbyterian Church of Scotland has a small mission-station at Udaipur city.

CHAPTER VII.

JAIPUR.

JAIPUR is a place of great interest, being the capital of the most important of that group of independent states known as Rajputana. The state of Jaipur contains an area of 14,465 square miles, and a population of nearly two millions, of whom about one-eighth are Rajputs, five-eighths other castes of Hindus, three-sixteenths Muhammadans, and about one-sixteenth Jains, who are a very influential and wealthy section of Rajput society.

The scenery of Jaipur is very fine, the country being crossed by ranges of lofty hills, and isolated peaks of a very striking character rising abruptly from the plain. There are vast and arid tracts of desert, in which some of the smaller rivers are absorbed. The hills to the north of the largest desert have been broken up by some remote geological disturbance, exposing deposits of alum, cobalt, copper, and nickel ore, some of their products being used in the manufacture of the fine Jaipur enamels which, with the cutting of carbuncles and garnets found in Southern Jaipur, forms one of the staple industries of the capital.

The Maharaja is the descendant of a long line of kings, founded in A.D. 967, by Rama, king of Adjodya, in Oudh. He represents the thirty-fifth generation. His father was one of the most public-spirited princes in India, who set aside the extravagant splendour of his predecessors in favour of expenditure for the benefit of his people at large. His memory is revered by all the population of the state. The military forces of the Maharaja consist of about 1,000 artillerymen, 4,500 cavalry, and 16,000 infantry. The income of the state is £1,200,000, of which more than half is devoted to religious grants of one kind or another. The city of Jaipur is about 1,500 feet above the sea; it is a delightful place. The temperature in winter is com-

THE FOUNTAIN SQUARE, JAIPUR.

paratively cool and pleasant, and the climate dry and healthy. It is the largest and most prosperous of all the Rajput capitals, and is undoubtedly the finest of modern Hindu cities. It is beautifully situated in an amphitheatre of rugged and precipitous hills, whose summits are crowned by picturesque fortifications, the chief of which, the Tiger fort, dominates the city on the top of an inaccessible scarped rock. A solid crenellated wall, twenty feet high, and nine feet thick, surrounds the whole city, pierced with seven gateways, strengthened by screen walls. At intervals, in the walls, are bastions and towers armed with old-fashioned cannons.

Jaipur is remarkable for its fine wide streets. The main thorough-

IN THE BAZAR, JAIPUR.

fares are 111 feet wide, the side streets 55 feet, and even the back lanes and slums are 28 feet; all running at right angles to each other.

The streets are crowded with a stalwart race of men, superior in every way to the poor, ill-fed people of so many districts of Bengal or Bombay. There are signs of wealth on every hand. The scene from the fountain, where the four great thoroughfares of Jaipur converge, is one of the most picturesque in the world. The great open space is filled with stalls of fruit, vegetables and cereals; gay piece goods from Cashmere, Cawnpore, or Manchester are displayed from others; thousands of pigeons walk in and out on the pavement, taking the greatest interest in the gaily dressed bargainers in front of every stall.

A continual stream of traffic flows up and down each broad roadway, foot-passengers mingling with smartly caparisoned elephants, trains of camels, white donkeys, and bullock-carts; the syces, or running footmen of some Rajput noble, cry passage for their master, who prances gravely in from the country on his white horse, with green and gold saddle, himself armed to the teeth with musket, pistol, sword and dagger; or some groom of the Maharaja comes along, leading a muzzled panther or leopard.

The houses are all washed rose colour, and glow warmly in the bright sunlight against the deep cobalt of the sky. On the roofs are smart groups of women and children, clad in wondrous colours, with flocks of parrots, pigeons, and crows sweeping round them, fluttering about the eaves, or perched on every corner.

In the shops below every possible handicraft is carried on, for nothing is done by machinery in India. Here are women in bright red dresses grinding at the mill, and singing as they work. Men, all the colours of the rainbow, stand in front of the dyers, waving long strips of green, red, or blue cloth in the drying sunshine. Others squat on the side walk being shaved, or wash themselves at the gutter with bright brass basins full of clean water. Cotton ginning, wheat winnowing, copper smelting, the potter's wheel, the spinning wheel, the gem-grinder's wheel, the gold-wire drawer, the silversmith, the shoemaker, with fifty other trades and their tools, clattering and noisy, make the busy scene a mass of moving colour and life such as I have never seen equalled elsewhere.

There is a good town bungalow at Jaipur, as well as two or three hotels, of which the Kaiser-i-Hind is the best. Good carriages may be hired by the day, and there are two or three reasonably intelligent guides. The traveller, immediately on arrival, should write a note to the British Resident, asking for permits to see the old Palace of Amber and the palace and stables of the Maharaja. The note should be left, with cards, at the residency, and the orders will be sent to the hotel

THE HALL OF THE WINDS, JAIPUR.

during the day. If only a short visit is being made to Jaipur, it will be better to write a day or two beforehand.

There is nothing of historical or archæological interest in Jaipur, the main charm of the place consisting of the wonderful picturesqueness of the people and the streets.

The palace and gardens of the Maharaja lie in the angle formed by the two main streets, covering a seventh of the area of the entire city. The grand entrance to the Palace, the Siran Deorhi, is opposite the College, in the most central part of the city. The only portion of the palace visible from the street is the singularly beautiful building called the Hawal Mahal, or Hall of the Winds, described by Sir Edwin Arnold as "a vision of daring and dainty loveliness, nine stories of rosy masonry and delicate overhanging balconies, and latticed windows, soaring with tier after tier of fanciful architecture in a pyramidal form, a very mountain of airy and audacious beauty, through the thousand pierced screens and gilded arches of which the Indian air blows cool over the flat roofs of the very highest houses. Aladdin's magician could have called into existence no more marvellous abode, nor was the pearl and silver palace of the Peri Banou more delicately charming."

This building is part of the quarters assigned to the ladies of the Zenana. Much of it is a mere mask of stucco, and most critics would refuse to accept Sir Edwin Arnold's poetic tribute to its beauty. It is, however, a unique bit of Indian architecture, well worth careful observation.

In the first great square, after entering the palace gates, is the largest of the five great observatories erected early last century, by Jai Singh, the celebrated Hindu astronomer and mathematician. It contains dials, azimuth masonry, altitude pillars, astrolabe, and a double mural quadrant, of enormous size and height, built of massive masonry smoothed with plaster, on which the gradations have been carefully marked. Passing on, the Diwan-i-Khas, or Private Audience Hall, is reached, a great marble building, beyond which is the Chanda Mahal, or "Silver House," the great palace of the Maharaja himself, seven stories high. Some favour or influence is required to gain admission to the apartments, which are furnished with the usual garish splendour of modern Indian palaces, the only thing worth seeing being the magnificent view from the roof, and a fine illuminated manuscript of the time of Akbar in one of the rooms of the ground floor.

A very pleasant hour may be spent in the lovely and well-kept gardens of the palace, especially if the Maharaja's band, carefully trained by an experienced European band-master, should be playing. All about the courtyards, and on the steps of the Diwan-i-Khas, lounge picturesque smartly dressed groups of the innumerable servants of the Maharaja, who seem to spend an easy and idle life. Leading from the central quadrangle is a long bazaar, where food and other necessaries are retailed to these retainers.

The fine tower, just outside the main entrance to the palace, which dominates the street, is called the Ishwari Minar Swarga Sul,—the minaret which pierces the sky. It is not permitted to ascend this tower, but the view cannot be finer than that obtained from the roof of the palace.

The Maharaja's College is a pretty and interesting sight when school is in session, and its thousand brightly attired lads are all assembled in their classes, grouped on the floors and verandahs of the great courtyards. Several of the professors and teachers speak English fluently, especially the accomplished Professor of History, Mr. Amritalal Dé, and, justly proud of their institution, they gladly show it to visitors, putting their clever students through their paces. This college was opened in 1844 with forty pupils, and now has upwards of 1,000 on its register.

The scholars are mostly Hindu. The college staff consists of fifteen English-speaking teachers, twelve Maulavis or Persian teachers, and four Hindu pundits, with others. Many of these gentlemen are graduates of Calcutta University, with which the college is affiliated. The other schools of Jaipur worth visiting are the High School for the sons of Rajput nobles; any of the thirty-three elementary schools for boys; and the charming female schools which the late Maharaja, with great liberality, has established, and which contain 700 or 800 pupils. The best of these is in the handsome house of Nattani, a former Minister of State.

One of the finest buildings in the city is the School of Art. with remarkably well-appointed technical classes, in which a large number of young men receive instruction in drawing, carpentry, iron-work, electroplating, engraving, metallurgy, gold and silver work, damascening, gem grinding and setting, enamelling, watch-making, wood-carving, sculpture, embroidery, weaving, and all those other native arts for which India in time past has been famous, but which have in some cases died out before European machinery and competition.

The public garden of seventy acres is extremely beautiful, and is partly zoological and partly botanical. The handsome building of white stone with a lofty clock tower at the entrance of the garden on the city side, is the Mayo Hospital with a hundred beds, an excellent and well-appointed institution built by the late Maharaja in memory of his fast friend, the Earl of Mayo. In the centre of the garden is the museum, one of the noblest modern buildings in all India, in which is an interesting collection of Indian and European art. Here are cases of objects illustrating every variety of Indian arts, industries, and antiquities; loom work of all kinds, carpets, sculptures, brass, silver and gold work, glass, enamels, jewellery, and natural products, gathered together at great cost from every corner of India. This museum is a favourite resort of the people, 150,000 passing its turnstiles during the year.

The public garden cost 400,000 rupees to lay out, and 30,000 rupees a year are spent to keep it up. The fine bronze statue is that of the Earl of Mayo.

All these splendid institutions are monuments to the enlightened and public spirited prince, who has by their aid raised his little capital to the position of one of the most modern and civilized cities in the world.

The menagerie is near the north gate, and here are ten or twelve huge man-eater tigers, confined in strong cages, fed at the Maharaja's expense. The amiable creatures to which we are accustomed at home, at Regent's Park or in Sanger's menageries, are quiet tabby cats compared with these horrible monsters, who shake the strong bars of their cages with impotent rage and fierce glare, growling with every tooth exposed, at any person who approaches. One huge brute is known to have killed and eaten fifteen human beings, another ten, and a third seven. These tigers are trapped in pitfalls, where they are left for many days until they have been starved into extreme weakness; then they are dragged off to imprisonment for life.

Mr. G. P. Sanderson writes thus of man-eater tigers in his "Thirteen Years among the Wild Beasts of India:" "This truly terrible scourge to the timid and unarmed inhabitants of an Indian village is now happily becoming very rare; man-eaters of a bad type are seldom heard of, rarely survive long. Before there were so many European sportsmen as there are now, in the country, a man-eater frequently caused the temporary abandonment of whole tracts; and the sites of small hamlets abandoned by the terrified inhabitants, and which have never been reoccupied, are not uncommonly met with by the sportsmen in the jungles. The terror inspired by a man-eater throughout the district ranged by him is extreme: the helpless people are defenceless against his attacks. Their occupations of cattle-grazing or wood-cutting take them into the jungles, where they feel that they go with their lives in their hands. A rustling leaf, or a squirrel or bird moving in the undergrowth, sets their heart beating with a dread sense of danger. The only security they feel is in numbers. Though the bloodthirsty monster is perhaps reposing with the remains of his last victim miles away, the terror he inspires is always present to every one throughout his domain. The rapidity and uncertainty of a man-eater's movements form the chief elements of the dread he causes. His name is in every one's mouth; his daring, ferocity, and appalling appearance are represented with true Eastern exaggeration, and until some European sportsman, perhaps after days or weeks of pursuit, lays him low, thousands live in fear day and night. Bold man-eaters have been known to enter a village and carry off a victim from the first open hut. Having lived in a tract so circumstanced until I shot the fiend that possessed it, and having myself felt something of the grim dread that had taken hold of the country-side, where ordinary rambling about the jungles, and even sitting outside the tent after dark except with a large fire, or moving from the encampment without an escort, were unsafe, I could realise the feelings of relief and thankfulness so earnestly expressed by the poor ryots when I shot the Jezebel that had held sway over them so long.

"The man-eater is often an old tiger (more frequently a tigress), or an animal that, through having been wounded or otherwise hurt, has been unable to procure its usual food, and takes to this means of subsistence. It is invariably an ex-cattle-killer that, from constant intercourse with man, has become divested of its natural dread of our race, and interference with whose kills has caused collisions between itself and cow-herds which have finally led to its preying upon the hitherto dreaded man when other food fails. The man-eater is as cowardly as it is cunning, fleeing before an armed man, between whom and a possible victim it discriminates with wonderful sagacity. The slightest sound of any one in pursuit of it, even the whisper of a single sportsman with one or two trackers in its haunts, starts it at once; it will then probably travel for miles, though even whilst fleeing it may pounce upon some unwary victim, as I have seen an ordinary tiger seize a bullock when itself the object of hot pursuit. This combination of cowardice and audacity constitutes the difficulty there always is in bringing a man-eater to bay.

"Though the belief that some tigers confine themselves entirely to human flesh is undoubtedly erroneous, a man is so much more easily overcome than any other animal that man-eaters frequently seize cowherds in preference to the cattle they are in charge of. It is this which has led to the belief that, after having once tasted human flesh, the tiger prefers it to any other. The reason why tigresses should be more frequent offenders than their lords is difficult to conjecture. Perhaps it is that when their cubs are young they are often put to great straits to obtain food for them, or urged to acts of boldness in their defence; or the fact that tigresses are as a rule more vicious, sly, and enterprising, as also more ferocious when pushed to extremities than tigers, may partly account for it. This may seem an ungallant representation by a sportsman (and who is more tender-hearted, more ready to overlook the sex's failings than the true sportsman ?), but it is the truth.

"How the belief arose that man-eaters are usually mangy animals it is difficult to understand. I do not remember to have read of a single instance of any sportsman finding this to be the case. Were tigers apt to lose their hair, or to become lean in old age, a foundation for the belief might exist; though to say that this was the result of eating human flesh would be erroneous. But old animals merely become lighter in colour, the black stripes narrowing and becoming further apart, and very slightly mixed with grey hairs, whilst the yellow turns to a paler hue than in youth. As far as my own experience goes, I have never seen a mangy or lean tiger."

The Maharaja's stables are worth seeing. Here are kept many varieties of carriages, some of which are ancient and curious; also a fine stud of three hundred horses, about fifty elephants, and a number of cheetahs and hunting leopards.

There are many interesting excursions into the suburbs of Jaipur. The alligator tank is a shallow lake just outside the walls, in which are a considerable number of these loathsome reptiles. As visitors approach the bank, the native cadgers who haunt all places of resort in India come forward. One goes off to the slaughter-house, to fetch a mass of the inwards of a bullock, while the others run to the margin of the tank, uttering shrill and weird cries. Presently the surface of the water is broken by the serrated backs of alligators, who in response to the yells of the loafers, emerge from their mud, seeking what they may devour. They swim slowly to the bank, sticking out expectant snouts, and gaping their white mouths and cruel jaws. Presently, the sky is almost obscured by kites, also attracted by the cries of the men. Now comes the messenger, with a lump of lights and offal, and a long rope. This is twisted round and round the bait, and thrown among the alligators, who fight for its possession—the kites swooping in at every gap, snatching off bits of meat. The lucky one slowly bolts it down, rope and all, when, with screams of joy, a dozen loafers seize the rope, and the tug-of-war begins. By degrees the huge monster, fifteen or sixteen feet long, is slowly

THE JAI SINGH SAWAI, JAIPUR.

dragged out of the water, snapping and snarling, till the rope breaks, the loafers fall back in a yelling heap, and the alligator sails slowly away, with six feet of rope waving behind him like a following snake, to digest his meal of hemp and offal at his ease. It is a gruesome spectacle, and hardly worth the couple of rupees which the loafers expect for their pains. It is, however, a very pretty sight to watch the kites swoop down with wonderful grace, catching bits of meat thrown up into the air, eating them as they hover, waiting for more.

The cenotaphs of the Maharajas are placed in charming gardens, just outside the north-east wall. The trees are full of monkeys, which abound all round the suburbs of Jaipur. The finest of these cenotaphs is that of Jai Singh Sawai, of the purest white marble—a dome supported by an octagon of eight beautifully carved pillars. The cornice is finely decorated with scenes in alto-relievo from the Hindu mythology, and the slabs round the base are groups of soldiers on elephants and horses, and other striking subjects. There is an excellent model of this beautiful work of art in South Kensington Museum.

A pleasant morning excursion may be made to the Temple of the Sun, and the sacred shrines of Galta. The Sun Temple is on the top of a hill about 350 feet high, two miles and a half from the hotel. The road is too bad for carriages, but a bullock-cart can go the greater part of the way, and will furnish a new experience in locomotion. The temple is a very ordinary affair, but the view over the plain, with the minarets and gardens of Jaipur glistening at the foot of the hill, is well worth the climb. It is interesting to note how the sand of the great Rajputana desert is encroaching upon the town. The houses and gardens of a near suburb lie deserted and almost buried in the sand, which has blown up the ravines of the hills, scores of feet deep.

The road descends rapidly from the Temple of the Sun into a dark gorge, narrowing into a pass about twenty feet wide, at the end of which is a group of ancient temples surrounding two deep pools of water. These temples are greatly venerated, and at times great hosts of pilgrims resort to them. Below the second tank are some minor temples and priests' houses, beyond which is the wide plain, dotted with rocks, some of which are crowned with old fortifications.

The old Palace and Temple of Sanganer is distant a pleasant drive of seven miles from Jaipur. The town is entered by a gateway, beyond which are two Tirpauliyas, as they are called—gateways with three openings and three stories; they are in a somewhat tumble-down condition. Passing two temples, dedicated to Krishna and Sitaram, the palace is reached—a vast wilderness of ruins, with some lovely fragments here and there.

In one of these the doors are panels of sandal-wood inlaid with ivory, leading into a charming courtyard with a ruinous old garden and fountains, that is very picturesque. Beyond the palace is the Sanganer Temple, dating from the 9th century. In a hollow of the outer wall is a rude stone idol covered with vermilion, called Bhojaji, supposed to be thousands of years old. The main entrance to the temple is of fine white marble. The inner courtyard is about sixty feet by forty, ornamented by rows of pillars with elaborately carved struts, surmounted by figures of gods.

The gateway leading into the inner court is also of marble, and is one mass of sculptured decoration; the sill is held up by heads of fearsome demons. Within this inner court is a shrine, into which none but the faithful may enter. Under a canopy sit three white marble figures of Parswanath, with six smaller black figures in front.

There are several other temples, Hindu and Jain, worth visiting, and two or three hours may be pleasantly spent in wandering about this decayed old city.

The greatest of all the attractions to Jaipur is AMBER, the ancient, but now deserted and ruined, capital of Jaipur. An early start, not later than six o'clock, should be made on the day for which permission has been obtained through the Resident. The route from the hotel passes through the city, out on the other side into a road lined with the handsome gardens and mansions of Rajput nobles; presently a fine spacious lake is reached, in the centre of which is a deserted palace, only accessible by boat. Basking on the banks and small islands are a number of enormous alligators, while others swim slowly about with their ugly backs just above the water. Two miles beyond this lake, and six from the hotel, the foot of the hill leading up to Amber is reached, where two or three elephants in smart trappings have been sent to meet the party, by the kindness of the Maharaja. These are placed by him at the disposal of every stranger who obtains a permit through the Resident; the mahouts expect two or three rupees as a present. The elephants take the visitor up to Amber—a distance of two miles, in about an hour, wait while the palace is visited, and then make the return journey.

The city of Amber is quite deserted, except by a number of fakirs or Hindu ascetics, who have taken possession of the empty houses. It is a weird looking place enough, and as the huge elephants plod slowly through its streets, no human being is met with, except some unkempt and ash-strewn creature looking silently out of a window or over the edge of a roof. There is nothing stranger in all India's past than the desertion by some monarch, for reasons now lost in obscurity or only guessed at, of his splendid palace and well-built capital, taking not only his court, but the entire population with him.

The palace is a fine pile of buildings of the later period of Musalman art. Its situation is extremely picturesque, being built along the slopes of a lofty hill, immediately over the lake, the summit being crowned with a powerful fortress. The surrounding hills are topped with smaller castles, linked to the fort by long walls of thick crenellated masonry. The old deserted garden of the palace, stretching far out into the lake, is a place of wondrous beauty, and its rich dark green foliage throws up in strong relief the whole façade of the great range of white and yellow buildings. Reproduced in the mirror of the still lake, it makes a picture not easily to be forgotten.

The elephants wind slowly up the steep slopes which lead to the entrance of the palace, which is defended by a narrow and curtained approach with three massive gateways, the last of which opens on a great desolate square, where the visitor dismounts, if "elephant-sickness" has not dismounted him earlier. I have obtained permission to quote at length the description of this marvellous palace, given by Sir Edwin Arnold in his "India Revisited":—

"A rich *nakâr-khana*, with brass doorways and alcoves of embroidered marble, opens the way into a second courtyard, paved with white and red stone, and surrounded by the most graceful buildings imaginable. One is the Diwan-i-Khas, a pavilion formed by columns of white marble and red sandstone, its inner walls of laced and pierced stonework, and its roof delicately embellished with colour. On another face of this 'Court of Honour' rises magnificently the gateway of the Mardana or 'Men's Abode,' which has been pronounced the finest portal in the world. It is in truth too lovely in tints, material, artistic labour, and *ensemble* to be described—a matchless portico, such as might provide the door to Paradise. Through this you reach across a green and cool garden—the Jey Mandir, or 'Hall of Victory,' adorned by panels of alabaster, inlaid with birds, flowers, and arabesques in various colours, the roof glittering with the mirrored and spangled work for which Jaipur art is renowned. There are bathing-rooms here, all of pale, creamy marble, looking forth upon the dead city and the fair valley through screens of fretted stone; chambers painted with curious pictures of towns, temples, and hunting or mythological scenes; and one beautiful apartment entirely lined with plates of mica let into the white walls and vaultings, between lines and floriated ornaments of

THE PALACE, AMBER.

grey, the effect being as though this royal retreat were filled with moonlight. Then we traverse the tiny but elegant chambers of the zenana—for the palace is at present empty—shut from the world by a jealously high wall, in which pierced lattices permit the imprisoned ladies to gaze upon the world without. There is a delicious little pavilion above this, on the roof of the great gate, styled *Sohag Mandir*, from which those secluded princesses could watch the Durbars in the square of the Diwan-i-Khas; and over the 'Hall of Victory' is built a *Jas Mandir* or 'Alcove of Light,' which literally glows with bright and tender colours and exquisite inlaid work, and looks through arches of carved alabaster and clusters of slender columns upon the sleeping lake and the silent mountains. If this portion of the palace must be regarded as a prison, it is the most beautiful gaol imaginable; and the grey old Rajput in charge explains that when the Maharaja's court is here, the men are sometimes all excluded, and the princesses have the run of the entire edifice.

"Yet the palace is not quite empty even to-day. At the side of the main entrance, beneath the ramp, exists a temple dedicated to Devi, and here it is the custom every morning in the year to sacrifice an animal. At the Durga festival, a whole herd of buffaloes and a flock of sheep are offered to the dread goddess, but the daily tribute is a goat, which replaces, it is said, the human victim whose life used to be taken every morning in this gloomy fane before the times of our British Râj. It chanced that we entered the temple just at the hour of sacrifice, and, although the ladies would by no means view the sanguinary ceremony, a brief conversation with the attendants induced them to admit Dr. Hendley and myself, to the presence of the goddess. She sat—the awful blood-loving *Kali*—all black and red, upon a platform inside the darkest part of the adytum of the temple, with eyes of glittering mother-o'-pearl and a necklace of skulls. At the foot of the platform was a heap of sand, and near it some wide-mouthed brass vessels, and a broad heavy-bladed sword. A Rajput was worshipping in the corner, and the priest, with two assistants, moved grimly about, arranging for the matutinal rite. The victim, a black goat, stood placidly enough upon the heap of sand, sniffing curiously at the edge of the stone platform where so many of his predecessors had perished. Suddenly a bell was touched, and the priest took the heavy sword and laid it in front of the image, while he made the 'ashtanga' or eight-fold prostration, and repeated the *mantra* of expiation. Then the two attendants laid hold of the goat quite gently, one steadying it at the tail, and one keeping its head straight with a cord lightly fastened round the neck and ears. The poor animal, quite unalarmed and unconcerned, stood perfectly still, while the priest bared his right shoulder and squared himself athwartwise; the sword, grasped by both hands, balancing under the goat's neck. Abruptly he raised it, swung it back far behind him, and then brought it whistling round with a blow which combined the cut and draw. There was a slight sound, as when a soft stick is chopped, and the blade had shred clean through the goat's neck-bone and neck, so that the boy with the cord caught up the severed head into the air before it could touch the earth. The body of the victim fell sideways, guided by the other attendant, who directed the bleeding arteries into one of the brass vessels. Taking the goat's head, the priest then laid it on the platform, before the glaring eyes of the goddess, and placing his brow on the earth, repeated the prayer prescribed. Thus the horrid propitiation ended, but we learned that the priests of the temple, being of a special caste, themselves ate daily five seers of the goat's flesh, and had the right to sell the remainder in the bazaar. The palace pays seventeen rupees monthly to the contractor who supplies these innocent victims. The priest said that the goddess would be very angry if the goat were not decapitated at a single blow, and that he could cut off the head of a buffalo with equal certainty in one attempt."

A CORNER OF THE DIWAN-I-KHAS, AMBER.

The excursion to Amber takes about six or seven hours to go, stay for two hours, and return. The student of architecture, the sketcher or photographer, will not, however, be content with so short a visit, and it is better to set aside a whole day for Amber, taking luncheon from the hotel.

Jaipur, like all native capitals, is a great place for processions. While I was there, in the winter of 1888, a new British Resident had come, and the Maharaja paid him a state visit, with full processional honours. The first indication of his leaving the palace was an enormous elephant, painted all over with gorgeous devices in brilliant colour, on whose back was a trumpeter, and another man bearing aloft a great flag. This beast was a "trotter," and went lumbering by at eight miles an hour, to clear the way for his Highness. The procession followed hard after. It was led by about fifty camels, each mounted with soldiers armed with big guns, that threw a 6 or 8 oz. ball. Following these was a company of artillery, then a group of horsemen beating big drums, the king's horse-guards, tall fierce Rajputs, bearing lances with bright pennons, and the Maharaja himself, a resplendent object encrusted with jewels, in an open barouche drawn by four horses. Behind him rode a regiment of cavalry, another of mounted police, carriages containing his diwan, his ministers, the members of his council, and a large number of nobles who had come in from the surrounding country. The whole procession was closed by a number of fine elephants with splendid trappings, and several cart-loads of Nautch girls! It was a brave and imposing spectacle.

Jaipur is a great centre for the manufacture, as well as the distribution, of Indian artistic workmanship. Makers of enamels, damascened work, shawls and chuddars, state umbrellas and chauris, marble, wood, and ivory-carving, printed muslins and chintzes, and every description of native jewellery, may be seen at work in Jaipur, in its various bazars and back lanes.

The Jaipur enamels are exceedingly beautiful, in depth, translucency, and purity of colour, ranking before all others in the world. Its principal form is that known as *champlevé*, in which the pattern is cut out of the gold or silver vessel, or jewel, and filled in with the enamel, which is fused on to the metal. The trinkets thus produced are plates, dishes, cups, saucers, spoons, bowls, boxes, inkstands, and jewellery. In all cases the more costly specimens of the art are embellished with precious stones, and the enamels are as lustrous and transparent as the emeralds and rubiès set in their midst. Sometimes the art is used with much effect in the hilts of the swords every true Rajput chief still feels bound to carry about with him whenever he goes abroad.

If the visitor wishes a modest specimen of this beautiful Jaipur enamel, he cannot do better than buy a ring. They are made of pure

WAITING FOR THE MAHARAJA, JAIPUR.

gold, from Mohurs, in pretty designs, such as twisted snakes, or clasped hands, costing from 20 to 40 rupees, or double that amount if precious stones have been used. There are also many other specimens of enamelled jewellery made, such as ear-rings, pendants, and necklaces. Some very effective and brilliant enamelled trinkets may sometimes be purchased at Jaipur, which are manufactured at Partabghar, in southern Rajputana, described in a later chapter (*see* "Bhopal—Indore").

Jaipur is celebrated for its garnet jewellery, which is manufactured very largely here. It is very effective and cheap. The principal manufacturer is Mr. Saith Mull Chand Golcha, who also keeps a large stock of enamels and other Rajput jewellery. He is a very accomplished gentleman, and speaks English fluently. If any visitor who calls upon him is really interested in art manufacture, Mr. Golcha, or his secretary, Mr. Ganput Lal, will show him all sorts of beautiful things.

The Damascened work of Jaipur is very inferior to that of Kashmir, Gujarat, and the Panjab, and is confined mostly to the decoration of shields, spears, swords, and other weapons, familiar in London shop-windows, and altogether unworthy of the connoisseur's attention.

The beautiful white marble, so plentiful in Jaipur State, is worked up into carved elephants, tigers, and other animals, and Hindu gods and goddesses, the marble being richly painted in a very effective way.

The weaving, dyeing, and printing of cotton fabrics is one of the great features of bazar life, and the printed muslins and cotton cloths of Jaipur are sold all over India for the purity and brilliance of their dyes. There is no better market anywhere for the traveller who wishes to purchase specimens of the skill of Indian weavers, dyers, and cotton-printers. Here are made large cotton *daris*, striped in various colours, gold and silver-printed muslins, turbans, bed-covers, and many other beautiful cotton fabrics. A day or two may be well spent in Jaipur in the study of all these various native industrial arts, where everything is made by hand, machinery practically unknown, and where the methods and processes have been virtually the same for a thousand years. The ordinary hotel guide is not much use, as he has no ideas beyond the rubbish sold on the verandah, or the small dealers who will give him a commission.

The only Christian Mission in Jaipur was established in 1866 by the United Presbyterian Church of Scotland. There are two British agents, several native preachers, and some excellent schools well worth seeing.

A day may be spent while at Jaipur, in visiting the interesting salt lake at Sambhar. A convenient train leaves Jaipur at 6.0 a.m., reaching Sambhar at 8.20; returning thence at 3.40, arriving at Jaipur at 7.10. The manager of the hotel at Jaipur will, if instructed, write the day before, ordering a conveyance to meet the train on arrival at Sambhar—probably a bullock-cart. The lake is an irregular sheet of water 20 miles long, very shallow, nowhere more than four feet deep. It is surrounded by arid rocks, abounding in lime and salt, and, during the rains, the water pouring down the sides of these hills becomes strongly impregnated with salt. As soon as the dry season sets in, the water of the lake begins to evaporate, and a crust of salt forms on the surface of the black mud which forms the bottom. This salt is red and blue, as well as white, the colours being caused by the presence of subaqueous microscopic plants. The harvesting of this salt goes on from October to March. Hundreds of men and women are employed in wading out through the mud to break off large cakes of this salt, bringing it in baskets to solid ground, where they load it into country bullock-carts to be taken to the railway-station. The evaporation of the lake is six inches in fifteen days.

There are one or two rickety boats, if adventurous visitors choose to run the risk of being upset in two feet of water and one of plastic mud; but nothing is to be seen thereby that cannot be equally well contemplated from the shore. The mud smells strongly of carburetted hydrogen.

The lake is in Rajputana, one shore belonging to Jaipur, the other to Jodhpur, but it is leased to the British Government. The average out-put of salt is about 4,000 tons, and supplies nearly all the markets of Rajputana, the Panjab, the North West, and Central India.

If time permits, after visiting the lake, an excursion may be made to Naren, the headquarters of the sect of Dadu Panthis, where there are some fine temples, a tank, and some magnificent specimens of *Ficus indica*, one of which measures nearly sixty feet in circumference round the trunk four feet from the ground. There is also a mosque built of the ruins of an old Jain temple, and a handsome gateway with an arch forty feet high.

CHAPTER VIII.

ULWAR.

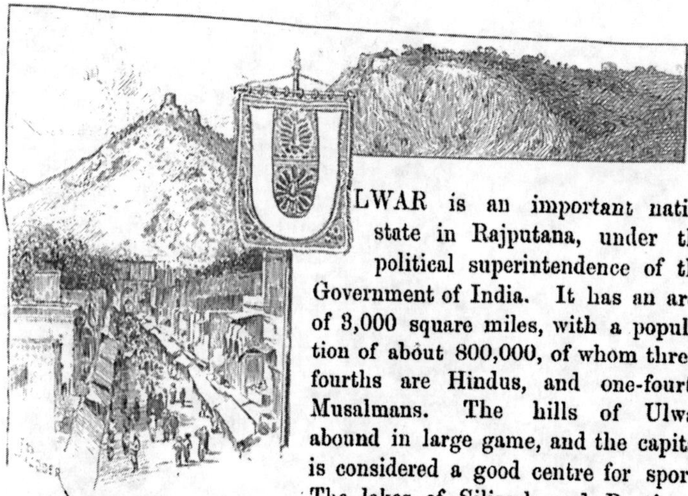

ULWAR is an important native state in Rajputana, under the political superintendence of the Government of India. It has an area of 3,000 square miles, with a population of about 800,000, of whom three-fourths are Hindus, and one-fourth Musalmans. The hills of Ulwar abound in large game, and the capital is considered a good centre for sport. The lakes of Siliserh and Deoti are full of fish, and also abound in teal and other wild fowl. Tigers and panthers are to be found in the hill jungles; and sambhar, nilghai, black buck, and pig in the plains.

The Raja has a revenue of about £250,000, and maintains an army of 2,000 cavalry, 5,500 infantry, and 800 artillerymen. He is an enlightened prince, on excellent terms with the British Government.

The city of Ulwar is well deserving of the traveller's notice, and if time presses, may be visited *en route* from Jaipur to Delhi in a single day. The mail-train leaves Jaipur at 7 a.m., reaching Ulwar at 11.30, a slower train leaving for Delhi at 4.30 p.m., giving five hours at Ulwar.

Ulwar is a picturesque town of 50,000 inhabitants. It is protected

THE TANK, ULWA

by a rampart and moat on all sides, except that which is closed in by the lofty rock crowned by the fort. There are five gates, and the streets are well paved and clean. The Dak Bungalow is a few yards from the station, and a note posted the day previously will secure breakfast being ready on arrival of the train, though that meal may be had at Bandikui at 9.30, the mail stopping for the purpose.

The conspicuous building near the station is the tomb of one Fath Jung, and dates from 1547. It has a fine dome, and has lasted longer than the memory of him in whose honour it was erected, for nobody in Ulwar, or anywhere else, appears to know who Fath Jung was or what he did.

The town is about a mile from the station. The fine temple in the market-place is in honour of Jagannath, and the curious ancient tomb which crosses the main street is called the Tirpolia, and dates back to about A.D. 1350. Tarang Sultan, brother of Firoz Shah, lies buried there.

The Banni Bilar palace is a handsome modern building, with very beautiful gardens, and a fine Durbar Hall, from the roof of which a splendid view is obtained of the fort, the temples, the cenotaphs, and the tank. This pavilion is of white marble, its roof and walls decorated with pietra dura.

Close at hand is the Raja's modern palace. The library is very rich in Oriental manuscripts of great rarity, some wonderful illuminated scrolls, ancient Korans, and one book, a copy of the Gulistan, valued at 500,000 rupees, whose pictures are a marvel of delicate colour. The librarian is always willing to show them to appreciative strangers. In the courtyard are two cenotaphs of white marble, adorned with pierced lattice-work, and further on are some marble temples to Vishnu, and the elegant cenotaph of Maharaja Bakhtawar Singh. The view from the pavilion of this cenotaph is one of the most beautiful in India. Sir Edwin Arnold writes of it:—

"You look upon this bright landscape, full of old legend and busy traffic, from balconies of pierced marble—delicious little bowers of carved and fretted embroidery, where the satin polish of the stone, the cool, smooth floors, the light filtering through sheeny windows of close and complex patterns; the tinkle of fountains falling on the pavement, the breeze sighing through the feathers of the palm trees, and the broad flags of the banana, make up a sense of luxury and graceful life, which words cannot convey . . . . . . There is no dead king's spirit which might not be proud of such a tomb, and no artist who would not confess it a perfect subject for his pencil, with the wild peacocks dropping their gorgeous trains down its white walls, and the water reflecting every line and angle of its noble contours."

In the armoury will be found a remarkable collection of ancient swords, with hilts of gold, decorated with jade, pearls, enamels, and other jewelling. Ulwar has always been famous in Indian art, for its

BAKHTAWAR SINGH'S CENOTAPH, ULWAR.

fine workmanship in steel. The weapons and armour of Bani Singh, grandfather of the present Raja, are those of a man of great proportions, his coat of mail weighing sixteen and a half pounds—the whole set are studded with diamonds.

The *Treasure House* contains great teak chests of gold mohurs and costly jewels, an emerald cup cut out of a large single stone, another like it of ruby, magnificent strings of pearls, and a diamond valued at 100,000 rupees. Ranged round the walls are gorgeous trappings for elephants and horses, costly robes and shawls, and cupboards stored with priceless perfumes for the Zenana ladies.

The *Shish Khana*, or Hall of Mirrors, is furnished with a table of silver, with quaint crystal channels, in which coloured crystal fish are placed.

The stables are the Maharaja's special pride, for he is passionately fond of horses, and keeps up a fine breeding stud of the best Indian and English thoroughbreds. The cavalry of Ulwar, are the best mounted troops in India. Just beyond the stables are the kennels, where are kept lithe hunting-leopards, lynxes, and cheetahs, for chasing black buck, and other wild deer, as well as some handsome falcons.

All these places may be inspected by any reputable European traveller, but if his visit is to be a short one, he will do well to write for permission a few days beforehand, to the Diwan of Ulwar, or to the Maharaja's secretary.

The best time to see the Fort is early in the morning—it is a stiff climb, but litters or jhampans can easily be obtained by ordering them over-night through the mess-man of the Dak bungalow. There is nothing worth seeing in the fort itself, the magnificent view of the city and surrounding country being the only reward for the fatigue, except some curious old cannons. The ramparts run along the hills for a circle of two miles.

The streets of Ulwar are full of interest, and the bazars well worth strolling through; the people are tall and stately, the women wearing gay dresses of crimson and yellow, with saris embroidered with little round bits of looking-glass, which glitter like diamonds. In one of the squares is a small menagerie, with the usual cages of savage, man-eater tigers, and some other wild beasts. A short distance off is the famous elephant carriage, used by the Rajah at the feast of the Dasara. It is drawn by four elephants, will carry fifty persons, and is two stories high; it is a piece of barbaric splendour, of no artistic merit or interest.

A pleasant drive of about eight miles, through cotton fields, and between rocky hills, leads to the fine lake of Seliserh, where the Maharaja has built a pretty palace, and keeps a small steam-launch. The lake is an artificial tank about a mile long, embanked within the hills of a green valley. It not only supplies the capital with pure water, but irrigates much of the surrounding country.

The United Presbyterian Church of Scotland has a mission and schools at Ulwar.

REWARI. This station is the junction for the Rewari-Ferozpur section of the B. B. & C. I. Railway.—Travellers intending to go through to Lahore, will save about six hours by taking this route. The line runs through alternate tracts of sandy waste, and rich wheat and rice lands; the only towns of any importance being Hisar, Sirsah, and Ferozpur. At the two former there are extensive ruins of Mughal cities, but they are not worth stopping to see. Ferozpur is a comparatively modern place; a military cantonment, and the principal arsenal of the Panjab. The battle-field of Sobraon is twenty-four miles from Ferozpur, by a bad road only fit for country carts.

A very interesting cross-country journey may be made from Ferozpur to Lodiana, by a good road through the finest wheat district in India.. The distance is sixty-four miles, and the whole route is alive with busy country life, and studded with large, prosperous villages. There is a good Dak bungalow half way at Jagrama.

CHAPTER IX.

DELHI.

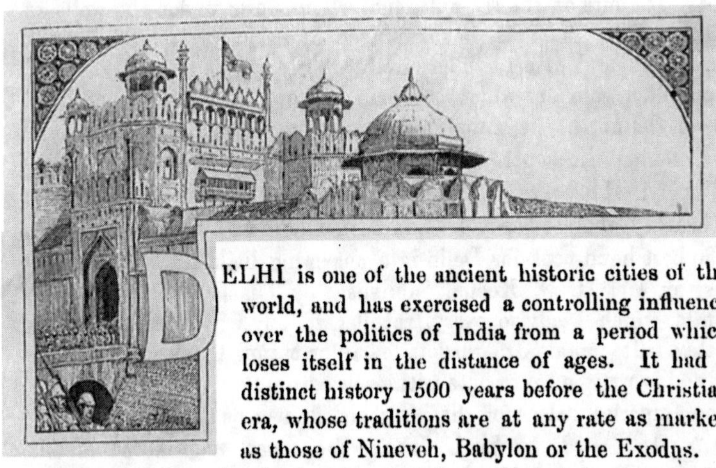

DELHI is one of the ancient historic cities of the world, and has exercised a controlling influence over the politics of India from a period which loses itself in the distance of ages. It had a distinct history 1500 years before the Christian era, whose traditions are at any rate as marked as those of Nineveh, Babylon or the Exodus.

Seven ancient and ruined cities, with colossal fortresses, splendid palaces, stupendous wells, magnificent temples and mosques, and gorgeous tombs stretch for twelve or fifteen miles on the great plain which lies between the Ridge and the river Jumna. Delhi may rank, for architectural beauty, historical associations, or present social interest with Rome, Athens, Cairo, Venice, or Constantinople.

Delhi cannot be seen in a day. It undoubtedly competes with Agra and Benares, for the right to be considered the most historical and profoundly interesting city in India.

Delhi has plenty of hotel accommodation. The hotels are mostly the property of natives, who rent them furnished to a caterer. The management changes continually, and the traveller must find out from Thomas Cook & Son, or from another traveller, which hotel has the best reputation at the time. There is now no Dak bungalow—it has become an hotel. For those who don't mind the noise of a railway station, the railway refreshment-rooms will be found central and comfortable, with good bed-rooms.

The guides who hang about the hotels are very ignorant, and few can speak more English than is sufficient to get themselves engaged. It is always best to settle a programme for a morning or afternoon, and get the hotel-keeper to give clear instructions to the driver of your carriage.

The modern city of Delhi is called Shahjahanabad, or else New Delhi. It abuts on the river Jumna, which flows under the walls of its famous fort. The city is surrounded by a lofty wall, strengthened with a ditch and *glacis*. The circuit of the wall is about six miles; there are ten gates, of which the principal are the Kashmir and Mori gates on the north, the Kabul and Lahore on the east, and the Ajmir and Delhi on the south. The population is about 180,000, pretty equally divided between Hindu and Muhammadan, who hate each other very heartily, and are ready to show their hatred at a moment's notice.

The best hand-book for Delhi is a charming little volume of eighty pages, by Mr. H. G. Keene, published by Thacker, Spink & Co., Calcutta, which I advise every traveller to buy who intends making any stay. It contains more detailed information than I am able to give, and is written up to date with each edition.

The Imperial Palace of the Mughals, known as the fort, was built in A.D., 1628—58, by Shah Jahan, the most magnificent of the imperial builders of India. In its glory, it was probably the most splendid palace in the world. As its massive and lofty red-sandstone walls, towers, and noble gateway burst upon the view on entering the Maidan in front, it is as impressive as the first sight of Windsor Castle from the Thames. The area within these walls is more than 1,000 yards long by 500 yards wide, and contains many buildings of unique beauty and interest, though many others have been cleared away by the ruthless exigences of a British military barracks. The Lahore, or as it is now called, the Victoria gate, is the main entrance, and faces the Chandni Chowk, separated from it by a fine park planted with trees. It is a singularly beautiful building, soaring 140 feet above the plain, its interior being a vaulted hall, 375 feet long, which Mr. Fergusson says forms the noblest entrance known to belong to any existing palace, presenting very much the effect of the nave of a gigantic gothic cathedral. There is a magnificent view of the city and surroundings from the top. Passing on through a bazar, in which stores of various kinds are sold, chiefly to the troops stationed in tho fort, the vast court of the palace opens out. The homely brick buildings right and left, are the modern barracks of English soldiers, and greatly mar the beauty of this marvellous palace. A ground plan of the whole fort, as it existed in Shah Jahan's time, will be found, with explanations, on page 592 of Fergusson's *Indian Architecture.*

The first of the original buildings is the Diwan-i-am, or public hall of audience, a beautiful colonnaded structure of red sandstone and inlaid marble. In the centre of the back wall is the royal throne and canopy, of white marble, decorated with *pictra dura*, representing flowers, fruits, birds, &c. Many of the bits of precious stone have been picked out and stolen. About one hundred yards further on a long range of buildings is reached, whose backs look over the Jumna. These are, beginning on the left, the Moti Masjid, the Akab baths, the Dewan-i-Khas, the Rung Mahal and the Zenana. A gateway under the Zenana leads out to an exercise ground on the river's bank, from which a good view of the whole line of buildings may be got. The Dewan-i-Khas was the private hall of audience. It is a building of pure white marble, ornamented without and within by inlaid work. The ceiling is richly decorated in gold and colour, and at one time was plated with silver, coined into rupees by the Maratha invaders in 1760. In the centre of this hall stands a white marble daïs, on which was once placed the famous peacock throne, a seat between two peacocks, whose spread tails were encrusted with sapphires, diamonds, rubies, emeralds and other precious stones, in imitation of the natural colours; over the back was a parrot, said to have been carved from a single emerald. This throne is reputed to have cost three to five millions sterling; it was realised by Nadir Shah in 1739. Over the north and south arches of the hall is a Persian inscription, raised and gilt, which may be translated: "If there be a paradise on earth, it is this, it is this, it is this." This hall is probably the most beautiful of all Shah Jahan's costly buildings, always excepting the Taj Mahal. In design, proportions, and decorations, it is choice to perfection. It measures ninety by seventy feet. The Akab baths lead out of the Dewan-i-Khas. They consist of three large rooms, lined and floored with white marble, delicately inlaid in patterns of *pictra dura.* They are crowned with marble domes, and are lighted from the roof. These chambers have been recently restored.

A courtyard on the other side leads into the lovely Rung Mahal, the entrance to which is one of the most perfect specimens of pierced marble screen work in all India. There is a small window in the centre of the screen, above which is the symbol of a pair of scales.

THE PEARL MOSQUE, DELHI.

The building contains a charming suite of rooms, with the usual *pietra dura* decoration, the arches of the doors leading from one to the other being inscribed with Persian couplets. The other buildings connected with the Rung Mahal are now used as officers' mess rooms, and a very horrible mess has been made of all their charming details! Opposite to the Akab baths is the jewel-like Moti Masjid, or Pearl mosque, sixty feet square, the daintiest little building in all India, a veritable "pearl of price." It was built in 1635 A.D. by Aurangzeb. The arches are Saracenic, and it possesses a bronze door of remarkable beauty.

Ex pede Herculem! From these brilliant remnants of this truly imperial palace, we may form some feeble idea of what it was in all its original glory, when the *Burj-i-Shameli*, the great marble bath-room, the *Metiaz-Mehal*, a huge quadrangle of palaces enclosing a garden 300 feet square, the *Nobatkhana*, or Music gate, the Golden mosque, the Hareem courts, and fifty other lovely pavilions, fountains and gardens, were thronged with the courtiers and retainers of the mighty Mughal emperors. These, and other glories of the palace, have all been swept away by successive barbarians. Nadir Shah, Ahmed Khan, and the Maratha chiefs, were content to strip the buildings of their precious metals and jewelled thrones; to the Government of the present Empress of India was left the last dregs of Vandalism, which, after the mutiny, pulled down these perfect monuments of Mughal art, to make room for the ugliest brick buildings from Simla to Ceylon.

Mr. Fergusson, commenting on this in his "Indian Architecture," says, "the whole of the Hareem courts of the palace were swept off the face of the earth to make way for a hideous British barrack, without those who carried out this fearful piece of Vandalism thinking it even worth while to make a plan of what they were destroying, or preserving any record of the most splendid palace in the world. Of the public parts of the palace all that now remains is the entrance hall, the Nobut Khana, the Dewani Aum, the Dewani Khas, and the Rung Mahal, now used as a mess-room, and one or two small pavilions. They are the gems of the palace, it is true; but without the courts and corridors connecting them they lose all their meaning, and more than half their beauty. Being now situated in the midst of a British barrack-yard they look like precious stones torn from their settings in some exquisite piece of oriental jeweller's work, and set at random in a bed of the commonest plaster."

The Jama Masjid is without rival among mosques. Nothing in Cairo can be ranged with it, and the great Constantinople mosque is only the converted Christian church of St. Sophia. It stands grandly isolated on a plateau of rock between the fort and the city, and is built of red sandstone, inlaid with white marble. It was begun by Shah Jahan in the fourth year of his reign, and finished in the tenth. There are three stately gates, approached by great flights of forty steps, the lowest of which is 150 feet long, on which hundreds of Musalmans lounge in picturesque groups. The principal gateway is finer than the other two, and faces the east; they lead into a vast courtyard, 450 feet square, surrounded by a cloister arcaded on both sides. The roof of this cloister is worth notice, being formed of sandstone slabs fifteen feet long. The court is paved with granite inlaid with marble. At one end is the mosque, 260 feet long and 120 feet wide. It is entered by a flight of marble steps, leading up to the great central archway eighty feet high. It is crowned by three domes of pure white marble, with two lofty minarets of marble and sandstone in alternate stripes. The best view of Delhi

THE JAMA MASJID, DELHI.

is obtained from their summits. The floor of the mosque is paved with slabs of white marble, with a border of black marble; each slab is three feet long by one and a half broad, and forms a "pew" for one person on Friday, when the mosque is thronged at noon with ten thousand devout Muhammadans.

The only other mosque in Delhi, with any architectural interest, is the Kalan Masjid, or Black mosque, near the Turkman gate. It was built in A.D. 1386 by Firoz Shah Tughlak, and was part of the city of Firozabad. It is a massive, undecorated building, though the openings of the walls are filled with some fine screen work in red sandstone. It is worth studying as an excellent and characteristic specimen of the Pathan architecture of the 14th century.

The mosque of Roshun-ud-Daula, with its three golden domes, is near the Northbrook fountain in the Chandni Chowk. Its interest is only historical, being the mosque from which Nadir Shah witnessed the terrible slaughter of the inhabitants in 1732. Near by is the Kotwali mosque, where Hodson exposed the dead bodies of the Delhi princes.

There are no Hindu temples worth visiting in Delhi city, but the beautiful Jain temple described and illustrated on page 259 of Fergusson's "Indian Architecture," situated up some winding lanes behind the Jama Musjid, may be viewed from 4 to 5 P.M.

The celebrated Chandni Chauk, or Silver street, the main thoroughfare of Delhi, is one of the most striking and picturesque streets in all India. It is nearly a mile long, and seventy-four feet broad. Down the middle runs an old aqueduct, now used as a footpath, shaded by a double avenue of neem and peepul trees. It is lined on both sides with the shops and handsome dwelling-houses of merchants, whose touts are the scourge of Delhi, swooping down upon every stranger like swarms of flies, pestering him to come and see their wares, cramming cards and circulars into his unwilling hands, screaming in the same breath the praises of their own shops, and the most terrible slanders of their opponents. These pests wake you in the morning, hang about you at breakfast, swarm round the hotel doors and verandahs, ride on the steps of your carriage, take short cuts, and come upon you unawares when you fondly hope you have got rid of them at last, and finally assemble at the railway station to curse you when you leave. Stony indifference is the only treatment.

The shops in the Chandni Chauk are full of Cashmere shawls, chadars, kincobs, brocades, gold and silver embroidery, wonderful loom-work, painting, jewellery, metal-work, enamels, carpets, pietra dura, pottery, weapons, armour, and all the other artistic melangerie for which India is famous. Travellers will do best in the long run by asking their bankers to recommend some firms of known respectability, and buy only from them. Manick Chand, for shawls, embroideries, and loom work generally, and the well-known firm of Ram Chand and Hazari Mull, for jewellery, are substantial men of good character and reputation. I have had satisfactory dealings with both firms. If a buyer tells them to ask a fixed price and stick to it, absolutely refusing to bargain, they will be reasonable enough. If, however, bargaining should be preferred, *Caveat emptor*, and he will eventually buy at one third less than the price asked, and a trifle more than he would have done on fixed price. With regard to the ruck of smaller men, no European or American can approach them in wiliness, or staying power in a bargain.

The visitor will pass repeatedly through the Queen's Gardens, which lie between the railway and the Chandni Chauk. These are well laid out with beautiful trees and shrubs, and abundant water from a branch of Ali Mardan's Canal. There is a small collection of wild beasts. The fine building facing the Chauk is the Institute, which contains the station library, a reading-room, the municipal-offices, a museum, public-hall, and a pleasant suite of rooms, used for dances and other social reunions of the English residents. Visitors find admission to all its privileges easy enough, through their bankers or any resident European.

Just outside the building, in the gardens, is a huge stone elephant, of considerable but unknown antiquity, brought here from Gwalior by Shah Jahan in 1645. The stone figures in the verandah of the museum, are those of two notable Rajput generals named Jaimal and Patta, who were slain by Akbar at the siege of Chitor. Keene's Guide contains a careful chapter on these ancient sculptures. There is not much to be seen in the museum. There is a fine clock tower opposite, in the Chandni Chauk, 128 feet high, built by the municipality at a cost of 25,000 rupees.

The handsome native hotel, called the Queen's Serai, is in the Queen's Road, near the railway-station, and well deserves a visit. It is a huge quadrangle of separate rooms or small buildings, in each of which some native commercial traveller or merchant is located. There are strangers from all parts of India to be seen here at times. The fine church in the same road, is St. Mary's, Roman Catholic.

The old fort of Salimgarh, lies on the river between the Fort and the bridge. It was built about 1530, and possesses no features of special note.

The cemetery is near the Kashmir Gate, and contains many interesting tombs and monuments. Among them is that of the hero of the siege of Delhi, during the mutiny, General John Nicholson, who, leading the assault, was struck down mortally wounded at the moment of victory. There is an older grave-yard hard by, filled with nameless graves. A pretty cross, twenty-five feet high has been erected, with an inscription to the memory "of those whose nameless graves lie around."

The Memorial Church of St. James is in the same neighbourhood, in a charming and well-kept garden. It was built by Colonel Skinner, at his sole cost, as stated on a tablet facing the altar, "in fulfilment of a vow made, while lying wounded, on the field of battle, in grateful acknowledgment of the mercy of Divine Providence, and in testimony of his sincere faith in the truth of the Christian religion." Round the walls of the church are many memorial tablets, chiefly to those who were murdered during the horrors of the mutiny.

The Kaṣhmir Gate, and its story, are too familiar to Englishmen to require any lengthy comment. It is a plain double-arched gateway in the city wall, left in the semi-ruined condition of the siege, great holes pounded by cannon-balls being visible not only in the gate itself, but in the wall on each side.

Few Englishmen will care to leave Delhi without visiting all the scenes of the famous siege of 1857. The best general view of the British lines is obtained from the Mutiny Memorial, on the top of the Ridge, a mile or so outside the Kashmir or Mori Gates. This is a beautiful monument, 110 feet high, from the summit of which an expert can point out all the various batteries and other details of the siege operations. Keene's excellent little Guide Book gives all the needful information, with some simple maps giving the positions of the contending forces. It would not be possible for a civilian to write any adequate description of this heroïc and historic struggle; but the traveller who wishes to visit all the battlefield, and master its smaller details, will find the information he requires, in the book-shelves of the Institute Library.

Having exhausted New Delhi the traveller will want to make arrangements for visiting Ferozabad, Indraput, Siri, Jahanpuna, Lalkot and Tughlakabad, all of which were in their turn Imperial cities, and together form the district, some thirty square miles in area, now known as "Old Delhi."

If time presses they can all be visited in a day, by sending a spare pair of horses over night to Lalkot, and starting at daybreak. It is, however, hurried work, and leaves very little time for detailed observation. It is better to take two days, spending the night at the comfortable bungalow under the Kutab-Minar at Lalkot, and making a special morning excursion some other day to Ferozabad and Indraput, which are only a mile or two outside the city wall.

The road to the far-famed Kutab-Minar is quite an Indian

"Appian Way," both sides being lined with tombs and mausoleums, the bulk of which, however, have no architectural or historical interest.

The first important building is the "Jantar Mantar," one of the huge observatories built by Jai Singh, Rajah of Jaipur, 1730 A.D.

The largest of the group is an enormous equatorial dial called the *Semrat Yantar*, or "Prince of Dials." The dimensions of the gnomon, which may be ascended by sixty-six steps, are :—

Length of hypothenuse	. .	118· 5 feet.
,, base	. . . .	104· 0 ,,
,, perpendicular	. .	56·75 ,,

The building is rather dilapidated, and is only of interest to those who have some rudimentary knowledge of the uses of an observatory.

There are also structures for taking observations of the stars by means of converse globes, an astrolabe, and others.

Three miles further on, the mausoleum of Safdar Jang is reached, standing in a walled inclosure about 900 feet square. It is raised to the memory of a successful general and vizier, who died A.D. 1753.

It is built of red sandstone and white marble, and contains a richly decorated sarcophagus. It is a good specimen of the degraded Moghal architecture of the last century.

Half way on the cross road between this mausoleum and Humayun's, is an interesting group of four tombs and a mosque, the exact date of which is lost in controversy. By some authorities they are of the Lodi period, 15th century, while others maintain they are much older; I can only state that I found them very beautiful both in design and surroundings, and well worth visiting if time permit.

After leaving Safdar Jang's tomb, a building is seen across the fields to the right of the road. This is the tomb of Firoz Shah, who died A.D. 1388. It is placed on the bank of a still more ancient tank, 100 acres in extent, constructed by Ala-ud-din in the 13th century. This tank is now quite ruined and dry, the bottom being under cultivation. There is no road to it, but it can be reached by walking one and a half miles.

On the left, about a mile short of the Kutab-Minar, are scattered the ruins of Muhammed Toglak's city of Jahanpuna, about A.D. 1330, and Siri, built by Sultan Ala-ud-din A.D. 1300. Both these cities have been used as stone-quarries for 500 years, and there is nothing left of Jahanpuna but huge mounds of rubbish and a section of the city wall. At Siri, the remnants of the old fortress of Shahpur, within which was the famous palace of Hazar Minar, or the thousand minarets, of which enough details are still distinguishable to give some faint idea of the splendour of Ala-ud-din's city.

Another mile, and the glory of Delhi, the soaring Kutab-Minar, is reached. This magnificent tower is 238 feet high, twice the height of the Duke of York's Column, tapering from nearly fifty feet in diameter at the base to nine feet at the top. It is divided into five stories. The lower story is ninety-five feet high, and consists of twenty-four faces in the form of convex flutings, alternately semicircular and rectangular. In the second story, which is fifty-one feet high, these projections are all semicircular; in the third floor, forty-one feet, they are all rectangular; the fourth, twenty-six feet, is a plain cylinder; the fifth, twenty-five feet, is partly fluted and partly plain. Each story is divided by a boldly projecting gallery running round the tower. The whole structure is encrusted with chapters from the Koran sculptured in low relief. A circular staircase of 375 steps leads to the top, and no traveller, who is equal to the exertion, should forego the view to be obtained from it. Spread out like a map is the whole Delhi plain, on which may be picked out the well-defined walls limiting the great fortified palaces and citadels which have one by one disappeared with the successive dynasties which created them, leaving only Titanic ruins as the memorials of their

THE KUTAB-MINAR.

vanished empires. The Kutab-Minar is supposed to be the most perfect, as well as the second loftiest tower in the world. Its carvings are as fresh as though they were of yesterday's date, though it is 650 years since it was finished. Its beauty of form and colour—red sandstone and white marble, contrasted with the intense blue of an Indian sky—cannot be described at all. I do not know of anything that can be compared with it for beauty of design and perfection of proportion, except that wonderful masterpiece of Italy's great architect, the Campanile of Giotto, at Florence, which was erected about the same period, and which is thirty feet higher. The Kutab-Minar was commenced by Kutab-ud-din, in the latter part of the 12th century, and finally completed by Altamsh, his successor, about A.D. 1210—20. It is a Tower of Victory, and has looked down upon the Hindus conquered by its founder, under an unbroken Muhammadan sway, from its completion, until the Mutiny in 1857.

About 150 yards from the Kutab-Minar, a second tower of twice its dimensions was begun by Ala-du-din, Altamsh's successor, but the project was abandoned before it had reached a height of fifty feet. It stands on the opposite side of the Delhi road.

The Kutab-Minar rises from the centre of the old Hindu fortress of Lalkot, built about A.D. 1060, whose massive walls, thirty feet thick, still surround it in sufficient preservation to enable the spectator to trace them distinctly from the summit of the tower. Considerable sections are still standing, sixty feet high, with great bastions at the angles. In the west wall portions of two or three gateways can still be made out. The inner walls are altogether two and a quarter miles in circumference. The outer walls, which extend further into the plain, belong to a later fortification, built during the following century by Raja Pithora, the last champion of Hindu independence in Upper India, who was defeated by Muhammad of Ghor, A.D. 1191, in a great battle under the walls of the fortress which still bears his name, and put to death afterwards in cold blood.

The group of buildings surrounding the Kutab-Minar possess, like the "Two and a half days" Mosque at Ajmir, built also by Altamsh, the peculiar features of a Muhammadan mosque constructed from the spoils of Hindu temples. This mosque of Altamsh at Lalkot has all its walls of Musalman architecture, while its columns are Hindu. The pillars are very elaborate, though much injured by iconoclasm; but figures of Jain saints may be seen here and there in the roof and obscure corners. The great central range of arches, extending about 380 feet, consists of three large and eight smaller arches, the central

MOSQUE AND IRON PILLAR, LALKOT.

one being fifty-three feet high and twenty-two feet wide. The great central arch is in excellent preservation, but the smaller ones are much dilapidated.

In the centre of the courtyard of this mosque an ancient iron pillar stands, which is one of the most curious things in India. It stands twenty-two feet above the ground, and its base, which is bulbous, is rivetted to stone slabs two feet below the surface. Its diameter at the base is 16·4 inches, and at the capital 12·05 inches. It is a malleable forging, welded together in sections. The iron is quite pure, without alloy. There are six lines in Sanscrit inscribed upon it; it is dedicated to Vishnu, and is a memorial of victory, erected by one Raja

ALA-UD-DIN'S GATEWAY, LALKOT.

Bhava, to commemorate "the defeat of the Bahilkas, near the seven mouths of the Indus," which fixes the date of its erection as A.D. 360—400. It weighs about six tons, and it is a striking fact that the Hindus, so long ago, could forge a bar of iron larger and heavier than any that have been forged, even in Europe, until a very recent date.

Just outside the north-west corner of the mosque stands the tomb of its builder, Altamsh, who died A.D. 1236. It is very beautiful in its details, especially in its interior decorations. It was built by his son and daughter, and is the oldest Musalman tomb known to exist in India. The roof has gone, but it is otherwise in fair preservation.

The noble southern gateway of the mosque was added by Ala-ud-din, seventy or eighty years later, and is supposed to be the finest specimen extant of the early Pathan style of architecture. The whole of this wonderful group of buildings which include and surround the Kutab-Minar, is fully described in Fergusson's "Indian Architecture," pp. 500—510.

About half a mile to the south-west of the Kutab-Minar, are the beautiful white marble tombs of two Maulavis, called Jamala and Kamalu; the side walls are richly decorated with coloured glazed tiles. The mosque of Faizullah Khan is close by, and is worth seeing.

On the road to the neighbouring village of Maharoli, is the tomb of Adham Khan, one of Akbar's generals, now a police station. At Maharoli, a mile distant from the Dak bungalow, are a collection of tombs of kings and nobles about and after the time of Aurangzeb, the ruins of a palace and gateway, some tanks, and other picturesque remains. But it is impossible even to mention all the numerous and splendid ruins, which are scattered about the plain within a radius of two miles from the Kutab-Minar.

The vast and desolate fortress of Tughlakabad, the stronghold and capital of the Emperor Tughlak, lies about four miles from the Kutab bungalow. This cyclopean group of buildings was erected A.D. 1321, and consists of a citadel, a vast enclosing fortress with thirteen gates, and a huge hexagon of outer walls including an area five miles in circumference. Tughlak Ghazi Khan was a successful military adventurer, whose life was one of those topsy-turvies only possible in oriental empires. He started life as a Turki slave, who, after being raised by his master, a renegade Hindu Emperor, to the position of Governor of the Punjab, rose in revolt against him, murdered him, and seized the throne. His dynasty, a series of ferocious ruffians whose kingdom was in continual revolt, lasted nearly 100 years, and was finally wiped out by Tamerlane A.D. 1398. Timur stormed Tuglakabad, had a five days' slaughter of the inhabitants, after the manner of the times, and left the city in ruins, the abode of the vulture, the panther and the jackal, whose descendants are the sole inhabitants to-day.

"The fort of Tughlakabad may be described with tolerable accuracy as a half-hexagon in shape, with three faces rather more than three-quarters of a mile in length each, and a base of one mile and a half, the whole circuit being only one furlong less than four miles. The fort stands on a rocky height, and is built of massive blocks of stone, so large and heavy that they must have been quarried on the spot. The largest stone which I observed measured fourteen feet in length by two feet two inches, and one foot ten inches in breadth and thickness, and must have weighed rather more than six tons. The short faces to the north-west and east are protected by a deep ditch, and the long face to the south by a large sheet of water, which is held up by an embankment at the south-east corner. On this side the rock is

TUGHLAK'S TOMB.

scarped, and above it the main walls rise to a mean height of forty feet, with a parapet of seven feet, behind which rises another wall of fifteen feet, the whole height above the low ground being upwards of ninety feet. In the south-west angle is the citadel, which occupies about one-sixth of the area of the fort, and contains the ruins of an extensive palace. The ramparts are raised as usual on a line of domed rooms, which rarely communicate with each other, and which no doubt formed the quarters of the troops that garrisoned the fort. The walls slope rapidly inwards, even as much as those of Egyptian buildings. The rampart walls are pierced with loopholes, which serve also to give light and air to the soldiers' quarters. The parapets are pierced with low sloping loopholes, which command the foot of the wall, and are crowned with a line of rude battlements of solid stone, which are also provided with loopholes. The walls are built of large plainly dressed stones, and there is no ornament of any kind; but the vast size, the great strength, and the visible solidity of the whole give to Tughlakabad an air of stern and massive grandeur, that is both striking and impressive. The fort of Tughlakabad has thirteen gates, and there are three inner gates to the citadel; it contains seven tanks of water besides the ruins of several large buildings, as the Jama Masjid and the Burj Munder. Tho upper part of the fort is full of ruined houses, but the lower part appears as if it had never been fully inhabited."—*Cunningham.*

The tomb of Tughlak is opposite the fort, in a small but strong citadel, surrounded by what was once a lake, but which is now dry and grass-grown; the causeway by which the tomb was reached, still remains. It is a solid, simple but very impressive building in much better preservation than the fortress. Inside the mausoleum are the tombs of Tughlak himself, his queen, and his son and successor Muhammed, who built the fortress on the opposite hill of Adilibad.

The powerful rock-like sloping walls, and massive towers, which surround the tomb, and the stern uncompromising architecture of the mausoleum itself, are fitting surroundings to the last resting place of this fierce warrior king. Very few travellers visit Tughlakabad. Guides and drivers look upon it only as added trouble, and are dissuasive. I passed it by myself on my first visit to Delhi, but afterwards spent a day wandering through its desolate streets, and deserted fortifications. It has made as lasting an impression on my memory as anything in India.

Humayun's tomb is about four miles from Delhi. It was built by Akbar the Great about 1560 A.D. in memory of his father the Emperor Humayun. It took sixteen years to build, and cost fifteen lakhs of rupees. It stands in the midst of a great garden of eleven acres, now a tangled waste, raised on a lofty double platform adorned with arches. It is built of red sandstone, decorated with marble inlay, crowned by a superb dome of white marble, estimated at three fourths the size of that of St. Paul's, London. The tomb itself is a large octagonal chamber. Four sides are occupied by doorways, and the other four lead into small octagonal chapels, rendering the building nearly square on the outside dimensions. It is about sixty-five feet in diameter, and seventy feet high to the top of the dome.

The enclosure is surrounded by a wall, the main gateway being a lofty and fitting entrance to this splendid tomb. Humayun's mausoleum has a special interest, from being the first of that succession of royal mausoleums for which India is renowned, of which Akbar's tomb at Sikandra, and the Taj Mahal at Agra are the more excellent sequels. Five of Humayun's successors to the crown of Delhi lie buried here, as well as eleven other viziers, generals and statesmen, deemed worthy of interment under the same royal dome. Some of the tombs are finely carved, and there is much beautiful pierced marble and stone-work throughout; it is undoubtedly one of the most striking buildings in all India. It was to this building that the two sons of the last king of Delhi fled, after the storming of the city in 1857. They were discovered by Hodson, who shot them afterwards.

THE TOMB OF HUMAYUN.

The beautiful cemetery of Nizam-ud-din is a short distance from Humayun's tomb, where lies buried the brilliant Shah Nizam-ud-din, Ala-ud-din's general, reputed to be the founder of Thuggism, and the murderer of Tughlak, whose tomb, hoary and time-worn, is enclosed in a very finely-pierced marble screen, surrounded by a verandah of white marble; the roof of the verandah is painted in a flower pattern. This singular and remarkable tomb is surrounded by many others of great beauty, notably those of the poet Khusru, the laureate of Tughlak's court, whose songs are still popular in India; of Muhammad Shah, Emperor of Delhi from 1719 to 1748; of Jahanara Begum, daughter of the Emperor Shah Jehan, whose inscription begs that nothing but grass may cover her, a wish still respected, and the lovely modern tomb of Mirza Jahangir.

NIZAM-UD-DIN'S TOMB.

Nizam-ud-din's Baoli, or well house, is within the enclosure, and the idlers of the place jump into the water, feet foremost, a height of seventy feet, for the pleasure of visitors, and for half rupees for themselves.

Indrapat, or Purana Kila, is the most ancient of all the dead cities of the Delhi plain. It was founded 2000 years B.C., by Yudisthira, first king of the Pandu dynasty of Indraprastha, whose subjects were the earliest Aryan immigrants into India. He was succeeded by thirty generations of successors to the throne, until his line was extinguished by the usurpation of Visarwa, prime minister of the last king. Indrapat, neglected and allowed to fall to decay by its Musalman conquerors, was at last rebuilt by Humayun, whose capital it became. Most of the walls and the citadel date from his time, but portions are still pointed out, which antiquarians allege are as old as 1500 B.C. Every gateway is now built up except the one illustrated below. Passing through its portals, and continuing through a squalid village, the singularly beautiful, but now desolate, mosque of Shir Shah, A.D. 1541, is reached. The fine octagon of red sandstone, seventy feet high, beyond the mosque, is called the Shir Mauzil, and was Humayun's library. The little chapel near the bazar is a station of the Baptist mission at Delhi.

INDRAPAT.

The ruins of Firozabad lie about a mile outside the Delhi gate on the banks of the Jumna. There is hardly one stone left upon another of the old capital built by Firoz Shah Tughlak, A.D. 1351–88. The only building not in absolute ruins is the Kotila, a three-storied house erected as a platform for the famous Stambha or Lat of King Asoka. This remarkable pillar is a monolith of pink sandstone, 42 ft. 7 in. long, and about 3 ft. 6 in. in diameter. The inscriptions on the pillar are mainly the edicts of Asoka, promulgating his religion of reformed Buddhism. A careful explanation of the Lats of Asoka, which are found at Allahabad, Tirhut, Sankisa, and many other places, will be found in *Fergusson*, pp. 52—56.

I have now briefly described the chief points of interest in this great plain of ruined cities. If my readers wish for more detailed information than can be found in these pages, which will probably be found sufficient for the ordinary traveller who is not a student of architecture, he will find it in the pages of Fergusson, or in the more extended writings of General Cunningham, the great authority on Delhi archæology. His works will be found on the shelves of the Institute Library in the Chandni Chauk.

Delhi is a city of merchants rather than handicraftsmen, but it enjoys a high reputation for gold and silk embroidery, jewellery, ivory painting, and carving, and other ornamental goods of fine workmanship, and its glazed pottery is only second in quality to that of Peshawar. The foundation of its art manufactures, especially loom fabrics, was laid by Akbar, who brought together at Delhi the best workmen he could get from various parts of India, Persia, and even Europe. Sir George Birdwood writes, in his Industrial Arts of India:

"It has been through the encouragement given by the great native princes and chiefs, and the cultivated taste of the common people, that the sumptuary arts of India have been brought to such artistic perfection. From the *Ayin Akbari, or Institutes of the Emperor Akbar*[A.D. 1556—1605], written by Abdul Fazl, Akbar's great minister, we learn that the Mogol emperors of Delhi maintained in their palaces skilled workmen from every part of India. It is said that Akbar took a great delight in painting, and had in his service a large number of artists, in order that they 'might vie with each other in fame, and become eminent by their productions.' Once a week he inspected the work of every artist, when in proportion to their individual merits they were honoured with premiums, and their regular salaries were increased. In the armoury also the emperor personally superintended the preparation of the various weapons which were forged and decorated there in every stage of their manufacture. In the workshop of the imperial wardrobe the weavers and embroiderers of every country were to be found, and whatever was made by them was carefully kept, and those articles of which there thus came in time to be a superfluity were given away in presents of honour. Through the attention of the emperor the manufacture of various new fabrics was established at Delhi. The skill of the imperial manufacturers increased also with their number, so that the cloths of Persia, Europe and China became drugs in the market. The emperor was very fond of woollen stuffs, particularly shawls; and the *Ayin Akbari* gives a list of all the varieties made in the palace, which were classified according to their date, value, colour, and weight. He had a vast establishment of jewellers, inlayers in gold, silver, crystal, and carnelian; damascene workers, chiefly for ornamenting arms; enamellers; plain workers in gold and silver; and pierced workers; embossers; 'inlayers with little grains of gold,' whose art will be further noticed in connection with the modern jewellery of Delhi; makers of gold and silver lace [*simbaft*] for sword-belts, &c.; engravers and workers in a sort of *nillo;* stone engravers, and lapidaries, and other artists. Sir John Chardin, who travelled in the East from 1664 to 1670, in his *Journal du Voyage* [London, 1686, Amsterdam, 1711], tells us that the kings and nobles of Persia also then maintained, as they do now, manufactures of all the arts and trades in their '*carconés*' [*karkhanas*] or workshops. He compares these factories to the galleries of the Grand Duke of Florence and of the Louvre.

"They entertain in these places a large number of excellent master-workmen who have a salary and daily rations for their lives, and are provided with all the materials for their work. They receive a present and an increase of salary for every fine work they produce. Their appointments were hereditary. This was formerly, and is now also, the case in India. In the Indian Museum collection of jade there is a large engraved bowl, on which a family of lapidaries, in the employ of the emperors of Delhi, was engaged for three generations. It is only in this way that artistic excellence in works of industry can ever be attained, and it is thus that the finest enamels and damascened work and shawls are still produced in India in the royal factories respectively of Jaipur, Hyderabad and Srinagar."

Delhi has always been a great centre for the manufacture of gemmed and enamelled jewellery. Its wealthy merchants, such as Ram Chand and Hazari Mull, will spread out on the floor of their house a stock of tiaras, aigrettes, head-ornaments, earrings, ear chains, nose rings and studs, necklaces of pearls, diamonds and other precious stones, cubes and tablets of gold set with stones on one side, and covered with brilliant enamel on the other, armlets, anklets, bracelets in gold and silver, of endless variety of form and beauty of decoration. The merchants, however, are very reluctant to show these exquisite specimens of native jewellery to Europeans, who, I regret to say, seldom buy them, while they will pay far larger prices for jewellery set and designed in European fashion, which is pretty and cheap enough in its way.

The exquisite miniatures, known as "Delhi paintings," are drawn in colours on ivory, with a fine pen. They are mostly portraits of famous Rajas and views of well-known buildings, but the artists will produce portraits from photographs, in which they manage at once to preserve the likeness and transform the subject into a Hindu. These pictures are very expensive if painted by really good artists, but are not of much real value, except as specimens of a unique art.

Delhi has always been famous for gem engraving. The old Delhi work in engraved and gem-encrusted jade of the Mughal period is of priceless value. There are some exquisite specimens in the Indian Museum at South Kensington. The modern imitation of this beautiful jewellery is very tasteful and pretty. Much of it is made in Delhi and also imported from Jaipur for sale by the Delhi jewellers. There are many clever carvers in ivory and wood in the bazars of the city, whose work is exposed for sale in the Chandni Chauk shops. There is no better place than Delhi in which to collect the native ornaments which make even the poorest Hindu woman look smart and well dressed. The large beads worn round the neck, and the bracelets and armlets of the humble folk in the bazars are generally lacquered wood, or bronzed, silvered or gilt. The silvering is produced by mixing tinfoil and lac together till they amalgamate; this, when thoroughly purified is boiled up into a solution, spread upon the wooden beads, and burnished when dry. The gilt is got by boiling myrrh, copal, and sweet oil together, and applying with a brush. The imitation of the genuine metal is excellent, but is often spoilt by having coloured glass stuck about the beads to imitate precious stones. I bought a biscuit-box full of the most charming and effective sham jewellery for a few rupees. They look very pretty, grouped with brass lotas and Indian glazed pottery, in a corner cupboard.

Delhi is famous for its leather work, and produces any quantity of cheap slippers, embroidered in pinchbeck and imitation silver, to the great detriment of the genuine gold and silver embroidered slippers of Lucknow. There is also a considerable manufacture of musical instruments, many of which are not only interesting as curiosities, but also remarkable for the beauty and variety of their forms.

Delhi is, after Calcutta and Bombay, the largest market in India for cotton goods, many Manchester houses finding it worth while to have resident agents to look after their trade. Manchester does not have all its own way, for there are two or three cotton-mills recently established, besides innumerable hand-loom weavers making every variety of native dress pieces. Delhi is noted for its muslin turbans, which are in great request all over India. I have bought most artistic pieces of native cotton fabrics, hand-printed, in the Delhi bazars for a few coppers. Delhi is a great depôt of the crafts of gold-lace weaving, spangle making, gilt embroidery, and all the trades connected with silver-gilt wire drawing, and gilt thread. The weavers, however, do not produce the rich and costly brocades and kincobs made at Ahmadabad and Benares, and inexperienced travellers should be very careful indeed in buying this description of loom work. Many of the cashmere shawls offered in the Chandni Chauk have been embroidered in Delhi with inferior tinsel thread. There is some very pretty cheap embroidery with coloured floss silk upon muslin, which is special to this city. The Delhi pottery, both glazed and enamelled, is excellent, and some good pieces may be picked up in the bazars. It is not, however, equal to that made at Lahore, Peshawar, or Multan. The traveller who is not able to go into the Punjab, yet wishes to take away with him some specimens of the finest loom-work and embroideries produced there, will find splendid and well-assorted stocks in the warehouses of the Delhi merchants, who indeed are able among them to produce good specimens of almost every art-manufacture in India, North, South, East, and West.

There are two extensive Christian missions at Delhi, in connection with the Baptist Missionary Society, and the Society for the Propagation of the Gospel in Foreign Parts. The Society for the Propagation of the Gospel has three missionaries, six or seven Cambridge Brethren, nine catechists, fourteen readers, twenty-eight schools of all sorts, eight churches and chapels, about 200 communicants, and 1,400 pupils in their schools. It also has an active Zenana Mission, consisting of fifteen ladies, and ten Christian native teachers. The beautiful memorial church used by the Indian adherents of this mission is in the very centre of the city, in the road leading from the railway-station to the Chandni Chauk; it possesses the unusual feature of two Baptisteries, a font for sprinkling infants, and a larger one for the immersion of adult converts who may prefer this method. There is always a crowded congregation at the Vernacular services on Sunday. This is one of the most interesting missions in India, and the Cambridge brethren are always glad to show the work to appreciative visitors.

The Baptist Mission and College are situated on the Maidan, a little beyond the Jama Masjid. There are four missionaries in charge of Delhi, three European and one Indian, and about twenty-six village stations in the district. There is also a well-organized Zenana Mission, under the superintendence of Miss Thorn, a lady of great ability and experience, assisted by six or seven Englishwomen, and several native teachers. The number of communicants is about 400, and the children in the various day-schools about 600.

The Baptist College is an institution for training native Christians for the Ministry. There are usually about twenty students, who receive a careful education in arts and theology. English services are conducted by the Baptist missionaries every Sunday in a handsome chapel in the Chandni Chauk, for the benefit of English residents in Delhi, and the garrison.

MEERUT is the principal military station of the North West, and is the military head-quarters of a division, including the garrisons of Delhi, Agra, Fatehgarh, Muttra, Dehra Dun, Landaur, Rurki, and Chakrata. The traveller who wishes to see something of Indian cantonment life, cannot do better than stay a day or two at Meerut, especially if he has introductions to residents there. There are good hotels and a Dak bungalow, a fine church seating 3,000 persons, but nothing of Indian interest. The Mall is accounted one of the most beautiful drives in India.

CHAPTER X.

SAHARANPUR.—SIMLA.—AMRITSAR.

SAHARANPUR is a well-built town, of 50,000 inhabitants, with a good hotel and Dak bungalow. There are some excellent agricultural and botanical gardens established by Government, an old fort used as a courthouse, and a few handsome tombs, but nothing worthy of serious attention. There is a vigorous and thriving American Presbyterian Mission. From Saharanpur there is a good carriage road to Dehra Dun and Mussooree—two popular hill stations. Mussooree is about 7,000 feet above the sea, and in popularity as a health resort, ranks next to Simla. The views of the snowy ranges of the Himalayas are very fine, but greatly inferior to Darjiling. Mussooree is much colder than Darjiling, and during the winter months is subject to heavy falls of snow. It is a twelve or fourteen hours' journey from Saharanpur. Dehra Dun is a very beautiful district, with an increasing tea crop on the slopes of the hills. It is a famous district for sport of all kinds, the Mahseer fishing being the best in India.

SIMLA is the summer capital of India. The "Simla exodus"

from Calcutta, as soon as the hot weather fairly sets in, is the great Anglo-Indian event of the year, the whole of the Government departments transferring their offices to this beautiful hill station. During the winter Simla is deserted. The town is seventy-eight miles from Ambala—an important cantonment and trading centre on the North Western Railway. The journey is made by Dak gharries or mail tongas, and takes about twelve hours to accomplish.

Ambala is a native walled city of 25,000 inhabitants, with a cantonment of about the same population, the garrison consisting of two regiments each of native and British troops, with three batteries of artillery. It is a good centre for sport. The American Presbyterian Board of Missions and the Church Missionary Society have stations here.

The traveller should, if possible, time his departure from Ambala so as to reach the foot of the hills by daybreak, that he may enjoy to the full the beautiful scenery which awaits him. There are good hotels at Kalka, thirty-eight miles from Ambala, nearly half way. Four hours' journey from Kalka is Kasauli, 6,300 feet above the sea, a popular hill station and sanitarium, situated in the midst of lovely scenery. Here is the Lawrence Military Asylum, a valuable orphan school maintained by the Government.

Twenty-seven miles beyond Kalka, by the longer route, is Solan, where there is a good Dak bungalow, from whence it is thirty miles more to Simla. From Solan the scenery is magnificent, the road twisting in and out between high rocks, and hanging over precipitous valleys. The shorter road passes through Haripur and Siri. It is best to go one way and return the other.

The population of Simla, in the winter, is about 15,000. This number is greatly increased on the arrival of the "Simla exodus," when the Government and all the departments come up from Calcutta. The mean elevation above sea level is 7,084 feet. It is very cold during the winter, and is often covered with a deep fall of snow.

"Lieutenant Ross, Assistant Political Agent for the Hill States, erected the first residence—a thatched wooden cottage, in 1819. Three years afterwards, his successor, Lieutenant Kennedy, built a permanent house. Officers from Ambala and neighbouring stations quickly followed the example, and in 1826 the new settlement had acquired a name. A year later Lord Amhurst, the Governor-General, after completing his progress through the North-West, on the conclusion of the successful Bhartpur campaign, spent the summer at Simla. From that date the sanitarium rose rapidly into favour with the European population of Northern India. Year after year, irregularly at first, but as a matter of course after a few seasons, the seat of Government was transferred for a few weeks in every summer from the heat of Calcutta to the cool climate of the Himalayas. Successive Governors-General resorted with increasing regularity to Simla during the hot weather. Situated in the recently annexed Punjab, it formed an advantageous spot for receiving the great chiefs of Northern and Western India, numbers of whom annually come to Simla to pay their respects to the British Suzerain. It also presented greater conveniences as a starting-point for the Governor-General's cold-weather tour than Calcutta, which is situated in the extreme south-east corner of Bengal. At first only a small staff of officials accompanied the Governor-General to Simla; but since the administration of Sir John Lawrence (1864), Simla has practically been the summer capital of the Government of India, with its secretariats and headquarters establishments, unless during exceptional seasons of famine on the plains, as in 1874.

"Under these circumstances the station grew with extraordinary rapidity. From 30 houses in 1830 it increased to upwards of 100 in 1841, and 290 in 1866. In February, 1881, the number of occupied houses was 1141. At present the bungalows extend over the whole length of a considerable ridge, which runs east and west in a crescent shape, with its concave side pointing southward. The extreme ends of the station lie at a distance of six miles from one another. Eastward the ridge culminates in the peak of Jako, over 8,000 feet in height, and nearly 1,000 feet above the average elevation of the station. Woods of deodar oak and rhododendrons clothe its sides, while a tolerably level road, five miles long, runs round its base. Another grassy height, known as Prospect Hill, of inferior elevation to Jako, and devoid of timber, closes the western extremity of the crescent. The houses cluster thickest upon the southern slopes of Jako, and of two other hills lying near the western end. The Viceregal Lodge, formerly named Peterhoff, stands upon one of the latter, while the other is crowned by a large building erected for an observatory, but now used as an ordinary residence. A new and more commodious Viceregal residence is now (1886) in course of erection on the Observatory hill, a little to the west of the present Government House. The church stands at the western base of Jako, below which,

SIMLA.

on the south side of the hill, the native bázár cuts off one end of the station from the other. The eastern portion bears the name of Chota Simla, while the most western extremity is known as Boileauganj. A beautiful northern spur, running at right angles to the main ridge, and still clothed with oak and rhododrendron trees, has acquired the complimentary designation of Elysium. Three and a half miles from the western end a battery of artillery occupies the detached hill of Jutogh. The exquisite scenery of the neighbourhood is unrivalled.

"The public institutions include the Bishop Cotton School, the Punjab Girls' School, the Mayo Industrial Girls' School, a Roman Catholic convent, a hospital, a dispensary, and a handsome town hall now [1886] approaching completion. The Government buildings comprise a district court-house and treasury, *tahsílí* and police office, post-office, telegraph station, &c. Until recently, the various offices were located in ordinary private houses, in many cases widely distant from each other. Since 1884 the offices of the Imperial Government have been concentrated in blocks of handsome buildings, centrally situated, and constructed at a cost of upwards of half a million sterling" (*Hunter*).

The commerce of the town consists mainly in the supply of necessaries to the summer visitors and their dependents; but a brisk export trade exists in opium, *charas* (an intoxicating preparation of hemp), fruits, nuts, and shawl-wool, collected from the neighbouring hills, or brought in from beyond the border, *viâ* Rámpur. Numerous European shops supply the minor wants of visitors, most of them being branches of Calcutta firms. The station has three English banks, a club, and several churches; and two European breweries are situated in the valley below. The great deficiency of Simla lies in its inadequate water supply. A water supply by means of pipes supplies Simla with water from the Mahásu range; but the constantly increasing population puts a strain upon the works which they are at times scarcely able to bear, and a further extension of the works, by the construction of additional reservoirs, is now well advanced towards completion. The springs are few in number, and several of them run dry during the summer months, when the demand for water is greatest.

There is a Baptist Mission in Simla, under the superintendence of Rev. James Smith.

Patiala.—This interesting city lies about an hour's railway journey from Rajpur junction. It is the capital of a Sikh state, the principal of the group of native states known as the "Country of the Cis-Sutlej." The state of Patiala has an area of 5,412 square miles, and a population of 1,600,000. The young Maharaja, Rajendra Singh, who came to the throne in 1888, is a cultured and enlightened ruler. His palace is a magnificent building, of modern Indian style, surrounded by fine gardens. The audience chamber is a gorgeous specimen of the very worst kind of decoration, ablaze with those glass chandeliers of which native princes are so inordinately fond. There are 100 huge chandeliers, and a vast glass candelabrum in the centre of the hall, in imitation of a fountain. This room is credited with an expenditure of over £100,000. The Maharaja's regalia is one of the costliest in India, one of his diamonds having cost £40,000.

SIRHIND.—At this place there are several interesting tombs of Afghan princes and others, many of them being finely decorated with coloured encaustic tiles; a large brick mansion, known as the Haveli, and a great Sarai of the Mughal Emperors, portions of which date back to the 10th century. These buildings, however, have not enough interest to detain the traveller; but to those who take any interest in public works, it is quite worth while to spend a day at Sirhind for the purpose of visiting one of the most important of the great irrigation canals of India. The Sirhind Canal draws its water from the Sutlej, near Rupar, and runs through the Ambala, Lodhiana, and Firozpur districts. Branches traverse some of the native states of the Punjab, including Patiala, Nabha, and Jind, terminating at Sirsa and Karnal. This magnificent work has cost nearly £7,000,000, part of which was contributed by native states, but mostly by the Indian Government. There are over 2,000 miles of channel, and it irrigates 800,000 acres of land.

LUDHIANA is a thriving town of about 50,000 inhabitants, principally Muhammadans. There are a large number of Kashmeri and Pathan settlers. It is a great central grain market, and maintains a considerable manufacture of shawls of the fine Rampur wool, cotton cloth, turbans, and other textile fabrics. There are some interesting Christian Missions here, under the charge of American Presbyterians, who also have a station at Jalandhar, but otherwise there are no attractions for the ordinary traveller.

JALANDHAR is a Musalman city of 60,000 inhabitants, which has a conspicuous place in ancient history. The only antiquities are a couple of tanks with some scattered ruins. There is a Cantonment here, with two regiments stationed.

AMRITSAR is the most populous, thriving, and wealthy city in the whole of the Punjab. It is not only of political and religious interest as the sacred city of the Sikh nation, but it is the seat of many artistic manufactures, and the great commercial gateway from India into the North Himalyan countries, and Central Asia. It is the 13th city in India as regards population, which is 152,000. The value of its imports and exports are about £4,000,000 yearly. Its merchants exchange the products of Bokhara, Khokand, Thibet, Afghanistan, and Persia, with those of Calcutta, Bombay, Manchester, and Birmingham. Its bazaars are thronged by a score of nationalities, and present a variety of type and dress only to be equalled by those of Peshawar.

There are three hotels and a town bungalow, the Amritsar Hotel being the best. It is pleasantly situated about half a mile outside the city, in a large garden. There is also a fair hotel near the railway station.

The great attraction to Amritsar is the famous Golden Temple, built by Ranjit Singh in the beginning of this century, in the centre of the sacred tank which gives Amritsar its name (literally, "the pool of immortality"). This temple has the double interest of its own intrinsic beauty as a work of art, and of being the heart of the Sikh religion.

The Sikhs are not a nation, but a religious sect bound together by the tie of military discipline. They are the product of a reformation of the 15th century, when Nanak Shah endeavoured to preach in the Punjab the doctrines of the great Bengal reformer, Kabir, whose aim was to found a unitary religion which would unite in the same faith, Musalman and Hindu, and whose teaching still survives in a small Hindu sect called "*Kabir-panthis*," whose headquarters are at Benares. The Sikh religion is grounded on Monotheism and moral purity. Their Bible, called the *Granth*, was commenced by *Guru* Nanak Shah, consolidated by his 5th successor, *Guru* Arjun, about A.D. 1600, and completed by the last *Guru*, the famous Govind Singh. The leading features of this Sikh Bible are the importance attached to moral precepts, and the ordering of worship stripped of every vestige of idolatry, raised to a high platform of simplicity and spirituality. The original copy of the *Granth* of *Guru* Arjun, is jealously preserved in the Golden Temple.

With the exception of Amritsar, which is the religious centre, and a few sanctuaries in places where *Gurus* and martyrs have lived or died, they have no holy places. Their temples are entirely houses for prayer and worship. Here they recite portions of the *Granth*, or sing hymns from the same sacred book. The congregation

THE GOLDEN TEMPLE, AMRITSAR.

separates after each person has partaken of the *Karah Prasad,* or "effectual offering," a cake consecrated in the name of *Guru.* They have no objection to well-conducted strangers taking part in the service, and even offer them participation in the *Karah Prasad.* An account of this interesting people will be found in Barth's Religion of India, pp. 238—251.

Few of the great cities of the world can boast such a noble square as that which surrounds the beautiful sacred tank in the centre of Amritsar. In the middle of the lake, reflected in its glassy surface, is the Golden Temple shining in the sunlight like some jewelled casket. All round the square are noble palaces, the dome-topped residences of wealthy Sikh princes and chieftains, white and dazzling amidst the dark green foliage of their gardens. High above them are soaring minars and lofty towers, while the white steps of the tank, the tesselated marble pavements of the terraces, and the causeway to the temple, are thronged with many-coloured pilgrims. The best view of this wonderful scene is obtained from the platform of the clock tower.

Visitors are met at the entrance gate of the Temple by an official guide; their shoes are removed, and their feet covered in canvas socks. A causeway, about seventy yards long, conducts to the temple itself. On both sides of the way are rows of beggars and musicians, to whom every worshipper gives a few grains of rice or other cereal. There are also nine curious gilt lamps on each side of the pier. The Golden Temple stands on a square platform surrounded with a handsome marble balustrade, except on the outer side, when the temple is flush with the tank and pierced by a handsome water-gate. It is not a large building, being only fifty-three feet square, but it is the most splendid temple in India, so far as richness of decoration is concerned. Its details, and indeed its general architecture, are disappointing; its charm consists more in the beauty of its surroundings, and the splendour of its colour.

The interior is richly carved and decorated with floral patterns. In the centre sits the chief priest, reading from the *Granth,* surrounded by pious worshippers who chant with him the verses from the sacred book. There is a small and beautifully sculptured pavilion on the roof. The domes, cupolas and the upper portion of the walls are covered with thin plates of gold, hence the name "Golden Temple."

In the handsome gateway, at the beginning of the causeway, whose beautifully wrought doors should be carefully observed, are kept the

THE ATAL TOWER, AMRITSAR.

various "properties" of the temple in a huge silver chest; gilt maces, a bejewelled gold canopy, and sundry necklaces and diadems of precious stones. These are used on processional occasions. In the Akal Bungah, a building in the outer courtyard opposite the gateway, is kept the sword of the mighty *Guru* Govind Singh, sundry other historic weapons, and an ark containing the vessels used for initiation into the membership of the Sikh Church.

Here the visitor will be presented with cups of sugar-candy, which he should carry conspicuously in his hand until he is clear of the premises, whatever he may do with them after.

In the beautiful garden of the temple, thirty acres in extent, well planted with orange, lemon, pomegranate and other flowering trees and shrubs, are several pretty pavilions, and the Atal Tower, 131 feet high, which may be ascended for the fine prospect of the city enjoyed from its summit.

On the other side of the temple square are the two lofty and imposing towers, called the Ram Garhuja Minars, 130 feet high, built 170 years ago by an ancestor of the Mangal Singh family. They are not fine specimens of Minar architecture, but their massive whiteness tells out against the blue sky, and adds variety and charm to this stately square.

The public gardens are about forty acres in extent, and in the centre is a pavilion which was used as a residence by Ranjit Singh, when he visited Amritsar.

The fort of Govindgarh was built by Ranjit Singh to dominate the town, and inspire the turbulent pilgrims who came to the sacred shrine, with some sense of the presence of authority. It is a place of no great interest, being merely a modern Indian fort of the present century. It is at present occupied by a small number of British troops.

If the traveller has a day to spare from the attractions of Amritsar, he will find it worth while to drive twelve miles to Taran-Taran, which was the city of *Guru* Arjun, and is counted only less sacred than Amritsar. Arjun constructed here a magnificent tank nearly 1,000 feet square, and built by its side a Sikh temple, decorated inside and out with frescoes.

The tank is said to possess miraculous healing powers, especially towards lepers, who are cured by swimming across it. Ranjit Singh greatly revered this temple, overlaying it with copper gilt, and richly ornamenting it. The tall column which stands by the tank is 140 feet high, and was erected by Prince Nao Nihal Singh. This city is famous in history as the stronghold of the Sikhs, and the country round furnishes most of the recruits of those Sikh regiments which are the flower of the native Indian army.

If any desire is felt to see Indian leprosy, there is plenty of it at Taran-Taran, in spite of the healing tank. One of its suburbs is inhabited by a tribe of hereditary lepers, who claim direct descent from *Guru* Arjun himself, whom tradition says was afflicted with this terrible disease. There is also, outside the town, a large leper asylum.

The *Serai* at Amritsar is one of the most interesting sights in India, and the hotel guides never dream of taking visitors to such places. It is a great open space, surrounded by small houses, in which are lodged the travelling merchants from Central Asia. In front of the houses are groups of various Asiatic nationalities, who have brought the produce of their country to exchange for Manchester piece goods, Sheffield cutlery, iron, copper, and other foreign commodities. Here are white-skinned Kashmeris, stout Nepalese, sturdy little Beluchis, stately but filthy Afghans, Persians, Bokharans, Khivans, Khokandis, Turcomans, Yarkandis, Kashgaris, Thibetans and Tartars, and even the ubiquitous Chinaman. These various types of the human race, with their strange national dress, cannot be seen anywhere else in India except Peshawar. They are all very good-natured, seem to like being stared at, and will show anything which may excite curiosity, such as the ingredients of a cooking-pot, their jewels and ornaments, their clothing, their babies, dogs, ponies, or their merchandise.

These people bring to Amritsar the raw material for the great staple manufacture of the city,—the soft fine down, or under-wool, of goats of the Great Thibet plateau and Kashmir, from which Kashmir shawls are woven. This craft is carried on by Kashmeris who settled here early in the century. In every side street looms are visible through the open fronts of the houses, and there are altogether upwards of 4,000 of them at work in the city. The weavers are delighted to show their processes to any stranger who is interested. If any time is taken up, a few annas should be given.

Besides the shawls of home manufacture, Amritsar is the chief emporium for those of a similar kind made in Kashmir. The great houses of London, Paris and Vienna have their resident buyers in Amritsar, and it is said that they pay as much as a quarter of a million sterling every year for these beautiful fabrics. A full-sized shawl, of the finest quality, costs £40 to £50, though smaller sizes, equally good as an example, can be bought as low as £10 to £15.

This craft, one of the most skilled in the world, is learned by the weavers from their earliest childhood. Those made in Kashmir are the finest in quality and pattern, as Amritsar has been somewhat corrupted by French designs and Magenta dyes. The Kashmir shawl craft is an ancient and important one, whether it be simple loom-weaving or embroidered with the needle on the plain fabric. The well-known cone pattern with its flowing curves and minute diaper of flowers, is the one most in vogue. Many other articles are made in Amritsar from the down of the Kashmir goat, as well as from camel's hair, which is even finer still; also from Kerman wool, which so closely resembles that of Kashmir and Thibet, that only an expert can detect the difference.

The plain shawls, white, blue, gray or crimson, known as Rampur chadars, are largely woven in Amritsar, and cost anything from 20 to 500 rupees, according to their fineness. They make charming presents to take home for ladies, old or young. These chadars are often embroidered along the border with the same needlework as the Kashmir shawls.

There is a large manufacture of silk goods at Amritsar. The silk piece goods are of solid worth, thick, strong and rich, a marked contrast to European silks, which have never been able to find a market in India. Here is woven the smart and gay striped silk, in common wear throughout the Punjab, called *gulbadan*. Pale green or dark green with scarlet stripe, yellow and crimson stripe, purple and yellow stripe, crimson and white stripe, white with various colours, are those mostly kept in stock. Other fabrics are shot with various colours, checked, or enriched with gold and silver fringes. There is a deep scarlet silk, with broad gold border, that is exceedingly beautiful, and also exceedingly costly.

Very choice carving in ivory may be procured at Amritsar, which is one of the chief places in India for its manufacture. The subjects are manifold, processions of Rajas, scenes from the Hindu mythology, hunting scenes, groups of birds, animals, trees and flowers, are carved in relief on combs and bracelets. Richly caparisoned elephants, state barges, palanquins, tigers, cows, peacocks, and other animals are carved as statuettes. They are wonderfully cheap.

Some of the finest carpets in India are woven at Amritsar. One dealer, just inside the first gate entered from the railway station and hotels, employs from 700 to 1,000 hands in carpet-weaving, at a wage of from three to six annas a day. He works mainly for three or four great London firms, and I have seen no worthier results in any of the carpet manufactories I have visited up and down India. No better opportunity will present itself to the traveller for studying this artistic and peculiarly Indian loom-work than this particular factory at Amritsar. Sir George Birdwood, in his "Industrial Arts of India," says—

"These pile carpets are called in India specifically *kalin* and *kalicha*. The foundation for the carpet is a warp of the requisite number of strong cotton or hempen threads, according to the breadth of the carpet, and the peculiar process consists in dexterously twisting short lengths of coloured wool into each of the threads of the warp, so that the two ends of the twist of coloured wool stick out in front. When a whole line of the warp is completed, the projecting ends of the wool are clipped to a uniform level, and a single thread of wool is run across the breadth of the carpet, between the threads of the warp, just as in ordinary weaving, and the threads of the warp are crossed as usual; then another thread of the warp is fixed with twists of wool in the same manner; and again, a single thread of wool is run between the threads of the warp, across the carpet, serving also to keep the tags of wool upright, and so on to the end. The lines of work are further compacted together by striking them with a blunt fork (*kangi*), and sometimes the carpet is still further strengthened by stitching the tags of wool to the warp. Then the surface is clipped all over again, and the carpet is complete. The workmen put in the proper colours either of their own knowledge or from a pattern. No native, however, works so well from a pattern as spontaneously. His copy will be a facsimile of the pattern, but stiff, even if it be a copy of his own original work. His hand must be left free in working out the details of decoration, even from the restraint of the example of his own masterpieces. If he is told simply, 'Now I want you to make something in this style, in your own way, but the best thing you ever did, and *you may take your own time about it*, and *I will pay you whatever you ask*,' he is sure to succeed. It is haggling and hurry that have spoiled art in Europe, and are spoiling it in Asia.

"Apart from the natural beauty of the dyes used, and the knowledge, taste, and skill of the natives of India in the harmonious arrangement of colours, the charm of their textile fabrics lies in the simplicity and treatment of the decorative details. The knop and flower pattern appears universally, but infinitely modified, never being seen twice under the same form: and the *seventi* and lotus, which have been reduced, through extreme conventionalisation, to one pattern. We have beside the shoe flower, and parrots, and peacocks, and lions and tigers, and men on horseback, or on foot, hunting or fighting. These objects are always represented quite flat as in mosaic work, or in *draps entaillés*, and generally symmetrically and in alternation. The symmetrical representation of natural objects in ornamentation, and their alternation, seems through long habit to have become intuitive in the natives of the East. If you get them to copy a plant, they will peg it down flat on the ground, laying its leaves, and buds, and flowers out symmetrically on either side of the central stem, and then only will they begin to copy it. If the leaves and flowers of the plant are not naturally opposite, but alternate, they will add others to make it symmetrical, or at least will make it appear so in the drawing. The intuitive feeling for alternation is seen in their gardens and heard in their music, and is as satisfactory in their music as in their decoration, when heard amid the associations which naturally call it forth. When the same form is used all over a fabric, the interchange of light and shade, and the effect of alternation, are at once obtained by working the ornament alternately in two tints of the same colour. Each object or division of an object is painted in its own proper colour, but without shades of the colour, or light and shade of any kind, so that the ornamentation looks perfectly flat, and laid, like a mosaic, in its ground. It is in this way that the natural surface of any object decorated is maintained in its integrity. This, added to the perfect harmony and distribution of the colouring, is the specific charm of Indian and Oriental decoration generally. Nothing can be more ignorant and ridiculous than the English and French methods of representing huge nosegays, or bunches of fern leaves tied together by flowing pink ribbons, in light and shade, on carpets, with the effect of full relief. One knows not where to walk among them. Continually also are to be seen perfectly shaped vases spoiled by the appearance of flowers in full relief stuck round them, or of birds flying out from them. Such egregious mistakes are never made by the Indian decorative artist. Each ornament, particularly in textile fabrics, is generally traced round also with a line, in a colour which harmonises it with the ground on which it is laid. In embroideries with variegated silks, for instance, on cloth, or satin, or velvet, a gold or silver thread is run round the outline of the pattern, defining it, and giving a uniform tone to the whole surface of the texture. Gold is generally laid on purple, or in the lighter *kincobs* on pink or red. An ornament on a gold ground is generally worked round with a dark thread to soften the glister of the gold. In carpets, however gay in colour, a low tone is secured by a general black outline of the details. All violent contrasts are avoided. The richest colours are used, but are so arranged as to produce the effect of a neutral bloom, which tones down every detail almost to the softness and transparency of atmosphere. The gold-broidered snuff-coloured Kashmir shawl in the collection of the Prince of Wales presents this ethereal appearance. Light materials are lightly coloured and ornamented, heavier more richly, and, in the case of apparel, both the colouring and the ornaments are adapted to the effect which the fabric will produce when worn and in motion. It is only through generations of patient practice that men attain to the mystery of such subtleties. It is difficult to analyse the secret of the harmonious bloom of Indian textures, even with the aid of Chevreul's prismatic scale. When large ornaments are used, they are filled up with the most exquisite details, as in the cone patterns on Kashmir shawls. The vice of Indian decoration is its tendency to run riot, as in Indian arms, but Indian textile fabrics, at least, are singularly free from it, and particularly the carpets."

CHAPTER XI.

LAHORE.

LAHORE is the capital city of the Punjab, and the administrative headquarters of Lahore division and district. Its population, inclusive of the military suburb of Mian Mir, is 150,000. The bulk of the inhabitants are Musalman, 86,000; there are 54,000 Hindus and 5,000 Sikhs.

Lahore is an ancient city, but did not attain any importance before the Mughal empire, when it was a place of considerable size and magnificence and its population probably twice or thrice that of to-day. Akbar enlarged and strengthened the fort, and surrounded the city with a strong wall, portions of which still remain, built into the modern fortifications of Ranjit Singh. Jahangir erected the Kwabgah, the Moti Masjid, and the Mausoleum of Anar Kalli, and Jahangir's own mausoleum is one of the most beautiful buildings in the Punjab. The Jama Masjid was the work of Aurangzeb.

Modern Lahore bears the stamp everywhere of the great Maharaja Ranjit Singh. His buildings are tawdry and in bad taste, and have very little artistic or architectural interest. Ranjit's city covers an area of 640 acres, is surrounded by a dull brick wall 30 feet high, and a moat, which has recently been filled up and planted as a garden.

There are 13 gates, connected on the outside of the ramparts by a good macadamized road.

The city itself is raised above the plain on the ruins of its predecessors. The streets are narrow and winding, forming a perfect labyrinth of quaint and picturesque scenes. The houses are lofty, many of them richly decorated. The bazars are densely crowded, very dusty and evil-smelling, but full of interest, like every Punjab bazaar.

The European quarter is handsomely laid out on the south side beyond the wall. The Mall, as the main thoroughfare is called, is

THE HAZURI BAGH, LAHORE.

about three miles long, studded on each side with public offices, private houses, fine shops, and churches. There are several good hotels in and near the Mall.

The principal group of ancient buildings in Lahore is the Fort and those clustering round it. The Fort is shorn of much of its former splendour, and what little is left does not suggest that in its palmiest days it would bear comparison with Delhi or Agra. It is entered by the Roshanai Gate, whose imposing façade is decorated with the coloured tiles so much in use throughout central Asia, introduced into the Punjab by Persian artizans.

The visitor is met inside the gate by an intelligent non-commissioned officer who acts as guide, pointing out and explaining the various objects of interest. The first building on the left is the Moti

Masjid, or pearl mosque, erected by Jahangir, A.D. 1598. Its arched entrances are now built up; the whole structure is desecrated by British whitewash, and used as the strong-room of the Government. A little farther on is a small modern Sikh temple, and beyond it is what is left of Akbar's palace, to which additions were made by Shah Jahan and Aurangzeb. The façade is quaintly decorated with enamelled tiles representing hunting and mythological scenes. In this group is a Shish Mahal, or palace of mirrors, a quadrangle about 130 feet by 100, and the Nau Lakha, a pavilion of white marble inlaid with pietra dura. The Shish Mahal has a sentimental interest as the place where the sovereignty of the Punjab was transferred to the British Government.

The armoury contains a singularly fine collection of old Indian weapons. The shield and battle-axe of *Guru* Govind Singh hangs on the wall, with other curious and historical armour, swords, guns, and harness. The view from the summit of Akbar's palace is superb, commanding the city on one hand, and on the other the vast fertile Punjab plain, dotted with tombs and villages, the river Ravi meandering through it like a silver ribbon.

The other buildings in the Fort are the Diwan i Khas and the Kwabgah i Kalan, both of which must have been splendid halls in their prime, but their beauty of decoration can hardly be discerned under their thick coat of whitewash, and their proportions have been shorn for the utilitarian purposes of a British barracks.

Leaving the Fort again by the Roshanai Gate, and turning to the right through a doorway, the Hazuri Bagh is entered. It is a dishevelled garden of surpassing beauty, in the centre of which is a pretty marble pavilion. On the right hand side of this garden is a lofty crenellated wall, in the middle of which is a fine gateway, now built up, which in Akbar's time was the entrance to the citadel. The towers of this gateway are remarkable. On the left of the garden is a desolate mosque, the Jama Masjid, desecrated by Ranjit Singh, who used it as an arsenal. It is now restored to the Musalmans as a place of worship, but it is little used and greatly neglected. The quadrangle, which is 530 feet square, is overshadowed by fine trees, the dark green foliage acting as a charming contrast to the deep, rich, warm red-sandstone. A splendid flight of twenty-two steps, ninety feet long at the base, leads up from the garden to the mosque, the minarets of which cut the sapphire sky

150 feet in height. The whole forms one of the most beautiful pictures to be found in all India.

The somewhat garish white building which glitters in bright contrast to the solemn and sombre mosque is Ranjit Singh's Samadh, or burning-place. The interior decoration of this building is fantastic, and is inlaid with convex mirrors. In the centre of the floor is a raised platform on which is carved a lotus flower, surrounded by eleven

RANJIT SINGH'S SAMADH, LAHORE.

smaller ones, marking the place where Ranjit Singh's body was burnt, with eleven ladies of his Zenana. The temple-tomb just outside the gate of the Huzuri Bagh is the shrine of Arjun, the fifth Sikh *Guru*; the Granth, of which he was the author, is read daily in Rangit Singh's Samadh.

There are some fine old mosques within the city walls. The mosque of Vazir Khan was built in 1634 by a Vazir of the Emperor Shah Jehan. The walls are richly decorated with coloured tiles. The courtyard is 130 feet square, the façade of the mosque being covered with carved inscriptions from the Koran. A climb of eighty feet reaches the summit of the minaret, from which a very fine view of this peculiarly oriental city may be obtained. In the centre of the mosque is the tomb of Abdul Ushak, a great resort for gossip and bargains. The streets in the neighbourhood of this mosque are very striking, the balconies of the houses and the frames of the doorways being richly carved. The finest house in Lahore is that of Raja Har Bans Singh, near the Masti Gate, which should be visited. It was built in the reign of Jahangir. The Golden Mosque (Soneri Musjid) is more modern, dating from 1753. It is finely placed at the angle of two streets, amid picturesque surroundings, its three golden domes glittering in the sunlight. Behind it is a curious well of great size, with a stone staircase descending to the water. In the open space called Hira Mandi throngs of gaily-dressed natives swarm, and many types of Afghans, Kashmiris, and other Himalayans and Central Asians may be observed. Driving a carriage through the streets of Lahore is no sinecure, and there is so much dust, dirt, and crowd that pedestrians who have come to stare about them are somewhat disagreeably, but not unkindly, jostled. The wonderful picturesqueness of the bazars is, however, ample compensation for the inconvenience.

The tomb of Anar Kali, now converted into St. James's Church, is near the Mall. Anar Kali (pomegranate blossom) was a lady of Akbar's court, who loved "not wisely, but too well" Salim, one of Akbar's sons. The tradition is, that, being detected, she was buried alive by Akbar, after whose death Salim erected this beautiful mausoleum to her memory. The sarcophagus, which stood in the centre of the building, has been removed to an ante-room, where it may be seen. It is one of the most beautiful and perfect specimens of carving to be seen in India. It is of white marble, and its decoration consists of the ninety-nine names of Allah, and an inscription stating that the tomb was erected to Anar Kali's memory, by Salim, or Jahangir.

The tomb with the fine blue-tiled dome is that of Sheikh Musa, called Ahanjar, or the Ironmonger. This tomb was once covered with Nakkashi tiling, but it has been almost all stripped off. A hundred yards off is a smaller tomb, the walls of which are much better preserved, and contain good pieces of this beautiful encaustic tile-work. Another building which gives a good illustration of coloured-tile ornamentation is that called *Chauburji*, or the Four Towers; it is the fine gateway to a garden, and is faced with green and blue encaustic decoration.

The chief public buildings of the European town are situated on the Mall; they do not call for much comment. The Punjab University, with its senate hall, is worth visiting; also the Oriental College, the Lahore Government College, the Central Training College, the Medical School, the Law School, the High School, and the Mayo Hospital, a fine building, with capacity for 110 beds.

The best-managed and most successful School of Art in India is at Lahore, under the superintendence of Mr. J. L. Kipling, C.I.E., who

TOMB OF ANAR KALI, LAHORE.

is also curator of the Lahore Museum. Mr. Kipling and his talented pupils have rendered great service in the completion of the collections in the India Museum at South Kensington, and many of the beautiful plates in "The Journal of Indian Art," published in London under the patronage of the Government of India, are contributed by them also. No traveller interested in Indian art should leave Lahore without a visit to the Mayo School of Art and the Museum.

The world-renowned Shalimar Gardens (the Abode of Love) are about six miles from Lahore. These beautiful gardens are about eighty acres in extent, entered by an imposing gateway, and surrounded by a lofty wall, with pavilions at each corner. The land slopes, and is divided into three terraces, connected by flights of steps; they were laid out by the Emperor Shah Jahan in A.D. 1637. Canals carry water to all parts of the garden, and in the centre is a large tank, with an island in the middle. There are innumerable small fountains everywhere. The buildings are rather mouldy, and the garden ill-kept, but in its day it must have been a lovely place.

There are other gardens in the neighbourhood, all of which will repay the searcher after picturesqueness. The best of these is the Gulabi Bagh (or Rose Garden), half-a-mile from Shalimar; this was laid out in 1655. It is entered by a well-preserved gateway of some beauty, being richly decorated with Nakkashi work—the coloured tiles already referred to as the ornamentation of the mosque of Vazar Khan, and the Roshanai Gate of the Fort.

The cantonment of Meean Meer is three miles from Lahore, and is a dull and dreary place. Here are stationed two batteries of artillery, one regiment of British infantry, one of native cavalry and infantry, and a regiment of Punjab Pioneers. The place is named after a Mussulman saint of the time of Aurangzeb, whose tomb stands in the centre of a square on a fine marble platform, a few hundred yards from the cantonment. It is a handsome domed building of red sandstone and white marble.

There are several other tombs in this neighbourhood, the most noteworthy being that of Pakdaman (the chaste lady), the holiest shrine in the Lahore district. She and her sisters, who are buried here with her, are said to be nieces of Ali, the successor of the Prophet; she died, A.D. 728, at the age of ninety. The tomb itself is an ancient and simple brick structure, thirteen or fourteen feet square. There are some curious old trees about the place, reputed to have more than 800 years' growth.

The magnificent mausoleum of the Emperor Jahangir is at Shah Darrah, four or five miles out of Lahore, on the right bank of the River Ravi. The road leads through a well-timbered country, across an interesting bridge over the Ravi. This tomb is placed, as usual, in the centre of a great walled garden, now a tangled wilderness, 1,600 feet square, entered by a fine gateway of white marble and red sandstone, some fifty feet high. (*See* chapter initial.)

The great feature of this remarkable mausoleum consists in a vast platform over 200 feet square, with a tesselated pavement of coloured marble. At each corner is a soaring minaret over 100 feet high, of singular beauty, and built of massive blocks of stone. Round the platform, originally, ran a richly-carved marble wall, which for some cause or other was destroyed by Ranjit Singh, who replaced it with the rubbishy substitute now standing. A splendid view of Lahore and the valley of the Ravi may be obtained from the topmost gallery of one of the minarets. The central dome of the tomb is small, and, in proportion to the noble platform and minarets, insignificant; the sarcophagus within is a good specimen of carving in white marble, the decoration being as usual the ninety-nine names of God.

To the west of Jahangir's tomb, through a doorway in the wall, is the tomb of Asij Jah, in the midst of a ragged and neglected garden. Judging from the beautiful fragments still remaining of the Nakkashi decorations of this building, it must have been one of the finest specimens of this art. The big ugly tomb farther to the west is that of Nur Jahan, and is not worth visiting.

If a somewhat prolonged stay is being made at Lahore, an interesting day's excursion may be arranged to Shekohpura, an ancient town twenty-two miles distant, which contains a ruined fort built by Jahangir, and a hugo brick palace, built by Ranjit Singh for one of his queens. Here is also a large disused tank, with a marble pavilion, and minaret over 100 feet high, of the time of Jahangir.

Lahore is a good centre for sport. Wolves, leopards, and nilgai are sometimes found in the wild country across the Ravi, and in the forest plantations antelope, deer, wild hog, hares, quails, sandgrouse, and peafowl are abundant. Ducks, geese, cranes, pelicans, and other wading birds are plentiful along the Sutlej, the Ravi, and other rivers, also crocodiles and alligators. There is good mahseer and other fishing to be had within easy distance.

There are four Missionary Societies represented in Lahore—the American Methodist Episcopal, the Church of England, the American Presbyterian, and the Indian Female Normal School and Instruction Society.

The Methodist Mission employs two missionaries, whose work lies chiefly among Europeans and Eurasians. Their church building is near the railway station.

The Church Missionary Society (whose headquarters for the Punjab are in Amritsar) began work in Lahore in the year 1867. At present there are two English missionaries and one native pastor connected with this mission. The former occupy the extensive premises enclosed by a high wall, which were once held by a wealthy Sirdar, and hence are known as "Mahan Singh's Garden." Within this enclosure are the mission-house, a hostel for native Christian young men coming to Lahore from other stations for instruction in the schools, or employment in the offices, and a pretty little chapel for religious services. Divinity classes were begun in 1869 by Mr. French (afterwards Bishop French). The English missionaries are engaged mainly in superintending the hostel, instructing classes in Divinity, and preaching in bazaar chapels. The native pastor ministers to a large community of native Christians, scattered through that part of Lahore called "Anarkali," whose place of worship, "Holy Trinity," is a well-built structure situated in a central position.

The American Presbyterian Mission here is the oldest in point of time, and strongest in point of numbers. At present there are six American missionaries and several native helpers. The mission was opened in 1849, with the approbation of the highest authorities (especially Sir Henry and Sir John Lawrence), by Messrs. Newton & Forman, who are still alive and on the field, esteemed and honoured throughout India. At that time the country was thought by many to be in an unsettled state, and new insurrections were looked for, the Punjab having just been annexed. The new missionaries were, therefore, advised by the civil authorities to desist temporarily from street preaching. This was carried on, however, after a few months, quietly, and then more openly, and from that time to this scarcely a day has passed without the voice of the preacher being lifted in the broadest thoroughfares, and before the great gates of the city. A day-school for boys was first started in the missionaries' house—at that time within the city. It opened with three pupils, all Hindu Kashmiris. Now there are about 1,100 boys and 400 girls in the various schools. In those days boys had to be bribed with books to come to study English—now nothing could bribe them to stay away, and English is of paramount importance. There is a Mission College, whose imposing buildings occupy a fine site granted by Government. There are now about 150 students preparing for the Intermediate and B.A. examinations, to whom, besides the regular University curriculum, daily instruction in the Bible and the Christian religion is given. When the missionaries first came to Lahore there were no native

Christians; now it is said that there are over 1,000 who claim to belong to one Christian denomination or another.

The Presbyterian native congregation worship in a neat brick building, which, with the Mission premises, are at Naulakka, near the railway station. English services are held every Sunday by the missionaries in the Presbyterian church in Anarkali.

The Indian Female Normal School and Instruction Society have been at work here nearly twenty-five years. At present they are represented by five ladies. Of these, two are engaged in the management of a large and flourishing boarding-school for Christian girls. The other three ladies devote themselves entirely to city and village work. They have the supervision of day-schools, in which are collected women and girls to the number of about 450. They visit, besides, nearly ninety zenanas, where instruction, especially in the Bible, is given.

PATHANKOT is reached by a branch line from Amritsar in about four hours. It is a quaint old place, with a fort built by Shah Jahan. Fifty-seven miles farther into the Himalayas is Dalhousie, a charming hill station, 7,700 feet above the sea, built upon three peaks, whose flanks are covered with beautiful forest. This is a very pleasant sanatorium, and the winter is less severe than at Simla or Mussoorie. The scenery is superb, especially at Chamba, twelve miles distant, the curious little capital of an ancient Hindu principality, which is surrounded by mountains from 14,000 to 20,000 feet high. The Kangra Valley, which lies between Dalhousie and Simla, contains some of the sublimest scenery in the world, but it cannot be visited during the winter, except with considerable difficulty and hardship.

CHAPTER XII.

RAWAL PINDI.—SEALKOT.—ATTOCK.—THE INDUS.—PESHAWAR.

RAWAL PINDI is a modern town, with a population a little over 50,000, pretty equally divided between Mohammedans and Hindus. It is a clean, bright, well-planned city, planted with fine trees, the head-quarters of a military division, with a garrison of three European and three native regiments, two batteries of artillery, and three mountain batteries. It boasts a handsome public garden, an extensive and singularly beautiful park, the favourite evening and morning resort of the European residents, a huge garrison church and the usual public offices and buildings pertaining to a commissioner's district of nearly 1,000,000 souls. Its situation is picturesque, at the foot of the Murree hills, sandstone buttresses of the Kashmir Himalyas clothed with magnificent forest trees of pine, oak, acacia and other hard woods. Leopards, wolves, hyenas, jackals, foxes, barking deer, ravine deer, hares, partridges, jungle fowl and pheasants, are plentiful all over the Murree hills, and good Mahseer fishing may be had in most of the streams. The popular hill station of Murree is thirty-nine miles from Rawal Pindi, 7,500 feet above sea level. There are several good hotels. This is one of the most beautiful of the Himalyan sanitariums; its cottages and bungalows, nestled in mingled forest and cultivation, enjoy a superb panorama of the sun-clad Kashmir mountains. The old town of Rawal Pindi is a group of narrow crooked bazaars, the population consisting of a mixture of Ghakkars, Bhattis, Awans, Khattris and Kashmiris.

The fort and arsenal is a strong pentagon, with a bastion at each angle, armed with heavy guns. It is designed to resist a siege by a fully equipped European army.

The missionaries stationed at Rawal Pindi belong to the American Presbyterian Board.

SEALKOT and JUMMOO are reached by a branch line just opened from Wazirabad junction.

Sealkot is a trading centre of rapidly increasing importance, with a large manufacture of paper. It has a population of about 30,000. The remains of the ancient fort of Raja Salwan crown a low circular hill in the middle of the town. The suburbs are very handsomely laid out. There is an interesting Sikh shrine, much resorted to by pilgrims, and the fine old Musalman tomb of Imam Alf-ul-hak. It is a military cantonment. The Church of Scotland and the American United Presbyterians have missions at Sialkot.

Jummoo is an ancient capital of Kashmir, once the seat of a Rajput dynasty, whose dominions extended over the plains of Sialkot. The town and palace are on the right bank of the River Tavi, and a grand old fortress overhangs the opposite bank on a cliff 150 feet above the water. It is a striking and picturesque place, with curious and interesting ruins scattered through the suburbs, giving evidence of its former magnitude and prosperity. The scenery in the immediate neighbourhood is very beautiful. There is no accommodation, but the Sealkot stationmaster will arrange for a railway carriage to be shunted for a sufficient time to enable visitors to see the place. The principal road to Srinagar, the present capital of Kashmir, starts from Jummoo, the distance being about 170 miles.

ATTOCK is the great historic fortress on the Indus, at its junction with the Kabul river. The fort, which was built by the Emperor Akbar in 1583 A.D., is an irregular polygon built on the end of a spur running down to the Indus. Ranjit Singh subdued Attock in 1813, the fortress remaining in the hands of the Sikhs till the British conquest of 1849. Before 1883, the Indus was crossed by a bridge of boats for eight months of the year, the rest of the time a good ferry

ATTOCK.

being maintained. There is also a curious tunnel under the river, a costly and useless piece of work. On the opposite side of the Indus is another massive fortress, Khairabad, the two places being now connected by the magnificent bridge of the Northern State Railway, which has a subway for carts and foot-passengers. The fort at Attock is a huge citadel, and, when built, must have been impregnable. It is one of Akbar's fortresses, and was built A.D. 1583. It is finely situated on the spur of a hill running down into the Indus. Attock is surrounded by mountains from 2,000 to 3,000 feet high, and the scenery ranks with the finest in India. The town is small, but very picturesque, especially the old Lahore gate; the population about 4,000, chiefly Muhammadans. The junction of the two rivers is about half a mile above the town, the Indus coming down from the Himalyas, a fine, clear, blue stream, the Kabul running into it at right angles, dark and turbid. Below the meeting of the waters, a whirlpool eddies between jutting precipices of black slate, known as Kamalia and Jalalia, from the names of two famous Roshanai heretics, who were flung, each from a summit, during the reign of Akbar, into the boiling pool below. Gold is washed out on the shores of the Indus and Kabul rivers above Attock, giving employment to about 300 men.

A very interesting excursion may be made by travellers who are prepared to rough it a little, by a boat voyage down the Indus from Attock to Dera Ismail Khan. Good native boats, with a deck-house of reeds or straw, may be hired for twenty or twenty-five rupees a day, and a polite note a week or two beforehand to the Assistant-Commissioner at Attock will, no doubt, be sufficient to get one of them engaged, and ready by the starting day, with a suitable crew and pilot. Some instalment of pay will probably have to be sent before the boat could be fitted up, but the A. C. will furnish the necessary information. The daily stages are Khushalgarh, Mokbad, Kalabagh, Kafir Kot and Dera Ismail Khan, five days in all, though so much depends on the state of the river, that it may be necessary to allow seven days.

Bukkur station, on the Sind Sagar Railway, is only a few miles by good road from Dera Ishmail Khan, and twelve hours by rail from Multan. It will be necessary to take provisions for the whole voyage, as supplies cannot be depended upon.

The scenery is very fine, and there are some formidable rapids here and there that lend excitement to the voyage. The Ghora Trap is a narrow gorge, about thirty yards wide, through which the river rushes with great speed. There is, however, no danger to the light

KHUSHALGARH.

passenger boat. All the way from Attock to Kalabagh the Indus runs through a succession of magnificent mountain gorges. At Khushalgarh, the military road to Kohat, Thal and the Kuran valley, crosses the Indus by a fine bridge of boats. The cliffs rise to a great height, and on the right bank are picturesquely crowned by an old fort. There is a good Dak road to Kohat (first class fare four rupees) at the foot of the Safia Koh and Afridi mountains. Mokbad is a thriving little town of over 4,000 inhabitants, a quaint old place, with a roofed bazaar, crowded with Afghan traders. There is a good road back to Attock from here, with a series of Dak bungalows; the distance is about 100 miles.

Kalabagh is a striking place. The old town is piled up the side of a steep hill of rock salt, like a great staircase, the roofs of one row of houses forming the street in front of the row above. A great cliff of rock salt towers above the town. There are important quarries of salt at Mari, just opposite to Kalabagh, where there are workable seams of pure salt lying between alternate *strata* of impure salt and marl. Between 3,000 and 4,000 tons are blasted out and sent away by the Indus during the year. There is also an alum industry in the neighbouring valleys, and a manufacture of iron implements of various kinds. A good road runs from Kalabagh to Piplan on the Sind-Sagar Railway, distant about seventy or eighty miles.

From Kalabagh to Dera Ismail Khan the river flows tranquilly through very beautiful river scenery, with fine views of the distant Suleiman Range. At Kafir-Kot there are some very interesting ruins built of huge blocks of smoothly chiselled stone, intermingled with ancient Hindù temples or sanctuaries. There are quaint carvings here and there representing idols. These ruins are placed on the crest of a spur of the Khisor hills, perched over the river bank. The towers are connected with the Indus by a wall. There is another ruined castle on the opposite bank. Their origin is lost in obscurity.

General Cunningham's Archæological Survey, which may be seen in any good Indian library, contains full particulars of these strange buildings, vol. xiv. p. 254.

Beyond Kafir-Kot, the Khisor range comes down to the water's edge in a precipitous mass, the peaks rising 4,000 or 5,000 feet above the plain. The banks are covered with patches of forest, and the tamarisk-covered islands are very lovely.

Dera Ismail Khan is a cantonment for three native regiments, and the administrative headquarters of a district. It is a new town of 25,000 inhabitants, and a favourite residence with Pathan and Multani nobles. The distance to the west is closed in by the two lofty peaks of Tukt-i-Suleiman, the highest of the great Suleiman range,

11,300 feet above the sea. It is a dull place, and the traveller will be glad to drive away from it by the excellent road which leads to Bukkur, a station on the Sind-Sagar Railway, 208 miles, or fifteen hours from Lala Musa junction northwards, and 147 miles, or eleven hours from Multan southwards.

PESHAWAR.—This ancient and historic city is situated in the midst of the "debateable ground" of our Indian Empire. Its traditions go far back into the earliest days of Aryan colonization. It was mentioned by the historians of Alexander's Conquest of India, and in the eighth century of the Christian era fell into the hands of the Afghans, since which it has been held by a score of successive conquerors, until in 1848 it became British.

The city and cantonment has a population of 80,000, of which 58,000 are Musalmans, 18,000 Hindus, 3,000 Christians, and less than 2,000 Sikhs. It is surrounded by a mud wall, built by the Sikh general, Avitabile, an Italian adventurer, which is pierced with sixteen gates, all of which are closed at sun-down.

The main street is entered by the Kabul gate, and is fifty feet wide, consisting of a double row of shops. This street is usually thronged with people, and is one of the most picturesque bazars in India. On each side of this main road are twisting narrow lanes opening out in small squares, in many of which are situated handsome mosques. The large building known as the Ghor Khattri was originally a Buddhist monastery, then a Hindu temple, and is now a native Serai or hotel, swarming with quaint and strange people from every part of Central Asia. A magnificent view of the entire Peshawar valley and its lofty snow-clad mountains may be obtained from the roof.

Just outside the walls is a quadrilateral fortress, called the Bala Hissar, on a hill completely dominating the city. Bastions stand at each corner, with a powerful armament of guns and mortars. The walls are of sun-dried brick, and rise nearly 100 feet from the ground.

The suburbs of Bnana Mari and Baghban are a succession of beautiful gardens, producing quinces, pomegranates, plums, limes, peaches, apples, and other fruit. North of Peshawar is a public pleasure-ground, the Bagh Shahi, or old royal gardens. Two miles west of the city lie the military cantonments and civil offices. The city was at one time completely surrounded by a chain of watch-towers, some of which are still standing, though most have become ruins.

Peshawar, from its geographical position, and from being a railway

THE BALA HISSAR, PESHAWAR.

terminus, ought to be the great emporium for all the trade between India and Afghanistan, Persia and Turkestan, but it has failed hitherto to become more than a halting-place on the great highway, and the traffic only streams through it. The bazars are, however, rendered very interesting from the variety of people passing through in charge of this trade, making Peshawar almost an Afghan city. The Afghan traders are extremely dirty, being dressed in loose coat and trousers of coarse cotton-cloth, never washed, with thick woollen or sheep-skin overcoats. Their shaggy unkempt black locks hang down beneath enormous turbans. They find their way through Peshawar to the most distant corners of India, hawking strings of weedy horses, raw silk, cochineal, drugs, fruits, and other miscellaneous products of their country. The little wooden boxes of yellow grapes packed in cotton, sold at every railway station in India, are all brought from Afghanistan by these wandering traders.

The local manufactures of Peshawar are cutlery and weapons, copper-chasing, embroidery, coarse cloth, and very beautiful *lungis* or scarves, for which Peshawar is famous. The dark blue *lungis*, with crimson edges, or ornamented with gold borders, are the most characteristic. They are made both in silk and cotton. The mass of the population is divided into petty trade guilds, recruited from miscellaneous tribes of every race in northern India and its adjacent countries; and almost every kind of art craft can be found at work in the bazaars of Peshawar.

The stony plain of Peshawar is the eastern mouth of the celebrated Khyber pass, which has played so conspicuous a part in the history of India, and especially in the series of wars between British India and Afghanistan, of which it is to be hoped we have seen the last.

It has been the great route into India for ages, whether for war, conquest, or commerce. The pass commences at the fort of Jamrud, ten miles from Peshawar, and twists for thirty-three miles through mountains 6,000 or 7,000 feet high, till it debouches on the plain of Jalalabad at Dhaka. The fort of Jamrud stands on a hill about 100 feet above the plain. It has three encircling walls of stone, and is a strong place. Three miles from Jamrud, at Kadam, a little village on the top of a hill, the pass is entered. The mountains close in, and in less than half a mile, the pass narrows to 150 yards, and a mile further, to about thirty yards, the rocks rising in sheer precipices of 60 or 100 feet, then sloping back. Six and a half miles from Jamrud,

Ali Masjid is reached, and here the width is fifteen yards only, the mountains on either side rising 1,000 to 1,300 feet sheer from the floor of the pass. The pass rises altogether about 1,700 feet to the summit of the pass at Landi Kotal. A permit must be obtained from the commanding officer of the cantonment at Peshawar, before the Khyber can be visited; indeed, at times it is necessary for visiting Jamrud, and under no circumstances can the pass be traversed beyond Ali Masjid. It is better to make application by letter a few days beforehand, as an escort is necessary beyond the British frontier.

The only Missionary Society for the male population engaged in Peshawar, is that of the Church Missionary Society, which was commenced in 1855, in response to a gift of Rs10,000 and an appeal from Major W. J. Martin, backed up by a very influential committee, held on Dec. 19th, 1853, under the chairmanship of the commissioner, Major [afterwards Colonel] Sir Herbert Edwardes.

JAMRUD.

The first Missionary was the gallant major himself, who severed his connection with Government, and was soon joined by the Revds. R. Clark and Dr. Pfander. There has ever since been a staff of two, three, or four Missionary Clergy, who live in the Mission clergy-house, close to the Cantonment Station, where there is a large and valuable library of some 4,000 volumes, not only on Theology, but on India, Afghanistan, Central Asia, Persia, Secular and Ecclesiastical History, Biography, Philosophy and the various Sciences.

The Mission is to Afghans, who believe themselves to belong to the Ten Tribes of Israel. Their tradition, history, customs, and physiognomy support the theory. The Afghans are a fine manly race of men, and whatever their faults are, hospitality is one of their greatest virtues, for which they will often go into debt. The hospitality the Missionary Clergy everywhere receive, is reciprocated by them in the guest-house they have erected in their compound, to which men of all classes come, from all parts of Afghanistan. They have also here a boarding-school for Afghan lads, representing many of the neighbouring tribes, and who attend as day-scholars the large Mission School in the city.

The Church of All Saints, which was erected in 1885 in the city of Peshawar to the memory of departed missionaries, is a very pretty oriental building, containing much handsome carving and decorated with Peshawar tiles. The Church, Pastor's house, library, &c., form one of the most complete places of Missionary energy in North India. The resident Native Pastor is always glad to show the church to visitors. Divine service is held every morning and evening in the vernacular.

The school, which is close by, opposite the Kohati Gate, while possessing no architectural beauty, is admirably adapted for the education of several hundred scholars in English, taking them up to the Panjab University Matriculation Examinations, under the superintendence of an English M.A. The scholars gathered from many nationalities, when assembled for the roll-call, seated on the large gallery, tier above tier, dressed in their many-coloured garments, is a very interesting sight. The school has been named after Sir Herbert Edwardes, whose memory is much revered for the great interest he always took in the mission, and for the immense pecuniary assistance he afforded.

The Literary Institute, called after the late Colonel Martin, is a building in the Pipal Mandi, containing a reading-room for educated Indians, and also a lecture-hall in which religious and scientific lectures are delivered, and evangelistic services are held.

The Church of England Zenana Missionary Society for women has several ladies working in connection with it: two for visiting native ladies and superintending girls' schools, and two for medical Missionary work. The latter have their head-quarters at Gorkhatri, in the highest part of the city, where they have a dwelling-house, and a small temporary hospital which H.H. the Duchess of Connaught, at her visit in Nov. 1884, has permitted to be called after her. The amount of good done is incalculable, but this tentative hospital is altogether too small for present exigencies, and subscriptions are now being received to build a commodious one on hygienic principles.

The American Presbyterian Society were once represented by the Rev. Isidore Loewenthal, a converted Polish Jew of great linguistic ability, but he was accidentally shot by his watchman in 1864. It is with reference to him that the story is told, that on his tombstone is inscribed: "He was shot by his chookidar; well done thou good and faithful servant." The fact is, this text does not appear, but "I am not ashamed of the Gospel of Christ." The story has, however, a substratum of truth, for in the Burial Register, that text is written underneath the record of his death. Although this story has been constantly refuted, it is a good one, and consequently dies a hard death. He was the first person to translate the New Testament into readable Pashto, the language of the Afghans.

The European garrison in cantonments is ministered to by Anglican Catholic, Presbyterian, and Roman Catholic chaplains. The members of the Church of England worship in the large handsome Church of St. John, where daily services are held; the Presbyterians in a barrack on Sundays; and the Romanists in their chapel on Sundays and week-days; the hours of service in each case varying with the season of the year.

CHAPTER XIII.

MULTAN AND SIND.

MULTAN, though of great antiquity and historic interest, is seldom visited by European tourists. It is only ten hours' journey from Lahore, and, although I have never been there myself, I strongly advise the traveller who has a margin of time to fill, to pay it a visit. Multan has had a continuous existence in history for 2,700 years, and is one of the most frequently besieged cities in the world. It made a desperate resistance to Alexander of Macedon, who, after subduing it, left a Satrap in charge of the province. The coins of the Graeco-Bactrian kings are frequently found in the neighbourhood of the city. Among its other famous sieges may be counted that of Sultan Mahmud in 1005, that of the Sikhs under Runjit Singh in 1818, and the storming of the city by the British in 1849, the crowning victory which led to the annexation of the Panjab.

Multan is built on a huge mound, the accumulated débris of previous cities, four miles from the present course of the river Chenab. It is surrounded on three sides by a ruined wall, the fourth side facing the dry bed of the old course of the river Ravi, which once flowed past the city, leaving two islands in its stream, the one that on which the city now stands, the other picturesquely crowned by the citadel. The suburbs of Multan are straggling and irregular, mingling with remains of the old fortifications, dismantled by the British in 1854. Within the city walls there is one broad street lined with shops called the

Chauk, made by the British in 1850. The other streets are narrow winding cul-de-sacs. The population is about 70,000, of whom more than half are Muhammadans. Multan is, and always has been, a great trading centre. Before the railway was made it was the collecting dépôt for the trade of the central Panjab, down the Ravi and Jehlam rivers, whence large quantities of produce were sent by the Indus flotilla to Karachi for shipment to Europe. The railway appears to have increased instead of diminished its prosperity, the exports and imports of Multan being over £1,300,000 annually.

The Fort is a massive group of buildings. Some of its most interesting details have been almost obliterated by the explosion of the powder-magazine during the siege of 1849, but many buildings remain with great artistic and picturesque interest, differing greatly from any others in India. The shrine of Ruku-i-Alam is an octagon of finely polished brick, fifty-two feet in diameter, topped by a smaller octagon, leaving a narrow passage all round, crowned by a magnificent dome. The whole structure is over 100 feet high. It is placed on the summit of the mound on which the citadel is built, and the whole outside surface is decorated with raised tiles of blue and white glaze. It was built by the Emperor Tuglak in 1340—50.

The great obelisk near by, seventy feet high, was erected to the memory of two British officers, whose treacherous murder by the viceroy of Multan in 1848, led to the war which ended in the annexation of the Panjab.

The tomb of Bhawal Hakk is another octagonal mausoleum within the walls of the citadel. It has been rather barbarously restored, and some of the original tiles, A.D. 1270, are still stuck about in the plaster. The sarcophagus is decorated with green tiles of fine colour and workmanship.

The only other ancient monument within the Fort worthy of notice is the ancient Hindu temple of the Narasinha Avatar of Vishnu, greatly injured by the explosion in 1849.

Within the city walls is the shrine of Muhammad Yusef, an ancient tomb of 1150 A.D., covered with encaustic tiles, excellent specimens of this beautiful ceramic decoration, and some other tombs of more recent date; and the fine mosque of Shah Gutlej.

The artistic crafts of Multan have held high position in India for centuries. Beautiful enamel work, similar in character to that of Jaipur, brilliant glass bangles, silk and cotton fabrics, especially

ENTRANCE TO THE SHAH GUTLEJ MOSQUE, MULTAN.
DECORATED WITH GLAZED TILES.

chintzes and scarves, figured and damasked silks, known as *Suja Khani,* are all to be seen in the bazaar, and possess peculiar characteristics.

The art of glazing earthenware has probably been possessed by Multan longer than any other district in India, and the city still maintains its supremacy. It dates from the earliest years of the 13th century, and is said to have been brought from China by Ghengiz Khan, after his invasion and conquest of that country. The following sentences are condensed from Sir Geo. Birdwood's "Industrial Arts of India":—

"It is said that the invasion and conquest of China by Ghingiz Khan, 1212, was the event that made known to the rest of Asia and Europe the art of glazing earthenware; but, in fact, the Saracens from the first used glazed tiles for covering walls, and roofs, and pavements, and of course with a view to decorative effect. The use of these tiles had come down to them in an unbroken tradition from the times of the 'Temple of Seven Spheres,' or Birs-i-Nimrud, at Borsippa, near Babylon, of the temple Sakkara in Egypt, and of the early trade between China and Egypt, and China and Oman, and the valley of the Tigris and Euphrates. Diodorus, describing (after Ctesias) the circular wall of the royal palace of Babylon, says:—'The whole portrayed a royal hunting scene, beautified with divers coloured forms of men and beasts, baked in the clay, and much like unto nature. . . . . There was Simiramis, killing a tiger, and by her side her husband Ninus, piercing his spear through a lion.' Glazed tiles had, however, fallen into comparative disuse before the rise of the Saracens, and it was undoubtedly the conquests of Ghingiz Khan, A.D. 1206—1227, which extended their general use throughout the nations of Islam. The glazed pottery of the Panjab and Sind probably dates from this period, and as we shall presently see, was directly influenced by the traditions surviving in Peria of the ancient civilisations of Nineveh and Babylon. It is found in the shape of drinking-cups and water-bottles (cf. pot, and Latin *poto,* I drink), jars, bowls, plates, and dishes of all shapes and sizes, and of tiles, pinnacles for the tops of domes, pierced windows, and other architectural accessories. In form, the bowls, and jars, and vases may be classified as egg-shaped, turban, melon, and onion-shaped, in the latter the point rising and widening out gracefully into the neck of the vase. They are glazed in turquoise, of the most perfect transparency, or in a rich dark purple, or dark green, or golden brown. Sometimes they are diapered all over by the *pâte-sur-pâte* method, with a conventional flower, the *seventi*, or lotus, of a lighter colour than the ground. Generally they are ornamented with the universal knop and flower pattern, in compartments formed all round the bowl, by spaces alternately left uncoloured and glazed in colour. Sometimes a wreath of the knop and flower pattern is simply painted round the bowl on a white ground.

"Mr. Drury Fortnum, in his report on the pottery at the International Exhibition of 1871, observes of the Sind pottery:—'The turquoise blue painted on a paste beneath a glaze, which might have been unearthed in Egypt or Phœnicia—a small bottle painted in blue or white—is of the same blood and bone as the ancient wares of Thebes. . . . But the tiles are very important. . . . They are in general character similar to, although not so carefully made as, the Oriental tiles known as Persian, which adorn the old mosques of Egypt, Syria, Turkey, and Persia. . . . The colours used upon them are rich copper green, a golden brown, and dark and turquoise blue. . . . The antiquary, the artist, and the manufacturer will do well to study these wares. As in their silk and woollen fabrics, their metal-work, and other manufactures, an inherent feeling for and a power of producing harmony in the distribution of colour and in surface decoration exists among the Orientals, which we should study to imitate, if not to copy. It is not for Europeans to establish schools of art, in a country the productions of whose remote districts are a school of art in themselves, far more capable of teaching than of being taught.'

"It is a rare pleasure to the eye to see in the polished corner of a native room one of these large turquoise blue sweetmeat jars on a fine Kirman rug of minimum red ground, splashed with dark blue and yellow. But the sight of wonder is, when travelling over the plains of Persia or India, suddenly to come upon an encaustic-tiled mosque. It is coloured all over in yellow, green, blue, and other hues; and as a distant view of it is caught at sunrise, its stately domes and glittering minarets seem made of purest gold, like glass, enamelled in azure and green, a fairy-like apparition of inexpressible grace and most enchanting splendour.

"The enamelled pottery of Sind and the Panjab is a sumptuary and not a village art, and is probably not older than the time of Ginghiz Khan. In all the Imperial Mughal cities of India where it is practised, especially in Lahore and Delhi, the tradition is that it was introduced from China, through Persia, by the Afghan Mongols, through the influence of Tamerlane's Chinese wife; and it is stated by independent European authorities that the beginning of ornamenting the walls of mosques with coloured tiles in India was contemporary with the Mongol conquest of Persia. But in Persia the ancient art of glazing earthenware had come down in an almost unbroken tradition from the period of the greatness of Chaldaea and Assyria, and the name *kasi*, by which the art is known in Persia and India, is probably the same Semitic word, *kas*, glass, by which it is known in Arabic and Hebrew, and carries us back direct to the manufacture of glass and enamels, for which 'great Zidon' was already famous 1,500 years before Christ. The pillar of emerald in the temple of Melcarth, at Tyre, which Herodotus describes as shining brightly in the night, 'can,' observes Kendrick, 'hardly have been anything else than a hollow cylinder of green glass, in which, as a Gades, a lamp burnt perpetually.' The designs used for the decoration of this glazed pottery in Sind and the Panjab also go to prove how much it has been influenced by Persian examples, and the Persian tradition of the ancient art of Nineveh and Babylon. The 'knop and flower' pattern, which we all know in Greek art as the 'honeysuckle and palmette' pattern, appears in infinite variations on everything.

"The old glazed tiles to be seen in India are always from Mahommedan buildings, and they vary in style with the period to which the buildings on which they are found belong; from the plain turquoise blue tiles of the earlier Pathan period, A.D. 1193—1254, to the elaborately designed and many-coloured tiles of the latter part of the great Mughal period, A.D. 1556—1750. Wherever also the Muhammadans extended their dominion they would appear to have developed a local variety in these tiles.

"It is the vigorous drawing, and free, impulsive painting of this pottery which are among its attractions. The rapidity and accuracy of the whole operation is constant temptation to the inexperienced bystander to try a hand at it himself. You feel the same temptation in looking on at any native artificer at his work. His artifice appears to be so easy, and his tools are so simple, that you think you could do all he is doing quite as well yourself. You sit down and try. You fail, but will not be beaten, and practise at it for days with all your English energy, and then at last comprehend that the patient

Hindu handicraftsman's dexterity is a second nature, developed from father to son, working for generations at the same processes and manipulations. The great skill of the Indian village potter may be judged also from the size of the vessels he sometimes throws from his wheel, and afterwards succeeds in baking. At Ahmedabad and Baroda, and throughout the fertile pulse and cereal-growing plains of Gujarat, earthern jars, for storing grain, are baked, often five feet high; and on the banks of the Dol Samudra, in the Dacca division of the Bengal Presidency, immense earthern jars are made of nearly a ton in cubic capacity. The clay figures of Karttikeya, the Indian Mars, made for his annual festival by the potters of Bengal, are often twenty-seven feet in height."

For the last thirty years the Church Missionary Society has maintained a weak mission in this place—the most important in the South of the Panjab. There are occasionally two missionaries on the spot, but the average since the commencement is one and a half. The Multan Mission district comprises an area of some 9,000 square miles, and a population of about 1,000,000.

In addition to the Church Missionary Society, the Society for Promoting Female Education in the East has two ladies in the station, who carry on a dispensary for women and children, and some schools for girls.

The mission houses are opposite to the Kutcherry in Civil Lines. There is a large mission school near the Husain Gui Gate of the city under, as head-master, Mr. William Khun Chand. This school prepares students up to the Entrance Examination of the Panjab and Calcutta Universities.

The mission church is situated in the compound of the mission school. Sixty-two miles from Multan, at Bahawalpore (capital of the native state of that name), is another mission school, containing 200 boys, and educating up to the middle school standard. This school has held its own in spite of the difficulties and opposition which arise in a native state, and some years ago when the Government started a rival school, and paid boys to come—while those in the mission school had to pay for coming—it was a common saying in Bahawalpore that if boys wanted scholarships they should go to the Government school, if teaching, they should go to the mission school.

What itineration work has been done has been principally in the district of Muzaffargarh, lying to the west of Multan.

From Multan to Karachi by the Indus Valley Railway is 611 miles. The time occupied on the journey by the mail-train is twenty-six and a half hours. Sind does not present great attractions to the general tourist, but as Karachi has, since the opening of the railway, become an important port for the arrival and departure of European passenger-steamers, this book would not fulfil its purpose if all information was omitted concerning the various points of interest on the line of railway.

The first place of any importance is Bahawalpur, the capital of a native state of the same name, on the western border of Rajputana, and on the edge of the vast sandy desert which stretches across to Bikaneer. The area of the state is 16,000 square miles, and the population 573,000. The nawab is an intelligent young prince, thirty years of age, ranking next to the Maharaja of Patiala on the list of Panjab chiefs.

The city of Bahawalpur has a population of about 15,000. It is surrounded by a wall four miles in circuit. The nawab's palace is a huge square pile, with towers at each corner. The great reception hall is sixty feet long, and fifty-six feet high; the vestibule of the palace is 120 feet high, and from the summit an extensive view may be had across the vast Bikaneer Desert.

Ruk Junction is the station for the Sind-Pishin Railway to Quetta. It has always been a regret to me that I have not been able during either of my journeys through India to visit Quetta and the Afghan frontier. My readers, however, are gainers thereby, as they have the advantage of the experience of one of the greatest authorities on Indian frontier questions—the Hon. George N. Curzon, M.P., who has been so kind as to condense his experience into the last chapter of this volume, where the traveller will find all the information he requires.

Larkhana is a busy town in the midst of the most fertile tract of arid Sind. There is nothing of special interest except an old fort and tomb, and the irrigation works.

Sehwan has a population of about 5,000, a large number of whom are professional beggars, supported by the charity of pilgrims to the great shrine of Lal Shahbaz, an old Musalman saint, whose tomb, dating back to 1356 A.D., is a beautiful specimen of encaustic tile-work. The fort is one of the most interesting relics in India, having been built by Alexander the Great. It is a huge artificial mound about 250 feet high, the summit of which is about 1,500 feet by 800, surrounded by a dilapidated wall; the remains of several towers are visible. Sehwan is probably the most ancient place in Sind. There is a good Dak bungalow.

A few miles from Sehwan is Manchhar Lake, which, when the Indus is in full flood, covers an area of twenty miles by ten, but in the dry season shrinks to about half its size. The space left by the receding water yields splendid crops of wheat and other cereals. The lake is full of fine fish, twelve or fifteen varieties, affording employment to hundreds of fishermen, who spear the fish, as the lake is too weedy for nets. The Government take one-third of the catch as royalty. During the winter months the lake swarms with every kind of waterfowl.

AT ROHRI.

Rohri and Sukkur are two towns on opposite sides of the Indus, with the Island of Bukkur lying between.

The Jama Masjid at Rohri was built about 1570 A.D.; it is a fine building of red brick, with handsome domes. The whole surface is covered with glazed encaustic tiles. The Idgah Masjid dates from 1593, and the War Mubarak, a building about twenty-five feet square, was erected by Prince Mir Muhammad, for the reception of a hair from the beard of the Prophet. This hair is set in amber, and enclosed in a gold case studded with precious stones. Rohri is very picturesque, many of the older houses being lofty brick buildings, whose flat roofs are surrounded by balustrades. The town is built on the top of a precipitous rock forty feet high, overhanging the river. There are some important irrigation works here, with powerful sluice gates, feeding a series of canals, which have cost over a million sterling. Sukkur is a modern town of no interest beyond the busy life of the river bank, crowded with river boats and steamers.

Five miles from Rohri is the ruined city of Aror, formerly the capital of the Hindu Raja of Sind, built on the old banks of the Indus. There is a fine old mosque in good preservation among the ruins, and a curious cave sacred to the goddess Kalka Devi, much resorted to by pilgrims.

Bukkur is a fortified island, composed of a great limestone rock 800 yards by 300 wide. The fortress covers the whole area of the island, which is surrounded by a double wall thirty feet wide. It has an ancient history, and has been fought for incessantly by rival states. There are two very pretty islands north and south of Bukkur, beatifully wooded, called Jind Pir, and Sadh Bela, on which are venerable and very holy shrines. A good steam ferry plies between Sukkur and Rohri.

Kotri is the station for Haidarabad, the capital of Sind, which is reached by steam ferry, and a short drive of three miles. Kotri has a population of about 10,000, and is practically the terminus of the downward traffic of the river Indus. The bank presents a lively scene, crowded with river craft of every kind, loading or discharging their various cargoes. Railway sidings are laid down to the river brink in zig-zags, so constructed as to do their work however low or high may be the river's level. The railway has greatly diminished the importance of Kotri.

Haidarabad is the old capital of Sind, with a population of 50,000. It is approached from the river by a very beautiful avenue of trees, and the town itself is finely placed on the hills of the Ganjo range, a site of great natural strength. The fort was a strong place when it was built, more than 100 years ago, but it has no modern improvements. It contains the arsenal of the province. It is irregular in shape, following the natural shape of the rock, surrounded by a Persian spear-head battlement, and approached by a bridge over a deep trench, leading to an intricate gateway. The whole building is very picturesque both as a whole, and in its details. The mosques, barracks and other buildings, which originally filled the interior, have all disappeared, with the exception of the palace of Mir Nasir Khan, now used by the commissioner as a residence. The "painted chamber" in this palace is a curious specimen of Indian decorative art. A splendid view is obtained from the massive circular tower that was the treasure-house of the Amirs of Sind.

On a hill near the city is a famous Musalman shrine dedicated to a saint, one Shah Makkai, a place of great resort for pious Moslem pilgrims. The Green Mosque is an interesting but dilapidated ruin.

The tombs of Gulam Shah Kalhora and those of the Talpur family

GATEWAY OF CARVED WOOD, HAIDARABAD.

are just beyond the market place of new Haidarabad. They are exceedingly beautiful mausoleums, of yellow marble, with finely carved and pierced windows, roofed with encaustic tiles. The old bazar clusters round the gateway of the fort, and is a busy scene full of life and trade. Many of the shops and merchant's houses are very quaint. The silver tissues of Haidarabad are noted all over India, and there is also a large manufacture of embroideries in silk and gold. In the days of the Amirs, this city was also famous for its enamelling and damascene work, chiefly employed in the decoration of swords, match-

THE GREEN MOSQUE, HAIDARABAD.

locks and other weapons. There are still interesting survivals in the bazar, and some fine specimens of enamelling on gold and silver may be obtained. They are, however, inferior to those of Jaipur, Partabgarh, and other Rajput enamels. There is also a considerable amount of seal-engraving carried on, and if the traveller is remaining a day or two, he may bring away as a memento a carnelian or silver seal, with his name engraved on it in Persian or Arabic, mounted on an enamel handle. The jewellery of Haidarabad is similar to that prevalent throughout the Panjab, and is mostly gold and silver. Solid silver torques, anklets and bracelets, of a severe style of rectangular construction and ornamentation are the usual forms.

The best of the lacquered wooden and papier mâché boxes and trays, now so familiar in English fancy shops, are largely made at Haidarabad. They are produced by laying variously-coloured lac in succession

OLD PAVILION, TATTA.

on the boxes, while turning on the lathe, and then cutting the design through the various colours. Other work is simply etched and painted with hunting scenes, natural or conventional flowers, animals, birds, &c., and then varnished. Furniture, such as chairs, and the legs of bedsteads are often lacquered in this way.

Haidarabad is a hot and dusty place, the average rain-fall in the year being only six inches.

Tatta is twelve miles from Jungchahi. It is a decaying and un-

TOMB OF MUZAR KHAN BALUCHI KURMATH, TATTA.

healthy town of about 9,000 inhabitants, mostly employed in the manufacture of the Tatta *lungis* or scarves, well known as among the best specimens of this class of loom work. They are thick, rich, variegated fabrics of cotton and silk. The only antiquities of any note at Tatta are Musalman. There is a series of remarkable tombs of the governors of Sind under the Mogul dynasty, built of brick and decorated with encaustic tiles in the

Persian style, of great beauty of pattern and exquisite harmony of colouring. These tombs date from A.D. 1500 to 1650, and are well worth a visit (*See* Fergusson, page 567). They are on the Makli hills, a mile from the town, and are undoubtedly the work of Persian artizans. They are all grouped behind an immense Idgah mosque. Some of them are built of yellow marble, carved with flowers and other decorations in low relief, and covered with domes of brilliant tiles. They are scattered over a vast cemetery six square miles in extent, said to contain a million tombs, and to have been a sacred burial ground for over twelve centuries.

The Jama Masjid is in the centre of the town. It was built by Shah Jahan A.D. 1647 and finished by Aurangzeb. It is a magnificent ruin 315 feet long and 190 feet wide, of brick, with a great central stone arch. The 100 domes with which the roof is surmounted are painted in different colours. The interior is beautifully coated with encaustic, the delicacy and harmony of the colours being very perfect.

Kalyan Kot is a venerable brick fortress, much dilapidated, ascribed to Alexander the Great. All that can be said on this point, however, is, that it was built before the invention of cannon. It is a curious old place, full of quaint ruins, the abode of countless pigeons.

KARACHI is a brand-new English seaport of about 90,000 inhabitants, which of late years, owing to the Indus Valley railway, has become a place of great importance, drawing most of the traffic from the Panjab away from Bombay. The distance by rail from Lahore being 820 miles, as compared with 1,304 from Lahore to Bombay. The rival ports meet at Saharanpur, so far as railway traffic is concerned.

In 1844, the first year of British rule, the trade of Karachi was only £122,000; in 1856 it had reached £1,235,000, and in 1889 its total was no less than £5,390,000. The town is handsomely built and well laid out, but apart from the interest of a great and thriving Indian seaport, it offers no attractions to the traveller. The British India Company run frequent steamers from Karachi to Bombay, a distance of 808 miles, and a voyage of three days.

The Sind stations of the Church Missionary Society are at Sukkur, Haidarabad, and Karachi, and they are also represented at Quetta and Bhawalpur.

CHAPTER XIV.

AGRA.

AGRA is the second city in the North-West Provinces, both in size and importance. Its population in 1881 was 160,000. It is finely situated on a great bend of the River Jumna, which is crossed by a fine railway bridge of sixteen spans of 142 feet each, and further up by a clumsy bridge of boats. The famous Fort is placed in the angle of the peninsula formed by this bend, on the very edge of the river, which in the rainy season, washes the base of its walls.

The old walls of the city encircle about eleven square miles, about one half of which is covered with houses. Agra is a well-built town, with a large number of thriving citizens, whose houses are better and handsomer than those of other cities of the North-West.

It is, without doubt, the most interesting place in all India. It marks, as no other city does, the crowning period of the Great Mogul Dynasty, which, beginning with Baber the Lion, sixth in descent from Timour the Tartar, has sat upon the throne of Delhi till it was finally cut off by Hodson in the tomb of Humayun, after the siege of Delhi. Akbar the Great removed the seat of his government from Delhi to

Agra, and in 1566 built the noble Sandstone Fort, whose red battlements stand uninjured to the present day.

The following is a brief summary of the history of Agra, from Sir W. W. Hunter's "Imperial Gazetteer of India."

"Before the time of Akbar, Agra had been a residence of the Lodi kings, whose city, however, lay on the left or eastern bank of the Jumna. Traces of its foundations may still be noticed opposite the modern town. Babar occupied its old palace after his victory over Ibrahim Khan in 1526; and when, a year later, he defeated the Rajput forces near Fatehpur Sikri, and securely established the Mughal supremacy, he took up his permanent residence at this place. Here he died in 1530, but his remains were removed to Kabul, so that no mausoleum preserves his memory amongst the tombs of the dynasty whose fortunes he founded for a second time. His son Humayun was for a time driven out of the Ganges valley by Sher Shah, the rebel Afghan governor of Bengal, and after his re-establishment on the throne he fixed his court at Delhi. Humayun was succeeded by his son Akbar, the great organiser of the imperial system. Akbar removed the seat of government to the present Agra, which he founded on the right bank of the river, and built the fort in 1566. Four years later he laid the foundations of Fatehpur Sikri, and contemplated making that town the capital of his empire, but was dissuaded, apparently, by the superior advantages of Agra, situated as it was on the great waterway of the Jumna. From 1570 to 1600 Akbar was occupied with his conquests to the south and east; but in 1601 he rested from his wars, and returned to Agra, where he died four years later. During his reign the palaces in the fort were commenced, and the gates of Chittor were set up at Agra. The Emperor Jahangir succeeded his father, whose mausoleum he built at Sikandra. He also erected the tomb of his father-in-law, Itmad-ud-daula, on the left bank of the river, as well as the portion of the palace in the fort known as the Jahangir Mahal. In 1618 he left Agra and never returned. Shah Jahan was proclaimed emperor at Agra in 1628, and resided here from 1632 to 1637. It is to his reign that most of the great architectural works in the fort must be referred, though doubtless many of them had been commenced at an earlier date. The Moti Masjid, or Pearl Mosque—the Jama Masjid, or Great Mosque—and the Khas Mahal, were all completed under this magnificent emperor. The Taj Mahal, generally allowed to be the most exquisite piece of

Muhammadan architecture in the world, commemorates his wife, Mumtaz-i-Mahal. In 1658 Shah Jahan's fourth son, Aurangzeb, rebelled and deposed him; but the ex-emperor was permitted to live in imperial state, but in confinement, at Agra for seven years longer. After his death Agra sank for a while to the position of a provincial city, as Aurangzeb removed the seat of government permanently to Delhi. It had often to resist the attacks of the turbulent Jats during the decline of the Mughals; and in 1764 it was actually taken by the Bhartpur forces under Suraj Mall and the Swiss renegade Walter Reinhardt, better known by his native name of Samru. In 1770 the Marathas ousted the Jats, and were themselves driven out by the imperial troops under Najaf Khan four years later. Najaf Khan then resided in the city for many years with great state as imperial minister. After his death in 1779 Muhammad Beg was governor of Agra; and in 1784 he was besieged by the forces of the Emperor Shah Alam, and Madhuji Sindhia, the Maratha prince. Sindhia took Agra and held it till 1787, when he was in turn attacked by the imperial troops under Jhulam Kadir and Ismail Beg. The partisan General de Boigne raised the siege by defeating them near Fatehpur Sikri in June 1788. Thenceforward the Marathas held the fort till it was taken by Lord Lake in October 1803. From this time it remained a British Frontier fortress, and in 1835 the seat of the government for the North-Western Provinces was moved here from Allahabad.

"The English rule continued undisturbed until the Mutiny of 1857. News of the outbreak at Meerut reached Agra on the 11th of May, and the fidelity of the native soldiers at once became suspected. On the 30th of May two companies of the Native Infantry, belonging to the 44th and 67th regiments, who had been despatched to Muttra to escort the treasure into Agra, proved mutinous, and marched off to Delhi. Next morning their comrades were ordered to pile arms, and sullenly obeyed; most of them then quietly retired to their own homes. The mutiny at Gwalior took place on the 15th of June, and it became apparent immediately that the Gwalior contingent at Agra would follow the example of their countrymen. On the 3rd of July the Government found it necessary to retire into the fort. Two days later the Nimach (Neemuch) and Nasirabad (Nusserabad) rebels advanced towards Agra, and were met by the small British force at Sucheta. Our men were compelled to retire after a brisk engagement, and the mob of Agra, seeing the English troops unsuccessful, rose at once, plundered the city, and murdered every Christian, European or native, upon whom they could lay their hands. The blaze of the bungalows was seen by our retreating troops even before they reached the shelter of the fort; the mutineers, however, moved on to Delhi without entering the town, and on the 8th partial order was restored in Agra. During the months of June, July, and August, the officials remained shut up in the fort, though occasional raids were made against the rebels in different directions. The Lieutenant-Governor of the North-Western Provinces (John Colvin), the seat of whose government lay at Agra, was one of the officers thus shut up. He died during those months of trouble, and his tomb now forms a graceful specimen of Christian sculpture within the fort of the Mughals. After the fall of Delhi in September, the fugitives from that city, together with the rebels from Central India, advanced against Agra on October 6th. Meanwhile Colonel Greathed's column from Delhi entered the city without the knowledge of the mutineers, who unsuspectingly attacked his splendid force, and were repulsed, after a short contest, which completely broke up their array. Agra was immediately relieved from all danger, and the work of reconstituting the district went on unmolested. The Government continued to occupy the former capital until February, 1858, when it removed to Allahabad, which was considered a superior military position. Since that time Agra has become, for administrative purposes, merely the head-quarters of a division and district; but the ancient capital still maintains its natural supremacy as the finest city of Upper India, while the development of the railway system, of which it forms a great centre, is gradually rendering it once more the commercial metropolis of the North-West."

The European quarter of Agra lies to the west of the city, beyond Laurie's Hotel, and contains the barracks of the garrison, the church, Havelock's memorial chapel, the judges' court, the Government college, and some handsome bungalows, all scattered through well-timbered *maidans*. The Catholic mission and orphanage is worth a visit, being one of the oldest missionary foundations in India, going back to the time of Akbar. Behind the mission is the old European cemetery, in which have been buried successive generations of Christians, some of the inscriptions being nearly 300 years old.

In viewing the city from the other side of the river, the great central object is the huge crenellated fortress of sandstone, with its vast red walls and flanking defences surrounded by the white marble domes and towers of its Royal Palace. This stupendous fort, impregnable at the time it was built, is a mile and a half in circuit, its frowning walls being 70 feet in height. During the mutiny in 1857, it sheltered within the walls of its barracks and palaces the whole European and Christian population of Agra and the district round, over 5000 in number. It commands the whole town, and also dominates every possible approach by the river. The *enceinte* is a later work, supposed to be by Shah Jahan.

The only entrance to the Fort is by the Delhi Gate, a splendid

DELHI GATE, AGRA FORT.

building of red sandstone, reached by a drawbridge which spans the wide moat. Passing through this gateway, which is guarded by tall Sikhs, a winding road mounts to the long flight of steps which leads to the entrance of the famous Moti Masjid, or pearl mosque, the private chapel of the court of the Mughal Emperors, occupying much the same relative position to the great palace of Agra as St. George's Chapel does to Windsor Castle. When the doors of the gateway are thrown open, the dazzling whiteness of this lovely mosque, standing in the full blaze of the noon-day sun, is simply blinding, and can only be seen through coloured glasses. Against the pure azure of the cloudless Indian sky, "all sapphire and snow," stands a corridor of three rows of beautifully-proportioned Saracenic columns and arches, roofed over with a row of exquisite cupolas, crowned by three lofty domes. These three aisles stand open to a great court-yard, surrounded by cloisters, formed by fifty-eight slender twelve-sided pillars on square bases, with a large fountain, or tank for ablutions, in the centre. Court-yard, cloisters, corridors, cupolas, windows and domes are all alike of the most beautiful white marble, enriched with fine carving in low relief. The mosque itself, *i.e.*, the three arched corridors, is 142 feet long by fifty-six feet deep, the courtyard being 100 feet wide from mosque to gateway. At each end of the mosque are marble screens of floriated tracery; the columns, arches, and vaults, exquisitely decorated, intersecting one another with infinite grace and beauty when viewed from the outer corners. The Moti Masjid was built by Shah Jahan in 1654, and the only ornament not strictly architectural is an inscription in black marble, inlaid in the frieze of the mosque. This inscription tells us that the mosque may be likened to a precious pearl, for no other in the world is lined throughout with marble. The gateway is exceedingly beautiful, and must not be overlooked in the dazzling beauty of the mosque. During the occupation of the fort by the British refugees at the time of the Mutiny, the pearl mosque was used as a hospital.

A few minutes' walk from the Moti Masjid brings us to the great square of the Fort, flanked on one side by the Diwan-i-Am, or public audience hall, built by Aurangzeb in 1685, 192 feet long by 64 feet wide, the roof being supported by a succession of colonnades of red sandstone, covered with plaster and painted white and gold. In the centre of this hall is a curious alcove of marble, inlaid with mosaics of precious stones, within which the Emperor sat, watching the administration of justice in the court immediately beneath him.

Here the Prince of Wales, the future Emperor of a vaster India than that of the Great Mughal, held a *durbar*, or public reception of native princes and nobles, during his visit to India in 1876.

The great square, now cumbered up with ugly British buildings, was where the Emperors held their jousts—elephant fights, and other sports of the period, the public being admitted to the cloisters which still surround three sides of it.

Passing through a small door at the back of the alcove within the Diwan-i-Am, a flight of steps leads into what is undoubtedly the most beautiful and unique monument of Saracenic art, the succession of buildings which form the palace of Shah Jahan.

The quadrangle first entered is the *Machhi Bhawan*, or Fish-square. A corridor runs all round, except on the side facing the river, where there is a wide terrace. From this terrace there is a splendid view of the Taj Mahal, reflected in the glassy surface of the Jumna. On the north side of the square is a small white marble mosque, which was reserved as a private chapel for the Emperor and his family. This dainty miniature house of prayer is entirely made of the finest and purest marble without gilding or inlaying of any sort. It is perfect in its way. The brass-pierced doorways are made from guns captured by Akbar at Chitor. Further on the same side of the

TERRACE OF THE MACHHI BHAWAN, AGRA FORT.

square, are a succession of apartments used by the court officials. Returning to the west side, passing the entrance door, two or three small chambers contain some chairs and a marble throne, relics of past Emperors. On the south side is a raised platform with a marble canopy, from which the courtiers used to angle, when the tank below, now dry and grass-grown, was full of clear water stocked with gold and silver fishes. On the terrace over the river, is a black throne, with a white seat opposite. The crack in the black throne is said to have occurred when the throne was usurped by a Jat invader.

At the south end of the terrace is the Diwan-i-Khas, or hall of private audience, consisting of two corridors, sixty-four feet long, thirty-four broad, and twenty-two feet high, built in 1637. There is nothing in India excelling the exquisite low relief carving of this building. The decoration of the pillars and walls is "pietra dura."

Most of this has been finely restored at the cost of Earl Northbrook, who found it much dilapidated by Indian and British Vandals.

Descending a few steps a two-storied marble pavilion is reached, surmounting one of the circular bastions on the river face, which possesses an unrivalled elegance and refinement, forming one of the most picturesque features of this marvellous palace. This is called the *Saman Burj*, or Jasmine tower, and is said to have been the boudoir of the chief sultana. The terrace in front is marked out in divisions of grey and white marble, and was used for playing *pachisi*, a kind of magnified draughts. Beyond this are a series of charming apartments, overlooking the Jumna, leading to the *Khas Mahal*, a small pavilion of white marble, the walls and ceiling of which were once richly gilt and coloured. A corner of the decoration has been recently restored. This pavilion opens out into the *Anguri Bagh*, the pretty garden of the Zenana, a fine quadrangle some 300 feet square. This is surrounded by various buildings, once devoted to the ladies of the Hareem, the most curious of which is the *Shish Mahal*, or palace of glass, an oriental bath, the walls and ceiling of which are decorated with thousands of small, circular, convex mirrors arranged in intricate patterns.

In another room are preserved the celebrated gates of Somnath, double emblems of conquest: firstly, when Mahmud of Ghazni carried them off from Somnath in Gujerat in the 11th century; and, secondly, when they were brought back as a trophy from Ghazni 800 years afterwards, and paraded through Northern India by a victorious British army. It is to be feared that our trophy is but a clumsy forgery, or, at best, the gates of Mahmud's sepulchre. It is even doubted if Mahmud ever took away any gates from Somnath at all. Archæologists, now-a-days, leave us none of our cherished myths. An Afghan horse-shoe, nailed on the middle of one of the doors, shows how wide-spread and venerable is the old superstition of luck connected therewith.

On the south side of the garden is a doorway leading to the oldest buildings within the Fort, the Jahangir Mahal, built during Akbar's reign as private apartments for the prince, his successor. These are built of red sandstone. The entrance gateway is exceptionally fine. The façade of the palace is decorated with relieving lines of white marble; the two inner courts, one of which is seventy feet square, are very massive, with carved brackets that at one time supported a

THE JASMINE TOWER, AGRA FORT.

verandah. Underneath these a moulding runs, carved with birds and lotus flowers. A flight of steps leads to the roof, on which is a handsome pavilion, surrounded by cisterns into which the water of the river was raised by a series of lifts, the remains of which may still be seen. This is the highest point in the fort, and affords a bird's-eye view of all the various buildings, and a good idea of its magnitude as a whole.

Some conception of the magnificence and luxury of the Mogul court may be got from the account given by a French traveller, M. Bernier, who visited India in 1663, during the reign of Shah Jahan. He writes as follows:—

"The king appeared sitting upon his throne, in the bottom of the great hall of the *Am-kas*, splendidly apparelled. His vest was of white satin, flowered and raised with a very fine embroidery of gold and silk. His turban was of cloth of gold, having a fowl wrought upon it like a heron, whose foot was covered with diamonds of an extraordinary bigness and price, with a great oriental topas, which may be said to be matchless, shining like a little sun. A collar of big pearls hung about his neck down to his stomach, after the manner that some heathens wear their great beads. His throne was supported by six high pillars, or feet, said to be of massive gold, and set with rubies, emeralds and diamonds. I am not able to tell you aright neither the number nor the price of this heap of precious stones, because it is not permitted to come near enough to count them, and to judge of their water and purity. Only this I can say, that the big diamonds are there in confusion, and that the throne is estimated to be worth four *kouroures* of roupies, if I remember well. I have said elsewhere that a *roupie* is almost equivalent to half-a-crown, a *lecque* to a hundred thousand roupies, and a *kourour* to a hundred lecques: so that the throne is valued forty millions of roupies, which are worth about sixty millions of French livres. That which I find upon it best devised are two peacocks covered with precious stones and pearls. Beneath this throne there appeared all the Omrahs in splendid apparel, upon a raised ground covered with a great canopy of purfled gold with great golden fringes, and enclosed by a siver balistre. The pillars of the hall were hung with tapestries of purfled gold, having the ground of gold; and for the roof of the hall there was nothing but great canopies of flowered satin, fastened with red silken cords that had big tufts of silk mixed with threads of gold hanging on them. Below there was nothing to be seen but great silken tapestries, very rich, of an extraordinary length and breadth. In the court there was set abroad a curtain tent, as long and large as the hall, and more. It was joined to the hall by the upper part, and reached almost as far as to the middle of the court: meantime it was all inclosed by a great balistre covered with plates of silver. It was supported by three pillars, being of the thickness and height of a barge-mast, and by some lesser ones, and they all were covered with plates of silver. It was red from without, and lined within with those fine *chittes*, or cloth painted by a pencil of Masulipatam, purposely wrought and contrived with such vivid colours, and flowers so naturally drawn, of a hundred several fashions and shapes, that one would have said it was a hanging parterre. Thus was the great hall of the *Am-kas* adorned and set out. As to those arched galleries which I have spoken of that are round about the courts, each Omrah had received order to dress one of them at his own charges; and, they now striving who should make his own most stately, there was seen nothing but purfled gold above and beneath, and rich tapestries under foot."

From every window and terrace of the palace fortress at Agra, the view closes in with the shining domes and minarets of the sublimely beautiful tomb erected by Shah Jahan over the body of his beloved wife, Arjamand Banu, who died giving birth to her eighth child. It was completed A. D. 1648. The famous Taj Mahal is probably the most renowned building in the world. Like that other great tomb, the Pyramid of Cheops, the enjoyment of its wondrous loveliness is marred by the recollection that it was built by forced labour, and reared on the lives of hundreds of its makers. 20,000 workmen were employed for seventeen years in building and decorating the Taj Mahal. They were half starved, and their families wholly starved, producing great distress and mortality. The total cost is estimated at over £4,000,000 sterling.

The road to the Taj from Agra passes the ruins and *débris* of many ancient palaces, and leads up to a superb gateway of red sandstone, inlaid with floral designs and passages from the Koran in white marble. This gateway is, in itself, one of the most beautiful buildings in all India. The roof is adorned with Moorish cusped arches, kiosks, and pavilions. A magnificent view of the Taj itself, with its surrounding gardens and the Jumna flowing beyond, is obtained from the roof. Passing through this splendid entrance, which is 140 feet high and 110 feet wide, and pausing on the top of a

ENTRANCE GATE OF TAJ MAHAL, AGRA.

flight of wide steps, the eye travels down an avenue of sombre cypresses, the floor of which is a long tank of white marble, covered with water about a foot deep, and reaching away for 300 or 400 yards. This lovely vista closes in with a vast dome of white marble, posed on a building whose perfect symmetry and absolute finish of every detail, flashes like some priceless jewel in the glorious blue setting of the Indian noon-day sky. Words are worthless in describing a building which, as a whole—whether in its details, its surroundings, its exterior, or its interior—is absolutely faultless.

The enclosure in which the Taj is placed is a great garden in which orange and lemon trees, pomeloes, pomegranates, palms, flowering shrubs and trees, with marble fish ponds and fountains, speak of the East in every whisper of their leaves and plash of their waters. This garden is a third of a mile square, surrounded by a wall of rich beauty. The marble-paved avenue of cypresses runs through its entire length, closed at one end with the dazzling white tomb, and at the other with the rich red gateway. The Taj Mahal is 186 feet square, and 220 feet high to the top of the dome. It is raised upon a plinth of white marble 313 feet square, and 18 feet above the level of the garden. At each corner of the plinth stand four tapering minarets 137 feet high. At each side of the Taj, 400 feet back across a great court flagged with marble, are splendid mosques of red sandstone richly decorated with mosaics of white marble, topped with three marble domes, only inferior in beauty to that of the Taj itself. These mosques are among the finest in India, and are apt to be overlooked in the all-entrancing beauty of the tomb to which they are complementary. I never saw a prettier picture than a picnic party of thirty or forty Hindus in every variety of bright holiday attire, grouped against the sunlit brightness of the marble pavement of the yard in front of one of these mosques.

Inside the Taj the emperor Shah Jahan and his beloved queen lie buried side by side in marble tombs, inlaid with rich gems, lighted by double screens of white marble trellis-work of the most exquisite design and workmanship, one on the outer, the other on the inner face of the walls. In England a building thus lighted would be gloomy and dark; under the blazing sun of India it only tempers a glare that would otherwise be intolerable, while giving light enough to see the infinite lace-like details of the wonderful screen of open tracery surrounding the cenotaphs.

The Taj is even more beautiful in the silver dress of moonlight than in the golden robes of the noonday sun. By day or night alike it makes an impression on the memory that nothing can obliterate.

Many hours may be spent in studying the details of the decoration of the Taj and its adjacent buildings. The lower walls and panels are covered with tulips, oleanders, lilies, and other flowers carved in low relief on the white marble. The *pietra dura* inlaying is equal to the finest Florentine, and is probably the work of a European artist, Austin of Bordeaux. The whiteness of the great mass of marble is thus broken with carving and inlaid flowers done in precious stones, combined in wreaths, scrolls, and frets. These are brilliant enough

A PANEL OF THE TAJ.

when looked at closely, but at a distance blend and tone the whiteness, giving a delicate suggestion of colour without losing the all-prevailing sentiment of pearliness, quiet and calm.

I am so sensible of my own impotence to do any measure of justice to this wonderful "dream in marble," that I have obtained permission from the poet of India, Sir Edwin Arnold, to quote both a prose and verse description from his ever facile pen:—

" . . . . . the wonder of Agra and the 'Crown of the World,' the Taj, the Peerless Tomb, built for the fair dead body of Arjamand Banu Begum, by her lord and lover, the emperor Shah Jahan. In truth, it is difficult to speak of what has been so often described, the charm of which remains, nevertheless, quite indescribable. As a matter of course, our first hours in Agra were devoted to contemplation of that tender elegy in marble, which, by its beauty, has made immortal the loveliness that it commemorates.

The Tarter princes and princesses, from whom sprang the proud Lion of the Moguls, were wont in their lifetime to choose a piece of picturesque ground, to enclose it with high walls, embellish its precincts with flower-beds and groves of shady trees, and to build upon it a *Bara-duri*, a 'twelve-gated' Pleasure House, where they took delight during the founder's life. When he died, the pavilion became a mausoleum, and never again echoed with song and music. Perhaps the fair daughter of Asuf-Khan, Shah Jahan's Sultana, had loved this very garden in her life, for her remains were laid, at death, in its confines, while the Emperor commissioned the best artificers of his time to build a resting-place for her dust worthy of the graces of mind and body which are recorded in the Persian verse upon her grave.

"In all the world no queen had ever such a monument. You have read a thousand times all about the Taj; you know exactly—so you believe—what to expect. There will be the gateway of red sandstone with the embroidered sentences upon it from the 'Holy Book,' the demi-vault inlaid with flowers and scrolls, then the green garden, opening a long vista over marble pavements between masses of heavy foliage and mournful pillars of the cypress, ranged like sentinels to guard the solemnity of the spot. At the far end of this vista, beyond the fountains and the marble platform, amid four stately white towers, you know what a sweet and symmetrical dome will be beheld, higher than its breath, solid and majestic, but yet soft and delicate in its swelling proportions and its milk-white sheen. Prepared to admire, you are also aware of the defects alleged against the Taj, the rigidity of its outlines, the lack of shadow upon its unbroken front and flanks, and the coloured inlaying, said to make it less a triumph of architectural than of mosaic work, an illustration somewhat too striking and lavish of what is declared of the Moguls, that they 'designed like giants, and finished like jewellers.' You determine to judge it dispassionately, not carried away by the remembrance that twenty thousand workmen were employed for twenty-two years in its construction, that it cost hard upon two millions pounds sterling, and that gems and precious stones came in camel-loads from all parts of the earth to furnish the inlayers with their material. Then you pass beneath the stately portal—in itself sufficient to commemorate the proudest of princesses—and as the white cupola of the Taj rises before the gaze and reveals its beauty—grace by grace—as you pace along the pavemented avenue, the mind refuses to criticise what enchants the eye and fills the heart with a sentiment of reverence for the royal love which could thus translate itself into alabaster. If it be time of sunlight, the day is softened to perpetual afternoon by the shadows cast from the palms and peepuls, the thuja trees, and the pomegranates, while the hot wind is cooled by the scent of roses and jasmine. If it be moonlight, the dark avenue leads the gaze mysteriously to the soft and lofty splendour of that dome. In either case, when the first platform is reached, and the full glory of the snow-white wonder comes into sight, one can no more stay to criticise its details than to analyse a beautiful face suddenly seen. Admiration, delight, astonishment, blend in the absorbed thought with a feeling that human affection never struggled more ardently, passionately, and triumphantly against the oblivion of death. There is one sustained, harmonious, majestic sorrowfulness of pride in it, from the verse on the entrance which says that 'the pure of heart shall enter the Gardens of God,' to the small, delicate letters of sculptured Arabic upon the tombstone, which tell, with a refined humility, that Mumtaz-i-Mahal, the 'Exalted of the Palace,' lies here, and that 'Allah alone is powerful.'

"The garden helps the tomb, as the tomb dignifies the garden. It is such an orderly wilderness of rich vegetation as could only be had in Asia, broad flags of banana belting the dark tangle of banyan and bamboo, with the white pavements gleaming crosswise through the verdure. Yet if the Taj rose amid the sands of a dreary desert, the lovely edifice would beautify the waste, and turn it into a tender parable of the desolation of death, and the power of love, which is stronger than death. You pace round the four sides of the milk-white monument, pausing to observe the glorious prospect over the Indian plains, commanded from the platform on that face where Jumna washes the foot of the wall. Its magnitude now astounds. The plinth of the Taj is over 100 yards each way, and it lifts its golden pinnacle 244 feet into the sky. From a distance this lovely and aërial dome sits therefore above the horizon like a rounded cloud. And having paced about it, and saturated the mind with its extreme and irresistible loveliness, you enter reverently the burial-place of the Princess Arjamand, to find the inner walls of the monument as much a marvel of subtle shadow and chastened light, decked with delicate jewellery, as the exterior was noble and simple. On the pure surface of this Hall of Death, and upon the columns, panels, and trellis-work

THE TAJ, AGRA. VIEWED FROM THE SUMMIT OF THE GATEWAY.

of the marble screens surrounding the tomb, are patiently inlaid all sorts of graceful and elaborate embellishments — flowers, leaves, berries, scrolls, and sentences—in jasper, coral, bloodstone, lapis-lazuli, nacre, onyx, turquoise, sardonyx, and even precious gems. Moreover, the exquisite Abode of Death is haunted by spirits as delicate as their dwelling. They will not answer to rude noises, but if a woman's voice be gently raised in notes of hymn or song, if a chord is quietly sounded, echoes in the marble vault take up the music, repeat, diversify, and amplify it with strange combinations of melodious sounds, slowly dying away and re-arising, as if Israfil, 'who has the sweetest voice of all Allah's angels,' had set a guard of his best celestial minstrels to watch the death-couch of Arjamand. For under the beautiful screens and the carved trellis-work of alabaster is the real resting-place of the 'Exalted One of the Palace.' She has the centre of the circular area, marked by a little slab of snow-white marble; while by her side—a span loftier in height, because he was a man and emperor, but not displacing her from the pre-eminence of her grace and beauty—is the stone which marks the resting-spot of Shah Jahan, her lord and lover. He has immortalised, if he could not preserve alive for one brief day, his peerless wife; yet the pathetic moral of it all is written in a verse hereabouts from the *Hudees*, or 'traditions.' It runs, after reciting the styles and titles of 'His Majesty, King of Kings, Shadow of Allah, whose Court is as Heaven':—'*Saith Jesus (on whom be peace), This world is a bridge! pass thou over it, but build not upon it! This world is one hour; give its minutes to thy prayers; for the rest is unseen.*'

For, through the vaulted door, opens to sight
A glorious garden—green, for ever green,
Since hither comes no harsh nor biting time
To strip the buds, but, all the warm year through,
The palms rise feathered, and the pipal-boughs
Whisper men's doings to the listening Gods
With watchful leaves; citrons and rose-apples
Keep their bright blossoms and their jewelled fruits,
And broad bananas flaunt their silken flags.
The spacious Pleasaunce shows on either hand
Dark verdant banks of various foliage—
Cooling the eyes, and quieting the heart—
With parterres interspersed, and rose-thickets,
And sheets of fiery Indian marigolds,
Moon-flowers, and shell-flowers; crimson panoply

Of the silk-cottons, and soft lilac light
Where sunbeams sift through Bougainvilliers:
Pink oleander-sprays you mark, fig-blooms,
Stars of the champak, tulip-cups, and spikes
Of silver-studded aloes, with red gold
Of peacock-bushes, and fair deadly bells
Of white datura. What most holds the eye,
Leading it onward towards the sight of sights,
Is yon black avenue of thuja-trees
With cypress intermixed ranged, all the way,
On either border of the broad-paved path,
Like sentinels of honour. From the gate
Straight to the threshold, of the Taj-Mahal
Those trees of mourning marshal you! Between
Gleams the paved way, laid smooth in slabs of white
River-like running through the banks of green;
And, on this middle pavement—all its length—
Wan water lies entanked, its crystal face
Rippled with gliding fish, and lotus-leaves
By the wind rocked, and rain of fountain-drops;
For—all its length—jets of thin silver dart
Into the Blue, and sparkle back to the Blue
Reflected in those marble-margined pools.
Led thus by sombre cypresses, and lines
Of dancing water-jets, and lilied tanks,
And glittering garden-causeway, the gaze lights
On that great Tomb, rising prodigious, still,
Matchless, perfect in form, a miracle
Of grace, and tenderness, and symmetry,
Pearl-pure against the sapphire of the sky
Enchanted, the foot follows the fixed gaze,
Which marks no more the garden's wealth, the pools,
The tall, dark sentry-trees, the shining path,
The enlaced and rustling bamboos, the plumed palms
With doves and sun-birds in their swinging crowns;
Only it dwells on that strange shape of grace
Instinct with loveliness—not masonry!
Not architecture! as all others are,
But the proud passion of an Emperor's love
Wrought into living stone, which gleams and soars
With body of beauty shrining soul and thought,
Insomuch that it haps as when some face
Divinely fair unveils before our eyes—
Some woman beautiful unspeakably—
And the blood quickens, and the spirit leaps,
And will to worship bends the half-yielded knees,
While breath forgets to breathe: so is the Taj;
You see it with the heart, before the eyes

THE TAJ BY MOONLIGHT.

Have scope to gaze. All white! snow-white! cloud-white!
Like a white rounded cloud seems that smooth dome
Seated so stately mid its sister-domes,
Waxing to waist, and waning to wan brow;
White, too, the minarets, like ivory towers,—
Four tall court ladies tending their Princess—
Set at the four shorn corners. Near and far
The garden clasps the Sanctuary in folds
Of rounded verdure; on its right and left
Rise fair two Musjids, chapels of the shrine,
Themselves in other spot majestical:
The one which looks to Mecca is for prayer,
This other, the Juwab—for symmetry—
Offers a resting-house where men may sit
And hear the Bulbul singing to the Rose,
And talk of Arjamand, and Love and Death.
Behind the glorious Tomb a court, a wall,
A bank which drops to Jumna, and, beyond—
Over the river, where her emperor died—
Brindaban, and a hundred leagues of plain.

Hushed, you advance—your gaze still fixed! heart, soul
Full of the wonder; drinking in its spell
Of purity and mystery, its poise
Magical, weird, aërial; the ghost
Of Thought draped white—as if that Sultan's sigh
Had lived in issuing from his love and grief
Immense, and taken huge embodiment
Which one rash word might change from Tomb to Cloud.
But mount the first great platform—sandstone, red,
A thousand feet each way—and, coming nigh,
You shall perceive the sovereignty of this
Which utmost loveliness did somewhile hide.
Now grows the mighty greatness of the Taj
Plainer! 'tis eighty feet of marble snow
From the embroidered fillet of yon Dome
To its gold Crownal, glittering in the sky
A hundred "yards of Akbar" from the ground.
Under that Saracenic entry-arch
These palms might grow, nor brush a topmost plume
Against the key-stone. Hence, too, shall you see
As if the Empress' self drew near, and near,
Till her blue veins showed, and her brows, and gems,
How opulent the unsullied marble spreads
With ornament, how decked with precious work
Of scroll and spray, volute and chasery,
And grave texts written clear in black and red
Inlaid upon the white; not marring it

More than those blue veins mar a lady's neck;
More than her pencillings of lash and brow
Break totalness of spotless skin and limb.

Mount, now, this second stair, arriving so
On upper platform, paved with marble pale,
Each way three hundred feet. Here stands the Taj!
This is the snowy table-land wherefrom
Rises the House of snow, mountainous, pure,
As any topmost peak of Himalay!
A massy square; the angles shorn; each face
Pierced with a vaulted entrance, parted off
From too keen worship of the Sun—who loves
Arjamand's bed—from too direct a ray
Of Indian moonlight, by those panelled doors
Of lace-cut alabaster. Nearer draw
And note their wond'rous toil—the white rock wrought
To exquisite, entangled, tracery
Intricate-patterned; knit, like midnight dreams
Of some geometer, in governed curves
Cissoid, parabola, and lemniscate,
Rhombus, and rhomboid, cirque, trapezium,
Each absolute, if eye shall follow them;
Strong as cast steel, but delicate as veil
Of filmy web from Dacca's patient loom
Ten folds whereof left Akbar's daughter bare,
So that the Mogul cried: "Com'st thou unclad?"
Thus by a hundred marble lattices
Passes the daylight to their place of rest,
Shorn of its glare; but you—before you pass—
Note, too, this diaper-work of branch and leaf
On door-post, lintel, and long cornices;
And how the black embroidering lines and texts,
Strict marshalled from the Arab alphabet,
Serve the broad beauty of the pearly walls
For softening shadows, how the Finial—
Pointing with gold the moon-round cupola—
Crowns with thin crescent its fair-lifted swell;
How—near approached—faint stains and wandering veins
Show on the marble-azure, saffron, rose—
So that it hath not coldness, like to snow,
But in large purity, takes glad the sun,
And answers him with tender tint and glow,
As if the milky marble lived, indeed.

You enter, reverent:—for a Queen is here,
And the dead King who loved her; and Death's self
Who ends all—and begins all; and Love's might

Which greater is than Death, and heeds him not.
White! white! tenderly, softly, white—around,
Above, beneath, save that the praying floor
Is laid in dark squares, and the architrave
Runs comely with adornings staid and script
Of Toghra text.

* * * * * *

Four tombs
Of Princes and Princesses—kindred bones—
Surround the shrine; here, in the heart of all,
With chapels girdled, shut apart by screens,
The shrine's self stands. White, delicately white!
White as the cheek of Mumtaz-i-Mahal
When Shah Jahan let fall a king's tear there,
White as the breast her new babe vainly pressed
That ill day in the camp at Burhanpur,
The fair shrine stands, guarding two Cenotaphs:
For when the trumpet of Serafil blows,
They shall not rise herefrom; their happy dust
Sleeps in one earth beneath, where two plain stones
Hers in the midst, and his—raised half a span
[For lordliness of sex and Empery]
But close beside it—mark their very graves.
This is but record of them, two Death-chests
O'er-flowered upon white marble with bright sprays
And coloured buds and blooms, posies of Death
Softly enamelled: on the Emperor's bier
The Kalamdan, noting a Mussulman
Dead in the Faith; on hers verses in black
Praising the name of Allah, and her name,
And when she lived and died—of all that time
The Glory, and the Cynosure, and Pearl.

All which rare work is over-canopied
With vaulted inner roof of milk-white blocks
Contracting, tier by tier, 'till far above,
A cap-stone shuts the canopy, so high
Those letters of the "Throne verse" cubit-long
Show like the little writing on a gem.
And ever, in the womb of that white roof,
Echoes sigh round and round, low murmurings,
Voices aërial, by a word evoked—
A foot-fall. Yet it will not render back
Ill noises, or a rude and scurril sound:
But if some woman's lips and gentle breath
Utter a strain, if some soft bar be played,
Some verse of hymn, or Indian love-lament,

Or chord of Seventh, the white walls listen close,
And take that music, and say note for note
Softly again; and then—echoing themselves—
Reverberate their melting antiphones,
Low waves of harmony encountering waves
And rippling on the rounded milky shores,
And making wavelets of new harmonies.
Thus—fainter, fainter—higher, higher—sighing
The music dieth upwards; but so sweet,
So fine and far, and lingering at the last,
You cannot tell when Silence comes: the air,
Peopled by hovering Angels, still seems full
With stir celestial, with foldings down
Of pinions; and those heavenly parting notes
As tender, as if great Israfil's self—
Who hath the sweetest voice in all God's worlds—
Still whispered o'er the tomb of Arjamand!

The milk-white marvel of this inner shrine
Is carved in Jali-work of tracery—
One panel of the tracery a slab
Five cubits every way, fretted and pierced
To marble gauze—so that the sunbeams, dimmed,
Steal, like gold twilight, to their mighty names
And show them well-nigh as if whispering them.
But yet a greater wonder! for its sides—
Where the wan stone spreads whole—holds inlaid wealth
Of fair delicious fancies, wreath and sprig,
Blown tulip, and closed rose, lilies and vines,
All done in cunning finished jewellery
Of precious gems—jasper and lazulite,
Sardonyx, onyx, blood-stone, golden-stone,
Carnelian, jade, crystal, and chalcedony,
Turkis, and agate; and the berries and fruits
Heightened with coral points and nacre-lights
[One single spray set here with five-score stones]
So that this place of death is made a bower
With beauteous grace of blossoms overspread;
And she who loved her garden, lieth now
Lapped in a garden.

And all this for Love!

A visit to the mausoleum of Prince Itmad-ud-Daulat provides a pleasant morning's drive across the Jumna by the old bridge of boats; a gay and busy scene, thronged with bull-carts from the country, the gravelly banks of the river on each side crowded with washermen and water-carriers. The tomb of Itmad-ud-Daulat stands on the margin of the river, a mile or so above the bridge. This prince was the father-in-law and prime minister of the Emperor Jahangir, and his mausoleum is one of the most beautiful tombs in India, a masterpiece of pierced and carved marble and *pietra dura*. It stands in a lovely garden overhanging the river. It consists of two stories; the lower one is inlaid on the outside with precious stones in geometrical patterns, diagonals, cubes, and stars. The numerous niches in the

TOMB OF ITMAD-UD-DAULAT.

walls are decorated with enamelled paintings of vases and flowers. The principal entrance is a marble arch, groined, and finely carved with flowers in low relief. The interior is decorated with brightly-coloured enamel paint. The upper story, surrounded by four towers, is reached by a staircase; it consists of pillars of inlaid marble, and a series of perforated marble screens stretching from pillar to pillar, the whole being roofed over with a canopy of marble.

The well-kept garden is entered by a great gateway of red sandstone. From the terrace, a fine extended view is obtained of the River Jumna, and some amusement may be found in watching the enormous turtles swimming about under the walls. Some of these are four or five feet long, with great horny beaks; they have been known to attack men swimming across the river, and pull them under water.

There are one or two other tombs further up the river, worth visiting, if the traveller has plenty of time on his hands. The most interesting of these is the Chini-ka-Roza, or china tomb, so called from its ornamentation, a sort of coarse enamelling on the plaster which has a look of porcelain. It is the resting-place of Afzul Khan, one of Jahangir's ministers of state.

The Ram Bagh, or Garden of Repose, close by, is extensive and well kept. The patched-up palace on the edge of the river was the residence of the Empress Nur Jahan, though it is doubtful if much of the original building remains. It is said the Ram Bagh was first laid out by Baber, the founder of the Moghul dynasty.

The Jama Masjid of Agra was constructed by Shah Jahan in 1644, in honour of his devoted daughter Jahanara, whose tomb lies side by side with the poet Khusru, in the beautiful cemetery of Nizam-ud-din, near Delhi. The main building of the mosque is divided, as usual, into three compartments, each of which opens on the courtyard by a fine archway, roofed by a low dome curiously built of white and red stone in oblique courses. The mosque is a stately building, 130 feet long by 100 wide, and anywhere else but Agra would attract the attention it deserves.

The Kalan Masjid is the oldest mosque in Agra, having been built by Sikandar Lodi, and is a fine, though somewhat dilapidated, specimen of the earliest style of Hindustani art.

The only other buildings in and round Agra worth noting are the usual modern surroundings of an important Indian city. There are two or three churches in the cantonment, and the Havelock memorial chapel.

The Roman Catholic church and convent are about half a mile from the fort, not far from the Central Jail, which is one of the largest in India, containing generally about 2,500 prisoners. Some of the finest carpets in India are made here. The Government College is in Drummond Road.

Firoz Khan's tomb is three miles on the Gwalior road. It is a beautiful building of Akbar's period, decorated with coloured encaustic tiles and fine sculpture of animals.

The only art-craft of importance in the Agra bazaars is that of inlaying on marble, inferior specimens of which are offered for sale on the verandahs of the hotels. This mosaic work is somewhat akin to that of Florence, but its best work is very inferior to the modern Florentine. It is produced by an inlay of various precious stones upon white Jaipur marble, consisting chiefly of agates, carnelians, chalcedonies, bloodstone, jasper, and lapis lazuli; but the costlier specimens are worked up with pearls, topazes, crystals, turquoise, garnets, coral, amethysts, and even sapphires. It is applied to various household trinkets, trays, boxes, paper-weights, inkstands, and table-tops. This beautiful craft was brought into Agra by Austin de Bordeaux, the reputed architect of the Taj Mahal, and has been greatly revived of late years under the influence of Dr. J. Murray, late Inspector-General of Hospitals for Bengal. In purchasing specimens it is necessary to avoid those which pander to European decoration, and buy only those which illustrate purely Indian ornamentation. A careful study of the Mosaics of the Taj and the fort will assist the traveller in making a wise selection.

SIKANDRA.—The tomb of the Emperor Akbar at Sikandra is, after the Taj, the noblest mausoleum in all India. The early morning is the best time of the day to visit Sikandra, which is six miles distant from Agra cantonments. The road is bordered with tombs, more or less ruined. The most interesting group will be found in a field about half way. One of them has an adjacent hall of sixty-four pillars, and commemorates one of Akbar's generals, a nephew of Etmad-ud-daulat. Not far off, close to the road, is a large *baoli*, or series of chambers built round a well, as a cool retreat in hot weather.

The pillars which stand by the wayside every two and a half miles are *kos minars*, or milestones (1 kos = 2 miles, 4 furlongs, 158 yards), built by Jahangir on the Imperial highroad to Lahore. Four miles from Agra, in front of a lofty arched gateway, is an old stone horse, supposed to have been placed there by Sikandar Lodi of Jaunpur, who founded the village of Sikandra, and built a palace there in 1495, the *Barah-dari*, now used as part of the buildings of the Famine Orphanage of the C. M. S.

Half a mile farther on is the Guru-Ka-Tal, a fine tank of red sandstone, now dry and weed-grown, with a mausoleum said to be Sikandar Lodi's tomb. This tomb is generally known as that of the Begam Mariam, the Portuguese Christian wife of Akbar, who was buried here.

Her tomb is in the vault below, and the cenotaph in the upper chamber. Close to Sikandra, a handsome gateway of carved stone leads into an enclosure in which is an elaborately sculptured red sandstone building of the period of Jahangir.

Fergusson speaks of the noble mausoleum at Sikandra as the most characteristic of all Akbar's buildings, quite unlike any other tomb built in India before or since, and of a design borrowed from a Hindu, or more correctly a Buddhist, model. It stands in a desolate but charming walled garden filled with fine trees, 150 acres in extent, entered by a splendid gateway of red sandstone, adorned with a wide scroll of Tugghra writing. At each corner of its roof rise white marble minarets sixty feet high, disfigured by the absence of their upper portions, which are said to have been shot off wantonly by cannon balls, during the sacking of Agra by the Jâts.

The view from the roof of the gateway is magnificent; not only because it is the best point from which to get a general view of the garden and tomb, but for the splendid prospect it affords of the surrounding country; the river Jumna winding through the fertile plain like a blue ribbon, the domes and minarets of the mosques and palaces of Agra and the Taj Mahal glistening like precious beads in its great loop, and the towering entrance of Fatehpur Sikri cutting the horizon in the far-away south.

Passing through this gateway, a broad paved road 150 yards in length leads through the garden to the tomb itself.

This building has five stories, or arched causeways of hewn stone richly carved, the bottom story being 320 feet square, with towers at each angle; it is thirty feet in height, with ten lofty arches in each face; the entrance to the tomb being about sixty feet high, topped with an exquisite marble cupola. The grand simplicity of this vast platform forms the best of settings for the more ornate terrace which stands upon it, measuring 186 feet each way, and fifteen feet in height. Upon this stand a third and fourth story of similar design, the whole building so far being of red sandstone elaborately carved. The fifth story is of the purest white marble, a cloistered quadrangle within, surrounded with marble trelliswork of the most intricate and beautiful designs, through which the blue of the sky and the dark green of the tangled garden gleam like some jewelled mosaic. Dainty cupolas crown the angles. In the centre is the cenotaph of Akbar, decorated with Arabesque tracery. A few feet from the monument

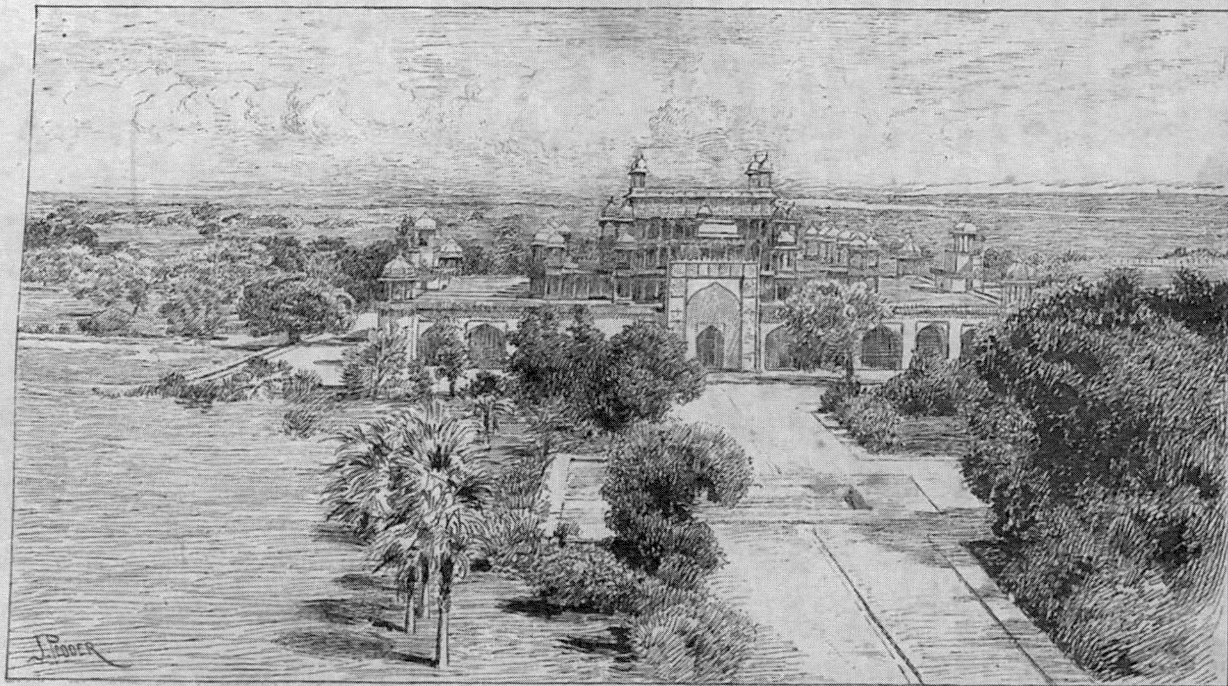

TOMB OF AKBAR, SIKANDRA.

stands a marble pillar containing a receptacle, in which it is said the Koh-i-noor was kept.

In the heart of this stupendous pile of arched terraces lies the grave of the mighty Akbar, in a gloomy domed chamber, into which the light of day faintly struggles through narrow apertures in the walls. This huge mausoleum took twenty years to build, and is said to have employed 3,000 workmen the whole time. The total height of the building is about 100 feet.

The Baptist mission at Agra, under the superintendance of Rev. Daniel Jones, is just opposite Laurie's Hotel. There are three European agents, nine native evangelists, sixteen teachers of 300 scholars in vernacular schools, with forty-five communicants. The Havelock Memorial Chapel, built by subscription to the memory of Sir Henry Havelock, who was a Baptist, is managed by the mission. Services are held there on Sunday for the benefit of English residents and soldiers, and part of the building is devoted to a soldiers' institute and reading-room.

The Church Missionary Society has extensive premises, consisting of St. John's Church and schools, and St. John's College. The church is under the care of a native clergyman, Rev. W. Seetal, and the congregation is about 500, with 180 communicants. The principal of St. John's College is Rev. G. E. A. Pargeter, and the vice-principal, Rev. T. F. Robathan. This is one of the best managed colleges in India, and prepares students for Calcutta University with very great success. The sons of most of the influential citizens of Agra are educated here, and there is, besides, a boarding-house for fifty Christian students.

CHAPTER XVI.

FATEHPUR SIKRI.

FATEHPUR SIKRI.—The deserted city of Fatehpur Sikri is a place of singular interest and beauty. No traveller should pass it by, however much he may be pressed for time. It is distant from Agra twenty-three miles, and it is necessary to order a carriage the day before, that relays of horses may be sent forward. There is, however, so much to be seen that if time permit, it is better to take two days for this excursion, spending the night in Akbar's record house, which is now fitted up as a Dak bungalow. There is also a messman and four beds at Birbul's House, within the palace courtyard. In either case, it is better to send word a day or two previously, that food may be procured.

The drive to Fatehpur Sikri takes about three hours and a half, the road passing through a richly-cultivated country and several large villages. If it is intended to go and return the same day, the start should not be later than daybreak. The scenes along the road are full of interest and variety, and much of the abundant animal life of India may be observed. The minas and other small birds hardly take the trouble to hop out of the way of the horses' feet. Vultures and crows, the village scavengers, roost about on stumps and rocks, letting one come within a few feet, when they fly lazily away to the next mound. At every wayside pond, handsome storks, cranes and other waterfowl abound. Wild peacocks strut about the fields, pheasants run across the road, pigeons, ringdoves, hoopoes, woodpeckers, and bright green parrots, fly from tree to tree, and the ubiquitous and ever-delightful palm squirrels, so full of cheerful impudence, frisk all over the place, playing in the dusty road or chasing each other up trunks of trees, on walls, or the roof of some village hut.

Fergusson tells us that it is at Fatehpur Sikri, more than any-where else, that Akbar the Great must be judged of as a builder. He was the first to occupy the spot, and apparently the last to build there, no single building being identified with any other emperor. It is a veritable romance in stone, the reflex of the mind of the great man who built it.

Akbar, the real founder of the great Mughal Empire as it existed for two centuries, came to the throne in 1556, and died in 1605, reigning nearly fifty years, covering the entire period during which Queen Elizabeth sat on the throne of England. Inheriting from his father, Humayun, but a small remnant of his kingdom, scarcely extending beyond Agra and Delhi, he reconquered the Punjab in 1556, annexed the Rajput kingdom in 1561—8, Gujerat in 1573, Bengal in 1576, Kashmir in 1586, Sind in 1592, Afghanistan in 1594, Khandesh in 1601, passing on to his son Jahangir an empire stretching from Persia to Burma, and from the Deccan to the crest of the Himalayas. Akbar removed the capital of the Mughal Empire to Fatehpur Sikri in 1570, with a view to the permanent establishment there of his court. But within fifty years of its foundation, it was abandoned in favour of Delhi by his successor, driven away, so it is said, by the badness of the water supply. The whole of the buildings of Fatehpur Sikri were therefore erected within a period of about thirty years, 1570—1605.

The road stops in an outer courtyard surrounded with red sandstone buildings, of which the principal is the Dak bungalow. Two or three guides are generally hanging about the door. These are all supposed to be lineal descendants of Sheikh Sulim Chisti.

The visitor should go at once to the great gateway, and work back through the mosque to the palace buildings. This superb entrance is called the Buland Darwaza (or high gate), and must not be taken as any part of the architectural scheme of the noble mosque, to which it forms the entrance. It is really a triumphal arch, erected many years after the mosque, in commemoration of conquest, as the inscription on the left hand of the gate entering the quadrangle states:—

"His Majesty, King of Kings, whose place is as Heaven, Shadow of God, Julal-uddin Mohummud Khan, the Emperor. He conquered the Kingdom of the South . . . . in the 46th year (of his reign), corresponding to the Hyree, 1010. Having reached Fatehpur, he proceeded to Agra." This fixes the date of the Buland Darwaza as 1601 A.D.

THE BULAND DARWAZA, FATEHPUR SIKRI.

The corresponding inscription, on the other side of the entrance, is translated thus :—

" Jesus, on whom be peace, said, the world is a bridge, pass over it, but build no house there ; he who hopeth for an hour, may hope for eternity. The world lasts but an hour, spend it in devotion ; the rest is unseen." A similar inscription is on the Taj.

The other inscriptions are pious proverbs, brief prayers, exhortations to good works, and such like.

Descending the broad flight of steps, ascending to the roof of a ruined Hammam, or bath-house, the whole of this superb monument may be seen to the best advantage. The plan is 130 feet long by eighty-five feet wide, and 130 feet high from the platform at the top of the splendid stairway. The façade is richly decorated and inlaid, pierced by a huge concave doorway, which is said by architects to be the most successful effort in the world to give dignity to a doorway in a great building used by men six feet high.

The doors themselves are not out of proportion for human beings to use, but being placed at the back of a semidome, to which the rest of the building is subservient, being not much more than its door-posts and lintels, their smallness is lost, and the full impression is conveyed that, in spite of its size, the gateway is fit for the use of ordinary people, and was not built for Anakim. The gateway is slightly out of the perpendicular.

At the side of the Buland Darwaza is a large tank about thirty feet deep, into which men and boys leap from the wall of the mosque, seventy feet above the water, running wet and breathless up the steps after their dive to beg for annas from good-natured visitors. This is one of those tanks or wells to be seen in most of the Mughal palaces, which were used as cool retreats during the heat of summer.

It is worth while ascending the gateway for the bird's-eye view of the mosque and palaces, and the wide prospect of the surrounding country. The guide, if asked, will point out the vestiges of the great market, or bazar, the flint pavement of which can still be traced for more than a mile in length. The ancient wall of the city still stands, seven miles in circumference, though little of its buildings remain outside the precincts of the mosque and palace.

The glorious quadrangle, to which the Buland Darwaza forms the entrance, is 433 feet long by 366 feet wide, including the mosque and cloister; the outside measurement is 550 by 470. The mosque occupies the greater part of the west side, the other three being surrounded by a beautiful cloister of red sandstone, in which are a succession of cells for pilgrims. The inscription on the main arch of the mosque states that it was built in the year A.D. 1571.

The mosque is crowned with three beautiful white marble domes. It is seventy feet high. The wings are of red sandstone, with lofty Hinduized pillars. The centre has a fine vaulted roof, is paved with white marble, and is quaintly decorated in geometric patterns.

Passing through a door at the back of the mosque is the tomb of the infant son of the Sheik Sulim Chisti, and some other interesting

TOMB OF SHEIK SULIM CHISTI, FATEHPUR-SIKRI.

buildings, including the house in which the Emperor Jahangir was born, a curious mosque with S-shaped brackets built by a stonemasons' guild for the Sheik, and the portico under which he taught his disciples. This group is older than the buildings of Akbar.

On the north side of the quadrangle are two of the finest tombs in all India; one is of carved red sandstone, and the other of white marble whose pierced screens look at a distance like fine lace.

The latter is the tomb of Sulim Chisti, the holy fakir, who exercised such influence over the Emperor Akbar as to have been almost his *alter ego*. If half the legends of this singular man are true, he must have been a shrewd and able statesman. The emperor's son, Jahangir, was named after this saint, bearing the title of Prince Sulim until he came to the throne. The tomb is elaborate and somewhat fantastic, the chamber being surrounded by a deep marble cornice, supported by curious twisted brackets of very elaborate design. Inside the building is a canopy like a four-post bed, encrusted all over with fine mother-of-pearl inlaid work, under which the saint reposes. Sulim Chisti died in 1572, and his tomb was completed in 1581 A.D. Half the village claims descent from this holy Fakir, and I believe the guides have some right to do so.

The neighbouring tomb is that of Islam Khan, a grandson of Sulim, who was a distinguished minister of Jahangir; it is very harmonious in all its details, a marked contrast to the exaggerated design of its companion.

There are many other interesting tombs on the north side of the quadrangle, including those of the ladies of Akbar's Court.

The fine gateway on the east side of the quadrangle is the Badshahi, or "Royal Gate," about sixty feet high. Passing through, descending the flight of steps, and turning to the left, the pretty houses of Abul Fuzl and his brother, Faizi, are reached, inside a courtyard. These buildings are now used as an Anglo-Vernacular boys' school, the scholars forming bright and picturesque groups round their masters in different corners of the open yard. The lads are very proud of their English, which they show off to any visitors who give them the opportunity.

The vast range of buildings which comprise the palace of Akbar is now entered through the stable-yard, in which over 100 horses and a large number of camels were kept. The fittings are still intact, being of carved stone. The next courtyard is that known as the palace of

BIRBUL'S HOUSE, FATEHPUR SIKRI.

Jodh-Bai, a princess of the royal house of Jodhpùr in Rajputana, wife of Akbar, and mother of Jahangir. This quadrangle measures 177 feet by 157, and is entered by an imposing and richly sculptured gate. On the north and south sides are suites of rooms roofed with stone slabs, enamelled a deep blue, in rich contrast to the sober red of the sandstone of which the palace is built.

On the stone terrace in front of the palace of Jodh-Bai are a series of small houses of the most delicate beauty, the most notable of which is the apartment of Birbul, one of Akbar's Hindu ministers. It contains eight rooms, each fifteen feet square, or two stories of four rooms each. Not a particle of wood or iron is to be found in the entire structure, which is massively built of red sandstone. The minuteness of the sculptured decoration covering every inch of surface inside and out, is more like the work of some Japanese carver in ivory than that of a stonemason. The ceiling of the rooms on the ground floor is made of long slabs of sandstone, fifteen feet long by one foot wide, resting on bold cornices, richly carved. The rooms on the upper floor are crowned by massive domes, got by putting a capstone on the top of sixteen sloping slabs, each of which stands on an abutment, the whole supported on eight sides, rising from the four walls of the room.

On the opposite side of the terrace is the pavilion known as Mariam's, or the Christian lady's house. This is said to have been built by Akbar as a present for a Portuguese wife, and some of the panels over the door, defaced by the iconoclastic zeal of later Mussulmans, represent an Annunciation, and other Christian subjects. Modern sceptics question whether Akbar ever had a Christian wife, but it is no concern of mine to throw doubts on any legend which may shed a halo of romance over anything I write about. It is better to believe a pretty and quaint tradition, than to quibble over it.

Between Birbul's and Mariam's houses, are placed some gardens with a charming little mosque, no doubt the private chapel of the ladies of the Zenana. Close by, is the Panch Mahal, a five-storied colonnade, sixty-five feet high. The ground-floor has fifty-six columns, the first floor thirty-five, the third fifteen, the fourth eight, while the fifth, or top story is a dainty little domed pavilion, resting upon four columns. The capitals of the columns vary in design. The guide points out one which is formed of two elephants with interlaced trunks, and another of a man plucking

THE PANCH MAHAL, FATEHPUR SIKRI.

fruit from a tree, which is said to be a fragment of some ancient Buddhist temple.

The Khas Mahal is a flagged courtyard, 210 feet by 120, with a pretty tank in the middle, in which fountains used to play.

The buildings on the south side are surmounted by a small and simple chamber, known as *Akbar's Kwabgah,* or sleeping-place. The walls are decorated with Persian inscriptions, which are mostly couplets in honour of the Emperor. In one of the angles of the Khas Mahal, is one of the most beautiful buildings in Fatehpur Sikri, known as the house of the Stambuli Begam, one of Akbar's wives, who is said to have come from Constantinople. Running round the walls of this pavilion are a series of elaborately-carved panels, about four feet high, the subjects of which are all drawn from nature, birds, beasts, trees, flowers, one panel being an elaborate and realistic jungle scene. Many of the pillars are also decorated with foliage and flowers.

The Diwan-i-Khas stands at the end of a large quadrangle, 210 feet by 120 feet, the floor of which is marked out in tesselated squares for the game of Pachisi. It is a curious and fantastic building, appearing from without to have two stories, but on entering it is found to be open from floor to roof, with an extraordinary pillar in the centre rising to the height of the upper windows. This column has an immense, elaborately-carved capital, from which four stone causeways lead to the four corners of the building, where they meet a landing-place, reached from the ground by a flight of steps. An accurate model of this column and capital stands in the India Museum, South Kensington. It is one of the queerest buildings I have ever seen, and none of the many conjectures of architects as to its original use appears to me to be satisfactory explanations. I can only look upon it as some costly freak. A colonnade, somewhat dilapidated, leads from the Diwan-i-Khas to the Diwan-i-Am, a small building of no great interest, placed in a vast colonnaded quadrangle, probably devoted to pageants and wild-beast fights.

The only other building within the precincts of the palace worthy of special notice is the Ankh Michauli, or, as the words mean, "the hide-and-seek place." My guide said that here Akbar and his friends played blind-man's buff, and other games, while others maintain that it was built for a playing-house for little Prince Sulim. It is more probable that it was the treasure-house of the palace, as an examination of the doorways show hinge-holes for massive stone doors. In front of this building, is an interesting little pavilion of pure Jain architecture, each of the architraves being supported by two struts coming from the mouths of monsters, and meeting in the middle like the apex of a triangle.

There are many minor buildings scattered about in the villages of Fatehpur and Sikri, that are of interest to the archæologist, the most important of which lies just outside the boundaries of the palace, of which indeed it is the chief outer gateway, the Hathi Pol, or elephant-gate. It obtains its name from the two colossal elephants which flank the spandrels of the main arch, one on each side. They were decapitated by Aurangzeb in a fit of Musalman iconoclastic zeal. Their trunks originally were interlaced, surmounting the keystone of the arch. A viaduct leads to a closed gallery from the Jodh-Bai to the rooms over the Hathi Pol. Adjoining this gateway is a great bastion, Sunjia Burj, the beginning of a series of massive fortifications begun by Akbar, but never carried out. Below the Hathi Pol is the Hiran Minar, or deer-tower, seventy feet high, studded with imitations of elephants' tusks, an ugly structure past which bucks and other game were driven for the Emperor to shoot.

The great square enclosure below the bastion is the Serai, built for the accommodation of merchants whose caravans brought their costly wares to Akbar's court.

CHAPTER XVII.

GWALIOR.

GWALIOR.—This historical city may be most conveniently visited from Agra. The Sindhia State Railway runs one train daily each way. It leaves Agra 4.30 P.M., reaching Gwalior 8.30 P.M., returning next morning about 7 A.M.; it is therefore necessary to stay two nights at Gwalior. There is a Dak bungalow at Morar, but since the departure of the garrison, it has not been well kept up, and may now be discontinued altogether. If that be so, the traveller should arrange with the station-master at Agra for the use of a carriage, which can be dropped off and shunted at Morar Station, to be picked up on the return journey. The night may be thus comfortably spent in a railway-carriage. Of course, cooked provisions must be taken.

Halfway between Agra and Gwalior is Dholpur, the capital of a native state of that name in Rajputana, with an area of about 1200 square miles, and a population of 230,000; the whole country is agricultural. There is a small town bungalow in Dholpur. The railway crosses the river Chambal by a fine sandstone bridge, 2,700 feet long, about five miles from the town. The piers of the bridge are sunk sixty-five feet below the bed of the river, and rise more than a hundred feet above it. In dry weather the Chambal is only a trickling stream, but in the rains it rises seventy feet, and runs more than half a mile wide.

The palace of the Rana was built about seventy years ago, and is a handsome building of no great interest. A short distance from the town is a beautiful tank, about half a mile square, dotted with pavilion-covered islands, and surrounded with 114 Hindu temples of various periods, from the 15th century to the present day. The lake is full of alligators. It is a great resort of pilgrims; Melas are held in May and September. There is a fine bridge of boats across the Chambal near Dholpur.

The station for Gwalior fort is Morar, where, until 1886, a British garrison 2,000 strong was stationed. In that year, however, the fortress of Gwalior, and the Cantonment of Morar, were restored to the Maharaja Sindhia, after having been held by British troops since the Mutiny in 1858. Jhansi is now the head-quarters of the military division of this part of India. Morar is connected with the fort of Gwalior by a good road, shaded by an avenue of fine trees.

GWALIOR is the capital of the great Maratha chiefs of the house of Sindhia, their scattered territories lying between the Jumna and the Narbada rivers, of which the Gwalior district is the largest, covering an area of nearly 30,000 square miles, with a population of three and a quarter millions, inhabiting more than 10,000 towns and villages. The people are mostly Hindus, not more than five per cent. being Musalmans. The total revenue of the State is £1,200,000. The Maharaja Sindhia is a staunch friend to the British Government, and displayed great courage and unswerving loyalty during the Mutiny. He is an Honorary General in the British Army, a Knight of the Grand Cross of the Bath, and a Grand Commander of the Star of India. His army consists of forty-eight guns, 6,000 cavalry, and 5,000 infantry. The founder of his family was a Maratha named Ranoji Sindhia, who began his career last century as slipper-bearer to the Peshwa Ranoji, by whom he was promoted to the head of the body-guard. Ranoji then became a leading Maratha raider, and died prince of the territories which have been handed down intact to his living descendant. Gwalior and the Sindhia family have played a leading part in the history of

British India, and their orange flag with its cobra has carried terror into many an Indian battle-field. Gwalior is an intensely interesting city. As the fortress capital of one of the leading native princes of India, it would naturally command the attention of the traveller, without the added interest of its beauty of situation, its fine architecture of the best Hindu period (1486—1516), its ancient temples, and its rock-cut Jain sculptures. The great fortress stands out of the surrounding plain on a mighty isolated rock of yellow

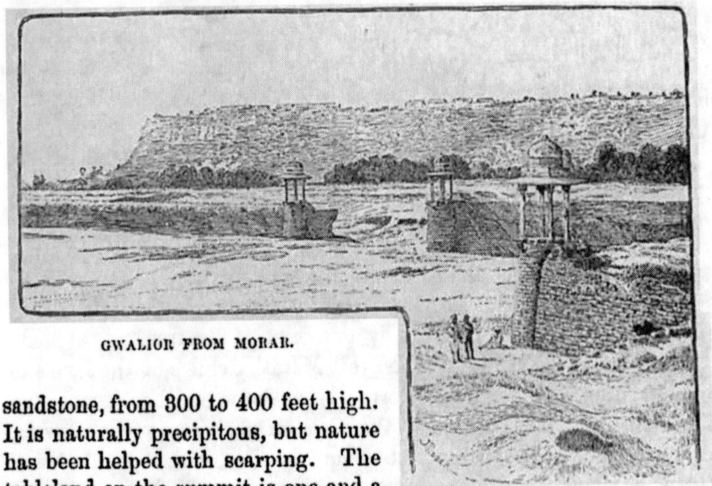

GWALIOR FROM MORAR.

sandstone, from 300 to 400 feet high. It is naturally precipitous, but nature has been helped with scarping. The tableland on the summit is one and a half miles in length, and 300 yards wide. On the eastern side of the rock, some colossal figures have been cut in bold relief. A rampart surrounds the fort which is reached by a vast staircase of successive slopes and steps, nearly half a mile in length, protected on the outside by a massive wall, and swept with guns. This long ascent is defended by six gates, all of them remarkable: the first is called *Alamgiri*, built in 1660, it has no special features; the second is *Badalgarh*, 100 years older, the work of Badal, an uncle of Man Singh, and a very fine specimen of the Hindu architecture of its time; the third is *Bhairon*, and bears the date 1485; the fourth is *Ganesh*, built about 1440; near this gate is an old temple, sacred to the hermit Gwalipa, who gives his name to Gwalior; the fifth is the *Lakshman*, and just before it is reached a temple is passed, hewn out of the solid rock, with an inscription fixing its date as A.D. 876. Above the gate, on the surface of the rock, are carvings of Mahadeo and his wife, and a huge sculpture of the Boar incarnation, probably one of the oldest in Gwalior; the sixth is the *Hathija*, or elephant-gate.

The citadel stands at the north-eastern corner of the enclosure, and presents a very picturesque appearance. This venerable fortress has been the cockpit of Central India; it has stood many a siege, and been stormed or starved into submission a dozen times at least. The rock was originally fortified in A.D. 773 by Surya Sen; in 1023 it was unsuccessfully besieged by Mahmud of Ghazni; in 1196 it was captured by Mahmud Ghori; in 1211 the Musalmans lost it again, but Altamsh, King of Delhi, won it back in 1231, after a year's siege. Narsinh Rai, a Hindu chief, seized Gwalior in 1398, and the Musalmans never regained it for 120 years, Ibrahim Lodi, the Pathan Emperor, recovering it for the Delhi throne in 1519. In 1526, Baber took it by stratagem, and in 1543 his son Humayun lost it again to Sher Shah, to be recovered in 1556 by Akbar the Great, who made it a prison for persons of rank. In the dismemberment of the Delhi Empire, Gwalior was seized by the Jat Rana of Gohad; then it fell into Sindhia's possession, who in his turn lost it to the East India Company in 1780, who entrusted it once more to the Rana of Gohad. Sindhia promptly retook it, and with the exception of two years, 1803-5, it has remained with the Sindhias to this day.

Gwalior owes its strength almost as much to its never-failing water supply, as to its steep rock; the fort is full of tanks, cisterns, and wells.

There are several palaces in the fort, of which the *Man Mandir* is the most important, being the most interesting example of early Hindu work in India. It was built by Man Singh about A.D. 1500. It measures 300 feet by 160, and on the east side towers 100 feet into the air. It is perched on the edge of the cliff, and the façade is relieved by a series of noble towers, crowned by open-domed cupolas, originally covered with gilt copper, joined together by a very fine lattice-work screen; the interior consists of two courts of considerable beauty, with rooms leading out of them. Man Singh's successor, Vikramaditya, added a still larger palace in 1516, and the Emperors Jahangir and Shah Jahan in their turn added a couple more. Shah Jahan's palace overhangs the city on the brink of a steep cliff, and is an oblong 320 feet by 170. The Gujarni palace is in an outwork at the foot of the fort, and was built for the Queen of Man Singh; it is a long two-storied building, much dilapidated.

There are about a dozen ancient Jain and Hindu temples on the

MAN MANDIR PALACE, GWALIOR.

rock of Gwalior, of which the two most important are the Sas Bahu, a Jain, and the Teli-Ka Mandir, a Hindu temple.

The Sas Bahu is dedicated to the sixth Tirthankar, Padmanatha, and Fergusson fixes the date at A.D. 1093. All that remains standing is the cruciform porch, measuring 100 feet through, and sixty-three feet across the arms. Of the rest of the building only the foundation

SAS PAHU TEMPLE, GWALIOR.

remains. The porch itself is somewhat dilapidated, but most of it remains intact, a charming and beautiful work of the mason's art. Its surface is covered with sculptures of figures, animals, flowers, and

TELI-KA MANDIR, GWALIOR.

diapered ornamentation. The central hall is thirty feet square, with four stupendous pillars bearing the great pyramidal roof. This roof is elaborately decorated.

The Hindu temple, Teli - Ka Mandir (the Oilman's temple) is a square of sixty feet each way, rising in a succession of sculptured stories to a truncated platform eighty feet high and thirty feet across. The fine doorway is thirty-five feet high. It was originally dedicated to Vishnu, and afterwards altered for the worship of Siva in the 15th century. The date of its erection is put by Fergusson in the 10th and 11th century.

The most striking of the Jain work at Gwalior, are the succession of rock-cut sculptures excavated all round the face of the cliff, about 100 in all, varying in size from a huge colossus fifty-seven feet high, to ordinary life-size figures. These were all excavated during the thirty-three years from A.D. 1441—74. Eighteen of these figures are over twenty feet high. The most of the statues are representations of Adinath, the first Jain pontiff. They may be known by his symbol on the pedestal, a bull. A seated figure of Nemnath, the twenty-second pontiff, is thirty feet high, his symbol being a shell.

The old town of Gwalior is a rambling dirty conglomeration of flat-roofed houses, crowded together at the eastern base of the rock. It contains the singularly beautiful tomb of Muhammad Ghaus, built in the early part of Akbar's reign, of yellow sandstone, grey and hoary from time. It is a square of 100 feet, with towers at each corner, roofed by a lofty Pathan dome, to which a few of the rich blue encaustic tiles which originally covered it, still adhere. The tomb stands on a lofty platform, and is surrounded by stone lattices of intricate pierced work, and a projecting porch on each face, crowned by a cupola. It is a finely proportioned building, and one of the noblest mausoleums of Akbar's time.

The tomb of Tansen, a famous musician, is hard by, and is a square building on twelve pillars.

The Jama Masjid, a very lovely mosque of white sandstone, in excellent preservation, is near the Alamgeri gate at the entrance to the fort. It was built in A.D. 1665.

The new town of Gwalior is called Lashkar, with a population of 90,000. Here is the fine new palace of the Maharaja, and a beautiful modern temple and cenotaph built by his mother.

BUNDELKHAND.—The extension of the Indian Midland Railway from Gwalior to Jhansi opens up to the traveller the interesting district of Bundelkhand, a tract of country comprising five British districts, and three small native treaty states, Orchha, Datia and Samthar, with about thirty other smaller states subordinate to the Central Indian Agency. This group of native states has a total

TOMB OF MUHAMMAD GHAUS, GWALIOR.

population of 1,749,000, ranging from 311,000 in Orchha to 800 in Dhurwai.

A college has been established at Nowgong for the education of the sons of the various Rajas, in memory of Lord Mayo, attended by some twenty or more of these young chiefs.

The whole province is full of ruins, large tanks, magnificent temples and ancient fortresses, built chiefly of granite and carved sandstone, dating from the time of the Chandel Rajputs, who ruled the country in the 11th and 12th centuries.

The best centre from which to explore Bundelkhand is

JHANSI, the administrative head-quarters of the British district of that name. It is now an important military contonment, taking the place of Morar, near Gwalior. There is a good Dak bungalow under the management of the deputy commissioner, and other accommodation may be had in a large building known as the Rani of Jhansi's palace. A letter should be written beforehand to the deputy commissioner. The fortress is occupied by British troops, and a beautiful winding drive has been constructed by the civil authorities round the ramparts, from which extensive views of the surrounding country and the old town of Jhansi in Gwalior territory may be obtained. There is plenty of large and small game in the neighbourhood, and any traveller who can get introductions may have a good time. The scenery is fine, the plains of Bundelkhand being diversified by a series of granite and sandstone hills 1 to 2,000 feet high, with scattered hills at the base of the ranges, abrupt and isolated, on which, as at Kalinjar, Ajaigarh and others, strong scarped forts have been erected, which in time past enabled the inhabitants of Bundelkhand to set at defiance the great Empires of India. These hill ranges have innumerable tanks for irrigation purposes, some of which are very ancient.

BARWA SAGAR.—Twelve miles from Jhansi, on the Nowgong road, is the village of Barwa Sagar, with a population of about 6,000 Hindus. This village is picturesquely situated at the foot of a rocky ridge, on the banks of a beautiful lake, in the middle of which are two craggy wooded islands. This lake is formed by an embankment three-quarters of a mile long, from which flights of steps descend to the water's edge. The plain below this embankment is planted with mango and other trees, many of which are of great size and age. This work was constructed by Udit Singh between 1705—37. Above the lake rises one of the finest old castles in India, also built by Udit

Singh, Raja of Orchha, in which some rooms have been fitted up as a Dak bungalow. Near Barwa Sagar is a venerable Chandel temple of the 10th century, built of massive stone blocks, finely sculptured with

UDIT SINGH'S CASTLE, BARWA SAGAR.

the figures of Hindu gods. The village is divided into three sections separated by stretches of cultivation, and the houses are embosomed in luxuriant foliage. Barwa Sagar is one of the most picturesque spots in India.

ORCHHA.—The old capital of Orchha state is within an easy drive of

RAJA'S PALACE, DATIA.

Jhansi. The present capital is Tehri, forty miles distant, where the Raja now lives. The gross revenue of the state is £90,000. The population of the state is 311,000, and of the town of Orchha, about 20,000. The interest of Orchha centres in its magnificent fortress palace, built for the accommodation of the Emperor Jahangir. The fine bridge leading across the river to the main gateway, its carved balconies, fluted domes, and gilded cupolas, with the rich foliage of the surrounding trees, make up a charming picture. There are some fine mausoleums of Bundela chiefs, and a very fine Hindu temple.

Datia.—The chief town of Datia state is twelve or fifteen miles north of Jhansi, on the railway to Gwalior. It is a most quaint and picturesque city of about 30,000 population, nobly placed on a rocky eminence, surrounded by a stone wall thirty feet high. The streets are narrow and intricate, but contain many fine old houses, the residences of neighbouring chiefs. The Rajá's palace stands boldly on the banks of a small lake, within the walls of a charming garden, planted with avenues of oranges, pomegranates and other trees. This garden is entered by a handsome gateway, and surmounted at each corner by embattled towers. Within the precincts is an octagonal building surrounded by a reservoir, containing a fountain composed of four elephants from whose trunks arises a jet of water. There are two other noble palaces at Datia, remarkable for great size and strength, as well as for the beauty of their architecture. On the banks of the lake, opposite the palace, are several fine tombs, and at Sonagir, a sacred hill four miles away, are some fine old Jain temples.

CHAPTER XVII.

MUTTRA.—BINDRABAN.—GOVERDHAN.—BHARTPUR.—ALIGARH.

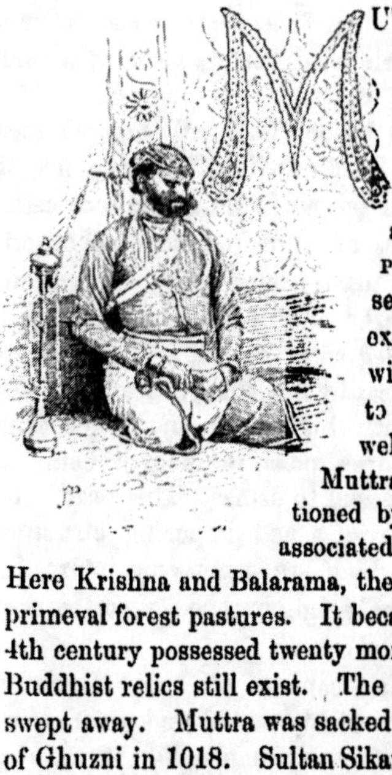

MUTTRA.—A delightful day's excursion may be made from Agra to Muttra, the birthplace of Krishna, and one of the seven holiest cities of Hindustan. A train leaving Agra at 6·30 A.M. arrives at Muttra at 10·0 A.M., and one returns from Muttra at 5·0 P.M., reaching Agra at 8·30 P.M. A second day, spending the night at the excellent town bungalow at Muttra, will be necessary if the traveller wishes to see the temples at Bindraban as well.

Muttra is a very ancient place. It is mentioned by Ptolemy, Arrian, and Pliny, and is associated with the earliest Aryan period. Here Krishna and Balarama, the divine herdsmen, fed their cattle in primeval forest pastures. It became a centre of Buddhism, and in the 4th century possessed twenty monasteries with 3,000 monks. Many Buddhist relics still exist. The ancient Hindu temples have all been swept away. Muttra was sacked with horrible atrocities by Mahmud of Ghuzni in 1018. Sultan Sikandar Lodi, in 1500, utterly obliterated all the Hindu shrines and temples; in 1636 Shah Jahan appointed a governor with express orders to suppress sternly all Hindu idolatry, which was again making headway, and in 1670 Aurangzeb rubbed out completely anything that was left over. The Hindu buildings of Muttra are therefore comparatively modern, and without architectural interest. The population is about 60,000, mostly Hindu, though at festival times it is swelled by tens of thousands of pilgrims from various parts of India.

Muttra abuts on the river Jumna. There is a wide street running along the bank the whole length of the city, with a succession of bathing ghats or flights of steps leading down to the river, surmounted by ornamented platforms and picturesque pavilions. These are best seen from the river itself, and boats for the purpose are to be hired. On the city side rises a succession of temples, palaces, and mansions, some of which are beautiful in design and elaborate in detail. They are generally built of fine white stone; the most remarkable of these buildings are, the Tower of Sati Burj, built in 1570, to commemorate the *Sati* of the wife of Raja Bhar Mal of Jaipur; the house of Guru Parshotomdas; that of Balamdas, a wealthy Gujerati; the temple of Parasnath; and the great palace and temple of Lakshman Das, a Muttra Seth, reputed to be the richest man in India. A good view of the city is obtained by crossing the bridge of boats to the other side of the river.

The Katra is a vast enclosure 800 by 650 feet, with two terraces, on the upper of which is a mosque. This was the site of the magnificent pagoda of Muttra, once the finest temple in India, but completely destroyed by Aurangzeb. Its walls, of hard red sandstone, still remain, with visible traces of their plaster modelling and graceful ornamentation. The Katra also marks one of the oldest religious spots in India, for it has been identified with the site of the ancient Buddhist monastery of Upagupta. Near by is the magnificent masonry tank known as the Patara-Kund, with high walls and steps rising about fifty feet from the water, on three sides, the fourth being an inclined plane, down which horses descend to drink. There are some very fine trees surrounding this curious and imposing structure. There is a museum at Muttra, in which are some very interesting Buddhist sculptures discovered in the neighbourhood, reported upon at great length by Cunningham, Vol. III.

The bazars are full of interest. The bankers and chief merchants are very wealthy, and their houses are richly carved and ornamented, rendering Muttra one of the most charming cities in India. Swarms of monkeys infest the streets, and the river is full of great turtles, both being fed by pious Hindus.

The only Musalman building of any importance is the Jama Masjid, recently restored with white chunam and encaustic tiles. It would hardly be worth a visit, were it not for the splendid view obtained from the minarets.

The general characteristics of Muttra are the same as those of Benares, but inferior in every way, and though it is full of Hindu features, the traveller who is limited as to time, and is including Benares in his tour, may leave it out of his arrangements without much loss.

Six miles from Muttra is the village of Gokul, the scene of Krishna's childhood, where there are many ruins of ancient Hindu temples and fortifications. The most interesting is a covered court, called Nanda's Palace, or the Assi Khamba (eighty pillars). "It is divided by five rows of sixteen pillars, each into four aisles, or rather into a centre and two narrower side aisles with one broad outer cloister. The external pillars of this outer cloister are each of one massive shaft cut into many narrow facets, with two horizontal bands of carving, the capitals decorated either with grotesque heads, or the usual four squat figures; the pillars of the inner aisles vary very much in design, some being exceedingly plain, and others as richly ornamented with profuse and often graceful arabesques."

The Methodist Episcopal Church Mission commenced operations in the city of Muttra in 1887, by appointing William Plomer, an ordained native Catechist, under the superintendence of the Rev. W. R. Clancey, then missionary in charge at Agra. In January of the following year, the Muttra circuit was formed, embracing the towns of Muttra and Brindaban in the Muttra district, and Hathras and Sikandra Rao in the Ali Sarh district, as centres of work, and the Rev. J. E. Scott, Ph.D., was appointed in charge. Both educational and evangelistic work was at once commenced and carried on during the year, resulting in the organisation of thirteen secular schools with an attendance of 336 pupils, and seventeen Sunday Schools, involving nearly 1000 scholars, and the baptism of about a dozen converts. Land was secured, and a mission-house erected thereon. In January, 1889, the mission was further strengthened by a Deaconess House and Training School. Miss F. J. Sparkes is superintendent, and is supported by a staff of assistants. A Medical Mission was also opened early in the year by Miss Kate McDowell, M.D., which has proved a great help in the work. Throughout the year almost every form of mission work is carried on. Ten Catechists, occupying six different centres, including Muttra, Brindaban, Hathras, Sikandra Rao,

Mohaban and Gokul, are constantly preaching at the fairs and in the bazars.

Zenana work has also been carried on at those centres, partly under the superintendence of Mrs. Scott, and partly under the direction of Miss Sparkes. Schools, both for boys and girls, the latter managed by Mrs. Scott, have been kept up throughout the circuit. Evangelistic services have been held regularly in the city of Muttra. A book-shop is kept supplied with both secular and religious books, and the sales are encouraging. About 2000 Urdu and Hindi tracts are distributed gratuitously every week. In addition to this work several services are held weekly for the benefit of the Nonconformist troops of the station. A chapel is being erected for their accommodation. During the year 1889, there have been gathered on the entire circuit about 100 converts, the most of whom have been from the lower castes.

BINDRABAN.—Bindraban is another sacred city on the banks of the Jumna, six miles from Muttra in the opposite direction from Gokul. It has a population of 22,000, of whom 21,000 are Hindu. It contains a large number of temples and shrines, one of which, the temple of Gobind Deva, built by Rajah Man Singh of Amber, is among the most notable buildings in India. Mr. Growse, who is the authority on the architecture of the district of Muttra, contends that it is the most impressive religious edifice that Hindu art has ever produced. It dates from 1590 A.D. The body of the building is in the form of a Greek cross, being 100 feet through the nave, and the same through the transepts. The four arms of the cross are roofed with vaulting equal in design and execution to that of the best period of Gothic art. The centre is crowned by a beautifully proportioned dome. The effect produced is very similar to that of a Gothic cathedral of a late period. The external design of the temple is very fine. It is somewhat dilapidated, and the domes are gone. It probably suffered considerable injury at the hands of Aurangzeb.

There are three other temples at Bindraban of the same period, those known as Gopi Nath, Jugal Kishor, and Madan Mohan. They are of the same style as the Gobind Deva, but inferior in proportions, and in a much more ruinous condition. The gorgeous modern temple which dominates the town of Bindraban was built by two brothers, Muttra Seths, Govind Das and Radha Krishnu. The former retired from the world and became a religious devotee in 1874, devoting himself to worship and almsgiving. Every day more than 100 persons are fed at this temple. The great court is 500 feet by 400, and the temple, which fills up the centre, leaves a passage all round about fifty feet wide. There are three gopuras or gate-towers in the outer wall, eighty feet high, covered with sculptures of very inferior workmanship. The outer court, which is 773 feet long by 440 broad, not only encloses the temple and inner court, but a fine garden and tank, with steps leading down to the water on all four sides. The main entrance to the outer court is through a pavilion ninety-three feet high,

TWO FAKIRS, BINDRABAN.

the most beautiful portion of the whole structure. In front of the god is a huge pillar of copper, gilt, rising sixty feet, and sunk twenty-four more in the ground. There is 10,000 rupees' worth of copper in this pillar. This temple was begun in 1845, took six years to complete, and cost about £500,000 from first to last.

Two days may be well spent in a delightful excursion through the Rajput State of Bhartpur, by laying a Dak from Muttra through Goverdhan, Dig, and Kumbher, to Bhartpur city, the distance being forty-three miles.

Muttra	—
Goverdhan	14 miles.
Dig	8 "
Kumbher	10 "
Bhartpur	11 "

There is a good well-metalled road all the way. The night must be spent at Dig, in the Gopal Bhawan, a palace placed at the disposal of travellers by the Maharaja of Bhartpur, who also supplies them with food and other necessaries. It is necessary to write to the political agent at Bhartpur for permission to use it.

GOVERDHAN is in British territory, but contains the cenotaph of the Royal family of Bhartpur, which, with temples, tombs and ghats, surround two large masonry tanks. The cenotaph of Buldeo Sing has a curious painted roof, full of pictures of the battles between Lord Lake and the Thakur Ranjit Singh in the siege of Bhartpur, in which the English are being slain hip and thigh.

"One mile further eastward, in the depth of a wild, wooded country, is the cenotaph of Suraj Mall, the virtual founder of the Bhartpur state. It is a beautiful building marking the spot where the Thakur's ashes were deposited. On every side of the reservoir that fronts it, handsome landing-places run out into the still water, with deep and wide staircases between; a venerable banyan-tree shades the south side, and sends its pendant shoots towards the water; apes swarm on its boughs, and, from time to time, a kingfisher quivers his flashing colours over the lake before he strikes a fish, or a great crane makes a swoop from one side of the woods to the other. The spot is singular in its repose, its silence, and its irregular charm. This is the *Kusum-sarowar*, or lake of flowers, one of the stations in the ban-jatra or autumn perambulation of the groves sacred to Krishna and his companions."—*Keene.*

This beautiful sheet of water is 400 feet square; the tombs of Suraj Mall and his two Queens, with many other charming little kiosks and temples, crown the lofty terrace which runs along the east side. The town of Goverdhan clusters round a vast tank called the Mansi Ganga, where a great religious fair is held every autumn, resorted to by as many as 100,000 pilgrims.

DIG is reached by a long causeway above a low flat country. It is a town of about 15,000 inhabitants, and is a place of great antiquity, being mentioned in the Puranas. Its commanding fort was

SURAJ MALL'S CENOTAPH, GOVERDHAN

dismantled by the British after the capture of Bhartpur by Lord Combermere. The great feature of Dig is the superb palace, or rather series of palaces, the work of Suraj Mall, the founder of the Bhurtpur dynasty, A.D. 1725—63. The palace at Dig is rightly considered the most perfect of all the many beautiful palaces of Rajputana. It is also the last erected palace in India of the Great Mogul period of architecture, all the Royal residences which have since been built being bastard examples of European styles, mostly Italian.

The Gopal Bhawan, where travellers who have obtained permission are lodged, is built on the brink of a lovely tank, full of fish, about 400 feet long by 300 broad. The other pavilions are the Nund Bhawan, a fine marble hall over 100 feet long; the Suraj Bhawan, about the same length, and the oldest of the group—it has a beautiful floor of inlaid marbles; the Sawun Bhawan and the Kishun Bhawan.

These buildings are most elegant in design, and richly decorated; with their annexes, they surround an area about 700 feet square filled in with fountains and parterres, in true Mughal style.

The special architectural interest of these beautiful buildings centres in their double cornices, which Fergusson says, "for extent of shadow and richness of detail, surpass any similar ornaments in India, either in ancient or modern buildings."

All round the palace are beautiful gardens, planted with fruit-trees and flowering shrubs, with abundant water. The bird life of these gardens is plentiful and various: peafowl, parrots, pigeons, mynas, kingfishers, and twenty other gay-plumaged birds fly and hop about with charming tameness.

A pleasant walk along the Rup Sagar Lake leads to the fort, a strong moated building with twelve principal bastions, covering about twenty acres. A good view of the town and neighbourhood can be obtained from the top of one of the bastions.

KUMBHER.—Halfway from Dig to Bhartpur is the town and fortified palace of Kumbher, founded at the beginning of last century by the Raja of Jaipur. It is a small town of 7,000 inhabitants, situated in a plain and fortified by a mud wall and ditch. The fort stands on a low hill commanding the surrounding country. The large palace within the fortress was built by Budan Singh, and is in good preservation. It is never used as a residence, and is full of bats and other vermin. The place is very picturesque.

The road between Dig and Bhartpur is the main highway of the

State, and full of interest. The native travellers are quaintly dressed in dark green quilted cotton clothes, looking brave and warlike with ancient matchlocks over their shoulders and swords stuck in their belts, worn only for harmless swagger. The women wear gay clothes and profuse jewellery, some of which is worth purchasing in the bazars of Dig or Bhartpur.

BHARTPUR.—The traveller will stay at the Maharaja's Dak Bungalow, where His Highness provides lodging and entertainment free for twenty-four hours, treating his visitors with generous hospitality. Bhartpur is the capital of the native Rajput state of that name. It is seventy-seven miles long and sixty-three wide, with a total area of

OLD FORT, BHARTPUR.

about 2,000 square miles, and a thrifty and industrious population of about 700,000. The country is flat, and with few natural advantages, being short of water, none of the rivers being navigable or perennial. The country is thought much of by religious Hindus, being popularly known as Brij, or the land of Krishna.

Its main human interest lies in the fact that it is the only Jat principality of any importance in India, and that a great proportion of the people are also Jats, thus belonging to the same ancient people as their nobles and princes.

The Jats (Getæ) are the survival in India of the great Scythian invasion of the first century A.D. There are nearly five millions of them in the country, mostly in the Panjab, where they form the most numerous and valuable element in the agricultural population.

During the anarchy which followed the death of Aurangzeb, a band of this hardy and brave people, under a chief named Churaman, seized territory in Bhartpur and fortified themselves upon it. Churaman was dispossessed by his brother, Badan Singh, who built Kumbher and Bhartpur fortresses, and his son, Suraj Mall, enlarged his bounds and built the fort and beautiful palace at Dig. The Maharajas of Bhartpur have been twice in serious collision with the British power; in 1805, when Lord Lake unsuccessfully besieged their capital, and

OLD PALACE, BHARTPUR.

in 1826, when Lord Combermere carried it by breach and assault. However, they managed through all to keep their throne and increase their territory. The present Maharaja holds in unbroken succession from Badan Singh, and is in offensive and defensive alliance with the British Government.

The revenues of the State are about £300,000 a year, and the Maharaja coins his own money. The army consists of about 1,500 cavalry, 8,500 infantry, and 250 artillery, whose guns, however, are only good enough for salutes. The State is well administered, and the present Maharaja, Jaswant Singh, is an enlightened and cultured prince.

Bhartpur is a fine Hindu city of 60,000 inhabitants, with clean, bright, prosperous bazars. It is surrounded by a wall and a dry moat. Its name is derived from Bharat, a legendary character in Hindu mythology. The fortress is surrounded by a canal, and is exceedingly picturesque; there is a fine view from a bastion of the inner fort called the Jawahar Burj. The palace is within the fort, and is a modern building with a magnificent stone staircase; it is furnished with tawdry European magnificence. The old palace is a very interesting building. There are some handsome Hindu temples in the city, and a mosque built by the State for the use of its Musalman subjects.

Bhartpur is famous for its manufacture of *Chauris*, or fly-whisks. The craft is confined to a few families in the employ of the Maharaja, and the process by which the tails are made is kept a profound secret. These tails are bunches of long straight fibres of ivory or sandal-wood, as fine as ordinary horsehair, from which chauris are usually made. The handles are of beautifully carved sandal-wood, ivory or silver.

A train at five o'clock P.M., from Bhartpur, reaches Agra before eight P.M., ending one of the most delightful little excursions in all India, which may be accomplished in three days, or spread out into a pleasant week, at the traveller's will.

ALIGARH.—The fort and civil station of Aligarh form a suburb to the ancient city of Koil, which has played a conspicuous part in the history of India for the last 1500 years. It is situated in the midst of a fertile plain lying between the Ganges and the Jumna, known as the Doab, an almost uninterrupted sea of green and smiling cultivation. The station is one of the prettiest in India, and the roadways are avenues of nim, mango, peepul, mowra, and other fine trees. The town bungalow is near the railway-station. The native town of Koil, is handsome and well-placed, surrounding a high mound, once the site of an ancient Dor fortress, but now crowned by Sabit Khan's beautiful mosque, which though built during the last century, is getting somewhat dilapidated. The only other mosque worth notice is a small Moti Musjid; the tombs of Gisu Khan and Hai Baksh are handsome in their way. There is a very beautiful tank in the city, surrounded by temples, pavilions, and magnificent trees, in which countless monkeys live. These mischievous animals are a great nuisance to the inhabitants, who are compelled to put iron gratings over the windows of the houses to keep them out; being sacred, they cannot be dealt with, either by slaughter or deportation.

The fort of Aligarh is about two miles from Koil, and has no features of interest; it is surrounded by a wide, deep moat, full of fish. It is a strong native fortification.

The main interest of Aligarh is the fine Musalman College for the sons of Muhammadan gentlemen, established by the energy and patriotism of Sir Syed Ahmed, K.C.S.I., who also founded the Aligarh Institute, with its library, news-rooms, and printing-press.

The Muhammadan Anglo-Oriental College differs from most

SABIT KHAN'S MOSQUE, ALIGARH.

other colleges in being the expansion of a political rather than a purely educational impulse. To this feeling, the feeling that national interests depend upon the principle it asserts, is due the support it has received, and the extreme interest with which it is watched, not only by the advanced school of Muhammadans, but by the British Government. In a country under foreign rule, a knowledge of the language and thoughts of the rulers is an absolute necessity not merely for the progress of a people, but for the maintenance of a state of civilization. The learned professions, government appointments, trade, in fact all the sources from which an aristocracy and a middle-class derive their means of subsistence, have a natural tendency to pass into the hands of those who have the best acquaintance with the ruling language. The Muhammadans, partly from instincts of pride and conservations, partly from religious motives, have hitherto held aloof from English learning, so much so that even at the present date less than five per cent. of the students of colleges belong to this formerly dominant race. Having been accustomed to the position of rulers, with the income of the state very largely at their disposal, occupying the most prominent posts, civil and military, with the numerous emoluments that in an Eastern state accompany power, they find themselves deprived of all their sources of revenue, while saddled with the expensive tastes inherited from their forefathers. The consequence has been national bankruptcy, and a loss of influence, of civilization, and of learning, that is one of the most lamentable spectacles that can offer itself to a patriotic mind. The mutiny of 1857 achieved at a stroke results as calamitous to the Musalman gentry, who when anarchy set in rushed like a high-spirited race into the fray, as many years of decadence. The spectacle of the ruin of so many noble Musalman houses aroused Sir Syed Ahmed, who during the mutiny had protected the English of his district with the most intrepid gallantry, to devote his life to the amelioration of his people. After years of thought he came to the conclusion that the acquisition of English education was the only remedy for his nation, and seeing that the Government colleges being secular and one-sided in their education failed to attract his people, he determined to found a college which should meet the peculiar needs of Muhammadans. Being himself without property, though belonging to one of the most illustrious of the old Muhammadan families, the enterprise seemed hopeless. But the extraordinary talents he brought to the task, coupled with an indomitable perseverance, have achieved a success far greater than the expectation of his supporters, who knew the lethargy and the poverty of the Muhammadans, had dared to anticipate.

The college was started in 1875 as a small school, and has now, in 1890, some 200 boys in the school, and about eighty students reading for their degrees in the college department. It has a staff of four Englishmen, three of them Cambridge graduates, and several native professors and teachers, Mr. Theodore Beck, M.A., being the principal, to whom much of the great success of the college is undoubtedly due. The subjects it teaches are English literature, mathematics, philosophy, history, Arabic, Persian, and Sanscrit. It differs from the colleges started by the State in two essential principles. In the first place provision is made for the religious instruction of the Muhammadans reading in its school and college departments. Five times a day the melodious cadences of the call to prayer summon the students from all parts of the capacious quadrangle, in which they live, to worship in the mosque according to the faith of their ancestors. The punctilious observation of the fixed times of prayer is regarded as the most essential characteristic of a devout Muhammadan, but the discipline necessary for the enforcement of this at first irksome practice, on boys and young men in whom the religious instinct is not strongly developed, is one of the most difficult tasks in the management of a large Musalman institution; but scarcely anything is valued so highly by the public, and no cause of complaint is heard so loud against the youths, educated in government institutions, as their neglect of this distinguishing mark of Islam. In addition to the enforcement of prayers, reading of the Koran and of books of theology and morality form part of the college curriculum. By these and other means it is hoped that the students who leave this college will serve to engraft the new learning on the ancient traditions, thereby winning over the most bigoted and the most conservative of the old school to a willingness to march with the times, and to adopt the only way open to them of rescuing their nation from its present depressed conditions.

The second principle, in which this college differs from the Government institution is, while the latter devotes attention solely to the intellectual aspect of education, and is of necessity mechanical in its methods, the Aligarh College is based on the model of the colleges of the English universities, the students living together in a large quadrangle, dining together, enjoying a healthy college life, and coming into constant contact with their English professors. It would be difficult to find in any country an institution inspiring a stronger *esprit de corps*. To all the natural sentiments an *alma mater* is capable of exciting the motive of patriotism is here added. The hopes of the nation are bound up with the success of this institution. It is the one great effort made towards progress and reform by a nation in which adverse circumstances have engendered a melancholy resignation to fate, and have sapped the springs of action. Hope finds its birth in this community of energetic and high-spirited young men. All the influences which give vitality to centres of education, have been set on foot here by the energetic old man whose mind conceived the scheme. The cricket team of the college holds the palm among native teams throughout Upper India, and holds its own with the best English station elevens. The debating society, founded on the model of the Cambridge Union, trains the youths in the art of public speaking and in the English method of conducting public business. College feasts and entertainments, religious festivals, poetic contests, cricket, football, and athletic sports help to diversify the lives and call out the varied talents of the young Musalmans. To all this an additional charm is added by the absence, as between teacher and pupil, of any feeling of distance or prejudice arising from difference of race. There is to be seen in Aligarh a frankness and intimacy of social intercourse between Englishman and Indian rarely met with in India. The English ladies and gentlemen of the station entertain the college students at lunch, and accept their invitations to dine with them in the college hall. The basis is thus laid of feelings of goodwill which, if it spread, will be of incalculable advantage both to the people of India and to the British Rule. On such occasions the venerable old Syed has frequently uttered with impassioned earnestness the wish of his heart that the Englishman and the Muhammadan may become sincere friends and fellow-workers, and has pointed to the college banner of a cross supported on a crescent.

The college at Aligarh is still in its infancy. It is still beset with enemies who resist all change in the established culture of Islam. Its buildings are not half erected for want of funds. In all ways its existence is a struggle against financial difficulties. If any generous persons feel drawn towards assisting this struggling institution of the 50,000,000 Muhammadan subjects of the Queen, they might remember that "Aligarh, India," is a sufficient address to secure finding the old Syed. But in spite of the incompleteness of the task the college has set itself, the scarcely perceptible direct effect it has been able as yet to exert on the fortunes of the Indian Muhammadans, it is difficult to exaggerate the moral influence Sir Syed's work has had on the Muhammadan community. It has deeply implanted in them the idea that without education they can do nothing, that a thorough knowledge of the English language is the first condition of their progress. It has led the way towards other humbler efforts being made in many other parts of the country. It has taught the Muhammadans that though depressed they are not powerless to work out their own improvement. It has led them to rely on their own efforts rather than on the Government, and to accuse themselves and not their rulers for their misfortunes. And if, as its aspiration is, the college at some future time develop into a great Indian Muhammadan University, the Oxford or Cambridge of Islam, it will be Sir Syed Ahmed and Mr. Theodore Beck to whom the future historian of India will point as educational saviours of the greatest and most illustrious of the nationalities of that continent.

CHAPTER XVIII.

CAWNPUR.

CAWNPUR.—The journey from Agra to Cawnpur is one of eight hours. There are three trains daily each way. Half way is the town of Etawah, little visited by travellers, but a place of much interest, well repaying a break for a few hours. The mail leaves Agra at 8.30 P.M., reaching Etawah at midnight. There is a good Dak Bungalow, and a possible bedstead in the station, where there is a refreshment-room. A train leaves Etawah for Cawnpur the next day at 5 P.M., giving ample time to see the town and its buildings. The population is 35,000, of whom 24,000 are Hindu, and 10,000 Musalmans.

The town is picturesquely built on a series of ravines running down to the bank of the River Jumna. The groups of buildings nestle among fine trees, and from the top of the Jama Masjid the city looks like a great garden. In the centre of the city is Hume Square, a fine open space containing market-place, public offices, the magistrate's court, a mission-house, police station, dispensary, and the Hume high school. The square is crowded with bright groups of corn, cotton, indigo, and other produce merchants, for rail and river make Etawah a busy and thriving centre. A fine *seraï*, with a handsome gateway, adjoins the market-place.

ETAWAH is an ancient city, dating back long before the Musalman invasions; it afforded rich plunder to Mahmud of Ghazni.

The banks of the Jumna are lined with bathing ghats, temples, and shrines, some of which are very ancient. The finest is the *Bisrant* Temple, more than 400 years old. A modern Jain building, with a beautiful white spire, is worthy of notice.

The *Jama Masjid* is a curious old building, patched up nearly 500 years back from a Buddhist temple. It contains many interesting fragments of early Hindu architecture.

The *Asthal* is one of the finest modern temples in India. It was built about 100 years ago by a rich Brahman of Etawah, and is very richly endowed.

The fort was built by the Thakur Samersi in the 11th century, and is a striking ruin placed on the top of a hill overlooking the river. It is reached by an underground passage. There is no detail of any interest, except a very deep well, and some underground chambers.

CAWNPUR.—This is a large modern native city, with British cantonments, whose population is over 150,000. Apart from the events of the Mutiny, it has no attractions to the traveller. There are several hotels, and comfortable quarters for a night may be had at the refreshment-rooms at the railway station.

The following concise description of the city, from Sir W. W. Hunter's "Gazetteer of India," will suffice to remind my readers of the incidents which give the ghastly interest clinging to this otherwise prosperously dull commercial city and railway junction :—

"The cantonments and civil station of Cawnpur lie along the right bank of the Ganges, while the native city stretches inland toward the south-west, and also fills up the space between the military and civil portions of the European quarter. Starting from the east, on the Allahábád road, the race-course first meets the eye of the approaching visitor. The native cavalry lines succeed to the westward, after which comes the brigade parade-ground. North-east of the latter lie the European infantry barracks and St. John's Church; while the intervening ground, between these cantonments and the river bank, is occupied by the Memorial Church, built on the site of Wheeler's entrenchments in 1857, the club, the artillery lines, and the various military offices. The city covers the plain north of the parade-ground; and the Ganges shore is here lined by the Memorial Gardens, enclosing the famous well. The gardens cover nearly fifty acres, and are prettily laid out. Over the fatal well a mound has been raised, which slopes upwards until it is crowned by a handsome octagonal Gothic wall, with iron gates. In the centre of the inclosure is the figure of an angel in white marble by Marochetti, with arms crossed on her breast, each hand holding a palm branch. Over the archway of the gate is inscribed: 'These are they which came out of great tribulation;' and around the wall which marks the circle of the well: 'Sacred to the perpetual memory of a great company of Christian people, chiefly women and children, who near this spot were cruelly murdered by the followers of the rebel Náná Dhundu Panth of Bithur, and cast, the dying with the dead, into the well below, on the xvth day of July, MDCCCLVII.' The expense of the construction of the gardens and memorial was defrayed partly out of a fine levied on the city after the suppression of the rebellion. A Government grant of £500 a year is made for the maintenance of the gardens, which are irrigated from the Ganges Canal. In the gardens, south and south-west of the well, are two graveyards, with monuments to those who were massacred or died at Cawnpur during the Mutiny. Further to the west stands the civil station, with the Bank of Bengal, Christ Church, the theatre, and other European buildings. Old Cawnpur lies three miles farther along the river-side, separated from the present city by fields and gardens. The modern origin of Cawnpur deprives it of architectural attractions; and it cannot boast of such ancient palaces or handsome mansions as adorn Agra, Benares, and other historic capitals. The few buildings with any pretensions to beauty or elegance have been erected during the last fifty years by bankers, merchants, or pleaders. The native city was built according to no plan, and is badly laid out, abounding in narrow streets and passages. Except on the undulating margin of the Ganges, or where indented by ravines, the sites of the city, cantonment, and civil station, are alike flat and uninteresting. The principal landing-place on the Ganges is that known as the Sarsiya *Ghát*, a noble flight of steps, surrounded by a vaulted arcade of brick and stone. Cawnpur also contains, besides the buildings mentioned above, two Roman Catholic chapels, a Union church, a fine market-place, high school, club, and two racquet courts, etc.

"Cawnpur possesses no historic interest in early times, being a purely modern creation to meet the military and administrative needs of the British Government. The city first arose after the defeats of Shuja-ud-daula, Nawab Wazir of Oudh, at Buxar, in October, 1764, and at Kora, in May, 1765. The nawab then concluded a treaty with the British, granting them the right of stationing troops at two places in his dominions, Cawnpur and Fatehgarh. One of the detachments, however, was at first quartered at Bilgrám; and it was not till 1778 that the present site became the advanced frontier post in this portion of the newly-acquired territory. From the location of a large body of troops in Cawnpur, the town sprang rapidly into importance as a trading mart, and has now developed into a commercial city of the first rank. In 1801, the surrounding country came finally under British rule, by cession from the Nawab Wazir, and the headquarters of a district were fixed in the city. No events of historical note occurred between the annexation and the Mutiny of 1857; but in that year Cawnpur was rendered memorable by the leading part which it played in the operations of the mutineers. The struggle with the rebels lasted from May to December, but the station itself was never lost for more than a few days.

"News of the outbreak of the troops at Meerut reached Cawnpur on the 14th of May. Eleven days later, the Nana Dundhu Panth of Bithur, adopted son of the last Peshwa, Baji Rao, was placed in charge of the treasury; and, on the 30th of May, the entrenchment of the European barracks began. On the 6th of June the native troops mutinied, sacked the treasury, broke open the jail, and burnt the public offices. Next day the Nana opened fire on the entrenchments, which had no other fortifications than a mud parapet, five feet in height. After three weeks' cannonade the position became untenable, and the garrison capitulated under a promise of personal security and safe conduct to Allahabad. On the 27th they embarked in boats on the Ganges for Allahabad, at the Sati Chaura *Ghat*, a landing-place near the spot where the Memorial Gardens now stand. Before they could put off, they were treacherously fired upon from the bank, and all destroyed or captured, except one boat-load, which escaped for the time into Fatehpur district. The prisoners, including women and children, were crowded into a house at Cawnpur, and finally massacred by the Nana's orders in the Savada Kothi, near the East Indian Railway, and their bodies cast into the now historic well, noticed above. On the 16th of July, Havelock's small force entered the city, and the Nana fled precipitately to Bithur.

"Four days later General Neill arrived with an ample reinforcement of 400 Europeans. Havelock thrice advanced unsuccessfully into Oudh, and retreated at last to Cawnpur, on the 10th of August. Shortly afterwards, General Outram reached the city, and marched on to the relief of Lucknow, which was successfully accomplished on the 25th. Lord Clyde's and Colonel Greathed's columns passed through on different occasions in October; and on the 26th of November the Gwalior mutineers approached Cawnpur. General Windham attacked and defeated the rebel force, but, being strengthened by Oudh insurgents, they again assaulted the city, which they wrested from us on the 27th. They held it, however, only for a single night, as Lord Clyde's army marched in on the evening of the 28th, drove out the mutineers, and utterly defeated them next day, outside the city, with the loss of all their guns. After the reorganisation of the district the site of the massacre was laid out as memorial gardens, and an ornamental building was placed over the well into which the bodies were flung. The surrounding wall is pierced with rows of lancet windows or openings, having trefoiled mullions, and handsome bronze doors close the entrance. Within stands the marble angel of Marochetti, already described. This forms the chief object of interest to visitors in a city otherwise devoid of historical interest. A memorial church also occupies the site of General Wheeler's entrenchments in the cantonment. The style is Romanesque, and the material consists of massive red brick, relieved by buttresses and copings of buff freestone."

Cawnpur is famous for its conjurers and snake-charmers. An idle hour may be pleasantly whiled away by sending for a group of these clever and amusing jugglers, who, for a few rupees, will perform any number of wonderful tricks.

The Society for the Propagation of the Gospel has a station at Cawnpur with two European missionaries, 130 communicants, and schools with 820 pupils. The American Episcopal Methodists are represented by three agents, but I have not been able to procure any recent returns of their work.

The Ganges forms the natural waterway for the traffic of Cawnpur, and still carries a large portion of the heavy trade. The Ganges Canal, which passes just south of the city, is also navigable, and affords means of communication for a considerable number of country boats. The East Indian Railway from Allahabad to Delhi has a station about a mile west of the city; and the Lucknow branch of the Oudh and Rohilkhand Railway, after crossing the Ganges by a girder bridge, passes between the native quarter and the cantonments, and joins the East Indian line a little west of the Cawnpur station.

The Grand Trunk Road from Calcutta to Delhi also runs through the city and military lines, while other roads branch off southward to Kalpi and Hamirpur, and northward, over the railway bridge, to Unao and Lucknow.

The chief industry of Cawnpur consists in the manufacture of leather goods, which is rapidly developing from year to year. A large Government tannery and leather manufactory is situated in the old fort, together with a steam flour-mill. Two large steam cotton-mills give employment to a considerable number of operatives, who manufacture yarn, cloth, and tents, and supply the native weavers with material for their craft, and several cotton - presses, both European and native. These two items of leather and cotton goods make up the principal export trade of Cawnpur; but the city also forms a great grain mart, where agricultural produce from Bundelkhand, Oudh, and the middle Doab is collected for dispatch by rail. The commerce of Cawnpur has steadily increased for many years past, somewhat to the detriment of Fatehgarh, Mirzapur, and other local trading centres, but the development of the railway system in Upper India is already acting so as to decentralise the trade, by creating intermediate marts.

CHAPTER XIX.

LUCKNOW.—JAUNPUR.—AJODHYA.

LUCKNOW, the capital of the comparatively recent kingdom of Oudh, is a terribly familiar word to every Englishman. The romance of the awful struggle of the Mutiny centres around the ruins of its Residency, sacred to the eternal memory of its heroic defence by the British garrison in 1857, and its two equally heroic reliefs under Havelock, Outram and Colin Campbell.

Lucknow is quite a modern city; after Calcutta, Madras, and Bombay, it is the most populous in India, city and cantonments together numbering nearly 300,000 souls, of whom one-half are Musalmans. Thirty-five years ago, it was the capital of a great Muhammadan kingdom, and is now the centre of administration, and the focus of the commerce, of an important British province. Lucknow attracts to itself much of the native Musalman aristocracy and learning, and undoubtedly exercises more potent influence in Muhammadan society than any other city in India, except perhaps Haidarabad. Lucknow is wealthy and prosperous, presenting an outward appearance of magnificence and splendour, though its architecture, with one or two exceptions, is, beyond all expression, execrable. Placed in the centre of a province justly called "the Garden of India," the suburbs are extremely beautiful; viewed from any vantage point, the city is wonderfully picturesque, the debased and degraded architecture being toned by distance, its lofty minarets and gilded domes alone visible among the luxuriant foliage in which the whole city appears embosomed. Nowhere in India are there more beautiful avenues, parks, and gardens; nowhere in India are there uglier palaces, mosques and mausoleums.

Lucknow has one quality that will be appreciated by the traveller, weary of Dak bungalows and railway rest-houses—Hill's Hotel is one of the best in India, centrally situated, in handsome buildings once the

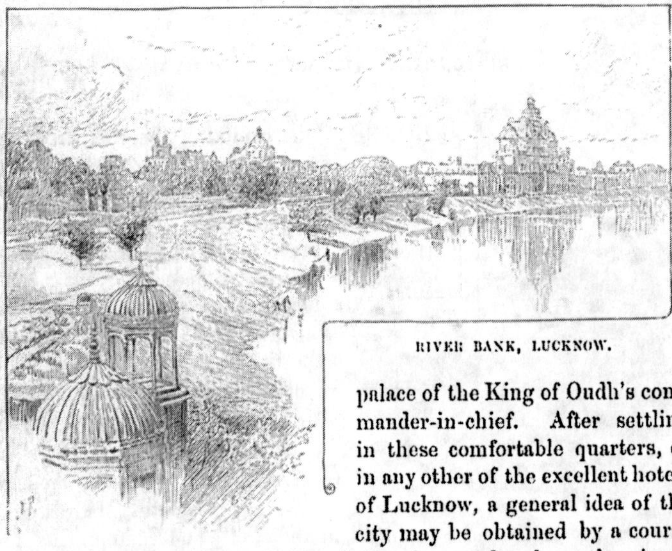

RIVER BANK, LUCKNOW.

palace of the King of Oudh's commander-in-chief. After settling in these comfortable quarters, or in any other of the excellent hotels of Lucknow, a general idea of the city may be obtained by a course round the Outram, Aminabad, and Canning roads, along the river's bank to the two bridges, and back through the native bazars: as charming and beautiful a drive as can be found in any city in the world.

The royal palaces of Lucknow are, without exception, the worst specimens in all India; costly and extravagant, tawdry and tinsel, bad in architectural design, worse in decorative treatment, but worst of all in the smear of Oriental vice and degradation that still seems to cling about them. The principal of these is the *Kaisar Bagh*, built in 1848—50, at a cost of ten millions of rupees. It is difficult to imagine where so much money is to be found in this hideous quadrangle of stucco rubbish, but probably every official, from the Prime Minister to the clerk of the works, had their share of it before it reached the actual buildings. These are already beginning to decay, and it is to be hoped that the Government will give all the assistance in their power towards their final destruction, and so make some amends for their Vandalism at Delhi, Bijapur, and elsewhere. Every courtyard and pavilion is redolent of the debauched king who built them, of his ferocious Begam, and his tribe of concubines. The Kaisar Pasand, in the south-west angle, the worst specimen of the group, has historic interest from having been the prison of Sir M. Jackson and his party, previous to their massacre.

The *Chattar Manzel*, or umbrella house, is another palace of the same bizarre and debased sort, so called from a fantastic gilt umbrella or canopy which crowns the roof. This was built 1827—37 by Nasir-ud-din for his huge hareem, and was originally surrounded by a lofty wall, which made it a strong place for the rebels during the Lucknow mutiny. This palace is now handed over to the United Service Club, which opens its doors readily to any well-introduced stranger.

There are many other smaller palaces and mausoleums scattered about Lucknow, all of which present a wearisome monotony of badness. They are to be avoided rather than looked for.

The only group of buildings in Lucknow of noble proportions and architectural interest is that made up of the Great *Imambara*, and the really beautiful Jama Masjid or cathedral mosque. The Great Imambara, though its details will not bear too close an examination, is however conceived on so grand a scale, as to entitle it to rank with the buildings of an earlier age. The principal apartment is 162 feet long, by 53·6 wide; on the two sides are verandahs, respectively 26·6 and 27·3 wide, and at each end an octagonal apartment fifty-three feet in diameter, the whole interior dimensions being thus 263 feet by 145. This immense building is covered with vaults of a very simple form and still simpler construction, being of a rubble or coarse concrete several feet in thickness, which is laid on a rude mould or centering of bricks and mud, and allowed to stand a year or two to set and dry. The centering is then removed, and the vault, being in one piece, stands without abutment or thrust, apparently a better and more durable form of roof than our most scientific Gothic vaulting; certainly far cheaper and far more easily made, since it is literally cast on a mud form, which may be moulded into any shape the fancy of the architect may dictate (*Fergusson*).

The word *Imambara* signifies the "Patriarch's place," used in the Musalman feast of the Mohurram, in celebration of the martyrdom of the sons of Ali, the immediate descendants of Muhammad. This huge building was erected by Asaf-ud-Daula in 1784 A.D., as a relief work during the terrible famine of that year. Its mosque, part of the original design, is a handsome and stately building.

The lesser Imambara is a florid horror to be escaped from as quickly as possible. It was erected by Muhammad Ali, 1837—41.

The *Jama Masjid*, or cathedral mosque, is the most beautiful building in Lucknow. Its towering minarets are a conspicuous object in the landscape for miles round. It is the only building in all Lucknow, with the exception of the Great Imambara, worth looking at a second time.

All round Lucknow are riverside pleasure-houses, walled gardens, tombs, and mansions, many of which, such as the Moti Mahal, the Sikander Bagh, Kadam Rasul, Najaf Ashraf, Khurshed Manzal, the Lall Baradari, the Musa and Alam Bagh, the Dil Kusha, and the ruined fort of Jalalabad, are associated with striking incidents of the defence and relief of Lucknow; their details hardly belong to a book devoted rather to the picturesque than to history, but they are admirably set out in Mr. Keene's clever little handbook of Lucknow, which may be purchased at any of the leading shops near Hill's Hotel.

In the Alam Bagh, a beautiful walled garden a third of a mile square, is the tomb of General Sir Henry Havelock, surmounted by an obelisk.

Wingfield Park is a pretty garden, of some forty acres, laid out with much taste and skill. It is famous for its roses, and other flowers. It is adorned with statues and little marble pavilions and fountains.

The Martinière is a college for boys, founded by General Martin, one of the many European military adventurers of the last century, who took service with the Indian princes. He was a Frenchman who in Clive's day enlisted in the British army, rising to the rank of captain, when he entered the service of the Nawab of Oudh, succeeding to the command of his army, and accumulating a vast fortune. He built the Martinière, a huge bizarre building with every imaginable style of architecture jumbled up together. Dying just as it was finished, he left money for its completion, and its endowment as a school. About 150 boys are educated there free of cost. It is one of the "sights" of Lucknow. A large number of the boys took a manly part in the defence of the residency, as hospital attendants, signallers, and even in active combat.

The great brick bridge of thirteen arches which spans the river, was built in 1780 by Asaf-ud-Daula, and is a very quaint and picturesque structure.

JAMA MASJID, LUCKNOW.

The Residency is of course the spot which, more than any other object of interest in Lucknow, attracts the British tourist. Apart from their romantic history, the ruins and surrounding garden form a beautiful picture. It is impossible for the most callous to wander unmoved through its pathetic cemetery, gay with flowers and shadowed by feathery bamboos. Every inscription brings to mind some fresh incident of the awful defence and relief of Lucknow. Here rests Henry Lawrence, "who tried to do his duty;" here are the graves of the chaplain and his only child, of twelve brave women and eight little children struck down by shot and shell, with two thousand officers and men who perished by war and massacre during the mutiny of 1857.

I leave each of my readers to select from the abundant literature of these terrible times such books as may enable them to make an intelligent inspection of the scenes of all the incidents of the defence of Lucknow. In my opinion Malleson's "History of the Mutiny" is the clearest and most graphic. The professional guides know all the spots by name, especially those in and round the Residency itself. The following extract from the *Imperial Gazetteer* will, however, suffice to bring to mind the main surface facts of the Mutiny narrative. A visit to the Museum, where there is a large model of the Residency, will also be found very helpful.

"A couple of months before the outbreak at Meerut, Sir Henry Lawrence [20th March, 1857] had assumed the Chief Commissionership of the newly annexed province of Oudh. The garrison at Lucknow then consisted of the 32nd [British] Regiment, a weak company of European Artillery, the 7th Regiment Native Light Cavalry, and the 13th, 48th, and 71st regiments of Native Infantry. In or near the city were also quartered two regiments of irregular local infantry, together with one regiment of military police, one of Oudh Irregular Cavalry, and two batteries of Native Artillery. The town thus contained nearly ten Indian soldiers to every European, or 7,000 to 750. Symptoms of disaffection occurred as early as the month of April, when the house of the surgeon to the 48th was burned down in revenge to a supposed insult to caste. Sir Henry Lawrence immediately took steps to meet the danger by fortifying the Residency and accumulating stores. On the 30th of April the men of the 7th Oudh Irregulars refused to bite their cartridges, on the ground that they had been greased with cow's fat. They were induced with some difficulty to return to their lines. On May 3 Sir Henry Lawrence resolved to deprive the mutinous regiment of its arms, a step which was effected not without serious delay.

"On May 12, Sir Henry held a *darbar*, and made an impressive speech in Hindustani, in which he called upon the people to uphold the British Government, as most tolerant to Hindus and Muhammadans alike. Two days earlier the massacre at Meerut had taken place, and a telegram brought word of the event on the morning after the *darbar*. On the 19th Sir Henry Lawrence received the supreme military command in Oudh. He immediately fortified the Residency and the Machi

Bhawan, bringing the ladies and children into the former building. On the night of the 30th May the expected insurrection broke out at Lucknow. The men of the 71st, with a few from the other regiments, began to burn the bungalows of their officers and to murder the inmates. Prompt action was taken, and early next morning the European force attacked, dispersed, and followed up for ten miles the retreating mutineers, who were joined during the action by the 7th Cavalry.

THE RESIDENCY, LUCKNOW.

The rebels fled towards Sitapur. Although Lucknow thus remained in the hands of the British, by the 12th of June every other post in Oudh had fallen into the power of the mutineers. The Chief Commissioner still held the cantonments and the two fortified posts at the beginning of June, but the symptoms of disaffection in the city and among the remaining native troops were unmistakeable. In the midst of such a crisis Sir Henry Lawrence's health unhappily gave way. He delegated his authority to a council of five, presided over by Mr. Gubbins, the Financial Commissioner, but shortly after recovered sufficiently to resume the command. On June the 11th, however, the military police and native cavalry broke into open revolt, followed on the succeeding morning by the native infantry. On the 20th June news of the fall of Cawnpur arrived; and on the 29th the enemy, 7,000 strong, advanced upon Chinhat, a village on the Faizabad road, eight miles from the Residency. Sir Henry Lawrence marched out and gave the enemy battle at that spot. The result proved disastrous to our arms, through the treachery of the Oudh artillery, and a retreat became necessary. The troops fell back on Lucknow, abandoned the Machi Bhawan, and concentrated all their strength upon the Residency. The siege of the enclosure began upon 1st July. On the 2nd, as Sir Henry Lawrence lay on his bed, a shell entered the room, burst, and wounded him severely. He lingered till the morning of the 4th and then died in great agony. Major Banks succeeded to the civil command, while the military authority devolved upon Brigadier Inglis. On 20th July the enemy made an unsuccessful assault. Next day Major Banks was shot, and the sole command was undertaken by Inglis. On the 10th August the mutineers attempted a second assault, which was again unsuccessful. The third assault took place on the 18th, but the enemy were losing heart as they found the small garrison so able to withstand them, and the repulse proved comparatively easy.

"Meanwhile the British within were dwindling away and eagerly expecting reinforcements from Cawnpur. On 5th September news of the relieving force under Outram and Havelock reached the garrison by a faithful native messenger. On 22nd September the relief arrived at the Alambagh, a walled garden on the Cawnpur road held by the enemy in force. Havelock stormed the Alambagh, and on 25th fought his way with continuous opposition through the narrow lanes of the city. On the 26th he arrived at the gate of the Residency enclosure, and was welcomed by the gallant defenders within. General Neill fell during the action outside the walls. The sufferings of the besieged had been very great; but even after the first relief it became clear that Lucknow could only be temporarily defended till the arrival of further reinforcements should allow the garrison to cut its way out. Outram, who had now re-assumed the command which he generously yielded to Havelock during the relief, accordingly fortified an enlarged area of the town, bringing many important outworks within the limits of defence; and the siege began once more till a second relieving party could set the besieged at liberty. Night and day the enemy kept up a continual firing against our position, while Outram retaliated by frequent sorties.

"Throughout October the garrison continued its gallant defence, and a small party shut up in the Alambagh, and cut off unexpectedly from the main body, also contrived to hold good its dangerous post. Meanwhile Sir Colin Campbell's force had advanced from Cawnpur, and arrived at the Alambagh on the 10th of November. From the day of his landing at Calcutta Sir Colin had never ceased in his endeavours to collect an army to relieve Lucknow by gathering together the liberated Delhi field force and the fresh reinforcements from England. On the 12th the main body threw itself into the Alambagh after a smart skirmish with the rebels. Sir Colin next occupied the Dilkusha palace, south-east of the town, and then moved against the Martinière, which the enemy had fortified with guns in position. After carrying that post, he forded the canal, and on the 16th attacked the Sikandra Bagh, the chief rebel stronghold. The mutineers, driven to bay, fought desperately for their fortress, but before evening the whole place was in the hands of the British. As soon as Sir Colin Campbell reached the Moti Mahal, on the outskirts of the city proper, General Havelock came out from the Residency to meet him, and the second relief was successfully accomplished.

"Even now, however, it remained impossible to hold Lucknow, and Sir Colin Campbell determined before undertaking any further offensive operations, to return to Cawnpur with his army, escorting the civilians, ladies and children rescued from their long imprisonment in the Residency, with the view of forwarding them to Calcutta. On the morning of the 20th of November, the troops received orders to march for the Alambagh ; and the Residency, the scene of so long and stirring a defence, was abandoned for a while to the rebel army. Before the final departure, Sir Henry Havelock died from an attack of dysentery. He was buried in the Alambagh, without any monument, a cross on a neighbouring tree alone marking for the time his last resting-place. Sir James Outram, with 3,500 men, held the Alambagh until the commander-in-chief could return to recapture the capital. The rebels used the interval well for the fortification of their stronghold to the utmost extent of their knowledge and power. They surrounded the greater part of the city, for a circuit of twenty miles, with an external line of defences, extending from the Gumti to the canal. An earthen parapet lay behind the canal; a second line of earthworks connected the Moti Mahal, the mess-house, and the Imambara; while the Kaisar Bagh constituted the rebel citadel. Stockade works and parapets closed every street, and loopholes in all the houses afforded an opportunity for defending the passage inch by inch. The computed strength of the insurgents amounted to 30,000 Sepoys, together with 50,000 volunteers, and they possessed 100 pieces of ordnance guns and mortars.

"On the 2nd of March, 1858, Sir Colin Campbell found himself free enough in the rear to march once more upon Lucknow. He first occupied the Dilkusha, and posted guns to command the Martinière. On the 5th, Brigadier Franks arrived with 6,000 men, half of them Gurkhas sent by the Raja of Nepal. Outram's force then crossed the Gumti, and advanced from the direction of Faizabad, while the main body attacked from the south-east. After a week's hard fighting, from the 9th to the 15th March, the rebels were completely defeated, and their posts captured one by one. Most of the insurgents, however, escaped. As soon as it became clear that Lucknow had been permanently recovered, and that the enemy, as a combined body, had ceased to exist, Sir Colin Campbell broke up the British Oudh army, and the work of reorganisation began. On the 18th of October, 1858, the Governor-General and Lady Canning visited Lucknow in state, and found the city already recovering from the devastation to which it had been subjected."

An interesting excursion may be made to the elephant stables of the Commissariat Department, about three miles from the hotel. There are over thirty elephants, and the whole stud is valued at about £10,000. These useful animals drag enormous loads, draw water, and perform a hundred other useful functions. They and their keepers are great friends, and they may be seen nursing the babies in a coil of their trunks, while the father prepares their food. They are fed on coarse loaves, or chowpatties, and are allowed a given number each. The elephant counts them carefully over, and if the keeper gives him short allowance, he protests with loud trumpetings till his tale is made up. They will search for and find with their trunks two-anna silver bits, handing them to their keepers when found, with much gravity of demeanour.

The native city of Lucknow affords ample opportunity for studying all the handicrafts of India. The bazars of any Indian native town are full of unwearying interest, especially in cities where, as in Lucknow, artistic manufactures have been stimulated by the presence of a wealthy Indian Court. Although the royal family of Oudh is fast vanishing into obscurity, Lucknow is still the favourite residence of its princes, as well as of the numerous wealthy nobles and Talukdars of Oudh. These, with the many rich merchants and the growing stream of English visitors, foster and encourage the shops and art-workmen of the bazars.

Different trades occupy various quarters of the Great Bazar, which is a narrow winding street running from one end of the native city to the other. The leading men of each craft occupy the front shops, the smaller fry crowding into the narrow lanes and alleys behind. The roadway is filled with a busy clamorous throng of Indians in gay dresses and bright turbans; so dense, indeed, is the crowd, that for many hours in the afternoon all vehicular traffic is forbidden by the authorities, as well as elephants, camels or horses.

To see any Indian bazar to advantage, a good intelligent guide is necessary. In Lucknow, the professional *valets-de-place* have got such a low ideal of what an Englishman is likely to want to see, that they are not much use. If possible, the traveller should get an introduction to some Indian gentleman, merchant, pleader, schoolmaster or doctor, who can speak English fluently, and persuade him to spend an afternoon as guide through the Lucknow bazar. It will be one of the most interesting experiences he is likely to have during his whole journey, and will give a thorough insight into the native life of India.

The entrance of the Great Bazar is occupied by the silversmiths, pale-faced Kashmiris who have formed colonies of their own in almost every city of Oudh, the Punjab and the North-West. They sit gravely on the floor of their open shops, chasing exquisite patterns of floral or animal subjects on silver teapots, cream-jugs, basins, cups, vases, bowls, rose-water bottles, boxes and other pretty trinkets. These are sold for a certain weight of rupees. The finest designs fetch double their weight, and simple patterns can be had for a fourth more than their weight. The ancient craft of gold and silver smiths has existed in India for thousands of years. The oldest piece now in existence is a beautiful and delicate Buddhist relic casket belonging to the India Office Library, found about forty years ago in a tope near Jalalabad in Afghanistan, dating from about 50 B.C. The gold and silver workers of Lucknow maintain a well-deserved reputation for the excellence of their work. The best known is the pencil-gilt silver-work, which is mainly used in the production of *Sarais*, or water-bottles. Their elegant shapes and delicate tracery, graven through the gilding to the dead white silver below, which softens the lustre of the gold to a pearly radiance, gives a most charming effort to this refined and graceful work. It is said to be a Mongolian art, but influenced and refined by the superiority which the Kashmiris possess over all other Orientals in elaborating decorative details of good design, whether in metal hammered or cut, enamelling or weaving. Cups

GOLD AND SILVER SMITH, LUCKNOW.

are also made in this work, and trays of a very pretty four-cornered pattern, the corners being shaped like the Muhammadan arch. The Kashmir origin of the art is manifest by the constant introduction of the well-known cone pattern so familiar in embroidered Kashmir shawls. No prettier present can be taken home from India than one of these lovely pencil-gilt cups or sarais, or the cheaper but not less beautiful engraved silver-work. Any traveller interested in the history of the silversmith's art in India, should consult the chapter on "Gold and silver plate," in Birdwood's "Industrial Arts of India."

Lucknow is famous for its *Hukas*, or tobacco-pipes, the smoking of which is so essential a part of every Indian bargain. The clay bowls are manufactured in the same quarter as the deftly-modelled and brightly-coloured clay figures which are sold in the same shops. This is the potters' quarter, where every kind of earthen vessel, from the common unglazed lota and water-jug, to turquoise imitations of the finest Persian glazed wares, are manufactured in the sight of every passer-by. Figures in clay representing faithfully and with much spirit the domestic servants and handicraftsmen of the city, and the different races, tribes and castes of Oudh and the North-west, dressed up in muslins, silks and spangles, are sold in the potters' bazar for two, three or four rupees a dozen, according to size and quality. It is possible also to procure from some of the finest modellers in clay, turbaned heads representing with great fidelity the facial type and head-dress of literally hundreds of differing races, castes and trades all over India. The coloured clay models of fruit are often used by the natives as a practical joke, and I have more than once been taken in by their striking fidelity to nature. The more costly potter's work of Lucknow is garish, flaunting and debased, not worth the notice of any European customer. It bears about the same relation to the beautiful glazed pottery of the Panjab, as the Chatter Manzil does to the Taj Mahal.

The jewellery bazar of Lucknow was, during the time of the Nawabs, one of the most famous in India, but now, though still important, it ranks far behind Jaipur or Delhi. The jewellers lost all their capital during the Mutiny, and are only now beginning to recover something of their old position. The table and rose diamond is cut here to a considerable extent. The finest and most elaborate jeweller's work can be had in Lucknow for about six or seven per cent. on the cost of the gold and precious stones. The very best artists will work for a rupee a day. The gold-enamelling of Lucknow ranks only next to that of Jaipur, to which it is very similar. With the exception of the well-known diamond-cut pattern of silver bangles, there is no specially distinctive jewellery of Lucknow; it is mainly gemmed and enamelled gold, similar to that of Delhi. It is a pretty sight to watch a gem-setter arranging his stones on a white cloth, picking them out, one by one, into patterns for which the gold and silver smiths make the setting. A clever guide may perhaps unearth some of the engraved gems, or gem-encrusted jade, for which Lucknow was famous in the days of the Nawabs.

The craft for which Lucknow has the greatest reputation throughout India is that of gold and silver wire-drawing, with its complementary trades of gold and silver lace, brocades, and embroidery. There are about 1000 artisans employed in this industry. The basis of these fabrics is gold, silver, or silver-gilt wire drawn out by hand, or rather by that extra hand possessed by every Indian, the foot, to an extreme thinness; sometimes used round, at other times flattened out into fine metal ribbons, or cut into spangles

GOLD LACE MAKERS, LUCKNOW.

of various patterns: a rupee can be drawn out to 800 yards of wire. These products are far superior to anything of the kind produced in Europe by machinery; the wire is used largely in Ahmadabad, Benares, and indeed all over India in the manufacture of kincob brocades. The principal kinds of lace made at Lucknow from gold and silver wire are called *lachka*, *kalabatu*, and *lais*. In *lachka* the warp is of silver-gilt strips, woven with a woof of silk; it is often stamped with patterns in high relief, and is mostly used for edging turbans and petticoats. *Kalabatu* consists of strips of gilded silver twisted spirally round threads of yellow silk, and then woven into a ribbon similar to *lachka*. In *lais* the woof is of wire, and the warp of silk. This industry reappears in the shoe and slipper bazar,

TAILOR, LUCKNOW.

where beautiful embroidered velvet and leather slippers may be purchased. The native kings of Oudh prohibited the embroidery of slippers with anything but pure gold wire, but the bazars of Lucknow are now mainly filled with pinchbeck frauds from Delhi. It is, however, possible to pick up very beautiful specimens of these old gold-embroidered shoes of Lucknow, from some of the dealers in curiosities who frequent the verandah of Hill's Hotel, who must not be judged by the cheap rubbish they offer at first, for they can produce things worth seeing and buying to anyone whom they think a likely customer. The tailors' quarter is hard by the lace bazar, and a tailor clad in striped muslin, with a jaunty green cap on his head, and a gay *huka* by his side, stitching silver lace on a blue velvet coat, made a quaint and pretty picture which a friend secured for me with a "detective" camera, and which Mr. Pedder has reproduced on the previous page. Gold embroidery is used to adorn gorgeous velvets called *makhmal*, which is made into costly State canopies, umbrellas of dignity, elephants' cloths, horse trappings, and other State caparisons. The sumptuous gold scroll-ornamentation is in design distinctly of Italian 16th century origin, brought over, no doubt, by the skilled Italian workmen who flocked to the court of Akbar and his immediate successors. The embroidered native coats of Lucknow have a great reputation all over India.

The Lucknow cotton-cloth bazar is a famous one. There is of course a large importation from Manchester, but there is still a solid survival of the ancient weaving industry of Oudh. There are about 1500 looms still at work in the city; cotton printing by small hand-blocks is a very successful trade, and the native chintzes, owing to the great superiority of their colour and their freedom from sizing, command nearly double the price of Manchester goods. Some of the most beautiful cotton fabrics and stuffs of India are produced at Lucknow, owing more to the strength and brilliance of their natural dyes, than to the fineness or softness with which they are woven. It is estimated that in spite of the enormous and increasing imports of Manchester cotton-prints into India, that the domestic manufacture not only far exceeds it, but is almost equal to the entire export trade of Manchester itself. Anyone who will take the trouble to turn over the stock of some large dealer in native-dyed cotton fabrics, will be well rewarded in the beautiful and harmonious masterpieces of textile art he will be able to purchase, for a few annas each.

The whole of the mile-and-a-half to which the central bazar

stretches, is one picturesque jumble of trades, following each other in quick succession. In the fruit bazar are stalls piled with oranges, pomeloes, tamarinds, limes, guavas, grapes, pears and apples, many of which are brought by Afghan merchants from Kabul, who lounge about in their dirty loose clothes and sheepskin caps.

A savoury smell filling the whole air heralds the food bazar. Here are stalls of hot frizzling kabobs, piles of sweetmeats made of honey, flour and ghee; bakers busy with chapatties, the flat cakes which are the universal bread of India, and which are baked brown in two

DYER'S SHOP, LUCKNOW.

minutes on flat sheets of iron over little charcoal fires; piles of yellow turmeric and scarlet chillies for curry; women grinding corn, dhal and other cereals.

Now the loud clattering of pots and pans announces the coppersmiths' quarter, where brassworkers and tinsmiths congregate. The work of the former, being an ancient craft, is as good as the latter, a 19th century importation, is bad. Everybody is familiar with the beautiful brass work of India, so much used in England for household decoration; its makers will use nothing but the finest material for their artistic labours. The tinsmiths, however, are content to work up disused petroleum and castor-oil canisters, and their work is on a par with their material. Nothing is more curious in an Indian bazar than the rapid transition from a workshop turning out the most

U 2

perfect and artistic results, to another whose jerryness and inefficiency have no rival anywhere in the world.

A group of shops piled with rough pink lumps of mineral, like inferior gypsum, form the salt bazar, a Government monopoly which brings in a revenue all over India of some £7,000,000 every year. Here and there throughout the bazar are little shops whose entire stock consists of a small lump of greenish pudding, which is being retailed out in tiny cubes. This is another "Government monopoly" and is *Majoon*, a preparation of the deadly *Bhang* or Indian hemp known in Turkey and Egypt as *Hasheesh*, the most horrible intoxicant the world has yet produced. In Egypt, its importation and sale is absolutely forbidden, and a costly preventive service is maintained to suppress the smuggling of it by Greek adventurers; but a Christian Government is wiser in its generation and gets a comfortable income out of its sale. When an Indian wants to commit some horrible crime, such as murder or wife mutilation, he prepares himself for it with two annas' worth of *Bhang* from a government majoon shop. The little rooms, open to the street, of which the sole furniture is some matting and a few *Hukas*, are *Churras* or *Chandu* shops, farmed out by the government of India to provide another form of Indian hemp intoxication which is smoked instead of eaten. The wide and spacious shops in front of which are strewn broken potsherds, and whose contents are two or three kegs and a pile of little pots, are the Government liquor-farmers' establishments. The groups of noisy men seated on the floor are drinking ardent spirits of the worst description, absolutely forbidden to the British soldier, but sold retail to natives at three farthings a gill, of which two farthings go to the Exchequer. No Hindu will drink from the same vessel as any one else, which explains the pile of little pots, and the broken sherds in the street outside.

Here and there a large native house is passed through the door of which streams in and out a swarm of customers. It is perhaps three o'clock in the afternoon. Entering with them, you will find yourself in a spacious but very dirty courtyard, round which are ranged fifteen or twenty small rooms. The stench is sickening, the swarm of flies intolerable, and there is something strange and weird in the faces of those coming in from the street. This is the establishment of another Government contractor, the opium farmer. At the entrance sits a comely well-dressed native woman, whose husband is busy sorting

OPIUM DEN, LUCKNOW.

(From a Photograph taken specially for this purpose

the arriving customers into the least crowded of the side rooms. Before her is a table on which are large bowls rapidly filling up with copper coins; like Matthew of old, she sits at the receipt of custom, for half these coins go to the Government treasury at Calcutta, the other half going into the pocket of the Government tax-collector, the opium farmer. Enter one of the small rooms. It has no window, and is very dark, but in the centre is a small charcoal fire, whose lurid glow lights up the faces of nine or ten human beings, men and women, lying on the floor like pigs in a sty. A young girl some fifteen years of age has charge of each room, fans the fire, lights the opium pipe, and holds it in the mouth of the last comer, till his head falls heavily on the body of his or her predecessor. In no East-end gin palace, in no lunatic or idiot asylum, will you see such horrible destruction of God's image in the face of man, as appears in the countenances of those in the preliminary stages of opium drunkenness. Here you may see some handsome young married woman nineteen or twenty years of age, sprawling on the senseless bodies of men, her fine brown eyes flattened and dull with coming stupor, and her lips drawn convulsively back from her glittering white teeth. Here is a younger girl, sitting among a group of newly-arrived customers, singing some lewd romance, as they hand round the pipes. There is a bonny little lad of six or seven, watching his father's changing face with a dreadful indifference. At night these dens are crowded to excess, and it is estimated that there are upwards of 12,000 persons in Lucknow enslaved by this hideous vice. Green hands can get drunk for an anna, or even less, but by degrees more and more opium is needed, till hardened sots require 200 or 300 drops of thick opium mixed with tobacco, to secure complete intoxication. An opium sot is the most hopeless of all drunkards. Once in the clutches of this fiend, everything gives way to his fierce promptings. His victim only works to get more money for opium. Wife, children, home, health and life itself at last, are all sacrificed to his degrading passion.

In the city of Lucknow in 1889, there were thirty distilleries of native spirits, 201 liquor shops, twenty-four opium dens, and ninety-two shops for Bhang, Churras, and other maddening and intoxicating drugs. These bring in a substantial and steadily-increasing profit to the Indian exchequer. The receipts of the North-West Provinces and Oudh from the retail sale of opium, Bhang and such poisonous drugs is about £70,000 and steadily increasing, while the revenue from spirits is nearly £600,000, having doubled itself during the last seven years.

But this is not "picturesque India." Let us get away from the reeking atmosphere of liquor shops and opium dens to the cheerful brightness of the Nakhas, or bird bazar, where live birds of all sorts are sold, not for the table, but for sport or pets. Here are cages of rare gamecocks, and pigeons trained to tumble in the air for wagers; little open boxes of fighting quails, kept severely apart till their duels are fought, for quail-fighting is the popular sport of Musalman Lucknow; parrots and minas trained to talk; larks and doves, weaver-birds, bulbuls, avadavats, and other singing-birds; tiny young partridges, mere balls of down, to be trained as they grow into household pets; hawks and falcons for the chase; peafowl, herons, storks, and waterfowl for the ponds of native gentlemen's gardens. Hundreds of small birds, of no value either as pets, songsters, or fighters, are bought by pious people every morning, to be set at liberty again as a work of merit, pleasing to the gods, or to serve the purpose of some other superstition. There is no prettier sight anywhere than the Nakhas Bird Market of Lucknow, if the eyes are discreetly closed to much ill-treatment and cruelty to these unfortunate feathered captives.

Nothing is more surprising to an Englishman, in visiting an Indian bazar, than the microscopic bargains which are made by the poorer buyers, as, for instance, the various condiments that are needed to make up a curry. The anna, in the Lucknow Bazar, can be divided up into 912 fractions, perhaps the smallest currency in the world, unless it be in the remoter parts of inland China. The money table is as follows:—

4 Cowries	=	1 gunda.
19 gundas	=	1 pie.
3 pies	=	1 pice.
4 pice	=	1 anna.

The money-changers will, for a tiny commission, change an anna into any or all of these sub-divisions.

The Christian missions at Lucknow are in the hands of the Church Missionary Society, the American Episcopal Methodists, and the English Wesleyan Methodists.

The Church Missionary Society is under the charge of the Rev. A. J. Birkett and a native colleague; there are about 100 communicants, and 400 children in the schools.

The Wesleyan Methodists have a chapel for English people, with thirty-seven church members, largely attended by soldiers, and a vernacular chapel with thirty-three members. The schools have an attendance of about 600 children. The Rev. W. D. Frater and the Rev. J. Parsons are in charge respectively. There is a small theological training school, with seven or eight students.

The American Mission is the most important of the three, having four or five American and as many more native ministers. They have nearly 200 communicants, and over 1,000 pupils in their various schools, most of which are Anglo-Vernacular.

The Oudh and Rohilkhand Railway runs north-west from Lucknow to Saharaupur junction, on the North Western, through Shahjahanpur, Bareilly, and Moradabad, none of which towns present any features of interest that need attract the tourist, or which call for any description in this book. The pretty hill station of Naini Tal, greatly resorted to by Europeans from Oudh and the North-West Provinces, is a long day's journey of seventy-four miles from Bareilly. It lies on the banks of a very beautiful lake, about a mile long, 6,500 feet above the sea. It is not, however, worth the time needful for a visit, being inferior in grandeur and beauty of surroundings to either Darjiling, Mussoorie, or Simla.

Southward, the Oudh and Rohilkhand Railway passes through a rich and fertile country, through Faizabad, Jaunpur, and Benares to its terminus, Moghal Serai, on the East India Railway.

JAUNPUR is an important town and administrative headquarters of about 50,000 inhabitants. It has borne an important part in Indian history. Fragments of ancient Buddhist and Hindu buildings are found in the walls of the Fort of Firoz, and there is no doubt that Jaunpur held an important place in the kingdom of Ajodhya. The splendid architectural monuments with which the city abounds, belong to the Pathan period, 1360—1560. The Sharki dynasty founded their capital at Jaunpur in 1394, and it remained in the hands of successive Musalman dynasties until 1775, when it passed into the hands of the East India Company.

The Fort of Firoz was built by the Emperor Tuglak in 1360. The fine gateway was once decorated with glazed yellow and blue bricks, of which some portions may still be seen. Within are several ruined buildings of some interest: a small mosque, a curious Jain pillar in three stories, with an ornamental spire, a round tower, and a bath.

The river face of the fort is very fine, the battlements being 150 feet above the surface of the water. A splendid view of the city and surrounding country may be obtained from the top. The greater portion of the interior structure of the fort was blown up and destroyed after the Mutiny. The mosque in the fort is the oldest in the town; the front rows of pillars have evidently been plundered from an older Hindu temple; they are very richly sculptured.

One of the finest old stone bridges in India spans the Gumti at Jaunpur. It was erected, 1569—73, by Munim Khan, measures 712 feet in length, with four central arches, and six of smaller span on each side. There used to be shops on each side of the roadway, but they were all swept away by a great flood 100 years ago.

The Jama Masjid is a very noble mosque, begun by Shah Ibrahim A.D. 1419, and finished in the reign of Husain, 1451—78. The courtyard measures 220 by 214 feet; on the western side is a range of buildings, the centre one being covered by a finely-proportioned dome. The front is a very remarkable pyramidal gate, like an Egyptian *propylon* in mass and outline, rising to a height of eighty-six feet. The three sides of the court were originally surrounded by double colonnades, two stories high inside, and three outside, the floor of the yard being raised to the height of the first storey. On each face was a handsome gateway, but the greater part of this lovely quadrangle has been taken down by the British authorities, being used by them as a stone-quarry for general purposes.

The Atala Mosque is a highly-ornamented and very beautiful building; the colonnades are four storeys deep, the outer columns on both sides being double square pillars. The lovely gateways are pure Saracenic, and the western face is broken by three pyramidal gateways, not so lofty as, but much finer in decoration than, the one at the Jama Masjid. Fergusson considers the interior domes and roofs superior to any other specimen of Muhammadan art of so early an age. They exhibit the arched style of the Saracenic architects in as great a degree of completeness as it is exhibited at any subsequent period.

The Lall Darwaza Mosque has a richly-decorated gateway, handsomely carved, with panels containing bells and lotus flowers. This gateway is boldly massive, and is a curious mixture of Hindu and Musalman styles. There are many other beautiful mosques and buildings at Jaunpur, the principal of which are the Jinjiri Masjid, with large piers upholding a screen of much beauty, built by Ibrahim; the Dariba Mosque, and the Idgah.

FAIZABAD is a city of about 40,000 population, half way between Lucknow and Benares. No special interest attaches to this city, and the only inducement for the traveller to halt there is to see Ajodhya, an ancient Hindu city of great holiness, five miles distant. There is a good Dak bungalow at Faizabad, which is a modern town. The only building possessing any architectural interest is the tomb of Bahu Begam, who lived and died here. It is said to be the finest mausoleum in Oudh.

AJODHYA is one of the seven sacred cities of Hindustan, a pilgrimage to which secures eternal happiness. These seven cities are Ajodhya, the city of Rama; Muttra, the city of Krishna; Buddh Gaya, the city of illusion; Benares, the city of Siva; Conjeveram, Avani, and Dwarka in Kathiawar. The interest of Ajodhya centres in its ancient history: the scenes described in the great Hindu epic poem of the later Vedic age, B.C. 500–300, the "Ramayana," or the adventures of Rama, are laid in and round Ajodhya. Rama Chandra ruled in great pomp at Ajodhya, and his epic covers the whole period of the rise and establishment of Buddhism, and of the earlier history of the Brahminical revolt against its influence. The beautiful description of Ajodhya in its prime, given in that unique and fascinating poem, "The Light of Asia," by Sir Edwin Arnold, are faithful transcripts from the pages of the Ramayana. They furnish striking pictures of the city, court and country life of the Buddhistic state of Kapilavastir long before the birth of Christ. When the Raja of Jaipur prepared his magnificent reception of the Prince of Wales in 1876, he planned his decorations of the city and the whole ceremonial from these wonderful descriptions of Ajodhya in the Ramayana. At this time Ajodhya was the capital of the Aryan Empire, the most magnificent city in India, and was probably unrivalled in all Asia. It is said to have covered an area of ninety-six square miles. Nothing is left now but heaps of ruins.

Ajodhya was restored on the revival of Brahmanism by King Vikramaditya, A.D. 57. The antiquities of the place are all identified with this period. *Ramkot* is the ancient fortified palace of this king, an oblong building about 200 feet long, with thick solid walls, now used as a temple sacred to Ram. It is, however, very doubtful if any portion of the original building exists. It marks the spot where

Rama Chandra was born. The Mani Parbat is a sacred mound or stupa attributed to Asoka, built on a spot where Buddha preached. There are two other mounds of the same kind called the Kuver and Sugriv Parbat. There are a great number of temples and shrines, to which some 400,000 pilgrims repair at the time of the great Ramnaumi Mela. There is also a singularly fine old mosque, built by Baber, somewhat neglected, but one of the most picturesque ruins in all Oudh.

AN AJODHYA FAKIR.

CHAPTER XX.

BENARES.

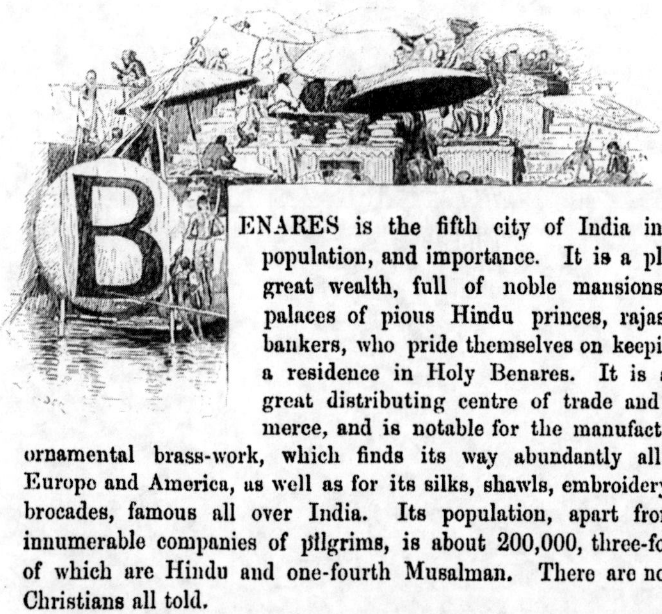

BENARES is the fifth city of India in size, population, and importance. It is a place of great wealth, full of noble mansions and palaces of pious Hindu princes, rajas, and bankers, who pride themselves on keeping up a residence in Holy Benares. It is also a great distributing centre of trade and commerce, and is notable for the manufacture of ornamental brass-work, which finds its way abundantly all over Europe and America, as well as for its silks, shawls, embroidery, and brocades, famous all over India. Its population, apart from its innumerable companies of pilgrims, is about 200,000, three-fourths of which are Hindu and one-fourth Musalman. There are not 300 Christians all told.

Benares is the metropolis of the Hindu faith. It is probably the most ancient city in India, and is supposed to date back to the first Aryan colonization. It is certainly coeval with the earliest days of Hinduism, and has held the first place of all in the hearts and affections of Hindus through every century of their history. To the pious Brahman Benares is what Mekka is to the Musalman, Jerusalem to the Christian. The longing of his whole life is to visit this place of spotless holiness and wash away his blackest sins in the sacred Ganges before he dies. The palaces which fringe the river are full of the aged relatives of their owners, come together from all parts of India, waiting with calm, patient, ecstatic happiness the summons to *Swarga* of the angel of death, for Benares is, indeed, the very gate of heaven.

Benares is equally revered by that other great religion of the East, the Buddhist. Twenty-five centuries ago Buddha preached his first sermon here, and made it the centre from which he sent forth his missionaries to Ceylon, China, Japan, Burma, Nepal, and Thibet, until half the human race came under the sway of his doctrine. Benares was even then so great a centre of religious thought and influence, that Buddha naturally selected it as his centre of operations, and endeavoured first of all to secure the countenance and support of its learned pundits and teachers. Tradition avers that it was from Benares Solomon procured his "apes and peacocks," both of which are still held sacred, in the Hindu temples of the city. It is also said that one of the wise men of the East, who brought presents to the infant Jesus at Jerusalem, was a Raja from Benares. However that may be, there is probably no sacred city in the world with so ancient and unbroken a record, or which even to-day exercises its sway over so many millions of devotees; dear alike to that religion which, above all others, is saturated with idolatry, and to its great rival which, scorning idolatry and polytheism, teaches that every individual man, by a holy life, can lift himself into and become part of the Divine.

Modern Benares is wholly given to idolatry. Buddhism has long since succumbed to Brahmanism, and been swept out of India altogether. Nothing remains but the ruins of its topes, temples, chaitya halls and Viharas, the most important group being at Sarnath, five miles from Benares.

Benares is without question the most picturesque city in India. It lies on a bend of the Ganges, along the crest of a hill about 100 feet above the water. Viewed from the river, it presents a panorama of palaces, temples and mosques, surmounted by domes, pinnacles and minarets, stretching three miles along the top of the bank. From these descend great flights of stone stairs, broken into wide platforms, on which are built exquisite Hindu shrines, bathing-houses, and preaching canopies. Long piers project into the river, on which sick people lie, carefully tended by their relatives, to get the beneficent healing of the great mother Ganges. Ghats, platforms and piers are alive with pilgrims from every part of India, in every variety of costume, and every stage of dress and undress, grouped under huge straw umbrellas, sitting at the feet of some learned mahant or preacher, gazing at holy ascetics, jostled by sacred bulls, crowding in and out of the water, drying themselves with towels, prostrate at the margin telling beads. Crows, kites, pigeons and parrots circle round the heads of this kaleidoscopic crowd. Up and down the ghats, all day long, but especially in the early morning, stream the endless course of pilgrims, ragged tramps, aged crones, horrible beggars, hawkers, Brahman priests, sacred bulls and cows, Hindu preachers, wealthy rajas or bankers in gay palankins, Fakirs, pariah dogs, and scoffing globe-trotters from Europe and America.

A pathetic feature of this jostling, bellowing crowd is the large number of tottering aged women, with scanty white locks, coming out of the cold river, crawling feebly up the steep steps with their wet clothes clinging to their poor shivering lean legs, shrinking into some recess lest the shadow of a passing Englishman or Musalman should fall upon them, a calamity that spoils the effect of the sacred cleansing and renders it needful to creep back once more to the chill water. Hundreds of aged creatures of both sexes are always in Benares, having left home and family, perhaps a thousand miles away, never to return, happy and glad to chill themselves slowly into heaven in the sacred waves of the Ganges.

Nothing in all their religion is so dear to the devout Hindu as their beloved mother Ganges. The ice-cavern in the mysterious Himalya which is her birth-place, is the fifth head of Siva. For 1600 miles her gracious course is hallowed by the haunts of gods and heroes. The most pious act a Hindu can perform is the six years' pilgrimage from source to mouth and back again. Pilgrims to her banks carry back bottles of the precious water to their kindred in far-off provinces; to die and be burnt on her sacred margin, and have their ashes borne away to the ocean on her loving bosom, is the last wish of millions of Hindus. No river in the world does more to justify the reverence of the people, blessed, fed and sustained by the water she brings down to the fertile plains from the "roof of the world."

Every morning, during his stay at Benares, the European traveller should take boat and row slowly down in front of the ghats. The

BATHING GHATS, BENARES.

guides belonging to Clark's Hotel, which is the best in the city, will make all necessary arrangements.

It is a great advantage to secure introductions in Benares to some educated Hindu gentleman, or missionary who has been for some time resident in the town. The professional guides all over India are very inferior, and cannot do more than show the way through the bazars, point out notable buildings, and keep a sharp eye on tips and commissions. Every turn of the street, every step of the ghat, every group on the platforms present some incident exciting the greatest curiosity, which can only be satisfied by someone versed in the customs of the Hindu religion.

Along the whole length of the city, there are altogether about fifty principal ghats. Boats generally embark at tho Dasasamedh ghat, or the Raj ghat, near the railway bridge. The boatmen prefer the former, as it gives them a row down stream, but it is better to start from the Raj ghat and row up, the slower pace of the boat giving more time for observation.

The magnificent steel bridge of the Oudh and Rohilkhand Railway is one of the finest in India, and has a total length of about 1200 yards. Passing under this fine work, the first ghat of interest is the Trilochana. The water between the two turrets on this ghat has a special sanctity, and every pilgrim bathes there. The houses above belong to some Delhi merchants.

Next to it is the Gau, or Cow ghat, so called from a stone figure of a cow, and that it is the drinking-place of the many sacred zebus which frequent the city.

The next two ghats are dedicated to Mahadeva and Durga; passing these the Panchganga, where five rivers are supposed to meet underground, leads up a magnificent flight of steps to the noble mosque which the iconoclast Aurangzeb reared on the site of the magnificent Krishna temple which he utterly destroyed.

It will be well to land here, and ascend the soaring minaret for the marvellous bird's-eye view it affords of the ghats, the whole city, and the sweeping mother Ganges bearing away the sins of her faithful and devoted children to be merged in the mighty ocean. This mosque is the finest building in Benares, and, in many respects, is unique. Its solid foundations, laid deep below the river's bed, rise from its level in huge stone breast-works, on the top of which rest the four walls and domes of the mosque. Springing lightly into the air, like the tall stems of

MOSQUE OF AURANGZEB, BENARES.

X

some beautiful flower, are two exquisite and graceful minarets, 150 feet from the floor of the mosque. These slender pinnacles are only eight and a quarter feet in diameter at the base, tapering to seven and a half feet at the summit. The river is 150 feet below the mosque, so that the whole building rises 300 feet, almost sheer from the water's edge, forming the very crown of the city. Muhammad, the theist and the idol breaker, thus appears to dominate with lofty and desolate scorn the 1400 temples of that ancient Brahman faith, which survives alike the precepts of Buddha, the fierce persecutions of Aurangzeb, and the mild and gentle teaching of Jesus. To sit in the air, on the topmost balcony of one of these slender minarets, with the city and river at one's feet, the pigeons and parrots whirling between, is an experience never to be forgotten.

Returning to the boat, the next ghat reached is the Ram, sacred to that deity, whose temple stands above it. Three or four others of no special interest are passed by, above one of them rising the great turreted palace of the Raja of Nagpur. The massive ghat which appears to be crumbling into the river is Sindhia's (the Maharaja of Gwalior).

We now reach the Manikaranika, the most sacred of all the ghats, leading down from the famous well dug by Vishnu. Here also is the Tarakeswar Temple and the Charana-paduka.

The next ghat of any importance is the Nepal; this handsome stairway is surmounted by the strikingly beautiful Nepalese Temple, the most picturesque in all Benares, differing altogether from the Hindu shrines. Above this is the famous Golden Temple; immediately beyond is the Burning Ghat, and here may be observed corpses undergoing cremation. The pairs of stones set up on end are monuments to widows who in time past were burnt alive with their husbands. These suttee stones are to be found all along the whole range of the ghats, but they are more plentiful just here. At Bhairava Ghat, hawkers sell peacock fans, warranted to blow away fiends and evil spirits; at the top of the steps is a goddess with a silver face, who protects her devotees from smallpox. The Man Mandir Ghat leads up to Jai Singh's observatory, the lofty building which towers above it.

Dasasamedh is one of the five specially sacred bathing-ghats. Here Brahma made his celebrated sacrifice of ten horses, which gives the ghat its name. There are some twenty or more ghats above

BURNING GHAT, BENARES.

Dasasamedh, most of them leading up to noble mansions. The finest of these is the Munshi Palace, built by a Diwan of the Raja of Nagpur, that of the Rana of Udaipur, and the Raja Ghat, leading to a large *serai* built by Raja Amrit Rao. Here is a huge stone effigy, which is said to be carried away in the rains by Mother Ganges, but reverently placed back in its ghat before the dry season sets in. At the Kedar Ghat is the holy *Well of Gauri*, which cures various diseases, dysentery in particular. In a tank close by is the wonderful stone called Mansovar, which grows the breadth of a millet seed every day. The last of all is the Ashi Ghat, one of the five sacred bathing-places, where the river Ashi adds its quota to the Ganges.

Having thus taken a general view of Benares, the traveller will wish to see all the various temples at which the pilgrims love to worship or idle, when not engaged at the bathing ghats. It is said there are nearly 1,500 Hindu temples and shrines altogether within the city and in the immediate suburbs, but, beyond a passing glance, very few of these are worth serious attention. The round of the principal temples, as taken by every pilgrim, is, however, after the ghats, the most curious and interesting sight in Benares. The interest is increased tenfold to him who is able to secure the guidance of an intelligent English-speaking Hindu resident or experienced missionary. Failing these, I will endeavour to give such help as may be possible in the pages of a descriptive book.

It is only when face to face with the eager crowds from every part of India, which throng the ghats and temples of Benares, that we realise to the full the latent power which still lives in the Hindu religion, and makes its votaries the most pious and devoted in the whole world. These pilgrimages to their holy places have a deep effect on the religious temper of India, and the worship which goes on here from day to day, year by year, is the very vital force itself of Hinduism. The Hindu at home is isolated within his own sect, and practises a very perfunctory religion; but on the great occasions of his life, when he visits one or other of the seven sacred cities, he realizes that he is after all a member of a vast religious community. He first visits the temples and shrines connected with his own particular faith, but that accomplished, he goes the round of all the sanctuaries in general. If he is a follower of Siva, he presently finds himself blended in sympathy with a disciple of Vishnu, and in turn finds his way to and worships at the shrines of Indra, Agni, Brahma, Saraswati, Lakshmi, Parvati, Ganesa, Krishna, and Hanuman.

The Holy of Holies at Benares is the famous sanctuary of the terrible Siva, the *Bisheshwar*, or Golden Temple. Siva is a lofty god; with his followers there is none like unto him. With every Hindu he is in the very front rank, none superior to him, except perhaps Vishnu. He sits enthroned on Kailasa, the fabulous mountain of the north, surrounded and waited on by innumerable spirits and minor gods, who get their orders through his trusty lieutenants, chief among whom are his adopted son, *Skanda*, the god of war, and the foster-child of the Pleiades; *Ganesha*, the chief of the troops, the god with the elephant's head, the inspirer of cunning devices and good counsel, the patron of learning, whose image appears on every school-house door; *Kuvera*, the god of treasures; *Virabhadra* (the venerable hero), the personification of fury in battle. Siva's birth is variously represented, but in reality he is eternal; he is *Mahakala* (endless time), which begets and devours all things. As creator, his symbols are the bull and the phallus, and his diadem is the moon. As destroyer, he is armed with a terrible trident, wears a gruesome necklace of skulls, and his attendants are skeletons. He is "Death;" the master of human cattle; the "master of victims." He is, more than any god, cruel, and exacts a bloody worship. He is the ruler of evil spirits, ghouls, and vampires, and at nightfall he prowls about in their company, in places of execution and where there are buried dead. He is *Bhairava*, the god of mad frantic folly, who, clothed in the bloody skin of an elephant, leads the wild dance of the Tandava. He is the god of the ascetics; this fearful sect go naked, smutty with ashes, their long, matted hair twisted round their heads; others follow hideous secret rites of blood, lust, gluttony, drunkenness, and incantations; others pose themselves in immoveable attitudes, till the sinews shrink, and the posture becomes rigid; others tear their bodies with knives, or devour carrion and excrements. These wretched beings lead wandering lives, and swarm at Benares, and all other holy places.

By the side of Siva sits enthroned *Uma*, his awful wife, the exact counterpart of her husband. Her most familiar designations are *Devi*, the goddess; *Parvati*, the daughter of the mountains; *Durga*, the inaccessible; *Sati*, the devoted wife; *Bhairavi*, the terror-inspiring; *Kali*, the black one; *Karali*, the horrible; all expressive of her twofold nature as goddess of life and death. Siva is the third person in the Hindu Triad (Brahma—Vishnu—Siva). Brahma is an abstract idea rather than a god, and for practical purposes the Hindu people may be divided into followers of Vishnu and Siva.*

Benares is the holy city of Sivaism, and the Golden Temple is its holy of holies. It is a small building, a quadrangle, covered with a roof, above which rises a very picturesque tower. At each corner is a dome, with a larger dome in the centre. These are all gilded with beaten gold, at the cost of Ranjit Singh. The guide will point out a shop near by, from the upper windows of which a fine prospect is obtained of this roof, and the spires and domes of neighbouring

* For further details, see Barth's "Religions of India," and Sir W. W. Hunter's "India," vol. vi. of the Imperial Gazetteer.

temples and mosques. It is not permitted to any but Hindus to enter the temple, but visitors may stand on some steps in the threshold, from which a sufficient view may be got of the interior of the temple. It is very crowded with pilgrims, priests, and sacred bulls and cows, the floor being filthy beyond description. Cheek by jowl with the temple of Siva is a temple to Mahadeva. The space between is a sort of belfry, in which is hung, with others, a beautiful

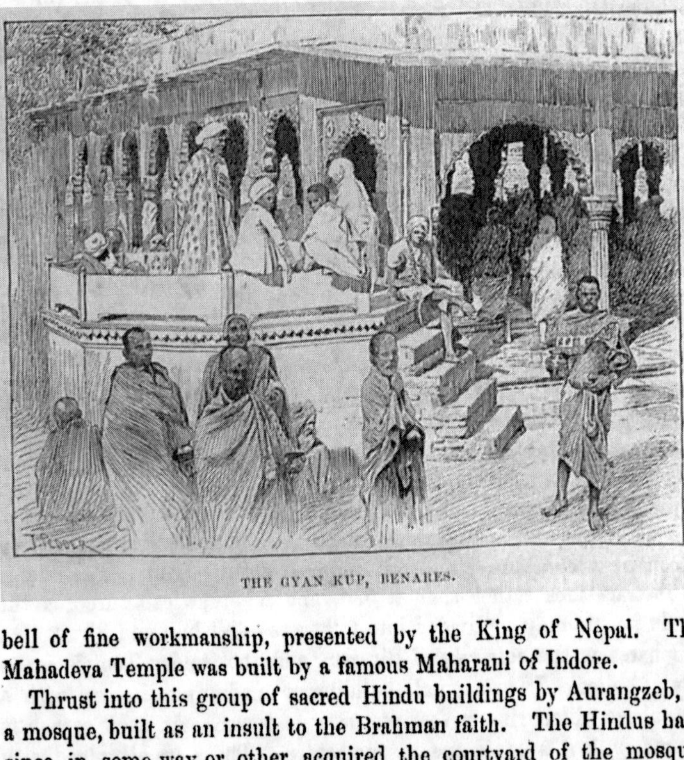

THE GYAN KUP, BENARES.

bell of fine workmanship, presented by the King of Nepal. The Mahadeva Temple was built by a famous Maharani of Indore.

Thrust into this group of sacred Hindu buildings by Aurangzeb, is a mosque, built as an insult to the Brahman faith. The Hindus have since, in some way or other, acquired the courtyard of the mosque, and Musalman worshippers have to find their way in through a side door. In the street outside is a curious shrine, called the Court of Mahadeva. Here have been collected images of Hindu gods in great numbers and variety, and others have been built into the surrounding wall. These are probably images collected together from the desecrated and broken temples which suffered from the fierce iconoclastic zeal of Aurangzeb.

Between the mosque and the Golden Temple is a courtyard, in the centre of which is the *Gyan Kup*, or "well of knowledge." Within this well is the choice residence of Siva himself. When the old temple of Bisheshwar was destroyed, the chief priest concealed the idol at the bottom of this well, which gives it unusual sanctity. The well is surrounded by a beautiful colonnade of forty pillars, presented in the year 1828 by a widow of the Maharaja Sindhia of Gwalior. The well is resorted to by every pilgrim, who drinks the precious water, handed to him in a sort of ladle by the attendant priests. This water is filthy and putrid from the rotted flowers thrown into the well by those who resort to the shrine. Neither the well nor the enclosure gives any suggestion of having been cleaned out during its existence.

Adjacent to the well is a fine bull, seven feet high, carved in stone, dedicated to Mahadeva by a king of Nepal.

All round the Golden Temple are a motley crowd of other temples and shrines, few of which, however, have any architectural interest, and are only worthy the attention of the student of the Hindu religion. The temple of *Anupurna*, the goddess of plenty, patroness of beggars and the poor, is worth visiting to see the groups of beggars sitting in front of the gate with their bowls, to catch the pinches of grain and rice thrown in by passing worshippers.

Within the temple are scores of sacred bulls and cows, many of them horribly diseased, fed by the pious devotees, who resort to Anupurna's shrine.

Close by is the temple of *Sakhi Bunjanka*, the witness bearer. Here pilgrims, on completion of their round of bathing and devotions, receive the crowning verification of it, and depart certain of entire cleansing and future bliss. At Shunkareshwar Shrine groups of expectant women may be seen praying for handsome and stalwart sons.

Near the old observatory, in the passage leading to its entrance, is a curious little temple sacred to the Rain God, who is drenched with water in dry weather to remind him of his duty, but who is neglected and encrusted with dirt in the rainy season. In times of great drought they put him overhead in a cistern, till he is aroused to a proper sense of responsibility.

The sacred spot of the followers of Vishnu is the *Manikarnika*, the famous "well of healing." Vishnu, the unconquerable preserver, is a great contrast to Siva the destroyer. He is a good fellow all round, and the familiar friend of man. In his incarnations of Rama and Krishna he lives in the hearts of his worshippers, in endless cherished legends, as a high-souled hero. The worship of Vishnu is, in one phase or other, the religion of the bulk of the middle and cultured classes in Hindustan. It is a graceful and pleasant religion, whose gods are heroes, bright friendly beings, who walk and converse with men.

"The God Vishnu dug this well with his discus, and, in lieu of water, filled it with perspiration from his own body, giving it the name of Chakra Push Karini. He then proceeded to its north side and

A CORNER ON THE GANGES, BENARES.

began to practise asceticism. In the meantime the god Mahadeva arrived, and, looking into the well, beheld in it the beauty of 100,000,000 suns, with which he was so enraptured that he at once broke out into loud praises of Vishnu, and in his joy declared that whatever gift he might ask of him he would grant. Gratified by the offer Vishnu requested that Mahadeva should always reside with him. Mahadeva, hearing this, was so flattered that he shook with delight, and one of his earrings fell into the well, giving it a double sanctity."

The well is four square, with steps going down for the use of bathers; the seven lowest steps are alleged to be without joining, thus furnishing evidence of the divine origin. The water is about three feet deep, horribly foul with the continual washings of the worshippers, and the stench fills the entire enclosure. After bathing, the devotees drink deep draughts of this filthy stuff, ladled out to them by priests in exchange for coppers. No matter how criminal or violent the life of the pilgrim has been, the stinking muddy water of Manikarnika cleans up the record of a lifetime, and sends him away absolutely pure and holy.

Below Manikarnika, on the edge of the river, is the graceful and beautiful temple of Tarakeshwar; the idol is kept immersed in a tank of water. Just above it is a large round slab let into the pavement, in the middle of which is a stone pedestal, the top of which is inlaid with marble. In the centre of this are two small flat spots, supposed to represent the two feet of Vishnu. It is held in great veneration, and at times great numbers flock to this *Charana paduka*, as it is called, to worship Vishnu's feet.

The temple of Bhaironath is that of the tutelary god of Benares, a sort of deified watchman, who drives evil spirits out of the city, and keeps a fatherly eye over all those who come to Benares to die in peace. The idol of this temple is a mighty stone cudgel, called Dandpan, with a small silver face on the thin end. The worshippers repair to this shrine on Tuesday and Sunday.

Close by Bhaironath is the richest temple in Benares for furniture and jewels, the *Gopal Mandir*, containing two gold images of Krishna. Near here also is the *Kal-Kup*, or Well of Fate. A square hole in the roof brings the rays of the sun upon the water exactly at noon, when the well is resorted to by those anxious about their futures.

One of the most curious and picturesque of all the Benares temples is that sacred to the goddess Durga, which is about two miles out of the city. The temple is a fine building, set off by a large tank in front, and surrounded by well-grown trees. Durga is the most terrific form of Siva's wife, and delights in all kind of bloodshed and destruction. When a Benares Hindu wants a meat dinner, he brings a goat or kid to the blood-bedabbled altar in front of the shrine, where its head is cut off by the officiating priest. This functionary levies toll on the carcase, and the votary then carries it off, and eats meat offered to idols to his heart's content. In the trees around this temple are hosts of monkeys, who peer round walls, and over pinnacles, or between the leaves waiting to be fed. These creatures are all gods and goddesses, and must not be molested. They are so mischievous that no one can live within half a mile of the temple, as all their household belongings would be destroyed by these monkeys, which number thousands. Some years ago they became such an intolerable plague that the authorities caught as many as they could, and deported them to a distant jungle. A few handsful of rice, scattered on the pavement surrounding the tank, will attract scores of them in a few seconds. These monkeys are sacred to Vishnu, and are kept up and revered as representations of Hanuman, the monkey god associated with Rama.

SACRILEGE!

What the monkeys are to Vishnu, the sacred Zebu is to Siva, and so the cow and bull are the objects of special worship to the Hindu; their slaughter is a horrible crime, and to eat their flesh is loss of caste in this world, and far worse in the world to come. It is a most meritorious act to dedicate bulls and cows to Siva, and to multiply around the god the living images of Nandi, his divine steed. These animals are always numerous in places sacred to the god, where they live in perfect freedom, pampered and fed by pious devotees, who tempt their appetites with dainties put out on the doorstep in a pot, and who let them wander unchecked into any shop they fancy, to help themselves to any grain or vegetables for which their souls may lust. The municipal authorities at one time used to kidnap them darkly at dead of night, and turn them loose on the opposite shore of the Ganges, but they generally swam back, and turned up holier that ever. In the Golden Temple fat old white bulls levy blackmail from every worshipper, who bring them cakes, rice flour, or a dainty bit of fruit.

Few travellers will care to thread the whole of this "labyrinth of Asiatic Theology" to its inmost recesses, and no possible guide-book can help him to do so. It would be the work of weeks, and could only be accomplished with the aid of some Brahman Guru.

The observatory of Jai Singh, entered near the Man Mandir Ghat, is the finest of all those erected by this scientific Raja of Jaipur. This curious building towers above the Dasasamedh Ghat, and, after Aurangzeb's Mosque, is the most conspicuous object in the general view of Benares from the river. It contains some structures for making astronomical calculations and observations, a single and double mural quadrant, an equinoctial circle of stone, and an enormous *Yantras amrat* (the prince of instruments), the wall of which is thirty-six feet long, and set in the plane of the meridian. One end is six feet four and a quarter inches high, and the other end twenty-two feet three and a half inches, sloping gradually upwards, pointing to the north pole. This is constructed to find out the distance from the meridian, the declination and ascension of any planet or star and the sun. The view from the top is magnificent, almost equal to that obtained from the minaret of Aurangzeb Mosque, and without the fatigue.

The *Arhai Kangura Mosque* is worth a visit, and will prove a pleasant change from the dirt and squalor of the Hindu pantheon. Its archæological interest lies in the fact that it was a Hindu temple of some magnificence long before the Musalman invasion of Oudh, and a portion of it is inscribed with a date corresponding to A.D. 1191. The mosque is crowned with a finely-proportioned and lofty dome.

The Raj Ghat fort, erected during the mutiny, but since abandoned, is on a small tongue of high land, dominating the junction of the Ganges and Burma rivers. It is supposed that in primeval times, Raja Banar's city was on this tongue of land. This is rendered more probable by the existence of two very beautiful Buddhist cloisters, the pillars and stone ceilings of which are richly carved and decorated. This interesting ruin has been much damaged by the Musalmans, who, till the mutiny, used this building as a mosque. On the way from the fort to the hotel the Bhairo Lât, one of Asoka's columns, is passed. There is only a few feet left of this Lât, which is covered with copper, and not visible. It stands on a terrace, in the middle of what was probably a Buddhist temple, of which there are only a few scattered and broken fragments left.

One of the prettiest sights in Benares is the girls' school established and maintained by the generosity of the Maharaja of Vizianagram, an enlightened and cultivated Hindu prince, a K.C.S.I., a Fellow of the Madras University, and a member of the Madras Legislative Council. Besides his Zemindary of Vizianagram, he has large estates in and around Benares. In this school some 600 girls receive an excellent education. Permission to visit must be obtained from Dr. Lazarus, whose beautiful bungalow is a few minutes' walk from Clark's Hotel, who may perhaps also give an order to see the Maharaja's palace and gardens at Belipur, if they are not occupied by guests.

The Government college is a handsome Gothic building in freestone. The Sanskrit college, founded by the Government in 1791, has been absorbed into the Government college. The late headmaster, Mr. Griffith, M.A., is considered to have made this admirable institution, with its 700 scholars, the best Government college in India. In this work he has been greatly assisted by the Anglo-Sanskrit professor, Mr. Arthur Venis, M.A., of Balliol College, Oxford, who is one of the most distinguished of living Orientalists. In the garden of the college is a curious monolith, thirty-one and a half feet high, with a Gupta inscription of the 4th century, and an interesting collection of carved stones brought from Sarnath and other places.

The Bazars of Benares form a narrow, winding wilderness of streets and lanes, shops, dwelling-houses, and temples being mixed together in the strangest medley. The artistic crafts are many and various, embracing almost every sort of Indian manufactures.

Benares is famous all over the world for its beautiful engraved brass work; it is the great Indian emporium for idols and temple furnishing, and contends with Ahmadabad for supremacy in silk brocades and embroideries.

Half the shops in the bazar are devoted to brass work of various kinds—water vessels, lotas dishes, bowls, candlesticks, lamps, boxes, rose-water sprinklers, bells, spoons, censers, images, gods, and fifty other domestic or sacred utensils, many of them most beautifully engraved, are displayed on stalls, behind which the craftsmen sit at work. Mr. Clark, the hotel proprietor, has the finest stock in all

Benares of this beautiful engraved brass work, and he has recently put up electroplating works, worth seeing, where he silvers the brass with great effectiveness and success.

This beautiful work has demoralized considerably of recent years, with most Oriental arts that become popular in Europe. It is very inferior to the engraved work of Ahmadabad, Tanjore, or Muradabad.

Sir George Birdwood says that Benares is the first city in India for the multitude and excellence of its cast and sculptured mythological images and *emblemata*, not only in brass and copper, but in gold and silver, and also in wood and stone and clay. These images of the gods are not made by a separate caste, but the carpenters and masons respectively make the large wooden and stone idols set up in the temples, the potters the clay idols consumed in daily worship, and the braziers, coppersmiths, and goldsmiths the little images in brass and copper, mixed metal, and gold and silver which are always kept in private houses. Brass is largely used in their manufacture, alloyed with six other metals, gold, silver, iron, tin, lead and mercury, making with the copper and the zinc of the brass, a mixture of eight metals, which is deemed a perfect alloy, and very highly prized. Idols of pure gold and silver are also made, and in the Sastras great praise is bestowed on those who worship graven images of these precious metals. The larger idols are always cast in moulds, and afterwards finished with the chisel and file. The gold images of Durga, Lakshmi, Krishna, Radha, and Saraswati, kept in private houses and worshipped daily, must not be less than one *tola* [nearly half an ounce] in weight, and they generally weigh three or four *tolas*. The images of Sitala [the goddess of small-pox] are always of silver, and weigh ten or twelve *tolas*. The images of Siva in his *lingam* form are made of an amalgam of mercury and tin, and are esteemed most sacred. They are always very small, and are kept in all houses and used in the daily worship. Copper images of Surya and of Siva riding on Nandi, and also, in many parts of India, of the serpent *Naga*, are kept in all houses and are worshipped daily. Brazen images of many of the gods are also kept in private houses and daily worshipped: and images of Radha, Durga, Lakshmi and Siva in mixed metal. The images of the gods made of this perfect alloy may also be worshipped either at home or in the temples. The images of all the gods and goddesses are graven in stone, but they are generally worshipped only in the temples; only a few very small ones being found in private houses, the greater number of those used in domestic worship being of the *lingam* form of Siva. The stone images seen in Bengal are generally of black marble, but there are some at Benares which are white. Wooden images are never kept in private houses, but only in the temples. The *nimba* tree, Melia Azadirachta, furnishes the temple images of Vishnu, Durga, Radha, Lakshmi, Siva, Garuda, and others. The mendicant followers of Vishnu always carry about a wooden image of him two cubits high. All images of clay are thrown into the river after being worshipped, and have therefore to be renewed daily. The figures made of Karttikeya for his annual festival in Bengal are often twenty-seven feet high. An immense manufacture of all these idols, and of sacrificial utensils, is carried on in Benares. The industry has sprung up naturally from the services of the numerous temples of this city, and has converted the precinct of every temple into an ecclesiastical bazaar. It was in this way that the seats of those who sold doves for sacrifice, and the tables of the bankers [*soukars* in India] who exchanged unholy for holy coins, were gradually intruded into the outer court of the Temple at Jerusalem; and that the "booths of Bethany" rose beneath the green branches on the opposite slopes of the Mount of Olives.

The *kincobs*, or gold brocades of Benares, are only rivalled throughout India by those of Ahmadabad. A specialty, however, of Benares, are the rich brocades wrought with figures of animals in gold and variegated colours. They are known by the name of *shikargah* (the happy hunting grounds). They were known to the Saracens as beast-hunts. They are probably the oldest survival of ancient loom-work extant, and are still the finest specimens the world can produce.

If Ulysses returned to earth again, he could probably get at Benares alone the exact outfit he would require to appear as he is described in the nineteenth book of the Odyssey.

> "In ample mode
> A robe of military purple flowed
> O'er all his frame; illustrious on his breast
> The double-clasping gold the King confest.
> In the rich woof a hound, mosaic drawn,
> Bore on full stretch, and seized a dappled fawn;
> Deep in his neck his fangs indent their hold;
> They pant and struggle in the moving gold.
> Fine as a filmy web beneath it shone
> A vest that dazzled like a cloudless sun."

The robe was clearly a Benares *shikargah kincob*, and the vest cut from Benares *soneri*, a rich cloth of gold without ornamentation. *Ruperi* is made in the same way, and is cloth of silver, even more

DHAMEK TOPE, SARNATH.

beautiful than *soneri*. According to Josephus, Herod was dressed in *ruperi*, when upon a set day, arrayed in royal apparel, he sat upon his throne, and made his last oration to the merchants of Tyre and Sidon.

Chand-tara (moon and stars), is another lovely brocade figured all over with representations of the heavenly bodies; *mazchar*, is "ripples of silver;" *dup-chan*, "sunshine and shade;" *halimtarakshi*, "pigeons' eyes;" *bulbul chasm*, "nightingales' eyes;" *murgala*, "peacock's neck." All these lovely kincobs are woven at Benares. But if you covet their possession, go not with an hotel guide to a tenth-rate dealer; go direct to Debi Parshad, in the Purana Chauk, but with money in your purse or excellent credit, for these goodly garments are worth their weight in gold.

Velvet carpets are made in Benares, but they are not specially fine, and the weavers are hardly worth hunting for. It is, however, a good place for purchasing those pretty pictures painted on talc, which are so common in all the cities of northern India.

SARNATH.—A hot and dusty drive of four miles leads to Sarnath. One of the four places most sacred to the memory of Buddha. *Bhuila* is his birthplace; *Sarnath* where he began to preach; *Gaya*, where he meditated; and *Kasia*, where he died. Here, surrounded by mounds of rubbish, stand the ruins of two great topes. The largest of these is called the *Dhamek*, which, it is said, was erected by Asoka, to mark the actual spot where Buddha preached his first sermon. Cunningham leans to the view that it was built in the 6th century, while Fergusson disagrees with both opinions, and fixes the date early in the 11th century. It is, however, certain that Hiouen Thsang, the Chinese pilgrim of the 7th century, speaks of a tope 100 feet high at Sarnath in his time. Whichever view is correct, this tope is one of the most interesting ancient monuments in India. The Dhamek is a solid dome ninety-three feet in diameter, and 110 feet high. Up to forty-three feet from the ground, it is built of stones, clamped together with iron. The lower part is relieved by eight projecting faces, each twenty-one feet six inches wide, and fifteen feet apart. In each is a small recess, in which, no doubt, figures of Buddha were originally placed. Encircling the monument, is an exquisite band of sculptured ornament fifteen feet wide, of which enough remains uninjured to give a good idea of what the whole must have been. The central part of this band consists of a geometrical pattern, with above and below a variegated border of fruit and flowers. The upper part of the tope is very dilapidated, and a crop of thick grass, with a tree, grows on the top. The tope is solid, with the exception of a very small chamber in the centre, and a narrow chimney running up the middle, through which the sky appears. A twisting passage less than five feet high, leads into this chamber. This floor is deep with sand, and anyone entering, must do so on hands and knees. No vestige remains of the rail and gateway which once no doubt surrounded this tope.

Half a mile away is another ruined tope of brick, called Jugat Singh's; not because it was built by that gentleman, but because he used it as a brick yard from which to build his palace. To the west of the Dhamek are the remains of a hospital, and farther on, those of a Vihara, or Buddhist monastery. The excavations of General Cunningham brought to light a large number of statues, bas-reliefs, sculptured columns, and other remains of the great city, which no doubt existed here more than 2,000 years ago.

The octagonal brick tower on the top of a steep hill near Sarnath, is a Musalman building of the 15th century. It is worth while to climb the hill for the view.

Sherring's little handbook of Benares (Newman, Calcutta), gives detailed particulars of these Buddhist remains, and much other useful information about Benares and the neighbourhood. It should be purchased by any traveller intending to stay in Benares more than a day or two.

There is rather a powerful force of missionary effort at Benares, the Church, the London, the Baptist, and the Wesleyan Missionary Societies being all on the field.

The Church Missionary Society has half a dozen European and about thirty Native agents engaged in preaching and teaching Christianity, and more than fifty secular teachers in their eight large schools, with nearly 1,500 pupils of both sexes. The superintendent is the Rev. B. Davis.

The London Mission is under the charge of Rev. J. Hewlett, assisted by Revs. Arthur Parker, T. Insell, and K. N. Dutt, with two Zenana ladies. Its leading feature is the College for Young Men, which prepares students for the Calcutta and Allahabad Universities.

The Wesleyan Mission also gives much attention to educational work, having about 850 scholars in their various schools, mainly elementary.

The Baptist superintendent is Rev. W. J. Price, who, with his Native evangelists, devotes himself mainly to preaching on the ghats and in the bazars.

CHAPTER XXI.

PATNA.

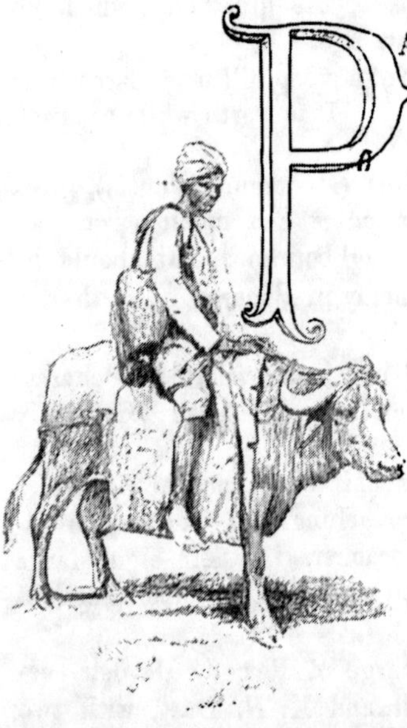

PATNA is well worthy of a day's visit, as a typical Bengal city. No accommodation exists there for Europeans, but there is a good town bungalow a few minutes' walk from the station at Bankipur, the western suburb and administrative head-quarters.

The population of Patna is 160,000, of whom 120,000 are Hindus and 40,000 Mohammedans. The city stretches nearly ten miles along the bank of the Ganges, the bazar, enclosed within the old walls, being about one and a half mile long by three-quarters wide, very closely built, most of the houses being mud with tiled roofs. A wide street twists through this part of the city, but all the rest is a bewildering labyrinth of narrow, crooked lanes and passages. There are no ancient buildings worth looking at, the old fortifications which surrounded the city, built by Azim, the grandson of Aurangzeb, having long since crumbled into mere rubbish heaps. Near the opium works, in the quarter called Gulzarbagh, there are two small temples of great antiquity, that have some interest, one of which is used by the Hindus, and the other as a mosque.

The main interest of Patna lies in its importance as an ancient trading town, owing to its position at the junction of three great rivers, the Son, the Gandak, and the Ganges; and the bustling activity of its inhabitants. The various marts or bazars of Patna are full of picturesque life, especially the central business quarter of Chauk, where cotton cloth is exposed for sale; the Marufganj, where seeds are traded in; the Mansurganj, the market for country produce; and the interesting riverside bazar of Colonelganj. All these may be visited in an open carriage in the course of a morning's drive, every yard of which will be replete with Indian characteristics. No less than £300,000 worth of Manchester goods alone pass through the Chauk in the course of the year, and a very large trade is done in wheat and other cereals, oil-seeds, cotton, tobacco, salt, timber, bamboos, hay and straw.

The only building of unique interest in Patna is the old Government granary, a high dome-shaped building, 430 feet in circumference round the base, with walls 21 feet thick, and an interior diameter of 110 feet. It is ninety feet high, with two winding staircases on the outside, reaching to the top, at which it was intended the grain should be poured into the building, to be extracted from the small doors which surround the base.

A swaggering Nepalese once rode his horse to the top, which is a platform ten feet wide, from which a fine view of the city may be obtained. On entering the building, the most bewildering echoes prevail, the foot-fall on the floor sounds like a trampling army; of a single note of music, sharply uttered, I counted thirty-two distinct echoes. A peal of laughter is repeated high up in the roof, deep down under the floor, and from every stone in the circular walls. A blow struck on an empty wooden case becomes at once a prolonged peal of thunder. It extinguishes St. Paul's as a whispering gallery, for the faintest murmur at one end is heard quite distinctly at the other. As the interior is pitch dark, the effects possible of production are infinite, and I think the Gola alone, as an unrivalled curiosity of its kind, would quite justify the traveller breaking his journey for a day at Patna. The following inscription is carved on a slab outside.

"No. 1. In part of a general plan ordered by the Governor General and Council, 20th of January, 1784, for the perpetual prevention of famine in these provinces, this granary was erected by Captain John Garstin, engineer. Completed the 20th of July, 1786.

First filled and publicly closed by ——," the blank remains, for the storehouse has never been used from that day to this, and is still "No. 1." It would contain 140,000 tons of wheat.

The largest of the Government opium factories is situated at Patna, and is well worth a visit. The superintendent is always glad to show visitors round the works. The raw opium arrives from the district where it is grown about the month of April, in sealed jars, each weighing one maund. Every pot is carefully tested for quality by an expert called a *purkhea*, who samples it both by touch and smell. Every tenth sample of each consignment is submitted to an English chemist for analysis and assay, and for the detection of adulteration. "Payment by result" follows, and the grower is paid by the mean result, whatever it may be.

The raw opium is then cast into big vats, an elaborate system of detection existing to prevent any of it sticking to the hands or bodies of the Indians who manipulate it. The pots when empty are carefully scraped, and smashed into a long heap by the river's brink, where quite an embankment has been formed by successive years of potsherds. These big vats hold about 2,000 maunds, sufficient to destroy the whole population of India. Having secured the mean consistence of each vat, the opium is then divided up into smaller vats, called "alligation" vats, of 250 maunds capacity, where it is worked up by the feet of coolies. As it is of the consistency of putty, the work is very severe, and the tramplers hang on to ropes, to enable them to free their feet the easier at each tread. It is then finally assayed, made into cakes, and is ready for market.

The manufacture is carried on through the summer months chiefly, and during the winter the opium is packed into chests, and distributed all over the East. At the close of the manufacture, the stock in the immense warehouses becomes nearly £4,000,000 in value. There are ranges upon ranges of these warehouses, each of which contains opium worth about half a million sterling.

The cake makers, some 250 in number, have for plant a flat board, a small square wooden box, a brass cup, an earthenware bowl, and a pile of dried poppy petals called "opium trash," worked into thin sheets, like leaf tobacco. A lump of opium of seventy consistence is carefully weighed out to each workman, with some *lewa*, thin opium of fifty consistence. The cake maker wets his brass cup with the *lewa*, tears his "trash" so that it fits the cup without a crease, soaks it in *lewa*, and fills in one after the other till his cup is lined with "trash" half an inch thick. He then drops the lump of opium into the centre, and works the "trash" deftly round with his supple hands until the opium is hermetically closed, and the cake, round and hard like a cannon ball, is ready to be packed and sent off to Calcutta, thence to China. Each cake takes about five minutes to prepare, and is worth 30 to 40 rupees.

The other great factory is at Ghazipur, near Benares. Their total production is between 50 and 60,000 chests a year, of which about one-twelfth is consumed in India, and the rest exported. The profit, which goes to the State as a government monopoly, is from five to six millions sterling.

The factory at Patna deals with all the opium grown in Behar, on an area of about 300,000 acres. The area under cultivation has been increasing of late years, being in

1883,	1884,	1885,	1886,	1887,
246,000.	250,000.	271,000.	283,000.	286,000 acres.

but the average of these five years is less than 1873—7. The consumption of pure opium in India every year is about 500,000 lbs.

The Baptist Mission has four European agents stationed at Patna and its suburbs, of whom the Rev. D. P. Broadway is the senior. A grandson of William Carey, the pioneer missionary of India, is in charge at Dinapur. The total number of church members in the district is about fifty.

GAYA is fifty miles distant from Bankipur Station, a railway journey of three hours. The neighbourhood of Gaya is full of holy places associated with the earliest beginning of Buddhism. There is a decent Town Bungalow here, about a mile from the station.

As a place for Hindoo pilgrimages Gaya is of modern date, and the temples are devoid of interest, historically or architecturally. There are forty-five sacred temples or shrines which have to be visited by the pilgrim in and about Gaya, round which he is personally conducted by a Brahman in a tour which lasts thirteen days, and costs a poor man about 20 rupees. About 100,000 pilgrims come yearly to Gaya. The British pilgrim will, however, find no great attraction in Gaya itself, which is only a fourth-rate holy city, but will push on to *Buddh Gaya*, a journey of about seven miles by carriage. Here is the celebrated temple which was erected A.D. 500 on the site of a still older one by a pious Brahman named Amara, to mark the spot where still existed the more celebrated Bo-tree, under whose shade Buddha sat for six years until he obtained complete enlightenment, B.C. 588. This building is a straight-lined pyramidal nine-storied temple, unique so far as India is concerned, though there are many like it of later date in China and Tibet. It differs entirely from the older and purer Buddhist architecture to be found near Bhopal and at Sarnath, near Benares, which are 600 or 700 years older. Its special historical interest comes from the fact that it was erected by a Brahman for Buddhist purposes at a time when the Buddhist and Brahman religions were in doubtful balance for supremacy in India.

This noble temple is 160 feet high. Its base is oblong and the top square. The wall of the tower is fourteen feet thick. The whole is built over a more ancient temple of the period of Asoka, B.C. 200, who surrounded it with a rail measuring 130 feet by 100, which still exists though very much ruined. Many of its fragments have been carefully collected from different portions of the surrounding country where they had been used for building purposes, and it now encircles the temple for three sides, tolerably complete. The pillars are about six feet high, and at the top and bottom of each are semi-circular slabs, decorated with carved groups of figures and other subjects. It is probably the most ancient sculptured monument in India, and is valued by antiquarians as furnishing examples of manners and illustrations of mythology at a most interesting period of Indian history. The domestic scenes represent feasting and love-making, and the religious subjects tree and serpent worship, dagobas, wheels, and other Buddhist emblems, and many strange mythological figures of mermaids, crocodiles, centaurs, and what not. The famous Bo-tree is planted on a terrace, raised thirty feet above the plain. It is very doubtful if this tree, venerable though it is, can claim to be the great original; but there can be no doubt about the genuineness of the Bo-tree at Anuradhapura in Ceylon. When Asoka sent his son and daughter into Ceylon as Buddhist missionaries, they took with them a branch of the celebrated tree at Gaya. The Ceylon Buddhists have worshipped this offshoot for more than 2,000 years.

A little distance from the great temple stands a smaller but much more ancient temple, in which is a figure of Buddha standing. The great temple has been rather barbarously restored. Mr. Stanton's illustration is drawn from a photograph in the India Museum, taken

BUDDH GAYA.

some years' ago, before the restoration took place. I refer the reader for more detailed information about Buddh Gaya to Cunningham's "Archæological Surveys," Vol. iii, and Fergusson's "History of Indian Architecture," both of which books will be found in any good library in India.

DEOGARH.—At Lakhisarai Junction the East Indian Railway forms a great loop, one side of which leads through Monghyr, Bhagalpur, and Rajmahal, following the course of the Ganges, the other, which is the route taken by the mail, through Deogarh and Raniganj; both meet at Burdwan, sixty-six miles from Calcutta.

Deogarh, on the main or chord line as it is called, is a place of great repute with the worshippers of Siva, and forms a centre of pilgrimage from all over India. Leaving Patna with the mail at 6 P.M., Baidyanath Junction is reached at 10.45 P.M., whence a short branch line runs to Deogarh in about twenty minutes. The group of temples dedicated to Siva are twenty-two in number, some of them being very ancient. The oldest is called Baidyanath, and contains one of the most ancient and venerated *lingams* in all India. The whole of the temples are surrounded by a high wall enclosing a large courtyard, paved with freestone at a cost of £10,000, given by a pious Mirzapur merchant. All the temples but three are dedicated to Siva in his form of Mahadeo. These three are sacred to his wife, Parbati.

The temples are connected from the topmost pinnacles with silk ropes, from which hang gaily coloured flags and tinsel. At one of the gates of the town are three very remarkable monoliths of contorted gneiss. They are placed like a cromlech, two upright and one across their tops. They are square cut, and twelve feet long, weighing about seven tons each. It is not known by whom this curious monument was erected, but it is probably the entrance to a Buddhist temple, as there are remains of an ancient Vihara, or monastery, close by.

PARASNATH is the sacred Jain mountain of Bengal. A railway journey of two hours from Deogarh, changing at Madhupur Junction, reaches Giridhi, whence Parasnath is distant eighteen miles, by a good metalled road. The mountain stands clear out of the plain, and is a narrow rocky ridge, the topmost peak of which is 4,488 feet above the sea. The summit is called by the Jains Asmid Sikhar, or the "peak of bliss," and is a tableland with scattered crags, on which are perched about twenty small Jain temples. There is a good Dak bungalow on the mountain, which was the officers' quarters when Parasnath was used some twenty years ago as a sanitorium. About 10,000 pilgrims visit the place every year, from all parts of India.

No less than ten of the twenty-four Jain Tirthankars attained *Nirvana* on this sacred mountain, which is called after Parsva the twenty-third, who is held with Mahavira, the twenty-fourth, to be the most worthy of adoration. Nineteen Tirthankars are said to be buried here. The temples are mostly modern, or at any rate so recently repaired or restored that nothing ancient can be discovered. Some of them are exceedingly beautiful, notably a choice little shrine of white marble, which cost £8,000.

The surroundings are extremely picturesque, the natural scenery enchanting, and the view from the summit superb. The ascent is by a good easy path, and there are plenty of coolies always at hand at the foot of the mountain for those who wish to be carried up.

From Parasnath to Calcutta there is nothing worth stopping for. The only places of importance being Raniganj where there are some important coal mines, and Burdwan, a populous modern Bengal town, devoid of interest.

Gaur.—This interesting ruined city was the old capital of Bengal, and is situated on a deserted channel of the Ganges, some thirty miles from Rajmahal, a station on the loop line of the East Indian Railway from Lakhisarai through Monghyr to Burdwan. The journey is full of difficulty, as two rivers, the Ganges and the Mahinanda, have to be crossed in ferry-boats. If any traveller wishes to visit Gaur, he should write a week or two beforehand to the magistrate at Maldah, the administrative head-quarters of the district in which Gaur is situated, who will let him know what accommodation and locomotion is possible. There is a comfortable bungalow at Maldah, under his charge, where visitors are sometimes put up.

The ruins of Gaur date from early in the 13th century, when the Musalmans conquered Bengal, and established their capital on this spot, down to A.D. 1575, when it finally disappears from history, abandoned by the court in consequence of the recession of the river Ganges, and the malarious condition of the city, which produced a terrible epidemic. It is said that in its prime Gaur had a population of three quarters of a million, and as its mass of ruins extends from Maldah to Maddapur, nearly twenty miles, this appears very probable.

Long before the Muhamedan invasion, Gaur was a Hindu capital, but no building of this period can be identified, except two isolated ruins outside the ramparts of the Musalman city, and the famous Sagar Dighi, a celebrated tank, whose banks, built of brick, are 1,600 yards long by 800 wide. The banks are surrounded with Muhamedan buildings, of which the best preserved is the tomb of Mukhdam Shah Jelal, a saint of great influence in the earliest days of Gaur. Not far from here is a great dry Ghat, leading down to what was once the course of the Ganges. Within the old site of the citadel, the most of which is now under cultivation, are two dilapidated mosques, which have still traces of their ancient beauty, and a fairly well preserved Jaya Stambha, or tower of victory. Chapter VII. of Fergusson's "Indian Architecture" is devoted to Gaur.

The Adina Mosque at Maldah, which was a suburb of Gaur, was erected A.D. 1358—67, by Sikandar Shah; it is a vast pillared court-yard 500 feet long and 300 wide. The Golden Mosque of Maldah is very beautiful still, and was built in 1566, just before the abandonment of the city.

PANDUAH is another ruined city, seven or eight miles from Maldah. The whole of these extensive ruins are smothered in jungle, with here and there small villages and patches of cultivation, which are increasing every year. There are plenty of tigers and other wild beasts in the district. Unless the traveller can spare a week at least, and is greatly interested in Pathan architecture, the journey to Gaur will hardly repay him.

CHAPTER XXII.

CALCUTTA.

CALCUTTA.—The best time to visit the capital of India is from December 20th to January 10th. Every Englishman in Bengal, civil or military, who can manage it, gets into Calcutta for Christmas and the New Year. Festivities, official and private, are the order of the day. This is the time chosen for the annual Calcutta Races, for charitable fêtes and fancy fairs, for the Viceroy's levee, drawing-room, ball, and garden-party. Every hotel and boarding-house is full to overflowing, and he is considered lucky who can get one of sixteen beds in a room at the Great Eastern Hotel, or Spence's. Travellers who reckon to reach Calcutta within the dates I name, should write at least two or three weeks beforehand for rooms. Ladies will be more comfortable at one of the many boarding-houses in and near the Chowringhi than at the hotels; and Thos. Cook & Son, the excursion-agents, will always secure accommodation, if written to in good time.

Calcutta is situated on the east bank of the Hugli, supposed to be the ancient course of the Ganges. It receives the traffic of the two mightest rivers of India, the Ganges and the Brahmaputra, as well as that of two great railway systems, the East Indian and the Eastern Bengal. It is the seat of the Government of India for more than half

POST OFFICE, CALCUTTA.

the year. Its population in the census of 1881 was 685,000, of which sixty-two per cent. are Hindu, thirty-two per cent. Musalman, and four and a half per cent.. Christian.

Calcutta takes its name from the ancient shrine of the goddess Kali, which has been a place of pilgrimage from very remote times. It is the sixth capital which Bengal has had during the last six centuries—Gaur, Rajmahal, Dacca, Muddea, and Murshedabad being its predecessors. It is just 200 years since the East India Company

THE HUGLI, CALCUTTA.

first established its factory at Calcutta, under the agency of Job Charnock, who hoisted the English flag, somewhere near the present mint, on the 24th of August, 1690. In 1710 the population was 12,000. In 1724 a municipality was established, with a mayor and nine aldermen. The Calcutta of to-day is a purely modern city, its oldest buildings of any importance being St. John's Church, A.D. 1790, and the Town Hall and Government House, both finished in 1804. The old fort, with its famous Black Hole, the Maratha Ditch, and all the other historic spots associated with Charnock, Dr. Hamilton, Holwell, Clive, and Warren Hastings, have lost their very identity, and are covered over with new public buildings. Calcutta is a brand-new European city, with fashionable drives, parks, bandstands, a Rotten Row, modern shops, a cathedral, and nonconformist chapels. Its public buildings are second-rate, greatly inferior, both in architecture and position, to those of Bombay, and none of them fit to compare with a good Lancashire town hall.

GOVERNMENT HOUSE is placed on the north side of the esplanade, in some six or seven acres of pleasant gardens, which look their prettiest when filled with gaily-dressed English ladies and native gentlemen in their very best and most sumptuous apparel, on the occasion of one of the Viceroy's garden-parties. The house itself is a noble palace, consisting of a great central building, in which are handsome suites of entertaining and reception-rooms. This is connected by galleries with four outlying blocks, in which are the private apartments of the Viceroy and his household.

To the west of Government House is the Town Hall, a fine Doric building, with a wide flight of steps leading up to the portico. The interior is without interest, and is used for public meetings, concerts, and other entertainments. Near by is the Legislative Council Chamber. the High Court, the Small Cause Court, and the Treasury. In Dalhousie Square, on the east side, is the Currency Office; on the south, the Telegraph Office and the Dalhousie Institute; on the west, the General Post-office, one of the handsomest buildings in the city; and on the north, the Writers' buildings and Police Office. The middle of the square is occupied by well laid-out gardens, surrounding a large tank. This beautiful open space may be considered the very centre of the city.

Between Dalhousie Square and the river lies the Custom House, in front of which are the busy jetties, crowded with ocean steamships, river barges, budgerows, and other native craft; a picturesque scene, closed in with the great Hugli Bridge. Following the road along the river's bank, several bathing ghats are passed, the Mint, and the Mayo Native Hospital; turning up Nimtolla Street, past the Free Church Institution, Beadon Square is reached, where missionaries preach or discuss on Sunday afternoon; then through Cornwallis Square, with its fine tank and the General Assembly's Institution facing it,

A CALCUTTA BUSTI.

following Cornwallis Street to College Square. Round this square are some fine educational institutions, the Presidency College, Hare School, Calcutta University, and Hindu College.

The Bow and Lall Bazars lead back to Dalhousie Square, and complete the round of the north part of the city. A large portion of this area, lying between the main streets, consists of colonies of natives; the working-classes congregating in Bustis, or native villages, crowded together in mud or straw huts, round a dirty tank, into which all the drainage runs, and in which they wash themselves and their garments. These become less crowded as the suburbs are reached, and little patches of garden, or a few cocoanut palms, reflected in the tanks with the brown huts, and the cotton-clad women and children, make pretty enough pictures.

Starting once more from Government House, the splendid Chowringhi road stretches along the east side of the magnificent Maidan, the glory and pride of Calcutta. The Theatre Royal, the Imperial Museum, the United Service Club, the Bengal Club, and many mansions and boarding-houses, face the Maidan, and in the streets behind are other handsome residences, in well-planted gardens, forming the wealthy quarter of the city. A drive of two miles reaches the cathedral and bishop's palace, and the end of Chowringhi road. Turning to the right, the race-course is passed; the road to the left opposite the race-course leads over Tolly's Nullah, to the Zoological Gardens, Belvidere, the beautiful park and house of the Lieutenant Governor of Bengal, and the Horticultural Gardens. From there, a short cross-road leads into Kidderpur Road, which returns over Tolly's Nullah by Canal Road to the Government Dock Yard. Thence, a magnificent riverside drive, thronged in the evening with open carriages full of English residents and wealthy natives, leads back past Fort William to Government House. All along this road, the river is crowded by a triple row of the finest sailing-ships in the world, whose masts and yards stand out sharp and clear against the evening sky, enhancing the natural picturesqueness of what is undoubtedly the most beautiful city drive in the whole world.

The suburbs of Calcutta are mostly mean and squalid groups of native villages, built of mud or straw wattles. They lie outside the Circular Road, which was made in 1742, with the soil thrown up from the "Maratha Ditch," constructed to protect the city from the Maratha invasion which overran Bengal that year. The ditch was filled up in 1801 by the Marquis of Wellesley. Garden Reach runs for two miles down the river bank to the jetties of the Peninsular and Oriental Steam Navigation Company. There are a number of fine houses with gardens in this suburb, which, however, of late years has been more or less deserted in favour of the district round the cathedral, which is now the fashionable quarter of Calcutta.

The only antiquity in Calcutta is the famous Kali Ghat, where the fearful wife of Siva has held her shrine and welcomed her horrid worshippers from time immemorial.

The present temple is 300 years old, and has no architectural pretensions. The way to it is a continuation of the Chowringhi, and it stands on the bank of Tolly's Nullah, with flights of steps going down to the water. Kali, or "the Black one," is a furious goddess, hideous in features, dripping with blood, gorgon-headed, with a necklace of human skulls. She sends pestilence and famine, and is only appeased with blood. In earlier days, human sacrifice was often her only propitiation, and as late as 1866, during the terrible famine,

KALI GHAT, CALCUTTA.

human heads, decked with flowers, were found before the altar of Kali. She is the goddess of the Thugs, who, sworn to mutual allegiance on her bloody rites, travelled through India disguised as merchants or pilgrims, strangling victims to her honour. The secret cult of Kali is too repulsive for description in these pages. This temple at Kali Ghat is the only place of public worship for Hindus in all Calcutta, though there are in almost every Hindu house or Busti domestic shrines called "Thakoor-bāri," where the household god or goddess sits enshrined. To Kali Ghat, on religious festivals, tens of thousands of worshippers repair: sacrifice goes on continuously, and the ghats and nullah are crowded with bathers. It is worth while to hire a boat, and be rowed up Tolly's Nullah from Hastings Bridge to Kali Ghat.

There are a good many Mosques in Calcutta, but none worth visiting. The finest is a new building in Dhurrumtollah Street, erected in 1842. It is resorted to by many hundreds of worshippers at noon and sunset, especially on Friday.

The wealthy Jain community of Calcutta have a beautiful place of worship in Halsi Bajan Road, called Buadri Dass' temple. It is in the centre of a charming garden, laid out in walks, parterres, and fountains, with statuary and pavilions. It has no architectural interest, but is well worth a visit.

The Burning Ghat on the banks of the Hugli, where the Hindus cremate their dead, is about a mile above the Hugli Bridge. This is a good opportunity for seeing the funeral customs of the Hindus; as the Ghat is constantly visited, no objection is raised to European visitors looking on, quietly and respectfully, while the cremation is proceeding. The funeral pyre is laid in dry wood, mingled with sandal-wood for the sake of its fragrance. The corpse is placed at full length on the pile, and then covered over with more wood, the head and feet only being visible. Passages suitable to the occasion are read by the officiating priest from the sacred books. The eldest son, or nearest living relative, having walked three times round the pyre, kindles it, and in about two hours the corpse is reduced to ashes, which are cast into the river. After the cremation is over, the relatives who have taken part bathe in the Hugli to wash away all impurity resulting from contact with the dead.

The Christian churches and chapels of Calcutta have no great attractions apart from what may be preached from their respective pulpits. They are all modern buildings, and from the Cathedral downwards are poor specimens of ecclesiastical architecture. In the grave-yard of St. John's Church are the tombs of Job Charnock, William Hamilton and Admiral Watson, the only surviving relics of old Calcutta, and some other tombstones removed from the old grave-yard when it was built over. Some of the older places of worship have associations connected with the earlier periods of missionary enterprise, that give them peculiar associations to many travellers, all of which will be found, with a mine of other general information about Calcutta, in a handy little volume of 250 pages, published by Newman and Co., the well-known booksellers, which I heartily commend to

THE BURNING GHAT, CALCUTTA.

anyone intending to stay more than two or three days in this dull capital, devoid of interest to any traveller without introduction to its charming and delightful society, or who is not a student of native institutions or missionary enterprises.

The archæologist will turn from these modern buildings, on the strength of which Calcutta impudently takes the title of "The City of Palaces," to the fascinating contents of the Indian Imperial Museum in Chowringhi. This splendid collection of Indian antiquities and art was founded by the Asiatic Society, whose journals and proceedings, filling fifty bulky volumes, are the rich mines from which almost

A BUDGEROW, CALCUTTA.

every authority on Indian antiquities, philology, literature and natural history has dug his ore. The museum of the society, taken over by the Government in 1866, has been housed and developed within the Imperial Museum, and the Society itself provided with free quarters forever within the same building. The Society, although parting so wisely with its museum, has retained its splendid library of 15,000 volumes, and its collection of Sanskrit, Arabic, Persian and Indian MSS.

The buildings of the new Imperial Museum were not completed until 1875. They are about 300 feet square, round a central quadrangle, colonnaded, and planted with tropical shrubs and trees. The elevation presents two lofty stories, and is a handsome specimen of Italian architecture. The rooms are beautifully lighted and entirely free from shadows. The museum is open from 10 A.M. to 4 P.M. every day, Sundays included, except Friday.

The archæological galleries contain a gateway and a considerable portion of the railing of the great Buddhist Stupa of Bharhut, the most important and interesting in all India, from an historical point of view, though perhaps not the finest in artistic merit. The gateway and rail, nearly 2000 years old, is richly sculptured with representations of the various births of Buddha, giving pictures of the weapons, dress, tools, furniture, buildings, worship and domestic life of the people of their time, 200—100 B.C.

Elsewhere are two colossal human figures from near Patna; ten bases of capitals from Muttra of the first century A.D.; in the centre of the same room is another remarkable sculpture from Muttra, carved on both sides with a Bacchanalian group, opinions being divided whether it is Scythian or Hindu. In this room also are many Buddhist sculptures of various kinds and a huge statue of Buddha.

To the right of the entrance to the west gallery is a finely carved marble slab from the Tope of Amravati, representing the dream of Maya, the mother of Buddha. In the cases round the walls of this gallery is a series of sculptures from the ancient Buddhist city of Ghandara, near Peshawar.

In another long gallery, 160 feet by 40, are a number of Buddhist sculptures arranged in recesses down one side, with Brahminical sculptures down the other. In the middle of the room is a series of casts of the sculptures of the Hindu temples of Orissa.

The sculptures brought from Sarnath are worth very careful examination. One of the slabs portrays the birth, temptation, teaching and death of Buddha. All through the galleries are glass cases containing smaller antiquities, stone and metal implements, ancient glass and pottery, jewels and such like, and a choice little collection of Musalman enamelled tiles.

In another room are casts of the friezes of the famous temples of Orissa, sculptures of the Asoka period, of the Sanchi Tope and other ancient monuments, many of which casts are also to be seen at the Indian Museum at South Kensington.

The Geological Museum is very complete. The natural history collections of every known beast, bird and reptile in India, and the fish and shells of the Indian seas, are intensely interesting.

There are several excursions to be made from Calcutta. The pleasantest is to the Botanical Gardens, which are situated beyond the village of Seebpur, on the bank of the Ganges; the drive over the Hugli Bridge, through Seebpur, is dusty and without interest, and the pleasantest route is by boat down the river to the Garden Ghat.

The garden fronts the river for a mile, and is 272 acres in extent.

THE GARDEN GHAT.

A pretty lake of ornamental water winds through the gardens, in which are every variety of indigenous water plants, and fine specimens of the great *Victoria regia* lily. The *palmetum* is singularly beautiful, and is well planted with a great variety of palms, not merely those peculiar to India, but others from all parts of the world. The orchid houses are renowned in horticulture, and well deserving of the praise bestowed upon them. In the hot season they are one mass of bloom.

There are many fine avenues of palms, mahogany trees, deodar trees and others. The great glory of the gardens, however, is the superb banian tree, one of the finest in the world. It is only 100 years old, yet its trunk is more than fifty feet in circumference, and nearly 200 air roots have descended to the earth beneath from its mighty branches. Its outside measurement is more than 800 feet in circumference. A large board fastened against the main trunk gives much useful and interesting information about this giant tree. Besides several conservatories and other plant houses, there is a remarkable collection of dried plants in a building near the superintendent's house, containing specimens of about 40,000 species.

VIEW IN BOTANICAL GARDENS.

Another pleasant excursion is up the river to Barrackpur Park, the country residence of the Viceroy. This is a mansion and park of 250 acres, beautifully wooded. The view from the house commands about six miles of the river. Those interested in missions may extend their journey to Serampur, opposite Barrackpur, and visit the chapel and college of the Baptist Mission, sacred to the memory of Carey, Marshman, and Ward, the venerated pioneers of Missionary enterprise in India.

Chandarnagar and Hugli are about three-quarters of an hour run by railway from Howrah Station. Chandarnagar is a French settlement, a place of some importance in the last century, but now a homely little town, still the official seat of a French sub-governor, whose office is a dull sinecure, with nothing to do but watch half a company of soldiers drill. Hugli was an old Portuguese factory from 1540 to 1631, when they were driven out by the Mughals. Afterwards it was the residence of Job Charnock. All historical buildings have long since disappeared. There is a handsome Mosque, Imambara and Serai, at Hugli.

There are no special art manufactures of any kind at Calcutta worthy of notice, except the jewellery workshops and show-rooms of Messrs. Hamilton & Co., who manufacture costly regalia and other gauds for the Indian Rajas and native princes. They do not, however, work to Indian patterns, but mainly from European designs. They are most polite in letting strangers walk through their shops and work-rooms.

I do not give any details of missionary work in Calcutta, as they are fully given in "Newman's Guide," being written up to date every year.

GROUP OF BOATS, TOLLY'S NULLAH.

CHAPTER XXIII.

DARJILING.

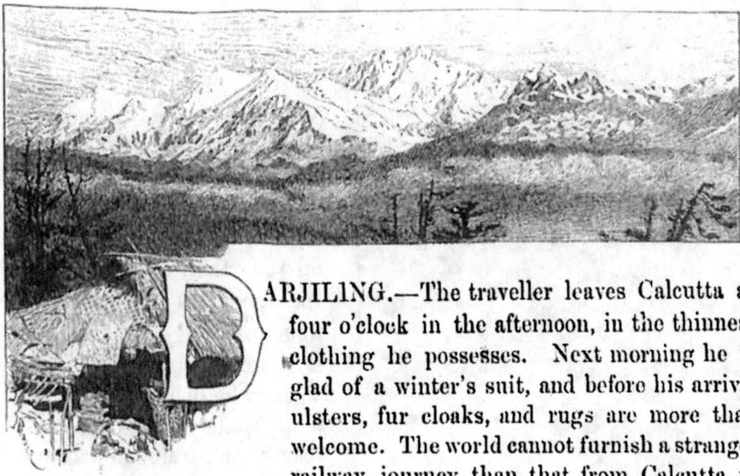

DARJILING.—The traveller leaves Calcutta at four o'clock in the afternoon, in the thinnest clothing he possesses. Next morning he is glad of a winter's suit, and before his arrival ulsters, fur cloaks, and rugs are more than welcome. The world cannot furnish a stranger railway journey than that from Calcutta to Darjiling. A five hours' journey on the usual gauge reaches the great Ganges river, which is crossed by a steam ferry; on the other side the train runs all night on a three-foot gauge; after breakfast, another transfer is made to a two-foot gauge, on which the locomotive crawls 7,400 feet up the Himalyas at a speed of six miles an hour. The total distance from Calcutta to Darjiling is 246 miles, and the "express" mail train does it in exactly twenty-four hours, or an average of ten and a quarter miles an hour. This, however, is better than thirty years ago, when passengers from Calcutta to Darjiling had to swelter for ninety-eight hours in Dak gharries.

The route from Calcutta to the foot of the hills is across the great fertile plain of Bengal, and nothing is lost by a night journey through its monotony; but the rise from the plains to Darjiling is probably the grandest railway journey in the world.

The railway is really a light tram, a Tee rail of about forty pounds per yard, laid for the greater part of the way along the old trunk road through Sikkim to Tibet. To increase the radii of the needful curves, many deviations have been made from the road, and practically there is now a pretty even gradient of one in twenty-eight from the foot of the hills to Darjiling. The line winds in and out along the hill sides, often running along the edge of tremendous gorges and precipices, now on one side, now on the other. At one spot the line rises in a complete figure of 8, at another a hill is climbed in a series of zigzags, on which the engine is alternately at the front and rear of the train, now drawing, now pushing. The locomotives are sturdy little engines weighing ten tons, built by Sharp, Stewart & Co.

ON THE DARJILING RAILWAY.

The open carriages hold six, in comfortable armchairs. A formidable break is provided for each. They are short four-wheeled bogies, for the line twists like a snake, and the curves are so sharp that the little train is in the shape of the letter S for two-thirds of the journey. A good shaking-up might reasonably be looked for, but the travelling is as smooth and steady as a trunk line in England. The road runs the whole distance through dense primeval forest, except where sunny spurs of mountains have been cleared for tea-gardens, making, with their bungalows and offices, a pleasant break in the landscape. At every turn fresh beauty reveals itself. Behind, stretching away to the horizon, is the vast fertile plain of Bengal, bathed in sunlight, with rivers meandering out from the mountain gorges like bright silver ribbons. Before, the first ranges of the Himalyas rising from 5,000 to 8,000 feet above the plain, forest clad to their summits. As the train commences the ascent, the line

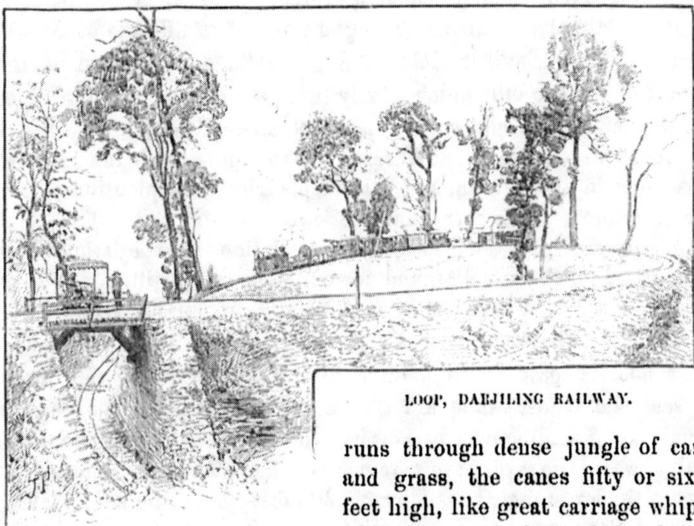

LOOP, DARJILING RAILWAY.

runs through dense jungle of cane and grass, the canes fifty or sixty feet high, like great carriage whips, while the grass beneath sends up blades fifteen feet, and seed-stalks twenty to twenty-five feet from the ground, with huge feathery tops. These impenetrable wildernesses are the haunts of tigers, rhinoceros, buffaloes, bears, sambhar deer, and wild hogs. As the train ascends, the jungle gives place to forest; oaks, banians, mimosas, acacias, fig, India-rubber, and mulberry trees are all plentiful for the first 2,000 or 3,000 feet of ascent, and these are interspersed with great clumps of giant bamboo sixty feet high, with culms as thick as a man's thigh. At 3,700 feet above the plain both peach and almond trees are in full blossom in January, and at 4,500 feet there are fine spreading chestnuts. At 5,000 feet appear the first of those beautiful Himalyan tree-ferns, fifteen or twenty feet high. A little further on a small tea plantation is passed, where the planter, in clearing his jungle, had spared some forty or fifty of these graceful trees, and very pretty they look standing out from the even spread of the low tea-bushes. 2,000 feet below the summit the train often enters a dense cloud, but on passing over and running down into Darjiling, clear weather is generally reached, the magnificent valley of the Ranjit and the snowy heights of Kinchinjanga bursting upon the sight in all the splendour of the setting sun.

Darjiling lives under the shadow of Kinchinjanga, in the heart of the great Himalyan Range. The giant mountain fills the window of the comfortable English Hotel, the "Woodlands," perched on the summit of a little hill, which is only twice the height of Snowdon or Ben Lomond. The station is 7,200 feet above Calcutta, yet when I was there in January, 1889, roses, nasturtiums, and lupins were blossoming in the garden, and wild raspberries were plentiful in the evergreen forest which surrounds the town.

No pen can give any adequate description of the stupendous magnificence of the situation and surroundings of Darjiling. It is at the end of a long wooded spur of Sinchul, a mountain about 9,000 feet high, which projects its steep sides out into an amphitheatre, whose floor is paved with modest hills 6,000 or 8,000 feet above the sea, and whose walls are the mightiest giants of the mighty Himalyas. Standing on Observatory Hill, the very end of the spur, looking west, the eye travels round the amphitheatre, dwelling in turn on the icy summits of Janu, 25,300 feet above the sea; Kabur, 24,000; Pandim, 22,000; Narsing, 18,200; Chomiamo, 23,300; Yakcham, 19,200; Kamhenjhan, 22,500; then a succession of unnamed snowy peaks lead on to Donkhia, 23,200, and other mountains of Bhutan. These fine sonorous words are fitting names for these Himalyan giants. Between these mountains, which stretch in a chain of over 200 miles in extent, are continuous successions of snow-fields and glaciers, and in the centre of the whole range rises their glorious monarch, Kinchinjanga, whose crown of ice rears itself five clear miles above the plain of Bengal. These mountains are from thirty to sixty miles distant from Darjiling, but their height is so immense that they could not be seen much nearer. Between Sinchul and Kinchinjanga, across the Ranjit Valley, stretches a chain of mountains from 10,000 to 12,000 feet. On this platform Kinchinjanga itself is raised. Its flanks are great granite

REVERSING STATION, DARJILING RAILWAY.

cliffs, rising sheer for 8,000 or 10,000 feet; above them are the vast snow-fields and glaciers, from which the granite again breaks in black stern peaks standing out against the dense blue sky.

At daybreak Kinchinjanga is usually buried under a dense mass of cloud, with clear blue everywhere else above. As the sun gathers strength, this mass of vapour slowly breaks up and spreads itself to the zenith. Presently the glittering ice-peaks show themselves through blue gaps, and by nine o'clock the upper clouds have melted, and the lower ones banked down into the Ranjit Valley, leaving the whole summit of Kinchinjanga clear, with its forty miles of snow-field and glacier, and its towering summits, a rich pale glittering yellow against the pure cobalt of the morning sky.

The Himalyan air is so rare and clear that every little detail of the mountain appears visible, and the whole stands out as distinct as the Monte Rosa range from the Riffel. Darjiling is 7,200 feet high, and although the summit of Kinchinjanga is forty-five miles distant as the crow flies, one must positively look up into the sky to see it. I estimate some of its glaciers to be at least fifteen miles in length, and on the other side of the mountain, looking north, are glaciers and snow-fields that are the largest in the world.

Darjiling is the great sanitarium of Bengal, and the town consists of a bazar or market, lying in a basin on the side of the mountain spur, round which are scattered the residences of the European inhabitants, and endless furnished villas let by the season. The most conspicuous buildings are an enormous convalescent home or general hospital, with accommodation for seventy or eighty patients, and the church, which tops the whole town. The villas are scattered all over three miles of hill-side, and suggest that some Himalayan giant had tipped a cart-load of them over the top, letting them settle on every projecting knoll. Every building is roofed with galvanized iron, which glistens among the dense foliage like silver, when the sun is high.

The temperature never rises above 80° in the height of summer, or falls below 30° in the depth of winter, so that it is an ideal climate for Europeans, whose bonny children present a marked contrast to the pale and wilted little creatures one sees in the plains. Children's diseases are almost unknown here. The bazar at Darjiling is quite the most interesting and amusing in India. Sunday is market-day, and throngs of Hill people and tea-coolies come into town, to do their

KINCHINJANGA FROM DARJILING.

marketing and have high jinks generally. The bazar consists of three large open spaces surrounded by stalls. The most familiar type of hill-man are the Lepchas, the Sikkim aborigines. Their features are distinctly Mongolian, their faces broad and flat, their eyes wide apart, and cheek-bones high. They are stalwart little chaps of five feet three inches or five feet four inches in height, with broad chests, mighty calves, and long sinewy arms. The men's faces are almost hairless, with seldom more than a few straggling hairs on lip or chin; but they make up for their want of beard by the most magnificent heads of coal-black hair, as thick and long as a horse's tail, which they plait into a pig-tail. The women wear two pig-tails, and are as lusty and strong as the men, carrying enormous weights on their backs. Their dress is much the same for both sexes, who are only distinguishable by their pig-tails and jewellery. It is a robe of striped coarse cotton cloth, crossed over the breast and back, leaving the arms free, and coming down below the knee; over this is worn, in winter a rough woollen coat with long, loose sleeves. They wear high boots of deerskin as protection from the terrible leeches which infest the woods in the rainy season. The Nepalese are gradually forcing the Lepchas out of Darjiling. When we took possession of British Sikkim, there were only some 200 Nepalese in the whole country, and now they form sixty-five per cent. of the population. The Lepchas are indolent, lazy, and fond of drink; while the Nepalese are a vigorous and prolific folk, excellent cultivators, who find ready employment in the tea-gardens.

The population of the whole district is 160,000, and is very mixed. Nepalese predominate, but there are also great numbers of Bhutias, Tibetans, Bengalis, and the Lepcha aborigines. About 40,000 labourers of these different nationalities find employment on about 200 tea-plantations, which is the flourishing and progressive staple industry of the district.

One of these tea-plantations ought to be visited, and the proprietors are always willing to show strangers round and explain each process. A good deal of cinchona is also grown in the Darjiling district.

The noise of the bazar at noon can be heard for a mile. The old proverb, "It takes two to make a bargain," has no honour here; it never takes less than twenty, and all feel bound to shout, push, struggle, and gesticulate. The crowd numbers many thousands, and these jolly Hill-men appear to be the most good-natured people in the world, rivalling in that respect even the Japanese. Every man carries a knife that would disembowel an elephant, but no one quarrels. Every woman is loaded with silver and gold jewellery, but no one is ever robbed. Here along a sunny wall are twenty or thirty barbers, busily engaged in cutting and trimming the unkempt locks of the men, mostly Tibetan traders who have tramped across the mountains, the hair lying in heaps in front of them, horribly suggestive of gregarines and other small game. Round the corner are a lot of Bhutia women, with great crocks full of snow-white curds, the favourite dainty of the place, which they serve out to their customers in square vessels ingeniously twisted out of plantain leaves. Near them are some Lepcha lads playing shuttlecock with the soles of their feet, which they turn upwards in the nimblest fashion. Then come some stalls for tea, which is boiled up with molasses, a gruesome compound. And now an open market is entered, where perchance one is jostled by a huge giant, a Buddhist Lama, who, followed by an acolyte as dirty as himself, bellows aloud for alms. All over the market are traders, squatted on the ground in front of their wares, the most heterogeneous assortment of goods imaginable—goats, pigs, poultry, tea, tobacco, beads from Venice, grain of all sorts, sweetmeats, cards, the bloodiest meat ever seen, killed at the back as required, and brought in dripping, piles of cotton and woollen goods, yaks' tails, brass Buddhas, ironmongery, pottery, old bottles, tinned meats, tape, cotton, needles, wooden spoons, oil, umbrellas, and feeding-bottles, all blent, with their vendors, in one great labyrinth of yelling confusion.

A noble sight indeed are the well-to-do Bhutia women who have come in to market. They are five feet six inches high, and about five feet broad, with great good-humoured faces, beaming like the rising sun through the brown varnish with which they paint themselves. Each has a great circlet round her head, formed of large beads of coral and turquoise, set alternately on a frame, the red and blue telling strongly against the mass of black hair. From their ears dangle enormous gold earrings, four or five inches long, pulling down the lobes of their ears. Four necklaces of amber, agate, coral, or big coarse turquoises, are the smallest number they can wear with any self-respect, and round their waist—well, where it ought to be—is a massive silver girdle with hanging ornaments, like a chatelaine. I scraped acquaintance with one of these ladies, and went marketing with her. She bought various bags of grain, mysterious flavourings,

A BHUTIA WOMAN.

a lump of pork, some cotton print, and two bottles of cheap brandy, which she tied up together in a huge cloth. She informed me that her jewellery had cost 3,000 rupees; she was quite willing to sell the lot, and begin collecting afresh.

Of course there are plenty of liquor shops in and around Darjiling. The Hill people drink readily enough, but the facilities for getting it are much too plentiful, especially among the tea villages. A few months ago the tea-planters of the Darjiling district held a large public meeting, attended by 150 out of 197, their total number, and unanimously adopted a strong memorial to the Government of Bengal, protesting against the almost universal establishment of out-stills, to the ruin of many of their coolies, and their own pecuniary loss. This out-still system is universally condemned, and its days are numbered.

The liquor sold in the bazar of Darjiling is mostly cheap fiery English spirit. In front of every shop is a board, "English soldiers cannot be supplied." The paternal Government of India takes care of its costly soldier, and protects him against the fiery poison of the out-still and the grog-shop, but Lepcha and Bhutia women may get as drunk as they please.

This cheap spirit is rapidly ousting the national drink of Sikkim, *murwa.* This is made from millet, soaked in yeast, and allowed to ferment slightly. When ready, it is put into a section of bamboo, and boiling water added. It is then sucked through straws. This liquor is wholesome, palatable, and nourishing, and so slightly intoxicating, that no one can possibly get drunk on it. No Lama ever goes from home without his bowl of murwa, and his bamboo cup.

There is a good trade with Tibet from Darjiling, which would be greater if a really good road were made through Sikkim. This may be one of the results of the recent expedition. From Darjiling sugar, rice, dried fruits, tobacco, spirits, madder, cotton goods, cloth, lac, ivory, and indigo are sent into Tibet, the indigo trade being very important and increasing. Tibet returns, in exchange, tea, salt, musk, coarse woollen fabrics, skins, sturdy and active ponies, cows, and sheep. The trade is carried on through the winter months, when the place is full of dirty Tibetans and their haggard flocks of sheep and goats.

Mount Everest, the highest mountain in the world, is not visible from Darjiling, but it may be seen in very fine clear weather from Tiger Hill, an excursion of six miles on ponies or in chairs. Sunrise is the likeliest hour of the day, and the journey may be made between *chota hazri* and breakfast. The views at sunset from Tiger Hill are wonderfully beautiful, and, if the visit can be timed for the full moon, the effect of the mingled light just after sundown upon the snows and glaciers of the Kinchinjanga range will never be forgotten.

During the winter, when the European traveller is likeliest to visit Darjiling, the many pretty cottages and bungalows are untenanted, the club and church deserted, the band-stand vacant. In the summer, however, when every rich family in Calcutta empties itself into Darjiling, the place is gay enough. The whole space on which the town is built is laid out in a succession of rides and walks, affording magnificent views. The best points of view are from the Observatory Hill above the church.

A LEPCHA TENT.

The Bhutia Busti, a quaint and picturesque village inhabited by Bhutias and Lepchas, is about a mile from the hotel. There are several groups of hamlets, in the middle of which is a Buddhist temple. As the ordinary tourist in India is not likely to find a Buddhist temple anywhere else in his travels until he reaches Ceylon, this opportunity ought not to be lost. This temple is Tibetan, differing entirely from the Cingalese. Two or three fat old lamas are generally found comfortably snoozing away their time, and will gladly exhibit their images and other treasures. In this village live all the curio dealers, who will exhibit prayer wheels, jewellery, relic boxes, turquoise necklaces, filagree work in silver and gold, studded with turquoises and jasper, and other Tibetan bric-à-brac. I bought on one of my visits some charming old Japanese crackle ware, and yellow glass, which had no doubt found its way through China and Tibet. These dealers come up to the hotel on Sunday mornings.

A pleasant excursion may be made on ponies or on foot to Rungarun, six miles distant, to see the botanical gardens of seventy-five acres. Here every kind of plant and tree, indigenous to this district of the Himalyas, has been got together.

A grand expedition may be made into the very heart of the snow mountains along the Singalia Range to Phalut, for which about four days are required. The stages are as follows :—

Darjiling to	
Jorpurki . . .	13 miles.
Tonglu	31 „
Sendukphu . . .	38 „
Phalut	51 „

There are good rest-houses at all these stations. By making an early start, reaching Jorpurki for breakfast, Tonglu may be reached the same night. The second day it is practicable to get on to Phalut by noon, and get back to Sendukphu the same night, returning the next day to Darjiling. This would, however, necessitate greater expense in pony and coolie hire than a four or five days' journey, and could only be undertaken by very robust travellers.

The road runs along the sky line of the lofty range of mountains on the left side of the great amphitheatre into which Darjiling is projected, and a guide will point out all the various stations named above, which are on peaks of the same name; Tonglu is 10,074, Sendukphu, 11,929, and Phalut, 11,811 feet above the sea. The views are superb, and not only is the great Kinchinjanga range visible all the way, but from the summits the whole of the vast Nepalese snowy range, including Chunlang (24,020 feet) and Mount Everest (27,799), with their lesser dependencies, any one of which would swallow up Mont Blanc.

Bedding and food must be taken forward to Tonglu by coolies, the rest-houses only supplying chairs and bedsteads. It is extremely cold at night. It is necessary to write a few days beforehand to the Deputy Commissioner at Darjiling to obtain permission to use the rest-houses.

Newman & Co., Calcutta, have published a very handy and intelligent guide book to Darjiling that it will be wise to buy beforehand, and those who intend spending some time, and taking any of the excursions I have suggested, will find Sir Joseph Hooker's charming book of travels in this district an invaluable companion.

If the traveller is not pressed for time, he will do well to return to Siliguri by the Tista Valley, instead of by rail, a delightful excursion of three days through the most lovely scenery, quite practicable for any lady who can stand the moderate fatigue of continuous pony riding. I have not been able to take this journey myself, but a lady and gentleman, friends of mine, some of whose beautiful photographs are the bases of illustrations in these pages, returned from Darjiling by this route the same week I was there; at my request, this lady wrote me a letter describing her experiences, and I cannot do better than reproduce it here:—

"*Nov.* 24, 1888.—My husband and I left Woodland's Hotel, Darjiling, about 9 A.M. on ponies, each with a syce, to ride down by the Tista Valley to Siliguri. Our provisions, which we took partly cooked (there was nothing to be bought on the road except goats' milk, which we got with difficulty at Kâligura), bedding, photograph-box, &c., had been packed on coolies backs and sent off earlier with our native servant, who was also mounted on a pony. It was a lovely clear bright morning when we started and rode to the Mall; there we took our last view of the snows, and began our descent into the valley, with the wooded heights of Senchal above us on our right. We went down a narrow stony path winding backwards and forwards, but always a steep descent, covered with loose stones and very fine dust, glittering in the sun like bits of glass. I rode the greater part of the way, having my pony led by the syce, but my husband walked down most of the way, taking every now and then short cuts. We ought to have started earlier, as, about ten, the sun got very hot, and for some time we had little shelter, though on the other side of the valley and beneath us were thick woods. We were thankful when we reached the shade of some trees, and the road began to be less steep. We passed through a good many tea plantations just beginning to flower, which smelt sweet, like new mown hay. We still kept going downhill, but now through thick woods, until about one o'clock, when we reached the Ranjit river, having ridden down about 6,000 feet in about eleven miles. The Ranjit is crossed here by a bridge, made by stretching two parallel canes across the river, from which are hung loops of cane, bamboos being put at the bottom for flooring; the bridge sways with the slightest movement, but we were told that the natives think nothing of crossing it with heavy loads on their backs. There is also a ferry, so that the bridge is only used when the river is in flood and too rapid for the boat, which is a large kind of canoe hollowed out of the trunk of a tree. Across the ferry is the shortest road into Sikkim, and a great many Lepchas and Bhutias, both men and women, many carrying loads of oranges, passed us while we were there. A number of small half-starved ponies were waiting for loads, and eating young bamboo leaves. After tiffin we rode on along a fairly broad and level road, cut through the thick and tangled jungle just above the river. It was a beautiful forest road, the tall trees and feathery bamboos forming an archway above our heads, beautiful creepers, some, though late, still in flower, strangling and completely covering the trees round which they clung, with large ferns and tropical plants with enormous leaves on each side. We neither saw nor heard any birds, but large black and dark blue butterflies occasionally crossed our path, while perfect stillness reigned, only broken by the river below us rushing swiftly between rocks. About four we reached a more open place where the Ranjit flows into the Tista, a bright green and more rapid river than the Ranjit; here our road turned to the right, and we followed the combined rivers, now called the Tista, passing near the junction of the rivers a few native huts. About half an hour farther on we came across our tiffin basket and other small things lying by the road side, and two of our coolies fighting with a stranger, our words not having much effect. We rode on to the Tista rest-house, which we reached about 4·30. Having sent our servant back to look after the missing properties, we began to look about us. The rest-house belongs to the engineers, from whom we obtained, at Darjiling, permission to use it; this is a one-storied building raised on posts from the ground only a few inches in front, but some feet at the back, with a broad verandah back and front. It consists of two fair-sized rooms, with a bedstead, a table, and a few chairs in each, and a very small dark bath-room, but without a bath. The verandah at the back looks over the river, and to the left is an iron suspension bridge. Just now the place is very busy, as this is the high road to Sikkim, and large quantities of stores are being sent up to the troops before the passes are blocked up by snow. Between the rest-house and the bridge are a few native huts and sheds for ponies, outside which our coolies and syces had lighted fires, and were squatting round cooking their evening meal. Bullock-carts were being unladen, and their contents packed on the backs of tiny ponies, which would take them two days' journey towards the front, the rest of the way they would be carried on by coolies. Presently our food arrived, and by the light of one lamp on a wall, and a candle stuck in a bottle, we had dinner, and soon after went to bed, somewhat tired with our twenty-one miles ride.

"*Nov.* 25.—After breakfast, at which we were joined by one of the

BHUTIAS AT BREAKFAST.

contractors looking after the transport, we left Tista and rode along still by the river. The road very much cut up by the ox carts, a number of which we met, some drawn by small, others by good sized oxen, but all requiring a good deal of prodding and shouting at to get them to drag their loads through the mud and mire. By eleven the sun was very hot, and the road so near the river's edge that there was in places very little shade, the jungle on our side still very thick, and the hills across the river covered also up to the summit with thick jungle. At 1·30, after eleven miles ride, we reached the rest-house of

Kâligura, very prettily situated under trees with the road and some native huts below on the river. To the right is an iron bridge, under which the Kâli, or Black river, now dry, flows to join the Tista. The Tista, here takes another bend, so that there are three valleys joining here, all alike, covered up to the top of the hills with thick jungle. We sketched and photographed, and after dinner sat outside watching the stars and talking to a native engineer who had just arrived, and who told us that the forests belong to Government and contained wild elephants, rhinoceros, and a few tigers, and that during the rains the valley is so feverish that even the coolies refused to work without extra pay. The Kâligura rest-house smaller than the one at Tista but better furniture and a bath.

"*Nov.* 26.—Up early and off by eight, riding still for some miles along the banks of the river, the country gradually getting more open and the hill lower. In about two hours we forded a small river in company with many ox carts, and found on the other side a good-sized village where huts of bamboos were being erected for the troops coming down from Sikkim. Here we left the Tista and the woods began to get much thinner until, at the end of an avenue of trees, we could see the plains. Several native villages were to be seen along the road, and we met a running postman taking mails for the troops. Under one of the last group of trees we had tiffin and then made up our minds to face the heat and finish our ride, although it was midday; and it was indeed hot, and the road had been most carefully made to avoid every bit of shade. We constantly saw villages ahead of us under clumps of trees, but our road took us always between them through fields of rice and quite straight across the hot plains. After about four miles we reached Siliguri and got off at the large Dâk Bungalow there, most thankful for the shade and some good tea which the Khansamah brought us. Were we to take the ride over again we should ride up instead of down, arranging for carriers and ponies to meet us on the arrival of the morning train from Calcutta and get the ride across the hot plains over before the sun was high; the steep path up at the end to Darjiling would be much pleasanter to ride up than down."

There are many interesting and beautiful excursions to be made from Darjiling, and since the British troops entered Sikkim, in 1888, much has been done to improve old and develop new roads. The principal road into Sikkim is good as far as Gnatong, seventy-two miles from Darjiling, and there are now Dak Bungalows all the way. The road is only fit for ponies, but the journey may be broken at the following stages—Peshok eighteen miles, Kalimpong thirteen, Pedong thirteen, Rongli twelve, Sedonchi eight, from whence to Gnatong is a final nine miles. The ups and downs are tremendous. In the first stage the drop from Darjiling to the Tista river is from 7,000 to 700 feet, while from Rongli to Sedonchi there is a rise of 10,000 feet in less than nine miles. The distance from Darjiling to Gnatong is forty miles across the map, but the ups and downs of the road stretch it out to seventy-three.

A short walk of three miles from Pedong brings the traveller to Dumsong, from which is obtained the finest of all the views of Kinchinjanga. Dumsong is only a Buddhist prayer wall, studded over with stone slabs engraved with inscriptions. The scene beggars description. Beyond a foreground of grassy slopes, great tree-ferns, and massy foliage, the most glorious snow mountain in the world hangs in the purple sky, a wonder of beauty! There is a good camping-ground at Dumsong, but for those who do not carry tents, almost as fine a view may be got from Rissum, five miles south of Pedong, where there is a good little bungalow, and lazy people may, if they choose, lie a-bed, and, through the window, watch the sun rise on Kinchinjanga.

At Rongli, where there is also a bungalow, good angling for Mahseer, and other fish may be had with spinning bait, a small spoon, gilt one side and silver the other, being the best.

Gnatong is a stone fort, crowded with poor wooden huts, embedded in hills. The scenery of the whole journey is the finest in the world. The Tista is a rushing torrent, with lofty wooded hills on each side, and at every summit of the way some fresh view of Kinchinjanga deepens the impression of its weird and massive beauty left by the views already enjoyed.

A pleasant digression may be made, if time permits, from Pedong to Guntok, the present residence of the Rajah of Sikkim. It is a hard day's journey of twenty-three miles, with two ascents of over 5,000 feet. The Rajah's name is Tootopewangel and his wife is Tenzamdrama. There is no accommodation at Guntok.

There is only one Protestant mission at work in Darjiling, that of the Church of Scotland, founded in 1870, and now carried on in four distinct branches, viz., (1) The Darjiling Division Mission, with its

IN THE TISTA VALLEY.

head-quarters in the town of Darjiling; (2) The Kalimpong Division Mission, with its headquarters at Kalimpong, twenty-six miles east of Darjiling, *via* the Tista Bridge; (3) The Scottish Universities Mission to Independent Sikkim, with its headquarters also at Kalimpong; and (4) The Darjiling Zenana Mission, with its headquarters at Darjiling.

The Darjiling Division field comprises the Darjiling Hill Territory, west of the Tista River, and the Darjiling Terai, at the foot of the hills, peopled, in the order of their predominance, by Nepalis who are Hindus, Lepchas (the aboriginal occupants) who are mainly demonolators, Bhutias (from Bhutan, &c.) who are Buddhists, and Plainsmen (from the plains) who are Hindus or Musalmans, Bengalis (Hindu or Musalman), and Dhangars (Hindu) from Chota Nagpore. The total population may be estimated at 150,000. The work among these people is superintended by the Rev. A. Turnbull, M.A., B.D. The Mission House, Darjiling, has a staff of eighteen native lay preachers at fifteen stations, including Darjiling and all the main places along the railway to Siliguri, where they are the virtual pastors of their respective Christian congregations, and the missionaries to their non-Christian countrymen; twenty-two native teachers, in one English-Hindi, one Bhutia and nineteen elementary Hindi schools with an attendance of nine hundred pupils; sixteen normal students, in the Training School at Kalimpong and in the Terai; a printing press, with sixteen employés; a colporteur; six book depôts, the one at Darjiling beside the Hindu temple, dealing in general as well as missionary literature; and two native doctors. The work is helped in the most catholic spirit by all denominations and classes of the European community, both congregationally and individually. In 1888 local European subscriptions amounted to 4,393 rupees, while the native Christians themselves contributed 737 rupees. The native Christians now number 580. In 1880 there were not eighty. All questions of admission to the sacraments, discipline, &c., are determined by a monthly Panchayat, consisting of the missionary, catechists, and adult members. There are two Sunday services in Darjiling, at the Mission House at 9.30 A.M. and 4 P.M., Sunday schools, Bible classes four evenings a week, and a prayer meeting one evening a week, at all the stations. There is of course also bazar preaching every Sunday in many of the bazars; in Darjiling, at the book depôt room from 11 to 2. The catechists itinerate during the week among the Christians and non-Christians of their districts. The printing press publishes Hindi and Bhutia schoolbooks, Nepali scriptures, Hindi, Nepali, Bhutia and Lepcha tracts, &c., and also does outside job-work. The Bible is being done into Nepali. The whole of the New Testament has been translated, and the Old Testament as far as Psalms; but only Genesis, Exodus, Proverbs, and from Matthew to Galatians has been published. Other publications which may be mentioned are, a monthly newspaper, a Handbook to the Bible, a Manual of Systematic Theology, a hymn-book, and Commentaries on Genesis, Exodus and Matthew, all in Hindi; and a Nepali grammar, and English-Nepali and Nepali-English vocabularies—all by the Rev. A. Turnbull. Hindi is the *lingua franca* of the mission. In 1885, in consequence of the threatening spread of drunkenness by the ubiquitous outstill and imported liquor shops established by the Government, a Total Abstinence Society was founded within the mission church, which now has over seventy members.

The Kalimpong Division field comprises all the British Hill Territory between the Tista River and the country of Bhutan, as well as the Dooars at the foot of the hills. This work also was begun in 1870, and is conducted in the same way as in the Darjiling Division. It is now supported by the Church of Scotland Young Men's Guild. Their first missionary, the Rev. J. A. Graham, M.A., who is now in charge, has under him five catechists, in four stations; eight teachers, in eight schools, with nine pupil-teachers and 230 pupils; fifteen students, in the training-school; and one native doctor. The number of native Christians (Lepcha and Nepali) is 560. A trip to Kalimpong is worth making.

The Scottish Universities Mission to Independent Sikkim was founded in 1886, and is supported by the missionary associations of the four Scottish Universities. Its missionary, the Rev. W. S. Sutherland, M.A., has under him one catechist, eight teachers, two pupil-teachers and 161 pupils, in six schools, and the training school at Kalimpong, with five teachers, and forty-one students, of whom eighteen belong to his own mission. The training school trains (just as the printing press at Darjiling prints) for all the three missions. The number of native Christians is fifty-five. Mr. Sutherland's headquarters are at Kalimpong, in British territory, until permission be obtained from the Rajah of Sikkim to build within Sikkim. The people proper of Sikkim are the Lepchas, but these are dominated in point of numbers and vigour by the Nepalis, and in point of political and religious influence by the Tibetans.

The Darjiling Zenana Mission, founded in 1886, and conducted by Misses Reid, Berry and Mackintosh, assisted by a native teacher, works in Darjiling among the native women of all classes. Its agencies are, Bengali and Hindi Zenana work, in as many houses as the agents can undertake; an English-Hindi elementary school; and a very successful Sunday school. Fees are received for all secular work, including music, singing and sewing; and the Bible is taught on every visit to the zenanas, and every day in the schools. It is in contemplation to extend the work to Kurseong, Tindharia and Siliguri. This mission is helped by the Darjiling branch of the Y.W.C.A.

Mission work is also being done by the Jesuits in Darjiling and out beyond Kalimpong; but no information of the operations of this body is, so far as we know, published.

English services are conducted in Darjiling every Sunday, both in the forenoon and afternoon; in connection with the Church of England by the chaplain, in St. Andrew's Church; in connection with the Nonconformists by the Rev. H. R. Brown, in the Union Chapel; and in connection with the Roman Catholics by the Jesuit fathers, in St. Joseph's. These three bodies have regular services also at Jalapur, the military cantonment, for soldiers. At Kurseong there is a Church of England chaplain and church for planters.

DACCA.—This important and interesting city may be reached in about fifteen hours from Poradaha Junction, on the railway between Calcutta and Darjiling. The mail from Calcutta to Dacca leaves at 9·30 p.m., arriving at Poradaha Junction 2·50 a.m., and Goalundo Ghat, at the junction of the Ganges and Brahmapootra rivers, at 5·40 a.m. Here the passengers are transferred to a comfortable steamer, which runs sixty-five miles down the mighty Ganges, swollen with its noble tributary, to the Dacca river, and which, after a further journey of forty-five miles more, arrives about 5 p.m., at Narayanganj Ghat, a little distance from Dacca city.

Dacca is the fifth largest city in Bengal, and has a population of 80,000, about equally divided between Musalman and Hindu. The town extends along the bank of the river for nearly four miles. With the exception of two main streets crossing each other at right angles, and the great square market-place, Dacca is the usual conglomeration of narrow, twisting lanes and blind alleys. Many of the native houses are built on a plan peculiar to this town, with a frontage of eight or ten feet, and side walls running back fifty or sixty feet. They are roofed over at back and front, the middle being a courtyard open to the sky.

In the last century Dacca was a place of first-class importance, and in the beginning of the present century boasted a population of over

DACCA.

200,000, and the suburbs extended for fifteen miles. All round the present city are ruins of good houses, mosques, and temples, smothered in jungle.

The old prosperity of Dacca centred in its muslins, which were famous all over the world, the trade sixty or seventy years ago reaching a quarter of a million sterling every year.

There are several large ruinous mansions along the river bank, which still bear melancholy witness to departed greatness: the tombs of the merchants who occupied them are in the pretty old cemetery near the commissioner's house.

The only buildings remaining from the reign of the Mughal Nawabs or Viceroys are the Katra, built in A.D. 1645, and the palace of Lal Bagh, A.D. 1690, both of which are more or less in ruins.

There is a motley Christian population in the district of about

9,000 or 10,000, the descendants of the old Dacca merchants, mostly Portuguese, Eurasians, Armenians, Greeks, and their admixtures: they are, as a rule, Roman Catholics. The Brahmo Somaj church is very strong, numbering about 1,000 adherents, and possessing a large hall.

The fierce competition of Manchester has pretty well destroyed the muslin weaving of Dacca, but there is still a survival, and the most beautiful specimens can be obtained in the bazars. The weavers are all Hindus, and the most highly-skilled craftsmen among them use no less than 126 distinct implements in the production of their finest fabrics. These are generally woven plain, but they are often embroidered, with great skill, in coloured silks, by a different class of workmen, who do not weave at all.

In the 17th century, Dacca muslin could be made fifteen yards long and one yard wide, weighing only 900 grains, the price being £40. Now the finest that can be got, of the same size, weighs 1,600 grains, and can be bought for £10. I doubt if muslin so fine as this can be got in the bazar, but the best hands will weave it to order. Among the presents to the Prince of Wales, when he visited India, were three pieces twenty yards by one broad, each weighing 1,680 grains = 3½ ounces. Tavernier, the Indian traveller (A.D. 1628—41), speaks of a muslin turban made at Dacca, thirty yards long, which was packed into a jewelled cocoanut. The names of these old muslins were *Abrawan*, or "running water," because it became invisible in water; *Subhnam*, the "dew of evening"; *Baft howa*, or "woven air," poetically suggestive of their exquisite fineness and delicacy. But although "woven air" cannot now be purchased, Dacca weavers still produce such beautiful specimens of plain, striped, figured, and chequered muslins as cannot be rivalled anywhere else in the world.

Dacca is also noted for its shell jewellery, bracelets and necklets being made from conch shells, the *Voluta gravis*, imported from the Maldive and Laccadive islands. They are sawn into semicircular pieces, which are joined together, carved, and inlaid with red composition.

Carved ivory fans, filagree work in gold and silver, gold and silver plate beautifully chased and engraved, are all largely produced at Dacca for the Calcutta market. There is also a manufacture of imitation jewellery, and a little time and trouble in the bazars, with a good guide, will secure, for twenty or thirty rupees, a charming collection, illustrative of all the patterns and designs used throughout Bengal.

The Brahmaputra is navigated by fine river steamers, with excellent passenger accommodation as far as Dibrugarh, on the extreme frontier of Assam. The voyage up takes four days, and the return journey three. The scenery in many places is very magnificent. Travellers who have spare time will find the journey very restful and replete with interest.

The Baptist Missionary Society is represented here by Rev. R. Wright Hay and Rev. T. H. Barnett, assisted by five native agents. There is membership of about sixty, and three good day schools.

CHAPTER XXIV.

ALLAHABAD.

ALLAHABAD is the administrative capital of the North-West Provinces and Oudh. It is built on the tongue of land formed by the junction of the Ganges and the Jumna. Its population is 150,000, of whom 100,000 are Hindu, 44,000 Musalman, and 6,000 Christian. There are several good hotels, of which Laurie's is the best. It is a military cantonment of some importance, the force generally consisting of two batteries of artillery, one regiment each of European and native infantry, and a regiment of native cavalry. The tongue of land on which Allahabad stands is singularly fertile, and nowhere in India are to be found such beautiful trees and gardens. All through the cold season roses and other flowers are abundant, and the civil station, with its wide streets, fine avenues, handsome bungalows, well-laid out compounds, and public gardens, covers six or seven square miles. The native town has no special characteristics, presenting the usual net-work of narrow lanes and alleys, branching out of a few principal streets. There are, however, some fine modern Hindu mansions, belonging to wealthy merchants and bankers. It is placed on the bank of the Jumna, just above the junction. A magnificent iron bridge brings the East Indian railway into the city from Calcutta.

Like so many other places in India, Allahabad is built on the departed greatness of previous cities, and has, as may be expected from the spot where the Jumna is absorbed by mother Ganges, a very ancient history. Here was the Aryan city, Varanavata, mentioned in the pages of the Mahabharata. Here was Prayaga, where Rama took refuge in exile: is it not written in the seven books of the Ramayana? Here Asoka reared one of his great stone lats. The Bhils ruled from Prayaga during the early middle ages; in 1575 A.D. Akbar the Great built the fort, renaming the city Allahabad (the abode of God), and in 1801 it became British.

The fort at Allahabad forms a striking object from the river: crowning the spot where the Ganges and Jumna meet, it marks the domination of Muhammad by its utter desecration of one of the holiest places of the Brahman faith. In Akbar's time it was one of the finest fortified palaces in India; but the ancient citadel is razed, the bastions have disappeared, and a sloping glacis has taken the place of the battlements. The buildings which the exigences of modern warfare have spared, have been converted into magazines, store-rooms, and barracks, and are covered with thick coats of British whitewash, or despoiled of their columns and verandahs for the repair of the fortifications. The great hall, of which, in its original beauty, there is an illustration on page 583 of Fergusson's "Indian Architecture," is now the arsenal. Its lovely colonnade has been filled up with a brick wall and the most uncompromising English windows; and whatever could not be cut away of its internal decorations, are hidden under plaster or whitewash. It was probably one of the most beautiful of Akbar's buildings, and it is a disgrace to the Indian government that it is not restored, as far as may now be possible. The noble gateway of the fort was destroyed to form the nucleus of one of the ravelins of the modern fortifications. There is not a single building of this once magnificent palace that can be looked at without sorrow and disgust.

One of the most interesting archæological remains in all India is the famous *Lat of Asoka*. These lats are stone columns which King

Asoka set up throughout his dominions in the thirty-first year of his reign, inscribed with summaries of the leading doctrines of the reformed Buddhist religion, of which he was the author. This remarkable man ascended the throne of Maghada (Behar) B.C. 260. Seven years after he became a convert to Buddhism, and did for that

BANIYA'S SHOP, ALLAHABAD.

faith what Constantine did for Christianity: established and endowed it as a State religion. He called a council of leading priests to settle a creed, appointed a State department to control it and watch over its purity, revised the Buddhist scriptures, and inscribed summaries of the creed on rocks, in caves, and on stone pillars throughout his kingdom. There are fourteen rocks, seventeen caves, and eleven lats, discovered by General Cunningham in different parts of northern India. The most accessible of the rock inscriptions is at Girnar, in

Kathiawar, and at Rupnath, near Jabalpur; and of the caves, those at Barabar and Nagarjuni, fifteen miles north of Gaya. Of the lats, two are at Delhi, one at Sanchi, near Bhilsa, at Rampuri, at Benares, one at Allahabad, and five scattered in less accessible places. Of them all, the one at Delhi, in Feroz Shah's palace, and that at Allahabad, are the best preserved.

The fourteen edicts of Asoka, inscribed on the Allahabad lat, and indeed on all the rocks, caves, and other lats, have been thus summed up by Mr. Robert Cust:—

1. Prohibition of the slaughter of animals for food or sacrifice.

2. Provision of a system of medical aid for men and animals, and of plantations and wells on the roadside.

3. Order for a quinquennial humiliation and republication of the great moral precepts of the Buddhist faith.

4. Comparison of the former state of things, and the happy existing state under the king.

5. Appointment of missionaries to go into various countries, which are enumerated, to convert the people and foreigners.

6. Appointment of informers (or inspectors) and guardians of morality.

7. Expression of a desire that there may be uniformity of religion and equality of rank.

8. Contrast of the carnal pleasures of previous rulers with the pious enjoyments of the present king.

9. Inculcation of the true happiness to be found in virtue, through which alone the blessings of heaven can be propitiated.

10. Contrast of the vain and transitory glory of this world with the reward for which the king strives and looks beyond.

11. Inculcation of the doctrine that the imparting of *dharma* or teaching of virtue to others is the greatest of charitable gifts.

12. Address to all unbelievers.

13. (Imperfect); the meaning conjectural.

14. Summing up of the whole.

The Allahabad pillar is rendered doubly interesting to the archæologist, from an inscription added to that of Asoka by Samudra Gupta (A.D. 380), detailing the glories of his reign and the great deeds of his ancestors. The column is about three feet wide at the base, diminishing upwards through its length of thirty-three feet to a diameter of two feet two inches at the top. The lat was originally crowned with a Buddhist emblem, but the collar only remains, and is formed of the well-known Assyrian honeysuckle ornament, familiar in the Ionic architecture of the Greeks. This makes it probable that the design for these lats came from Central Asia.

Close to the column is a dilapidated subterranean temple, dedicated to Siva, the traditional spot under which the Ganges, Jumna, and Saraswati rivers unite their streams. In this temple an ancient log is stuck into the ground, which the priest in charge claims to be a branch of the original *pipal* or Bo-tree, now at Gaya; but ribald men say that it is renewed every two or three years from the jungle. The pilgrims, however, are satisfied with it, and its genuineness is mainly their concern, not ours.

The Khusru Bagh is close to the railway station. This well-kept garden was the pleasure-resort of the Emperor Jahangir when Prince Salim. Khusru was his son, and played a part in history very similar to that of Absalom, coming, like him, to an untimely end after an unsuccessful rebellion. His tomb is in the centre of his garden, and is a large domed building in the Mughal style. The faded decorations of the interior are clever and spirited paintings on plaster of birds and flowers. The other two large tombs are those of Khusru's mother and sister. The garden is well kept up at the cost of the municipality, and is a favourite resort of the people of Allahabad. The house occupied by the head gardener is known as the Tamboli Begam's house. Here, it is said, Akbar's European-Turkish wife, the Stambouli Begam, lived, when the court was held at Allahabad.

There are some handsome modern buildings in the European town, notably the government offices, the law courts, the various churches, the Thornhill and Mayne memorial, the Mayo memorial hall, and the Muir central college, which is the chief educational establishment of the North-West Provinces.

Allahabad publishes the most important and influential paper in India, the well known *Pioneer*, edited with much skill and enterprise, attracting to its service the ablest young journalists in India, and keeping up a staff of correspondents in every important centre of influence throughout the country. Its politics are severely Conservative, and its bias all on the side of the Government, whose confidential organ it aspires to be. It is uncompromisingly hostile to the rising ambitions of educated Indians.

It is opposed by the *Morning Post*, another very clever paper, and both are sold at every railway station in the north-west. It is a curious fact that the Calcutta press has never had half the influence in India possessed by the *Pioneer*, which occupies in its way the same unique position as the *Times* in England, or the *Scotsman* in Scotland.

European travellers should manage, if possible, to visit Allahabad at the time of the great *Magh Mela*, which is at its height in January, at the new moon. This religious fair is held every year on the tongue of land where the Ganges and the Jumna, the two most sacred rivers of India, mingle their waters. At this time of the year the rivers are at their lowest, and a spit of sand, two miles long, and a mile or so wide, is left high and dry. To this spot hundreds of thousands of Hindus resort, to avail themselves of the double efficacy of the two rivers, and to wash away their past sins. They travel great distances by rail and on foot. When I visited the Mela in 1889, I saw a telegram from Puna to a Brahman at Allahabad, ordering nine priests and fakirs to accompany a rich pilgrim round all the shrines of the fair, and put him through his bathing and pujas properly.

The Mela is a great city of grass and reeds, the pilgrims living in rude, hastily constructed huts of wattles. The main street, a mile long, is taken up with booths, tents, and preaching platforms; Brahmans, hawkers, palanquins, missionaries, fakirs, beggars, six-legged cows, anti-cow-killing preachers, country carts, pilgrims, priests, musicians, devotees and scoffers, jostling along in one vast, noisy stream. On a little platform may be seen some horrible dwarf, who has the faculty of twisting all his joints about under his skin, till his arms and legs look like bags of eels; a dusty ringletted fakir, who has been standing for fifteen years, who has gone to sleep in the midst of the Babel, leaning on a board slung from a tripod of bamboos; another of his fraternity lies on his face in the dust, in yelling contortions; a dirty, ragged ascetic, who has crawled across India on his hands and knees, and another who has come down out of the Punjab, measuring his full length on the ground every three steps; another has not spoken to a soul for twenty years, and sits in still contemplation on a heap of ashes; yet another has his arm in the air, withered and rigid by long continuance. All are in rags, some are clad only in long, matted hair and ashes, and all are held in profound veneration by the people, who give them rice, grain, fruit, and small coins, which they accept with stony indifference.

There are thousands of beggars, displaying every possible form of hideous deformity, or leading about cows with six legs, or other excrescences, which appear to be doubly sacred. Brahman priests have set up small temples in which the gods, gaudy with paint and hideous with cardboard masks, are more repulsive than usual, surrounded by hundreds of devout worshippers, who give small change in payment for a spot of vermilion between the eyes, after doing their pujas to

A FAKIR.

the idols. On reaching the river the crowd becomes denser than ever waiting their turn for a place on the wooden platforms pushed out into the junction of the two streams, on which men and women together perform their ablutions.

On the three great days of the feast there are upwards of a million people congregated at this Mela, the main feature of attraction being the procession of all the fakirs, some 300 in number, down the main street to bathe in the river; they only go in up to their knees, and do not wash all over as they are too holy to need that.

I observed two missionaries who had tents at the Mela, preaching, and selling copies of the Scripture, Gospels, and tracts in the vernacular, but they did not appear to attract many people. They told me, however, that their sales were greatly increased year by year, and that whereas ten or fifteen years ago they gave away their books, generally to see them torn up and thrown about, now they are able to sell considerable numbers. The whole scene is very strange and curious.

There are agencies from four Missionary Societies at Allahabad. The Church Missionary Society under the charge of the Rev. H. M. Hackett and three others, has 140 communicants and four schools; the Baptist Missionary Society has four agents and twenty church members; the American Presbyterian Board is represented by the Revs. J. M. Alexander and J. J. Lucas, with several ladies devoted to Zenana work; and the American Episcopal Methodists are also in the field.

Mirzapur.—Mirzapur is a city of about 60,000 inhabitants. Till recent years it was the largest mart in Hindustan for grain and cotton, but it has been gradually displaced by Cawnpur, and by direct railway communication between Allahabad and Bombay. The town has a very handsome frontage to the Ganges, lined with stone ghats, behind which are fine mosques, temples, and substantial mansions with highly decorated façades and richly carved balconies and door-frames. Large and handsome wells occur in the principal streets. The view of the city from the river is very striking and picturesque.

Not far from Mirzapur, is a famous temple of *Parvati*, in her sterner and more destructive aspect of *Vindhyavasini*, "the dweller in the Vindhya Mountains," where human sacrifice, less than fifty years ago, formed part of her worship by the Gonds and Kols. At this temple, the blood of goats is never allowed to cease from flowing before the image of *Parvati*. Mirzapur is most familiar to the traveller as giving the name to the cheap Indian carpets manufactured chiefly in the jails, here and elsewhere, and which are steadily deteriorating the quality and art character of Indian carpets generally. Instead of, as formerly, striving his utmost to produce a carpet that should be a real work of art, the weaver has now to work up to the charges in the European markets, depreciated by the endless production of jail labour. These carpets are hawked on the railway platforms, at what seem to the uninitiated remarkably low prices. But the staple is short, the texture loose, and they stand no wear and tear. The Mirzapur carpets of twenty years ago, which made the reputation which still lingers round the name, are really fine loom work, and wear splendidly, but their cost was double that of these degenerate successors. The London Missionary Society have a station here, under Rev. D. Hutton.

Between Mirzapur and Moghal Serai, the famous fort of Chunar is seen, about two miles from the station of that name, in the midst of very beautiful scenery. It is built upon a sandstone rock, jutting out into the Ganges, the circumference of the walls being about one and a half miles. The present fortifications are Musalman, but there are abundant fragments of the ancient Hindu fortress in the sculptured stones used in the walls and pavements. Some of these date very far back, and bear traces of Buddhist workmanship, and the familiar bell and flower pattern. Well established tradition records a fortress here in the days of Vikramaditya, King of Ujain, B.C. 57. Chunar was a favourite residence with Warren Hastings, whose house still remains on the summit of the rock, and is used for a barracks for a small force of British infantry stationed here, guarding the State prisoners who are confined in the fortress. Near the rock is a lovely Musalman cemetery, with many beautiful tombs, the most important of which is that of a saint venerated alike by Muhammadan and Hindu. It is well worth while breaking the journey between Mirzapur and Benares for a few hours, to visit this historic and picturesque place.

MANIKPUR and BANDA.—Banda is one of the districts of Bundelkhand. There is now a railway to the town of Banda, part of the "Indian Midland" system, which branches off from Manikpur on the main line of the "East Indian." Leaving Allahabad at 11.10 A.M., Manikpur is reached at 3.0 P.M. The train for Banda leaves at 5.0 P.M., arriving at 9.30 P.M. The two hours' wait may be pleasantly utilised by a stroll or drive round Manikpur; a note to the stationmaster the previous day will secure a conveyance. Manikpur is a ruined city, and may be best described as a series of groves of trees, interspersed with picturesque ruined palaces, mosques, and tombs. The stones of many of the ancient palaces have been taken away to build others elsewhere. Some of the finest carvings have been worked into the great Imambara at Lucknow.

There is only one train daily each way on the Banda Railway, the return journey being at 10.30 A.M.; but if the traveller is out at daybreak he may see a good deal, and yet get away that morning. Banda is the chief town and administrative headquarters of the district. It is a straggling, ill-built town, with clean wide streets, and has a large number of dilapidated mosques, Hindu and Jain temples, some of which are worthy of notice. There are the ruins of a fine palace built by the Ajaigarh Rajas (1200—1300 A.D.); a well-preserved and handsome tomb of Guman Singh, Raja of Jaitpur; and across the River Ken the ruins of the fort of Bhurajgarh, stormed by the British in 1804.

The scenery on the short railway journey between Banda and Manikpur is very beautiful, and as the train takes about five hours to do sixty miles, plenty of opportunity is given for its leisurely enjoyment. It passes through a country of well-wooded hills, breaking into fine cliffs and deep ravines, in which antelopes, nilgai, black buck, and ravine deer find welcome shelter. The district is scattered over with immense boulders, the characteristic feature of the central Indian hills.

Manikpur Junction is reached at 3.0 P.M., meeting a train from Allahabad; arriving at Sutna 5.30, and Jabalpur 1.0 A.M.

Sutna is a small town and military cantonment, occupied by a detachment of Bengal Cavalry. It is thirty-one miles by a good road from Rewa, the interesting capital of the native state of Rewa, which is one of the most important in Central India, having an area of 10,000 square miles, and a population of 1,305,000.

The famous Buddhist Tope of Bharhut is nine miles from Sutna; its beautiful rail and gateway, probably the finest yet discovered, has been removed to the museum at Calcutta. The tope itself is now hardly visible, and the place is not worth visiting, except by those who are interested in Buddhist archæology.

CHAPTER XXV.

JABALPUR.

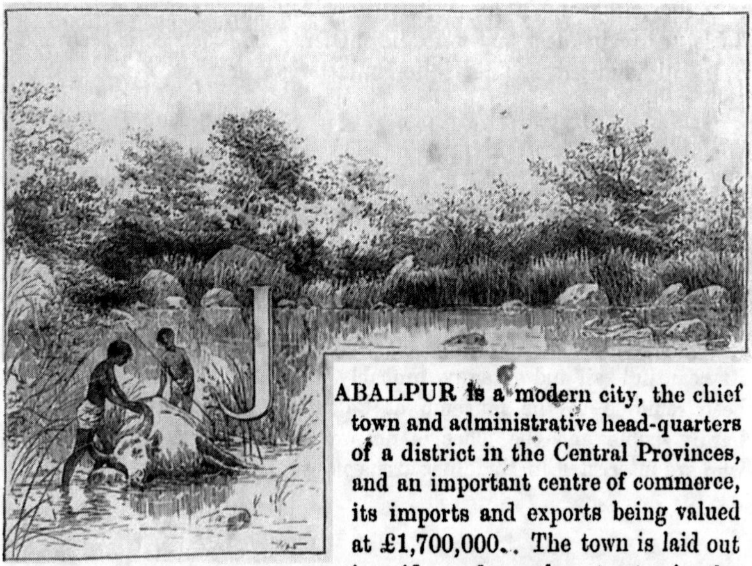

JABALPUR is a modern city, the chief town and administrative head-quarters of a district in the Central Provinces, and an important centre of commerce, its imports and exports being valued at £1,700,000. The town is laid out in wide and regular streets, in the centre of which is a beautiful tank surrounded by temples. There is a fine public garden. The garrison consists of a European and native regiment of infantry, and a squadron of native cavalry.

There is nothing of architectural interest at Jabalpur, and the main attraction to travellers is the beautiful scenery of the Narbada River at the Marble Rocks. The jail, however, ought to be seen, for here are detained in comfortable durance the last of that terrible tribe of murderous devotees known as Thags. The prison is under the charge of Colonel Hughes-Hallett, a distinguished jail administrator, who will give permission to visit it to any European traveller. It is better to write a day or two beforehand. Most of the older Thags are now dead, but when I visited the jail in 1889 I saw a venerable old gentleman, whose declining years are tinged with melancholy because he was "run in" before he had completed a hundred victims to Bhawani. He had reached ninety-nine, which makes his lot the harder to bear. He is watched with some care, as he is under strong and continuous temptation to round off his record somehow before he goes hence. He was, however, very decrepit and bed-ridden, and is probably now dead.

The Thags confined at Jabalpur are mostly informers and their descendants; the young people intermarry, and live in a walled village just outside the prison. The Government do not think it safe to allow even the grandson of a Thag to go abroad, lest he should be tainted with this fearful religion. There are only about 350 of them left, and those able to work are employed chiefly in tent-making and carpet-weaving. Colonel Hughes-Hallett manages matters so skilfully that the profits not only keep the aged and infirm in comfort, but leave a good annual margin of profit.

The date of the origin of this secret society of murderers is buried in the obscurity of the past, but it is probably one of the branches of the secret or "left-hand" cultus of the worship of Siva. Their murdered victims were offered to the goddess Kali, the black wife of Siva. Originally they were Hindus, and of one caste, but latterly they opened their membership to all castes, and even to Muhammadans. They trace their origin to primeval times, when the gods dwelt upon the earth, and consider that all the secrets of their society are depicted on the most ancient of the rock sculptures of Ellora. In these remote ages India was infested by a man-eating gigantic demon, who was so voracious that he threatened the extirpation of the entire population. The goddess Kali, in answer to prayers from her faithful worshippers, slew this demon; but from each drop of blood as it fell there sprang up a fresh demon. To deal with this man-eating brood Kali created two men, whom she taught to kill them by strangulation, so that no blood should be spilt. These two men extirpated the demons, and in gratitude the people thus delivered formed the cult of Thagi, and have ever since propitiated Kali by human sacrifice in which no blood should be spilt.

Membership was hereditary, and the admission of strangers was very cautiously observed. When the boys reached a certain age, they were initiated with terrible mysteries, the priest handing him the sacred handkerchief, and teaching him his business of successful and silent strangling. Sometimes their women were initiated, as they were found useful in decoying their intended victims, who were always travellers. They were suddenly strangled, their backbone being afterwards broken to make death sure, and their bodies, after being plundered, were carefully and deeply buried. The pickaxes used for interment were profoundly venerated, being made and consecrated to the service of Kali with many ceremonials. All women, poets, smiths, carpenters, Ganges water-carriers, oil vendors, dhobies, and musicians were, for sundry religious reasons, exempt from their murderous attentions. Their operations were conducted under a system of signs and passwords, by which Thags were bound to help one another in the committal and concealment of their murders.

It is now fifty years since Captain Sleeman, an able police officer, broke up this awful league, by means of arrests on suspicion and a clever system of cross-examination, and the extorted confession of informers. The whole network was at last discovered, and numbers of them met with the fate they deserved, and were executed. The informers, with the women and children, were of course spared, but have been caged up ever since at Jabalpur.

The suburbs of the city are remarkably beautiful. The gorges of the surrounding hills have been converted into a series of tanks, and planted with fine trees. The overhanging crags, and huge boulders scattered at their feet, add to the charm of the scenery.

Jabalpur is the centre of some of the finest natural scenery in India, surrounding the head waters of the River Narbada, which rises in a lofty flat-topped mountain called Amarkantak, and flows 800 miles to the sea, near Broach. The Narbada is one of the most sacred rivers of India, and its source is guarded by a little colony of priests, who have built a group of shrines in the midst of the wild and desolate region which surrounds it. The river bubbles up gently in a small tank in one of the beautiful glades of the mountain, meanders for two or three miles through green meadows, fed by countless springs, till it reaches the edge of the tableland which forms the summit. Here it falls over the black basaltic cliff in a cascade of seventy feet, called Kapila Dhara. A little farther on is another fall, known as Dudh-Dhara. The Narbada tumbles down the slopes and crags of Amarkantak in a succession of cascades, winds round the picturesque hills of Mandla, and under the walls of the great ruined palace of Ramnagar, a vast quadrangle round an open court, with a tank in the centre, built in the 17th century. From Ramnagar to Mandla the river flows in an unbroken expanse of clear blue water for several miles, between fine woods and under lofty hills, the home of the wild Gonds, Baigas, and Kols, and a notable country for tigers and wild buffaloes. Mandla is an interesting old town, surrounded by a bastioned wall, with a fine palace of the latter part of the 17th century, and a number of pretty temples along the river's brink. The district of Mandla is famous for its excellent sport, and the river affords first-rate mahseer fishing. The Narbada flows on through a forest country to within nine miles of Jabalpur, where it enters a narrow gorge of two miles in length, cut through a mass of marble and basalt, known as "the marble rocks," one of the most beautiful and unique bits of scenery in the world.

Only a hardy traveller could make the journey through the wild and romantic country between Mandla and the sources of the Narbada; but there is a good road of about thirty miles to Mandla itself, and the beautiful scenery of the Narbada round Mandla and Ramnagar amply repays the time spent in exploring it.

The Marble Rocks may be visited from Jabalpur in an easy day's excursion. It is fourteen miles to the comfortable bungalow, with a good driving road the whole way.

About six miles out of Jabalpur, a road turns off through a lovely wooded valley, strewn with huge boulders, leading to the Madan Mahal, an ancient Gond castle, perched on the summit of a hill about 600 feet above the plain. This hill is curiously formed of enormous granite boulders, piled one on the top of the other; great bolster-shape masses, many of which are seventy or eighty feet long. The hill is crowned with one huge boulder, the top of which has been levelled to form the floor of the Madan Mahal, built some 400 or 500 years ago by a Gond Raja for his favourite wife, who wished to dwell always in sight of the sacred Narbada, which may be seen in the plain below, winding like a blue ribbon among the trees. It is a well preserved ruin, interesting alike as a singular curiosity in Hindu architecture and for the superb view which it commands of the surrounding country. An early start from Jabalpur is necessary if this little diversion from the road is made.

It takes about four hours for a carriage and pair to drive from Jabalpur to the Marble Rocks Bungalow, visiting the Madan Mahal on the way. The return journey can be made in two hours or less. Four hours will be needed to do justice to the "Marble Rocks." If there be a moon, I advise that the night be spent there, as the scenery is wonderfully beautiful by moonlight.

THE MADAN MAHAL.

The bungalow is perched on the very edge of a precipitous rock, about 100 feet above the water, the verandah commanding a lovely view of the gorge itself, and the wooded banks of the river as it flows tranquilly away into the plains of Central India. There are plenty of

THE MARBLE ROCKS, JABALPUR.

comfortable boats, and the excursion through the gorge and back is one never to be forgotten. The river is blue, clear and transparent, and is as deep as the cliffs are high. These rise sheer from the water's edge, pure marble and basalt; now dazzling white against the deep blue sky, now creamy, yellow, red, or black veined with green.

On every coign, pigeons and parrots perch and flutter, alligators bask on rocks jutting out of the water, and monkeys chase each other in leaps from point to point. The narrowest part is called the "monkey's leap," and often these creatures may be seen clearing the river at a bound, 100 feet above the water.

Enormous bees' nests hang from every projection, and visitors are forbidden to smoke in the boats, or shoot birds and alligators, for fear of annoying the bees, which would swarm down and attack the obnoxious intruder. There is a grave near the bungalow in which a young engineer lies buried, stung to death in the river, into which he leaped in an unavailing attempt to escape these terrible insects. He was shooting pigeons at the time, when thousands of bees came swarming down upon the boat. Bees seem to be the only wild beast an Indian guide is afraid of; he cares nothing for tigers, panthers, alligators, or cobras, but if he walks under a bees' nest he is discreetly silent till he is well away. In 1877, Mr. Burgess, the well-known Indian archæologist, being attacked by bees at the caves of Ajunta, was driven into a tank, where, up to his neck in water, he fought for his life for hours, finally beating them off, but sustaining dreadful injuries which confined him to his bed for weeks. There is, however, no danger if the simple regulations laid down are adhered to.

Tradition says that this lovely channel was cut by the God Indra, and the footprints of his elephant are still pointed out and worshipped. At the head of the gorge is a beautiful waterfall called the Dhuandhara or "smoke sheet," where the Narbada falls thirty feet over a barrier rock into a fine pool below, a good spot for Mahseer fishing.

A long flight of stone steps leads to the summit of the hill above the bungalow, commanding a superb prospect; here stands an old Hindu temple, surrounded by a circular cloister ornamented with sculptures of Hindu gods. This has been much injured by the Musalman iconoclasm of Aurangzeb's time.

The Church Missionary Society have been at work in Jabalpur since 1854, and have also most interesting missions at Mandla, among the Gonds, and at Kherwara among the Bhils. Rev. J. P. Ellwood is the superintendent, and his work generally presents features of unusual interest, especially that among the Gonds at Mandla.

At Sohagpur and Hoshangabad, on the railway to Bombay, the Society of Friends are engaged in missionary enterprise, with much success.

Bhusawal—Nagpur—Bilaspur.—From Bhusawal Junction, where there is a good hotel and railway repairing shops, a branch line turns off to Nagpur, the headquarters of the Government of the Central Provinces, and Bilaspur. It will no doubt be eventually extended to Calcutta. This railway opens up and passes through the centre of the Haidarabad assigned districts, better known as Berar, a fertile district producing plentiful crops of cotton, and the district known as the Central Provinces.

Berar is a rich agricultural country, with some 3,000,000 acres under cereal crops, and more than 2,000,000 under cotton. The villages are populous, but the towns small and without any interest to the ordinary traveller, who will find nothing to attract him along the whole line.

Only one-third of the Central Provinces are under cultivation, a greater part of the land being covered with scrubby jungle. Some archæological and antiquarian interest may be found in the ruins of the time of the old Gond kingdom, but they are mostly buried in dense jungle, or lie in out of the way places like Deogarh, very difficult of access. The opening of the railway is attracting the attention of missionary enterprise to the aboriginal races of the Central Provinces, of whom the Gonds are the most numerous, being about two and a half millions, of whom many have embraced Hinduism; but at least one and a half millions still cling to their primitive religion, from whom hopeful converts to Christianity are made.

CHAPTER XXVI.

BHOPAL.—INDORE.

THERE is no place on the Great India Peninsula Railway of sufficient interest to stop the traveller between Jabalpur and Itarsi, the junction for the Bhopal State Railway, which extends by the Indian Midland Railway to Jhansi, Gwalior, Agra and Cawnpur.

BHOPAL is the capital of the native state of the same name. It is 1,670 feet above sea level, and is surrounded by a stone wall two miles in circumference, within which is a strong fort. The Begam's palace is outside the city walls, on a large rock called Fatehgarh, strongly fortified. The city is almost surrounded by two beautiful lakes, one of which is four and a half miles, and the other two miles in length. These lakes supply the town with water. The streets, bazars, mosques, and temples of Bhopal, are remarkably picturesque, though presenting no special features of interest to the archæologist.

The population of the state is 950,000, of which more than three-fourths are Hindu, one-eighth aboriginal tribes, and one-tenth Musalmans. The ruler of Bhopal is a woman, and the throne descends in the female line. The Begam is the only female potentate in India. She is an able and vigorous lady, with unredressed grievances against the British Government. She has an army 3,000 strong, but is not otherwise formidable. She has power of life and death in judicial matters, and her territories are not under the jurisdiction of

British courts. Her mother stood bravely by the British rule during the Mutiny, and the loyalty of the present Begam is unquestioned, in spite of her grievances. She is Musalman by religion, and has two sons and one daughter, the latter being the heir apparent, and married.

Twenty-six miles north of Bhopal, on the Indian Midland, in Gwalior State, is BHILSA, a small town of 7,000 inhabitants, protected by a

A STREET CORNER IN BHOPAL.

strong castellated fortress, surrounded by a ditch. In this fort is a handsome old brass gun, of the time of the Emperor Jahangir, about twenty feet long, with large rings held by dolphins. Some quaint Hindu temples are built in the bed of the river Betwa.

Five miles from Bhilsa is SANCHI, a small village, round which are scattered some of the finest Buddhist remains in India; including eleven topes, the finest of which is known as the Great Sanchi Tope, surrounded by four gateways and a rail, casts of which may be seen in the Indian Museum at South Kensington.

THE GREAT BUDDHIST TOPE AT SANCHI.

These topes are solid mounds or domes of brick, erected to celebrate some important event, or to enshrine a relic to the great Buddha, or of some notable Buddhist teacher or saint. They were generally plain structures, but surrounded by rails and gateways of the most elaborate sculptured decoration. They date from B.C. 250 to A.D. 300, and their inscriptions and sculptures furnish an ancient pictorial history of India as complete as that possessed by Greece or Rome. The most accessible of these topes, is that at Sarnath, near Benares, but the rail and gateways there have long since disappeared, and the great tope of Sanchi is so complete in all its ancient features that it is the one usually visited by the traveller interested in Bhuddist antiquities. Situated in a remote and thinly populated country, these remains have been spared the iconoclastic destructiveness of Musalman bigots, and have not been treated as brick-yards and stone quarries for neighbouring cities.

The great tope is well preserved, the rail and three of the gateways are still standing, the fourth gateway having been thrown down, but still lying on the ground.

The tope is a huge dome of bricks laid in mud, placed on a sloping circular platform, 120 feet in diameter, and fourteen feet high. The dome is 106 feet in diameter, and forty-two feet high. It will thus be seen, that a platform about six feet wide and fourteen feet high, surrounds the entire dome. This was originally surrounded by a sculptured balustrade, and ascended by two wide flights of steps. No vestige of either remains. On the summit of the tope is a flat space thirty-four feet in diameter, which was also at one time surrounded by an ornamental railing, and in the centre of which was a stone relic casket.

This tope, and most of the others at Sanchi, were probably erected during the reign of Asoka B.C. 250. None of them are supposed to be later than A.D. 100. There are many other very interesting topes at Sonari, Satdhara, Bhojpur, and Andher, villages within a radius of six or seven miles of Sanchi, but the ordinary traveller will be content with seeing the great tope and the other ruins in the immediate neighbourhood of Sanchi.

I do not venture on any treatise upon Buddhist architecture, or any detailed description of these marvellous and interesting monuments of this period of Indian art. My readers will find in my illustrations a sufficient suggestion of the latter, and will find the former in the first

WEST GATEWAY, SANCHI TOPE.

four chapters, Book I., of Fergusson's "Indian Architecture." The more earnest student had better purchase "The Bhilsa Topes," by Gen. Cunningham (Smith, Elder & Co.), and Fergusson's "Tree and Serpent Worship" (Allen & Co.), which contains the fullest particulars about the Great Sanchi Tope, as well as some fifty illustrations of its details.

KHANDWA is the junction for the Scindia and Nimach section of the Bombay, Baroda and Central India Railway.

Khandwa is a growing railway town of 15,000 inhabitants, a rest-camp for troops, with an excellent travellers' bungalow close to the station. The mound on which the town stands was anciently a seat of Jain worship, and the carved stones and pillars of the old temples may be detected in the more modern Hindu shrines, and in the Maratha Fort.

The town is surrounded by four ancient tanks, round which temples dedicated to Siva are grouped. One of these tanks bears a date corresponding to A.D. 1132.

EAST GATEWAY, SANCHI TOPE.

INDORE, Holkar's capital, is seven hours' journey by rail from Khandwa. It is a modern city of about 75,000 population, mostly Hindus. It is devoid of archæological interest, the only building of importance being the modern palace of Maharaja Holkar, a lofty and

VIEW ON THE KAHAN RIVER, INDORE.

imposing structure with a magnificent storied gateway. The Lal Bagh is a beautiful garden on the banks of the river, in which the Maharaja has built a handsome villa called the Barahdari, and keeps up an interesting menagerie. The Kahan river runs through the town, and is kept well filled with water by an embankment. There are some very pretty scenes along its banks. The native state of Indore has an area of 8,400 square miles, and a total population estimated at 1,200,000.

The Holkar dynasty dates from 1693, and remained loyal through the crisis of the Mutiny. The Maharaja is one of the wealthiest of the native princes of India, and his revenues are about £800,000. His military establishment is about 9,000 troops of all kinds.

MHOW is an important British cantonment, with a native population of 27,000. There is nothing to attract the traveller. The Canadian Presbyterian Mission has stations here and at Indore. From here, however, a very interesting excursion may be made to Mandu, the ruined capital of the old kingdom of Malwa, thirty miles from Mhow.

MANDU was founded about the 4th century, but rose to its greatness under Dilawar Khan and his son Hoshang, kings of Malwa about 1380—1420 A.D. The city is nobly situated on an extensive plateau, surrounded by a great ravine 300 or 400 yards wide, and about 200 feet deep. This plateau is surrounded by a wall, built on the edge of the cliff, and is twenty-eight miles in extent, following all the deviations and indentations of the ravine. The plateau is about five miles long by three wide, and is approached by a splendid causeway, defended by three gateways.

The finest building in the city is the Jama Masjid, built by Hoshang. The four sides of the courtyard consist each of eleven great arches, similar in design and size, supported by pillars cut out of single blocks of red sandstone. The side next the gateway has two arcades, the opposite side has five arcades, and is crowned with three great domes, forty-two feet in diameter. The other two sides have three arcades each. Every quadrangle of columns is roofed with a small dome, and the whole mosque measures 290 feet by 275. The tomb of Hoshang stands behind the mosque, and is a fine specimen of a Pathan mausoleum. On one side is a magnificent dharmsala, 230 feet long, with three ranges of pillars. This has evidently been built from the spoils of Jain and Hindu temples much older than the time of Hoshang.

The principal palace is called the Jehaj Mahal, or "ship palace," being built between two fine tanks, and so having the appearance of floating like a ship at sea. The principal apartment is a vaulted hall, about fifty feet by twenty-five, and twenty-four feet high, flanked by buttresses of enormous strength. At the end of the hall is a range of apartments three storeys high, with balconied windows, and beyond them a long range of vaulted halls, standing in the water. The whole series of buildings is very grand and massive, but its details are choked with jungle and vegetation, and are hardly visible. There are many other palaces, all more or less ruined, with spendid tombs and other buildings, scattered all over the plateau. Of this strange

THE JEHAJ MAHAL, MANDU.

deserted city Fergusson says: "In their solitude, in a vast uninhabited jungle, these buildings convey as vivid an impression of the ephemeral splendour of these Muhammadan dynasties as anything in India, and, if illustrated, would alone suffice to prove how wonderfully their builders grasped the true elements of architectural design."

The district round Mhow has many places of archæological interest. Dhar, the ancient capital of the native state of that name, is a walled town with many striking ruins, especially two mosques constructed entirely from remains of Jain temples. At Bagh, in a secluded ravine, are a series of Buddhist cave temples, of a period from 500—790 A.D., remarkable for their rock-hewn pillars, and the remains of frescoes of great beauty and brilliance of colour. Maheshwar, on the right bank of the Narbada, has some charming river scenery, and possesses the most beautiful ghat in all India, erected by Ahalya Bai, the widow of one of the Holkars, whose splendid cenotaph is hard by. There is also a very fine palace, built some sixty or seventy years ago. The country between these various places, which all lie within a radius of about thirty miles from Mhow, is very wild, and thinly populated. The journey must be taken on horseback, with tents and all necessaries, as no supplies can be got on the road.

A more easy and very interesting expedition may be made to MANDHATA ISLAND, seven miles by a good riding road from either Mortakka or Barwaha Station, between Mhow and Khandwa. There is a fair Dak bungalow at Barwaha, and the station-master will arrange for horses if written to beforehand. Mandhata is an island in the Narbada River, famous for its many temples, but pre-eminently for the great shrine of Omkar, a form of Siva. The island is about a square mile in area, and a deep ravine runs through it. The south and east faces terminate in bluff precipices, 400 to 500 feet high. The opposite bank of the river is equally steep, and between the two cliffs the Narbada flows in a deep still pool, full of alligators and huge fish, which are very tame, picking food off the lower steps of the sacred ghats. The rocks are of green slate, boldly stratified. The shrine of Omkar on the island, and Amreswar on the southern bank of the river, are two of the twelve great Lingams which existed in India when Mahmud of Ghazni demolished the temple of Somnath in 1024 A.D. As late as sixty years ago devotees of Siva and Kali flung themselves off the Birkhala cliffs, on the east end of the island, to be dashed to pieces on the rocks below. Here is the oldest of the Sivaite temples, consisting of a courtyard with verandah and colonnades, boldly carved.

All the temples on the island are dedicated to Siva or his associate deities, but on the main land, on both sides, are many other shrines and temples to Vishnu, and a very interesting group of Jain temples. The picturesque beauty of the river and the cliffs, and the fine carvings on these ancient shrines, some of which date back 700 or 800 years, make Mandhata one of the most attractive spots in Central India.

Travelling northwards from Indore, the first place of interest is UJJAIN, in Gwalior state, the terminus of a short branch line, fourteen miles from Fatehabad Junction. Ujjain holds a notable place in

MANDHATA ISLAND.

Hindu history and religion, being one of the seven sacred cities of Hinduism; it was also the capital of Vikramaditya (a very sun in prowess), the hero of the *Samvat* era, somewhere about the first or second century A.D., celebrated in song and verse for his legendary victories over the Scythian invaders, and who forms the central royal personage of the Hindu stage. His dynasty appears to have lasted to the 6th century, and then melted into the darkness of the 7th and 8th. His court was the resort of poets, musicians, and literati. A Musalman kingdom of Malwa, with Ujjain as its capital, was formed 1387 A.D., but was absorbed by Akbar in 1571. The modern city is surrounded by a masonry wall and round towers. The main bazaar is wide, and lined with good houses and shops. Sindhia has a handsome palace here, near which is an ancient gateway, which tradition assigns to Vikramaditya's fortress. There is also in the city one of Jai Singh's observatories, similar to those erected by him at Delhi, Jaipur, Benares, and Muttra. This observatory at Ujjain is the meridian of Hindu geographers. There is little left of the ancient city, whose ruins lie in heaps about a mile outside the walls.

DEWAS is the chief town of a small native state of 150,000 population, and is fifteen or sixteen miles from Ujjain. Here is a small conical hill, about 300 feet high, on which stands the temple of Chamunda Devi, reached by a long flight of unfinished masonry steps. The temple near the crest consists of a demi-spherical vault or cave, cut into the side of the cliff, having a huge figure of the goddess carved in relief. This little state has two chiefs, called the Baba Sahib and the Dada Sahib; the rule of each chief is distinct within his own limits. These potentates each maintain a standing army of about 100 horse and 500 foot.

RATLAM is the next town of any importance on the line of railway. It is the thriving capital of a little state, a great opium and grain market, with good bazaars and buildings, many of which are very picturesque. It has a population of about 32,000, that of the whole state being 90,000. The Raja of Ratlam, Jaswant Singh, is a Rajput of the Jodhpur family, and is thirty years of age. He is an enlightened prince, and has done much for the education of the people. There is a good college with 500 students. He has built himself a fine new palace. The Ram Bagh, or Maharaja's garden, is one of the most beautiful in India. There is a good Dak bungalow near the station, and conveyances are easily procured.

NIMACH is a small walled town and British cantonment in the state of Gwalior. There is a good Dak bungalow here. The only object in stopping at Nimach will be to visit the small Rajputana state of Partabgarh, and its ancient deserted capital, Deolia. The modern capital, Partabgarh, is thirty-two miles from Nimach by a fair road. There is also a good country road from Mandesar, a station on the line only nineteen miles distant, but I doubt if any conveyance better than a bullock-cart could be obtained there. The city of Partabgarh is surrounded by a loop-holed wall, and defended by a fortress. The old palace is in the middle of the town, and is now abandoned by the maharaja in favour of a pretty country residence a mile or so outside the walls.

A special kind of enamel ware is produced at Partabgarh, which is quite unique and cannot be met with anywhere else. This enamel is produced by melting a thick layer of green enamel on plates of burnished gold, and, while it is still hot, covering it with thin gold cut into mythological, hunting or other pleasure scenes, in which, amid a delicate network of floriated scrolls, elephants, tigers, deer, peacocks, doves, and parrots are the shapes most conspicuously represented. After the enamel has hardened the gold-work is etched over with a graver, so as to bring out the characteristic details of the ornamentation. In some cases it would seem as if the surface of the enamel was first engraved, and then the gold rubbed into the pattern so produced, in the form of an amalgam, and fixed by fire. The art of making this beautiful enamel is confined to two families, who jealously guard the hereditary secret. Enamels of a similar character, blue instead of green, and inferior in workmanship, are produced at Ratlam. (*See* Birdwood's "Industrial Arts," chapter on enamels.)

Deolia, the ancient capital, stands on a steep hill seven and a half miles west of Partabgarh, commanding the whole country round. It is quite deserted, and the fine old palace, built about 1650 A.D. by Hari Singh, is gradually falling to decay. There are several interesting temples, two of which are Jain, and some tanks, the finest of which was built about 1590 A.D.

From Nimach to Chitor there is nothing of interest.

CHAPTER XXVII.

ELLORA, DAULATABAD, AURANGABAD, AJUNTA.

ELLORA is forty-four miles from Nandgaon, on the Great India Peninsula Railway, which is the nearest station on that or any other route. It is in the territory of the Nizam of Haidarabad; the mail train from Bombay reaches Nandgaon at 6 P.M., and from Calcutta at 10.30 P.M. The town bungalow is a comfortable building of three rooms, a few yards from the station, and good meals may be obtained at the railway refreshment rooms.

It is necessary, a few days before the day of arrival at Nandgaon, to communicate with Messrs. Nusserwanji & Sons, mail contractors, Nandgaon, who will either lay a Dak to Ellora and back, or, for the longer journey, to Ellora, Daulatabad, and Aurangabad; they will also secure the bungalow, and order meals at the refreshment-rooms. They are civil and obliging Parsis. The conveyance supplied is a tonga, a low, flexible dog-cart, drawn by two ponies. They carry four persons, including the driver, and travel six or seven miles an hour. An early start is advisable. The first bungalow on the road is at Tarora, just outside the wall of the village, thirteen miles from Nandgaon, where breakfast can be had; twenty-two miles farther is Deogaon, the second bungalow, which should be reached about one o'clock. It is an excellent resting-place, with a good mess-man.

From here to Ellora is nine miles, which may be driven late in the afternoon.

There is no bungalow or any accommodation at Ellora; it is necessary to push on two miles farther, up a steep hill, to the village of Rozah. Picturesquely perched on the summit, with grand views over the western plains, are two bungalows. The largest belongs to the Nizam of Haidarabad, and has accommodation for seven or eight persons; permission to use it is very freely obtained by Europeans, on writing a few days beforehand to the Sadr Talukdar, Aurangabad. The smaller one, an ancient Muhammadan tomb converted to the purpose, belongs to the English officers' mess, who very willingly place it at the disposal of English visitors. Address the mess secretary of the Haidarabad contingent, Aurangabad; there is no mess-man at this latter place. The mess-men of all these bungalows profess to supply tea, milk, rice, and eggs; but my own experience of them was unfavourable, and I advise travellers to take with them tinned provisions enough for the time they mean to spend on this entire excursion. The bungalows are all well built and very clean. I found a small stock at the railway refreshment rooms at Nandgaon, from which it was possible to select enough for modest meals. No bread can possibly be got, so two or three tins of biscuits are necessary.

Ellora is a quaint and pretty village, embosomed in trees. The only object of interest is a fine tank surrounded by temples, by the road-side, between Ellora and Rozah.

Rozah is a small town, with a bazar; innumerable ruined tombs are scattered about outside the walls. The only one of any historical or architectural interest is that of the great Emperor Aurangzeb, which has a well-executed pierced marble screen, and a curious teak door carved in lattice-work.

Near the tomb is a mosque, in which is the shrine of a Muhammadan saint, who died more than 700 years ago. The Dargah of Shah Razu is a plain tomb of considerable antiquity, said to be nearly 600 years old.

The famous caves of Ellora are, on the whole, the finest and most perfect group of those marvellous temples and monasteries which have been cut out of the solid rock by the ancient people of this land of wonders. Scattered along the base of a range of beautiful wooded hills, rising some 500 feet out of the plain, are a succession of rock

THE GREAT KYLAS ELLORA.

temples, Buddhist, Hindu, and Jain. Their dates are obscure, but the oldest is set down by authority at 200 B.C., and the most recent at 1200 A.D. The smallest and most insignificant of them, if alone, would well repay the fatigue of the journey; but passing from one to another the traveller is struck dumb with amazement, as he enters a series of caves as big as churches; with huge images eight or ten feet high ranged round the walls, elephants, lions, tigers, alligators, rams, antelopes, swans, and oxen, or symbolical representations of them, larger than life; friezes of figure subjects as big as that of the Parthenon, varied by intricate wall sculpture of every description, and the whole dug and carved out of the solid rock without a single stone being introduced.

There are, at least, thirty principal Chaityas (temples) and Viharas (monasteries) cut out of the side of the hills, with short intervals between them, scattered along a distance of about two miles and a quarter, right and left of the splendid Kylas, the central wonder of the series, which was carved out by the Dravidians, A.D. 750—850. This greatest of these Titanic excavations cannot be called a cave at all. The architect has quarried a huge chunk of solid rock out of the hill side, leaving a mass in the centre, standing out alone from the lofty cliffs from which it has been cut. He has then taken this block in hand, hollowed it out into vast chambers, left great pinnacles and pagodas on the roof, and carved the whole surface, inside and out, with reliefs illustrating the history of his gods. In shaping the floor of the wide court in which his temple stands, he has left erect lumps and columns of rock, which he has fashioned into elephants, guards, and decorated towers. Every bit of the entire fabric is a mass of sculptured figures, beautifully finished in all their details. The Kylas, standing on its site, as excavated out of the solid rock, is an absolute monolith. The whole structure (it is in no sense a *building*) is 365 feet long, 192 feet wide, and 96 feet high. It is as though a fine English cathedral had been carved out of a mountain in one single piece, instead of being built stone by stone.

> "From one vast mount of solid stone
> The mighty temple has been cored
> By nut-brown children of the sun,
> When stars were newly bright, and blithe
> Of song along the rim of dawn,
> A mighty monolith!"

On the right hand of the entrance is a cistern of water. On each side of the great gateway there is a projection, reaching to the first story, with fine sculptured battlements; the gateway is spacious, with apartments on each side. Over the gate is a rich balcony, which was probably used as a music gallery. The pillars on the outside of the

GALLERY OVER THE GATEWAY OF THE KYLAS.

upper story are worthy of notice. The passage through the gateway is a mass of sculptured decoration.

The plan on the following page will give the visitor some idea of how to find his way through the wonders of the Kylas. He will first of all explore the great courtyard. Passing underneath the gateway (1) he enters the area (2), and proceeding under a small bridge, passes a solid square mass (3) which supports a huge Nandi Bull; the sides of this recess are profusely sculptured; passing on under another small bridge, beneath which are two gigantic figures, he arrives at the body of the grand temple (4), the excavation of which is in the upper story, reached by the two flights of steps (5).

The right hand side of the temple below is adorned with a wonderfully

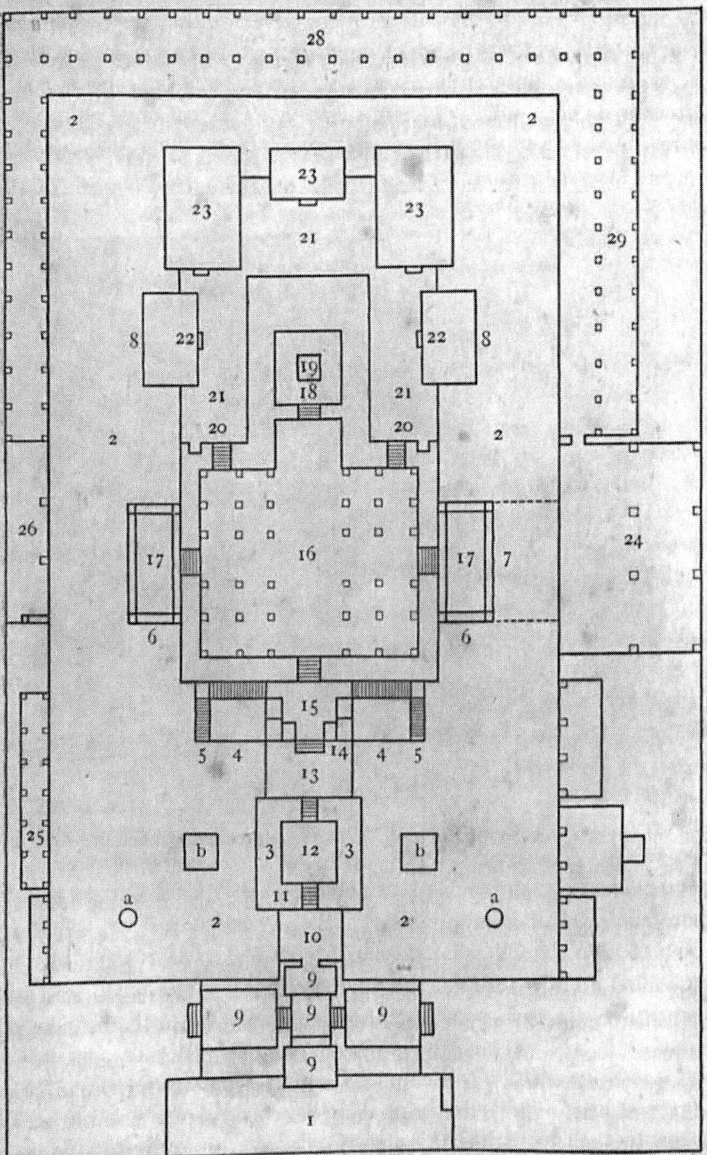

GROUND PLAN OF KYLAS.

complex battle scene; from this tableau the heads of elephants, lions and mythical animals emerge as though supporting the temple; then a projection (6) is reached, in the side of which, sunk in the rock, is a large group of figures, much mutilated. This projection was connected with the apartments on the right hand side of the area by a bridge (7) which has given way, and is now in ruins. It fell about 200 years ago.

Passing the projection of the main body of the temple, it lessens for a few paces, and then again expands (8), and after a very small space on the line of the body of the temple, it terminates in a smaller degree of projection still. The whole of the outside walls of this vast monolithic monument is one mass of sculptured scenes, supported from the base by huge figures of elephants and other beasts.

The gateway consists of three centre rooms and one on each side (9). From the centre rooms, crossing a bridge (10), you ascend by seven steps (11) into a square room (12) in which is the Nandi Bull. This room has two doors and two windows. Opposite the windows are two beautiful square towers or obelisks, thirty-eight feet high, graduated from the base to the capitals, which were originally crowned with lions (*b*). Two elephants, the size of life, have also been carved out of masses of stone left standing in the area (*a*).

From the Bull, the visitor crosses over the second bridge (13), and ascends by three steps (14) into a handsome open portico (15), supported by two pillars looking towards the bridge, and two pilasters that join it on to the temple, the grand apartment of which (16) is entered by four handsome steps and a doorway, guarded by two gigantic sentinels in stone. Advancing a few paces into the temple, which is supported by two rows of pillars, there is an intermission of two pillars, right and left, to open porticoes (17) projecting from the body of the temple.

The shrine (18) of the Lingam of Mahadeo (19) forms the termination of this superb chamber, every inch of which is elaborately sculptured.

Doors (20) on each side of the Lingam shrine lead to an open platform (21), having on each side of the great centre pyramid covering the Lingam two other recesses (22), which contain no image. Three other recesses (23) terminate the platform, all of them being covered with decorations of sculptured figures from the Hindu mythology.

The right hand side of the area has a number of excavations. At

(24) the end of the fallen bridge are three stories, the rooms of which probably formed the residences of priests.

On the left hand side of the area the excavations are more important. In an upper story, reached by steps, is a fine temple (25), at the end of which is a Lingam shrine, and near the entrance doorway is a Nandi Bull, with two huge sentinels leaning on their maces. This temple has singularly beautiful pillars. It is called *Pur Lanka.*

PUR LANKA, KYLAS.

Coming down again, you pass through a sculptured excavation (26) into a fine verandah (28, 29), which is devoted to a pantheon of Hindu deities. There are forty-three groups of principal figures, with surrounding panels illustrating their history.

To give any adequate description of all the cave temples and monasteries of Ellora, would require a book to itself, which Mr. Burgess has already provided, and I do not profess in this volume to go below the surface of things. I shall therefore content myself with indicating briefly a few of the most noteworthy examples.

Close to the Kylas, a path leads down to a house where Brahman guides must be procured, who will point out in succession the various objects of interest, and give a reasonably intelligent explanation. None of them speak English, and an interpreter is necessary.

The guides generally commence at the group of caves to the extreme

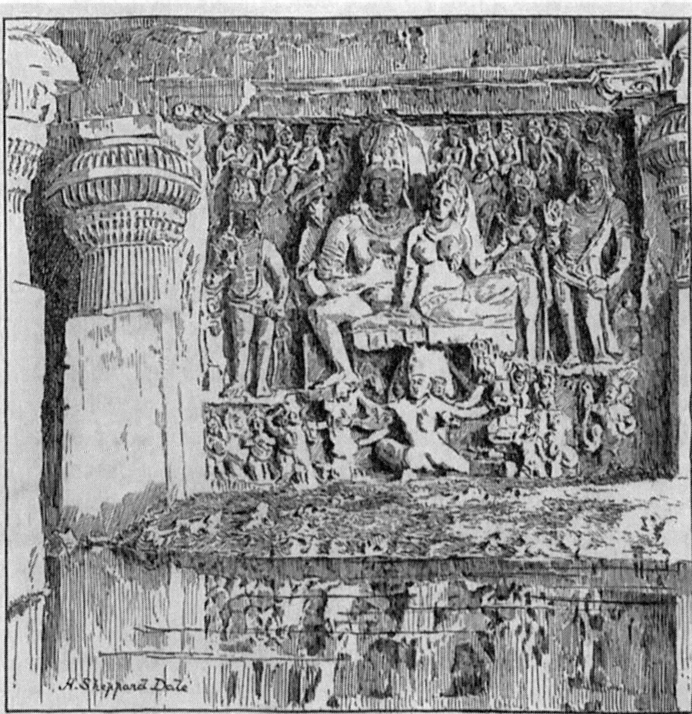

SCULPTURE OF SIVA AND PARVATI, ELLORA.

south, called the Dher Wara, or outcast's quarter, nine in number. These are Buddhist, the central hall having twelve beautiful columns with cushioned capitals, and two enormous sentinels. The largest cave is 104 feet long by sixty feet broad.

The Vishwa Karma, or Carpenter's Cave, is one of the finest in all India. It is a single excavation about eighty-five feet by forty-five, and thirty-five feet high. Above the richly-sculptured gateway is a balcony, which was used as a music gallery to the temple. The interior is not unlike a chapel with an arched roof. At the upper end, under a canopy, is the figure of the founder, who according to the legend, carved out the whole temple in one long night of six months.

A frieze, four feet deep, surrounds the nave between the pillars and the ribs of the roof, on the top of which is a line of figures called *Nagas*.

The date of this temple is said to be A.D. 1306.

The Do Tal, or two storeys, is a pillared cave, Buddhistic in all its details. The Tin Tal has three storeys, the largest chamber being 110 feet by 66 feet. The central pair of front columns are very remarkable, being representations of a vase of flowers. Some of the finest sculptured figures in Ellora are to be found within this monastery.

The next cave of any importance is Ravan Ka Khai, the first of the Brahmanical caves. It is full of spirited sculptures representing scenes from the history of Durga, Lakshmi, Prithwi, Vishnu, Sità, Kali, Ganpati, the Sapta Matra, Bhairava, Siva, Parvati, and other deities.

The Das Avatar is the oldest Brahmanic cave, and bears evidence of having been begun by Buddhists and finished by Brahmans. The great chamber is 103 feet by 45 feet, sustained by forty-six pillars, and surrounded by a series of recesses containing vigorous groups of figures similar in character to those in Ravan Ka Khai, but mostly drawn from Siva in his character of destroyer, and very gruesome and horrible they are.

The visitor now crosses the high road, passes the Kylas, follows a charming footpath under the hills for a mile or more, till he arrives at the beautiful group of Jain caves known as the Indra Sabha, and the Jagannath Sabha, the sculptured façades of which are remarkably beautiful.

The Indra Sabha is so called from the beautiful statues of Indra and his wife Indrani, undoubtedly the finest works of art in the whole series. Like all Jain temples, this group of caves is one mass of sculptured decorations, the details of which will bear hours, or even weeks, of careful study.

A very beautiful view of the surrounding country may be obtained from the hill immediately over Rozah, with the great rock fortress of Daulatabad in the distance, and the domes of Aurangabad beyond on the horizon.

I advise that not less than two days be spent at Ellora, if possible. But, if time be an object, it is possible to spend the morning of the second day in another visit to the caves, and reach Nandgaon in plenty of time for the 10.30 P.M. mail towards Bombay.

GOD OF THE WINDS, ELLORA.

A third day may be well spent in extending the Dak to Daulatabad, seven miles from Rozah, and Aurangabad, eight miles farther. The horses which make the final stage to Rozah, will do this journey (with two or three hours' rest under the trees at Daulatabad) between 6 A.M. and noon. The afternoon can be spent at Aurangabad, where there is an excellent town bungalow; and Nandgaon can be reached the next evening.

DAULATABAD is a huge fortress built on a lofty rock, standing out of the great plain like an island. Permission to visit it must be first obtained from the Sadr Talukdar at Aurangabad. The rock of Daulatabad is a huge cone of granite 500 feet high, with a perpendicular scarp all round from 80 to 100 feet. At the foot of the rock is a ragged collection of mud huts, all that is left of the old city. Daulatabad is one of the finest rock forts in all India, and dates back to the 13th century. The moat is about thirty feet wide, and is crossed by a narrow stone bridge. From the other side, a long tunnelled gallery winds up through the hill to the summit. Candles or torches are necessary, as the tunnel is very dark in places, and the pavement not too smooth. Emerging, the gate of the fortress appears, studded with sharp spikes to resist elephants, which were used in old times as battering rams.

The notable buildings inside the fortress itself are a Bastion with a fine balcony, an old Hindu temple, a large tank of masonry, a Hindu temple transformed into a mosque, a minaret about 120 feet high (clustered with hornets' nests, which make the ascent unsafe), said to have been erected to commemorate the first conquest of the fortress by the Muhammadans in 1294, and a cenotaph to the last King of Golconda, all more or less neglected and dilapidated. There is also a very fine old gun, twenty-two feet long, called "Kilah Shikan," or the leveller of forts.

Just beyond the gun lies the ditch or moat which protects the citadel; the only bridge being a narrow stone laid across. Except at this crossing, the rock is scarped away to a considerable height. The path leads by tunnelled passages up and down steps and slopes, crossing a platform looking over a pretty garden, the trees of which are full of huge hornets' nests, passing a shrine to the memory of a fakir, finally emerging on a pavilion, which commands a magnificent view of the hills of Rozah and Ellora, and the distant city of Aurangabad. Just below this pavilion is a fine tank full of clear water; another 100 steps must be climbed to reach the citadel itself, which stands on the very summit of the rock, on a platform not more than 200 feet across. Here are several large cannons.

The early history of this ancient and powerful fortress is lost in obscurity. In 1294, when it was the capital of the Yadava Kingdom (called Deogiri), it was beseiged by the Muhammadans under Ala-uddin, the fore-runner of the Musalman conquerors of India in the Deccan. The fort ran short of provisions, and was starved into surrender in three weeks. The Yadava Raja secured peace on

DAULATABAD.

pretty hard terms. He had to pay 48,000 lbs. of gold, 560 lbs. of pearls, 160 lbs. of rubies, diamonds, emeralds, and such like; 80,000 lbs. of silver, and 5,000 pieces of silk, with a yearly tribute.

His grandson, who revolted some thirty years later, had to pay a heavier ransom still for being defeated; he was flayed alive, and his skin hung up on the main gate of Deogiri.

Tughlak Shah made Deogiri the capital of the Muhammadan Empire, rechristened it Daulatabad, or the fortunate city, and removed thither the whole population of Delhi, a distance of 800 miles. Daulatabad has remained in the hands of the Muhammadans from that day to this. After the death of Aurangzeb in 1707, all the Mughal possessions in the Deccan became the kingdom of Asaf Jah, whose direct descendant is the present Nizam of Haidarabad.

Daulatabad is not now garrisoned, but is occupied by about 100 military police. It is one of the few places in India where grapes can be successfully grown.

AURANGABAD is eight miles from Daulatabad. There is a clean and comfortable town bungalow. The population is 21,000, who carry on a thriving trade in wheat, cotton, and general merchandize, over a large area of Northern Haidarabad. The town was the capital of the Emperor Aurangzeb, and contains many buildings of great interest, erected during his reign from 1650—70. It is surrounded by masonry walls, with bastions at the various angles. The most interesting building is a mausoleum, built by Aurangzeb in memory of a favourite daughter, Rabia Durani. He gave orders to his architect to reproduce an exact copy of the Taj Mahal at Agra, the tomb of his father Shah Jahan. It is, however, a very long way behind its celebrated pattern, though one of the most beautiful mausoleums in India. The government of the Nizam has recently restored the building, which had been allowed to fall into partial decay. The door of the great gateway is plated with brass, and along the edge is an inscription setting forth the date and names of the architects. The roof of the gateway has a curious and unusual decoration, consisting of rows of sculptured eggs, diminishing in size as they ascend to the centre. The garden, surrounding a large reservoir, is well kept, and very lovely; every step taken presents a fresh and charming picture. The mausoleum itself stands about 200 yards distant from the gateway, on a platform ten or twelve feet high, and some sixty yards square. On entering the building the tomb of the princess is seen, enclosed in an octagonal screen of pierced white marble, twenty-four feet in diameter.

A short walk brings us to the Pan Chakki, a shrine dedicated to a saint from Bokhara, Aurangzeb's favourite religious teacher. At the entrance to the gardens is a fine tank of clear water full of large

MEKKA GATE, AURANGABAD.

fish, beyond which is another tank, justly famous throughout India. It is 160 feet long by 80 wide, and is entirely supported by arches, and great pillars five or six feet thick. This tank forms the roof of a large hall, reached by a flight of steep steps two or three feet high. On the right of the tank is a mosque, which presents the peculiarity of its columns being alternate rows of wood and masonry. In one corner of this mosque, in a tiny garden, is the pretty shrine of the saint.

The Mekka gate and bridge are said to date from the fourteenth century. Inside the gate is a curious little mosque of black stone, built by Malik Ambar, an Abyssinian slave, who rose from that position to be regent of the kingdom of Ahmadnagar. The Municipal Hall and Government House are modern Indian buildings, rendered picturesque by tanks of fresh clear water. The decoration of the Barahdari, or Government House, is a lace-like tracery in white Chunam.

The Jama Masjid is hardly worth a visit, except to see the great *Ficus indica* which grows near it, whose foliage is some 300 feet from side to side.

Two miles out of town is a vast stone building, built by Aurangzeb as a Serai for the accommodation of travellers. It has no architectural pretensions, but its spacious courts give some idea of what an Indian hotel was in the days of the Mughals. There is also, a little way out on the east side, an Armenian cemetery, with tombs inscribed in Hebrew character. Two miles from the city, in a range of hills 500 feet high, are a series of Buddhist caves; but as they are very inferior to Ellora, and present no fresh archæological interest, it is hardly worth while visiting them.

A few English troops, a section of the Haidarabad contingent, are stationed at Aurangabad. Splendid gold embroidered velvets are woven here, used mostly by Indian Rajas for their costly state functions.

If the traveller has followed out my suggestions, he will have reached Aurangabad about two in the afternoon. By noon the next day he will have seen whatever there is of interest, and may start at 2 P.M. on his return journey to Nandgaon, a distance of fifty-six miles. This can be accomplished, but with some fatigue, in a single day's drive, but it is better to take an evening drive to Deogaon, twenty-one miles, where there is a good Dak bungalow, spend the night there, driving on the following forenoon the remaining thirty-five miles to Nandgaon, reaching there at midday, giving time for rest and a meal before the departure of the trains either way.

The distances for the round trip to Ellora, Daulatabad, and Aurangabad, from Nandgaon, are as follows:—

Nandgaon to	Tarora	13 miles.
„	Deogaon	35 „
„	Ellora	44 „
„	Rozah	46 „
„	Daulatabad	53 „
„	Aurangabad	61 „

The return journey:—

Aurangabad to Mitmátha	. . . . .	3 miles.
" Fathabad	. . . . .	13 "
" Deogaon	. . . . .	21 "
" Tarora	. . . . .	43 "
" Nandgaon	. . . . .	56 "

AJUNTA.—Travellers bound for the caves of Ajunta will stop at Pachora station, where there is a small waiting-room and Dak bungalow. The caves are thirty-five miles distant, and the road bad and rough, only fit for horseback or bullock-cart. The mail trains from Jabalpur arrive at 8.35 P.M., and from Bombay 7.50 A.M. The mamlutdar of Pachora will provide a country bullock-cart which, with a change of bullocks half-way at Sindurni, where there is no traveller's accommodation of any sort, will reach Fardapur, four miles from the caves, before dark the same day, if a very early start be made in the morning. At Fardapur there is a Dak bungalow of some sort, but no messman. It has two small rooms, and is under the care of the village *chaprasi*. Bedding and food must be taken. It is a rough, hard journey, and unless the traveller is an intelligent student of Buddhist antiquities, anxious to see both Ajunta and Ellora, he had better pass Ajunta by in favour of Ellora, a much easier expedition, and undoubtedly the more interesting, to the ordinary tourist, of the two great groups of cave temples. The bees at Ajunta are both troublesome and dangerous, while Ellora is comparatively free from them.

If, however, the journey both to Ajunta and Ellora is in contemplation, it will be better to arrange with Messrs. Nusserwanji & Son of Nandgaon for a round Dak from Pachora to Ajunta, Aurangabad, Daulatabad, Ellora, and Nandgaon, or *vice versâ*, writing at least a week beforehand. They will also arrange for the various bungalows on the route to be got ready. As I have never been to Ajunta myself, I cannot speak of the journey from experience; but Mr. Nusserwanji, when arranging for my Dak to Ellora, Aurungabad, and Daulatabad, told me it was a very hard journey, and quite unfit for the two ladies who accompanied me.

The defile up which the path winds from Fardapur to the caves is wooded, lonely, and rugged. The caves are excavated out of a wall of almost perpendicular rock, about 250 feet high, sweeping round a hollow semi-circle, with a stream below, and a wooded, rocky promontory jutting out from the opposite bank. Owing to the difficulty of access, these caves are little known or visited, and the loneliness is complete. A guide is necessary, as the path is often obscure. He may be got at Fardapur. These cave temples and monasteries furnish a continuous narrative of Buddhist art during 800 years, from shortly after the reign of Asoka to shortly before the expulsion of the faith from India, from 200 B.C. to 600 A.D. The chief interest of the latest lies in the nearness with which Buddhism had approximated to Brahmanism before the convulsions amid which it disappeared from India altogether. This, however, is equally manifest at Ellora, where the transition is carried forward still later into Jainism and modern Hinduism. I have not space for lengthy descriptions or illustrations of places not likely to be visited by my readers, whom I refer to the pages of Fergusson's "History of Architecture," where in the chapters on Buddhist architecture, they will find full particulars of this marvellous series of cave temples.

CHAPTER XXVIII.

NASIK.

NASIK is the Benares of the West, and plays the same part to the Godaveri river as Benares does to the Ganges. It lies four miles from Nasik Road station, where there is a good refreshment-room and bungalow; there are also two nice bungalows at Nasik itself. There are plenty of tongas waiting every train. The population, including the cantonment, is 27,000. The greater portion of the population is Hindu, and there are 1,300 families of Brahman priests making a good living out of the temples and pilgrims. There is a large manufacture of idols, chiefly in brass, as well as every sort of brass and copper ware, for which Nasik has a just reputation. Very pretty trinkets may be bought in the bazars; jewel caskets, inkstands, sweetmeat and spice boxes, rings, chains, lamps, and idols. Fine silk pieces, with borders of gold and silver, are woven here.

The city is built on both sides of the river; it is eighty yards broad, running through a succession of shallow masonry basins, with flights of stone steps for the use of bathers and pilgrims. The banks are lined with temples, shrines, cupolas, and platforms, and many others rise in the middle of the shallow river. The principal bazar is held on the north bank, and early in the morning the bazar, ghats, temples, and river, are thronged with the population of the city, and some of the many thousands of pilgrims who come to Nasik during the year. At the Singhast festival some 300,000 pass through in the course of two or three weeks. The streets of the town are narrow and crooked, but many of the houses have fine two-storied frontages, rich in well-carved woodwork. There is no wall round the city, but the main streets are entered by handsome gateways.

Nasik is the scene of some of the events described in the great Hindu epic poem, the Ramayana. Rama was the eldest son of Dacaratha, King of Ajodhya, and was a hero, a victorious warrior, and a slayer of monsters. His wife, Sita, was born from a furrow, and is the goddess of tilling and seed-sowing. His temple at Nasik is celebrated throughout all Western India. It is called Panchawati (the five banyans), and is situated on the eastern bank of the river, about half a mile outside the town. It stands under the shade of five magnificent banyan trees, and none but Hindus may enter it.

The Sundar Naryan temple is a very beautiful structure, built about A.D. 1710—20. None of the shrines at Nasik, though picturesquely grouped, have any special architectural interest. Most of them are dedicated to Siva. The oldest temple in the town is that dedicated to Kapeleshwar, the Skull god, one of the names of Siva. It is ascended by fifty steps, and is 600 years old. It is much frequented by pilgrims. The handsomest of the temples is that dedicated to Kala Rama, standing in an oblong enclosure with 96 arches, 260 feet long and 120 broad. The shrine in the centre is 93 feet by 65, and 60 feet high. It is about 100 years old, and is said to have cost 700,000 rupees.

The various stone basins through which the river passes are called *Kunds*. That on the Panchawati side is Rama's Kund, where the god was wont to bathe. The ashes of the dead are thrown into the river from its steps.

The arched buildings, roofed over, which rise from the bed of the river, are Dharmsalas, where fakirs and pilgrims lodge. There are a great number of these scattered about on the banks.

RAMA'S KUND, NASIK.

Half a mile down the river, and across the ferry, is a hill about 200 feet high, called Sunar Ali, from which a most interesting view of the whole city, river, and temples can be obtained. The hill close by with the square building on the top is Junagarh, or the Old Fort, which was built by Aurangzeb.

The source of the Godavari River is on the side of a mountain behind the village of Trimbak, and is reached by a flight of some 700 steps; the prospect is superb. Here is a small tank, into which the holy water of the source trickles from the lips of a graven image under a stone canopy. This tiny stream, though rising within fifty miles of the Bombay coast, flows 900 miles across India, and falls into the Bay of Bengal.

Trimbak is about eighteen miles from Nasik, but with a change of horses half way a good rider can go there and back in the day. The scenery is very beautiful, especially round Trimbak, where the mountains form a crescent of peaks 1,200 or 1,500 feet above the plain. There are many handsome tanks and pagodas by the road side. The temple of Trimbakeshwar is dedicated to Siva, Trimbak ("the three-eyed one") being one of his names. It is a large building, similar in design to the Sundar Naryan temple at Nasik, and was built about 1730 A.D. by Baji Rao Peshwa, at a cost of nearly a million rupees. Strangers may not enter, but may ascend a portico, which gives a good view of the court and shrine. Many pretty temples and groves surround Trimbakeshwar.

The Lena caves, a series of Buddhist Chaityas and Viharas, are six miles from Nasik on the Bombay road. Some of these are very remarkable, and date as far back as 50—150 A.D. They are in good preservation, especially the figures inside the caves. The largest is a fine hall, about eighty feet by sixty, with twenty-one cells. An illustration and description of the principal Chaitya caves will be found in Fergusson's "Indian Architecture," p. 115.

There is a vigorous mission station at Nasik under the care of the Church Missionary Society, whose agent, Rev. W. A. Roberts, M.A., was good enough to give me some particulars. It was commenced about fifty years ago. In the earlier days of the mission great attention was given to educational work in the town itself, nearly all the education being at one time in the hands of the Church Missionary Society's missionaries, one of whom was the father of Archdeacon Farrar, who was born at Nasik. In the year 1854 a settlement was planned at Sharanpur, one and a half mile to the west of Nasik, which gradually weakened the work in the town itself. As the necessity which then existed for the segregation of Christians has passed by, little is now made of the village of Sharanpur, though the mission schools and other premises are stationed there, and it is the centre of evangelistic and educational work for the Nasik district. Here is an orphanage and boarding-school containing about fifty children, to whom an elementary education is given, and who, out of school hours, make themselves useful on a farm attached to the orphanage, and which supplies food for the school. There is also a normal class, where vernacular teachers are trained for the Church Missionary Society's schools in Western India, and a poor asylum entirely supported by the residents of the station. Service is held for the Europeans of the station, to whom Mr. Roberts is honorary chaplain, in an excellent school-room. It is, however, intended presently to build a church, for which most of the money has been subscribed. The present staff consists of Mr. Roberts, six catechists and scripture-readers, and thirteen school-teachers. This staff is responsible both for the work at Nasik and at nine out-stations, where there are schools. There are altogether about 300 Christians attached to the mission.

The Indian Female Normal School is the only other society stationed at Nasik, and acts in sympathetic co-operation with the Church Missionary Society. The staff consists of two European ladies, two Bible-women, and four school-teachers, who work in three girls' schools, visit houses in Nasik, and preach to women in the surrounding villages.

From Nasik to Bombay the line runs through extremely beautiful scenery down the Thal Ghat, the distance being 117 miles. The descent begins at Kasara Station, 1,912 feet above sea level, and seventy-five miles from Bombay. The Thal Ghat Pass has two lines of communication running down it—the old mail road from Bombay to Agra, and the Great Indian Peninsula Railway. This latter descends by gradients often as steep as one in thirty-seven, by sharp curves as extreme as seventeen chains radius, and by frequent reversing stations. It reaches the bottom at Kalyan Junction, and from there to Bombay runs through a flat coast country.

Munmar is the junction for the Dhond and Munmar State Railway. There is an excellent waiting and refreshment room and a good Dak bungalow with a messman. About a mile distant is a remarkable pyramidal hill, 750 feet high, with a curious natural obelisk of trap-rock sixty feet high, perched on the top of it.

Thirteen miles to the north is the grand old fortress of Chandor, 4,000 feet high, in the midst of a fine range of lofty mountains. This fort is almost inaccessible, and of great natural strength. Five

GOLD WIRE-DRAWERS, YEOLA.

miles from Munmar, on the Dhond line, are two lofty precipitous hills crowned with ancient fortresses, 1,000 feet above the plain, known as Ankai and Tankai. The village of Ankai is deserted, its inhabitants having depended on the fort alone for a livelihood. In the sides of the hill, above the village, are a small series of seven or eight Buddhist cave temples, elaborately sculptured. Tankai, the hill to the eastward, is the best ascent, the greater part of it being steps cut in the rock. A magnificent view is obtained of very fine scenery. Between Yeola and Puntamba stations, numerous antelopes and buck may be seen from the train, as well as a great variety of bird life. Yeola is a town of some importance, well worth visiting, with a large silk-weaving and gold twist industry, employing 7,000 persons of both sexes. A very superior yellow silk cloth, called *pitambar*, and fine silk pieces with borders of silver or gold are made at Yeola.

AHMADNAGAR is a large military and civil station. It has a population of about 40,000. It was founded by Ahmad Nizam Shah, A.D. 1494, and has played a leading part in Deccan history for the last 400 years. It is surrounded by a clay wall about twelve feet high, with ruined gates and bastions, built A.D. 1562. The town is dull but prosperous, with good bazars. The chief industries of the place are the weaving of cotton *saris*, a trade which has a special bazar, the manufacture of carpets, which have a great reputation for durability, and copper and brass ware. Half a mile east of the city is the old fort, built of stone, circular in shape, half a mile in diameter, and surrounded by a wide, deep moat. It was built in 1599. In 1803 the fort was taken by the British; the breach is still visible, and a tree planted by Lord Wellesley, who commanded, still flourishes. British vandalism has not left much of the old Musalman architecture. A 16th century mosque has been converted into the collector's office; the judge's court was originally the handsome palace of a Musalman noble, built in the year 1600; the jail and civil hospital have been converted from other old buildings. There are still some old Musalman aqueducts to be seen outside the city.

There is a flourishing mission here in the hands of American Methodists, well deserving of a visit, and a most interesting college for the training of Christian schoolmasters, under the principalship of Mr. J. S. Haig, of the Christian Vernacular Society.

From Ahmednagar to Dhond there is nothing worthy of notice.

CHAPTER XXIX.

BOMBAY TO PUNA.

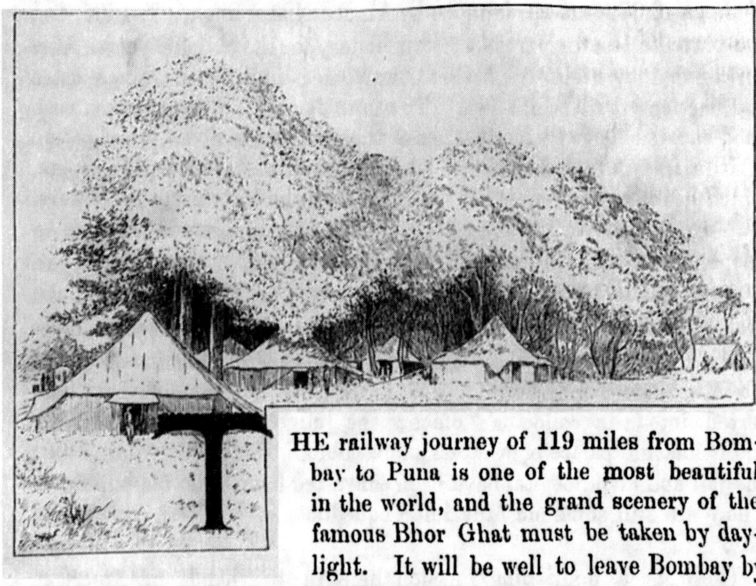

THE railway journey of 119 miles from Bombay to Puna is one of the most beautiful in the world, and the grand scenery of the famous Bhor Ghat must be taken by daylight. It will be well to leave Bombay by the 7.30 A.M. train, stopping for a few hours at Kalyan junction to see the curious old temple of Amarnath about four miles from the station. There is a small station at Amarnath itself, but it is better to drive from Kalyan. This temple is an unspoilt specimen of genuine Hindu architecture. An inscription on its face is dated A.D. 1060, and portions of it are 200 years older. The temple faces west, but the entrance hall has doors facing north and south also. Each of the three doors has a porch, approached by five or six steps, and supported by four square pillars. The entrance hall is 22·9 square, its roof supported by four very elaborately carved columns. In their details, no two are exactly alike; they are square at the base, becoming octagon about one-third of their height. The carving of these pillars is extremely beautiful and varied. The whole of the building (which is dedicated to Siva), outside and in, is finely sculptured with figures of Mahadeva, Parvati, Kali and Siva, with ascetics, monsters, and innumerable human figures and animals, carved with a skill not surpassed by any Hindu temple in India. Travellers visiting this temple should go the day before to one of the Bombay libraries, and read the interesting account given in Vol. III., p. 316, of the "Indian Antiquary," and Vol. XIV. of the "Bombay Gazetteer," pp. 2—8.

Kalyan is an ancient town, but with no antiquities left worth notice. It is now a thriving place, an important railway junction, with a population of 14,000, most of whom get their living by husking rice, the staple industry of the district.

Neral is the station for Matheran, a beautiful hill sanitarium, 2,460 feet above the sea, a favourite resort of Bombay Europeans. It is an eight mile climb to Matheran, but by writing the day before to an official known as "the Superintendent" at Matheran, ponies or palkis with coolies, will be provided to meet the train. The charge for ponies is two rupees each, and for palkis with twelve coolies, eight rupees. The path climbs up the face of the Ghat, skirting precipices, winding in and out among broken cliffs and leafy groves, with charming views at every turn. There are a great number of excellent hotels, the "Rugby" being on the highest ground, and the "Granville" the newest, with its windows open to the refreshing sea breeze that blows over Matheran. There are all the accessories of a well-established hill station: church, library, newsroom, lawn tennis, and gymkhana. All these nestle amid woods on a shallow tableland of about eight square miles, surrounded by a series of rocky promontories, which jut out into mid-air, their precipices falling 2,000 feet sheer into the valleys below. These promontories are called "points"—there are about sixteen of them, the most popular being known as Panorama, Louisa, Porcupine, Hart, Chauk, and Garbat points. The evening view from Panorama Point is exceedingly beautiful. It hangs over the level plain which stretches away to Bombay, forty miles off, whose towers and shipping, with the ocean beyond, are all golden in the setting sun.

The favourite excursion is to Prabal Point, where there is an ancient fort, thirteen miles off, perched on a rocky spur of a mountain, 4,000 feet high, in the midst of precipitous rocks of fantastic shapes. The path crosses a deep intervening valley, and affords an infinite variety of scenery.

From Louisa Point, in the rainy season, a splendid cataract, 100 feet

AT MATHERAN.

wide, falls into the valley in a single leap of 1,000 feet. All around Matheran Hill, 300 or 400 feet below the edge of the tableland, runs a plateau or terrace, clothed with richest verdure, with a ride running through the trees.

Matheran is a delightful place for the traveller who arrives at Bombay in October, after a fortnight's grilling in the Red Sea and the Indian Ocean.

Scattered about among the surrounding hills are little communities of Aborigines, Dhangars, Thakurs, Kathkaris, and other wild forest races.

At Karjat, sixty-two miles from Bombay, the ascent of the Bhor Ghat commences. The line rises 1,831 feet in fifteen miles; the average gradient being one in forty-eight. The total length of tunnelling is 2,535 yards. There are eight viaducts, varying from

52 to 168 yards in length, the highest of which is 139 feet. Some of the embankments are stupendous structures, one of which is seventy-four feet high. The cost of the incline was £41,188 per mile; a total of half a million sterling.

At 1,350 feet above the sea, the train stops ten minutes at the remarkable reversing station, to enable the powerful engines to pass to the other end. The view from this station, in the very heart of the Ghat, is superb. This marvellous engineering achievement is full of interest every yard of the journey; the time taken by the mail trains in climbing this railway ladder is an hour and twenty minutes.

Khandala, at the top of the Bhor Ghat, is a pretty summer retreat for the inhabitants of Bombay. There is a beautiful waterfall here, the upper cataract of which has a sheer drop of 300 feet. It is only worth visiting in the rainy season. The next station is Lonauli, where there are good waiting and refreshment-rooms, and a fair hotel. This is the best stopping-place to visit Kárli Caves, and good tongas with two ponies may be had by ordering beforehand from the station-master, or hotel-keeper, which will drive along the Puna road for four miles, and thence by a rough country track for about two miles more, to the foot of the mountains in which the cave is situated. An easy footpath, ascending about 600 feet, leads to the entrance. It is rather a tiring journey if taken in the heat of the day, but if the traveller sleeps at Lonauli, and makes an early morning start, so as to get the climb over before nine, there is nothing beyond the powers of an elderly lady in good health. I have left Lonauli at 7 A.M., spent two hours at the cave, and returned by noon.

The cave at Kárli is undoubtedly the largest and most complete Buddhist chaitya in India, and is so easy of access that it ought on no account to be omitted from the programme of an Indian tourist. A full description, with plans, sections, and views of the exterior and interior, will be found in Fergusson's "Indian Architecture," p. 116. For the benefit of those of my readers who have not been wise enough to provide themselves with a copy of this invaluable book, I append the following extract:—

"It is certainly the largest as well as the most complete *chaitya* cave hitherto discovered in India, and was excavated at a time when the style was in its greatest purity. In it all the architectural defects of the previous examples are removed; the pillars of the nave are quite perpendicular. The screen is ornamented with sculpture—its first appearance apparently in such a position—and the style had reached a perfection never afterwards surpassed.

"In the cave there is an inscription on the side of the porch, and another on the lion-pillar in front, which are certainly integral, and ascribe its excavation to the Mahárájá Bhúti or Deva Bhúti, who, according to the *Puránas*, reigned B.C. 78; and if this is so, they fix the age of this typical example beyond all cavil.

"The building resembles, to a very great extent, an early Christian church in its arrangements, consisting of a nave and side-aisles, terminating in an apse or semi-dome, round which the aisle is carried. The general dimensions of the interior, are 126 feet from the entrance to the back wall, by 45 feet 7 inches in width. The side-aisles, however, are very much narrower than in Christian churches, the central one being 25 feet 7 inches, so that the others are only ten feet wide, including the thickness of the pillars. As a scale for comparison, it may be mentioned that its arrangement and dimensions are very similar to those of the choir of Norwich Cathedral, or of the Abbaye aux Hommes at Caen, omitting the outer aisles in the latter buildings. The thickness of the piers at Norwich and Caen nearly corresponds to the breadth of the aisles in the Indian temple. In height, however, Kárli is very inferior, being only forty-two feet, or perhaps forty-five feet from the floor to the apex, as nearly as can be ascertained.

"Fifteen pillars on each side separate the nave from the aisles; each pillar has a tall base, an octagonal shaft, and a richly ornamented capital, on which kneel two elephants, each bearing two figures, generally a man and a woman, but sometimes two females, all very much better executed than such ornaments usually are. The seven pillars behind the altar are plain octagonal piers, without either base or capital, and the four under the entrance gallery differ considerably from those at the sides. The sculptures on the capital supply the place usually occupied by frieze and cornice in Grecian architecture; and in other examples, plain painted surfaces occupy the same space. Above this springs the roof, semicircular in general section, but somewhat stilted at the sides, so as to make its height greater than the semi-diameter. It is ornamented even at this day by a series of wooden ribs, probably coeval with the excavation, which prove beyond the shadow of a doubt that the roof is not a copy of a

ENTRANCE TO KARLI CAVE.

masonry arch, but of some sort of timber construction which we cannot now very well understand.

"Immediately under the semi-dome of the apse, and nearly where the altar stands in Christian churches, is placed the *daghoba*, in this instance a plain dome slightly stilted on a circular drum. As there are no ornaments on it now, and no mortices for woodwork, it probably was originally plastered and painted, or may have been adorned with hangings, which some of the sculptured representations would lead us to suppose was the usual mode of ornamenting these altars. It is surmounted by a Tee, and on this still stand the remains of an umbrella in wood, very much decayed and distorted by age.

"Opposite this is the entrance, consisting of three doorways, under a gallery exactly corresponding with our rood-loft, one leading to the centre, and one to each of the side-aisles; and over the gallery the whole end of the hall is open, as in all these chaitya halls, forming one great window, through which all the light is admitted. This great window is formed in the shape of a horse-shoe, and exactly resembles those used as ornaments on the façade of this cave, as well as on those of Bhaja, Bedsa, and at Násik. Within the arch is a framework or centering of work standing free. This, so far as we can judge, is, like the ribs of the interior, coeval with the building; at all events, if it has been renewed, it is an exact copy of the original form, for it is found repeated in stone in all the niches of the façade, over the doorways, and generally as an ornament everywhere, and with the Buddhist "rail" copied from Sánchi forms the most usual ornament of the style.

"The presence of the woodwork is an additional proof, if any were wanted, that there were no arches of construction in any of these Buddhist buildings. There neither were nor are any in any Indian building anterior to the Muhammadan Conquest, and very few, indeed, in any Hindu building afterwards.

"To return, however, to Kárli, the outer porch is considerably wider than the body of the building, being fifty-two feet wide, and is closed in front by a screen composed of two stout octagonal pillars, without either base or capital, supporting what is now a plain mass of rock, but once ornamented by a wooden gallery, forming the principal ornament of the façade. Above this, a dwarf colonnade or attic of four columns between pilasters admitted light to the great window;

and this again was surmounted by a wooden cornice or ornament of some sort, though we cannot now restore it, since only the mortices remain that attached it to the rock.

"In advance of this screen stands the lion-pillar, in this instance a plain shaft with thirty-two flutes, or rather faces, surmounted by a capital not unlike that at Kesariá, but at Kárli supporting four lions instead of one; they seem almost certainly to have supported a *chakra*, or Buddhist wheel. A similar pillar probably stood on the opposite side, but it has either fallen or been taken down to make way for the little temple that now occupies its place.

"The absence of the wooden ornaments of the external porch, as well as our ignorance of the mode in which this temple was finished laterally, and the porch joined to the main temple, prevent us from judging what the effect of the front would have been if belonging to a free standing building. But the proportions of such parts as remain are so good, and the effect of the whole so pleasing, that there can be little hesitation in ascribing to such a design a tolerably high rank among architectural compositions.

"Of the interior we can judge perfectly, and it certainly is as solemn and grand as any interior can well be, and the mode of lighting the most perfect—one undivided volume of light coming through a single opening overhead at a very favourable angle, and falling directly on the altar or principal object in the building, leaving the rest in comparative obscurity. The effect is considerably heightened by the closely-set thick columns that divide the three aisles from one another, as they suffice to prevent the boundary walls from ever being seen; and, as there are no openings in the walls, the view between the pillars is practically unlimited.

"These peculiarities are found more or less developed in all the other caves of the same class in India, varying only with the age and the gradual change that took place from the more purely wooden forms of these caves to the lithic or stone architecture of the more modern ones. This is the principal test by which their relative ages can be determined, and it proves incontestably that the Kárli cave was excavated not very long after stone came to be used as a building material in India."

There are other minor caves of the same character at Bhaja and Bedsa, both of which places are within easy riding distance of Lonauli, of which full particulars are given by Fergusson, pp. 110-116.

There is a Dak bungalow at Kárli Station, two miles from Kárli cave, five from Bhaja, and nine from Bedsa; but as no ponies or tongas can be obtained there, they must be ordered from Lonauli.

From Lonauli to Puna, a distance of forty miles, the line runs through a rough country, most of which is under spade tillage. Many of the battles of the Maratha wars were fought on this ground.

DECCAN COUNTRYMAN.

CHAPTER XXX.

PUNA.

PUNA is a handsome city of 130,000 population, the military capital of the Deccan, and the summer capital of the Bombay Presidency. Puna is comparatively modern, being known in Indian history as the capital of the Maratha Peshwas, the dynasty which ruled the Deccan from 1715 A.D. until 1818, when the seventh and last Peshwa, Baji Rao, watched from the horseshoe window of the temple of Parvati the final rout of his forces by the British on the Field of Kirki. His adopted son, Nana Sahib, wreaked a fearful vengeance on the British forty years afterwards. Sindhia, Holkar, and the Gaekwar of Baroda, are all offshoots of this great Hindu kingdom of the Marathas. The Peshwas were a dynasty of raiders and fighters rather than builders, and Maratha monuments are mostly impregnable fortresses and inaccessible castles, perched on the hills of the Deccan, rather than palaces or temples.

The European side of Puna is laid out in fine rectangular roads, wide and well made, shaded by avenues of trees. The bungalows of the residents are pretty and picturesque, with bright gardens and compounds. There are all the usual features of a first-class European station—clubs, libraries, gymkhanas, excellent hotels, of which the "Napier" is the principal, churches, livery stables, and shops. The Victoria Gardens are on a terrace, overlooking the Mula River, across which a weir has been thrown, keeping the water always at the same level throughout the dry season. The view up the river is picturesque in the extreme, being closed in by the beautiful hill of Parvati. Here a band plays in the evening three times a week, and hither resort the "beauty and fashion" of Puna.

The native city has all the characteristics of a prosperous Hindu community. It extends along the bank of the small river Muta, on high ground, for about a mile and a half. The only noteworthy buildings are the old palace of the Peshwas, which was burnt down in 1827, and is only a mound of ruins within the still standing fortified wall, and some fine mansions of Maratha nobles, one of which, the old Deccan college, with its double courtyards surrounded by carved teak galleries and pillars, is open to public inspection. The classes have been removed to a handsome modern building in the suburbs. The bazars are handsome and well stocked with shops; pretty little squares, nicely planted, occurring at frequent intervals. Puna, like Nasik and Ahmadabad, is famous all over India for beautiful brass-work of all sorts, especially idols. Here and there in the bazar may be picked up old swords, and other weapons of the fierce Maratha times.

In the jewellers' shops may be purchased the graceful head ornaments, in gold, silver, or lac, of which the Maratha women are so fond; armlets which, by a peculiar double bend, grasp the arm firmly; chain-like anklets, lighter and more refined than those of Gujarat. Figures in plastic clay, painted, and dressed up in muslin and silk, illustrating all the types and castes of the Deccan, can be obtained for a few annas, and are really beautiful works of art, if made by one of the better craftsmen. Throughout the leading bazars are shops whose occupants are engaged in making lovely sham jewellery of some sort of perfumed composition; bracelets, necklaces, chains, and anklets of various seeds, such as the scarlet and black seeds of *ganja*, the flat black seeds of the *turwar*, red seeds of the *rukta chandan*, the mottled seed of the betel nut, and the deeply furrowed seeds of the *rudraksh*, which latter are worn by Musalman fakirs. These pretty trinkets are ridiculously cheap. Peacocks' feathers are made up with cuscus grass, green beetles' wings and spangles, into fragrant, showy fans and mats; charming embroidered slippers may be purchased at the shoemakers' shops; weavers are at work on beautiful yellow silk

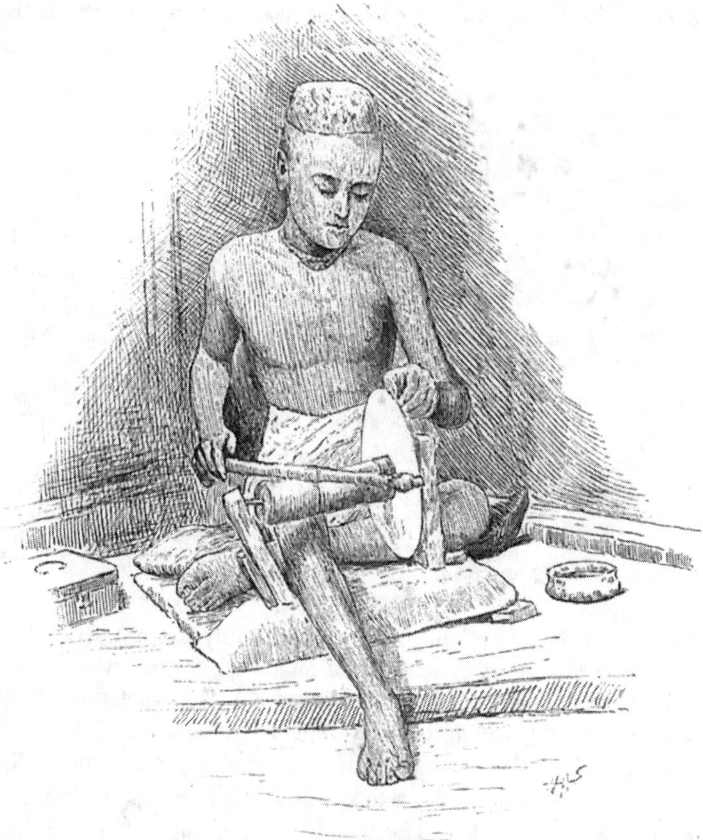

A TINSEL CUTTER, PUNA.

pitambars, worn by both sexes on sacred feast days; turban folders sit gravely among their wooden dummies.

A flourishing trade is carried on in gold and silver wire and thread, lace, and foil, and all manner of tinsel ornaments. It is in Puna that the richest and costliest border for *saris* is made, the famous *shikar*, or hunting pattern, woven in gold and silver threads into a woof of fine silk: all these, with the thousand and one other native handicrafts of a large Hindu city, render the Puna bazars specially attractive to everyone interested in Indian art and manufacture.

The most attractive suburb of Puna is that on the south side of the city, where lies the Hira Bagh, or Diamond Garden, and beyond it the

THE HILL OF PARVATI, FROM THE LAKE.

famous hill of Parvati. The garden is beautifully laid out with a lake and island, a villa built by one of the later Peshwas, a little mosque, and some pretty temples and summer-houses. The vegetation of the Deccan is seen to good effect in the Diamond Garden, which has been carefully planted with every variety of tree and shrub indigenous to the district. The borders of the lake are thick with grasses, rushes, and water plants of all sorts. The temple-crowned hill of Parvati rises almost from the edge of the lake. A long winding flight of wide steps leads to the summit in a gradual ascent, so scaled that elephants can travel by it. On the level summit is the fine temple to Parvati, built by the Peshwa Balaji Baji Rao in 1749, at a cost of a million rupees, within which is a silver image of Siva, with a golden Parvati and Ganesh on his knees. At each corner of the temple court are small shrines to Surya, the Sun god, Vishnu, Kartikaya, the War god, and Durga. Parvati is the wife of Siva, but at Puna she is worshipped for the more gracious side of her character, as *anna purna*, the food-giver, *uma*, the light, or *gauri*, the brilliant. Those who favour her terrible side, may worship at the lesser shrine of Durga in the corner of the courtyard. The Brahmans who hang about the steps to act as guides can generally speak English enough for their

TURBAN FITTERS, PUNA.

business. On the west side of the hill is a ruined palace of the Peshwas, injured by lightning sixty years ago.

The view from the hill embraces Puna, and all the country round, closed in by the blue Ghats in the dim distance.

Some pretty river scenery is to be found at the Sangam, where the Muta and the Mula rivers meet. Here are several well-built temples, sacred to Mahadeo, surrounded by well-planted gardens, affording a pleasant morning or evening stroll. The beautiful house and gardens of Sir Albert Sassoon, known as Garden Reach, are near the Sangam, and are worth visiting if permission can be obtained. The house is sumptuously decorated and furnished, and the gardens remarkably well kept up.

The Government house is reached by an easy drive of three miles, and is called Ganesh Kind. It is a handsome mansion, devoid of interest.

A MARATHA BRAHMAN.

Fourteen miles from Puna is one of the finest of the many old Maratha fortresses scattered throughout the Deccan.

Sinhgarh (the lion's fort) is situated on a rugged and isolated mountain, 4,162 feet above the sea. From the slopes of the mountain rises a great black wall of rock, forty feet high, on the top of which is placed the fort on a triangular piece of tableland, nearly two miles round. This plateau is surrounded by a strong wall flanked with towers. There are two gateways, the *Puna*, and the *Kalyan*. Within the walls are several bungalows to which the European inhabitants of Puna resort during the hot weather in April and May. This is a very ancient fortress. It was blockaded by the Delhi Emperor Tughlak in 1340, was captured by Ahmad Shah in 1486, was won by a bribe by Sivaji in 1647, who gave it its present name, and made it a very strong place. In 1565 Sivaji was blockaded out of it by a Mughal force, and in 1670 it was retaken by Tanaja Malrusa, its capture forming one of the most daring exploits in Maratha history.

In 1702 it resisted a siege by Aurangzeb for nearly four months, when it was betrayed by the commandant, to be retaken by the Maratha forces in 1706. It remained in their undisturbed possession till 1818, when it was stormed by British troops, and finally dismantled.

The journey is an easy one, as a good driving road goes from Puna to the foot of the mountain, where the carriage must be exchanged for a chair on poles, carried by coolies up the two and a half miles of winding pathway which leads to the summit. It is well to start before daybreak, that the ascent may be made in the cool of the morning. Ten miles from Puna, Lake Fife is passed, a fine reservoir that irrigates the country between its outlet and Puna, and also forms the principal water supply of the city.

The view from the fort is magnificent, stretching over the vast and fertile plain of Puna on the one hand, and commanding a fine panorama of the Ghats and their outlying spurs on the other. On one of these spurs, a few miles to the southward, may be descried another fortress called *Purandar*, which has also borne its part in Maratha warfare.

Jijuri, about seventeen miles from Puna, is famous for its great temple, picturesquely built on the top of an isolated hill, 250 feet high, dedicated to Khanderao, an incarnation of Siva. This temple was built 200 years ago by one of the Holkars. The road which winds up the hill is studded with pillars, gateways, carved images and other votive offerings. There is an enormous drum in the temple, which is heard for miles round when struck.

There are several educational institutions at Puna of some importance, the most notable of which are the Engineering College, the Deccan College, the first grade High School, the female Normal School and a training school for Anglo-Vernacular teachers.

Puna is a great centre of Brahmanic influence, and there are no less than 50,000 Brahmans in the Puna district.

The Free Church of Scotland has a flourishing mission in Puna, with 140 communicants and seven schools, with nearly 1,000 scholars; the Rev. John Small is the superintendent, who also conducts much religious work among the British troops in the cantonment. The Rev. R. A. Squires represents the Church Missionary Society, which has 100 communicants and two small schools.

MAHABLESHWAR.—The beautiful hill station of Mahableshwar is within an easy day's journey from Puna. A train leaves Puna by the Southern Maratha line at about 7.30 A.M., which arrives at Wathar

A WAI MARATHA.

about 1.30. Here there is an excellent refreshment-room, where a good tiffin may be had by writing the day before. Two-horse carriages may be arranged for through Mr. Ardasir Framji, mail contractor, Mahableshwar, who has an office in the Civil lines at Puna. The drive from Wathar station to Mahableshwar is through a very pleasant undulating country, with the mountains in the distance. The road being hot and dusty, some travellers prefer to leave Puna by the afternoon train, spend the night at the Wathar bungalow, and go on in the cool morning air, which blows fresh off the hills.

The distance is about forty miles, and the ascent begins at Wai, about half way. There is an excellent Dak bungalow at Wai, where tea may be had, and good meals by sending word beforehand to the messman. Wai is a lovely spot on the banks of the sacred Krishna, embosomed in trees, and surrounded by an amphitheatre of lofty hills.

The banks of the river are lined with pretty temples, stone ghats, bathing-houses and shrines, in the midst of beautiful foliage. The view from the bridge is one of the most picturesque in India, and a good panorama of all the riverside temples may be had from the garden of the Dak bungalow. A very beautiful temple is to be seen at Dom, five miles from Wai, with a splendid fountain of white marble, the edges of which are carved with lotuses, and a pillar of white marble, crowned with the five heads of Siva, with clusters of cobras round them. At Wairatgarh eight miles up the valley is one of the finest banyan trees in the country.

The road from Wai winds slowly up a steep ghat. With extra mules harnessed to the carriages, the ten miles to Panchgani are accomplished in about two hours. Here are several bungalows belonging to Europeans and Parsis from Bombay, and a good Dak bungalow. The remaining ten miles to Mahableshwar are along a good and fairly level road. Seven hours are usually taken to travel from Wathar to Mahableshwar.

There are several excellent hotels at Mahableshwar. I can speak well of the "Fountain," which affords a sublime view from its verandahs, and is very well managed.

Mahableshwar is a wide plateau, six or seven miles long and about three miles at its widest, the edge of which, seaward, is a vast, sharply-sloping precipice, verdure clad from top to bottom, except where great spurs of rock jut out into the air. The principal of these spurs are Lodwick, Sidney, Kate's, Olympia, and Elphinstone Points, from all of which superb prospects may be obtained.

The plateau is 4,500 feet above the sea, and is laid out with many miles of excellent drives and rides, leading to all the various "points," waterfalls, and other picturesque scenery with which Mahableshwar abounds. This sanitarium is, of course, chiefly resorted to during the hot weather, but it is uninhabitable during the rains of the south-west monsoon, from the middle of June to the end of September. It is at its best in October, November, April, and May. I had the Fountain Hotel to myself for a few days in January, 1889; the temperature averaged about 64°, 45° to 50° at night, rising to over

80° at midday. The air was clear as crystal, and the heavens at night beyond all description beautiful. The finest view is from Elphinstone Point, from the end of which there is a sheer precipice of some 1,800 feet; but all the points should be visited in succession, as each presents some feature differing from the rest. Lodwick Point is the best from which to view the precipice of Elphinstone, and the rocky mountain on the top of which is the old Maratha fortress of Partabgarh.

Near Elphinstone Point is the old village of Mahableshwar, where there are two or three very ancient and venerated Hindu temples erected over the source of the sacred river Krishna, to which god the temples are dedicated. The principal building covers a tank, surrounded by pillared recesses. At the head of the tank is a stone cow, from whose mouth holy Krishna trickles, in a stream of pure clear water, to gladden the land for 800 miles before he reaches the Bay of Bengal. The village and temples form a quaint group of buildings, embowered in trees of dark foliage. The falls of the Yena are at the head of a mountain gorge of singular wildness and beauty. The river tumbles over the edge of a cliff 500 feet deep. After the rains it is a magnificent sight, but in the winter it dries up to a slender stream, which, as it falls, is dissipated into thin, iridescent spray.

The great fortress of Partabgarh was selected for its unique position of impregnable strength by Sivaji, the founder of the Maratha power, in 1656. It lies about twelve miles from Mahableshwar, on an excellent road, which presents an infinite variety of magnificent scenery. There is a very charming and comfortable Dak bungalow at the foot of the hill, where chairs and coolies can be obtained for the steep and difficult ascent, which practised walkers can climb in about an hour and a quarter. The fort is 3,543 feet above sea level, the walls of the lower fort forming a sort of crown round the brow of the summit. The western and northern sides of the fort are gigantic cliffs with an almost vertical drop of 700 or 800 feet. The towers and bastions on the other side are thirty or forty feet high, on the edges of scarps about the same height. The main entrance is reached by a long, winding flight of steps cut in the solid rock, and in Sivaji's time Partabgarh must have been a hopeless task to a besieger, only to be conquered by treachery or starvation. It was through the latter it surrendered to the British forces in 1818.

HILL AND FORT OF PARTABGARH, FROM MAHABLESHWAR.

Sivaji, nicknamed by Aurangzeb, the Mountain Rat, has given legends to almost all these stern, old Maratha forts scattered along the spurs of the Western Ghats. It was from Partabgarh that he issued, after offering sacrifice to the horrid goddess Bhawani, to the committal of the most detestable act of treachery that stains the pages of Indian history. Under the pretence of making peace with the Brigadier-General Afzul Khan, who was besieging the fortress, he led him into a secluded place, and under cover of a fraternal embrace, ripped his bowels open with a weapon called *wagnak*, or the "tiger's claw," concealed in his left hand, and stabbed him, at the same time, to the heart with the *bichwa*, or "scorpion dagger," hid up his right sleeve. Sivaji is the great hero of the Maratha Hindus. His descendants are held in deep reverence, and these treacherous weapons, with other relics, are still religiously preserved at Kolhapur and Satara; his famous sword, Bhavani, being an object of profound worship to this day at Kolhapur.

In the Mahableshwar seasons, it is possible to return to Bombay by Partabgarh and Warra to Dasgaon, whence a steamer plies across the bay to Bombay; but in the cold season this route is closed, and the only way to or from Mahableshwar is by Wathar and Wai.

The return journey may however be varied by driving through Satara, to Satara Road station, through Irmal, Kilgarh, and Khinzir. Satara is thirty-one miles from Mahableshwar, and the road excellent all the way; Satara Road station forty-one miles. The scenery, especially about the Kilgarh ghat, is very fine, of the same nature as that from Mahableshwar to Wai.

SATARA.—The next station beyond Wathar is Satara Road, from which Satara city is distant ten miles. Tongas can be had by writing to the station-master beforehand.

Satara is the chief town of the district of the same name, with a population of 30,000. It is a clean town, with good, wide streets, at the foot of a steep, rocky hill, on the top of which is perched a strong fort, which possesses seventeen (*satara*) walls, towers, and gates, and thus gives the name to the town. Satara stands 2,320 feet above sea level, is exposed to the breezes from the sea, and is altogether a very pleasant and picturesque spot. There is a good Dak bungalow. The water supply is excellent, drawn from a large tank on a neighbouring hill, conducted by an aqueduct four miles long. The old palace of the Maratha chiefs is a plain, dull building, without any interest. It is the house of fighters who saw little of their homes, and cared less about them. The new palace is hard-by, a huge, rambling, building, with a vast hall 160 feet long by 50 wide, and a façade painted over with garish Hindu frescoes.

A Raja of the old family lives in a house near the palace, who still possesses the sword of Sivaji, the crown jewels of the Satara rajas, and some other family relics of antiquarian interest, which may be seen by arrangement with his secretary.

The fortress is an ancient one, dating from A.D. 1192, when it was built by a Raja of Panhala. The gate and walls are all that are left standing, the buildings in the interior having been destroyed. A good panorama of the Mahadeo hills and Sahyadri range is to be had from the fort. The special art crafts of the Satara bazars are ivory carvings, beautiful silk loom fabrics embroidered with gold borders, and gold and silver wire.

Three miles from Satara, at the junction of the Krishna and Yena rivers, is Mahuli, a picturesque place of much holiness, where the Hindu dead of the Satara district are brought to be burned. There are fifteen or twenty handsome temples on the brink of the two rivers, the oldest of which, built about 200 years ago, is a very fine specimen of Hindu architecture. Mahuli was a favourite spot for the widow sacrifice of *Sati*, before it became illegal.

Returning to Satara Road station, the next stopping-place of interest will be Miraj station, from which Kolhapur, the thriving capital of a native state of the same name, is distant thirty miles. Any traveller wishing to visit this interesting city should write to Mr. Dhamvati, mail agent, Kolhapur, who runs a daily tonga to and from Miraj.

KOLHAPUR is one of the Deccan group of native states, with an area of 2,816 square miles, and a population of 800,000. The Rajas trace descent from Raja Ram, a younger son of the great Maratha chief, Sivaji. The present prince is still a minor, a promising lad of about sixteen years of age. The revenue of the State is about £220,000, and the Raja's income £170,000.

The picturesque native capital has a population of about 40,000, and has been greatly improved of recent years, many costly modern buildings having been erected. It is a great centre of trade, its streets being thronged by merchants from a wide circle of country, dressed in their various distinctive attire. There is a good Dak bungalow in the cantonment.

Kolhapur has for centuries been held in esteem throughout the Deccan for the antiquity of its temples. Its origin was that of a religious settlement, clustering round the great temple of Mahalakshmi, the goddess of plenty and good luck. The extreme antiquity of Kolhapur is emphasised by the number of Buddhist remains discovered in the neighbourhood, and notably a crystal relic casket found in a tope, with inscriptions on the lid identifying its deposit with the 3rd century B.C. Small but very ancient temples have been excavated at Karavira, close to the city, which is believed to have been the site of the capital of the district at a remote period.

The fort was built by a king of Bijapur, A.D. 1560–70. The palace square is a fine group of buildings, entered through a stone gateway. Opposite the palace is the treasury, and the other sides of the square are occupied with Government offices, a gymnasium, and the high school. Behind these is the temple of the tutelary goddess of the town, Amba Bai, whose brass image is carried round the town in procession on festival days. This temple is about 150 feet square, built of black stone, and the height to the topmost pinnacle is over eighty feet. It is a mass of elaborate carving, inside and out, of the Jain style of decoration, and the date over the porch is the equivalent of A.D. 1218. The great bell of the temple is Portuguese work.

The entrance to the palace square is called the Nakar Khanah, or "Music Gallery;" it is a curious and somewhat bizarre structure.

The city is surrounded by a very strong wall, thirty feet high, with a wide, deep ditch in front. There are numerous fortified bastions, and six strong gateways, studded with iron spikes, to resist the battering by elephants. The entrances are over drawbridges. The palace is in the centre of the town, the main streets radiating from it to the walls, with circular lanes crossing them. In the suburbs are some fine cenotaphs of previous rajas in a pretty walled garden. The hill forts of Panhala and Pawangadh, with Joteba's Hill, are within ten miles of the city, and have much interest to the antiquarian.

There are several Buddhist caves, and many shrines and temples on Joteba's Hill, and Panhala was a strong fortress in the 12th century. Within its solid walls Sivaji built two stone granaries, still standing, 130 feet long, fifty-seven feet wide, and thirty feet high. One of the entrances is a fine *Tin Darwaza*, or triple gateway, richly decorated with sculpture. The building called Sadoba's Temple was once a pavilion for the ladies of the governor.

There are also two or three interesting tombs, and an old 15th century tank, in which a large number of Brahmani women drowned themselves, from fear of the British soldiers, when the place was stormed during the Maratha war. Panhala was one of Sivaji's favourite castles.

At Gokak, on the railway between Miraj and Belgaum, the Gatparba River tumbles headlong down a narrow gorge in a single leap of 180 feet. In the rainy season this is one of the most magnificent scenes in India, but in December and January, when the European tourist is at large, it shrinks up to nothing, its bulk in July being as nearly as possible 350 times the volume it is then. The falls are some miles from the railway. A polite note to the station-master at Gokak Road will get all necessary information with regard to conveyances and lodging.

Belgaum is the chief town of an important district, and a cantonment for about 4,000 troops. Its population is about 25,000. There is a strong fort, built in 1648, surrounded by a broad wet ditch, without any features of interest.

The special trades of its bazars are bells for bullocks, clay figures, and fruits, cotton-spinning and weaving, and red fancy pottery. There are two Jain temples of the early part of the 13th century and a good mosque. Belgaum is a popular and healthy station.

At Londa Junction, the branch line to Goa turns off, the terminus of which is Murmagao Harbour, whence ferry boats ply to Goa city, or Panjim, the capital of the Portuguese territory, where there is an hotel.

Goa is a Portuguese settlement, the oldest European colony in the East Indies. Its territory measures sixty-two miles long by forty miles at the widest part, with a total population of about 450,000. It is a mountainous country with several peaks from 3,000 to 4,000 feet above the sea. There is a fine harbour at Goa, with two good roadsteads, one called Alguada and the other Murmagao, at the terminus of the railway. The inhabitants are of three classes, Europeans, Eurasians, and natives. More than half the population are Roman Catholic, the rest Hindu. All the native Christians wear European dress, the women still wearing the sari, over a Europeanized garment.

The Archbishop of Goa is the primate of the East, exercising jurisdiction over the Catholics of all the Portuguese Colonies, and much of British India also.

There are now no religious orders, the churches being under secular priests, who are all Goanese. The Catholics of Goa are very devoted to their religion. All other creeds enjoy perfect liberty of conscience, and have their own temples and mosques.

The trade of Goa is the melancholy ghost of its former prosperity, and is still dwindling. There are no banks of any kind. Good roads prevail throughout the colony, and forty-nine miles of the railway from Murmagao runs through Goanese territory.

Goa has no navy, but it defends itself from all invasion with a standing army of 313 men of all ranks, and maintains its domestic government with a police force of 900 men. It enjoys one telegraph office at Goa city, or Panjim as it is called locally, of which the British Government pays half the cost. There are two good hospitals, and some excellent religious charities, one of which is as old as the days of D'Albuquerque. Education is fairly well provided for in all its branches. The revenue and expenditure balance, and amount to about £105,000.

The administration consists of a Governor-General, and a council composed of the Chief Secretary, the Archbishop, the High Court Judges, two military officers, and the heads of departments.

The history of Goa as a Portuguese settlement dates from A.D. 1510, when Alfonso D'Albuquerque, with twenty ships and 1,200 soldiers, took bloodless possession of it from the Bijapur kings of the Deccan. He was driven out a few months after, but, reinforced from Portugal, reconquered it by a horrible and bloody assault, after which he fortified it, and established a Portuguese Government which has lasted till to-day. After seventy or eighty years of constant fighting, conquest and reconquest, during which the celebrated Jesuit missionary, Francis Xavier, lived, died and was buried in the gorgeous church of Bom Jesus, Goa reached its summit of prosperity at the end of the 16th century. When English enterprise was struggling into barely tolerated existence in India, "Golden Goa" presented a scene of military, ecclesiastical, and commercial magnificence which has never been rivalled since, and to which modern Calcutta has no parallel.

It had no staying power. In 1603 the Dutch began to assert themselves in the East and blockaded Goa. This was the beginning of a struggle lasting seventy years, during which time, one by one, nearly all the Portuguese possessions fell into the hands of Holland,

and the power of Portugal was shattered and dismembered. For 200 years Goa has steadily deteriorated, with a few spasms of revival, until now it has become a pathetic wilderness of ruined churches and palaces, with not a twentieth part of the population which in its hey-day thronged its prosperous streets and quays.

Of the ancient Hindu city, not a trace remains. Old Goa, conquered by D'Albuquerque, built by the Musalmans in 1479, and virtually rebuilt by the Portuguese during the 16th century, is now a desolate expanse of ruins, in the midst of which, in decayed and melancholy splendour, some noble churches still remain, with a population surrounding them of less than 2,000 souls.

The oldest of these churches is the Convent of St. Francis, originally a mosque, converted into a church by the Portuguese. Its chief portal has been preserved intact, but the rest of the building was reconstructed in 1663. The cathedral was first built in 1512 by D'Albuquerque, on St. Catherine's day, to her dedication, being the day on which he entered Goa. This also was entirely reconstructed in 1623 in its present majestic proportions, 250 feet long, 180 feet wide, the front being 100 feet wide and 116 feet high. The chapel of St. Catherine was erected in 1551. The church of Bom Jesus was built as a shrine for the great Indian missionary, Francis Xavier, whose magnificent tomb of marble and jasper was the gift of the Grand Duke of Tuscany, and enjoys a world-wide reputation. Events in the life of the saint are represented in about thirty tableaux round the shrine.

The Convent of St. Monica was built in 1606, and the convent church of St. Catejan in 1665; the latter is an imitation of St. Peter's at Rome.

The once renowned palace of the viceroys has entirely vanished, and so has the great custom-house. But there are still the dilapidated ruins of the famous palace of the Inquisition, the colleges of St. Roque and St. Paul, the Hospital of St. Lazarus, the arsenal, and the ecclesiastical prison, as well as many churches and chapels. The gardens of these, and of the mansions of the Portuguese nobles, are now cocoanut plantations, the ruins smothered in jungle, and the streets grass-grown. Old Goa lives in the past, but is still dear to every pious Indian catholic, many of whom every year visit the sacred shrine of the great Eastern evangelist, whose memory lives, not in its pomp and splendour, but in the hearts of the million of

Christians in India who bear witness to-day of his success as a missionary.

Panjim, or New Goa, is a handsome little town, built about 120 years ago. From the river, it has a very picturesque appearance, with its stately row of public and private buildings, and the old fort, now converted into a viceregal residence. There are no antiquities, or buildings calling for notice for their architectural beauty. The British India Company's steamers call regularly at Goa for Bombay going north, and coast ports to Calcutta going south.

CHAPTER XXXI.

BIJAPUR.

BIJAPUR.—Returning from Goa by rail, the only through train in the day leaves Murmugao at 7.30 A.M., and joins the southern Maratha Railway at Londa Junction at 1 P.M., reaching Belgaum at 4.29. Most travellers, however, will not care to return to Puna, but will continue southward to Bangalore, or eastward, *viâ* Bijapur to Haidarabad, which latter course I shall take with my readers, as there is nothing of much interest to the average tourist between Londa and Bangalore. I may, however, note in passing on, that the new route opened up through Harihar is the best and quickest from Bombay to Mysore and Bangalore. The train leaves Londa for Hubli at 1.30, arriving there at 6.4 P.M. Hubli is a thriving town of 40,000 inhabitants, the centre of the cotton trade of the Southern Maratha country. It was once the seat of an English factory, plundered in 1673 by Sivaji.

There are a great number of ancient Jain temples in the neighbourhood of Hubli, and a fine old fort in the city itself, but nothing of a character that cannot be seen to better advantage elsewhere. There is a good Dak bungalow. I advise the traveller to push on to Gadak, which is reached at 8.55 P.M., where there are a number of interesting old Hindu temples, richly sculptured, some of which date as far back as the 10th century.

The only train in the day on the East Deccan line leaves Gadak at 7 A.M., and arrives at Bijapur 3.30 P.M. At Badami, on the way, there is a very interesting Jain cave temple, A.D. 650, three Brahmanic caves a little older, and two venerable and curious Dravidian temples, which will prove attractive to the archæologist. Some account of these will be found in Fergusson, pp. 261, 411, 439—444. Badami was the Chalukya capital of the district in the 6th century, when it was a place of some note, being visited by Hiuen Tsiang, the Chinese traveller, who gives a glowing account of its splendour.

The whole districts of Dharwar and Bijapur abound in old forts, sculptured temples, and religious houses of the Lingayat sect, many of which are now used as Dak bungalows. There is, however, no one building that is exceptional, and travelling is not very easy.

BIJAPUR is the headquarters of the district which now bears its name, but was formerly known as Kaladgi. The interest of the city lies in the superb remains of a great Musalman dynasty, distributed within and without its six miles of walls.

The founder of the Musalman State of Bijapur was, according to Ferishta, a son of Murad II., the Osmali Sultan, on whose death his son and successor, Muhammad II., gave orders that all his own brothers should be strangled. From this fate one only, named Yusaf, escaped by a stratagem of his mother. After many adventures, Yusaf is said to have entered the service of the King of Ahmadabad-Bidar, where he rose to the highest offices of state. On the king's death, he withdrew from Ahmadabad to Bijapur, and declared himself its king; the people readily acknowledged his claim. Yusaf reigned with great prosperity, and, extending his dominions westward to the sea-coast, took Goa from the Portuguese. His resources must have been considerable, as he built the vast citadel of Bijapur. He died in 1510, and was succeeded by his son Ismail, who died in 1534, after a brilliant and prosperous reign. Mulu Adil Shah having been deposed and blinded, after an inglorious reign of only six months, made way for his younger brother Ibrahim, a profligate man, who died in 1557. He was succeeded by his son Ali Adil Shah, who constructed the wall of Bijapur, the Jama Masjid, or great mosque, the aqueducts and other works. This ruler joined the kings of Ahmadnagar and Golconda against Raja Ram, the Hindu sovereign of Vijayanagar, who, with the exception of the Emperor of Delhi, was the greatest potentate in India. Raja Ram was defeated in 1564 in a great battle at Talikot on the river Dhon, and being made prisoner, was put to death in cold blood, and his capital taken and sacked. Ali Adil Shah died in 1579.

The throne then passed to his nephew, Ibrahim Adil II., an infant, whose affairs were managed by Chand Bibi, widow of the late King, a woman celebrated for her talents and energy. On Ibrahim assuming the government he ruled with ability; and, dying in 1626, after a reign of forty-seven years, was succeeded by Muhammad Adil Shah, under whose reign Sivaji, the founder of the Maratha power, rose into notice. Shahji, the father of Sivaji, had been an officer in the service of the King of Bijapur; and the first aggressions of Sivaji were made at the expense of that State, from which, in the interval between 1646 and 1648, he wrested several forts. Soon afterwards he took possession of the greater part of the Konkan. Muhammad, however, had a more formidable enemy in the Mughal Emperor, Shah Jahan, whose son and general, Aurangzeb, besieged the city of Bijapur, and was on the point of taking it, when he precipitately marched to Agra, whither he was drawn by intelligence of court intrigues, which he feared might end in his own destruction. After his departure, the power of Sivaji rapidly increased, and that of the King of Bijapur proportionately declined. Muhammad died in 1660, and was succeeded by Ali Adil II., who, on his decease in 1672, left the kingdom, then fast descending to ruin, to his infant son, Sikandar Adil Shah, the last of the race who occupied the throne.

In 1686 Aurangzeb took Bijapur, and put an end to its existence as an independent State. Its vast and wonderful ruins passed, with the adjoining territory, to the Marathas during the decline of the Delhi empire. On the overthrow of the Peshwa in 1818, they came into the hands of the British Government, and were included within the territory assigned to the Raja of Satara, who manifested much anxiety for the preservation of the splendid remains of Muhammadan grandeur in Bijapur, and adopted measures for their repair. Since the escheat of Satara in 1848, from failure of heirs, the Bombay Government has acted in the same spirit, having taken measures with the approbation of the authorities in England, for arresting the further progress of dilapidation in the buildings, as well as for collecting and preserving the relics of manuscripts, coins, copper-plate inscriptions, and other curious and interesting memorials of the past.

On the transfer of the headquarters of Kaladgi district to Bijapur, however, many of the old Muhammadan palaces were utilised for public purposes. In the process, the persons entrusted with the duty showed themselves vandals and utter barbarians. They made a Dak bungalow of the fine mosque attached to the beautiful tomb of Sultan Muhammad, running up partitions between the arches to make separate rooms, daubing the whole building over with whitewash. Another lovely mosque, with specially characteristic architecture and decoration, has been turned into a post-office, its archways filled in, British windows inserted, and, horrible to relate, a galvanized iron verandah from Wolverhampton run along the front. The Eidgat of Aurangzeb is a police station, the Mekka Masjid a courthouse, the mosque of the tomb of Ibrahim some other office, and the whole lot whitewashed in red, white or blue, according to the fancy of the Goth who conducted the operations. Nearly every bungalow used by the civil service is the ruined and desolated shell of some fine old Musalman building. One of the grandest ruined cities in the world has been smirched and disfigured, and only those more massive monuments that could not be adapted to a cutcherry or a central distillery, have escaped undamaged. The Vandalism is as bad as though Tintern Abbey were converted into a brewery, Kenilworth into a workhouse school, or York Minster into a cavalry barracks.

Bijapur is a magnificent and desolate ruin, only outrivalled in desolation by Fatehpur-Sikri. It represents a style of its own, a specially beautiful variety of Indo-Saracenic architecture only to be found in the Deccan; it is of all its period the only superb example left comparatively intact and unruined, except by the Vandalism just referred to. Bijapur in its glory covered as large an area as Paris; but little is left of the city itself, its palaces, gardens, mosques and tombs, outside the fort, being, with one or two exceptions, shapeless masses of jungly ruins. The walls of the fort still stand, and form an irregular circle about six miles in circumference, enclosing the citadel, whose palaces, mosques and Jain temples, with their grass-grown courts and tamarind trees, are tolerably well preserved, and extremely picturesque. The great number of carved and sculptured Hindu and Jain stones used in the building of the citadel, especially about the main gateway, attest to the importance and splendour of Bijapur before the Musalman dynasty. There are two or three ancient Jain temples still intact, with slight additions, showing that they have

JAMA MASJID, BIJAPUR.

been used as mosques. In one of these there is a very remarkable black stone pillar beautifully wrought in elaborate sculptures, which the guide will be sure to point out. The principal palaces in the citadel are the Sat Khandir, or house of seven stones, an extraordinary building of great loftiness, used as a pleasure palace by the ladies of the harem; the Anand Mahal, or joy palace, which was the apartment of the women of the household; the Gazan Mahal, or paradise palace, with three archways fifty feet high, the centre one being nearly seventy feet wide; the Mihtar Mahal, in front of which are two fine gateposts of stone; and the Suneri Mahal. The Mekka Masjid is a lovely little gem.

The Jama Masjid, which lies half way between the citadel and the Alipur gate, was commenced by Ali Adil Shah, A.D. 1557, continued by his successors, but never finished, the fourth side and the great gateway not having been commenced when the dynasty collapsed. It is one of the noblest mosques in India. The pillared, arched, and dome-cloistered court-yard is 331 feet by 257 feet, measured over all. The mosque itself is 257 feet by 145 feet. It is divided into forty-five squares, about twenty-four feet each, nine of which are occupied in the centre by the grand dome, forming a square measuring seventy feet each way. The dome is fifty-seven feet in diameter in the circular part, and is about 110 feet to the crown. This mosque is undoubtedly the finest in the Bombay presidency, and one must travel 1,200 miles to Ahmadabad to find anything to compare with it, or with its predecessor at Kalbargah.

Ali Adil Shah had great ambitions with regard to his own tomb, which he commenced on the colossal scale of 200 feet square. It is, however, almost level with the ground, for his successor, Ibrahim, did not go on with it, but gave all his attention to his own, which stands just outside the Mekka Gate. This is a singularly beautiful mausoleum, covered all over inside and out with elaborate and finely executed carving. It is said that the entire Koran is engraved upon its surface. The cornices are supported by elaborate brackets, and the windows filled with tracery; originally all this decoration was gilt on blue ground, and traces of this decorative treatment may still be seen. There are two apartments in the building, forty feet square, the stone roof of the lower one, perfectly flat, being supported by a projecting cove, forming the floor of the upper, which is within the dome.

Next to the tomb is an equally beautiful mosque, which has been barbarously converted into some office connected with the collectorate. In the surrounding garden are many kiosks, fountains, tanks, serais and other buildings, the whole forming a series of oriental pictures almost unique, even in India.

But the great glory of Bijapur is the stupendous domed mausoleum of Sultan Mahmud, which lies near the walls, a quarter of a mile to the right of the Alipur Gate. It is built upon a platform 600 feet square. The interior is a vast apartment 135 feet square, being the largest domed room in the world, more than 2,000 feet larger in area than the Pantheon at Rome.

At a height of fifty-seven feet from the floor line the hall begins to contract, by a series of ingenious and beautiful pendentives, to a circular opening ninety-seven feet in diameter. On the platform of these pendentives the dome is erected 124 feet in diameter, leaving a gallery more than twelve feet wide all round the interior. Internally the dome is 175 high, externally 198 feet, its thickness being about ten feet. The dome of St. Paul's, London, is sixteen feet less, and that of St. Peter's at Rome twelve feet greater in diameter, than that of the tomb of Sultan Mahmud. Fergusson gives a most interesting

SULTAN MAHMUD'S TOMB, BIJAPUR.

treatise on this marvellous mausoleum, with sections and diagrams, pp. 562—6 of his History of Indian Architecture.

The tomb of Khawas Khan and his Sheik Abdur Rajak, of Begam Sahibah, one of Aurangzeb's wives, and of Kishwar Khan, are fine buildings worthy of notice if time permit.

The Taj Baoli or Royal well, is just inside the Mekka Gate: there is a tank in front about 250 feet square, stocked with fish. There is a curious arcade to the right of the well, into part of which some public office has been jammed.

There are several fine old guns here and there round the walls, on the different bastions. On the Upari Burj, a tower over sixty feet high, there are two iron guns, the largest of which is thirty feet long with a twelve-inch bore.

On the top of the Lion Bastion, built in 1688, is a famous old gun of bronze, called the Malik-i-Maidan, or lord of the plain. It is fourteen feet long, and the same diameter from breech to muzzle, five feet, the bore being 2 ft. 4in. wide. It has not been fired off for sixty years, when it was charged with eighty pounds of powder by a Raja of Satara. It is probably as old as the bastion on which it is placed.

THE MALIK-I-MAIDAN.

Bijapur has a population of about 12,000, but apart from its buildings has no interest of any kind to the traveller.

Hotgi is a journey of six hours from Bijapur; it is the junction of the East Deccan Railway with the main line of the Great Indian Peninsular Railway. There is a good refreshment room with sleeping accommodation at the station.

Hotgi is devoid of interest; the next station westward towards Puna is Sholapur, a thriving town of some importance, with a population of 60,000. There is a good Dak bungalow close to the station. Sholapur has been a place of note in the Deccan for 700 or 800 years. Its fortress, small but very strong, was built by Hasan Gangu, the founder of the Bahmani dynasty in 1345. The walls of the city have been mainly destroyed to make room for its rapid growth during recent years.

Sholapur is an industrial town, noted for its silk and cotton cloth. A fine cotton mill has been recently built, with over 20,000 spindles, and some 200 looms.

Travelling east from Hotgi, the first place of importance is KALBARGAH, in the territory of the Nizam of Haidarabad. Its population is 24,000. In early times it was a Hindu city of great extent.

GREAT MOSQUE, KALBARGAH.

Hasan Gangu selected Kalbargah as his capital in 1347. His dynasty remained there till 1442, when the capital was transferred to Bidar, after which the mosques and palaces, which had been erected by successive kings, fell into ruin and decay. The outer walls and gateways of the old fort are now in a dilapidated condition. The citadel still stands almost intact. There are some curious old guns in the bastions; one of the largest has twenty rings on each side for lifting purposes. The temple of Raja Kalchand is in the fort. It is a vast pillared hall, with 100 columns thirty-five feet high. It measures 212 feet by 167.

The tombs of the Bahmani kings are about two or three furlongs outside the fort. The first king's tomb (Hasan Gangu) is a plain building about seventy feet square and 100 feet high. They are none of them remarkable for anything but dirt, being mostly used as stables and cow-houses, their only decoration being the fuel of the country, drying on their outer walls.

The only thing worth stopping to see at Kalbargah is the great Masjid, modelled after the famous mosque of Cordova in Spain, its chief peculiarity being, that, alone among the great mosques of India, its whole area of 38,000 feet is covered in, the light being admitted through the walls, which on three sides are pierced with arches. It is undoubtedly one of the most distinctive buildings in India, and quite one of the finest and most remarkable of the old Pathan mosques. There are full particulars with ground plan and sections in Fergusson, pp. 552—6.

The old bazar of Kalbargah is a unique building 570 feet long by sixty wide, a double row of sixty-one arches on each side, supported by pillars, with blocks of buildings at each end highly decorated.

There are other fine buildings and tombs scattered about the city, many of which are curious and different from the usual Musalman architecture of the period, but their history is lost in obscurity. One of the most interesting is of a later date than the rest, being a serai, mosque and college built by Aurangzeb.

CHAPTER XXXII.

THE NIZAM'S STATE.

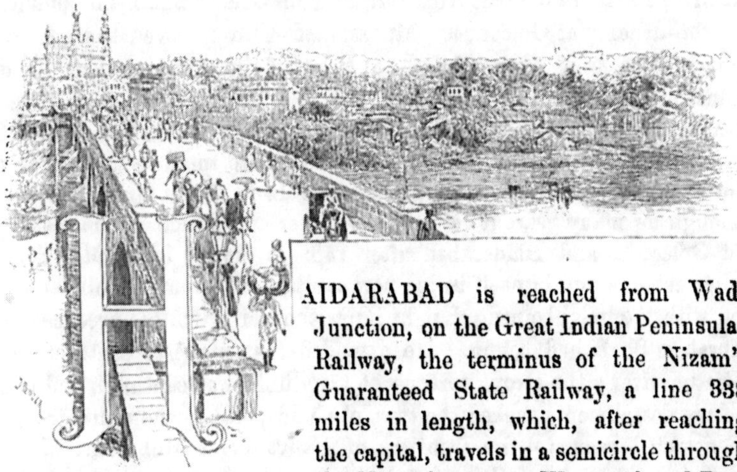

HAIDARABAD is reached from Wadi Junction, on the Great Indian Peninsular Railway, the terminus of the Nizam's Guaranteed State Railway, a line 338 miles in length, which, after reaching the capital, travels in a semicircle through the Nizam's state to Warangal and Bez-Wada, on the rich delta of the Krishna river, whence a rapidly extending network of canals communicate with the sea at Masulipatam, and with the Godavari through Ellore. There are three trains a day each way between Wadi and Haidarabad, one train only from Haidarabad to Bez-Wada. The average traveller, however, is not likely to extend his journey beyond Haidarabad. There is a good refreshment room, and sleeping accommodation at Wadi Junction.

The interest of Haidarabad centres in the fact that it is the largest native state in India, and that the Nizam is by far the most important of all the independent princes. His dominion, excluding Berar, which is assigned for the present to British administration, is 80,000 square miles, and the population in 1881, 9,846,000, of whom one tenth only are Musalman, a notable instance of the wonderful tenacity of Brahmanism on the Hindu mind. The revenues of the state are about £4,000,000. The Nizam Mir Mahbub Ali was born in 1866. He ranks as the first Muhammadan ruler in India, and is entitled to a salute of twenty-one guns. He maintains a standing army of 15,000 strong, besides a large body of irregular forces.

The following brief history of Haidarabad is taken from Hunter's Gazetteer :—

"Haidarabad was founded in 1589, by Kutab Shah Muhammad Kuli, the fifth in descent from Sultan Kuli Kutab Shah, the founder of the dynasty at Golconda. Muhammad Kuli removed the seat of government from Golconda on account of its want of water and consequent unhealthiness, and built a new city on the banks of the Musi river, seven miles from his former capital. He called it *Bhagnagar*, 'Fortunate City,' from his favourite mistress, Bhagmati; but after her death he named it Haidarabad, 'The City of Haidar,' though for many years it retained its former appellation. The history of Golconda and Haidarabad after 1589 is almost identical. Soon after establishing himself in his new capital, Muhammad Kuli carried on with the neighbouring Hindu Rajas the war which his predecessor Ibrahim Shah had begun. He extended his conquests south of the Kistne river; the strong fortress of Ganditoka was captured, and one of his detachments sacked the town of Cuddapah. Some of his troops penetrated even to the frontiers of Bengal, and Muhammad Kuli defeated the Raja of Orissa, and subjugated the greater part of the Northern Circars.

"In 1603, an ambassador from Shah Abbas, King of Persia, arrived at Haidarabad with a ruby-studded crown and other magnificent gifts. The palace of Dil-kusha was allotted to the envoy, who remained there six years, receiving from Muhammad Kuli £2,000 annually for his expenses. When the ambassador left for Persia, an officer of the court of Haidarabad accompanied him, bearing return presents, and amongst them some gold cloth manufactured at Paitan, which it took five years to make. In 1611, Muhammad Kuli died, after a prosperous reign of thirty-four years. The principal memorials of this monarch are the palace and gardens of Ilahi Mahal, the Muhammadi gardens, the palace of Nabat Ghat, the *Char Minar* or college, and the *Jama Masjid* or 'Cathedral' Mosque. According to the accounts of Mir Abu Talib, the king's private treasurer, £2,800,000 was expended on public works during the reign of Muhammad Kuli, and £24,000 was distributed every year among the poor. The king's example of liberality was followed by his nobility; and the number of handsome buildings throughout the dominions of the Kutab Shah monarch is unsurpassed, if not unequalled, in any other of the Muhammadan kingdoms of the Deccan.

"Muhammad Kuli was succeeded by his son, Sultan Abdulla Kutab Shah. The Mughals under Shah Jahan, the fifth emperor (1627—58), now make their appearance in Southern India. Aurangzeb, Shah Jahan's son, was sent as viceroy into the Deccan by that prince, who seemed bent on compensating for failures beyond the Indus by the subjugation of Bijapur and Golconda. The immediate cause of his attack upon the latter kingdom was an appeal from Mir Jumla, the prime minister, whose son had involved him in a dispute with the court. Mir Jumla finding himself unable to obtain such concessions as he desired from his own sovereign, determined to throw himself on the protection of the Mughal Emperor. Such an opportunity for intrigue suited Aurangzeb's character, and he strongly urged his father to entertain Mir Jumla's petition. Shah Jahan, influenced by this advice, issued a mandate to Abdulla to redress the complaints of his minister; but Abdulla was so incensed by this questioning of his independence that he sequestrated Mir Jumla's property, and committed his son, Muhammad Amin, to prison. Shah Jahan now despatched Aurangzeb to carry his demands into effect by force of arms. Under pretext of escorting his son Sultan Muhammad to Bengal, to wed the daughter of his brother Prince Shuja, Aurangzeb made a treacherous attack upon Haidarabad. The road from Aurangabad (the capital of the Deccan) to Bengal made a circuit by Masulipatam in order to avoid the forests of Gondwana, and thus naturally brought the viceroy within a short distance of Haidarabad. Abdulla Kutab Shah was preparing an entertainment for Aurangzeb's reception, when he suddenly advanced as an enemy, and took the king so completely by surprise that he had only time to flee to the hill-fort of Golconda, seven miles distant, whilst Haidarabad fell into the hands of the Mughals, and was plundered and half burned before the troops could be brought into order. Abdulla did all in his power to negotiate reasonable terms, but the Mughals were inexorable; and after several attempts to raise the siege by force, he was at last forced to accept the severe conditions imposed on him, viz., to give his daughter in marriage to Sultan Muhammad, with a dowry in land and money; to pay a crore of rupees (£1,000,000 sterling) as the first instalment of a yearly tribute; and to make up the arrears of past payments in two years. Mir Jumla remained in the service of the Mughals, and became a favourite general of Aurangzeb, and one of the most useful instruments of his ambition.

"Abdulla died in 1672, and was succeeded by his son-in-law, Abu Husain, who in his youth had been notorious for dissipated habits. He fell entirely under the influence of a Maratha Brahman, named Madhuna Panth, who became his prime minister. In 1676, at the invitation of this man, Sivaji, the founder of the Maratha supremacy, entered Haidarabad with a force of 70,000 men, on his way to the Karnatic. He also concluded a treaty with Abu Husain. Sivaji's reception at Golconda afforded grounds for a war with the state of Bijapur, but the invasion was resisted and defeated by Madhuna Panth. Sivaji died in 1610, and was succeeded by his eldest son, Sambaji, with whom Abu Husain also entered into an alliance. Aurangzeb was prevented from at once turning his arms against Golconda, owing to a convention made by his son, Prince Muazim. When in 1686, Khan Jahan was sent against that state, and found himself unable to oppose its army, he begged urgently for reinforcements; and Prince Muazim was despatched to his assistance. The leader of the Golconda troops proved unfaithful to his cause, and allowed the united forces to proceed unmolested to Haidarabad, where he joined the Mughals with the greater part of his troops. The king, Abu Husain, shut himself in the fort of Golconda; and Haidarabad was again left open to plunder. Madhuna Panth was killed in a popular tumult, and the king accepted such terms as he could obtain. A payment of two millions sterling in money and jewels was demanded. The treaty, however, was of short duration, for in 1687 Aurangzeb formally declared war against Abu Husain. The king bravely defended the fort of Golconda for seven months, and lost it at last by treachery, and was sent a captive to Daulatabad, where he resided until his death. Abu Husain was a very popular monarch, and many anecdotes of his virtues are still current in the Deccan. Aurangzeb immediately took possession of all the territories of Bijapur and Golconda, but his occupation was little more than military. The districts were farmed out, and were governed by military leaders, who received twenty-five per cent. for the expense of collecting the revenue.

"No event of any importance occurred at Haidarabad until 1707, the year of Aurangzeb's death. A dispute for the crown took place between his two sons, Prince Azím and Prince Muazim. The latter was victorious, and ascended the throne as Bahadur Shah. Prince Kam Bakhsh refused to acknowledge his brother as king; and Bahadur Shah, after attempting in vain to win him over by concessions, marched against him to the Deccan, and defeated him in a battle near Haidarabad (February, 1708), in which Kam Bakhsh was mortally wounded. Bahadur Shah then made a truce with the Marathas: and affairs in the Deccan remained quiet until the end of his reign in 1712. The vice-royalty was given to Zulfikar Khan, an adherent of Prince Azim; and the administration of the Government to Daud Khan, a Pathan officer, who had distinguished himself under Aurangzeb. The death of Bahadur Shah was followed by struggles amongst his sons. The incapacity of the eldest, Jahandar Shah, had given a great ascendancy to the second, Azim-us-Shan, who was supported by the army and the nobility. A battle ensued; Azim-us-Shan was repulsed and slain, and Jahandar Shah remained undisputed master of the throne. One of his first acts was to put all the princes of the blood within his reach to death. Among those whom he could not get into his power was Farukhsiyyar, the only son of Azim-us-Shan; but the cause of this prince was espoused by the Governor of Behar, Sayyid Husain Ali. The rivals met near Agra on the 28th of December, 1712; and on the 1st of January, 1713, Farukhsiyyar ascended the throne and conferred dignities upon all his adherents. Among these was Chin Khilich Khan, a noble of high rank, and a brilliant statesman, to whom was given the title of Nizam-ul-mulk Asaf Jah. Zulfikar Khan was put to death, and Sayyid Husain Ali appointed viceroy of Deccan in his stead. But the emperor was jealous of his powerful subject, and wished to get rid of him. He therefore wrote to Daud Khan, promising him the vice-royalty if he would attack Husain Ali on his arrival in the Deccan and destroy him. No more acceptable commission could have been offered to Daud Khan than that of revenging the death of his friend and patron, Zulfikar; and taking up a position at Burhanpur, he proclaimed himself viceroy, and awaited Husain Ali's appearance. A severe battle was fought, in which Daud Khan was on the point of victory when he was struck by a bullet and killed instantly (1716). Husain Ali immediately took the field against the Marathas, but was completely routed. He and his brother, Sayyid Abdulla Khan, the Wazir of the Deccan, now united their forces against Farukhsiyyar, whose schemes for the destruction of Husain Ali had proved abortive. In December, 1719, the allies advanced upon Delhi, and the emperor submitted to their demands, which became more exorbitant day by day, and ended in their obtaining possession of the royal citadel and palace, which were occupied by their troops. In February, 1719, Fàrukhsiyyar was deposed, and two months later put to death by order of Husain Ali and Abdulla Khan.

"The two Sayyids, as the brothers were called, selected as emperor Rafi-ud-daula, who died in a few months. He was succeeded (1719 to 1748) by Muhammad Shah, the last independent emperor who sat on the Delhi throne. The first great event in his reign was the overthrow of the two Sayyids, which was effected in great measure by a league between Asaf Jah and Saadat Khan, his coadjutor and rival, and afterwards the founder of the Oudh dynasty. Asaf Jah saw in the disturbed condition of the country an excuse for raising troops; and as he perceived the difficulty of establishing a permanent control at Delhi, he determined to lay the foundation of his power on a firmer basis, and turned his attention first to the Deccan. His plans against the Sayyids succeeded. In October, 1720, Husain Ali was assassinated, and at the end of the year Abdulla Khan was defeated and taken prisoner by Muhammad Shah; but the power of this monarch was rapidly declining. In January, 1722, Asaf Jah arrived at Delhi, and assumed the office of Wazir. He found the court in a state of utmost weakness; the emperor and his favourites were given up to pleasure, and after some months of mutual dissatisfaction, they devised plans to free themselves from the troublesome counsels of Asaf Jah. The Wazir was despatched against the refractory governor of Gujarat, but speedily returned, strengthened by the addition of a rich province. In October, 1723, shortly after this victory, Asaf Jah resigned his post as Wazir and set off for the Deccan, a proceeding amounting in reality to a declaration of independence. The emperor, although he graciously accepted Asaf Jah's resignation, and conferred on him the title of Lieutenant of the Empire—the highest that could be conferred on a subject—did not on that account abate his hostility. He sent orders to the local governor of Haidarabad to endeavour to dispossess the viceroy, and assume the government of the Deccan in his place.

"Mubariz Khan entered zealously on his task, and succeeded in gathering together a powerful army. Asaf Jah protracted negotiations for several months, and endeavoured to sow sedition among the adherents of the governor. At last he was forced to come to open war, and soon gained a decisive victory over Mubariz, who lost his life in the battle, fought in October, 1724. As the emperor had not avowed the attack which he had instigated, Asaf Jah, not to be outdone in dissimulation, sent the head of Mubariz to court with his own congratulations on the extinction of the rebellion. He then fixed his residence at Haidarabad, and became the founder of an independent kingdom, now ruled over by his descendants, who derive from him the title of Nizams of Haidarabad State."

There is no hotel at Haidarabad, and Europeans will not find it easy to get accommodated. At Secunderabad, four miles distant, there is a very comfortable hotel close to the station, as well as an excellent Dak bungalow.

Secunderabad is a British military cantonment, the largest station in India, the headquarters of the Haidarabad subsidiary force, which constitutes a division of the Madras army. There are usually stationed here about 3,000 European, and 5,000 native troops of all sorts. This force is maintained by the British Government by treaty with the Nizam, in lieu of certain contingent and auxiliary forces which had been previously raised by him to co-operate with the British army, but which had proved inefficient. The cost is defrayed out of the revenues of the assigned district of Berar. The cantonment covers an area of nearly twenty square miles, including the beautiful tank, the Husain Sagar, and the magnificent parade ground. A short distance from Secunderabad, at Trimalgiri, is a strong entrenched camp capable of accommodating all the Europeans in the district in case of need. Secunderabad is not a healthy station, except during the cold season.

The capital, Haidarabad, is encircled by a strong bastioned stone wall, six miles in circumference, pierced with thirteen fine gateways. The population within the city walls is 124,000, and in the suburbs 231,000 more; total 355,000. It stands in the midst of wild and rocky scenery, with isolated granite peaks. In the hollows are pretty tanks, some of which are very large, the one which supplies the city with water being twenty miles in circumference.

The buildings of the city are homely and without much architectural pretensions, but the bazars are picturesque beyond all description.

The Nizam, as the most important Musalman potentate possessed of an Asiatic capital, has attracted to his service, civil and military, Muhammadans from almost every part of Asia and even Africa, all of whom go about armed to the teeth with the quaint weapons of their countries, and wearing their distinctive dresses. Turks, Arabs, Moors, Afghans, Zanzibaris, Persians, Bokhariots, Rohillas, as well as Sikhs, Rajputs, Marathas, Parsis, Madrasis, and every variety of Hindu swarm in the chief streets of Haidarabad. The best way to see the city is from the back of an elephant. The only broad street runs from the Afzal gate right through the city.

Haidarabad, being a comparatively modern capital, has nothing of antiquarian and little of architectural interest to attract the traveller.

The Nizam's palace consists of three enormous quadrangles surrounded by buildings, handsome enough, but devoid of character.

These courtyards are full of armed retainers, servants, horsemen, carriages and elephants, and at busy periods of the day are very amusing. There is, however, nothing to be seen inside or outside the palace but the usual tasteless display of splendour characteristic of modern Indian princes. It accommodates 7,000 people of all sorts.

In the very centre of the city, at the junction of the four main streets, is the famous Char Minar, or four towers, built about A.D. 1600, upon four grand arches, above which are several storeys of rooms originally devoted to a college but now used as a store-house. The building is four square, each face being 100 feet, and the minarets soar into the air 250 feet above the level of the street.

This is the busiest spot in the whole city, and hours may be spent watching the amusing and picturesque scenes surrounding the Char Minar.

The Jama, or Mekka, Masjid, designed after the one at Mekka, is a very grand building. The pillars of the courtyard are lofty granite monoliths. Its minarets are very beautiful, and are about 100 feet high, it was built by Muhammad Kuli Kutb Shah about A.D. 1600.

Sir Salar Jung's palace, the Bara Dari, is a fine modern mansion

MAIN STREET OF HAIDARABAD, WITH CHAR MINAR.

of great size, surrounded by beautiful gardens; in the stables are several magnificent elephants and a fine stud of horses.

The suburbs of Haidarabad are remarkably attractive and beautiful. They are enriched by splendid gardens, magnificent pavilions, charming drives, tanks, bridges and deer parks.

Near the railway station is a pretty zoological garden, with some fine tigers and other animals and birds.

The British residency is situated in the suburb of Chander Ghat; it is one of the finest modern residences in India. It is on the banks of the River Musa, opposite to the Nizam's palace, communicating with it by the Oliphant Bridge.

The residency was built in 1808, and was constructed entirely by native workmen. The north front, which looks away from the river and city is adorned by a splendid portico, reached by a flight of twenty-two granite steps, the lowest of which is sixty feet long and flanked by huge stone sphinxes.

The hall is sixty feet long, thirty-three feet broad, and fifty feet high, and all the other rooms are in proportionate size. The staircase is the finest in India, each step being a single block of the purest granite. The whole building is richly decorated and handsomely furnished in a way likely to impress the oriental mind. The residency stands in beautiful pleasure grounds, surrounded by a grim wall of great strength with two gateways. The resident is not oppressed by all this splendour, but lives in a snug house of his own hard by within the grounds.

The Jahan Numa palace is in the suburb of that name; it is in the midst of rice fields crossed by a causeway. At the end of it a long street with houses on both sides, built for the accommodation of retinues of distinguished visitors, leads up to a large courtyard. At the end of this is the palace, an odd building with a terraced garden at the back as high as the topmost room. The palace is full of those mechanical nick-nacks of which Indian rajas are so inordinately fond, of the "drop-in-a-penny-and-the-machine-works" kind, and other curiosities; in the garden are cranes of various sorts and a few animals in cages.

The Mir Alam tank is a beautiful sheet of water about two miles long, embanked by twenty-one large and massive granite arches, laid on their sides, the arch abutting into the lake. At the west end of this lake, which is very picturesquely embayed, is a low wooded hill, on the top of which is the Dargah of Mahbub Ali. This is a charming little shrine, once covered with blue tiles, from which a fine view of the lake and surrounding country may be obtained.

The Husain Sagar tank spreads itself out on one side of the road from Haidarabad to Secunderabad, for a distance of two or three miles. A new palace for the Nizam is being built on the shores of this fine lake, and the whole way between the two towns will soon become a continuous line of mansions and bungalows, built by the Musalman nobles who resort to the court of the Nizam. This road is the fashionable evening drive and ride, the gayest in India; for the Haidarabad nobles pride themselves above all things on their stables and carriages.

Golconda is an ancient fortress and ruined city about seven miles west of Haidarabad. In former times Golconda was a large and powerful kingdom of the Deccan, which rose out of the ashes of the

GOLCONDA FORT.

Bahmani dynasty. Aurangzeb annexed it to Delhi in 1687, and it has been deserted ever since. It was the capital of the Kutub Shahi kings, who held their court here from 1512—1687.

The diamonds of Golconda, of proverbial celebrity, were only cut and polished here, being found at Partial close to the frontier. The plain in which Golconda is situated is stony and arid, with enormous boulders of granite piled one on the top of each other in strange and fantastic heaps. In the midst of these rises a solitary hill about 250 feet high crowned by a sombre fortress. Ranged along the foot, on the plain, are the tombs of the kings, a row of vast mausoleums, a

TOMBS OF THE KINGS, GOLCONDA.

veritable Necropolis, solitary and deserted. Not many years ago these tombs were overgrown with grass and jungle, but the late Sir Salar Jung has cleared it all away and done much towards the intelligent repair and restoration of these interesting monuments.

The tombs are similar in character though differing in size and height. Each tomb stands on a square terrace. It consists of a quadrangular arcade with minarets at the four corners. The body of the building rises squarely above the terrace of this arcade, flanked with smaller minarets, and from this level the magnificent dome springs into the air. They are built of the granite of the country, and in their pristine glory were decorated with stucco and encaustic tiles, of which some remain.

The finest tomb is that of Muhammad Kuli Kutb Shah, the builder of the Char Minar and the Mekka mosque at Haidarabad. It is 180 feet high, the dome being sixty feet high. There are some magnificent single blocks of granite worked into this tomb, especially the pillars and pilasters of the portals. This building was decorated with encaustic tiles, of which a few remain, suggestive of the beauty of the whole.

Although Haidarabad has no buildings that rank with the finer monuments of India, it is an intensely interesting and beautiful city, differing in its characteristics from every other native capital. Jaipur,

Baroda, Maisur, or Indore, are Hindu capitals, with Hindu customs. Haidarabad is a survival of dominant Islamism, with Musalman customs. It is a remnant of the gorgeous East, a page out of the "Arabian Nights." Haidarabad has never been brought under the heel of England. There are no Babu clerks, or college and high-school students, thronging the streets and bazars, but good valiant swashbucklers, bristling with daggers and matchlocks.

The civil service, as well as the military, is manned in all its ranks by Musalmans imported from Upper India, and the ever ubiquitous Bengali has no chance whatever. The nobles are feudal barons, with enormous estates, which they govern in their own fashion without much heed to the central authority, maintaining their fine palaces and princely hospitality in the capital. They are easy-going followers of the prophet, especially in the matter of champagne and other convivial accessories. Their hospitality is boundless, and any Englishman well introduced into Haidarabad, will want to stay as long as he can. There is the most cordial relationship between them and the many Englishmen resident in the city, visiting and entertaining each other with a freedom existing nowhere else in Musalman society. The English club admits native gentlemen as members, and the officers of the Nizam's forces dine at the messes of the British officers at Secunderabad. A Haidarabad native gentleman understands European manners and customs perfectly, and speaks English fluently. All the freedom, however, is confined to men, and the ladies of their households are as tightly secluded as in other Musalman communities.

The trade crafts of Haidarabad are much the same as those of other Deccan cities. There are, however, one or two special manufactures worth noticing. It is a great market for piece goods woven of silk and cotton mixed, known as *Mashru* or *Sufi*. It is not lawful for Musalmans to wear pure silk, so they mix the silk with cotton; hence the well-known Indian fabrics with a cotton warp, and the woof of soft silk in a striped pattern, having the lustre of satin; this is called *Mashru*, or "permitted." Some of the *Mashrus* are figured in gold or silver. The *Sufis* or "lawful" pieces are mixed in stripes and checkers, or figured; they have no satiny shine, but are more like glazed calico. They are glazed with a preparation made from quince seeds. There is also a considerable manufacture of *Makhmal*, the gorgeous and costly gold-embroidered velvets used for canopies of state, umbrellas of dignity, elephant and horse trappings and caparisons, whose sumptuous gold scroll ornamentation is Italian in origin, and no doubt was introduced by the Portuguese. Some of the best oriental pile carpets are made in Haidarabad, though better ones are produced at Warangal and the villages round. The very finest rugs exhibited at the 1851 Exhibition came from Warangal, their peculiarity being the exceedingly fine count of the stitches, about 12,000 going to the square foot; the colours were wonderfully blended,

ANCIENT GATEWAY, WARANGAL.

and kept in subjection by their judicious distribution and the extreme closeness of the weaving. The cost of these beautiful rugs was about £10 per yard, and they may be seen at the India museum at South Kensington. Persian competition has almost ruined the carpet trade of Haidarabad, but anyone who knows his way about an Indian bazar, can still find specimens in the Nizam's country that excel anything else to be got in India.

The red earthenware pottery of Haidarabad is well-known in the Eastern shops of London, and is very pretty and artistic. There is no place in India where it is so easy to get together a collection of armour and weapons. The service of the Nizam has for a long time attracted the warlike Musalman tribes of India and Central Asia, who have brought their weapons with them. Every kind of shield, sword, knife, dagger, matchlock, spear, battle-axe, pistol, helmet, and breast-plate, engraved, damascened, sculptured, or jewelled,—may be picked up in the Haidarabad bazar, and so, too, may very base imitations, manufactured on the spot, to snare the unwary traveller.

The Wesleyan Missionary Society is active in Haidarabad, having stations also at Secunderabad and other places in the Nizam's dominions. They have nine missionaries, a total membership of about 300, with some 1,400 scholars in twenty-eight schools. The Rev. Wm. Burgess is chairman of the district and general superintendent. The Society for the Propagation of the Gospel, the American Episcopal Methodists, and the American Baptists, also are in the field, the latter having a small station in Hanumancondah.

Warangal is eighty-seven miles from Secunderabad. The train leaves at 11.15 A.M., and reaches Warangal at 6.15, returning next day at 3.15 P.M. Warangal is a small town of about 4,000 inhabitants, interesting only to the antiquarian. It was the ancient capital of the Hindu kingdom of Telingane, which merged by conquest into the hands of the Bahmani kings. At Warangal there are four Kirte Stambhas, as they are called, facing one another, as though forming the gateways of a square enclosure. There is no trace of any wall, however, or of any building having been erected within the supposed enclosure. They were set up about 1150 A.D., by Pratapa Rudra, who built the Great Temple at Hanumancondah, a still older capital, six miles from Warangal. Fergusson looks upon these remarkable erections as lineal descendants of the four gateways at Sanchi, and they have probably been erected to replace some wooden structure fallen to decay.

The "thousand-pillared" temple of Hanumancondah is one of the most remarkable in India. It is a triple building with three large detached chambers, in front of which is a beautiful portico, supported by hundreds of pillars, dispersed in a complicated manner, with great beauty of detail, and differing in design. The windows are beautifully pierced stone slabs. The doorways are superb.

All round Warangal there are a great number of smaller temples and shrines, in the same style, and dedicated like it to Siva—they are mostly in ruins. At Warangal wild silk is spun and woven into very pretty fabrics. It is a long and weary journey from Warangal

PORTICO OF TEMPLE, HANUMANCONDAH.

to Bez Wada, the terminus of the Nizam's state railway. The distance is only 130 miles, but it takes nine hours to accomplish it. Bez Wada contains much that is interesting to the archæologist, including some rock-cut temples of the Buddhist period, and some very ancient Hindu pagodas. Bez Wada is on the banks of the Kistna river, which is here confined between two hills about 1,300 yards apart, through which it flows with considerable velocity, six and a half miles an hour in flood; below Bez Wada it widens out into a channel three or four miles wide, and has formed a wide and rich delta. It is estimated that the Kistna in flood carries past Bez Wada sufficient alluvial matter to form a deposit one foot deep over a surface of five miles. One of the most important irrigation works in India is at Bez Wada. The anicut is very massive, being nearly 1,300 yards long, 263 broad, and rising twenty feet above the river bed. The water thus caught is conducted by 254 miles of main channels to irrigate 226,000 acres, bringing in a revenue of nearly £100,000 a year. The daily train on the Nizam's railway leaves Bez Wada at 6 A.M., arriving at Warangal 3.15 P.M., Secunderabad, 9.40 P.M., and Wadi Junction, 6.15 A.M., making an average speed of sixteen miles an hour. In all probability the Bellary Kistna Railway will be open for passenger traffic before this volume is published. The traveller will then be able to proceed from Bez Wada through Nandial to Adoni on the Madras Railway, without coming back through Haidarabad (*see* next chapter).

CHAPTER XXXIII.

HAIDARABAD TO MADRAS.

FROM Wadi junction to Raichur the journey occupies about three hours. There is good sleeping accommodation at the refreshment rooms. Raichur is an old town and fortress in Haidarabad state. The present population is about 15,000. The fort consists of a citadel enclosed with a double line of fortifications. The inner wall contains an inscription in Sanscrit stating that it was built by King Vithala A.D. 1294. The gateway was built by Sultan Ibrahim Adil Shah, A.D. 1570. The citadel stands 290 feet above the plain, and is in remarkably good preservation. There are some interesting buildings inside the wall of the fort, including a pretty shrine. The view from the top is very extensive. There is a curious old gun on one of the bastions with the breech blown away, showing that it is made of longitudinal iron bars bound together by two wrought iron coils. The town is well-built, with good wide bazars. Raichur is noted for the excellence of its glazed pottery and embroidered slippers.

Raichur is the south-eastern terminus of the Great India Peninsula Railway, where it makes junction with the north-west line of the Madras Railway.

ADONI.—The first place of any importance on the Madras Railway is Adoni in the Madras Presidency, an ancient place with far-reaching traditions of over 3,000 years. It has been a strongly fortified position for many centuries. The fort, which is built on two hills called Barikala and Talibanda, 800 feet above the plain, has borne a conspicuous part in the history of the district. In its present form it dates from about A.D. 1570. It is now in ruins. The town has a population of about 25,000, with a large proportion of Muhammadans. There is a fine mosque. The bulk of the population are engaged in the weaving of cotton and silk fabrics and carpets. On the summit of Talibanda is a fine fig tree, which is visible for twenty or thirty miles in every direction. Adoni is a place of much picturesque beauty of situation and surroundings. Between Kosigi and Adoni the railway runs through singular rocky hills of fantastic shapes. Guntakal is the junction of the Madras and Southern Maratha lines. The line to Nandial extends for ninety miles, opening up the Karnul district and the Nallamalai Hills, a wild country famous for its tigers and other wild beasts, as well as every variety of Indian game.

BELLARY is two hours distant from Guntakal on the Southern Maratha Railway; it is the chief town of a large district in the Madras Presidency, and the headquarters of a brigade of the Madras army of a total strength of 3,000. It has a population of nearly 60,000, of which two-thirds are Hindu. The city stands in the centre of a vast treeless plain, broken by occasional masses of granite and huge boulders that spring abruptly from the soil, like islands in the sea. On one of these, 450 feet high, and about two miles in circuit is built the impregnable fortress of Bellary inaccessible in the face of the smallest defensive force. There is a lower and upper line of fortifications, both built of granite, and the crown of the hill within the upper line is the ancient citadel, within which is a singular granite pillar, thirty-six feet high, elaborately sculptured, and a queer old temple to Siva. This was one of the strongholds of Tipu Sultan.

The town of Bellary straggles all round the base of the rock on which the fort is built. It presents the ordinary characteristics of a prosperous and thriving centre of trade. The principal produce of the district is grain, cotton, oil seeds, and sugar. There is a fine cotton mill. Bellary is singularly bare of trees, but there are many specimens of the curious Phlomis indica, or umbrella tree, with its grateful shade and fragrant blossoms. The distinctive art crafts of the bazars are glass, bangles, carved teak, lacquered wood boxes, bracelets and toys, cotton carpets, silk and cotton cloth, pretty chintzes, printed on coloured grounds, black blankets, and coloured felts.

Forty-eight miles from Bellary is Hampi or Vijayanagar, a ruined city of great interest, covering nine square miles. Hampi was founded by two adventurers in 1336 A.D., and for 230 years was the capital of the Vijayanagar dynasty, the last great Hindu power of the south, who built magnificent temples and palaces, of which many specimens still remain in a fair state of preservation. Hampi is seven miles from Hospet station, where there is a Dak bungalow. There is also

UMBRELLA TREE AND GRANITE BOULDER, BELLARY.

one at Kamalapur, two miles from the ruins. There are good country carts on hire at Hospet, and the Tasildhar of Hospet is instructed to give every facility to European travellers. Its period of greatest prosperity was from 1508—42, when the finest monuments of the city were erected—the most remarkable of these is a temple dedicated to Vitoba, a local manifestation of Vishnu. It was erected A.D. 1530, and is still unfinished. It is wholly built of granite, and carved with great boldness and power. Though not very large, it is one of the most beautiful temples, and its porch one of the richest pieces of decoration in India. To the right of the entrance is a curious little building, cut out of a single block of granite. This is the car of the god, but the wheels are the only moveable part of it.

The palace buildings are detached and scattered; they bring before us the arrangements of a Hindu prince's residence before they fell under the sway of Musalman influence. They consists of pavilions, baths, audience halls, hareems, and other buildings, probably joined together by wooden arcades, long since vanished. The style of architecture is a mixture of Saracenic and Hindu, which is not met with often in India, and which is extremely picturesque.

Mr. J. Kelsall, in his "Manual of the Bellary District" (Madras,

CAR OF THE GOD VITOBA, HAMPI.

1872), says :—" Many of the buildings are now so destroyed that it is difficult to say what they were originally meant for, but the massive style of architecture and the huge stones that have been employed in their construction, at once attract attention. Close to Kamalapur there is a fine stone aqueduct, and a building which has, at some time or other, been a bath. The use of the arch in the doorways, and the embellishments used in decorating the inner rooms, show that the design of this building was considerably modified by the Musalmans, even if it was not constructed by them altogether. A little to the south of this is a very fine temple, of which the outer and inner walls are covered with spirited basso-relievos, representing hunting scenes and incidents in the *Ramayana*. The four centre pillars are of a kind of black marble, handsomely carved. The flooring of the temple, originally large slabs of stone, has been torn up and utterly ruined by persons in search of treasure, which is supposed to be buried both here and in other parts of the ruins. The use of another covered building close by, with numerous underground passages, has not been ascertained. It is also covered with basso-relievos, in one of which a lion is represented. At a little distance is the building generally known as the 'Elephant Stables,' and there seems no reason to doubt that it was used for this purpose. Two other buildings, which, with the 'Elephant Stables,' form roughly three sides of a square, are said to have been the concert-hall and the council-room. Both, but especially the latter, have been very fine buildings.

"Besides these, the remains of the *zanana* and the arena are still visible. But the huge monoliths applied to various purposes form perhaps the most distinctive feature of these ruins—one, a water-trough, is forty-one and a quarter feet long; another, a statue of Siva, thirty-five feet high. There are two fine temples, between which the road passes, but which are remarkable for nothing but the enormous size of the stones which have been used in their construction. Masses of cut granite, many of them thirty feet in length by four in depth, are seen high up in the wall, and no explanation can be given of the mode in which they were placed in their present position. There are also several temples in a fair state of preservation, notably one dedicated to Vishnu, about three-quarters of a mile from the palace, and close to the river. It is entirely of granite, and contains some splendid monolithic pillars richly carved. The inscriptions at Hampi have contributed materially to our knowledge of Vijayanagar history."

There is still a great annual festival here, although the village is insignificant in size, with a population of 693 in 1881.

The London Missionary Society commenced missionary work in the town of Bellary in 1810, and the first missionaries of the society spent much time and labour in translating the Scriptures into the Canarese and Telugu languages, as well as in writing and circulating Christian tracts, which they printed in the Mission Press.

Orphan schools for boys and girls were commenced in 1833, and in these schools many boys and girls have been trained, some of whom have occupied useful positions in the Mission.

Twelve years ago it was thought desirable to let the girls' orphan school die out as the boys had done, but the severe famine which then visited South India, left upon the Missionaries' hands so many orphan children, that it was found necessary to carry on the schools more vigorously than ever. There are now about forty girls and boys supported from funds obtained for this special purpose.

Bellary town is divided into two principal parts—Bruce Petta and the Kowl Bazar, between which lies the large tank, which is filled only when there is a good rain-fall.

An extensive and valuable site of about nine acres in Bruce Petta belongs to the Mission, and on this site now stand the chapel built in 1824, the English School, the Book Depôt, and many houses occupied by native Christians. In the Kowl Bazar there are, belonging to the Mission, a chapel built in 1868, two small school-rooms and several houses. In the Fort is a beautifully built chapel, the gift of a friend resident in Bellary, where English services are held.

The Canarese, Telugu, Tamil and Hindustani languages are extensively spoken in Bellary town. Christian services are conducted regularly in the three first. Canarese being the principal dialect of the district, most of the mission work is carried on in that language.

The Christian community connected with the London Missionary Society in the town numbers two hundred and forty-eight. The difficulty of obtaining suitable employment is the cause of many of the children of Christian parents going to other towns. No less than one hundred have left during the last ten years.

The large Anglo-Vernacular School, called the Wardlaw Institution, which now contains nearly 400 scholars, and which teaches up to the Matriculation Standard of the Madras University, was for some years the only school in the town where English was taught. The Government afterwards established an English school, which flourished under its care for many years, which is now managed by the municipality. A branch school, connected with the Wardlaw Institution in Kowl Bazar, and two vernacular boys' schools, are also worked by the Mission.

Work amongst the female population of Bellary is carried on in schools and by house to house visitation, by the wives of missionaries, an assistant lady missionary, and three Bible-women. There are two schools for Hindu girls, and the orphan school for Christian girls, containing in all 135 children.

In connection with the Bellary Native Church there is a vigorously worked branch of the Blue Ribbon Army, which numbers 140 members. The work of this society has extended to most of the out-stations also.

In the town of Bellary there are two churches belonging to the Church of England, Trinity Church in the Fort and the Garrison Church in the cantonment. The parade services are held in the latter. In the former a general service, attended by military officers and soldiers, the civilians and Eurasians. A military chaplain is in charge of this work.

There is also a Tamil Native Church, connected with the Society for the Propagation of the Gospel, which for many years was under the general supervision of the chaplain, but is now ministered to by a native clergyman, who is assisted by a catechist. The native services are held in Trinity Church.

The Protestant Orphanage, which was commenced by the London Missionary Society in 1811, and which is managed by a committee with the chaplain as secretary, has commodious buildings in the Fort, and is a most useful institution, where many Eurasian orphan children have found a home and been trained to earn a respectable livelihood. There is a workshop connected with the orphanage.

In 1877, Mr., now Bishop Taylor, of the American Methodist Episcopal Church, began work amongst the Eurasian population of Bellary. A small church, which was intended to be self-supporting, was commenced, and is ministered to by its own pastor. This church has become settled and worships in a chapel which was built in the Fort by local contributions.

The Roman Catholic Mission was begun in Bellary in 1775, and was in charge of Goa priests till 1837, when Government appointed a chaplain to minister to the Roman Catholic soldiers of the station. Then a new mission was virtually commenced.

The Goa priests retained charge of the chapel and congregation in the Fort, but carry on very little aggressive work. Most of the work is done by the chaplain and his assistants under the See of Madras.

There are two churches under the care of the latter—St. Lazarus's Church for native Christians, which was erected in 1847 by public subscription, is in the Kowl Bazar, and the Church of St. Mary's, which was built in 1866 by Government for the use of the soldiers, is near the European barracks. Near St. Mary's Church are school-rooms for boys and girls, an Industrial School, and the recently erected handsome structure called St. Philomene's School, in which European and Eurasian girls receive a good education from the nuns who live on the spot. There are usually two European and one native priest stationed in Bellary.

Returning from Bellary to Guntakal junction, the first place of interest on the Madras Railway is GOOTY, a rest camp for troops, and a flourishing little town of 6,000 inhabitants. One of the most important stations of the London Missionary Society has its great head-quarters here, under the charge of Messrs. W. W. Stephenson and B. Lucas. There are twenty-eight out-stations in the surrounding villages, and the society claim 2,400 native adherents. The work is mainly district preaching, though they possess fifteen small schools, with about 300 scholars.

The fort of Gooty, built in the early part of the 16th century, was a place of immense strength. It was the stronghold of the great Maratha guerilla chief, Morari Rao, who joined Clive in 1751 on the relief of Arcot. Originally belonging to a dependent of the Vijayanagar family, it formed one of the conquests of Mi Jumla, the Golconda minister, and a famous general of the Mughal Empire. Gooty was afterwards held by the Pathans of Cuddapah and Sawanur, from whom it was wrested in 1714 by the Gauripur family of Marathas, the most distinguished of whom obtained, in 1744, the Nizam's recognition of his territory as a Maratha state. In 1776 Haidar Ali besieged the town, which was forced to capitulate after a siege of four months, the water supply being exhausted. Haidar used this fortress as his head-quarters in several expeditions against the neighbouring *palegars*. Gooty was captured by the British in the Mysore campaign of 1799.

Wilks describes the fort as follows:—"The fort is composed of a number of strong works occupying the summits of a circular cluster of rocky hills connected with each other, and enclosing a level space which forms the site of the town. The town is approached from the plain by a single fortified gateway on the south-west, and by two small footpaths across the lower hills, communicating through small sallyports. An immense smooth rock, rising from the northern limit of the circle, and fortified by gradations surmounted by fourteen gateways, overlooks and commands the whole of the other works, and forms a citadel which famine or treachery alone can reduce. The rock is composed of granite, in which red felspar prevails. Its extreme height above the sea has been ascertained to be 2,171 feet, but notwithstanding this, the heat in April and May is intense. Its height above the plain is 989 feet. On the summit of the hill are several wells and reservoirs for water, and various buildings where state prisoners were confined.

"On one of the bastions, overlooking a precipice of about 300 feet, is a small building, called Morari Rao's seat. Here the Maratha chieftain was wont to sit and play chess, watching at the same time all that was going on in the town below, or as a spectator of the prisoners being hurled from the top of an adjoining precipice, and dashed to pieces on the rocks. Besides the fort, the most interesting features in Gooty are the choultry, tomb, and memorial well of Sir Thomas Munro, who died at Pattikonda in 1827."

TADPATRI is a small but thriving town of 9,000 inhabitants, founded 400 years ago by Ramalingam Nayadu, one of the governors of Vijayanagar. There is a good Dak bungalow in the town, and a refreshment-room at the station. There are three magnificent temples of the period of the Vijayanagar dynasty, which are among the finest in India. If, however, the traveller has been to Vijayanagar, or intends visiting Tirupati, at both of which places there are equally fine specimens of this type of Hindu architecture, he will hardly care to break his journey.

CUDDAPAH is a town of 20,000 inhabitants. There is nothing of interest except some old palaces of the Nawabs, now used as Government offices. At Madanapalli, a small town some miles distant, there is a fine pagoda and a beautifully carved monolith.

RENIGUNTA is the junction for the South Indian Railway, running eighty-three miles to Nellore from Tirupati. Fourteen miles from Renigunta, easily accessible by bullock-cart, is the curious and unique palace of the Telugu kings of Chandragiri, built entirely of granite, no wood having been used in any portion of the structure.

TIRUPATI, half-an-hour by rail from Renigunta junction, is a Hindu town of 14,000 inhabitants, celebrated for its hill pagoda, the most sacred in Southern India. The chief temple is six miles distant, at Tirumala (the holy hill), known to Europeans as Upper Tirupati, but the annexes and outer entrances of the ascent begin about a mile from the town. The chief temple is sacred to Vishnu, and is so holy that till quite lately no Christian or Musalman was allowed to enter. Difficulties are still raised, and it will be best to write a few days beforehand to the district magistrate at Tirupati, or to the collector's office at North Arcot, asking that notice may be given to the *Mahant* of the temple of the intended visit, and a note should also be sent to the Tirupati station-master for a conveyance to the Dak bungalow, some distance from the station. Thousands

TEMPLE TANK, TIRUPATI.

of pilgrims flock to Tirupati, with rich gifts for the idol, about 120,000 passengers alighting at the station every year, bound for the temple.

Up to 1843 the pagoda was under the management of the British Government, who derived much revenue from the offerings of pilgrims. Now, however, the whole revenues are handed over to the *Mahant*, or chief priest. The receipts are a little over £20,000 a year. The hill on which the great pagoda stands is 2,500 feet above the sea. It has seven peaks, and that on which the pagoda is perched rejoices in the name of Srivenkataramanachellam. The temple is said to have been built at the commencement of the Kaliyug, or present Hindu era, B.C. 3100, when it was prophesied that worship would continue for 5,000 years exactly, and that the end would be foreshadowed by a decrease in the temple revenues. The real date of the present building is lost in obscurity, but Fergusson thinks it is no later than the earliest kings of the Vijayanagar dynasty, who are very likely to have done some building at so sacred a spot. There is a deserted temple of great beauty on the banks of the river, a short distance from the other. It possesses two gopuras, or gateways, of a fine close-grained hornblende, whose sculpture is very elaborate, cut with great sharpness and precision, and with much taste. These are of the very best period of the Vijayanagar kings. Fergusson gives two full-page illustrations of their sculpture in the "History of Indian Architecture," pp. 376–7.

The natural beauty of Tirupati is very great, and the surroundings of these interesting old temples enhance their wonderful picturesqueness. The German Lutheran Church has a mission station here.

NELLORE is an important town of 30,000 inhabitants, with ancient traditions, and a temple-crowned hill. There is an excellent Christian high-school, under the charge of the Free Church of Scotland.

From Arkonam junction, a short line of thirty-two miles runs to Chingleput on the South Indian Railway. Half way is CONJEVERAM, an important Hindu town of 40,000 inhabitants, and a place of especial sanctity; the Dak bungalow is a good one. Conjeveram is one of the seven holy cities of India, a pilgrimage to which confers eternal happiness, and it is to the South what Benares is to the North. In ancient times it was a great Buddhist centre, and afterwards came under Jain influence. Jain nuns are still to be seen in the district. About the 12th century the place fell under Hindu predominance, and most of the finest buildings date from the period of the Vijayanagar kings, and were erected by them. The great annual fair in May is attended by 50,000 pilgrims.

The two towns of Great and Little Conjeveram possess groups of vast temples, Brahman choultries, or rest-houses, alms-houses, shrines, and all the other features of a first-class sacred city.

The huge temple at Great Conjeveram has some noble gopuras, or gateways, large mantapas, or pavilion shrines, the usual 1,000-pillared hall, or courtyard, some superb tanks with flights of stone steps, and all the features of an important Dravidian temple. The largest gopura has ten storeys, its height being 188 feet; it is as nearly as possible square at the base, each side being about seventy-four feet.

The summit affords a fine bird's-eye view of the entire temple and surrounding country, but is rather a fatiguing ascent, the steps being very high, and the passages so dark that torches are necessary.

Passing through the gateway, a large open space is entered, to the left of which is the hall of the 1,000 pillars, which, however, only count

PAVILION, LITTLE CONJEVERAM.

540. Most of the columns are beautifully carved; they are eight feet high, and support richly-decorated friezes. In the centre of the hall are a number of grotesque wooden figures used for processional purposes. Only Hindus may enter the idols' shrine.

The Vishnu temple of Little Conjeveram is about two miles distant from the Great Temple. Here is a very remarkable hall of pillars, ninety-six in all, carved at the bases into horsemen and hippogriffes. In front of the tank are two stambhas, or columns for flag staffs, one of which is covered with plates of gold, and a singularly beautiful pavilion, with a painted roof resting on four slender pillars. The treasury of this temple is rich in ancient jewels, which are shown by an attendant Brahman.

Last year, 1889, an important Medical Mission was established in this city by the Free Church of Scotland, under Dr. and Mrs. Walker with two native assistants.

The best way of visiting Conjeveram is to stay the night at Arkonam, where there is a good refreshment-room with bed-rooms up stairs, going on to Conjeveram by the train leaving at 6 A.M., arriving 7.10; the return train leaves 5.15 P.M., reaching Arkonam 6.25 P.M. A letter to the station-master will secure a conveyance to meet the train on arrival at Conjeveram.

CHAPTER XXXIV.

MADRAS.

MADRAS, the capital of the oldest presidency in India, straggles for nine or ten miles along the coast, covering an area of about thirty square miles. The population is about 430,000. Hindus number 320,000, Musalmans 55,000, Christians 45,000. There are some 3,500 Europeans, and 15,000 Eurasians. The proportion of Christians is higher in Madras city than anywhere else in British India. Tamil is the language chiefly spoken, though quite a fourth of the population is Telugu. English is widely understood, and all the well-to-do people speak it with ease.

Madras was founded in 1639 by Mr. Francis Day, who obtained a grant of the land on which the city now stands from the Raja of Vijayanagar, and constructed a factory.

In 1702 the place was unsuccessfully besieged by Aurangzeb's famous General Daud Khan. In 1741 it successfully resisted the Maratha power. The fort was extended and strengthened in 1743, and Madras became the most important city in Southern India. Traces of the old wall still exist, some of the bastions having been utilised as police-stations.

In 1746 Madras was taken by the French, who held possession of it for two or three years. The French under Lally again occupied Blacktown for a few months in 1758, but were beaten off by a British fleet before they could reduce the fort. Since then the history of the city has been uneventful, and its prosperity steady and progressive.

There are plenty of good hotels in Madras, the best of which are situated along the Mount Road. The Royal, Elphinstone, Albany, and Dent's Garden are all nice hotels in large compounds. Lippert's Hotel, opposite the pier, is good but noisy. The Madras Club is one of the best in India, and it is not difficult for travellers of "recognised position" to get elected, especially if they have already become members of any of the leading clubs in Bombay or Calcutta. There are some thirty or forty suites of rooms, and the visitor intending to remain any length of time in Madras will be much more comfortable at this club than at any hotel. It stands in a fine garden opposite Neill's statue in the Mount Road.

The harbour is the most interesting thing about Madras. It is protected by two huge breakwaters, reaching out like arms, enclosing a space about 1,000 yards by 830, with a maximum depth of water of seven fathoms. It is an immense work, containing nearly a million tons of huge concrete blocks. It has not proved a success. A terrible cyclone in 1881 breached and spread out nearly half a mile of breakwater. The western coast is at certain seasons swept by fierce hurricanes, and at all times the surf in Madras harbour is very great. In the finest weather great steamers pitch at anchor in the harbour, and the embarking of passengers is attended with much inconvenience and difficulty. The boat used is called a *Masula*; it is a large open boat of thin planks stitched with cocoa fibre to a strong frame. They are rowed by ten or twelve almost naked Madrasis, who beach them through the surf with great skill. Passengers are landed at an iron pier, which runs 330 yards into the harbour; they have to display much agility in jumping off at the rise of the wave, which in calm weather is seven or eight feet and in windy weather fifteen to twenty. The disembarking of twenty or thirty passengers and their luggage is a troublesome and often dangerous business. The native boat is the *Catamaran*, a hollowed out log with a projecting outrigger, or three logs of light wood lashed together and driven by a paddle, which is almost universal down the Coromandel coast.

THE BEACH, MADRAS.

The beach between the pier and the lighthouse is crowded with all sorts of native boats, and is full of busy life.

The lighthouse is a Doric column of granite 125 feet high, whose flash-light is visible from a ship's deck fifteen miles out to sea.

The esplanade, between the two roots of the breakwaters and facing the harbour, is an irregular terrace of large business premises, behind which is Blacktown, the usual name for the native city of Madras, as

MADRAS CATAMARAN.

distinguished from Whitetown, the suburb surrounding the fort, where the European residents and their shops are located. It is a busy crowded place, with wide streets, but lacking in all interest except human. The visitor will find his amusement in the quaint shops of the bazars, the groups of natives in the streets, and in the excellent general market, where all sorts of strange fish and beautiful fruits are exposed for sale.

The European quarter is prettily laid out, and richly timbered. The marine promenade is about two miles long, and is thronged towards sundown with English carriages, and crowds of well-dressed Indians, who come to hear the band play.

One of the most picturesque sights in India is the washing-ground on the River Adyar, where hundreds of *Dhobies* are busy with the garments of their European employers. Government House is an imposing mansion in the midst of a wide and well-planted park, noted for its beautiful palms.

There are several extensive tanks and lakes in the suburbs of Madras, of which Nangambakum, Spur, Perambore and Vasawalh are the principal. At Triplicane there is an ancient and very holy tank, said by its Brahmans to be equivalent to 10,000 baths in the Ganges, and to be able to save the soul even of a dead body dipped into its waters. It is much resorted to.

Beyond Triplicane, about six miles from the centre of Madras, is the Governor's country house, a charming bungalow in the middle of a

HACKNEY CARRIAGE, MADRAS.

deer park. The house is faced with white chunam, a hard plaster made from ground-up shells, which takes a high polish like the finest white marble. The gardens are famous for rare flowering trees and shrubs, and there are some fine specimens of the traveller's palm. The tank of Victoria Regia lilies alone is worth a visit. There are also many acclimatised trees from other parts of the tropics.

The People's Park is adjacent to Blacktown, near the central railway station, and is a great place of public resort. It makes a delightful stroll in the early morning, its area of 116 acres being laid out in shady walks and avenues six or seven miles in extent. It has eleven pretty lakes and ponds, a well-maintained menagerie and aviaries, a splendid public swimming bath, lawn-tennis courts, a band-stand lit up with electric light, and other minor attractions.

The Robinson Park at Royapuram is newly laid out, and was opened to the public in 1886. Its main attraction is its Botanical Garden, and a large fernery placed on an island reached by a light iron bridge of fifty feet span. The old Botanical Gardens are near St. George's Cathedral, and are somewhat neglected.

A pretty drive along the shore of Long Tank leads to Little Mount, sacred to all Indian Roman Catholics as the spot where St. Thomas the Apostle is said to have been martyred in 68 A.D. by Brahmans, who stirred up the people against him. After being stoned by the crowd, he was thrust through with a spear (see "Hunter's India," pp. 229—236). In the museum at Madras is a gold coin of Claudius, struck to commemorate the conquest of Britain, discovered in excavating a foundation near the city. Sir Edwin Arnold, with quaint poetic conceit, suggests that it came to India in the scrip of the Apostle! And why not? At the summit of the Little Mount is a chapel dedicated to St. Thomas; beneath, is a cave lighted by a narrow opening, through which the Apostle once squeezed himself, in a successful escape from pursuing Brahmans. There is also a little cell, said to have been his dwelling, with holes in the ground worn away by his knees in constant prayer.

Crossing the Marmalong Bridge over the Adyar River, alive with Dhobies, a drive of three miles brings the traveller to St. Thomas Mount, along a road shaded by banian trees. This is a hill of green stone, 220 feet high. The flat summit is occupied with barracks and their supplementary buildings. The topmost point bears an ancient Nestorian, now Armenian chapel. The present building was erected 1547 A.D. by the Portuguese; but at the back of the altar is a carved stone cross, dating as far back as 800 A.D. There is a pleasant view of the sea and the surrounding country from this chapel.

The most interesting public building in Madras is the old palace of the Nawabs of the Karnatic in the Chepak Park, now magnificently restored, and used as the offices of the Revenue Department and an Engineering College. It is a curious mixture of styles, Saracenic, Ionic, and Doric, veneered over and pulled together by restoration into a very fair specimen of modern Indian palace architecture. Within the same park is the Senate House of the Madras University and the Presidency College, whose architecture is in harmony with the palace. Fort St. George has very little left of the original buildings of 1670, except St. Mary's Church. The interior is occupied by rows of modern barracks, Government offices, and the arsenal. The arsenal contains a curious and interesting collection of trophies of the various wars in which the Madras Army has been engaged. Amongst these are two guns captured from Tipu Sultan at Seringapatam, some long guns with twelve feet barrels and only three inches in diameter, and other Indian weapons and war furniture.

The museum contains a collection of natural history, the most interesting portion of which is the exhibition of local fishes, sponges, corals, and shells, with a series of specimens illustrative of the pearl fisheries of Tuticorin. The great skeleton of a whale found dead on the Mangalore beach in 1874, fifty feet long, is said to be the most perfect specimen in existence; there is also a very large shark,

A MADRAS BARBER.

nineteen feet long. The departments of botany, economics, mineralogy, geology, and industrial arts are well chosen and kept up. In the archæological collection are some of the famous sculptures of the Buddhist Tope at Amravati, 400—500 A.D., of which some account is given in Fergusson, pp. 71—2, and 99—103. The industrial arts section is rich in Tanjore metal ware, the zincwork of Trichinopoly, Bidri ware, inlaid work from Vizagapatam, old jewellery, arms, lacquer-work, silver and gold smith's work, and fabrics from Southern Indian looms. The collection of coins is unusually fine, well set out, and chronologically arranged. The museum is popular with the Madrasis, about 400,000 persons entering its doors every year.

There are thirty-one Protestant churches and chapels, and fifteen

Roman Catholic churches in Madras. They are mostly very ugly and uninteresting. The oldest are, St. Thomé Cathedral, a spacious building erected over the tomb of St. Thomas by the Portuguese in 1606; the Church of the Assumption in Blacktown, 1640 A.D.; and St. Mary's, Church of England, the oldest in India, 1680 A.D. St. Mary's contains several interesting monuments of distinguished Englishman, Sir Francis Wittingham, Lord Hobart, Missionary Schwartz, Sir Henry Ward, and others. The inside has been gutted of its queer old wooden pulpit and galleries, which have stood for 200 years, in favour of very indifferent choir stalls and pews. St. Andrew's Church is handsome in its way, but mixed in its styles, like most modern Indian buildings; it has a fine dome, the interior of which is covered with chunam mixed with lapis lazuli, producing a very beautiful blue. The steeple over the vestibule is 165 feet high. The Armenian church in Blacktown is a quaint building of 1712 A.D.

The principal schools and colleges are, the Madras Christian College of the Free Church of Scotland, with 600 university students and 1,000 school pupils, one of the most famous educational institutes in India; the Society for the Propagation of the Gospel College, with 400 pupils, a boarding-house, and theological hall; the Teachers' College; the Medical College; the Civil Engineering College for candidates for the Public Works Department; and the Presidency Government College: all of which prepare students for the Madras University. Of schools there are a great number, mostly in connection with the various Christian missions.

There are many charitable institutes, hospitals, and asylums, but I cannot enumerate them. A complete list will be found, with much other useful information about Madras, in the excellent little guide-book published by Higginbotham & Co., Mount Road.

A whole book might be written about the various Christian missions in Madras. The Church of Scotland, the Church Missionary Society, the Wesleyans, the London Missionary Society, the American Baptists, the Free Church of Scotland, the Society for the Propagation of the Gospel, the American Methodist Episcopal Church, the German Lutherans, the American Board, are all hard at work, and full particulars of their various locations will be found in Higginbotham's guide.

The shops and bazars of Madras are full of Indian curiosities and beautiful specimens of industrial art. Messrs. Orr & Sons, Mount

Road, are the leading dealers in jewellery and curios, and are not unreasonable in prices. Some of the most beautiful pierced and hammered silver work is produced by the native jewellers of Madras; the work known as *swami*, is decorated with figures of the Puranic gods, in high relief, sometimes *repoussé*, sometimes soldered on the surface; they also produce superb gold and silver ornaments. The temple bells and sacrificial vases, made in this city, are distinguished above all others by their stately designs and fine workmanship. The handles of the bells are generally crowned with a group of gods, sculptured in bold relief.

OIL MERCHANT, MADRAS.

The blackwood furniture made in Madras differs from that of Bombay and Gujarat, by being exclusively of European design, but it is of excellent quality; there is also plenty of good sandalwood and ivory carving to be had. Highly elaborate and accurate models of the great Dravidian temples of Southern India are made of the pith of *Sola*, the same material as that used in making the sun-hats, or *Sola topis*. In the carpet shops may be purchased handsome Bellary felts, and the splendid coconada or Madras rugs, of uncontaminated native design and integrity of workmanship, woven in out-of-the-way villages on the Coromandel coast, by the Musalman descendants of Persian settlers.

I have always regretted, that when I visited Madras, I had not time to make the journey to Mahabalipur (or the seven pagodas), thirty-five miles south of Madras, one of the most interesting places in all India to the archæologist, presenting a series of architectural wonders, from B.C. 200—100, down to recent times, their lonely remoteness on a sea-washed island having contributed to their marvellous preservation.

The journey is a pleasant one, by the Buckingham Canal, lined with groves of cocoa-nut and other palms, chiefly cultivated for toddy. There are good boats, and the trip may be made during the night, with mattress and pillow, the temples viewed during the day, and the return journey accomplished by night. Supplies of food must be

TODDY TAPPING, MADRAS.

taken, as the village is very small and poor. The bungalow belongs to the Public Works Department, who will always lend it to respectable travellers.

The antiquities of the place may be divided into three groups: (1.) The five *raths* to the south of the village, belonging probably to the lates Bhuddhist period; (2.) The cave temples, monolithic figures, carvings, and sculptures, west of the village, probably of the 6th or 7th century, A.D.; (these contain some marvellous reliefs, ranking with those of Ellora and Elephanta): (3.) The more modern temples of Vishnu and Siva, the latter being washed by the sea. To these two, with five other pagodas, buried—according to tradition—by the sea, the place owes its English name. The following selections from Crole and Hunter describe these antiquities.* Mr. Crole writes:—

"The best, and by far the most important, of its class is the pastoral group in the Krishna *mantapam*, as it is called. The fact is, that it represents Indra, the god of the sky, supporting the clouds with his left hand, to protect the cattle of Bala from the

* See also Fergusson, pp. 134, 175, 274, 326, 330, 333.

fury of the Maruts or tempest demons. Near him, the cattle are being tended and milked. To the right, a young bull is seen, with head slightly turned and fore-foot extended, as if suddenly startled. This is one of the most spirited and life-like pieces of sculpture to be seen anywhere.

"A little to the north of this is the great bas-relief which goes by the name of 'Arjun's Penance.' It covers a mass of rock ninety-six feet in length, and forty-three feet in height, and is described by Fergusson as 'the most remarkable thing of its class in India.' 'Now' says he, 'that it is known to be wholly devoted to serpent-worship, it acquires an interest it had not before, and opens a new chapter in Indian mythology.' There seems nothing to enable us to fix its age with absolute certainty; it can hardly, however, be doubted that it is anterior to the 10th century, and may be a couple of centuries earlier.' . . . . .

"Near the stone *choultry* by the side of the road, and a little to the north of the rock last described, stands a well-executed group lately exhumed, representing a couple of monkeys catching fleas on each other after the manner of their kind, while a young one is extracting nourishment from the female.

"Near this point, a spectator, looking southward, may see, formed by the ridges on which the caves are cut, the recumbent figure of a man with his hands in the attitude of prayer or meditation. This figure measures at least 1500 feet long, the partly natural resemblance having been assisted by the rolling away of rocks and boulders. On the spot, this is called the 'Giant Raja Bali,' but it is no doubt the work of Jains.

"The whole of this ridge is pitted with caves and temples. There are fourteen or fifteen Rishi caves in it, and much carving and figuring of a later period. These are distinguished by the marked transition from the representations of the scenes of peace to scenes of battle, treading down of opposition and destruction, the too truthful emblems of the dark centuries of religious strife which preceded and followed the final expulsion of the Buddhists. Their age is not more than 600 or 700 years; and the art is poor, and shows as great a decadence in matter as in religion. The representations are too often gross and disgusting, and the carving stiff and unnatural—entirely wanting in ease and grace and truth to nature.

"Behind this ridge, and near the canal, are two more of the monolithic *raths*, and one similar in form, but built of large blocks of stone.

"The last period is represented by the Shore Temple, the Varahaswami Temple in the village, and by some of the remains in a village in a hamlet called Salewankuppen, two miles to the northward. In the two former there is little distinguishable in construction and general plan from similar buildings to be found everywhere in the south.

"Looking at the place as a whole, its architecture, its sculptures,

GRANITE BOULDER TEMPLE, MAHABALIPUR.

and its inscriptions, we would seem to possess here a complete religious history of the south carved in the imperishable rock; and, with all deference to the high authority of Mr. Fergusson (who, however, seems to have confined his study almost entirely to the monoliths), it is difficult to believe that the remains enumerated do not form a chapter in the story anterior to his earliest one, which he dates about the 6th century A.D. It would seem to be much more in accordance with the evidence to accept these remains as the records left by the Buddhist faith, and to assign to them an age nearly coeva with the zenith of Buddhist architecture and sculpture, or a period commencing a couple of centuries or so before the Christian era."—(Crole.)

"On the left side of the rock, which is divided by a deep natural cleft, the chief figure in the upper part appears to be the giant Raja Maha Bali Chakrabaritti, with his attendant dwarfs, five Rajas with their wives, four warriors, five ascetics, and a holy Rishi in his cave temple. The lions, tigers, cheetahs, and deer, in different parts of the sculpture, show that the people have travelled from a distance through the jungles.

"In the central part of the cleft, at the bottom, on the left, is a figure seated, which I take to be Buddha, with his five disciples in front of the cave temple, with the holy Rishi. The heads of three of the disciples have been broken off. . . . . In the deep recess formed by the natural cleft in the centre of the rock sculpture, is the lower part of the body and tail of the snake deity Vasuki, the Naga Raja; and below this is the entire figure of Ulupi, his daughter, with a canopy of three snakes rising over the head. The upper portion of the Naga deity had been broken off, and was said to be buried in front of the sculptures. I made search for it, found it, and got it dug up, set upright, and photographed; it is the figure of a man with his hands raised in prayer, and a canopy of seven snakes rising over a pyramidal head-dress, and with the usual emblems of the Buddhist religion. To the right of these are several Rajas and men, each accompanied by his wife; six dwarfs; and eight Barudas, or figures of men and women with the legs of birds; several monkeys; a cat doing penance, while rats are running near it; two large, and several small elephants; lions, tigers, geese, cocks, and hens. I thought at first, that all the figures were coming to do reverence or to worship the snake deity; but when we first took photographs of this rock sculpture, the whole of the central clept was overgrown with trees and brushwood, and the five disciples of Buddha were buried.

"Lord Napier, then Governor of Madras, visited the spot about a week after the snake deity was dug up, and had excavations made to the depth of seven or eight feet, which exposed a great number of figures and animals, and showed that the old road must have passed in front of the rock at a depth of five or six feet below the present level, the ground having been filled up chiefly with broken bricks and earth, with here and there large fragments of sculptured rocks, dressed stones, and cornices from the adjoining temples. The broken tusk of the large elephant was also found. To the left, and below the five disciples of Buddha, is a deer, in a very natural attitude, scratching its nose with its hind foot. The male and female elephants with their young behind them, and some of the figures of crouching tigers and cheetahs, are in a very natural and spirited style; and there is a great look of natural animation, movement, and bustle in the whole

MONOLITHIC TEMPLE, MAHABALIPUR.

group, of which Buddha and his five disciples appear to occupy the principal position and to attract the greatest attention, while the snake deity and his daughter are, as it were, in the background, and ascetics are scattered about in several parts. . . One point of great importance in these early large rock sculptures is, that they represent scenes of peace with men and their wives, a single wife accompanying each, and the animals, Barudas, and birds in pairs, while the Raja Mahabali is accompanied by dwarfs, and the other Rajas, whose rank is indicated by umbrella-bearers, have each his wife beside him. The ascetics, of whom there are five or six, have no wife. It appears to me that the story is one which represents the establishment of the

Buddhist religion, or one of peace, goodwill, toleration, and kindness to all men, and to animals and birds. Mr. Fergusson declared it to be, with the exception of the pagoda at Tanjore, the finest and most important *vimana* in the south of India. It is small, being not more than thirty feet square at the base, and sixty feet high; but it is free from all surrounding walls and gateways, which so detract from the grandeur of other pagodas. The same authority assigns the edifice to the 11th century, and the neighbouring excavations to the 13th or 14th.

"It is to be regretted that the inscriptions of Mahabalipur, as yet deciphered, furnish no clue to the date or history of these remarkable structures; though Dr. Babington explains one line as conveying the name of the founder, 'Atirana Chanda (he who in battle is furious), Lord of kings, built this place called Atiranachandeshwara.' It is equally a matter of doubt to what deity the sea-side pagoda was originally dedicated. In the chamber next the sea is a gigantic *lingam* of black polished stone, which would lead us to suppose it a temple of Siva. On the other hand, there is a gigantic figure of Vishnu, in a recumbent posture, in one of the verandahs. The uncertainty on all these points may, perhaps, heighten the zest of inspection."—(Hunter.)

Three miles or so beyond Mahabalipur, on the banks of the canal, is Sadras, the ruins of an old Dutch settlement of 1647, A.D. The fort is very dilapidated, but was evidently a place of great strength. There are some very curious Dutch tombs; the governor's house is fairly preserved, and is now a travellers' bungalow.

ARCOT is five miles from the railway station, on the line from Madras to Calicut. Its interest is mainly historical. The capture and brilliant defence of Arcot by Clive are among the most notable feats of the British arms in India. Little or nothing remains of the fortress. In the Delhi gate of the old city walls is still shown the chamber in which Clive lodged.

VELLORE is a thriving town of 43,000 inhabitants four miles from the station. The fine old fortress was built about 1274—83, and in spite of frequent sieges, is in remarkably good preservation, still exhibiting battlements adapted for matchlocks and bows, built before cannon came into general use. It is about a third of a mile in length, and a little less in breadth, surrounded by a strong masonry rampart, and a wide wet ditch.

Within the fort is one of the finest and most interesting temples in South India. The great seven-storied gopura is 100 feet high, with a handsome door of wood, studded with iron bosses. The porch, built in 1350 A.D., has recently been carefully restored by Government. On either side of the doorway are three Yalis, or grotesque figures carved from monoliths, acting as supports to a very beautiful cornice. These figures are finely sculptured. The ceiling of the portico is decorated with a singular centre-piece, representing a group of parrots hanging head downwards round some fruit. There are here several compound pillars of exquisite grace and beauty, which would alone repay a visit to Vellore. Every inch of detail in this beautiful pagoda is worthy of study. (*See* "Fergusson," pp. 370—2.)

The Chanda Sahib mosque is worth seeing.

Vellore is situated in the midst of beautiful hills, some of which are 2,000 feet above the plain. Sayer's Hill, about 1,000 feet high, immediately over the town, may be ascended in about an hour by a good walker; there is a ruined fort on the summit, from which a superb view may be obtained.

One of the leading industries of Vellore is the cultivation of sweet-scented flowers for the Madras market.

At Virinjipuram, eight miles from Vellore, there is a large temple visited by crowds of pilgrims. Malipati, the next station, is reached after crossing the Palar river, by a remarkably fine bridge; this place is famous for its good oranges. Jalarpet is the junction for the Mysore branch of the Madras Railway, 132 miles from Madras.

The American Reformed Church, under the superintendence of the Rev. W. W. Scudder, D.D., has stations at Vellore, Arcot and the district round. They have a large and competent staff of 18 American missionaries of both sexes, and 210 native assistants, forming one of the most powerful corps of missionaries in India. They have 2,000 communicants, and over 3,000 scholars in 103 schools.

SALEM is an important town of nearly 60,000 inhabitants, taking its name from the ancient monarchy of *Shelam*. It is pleasantly situated 900 feet above the sea, in a valley surrounded by the Shevaroy hills. An ascent of seven miles leads to the plateau on the summit of these hills, many of which are over 5,000 feet high, the highest point being 5,410.

Yerkad is the oldest of the hill settlements, as well as the nearest to Salem, and is surrounded by rugged peaks and finely timbered

THE SHEVAROY HILLS.

slopes. There are a large number of coffee plantations on the plateau, and limes, oranges, lemons and pomeloes grow plentifully. The inhabitants of these hills are Malayalis.

Salem is a very good specimen of a prosperous Southern India town, with wide streets, planted with rows of cocoanut trees, and lined with good two-storeyed houses. It is famous for its loom-work, principally linen, damasks, and silk pile carpets. The beauty and superior workmanship of the carpets made in Salem jail is well known. It is also famous for its cutlery and fine steel, worked in small charcoal furnaces in the surrounding hills. The London Missionary Society is here.

The railway journey from Salem to Erode junction is very picturesque. The old fortress of Erode was levelled as a relief work during the famine of 1877. Here a branch of the South Indian Railway from Trichinopoli joins the Madras Railway.

Podanur is an important junction, with good refreshment rooms. Hence a line runs to the Nilgiri hills and Coimbatore.

COIMBATORE is an important town of 40,000 inhabitants, the head-quarters of a district. It is built with very wide streets, and natural drainage, 1,437 feet above sea level. Three miles from Coimbatore, at Perur, is the temple of Mel-Chidambaram, celebrated for its sanctity, and remarkable as one of the three Hindu temples spared from destruction by Tipu Sultan. It presents the usual characteristics of a fine Dravidian temple. It was built in the beginning of the 18th century, and its carving is inferior in quality though similar in character to the temple at Vellore. The Animalei hills, above Coimbatore, are vast teak forests, full of wild elephants and other great game, including tiger, bear, wild cattle and ibex. There is no finer forest scenery to be found anywhere. They run from 3,000 to 6,000 feet in height, and are of much the same character as the Nilgiri hills.

At Tunakadu, some twenty miles from Coimbatore, is the head-quarters of the forest service, where a number of well-trained elephants drag and pile the timber with much intelligence.

Mettupalaiyam is the terminus of the branch line to the Nilgiri hills, a district dealt with at length in the next chapter.

The railway now runs through the Salghat valley, a remarkable gap in the great western mountain wall, twenty miles broad, and leading by an easy route, only 1,000 feet high, from the interior to the sea board.

Shoranur is the station where travellers bound to Cochin leave the railway. The journey is made by palki and coolies to Trichur, thence by boat along the lagoons, the total distance being seventy-two miles. A British India steamer from Calicut is, however, a pleasanter alternative, unless the traveller desires the novel experience of the lagoon boats. From Cochin, the lagoon journey may be continued to Quilon, eighty-eight miles further, and Trivanderam, the capital of Travancore, forty-one miles beyond Quilon. Few travellers will be able to spare the time so slow a journey will consume.

Calicut, the terminus of the railway, is a thriving seaport with a population of 60,000. It is the head-quarters of the rich and populous district of Malabar, and its imports and exports, including the sub-port of Beypur, amount to over a million sterling. The present town dates from the 13th century, and was the capital of a considerable dominion until the 15th century, under powerful rulers who were called Zamorins. It gives the name to the cotton cloth known as calico. Calicut is celebrated in history as having been the first port in India ever visited by Europeans, the Portuguese adventurer Covilham having landed here in 1486. Vasco di Gama arrived in 1498, but was inhospitably received. The town is beautifully situated in the midst of groves of palm, mango and jack trees. The Portuguese church was built by the Zamorin in 1525, and presented by him to the Portuguese. The British India steamers call at Calicut going north and south, every week. The missionary enterprise of Calicut is conducted by the Basle German Evangelical Society.

CHAPTER XXXV.

MYSORE STATE.

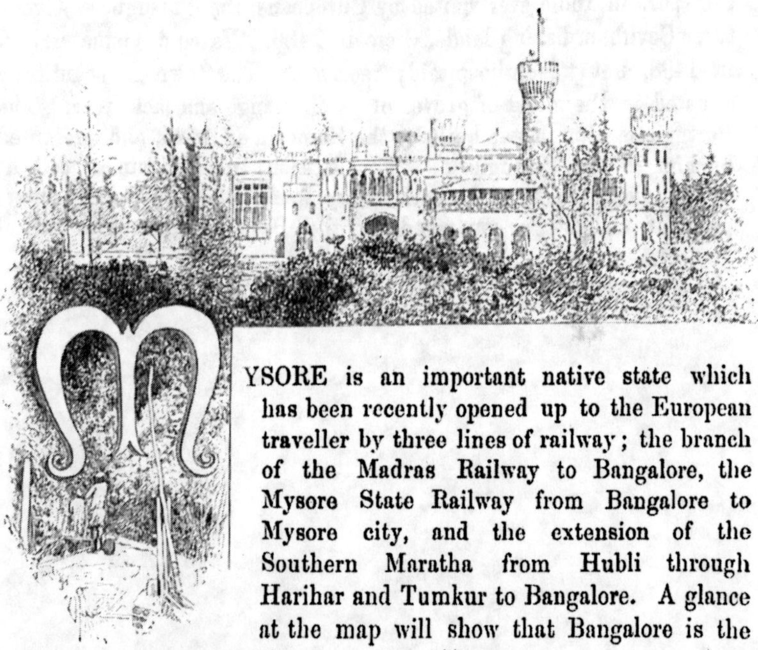

MYSORE is an important native state which has been recently opened up to the European traveller by three lines of railway; the branch of the Madras Railway to Bangalore, the Mysore State Railway from Bangalore to Mysore city, and the extension of the Southern Maratha from Hubli through Harihar and Tumkur to Bangalore. A glance at the map will show that Bangalore is the centre of this group of lines.

Mysore (Mahesh-uru, the city of buffaloes) is one of the most important native states in India. It is surrounded entirely by British territory. Mysore city is the capital, but Bangalore is the administrative head-quarters. The Maharaja divides his residence equally between the two. The cantonment of Bangalore is assigned to the British Government, and is a civil and military station under British administration. It is looked upon as the healthiest and pleasantest cantonment in all India.

The area of the state is 24,743 square miles, and its population 4,186,188. Its early history is obscure, but much light has been thrown upon it by recent discoveries of inscriptions on stone and copper throughout the State. At the beginning of the Christian era, Mysore appears to have been under Jain influence and supremacy, and many of the most interesting archæological remains are Jain. This religion was relinquished for Brahmanism about the 2nd century A.D., which has been the religion of the people of Mysore ever since, and of their kings with the exception of a short period in the 13th century, when they professed Jainism, leaving several beautiful temples as monuments of their sway.

The most conspicuous of the modern rulers of Mysore are the famous Haidar Ali, and his son Tipu Sultan. Haidar usurped the throne in 1763, and his son Tipu was defeated by the British and slain at the storming of Seringapatam in 1799, when the throne was restored to a representative of the Hindu Wodeyar dynasty, founded in 1610. This Maharaja grossly misgoverned the State, and was superseded by the British Government, who administered in his name, and after his death in that of his adopted son, until 1881, when he was formally installed as Maharaja, the chief commissioner handing over his office to his diwan. The present Maharaja, Chama Rajendra Wodeyar, who has had a liberal education under European tutelage, continues the government with great ability and success. He is aided by a council, which deals with all the more important administrative measures.

Mysore State is an undulating tableland, broken by ranges of rocky hills and deep ravines. The general elevation of the country is from 2,000 to 3,000 feet above the sea, with a fine pleasant climate. A peculiar feature in the scenery is the large number of isolated granite rocks called *droogs*, sometimes stupendous monoliths, sometimes huge boulders piled up, often rising 2,000 feet from the plain. Many of these are crowned with ruined fortresses, once the strongholds of robber chieftains, who domineered over the adjacent plains.

The mountain ranges of Mysore run as high as 6,000 feet above the sea, the highest peak being Mulaina Giri (6,317 feet). Their flanks are clothed with superb forests, the resort of wild elephants, bison, tigers, panthers, leopards, bears, sambhar, and spotted deer, jungle fowl and spur fowl. The summits are clear of timber, being grass downs, with wooded hollows. The open country of the State is well cultivated, watered by two great rivers, the Kistna and the Kaveri, while the streams which gather from the hill sides and mountain ranges are at every favourable point embanked into chains of tanks, varying in size from ponds to large lakes, dispersed throughout the country to the total number of 38,000. The largest is the Sulukere tank, a noble sheet of water forty miles in circumference.

The roads of Mysore are generally good, and the country breed of bullocks famous for speed and endurance. Travelling is done by bullock tongas, and long distances may be accomplished at a rate of four or five miles an hour.

The Maharajà pays great attention to the maintenance of the breeds of bullocks at his great cattle farm at Hoonsoor, whence first-class bulls are distributed to the large villages for the free use of their agricultural herds.

The best time to visit Mysore is during December, January and February, when the mornings and evenings are cold and bracing, with bright sunny days. The best season for sport is April, after the young grass has begun to grow. Sportsmen will find ample information in "Thirteen Years among the Wild Beasts of India," by Colonel G. P. Sanderson (Allen & Co., London), the officer in charge of the Government elephant-catching establishment of Mysore, one of the most fascinating books of sport I have ever read. The Kurubas, or wild hill people, live in the woods in small communities, their dwellings being mere hovels made from branches of trees. In January the Kurubas burn the dry jungle grass, which has grown to five or six feet and seeded, the burnt ground quickly producing a supply of sweet green herbage when the showers of spring have fallen on the ashes. These people live on succulent roots of various kinds, leaves, and *ragi*, a coarse grain grown in the plains.

They are black, ugly, and short in stature; their coarse hair grows to a great length, and is tied back with string. They are now beginning to take work on coffee plantations, and in the forest department as tree-fellers. They are fond of sport, and are thoroughly acquainted with the habits of all the wild animals of the country. They hunt with spear and net. The nets are first supported on upright light props set across a line of country. The jungle is then driven up to the nets, into which the animals gallop; their heads become entangled in the meshes, the net falls and wraps them, and they are speared in the midst of their struggles.

The cultivators of the plains are unsurpassed in skill and industry by any agriculturists of India. The main crop is ragi, which in appearance is very like turnip-seed. It is ground in the common double-stone handmill, boiled in earthen pots into a stiff pudding, made up into balls, and eaten with curried vegetables, or meat if it can be got. This is the chief food of the poor throughout Southern India, and is only about one-third the price of rice.

The other important crops are coffee, sugar, oil-seeds, areca or betel-nuts, cinchona and cardamoms. The number of coffee plantations held by Europeans is about 500, and there are probably 25,000 small patches cultivated by natives. These cover about 150,000 acres, altogether producing about 5,000,000 pounds of coffee. The out-turn of sugar is £160,000, and of areca nuts £180,000 in value every year. The rice and grain crops are large, reaching a total annual value of £350,000.

The revenues of the State are about £1,100,000, and the expenditure usually leaves a comfortable surplus. A yearly subsidy of £350,000 is paid to the British Government, for the maintenance of a force for the defence of Mysore. This force is all stationed at Bangalore, and consists of two European and four native regiments, with artillery and sappers.

Mysore city lies at the foot of the Chamundi Hill, an isolated peak rising 1,500 feet out of the plain. The streets are broad and regular, lined with substantial two- and three-storied tiled houses and some fine public buildings. The inhabitants are prosperous. The fort stands in the south of the city, and is a square of about 450 yards. It is devoid of interest as a fortification. It contains the Maharaja's palace, a modern Hindu building, tawdrily decorated with frescoes. In the front is the Dassara Hall, an open gallery supported by four curiously carved pillars, where the Maharaja shows himself on State occasions, seated on his famous fig-wood throne. This throne was presented to Raja Chikka Deva in 1699 by the Emperor Aurangzeb. The fig-wood of which it is made is overlaid with ivory, which has since been covered with gold and silver plating, wrought with figures from the Hindu mythology. Some of the rooms in the palace have doors richly inlaid with carved ivory and silver. The remainder of the area within the fort is covered with buildings for the use of the royal household.

The Jagan Mohan Mahal is a fine building erected by the late Maharaja for the entertainment of European guests. The upper storey is decorated with grotesque paintings of hunting scenes.

There is a very remarkable stone, Nandi or sacred bull, on a low hill near the town, one of the finest Nandis in all India.

A splendid view of the city may be got from the British residency gardens.

Mysore is notable for the excellence of its gold- and silver-smiths, who produce the most beautiful chased and embossed trays and dishes, decorated with flower and leaf patterns in low relief, or mythological subjects in high relief—*repoussé*. The beaten gold jewellery of Mysore is almost as thin as paper, but ornamented so beautifully and artistically as to give the appearance of great solidity. The most highly-finished jewels of beaten gold may be purchased at about one-fifth of the net weight added to the value of the gold. Sandal-wood carving and inlaying is largely carried on at Mysore, mostly figure subjects in very high relief against floral or leaf patterns in low relief, similar to the work of the gold- and silver-smiths. Some clever lacquer-ware is produced here, in imitation of the brilliant jewelled enamels of Jaipur; the ground is laid in transparent green on tin-foil, and the subjects are painted on this shining back-ground in the brightest opaque colours. The weavers make a curious silk cloth, interwoven with lace, which commands a very high price; a good deal of silver and gold lace is also made in the Mysore bazars.

SERINGAPATAM.—This old capital of the State of Mysore is situated on an island in the river Kaveri, ten miles from Mysore. It has a population of about 12,000. The name is taken from Sri Ranga, one of the forms of Vishnu, who is worshipped in the ancient temple within the fort, at which shrine tradition says Buddha himself worshipped. The greater portion of the building dates from the 16th century, though other parts are said to be as old as the 9th century. Many fragments of Jain temples are built into the walls. Seringapatam was the seat of the government of Mysore until 1799, when the fort was stormed after the historical siege, and Tipu Sultan slain in the breach. The residence of the restored Raja was removed to Mysore, and Seringapatam, which had a population of 150,000 at the height of Tipu's power, fell into the decay in which it still remains. The place is very malarious, like most ruined and abandoned cities. The fort is a huge mass of masonry, without architectural beauty, and its interest centres only in the historic struggle which was ended within its walls. The story is told in every history of India, and at full length in Colonel G. B. Malleson's "Seringapatam." Inside the fort are the ancient temple, the Jama Masjid, a fine mosque built by Tipu shortly before his death, and the

SACRED BULL, MYSORE.

ruins of Tipu's palace. Outside the wall is the Darija Daulat Bagh, (the garden of the sea's wealth), a decaying building handsomely decorated with arabesque work in rich colours. It was built by Tipu as a summer-house, and contains the celebrated pictures representing the defeat of the British forces at Conjeveram by Haidar Ali in 1780. They are quaint specimens of native art, the caricature of the British soldiers being extremely amusing.

At the lower end of the island is the Lal Bagh, containing the mausoleum built by Tipu for his father Haidar Ali, in which he himself lies buried also. It is a square building, with dome and minarets, surrounded by a pillar corridor of black hornblende. The double doors, inlaid with ivory, were a present from Lord Dalhousie. The inscription on Tipu's tomb states that he died a martyr to Islam.

Falls of the Kaveri.—Enclosing the Island of Sivasamudram are the celebrated falls of the river Kaveri, unrivalled in all India for romantic beauty. The nearest station is Maddur, half way between Mysore and Bangalore. There is a good refreshment room. The distance to the falls is thirty miles: there is a fair Dak bungalow. Arrangements for conveyance can be made by writing to the Maddur station-master. The river is split by the island, which is three miles long, and each stream makes a descent of about 200 feet in a succession of rapids and waterfalls. The island is malarious in the winter. At this time too, although the scenery is exquisitely beautiful, the river is narrow and shallow, dividing itself into a score of cascades. The best time to visit Sivasamudram is during the rainy season, when the river roars down the fall in an unbroken sheet 500 yards wide, with a horse-shoe recess in the centre, as at Niagara, to which it has been compared. The island is connected with the mainland by two solid stone bridges, accessible in the highest floods. Twelve miles from Sivasamudram is the ancient city of Talkad, on the left bank of the river. Its history is obscure, but tradition says that the last rani of Talkad cursed the city "that it should become sand," and then drowned herself in the Kaveri. At the present time the old city is buried under heaps of sand, with here and there the tops of pagodas sticking up. One fine temple is still uncovered, and another is kept open with great labour, for worship, by the surrounding inhabitants. The traveller who is exploring Mysore leisurely will find it worth while to push on ten miles farther to Somnathpur, celebrated for its two splendid old temples. That of Prasanna Chenna Kesava was completed in 1270 A.D., by a prince of that name. The whole building is elaborately ornamented, and the structure is completed by three pyramidal towers, or *vimanas*, surmounting the triple shrine. Round the exterior base, carved in relief, are leading incidents of the Ramayana, Mahabharata, and Bhagvata, the termination of each chapter and book being indicated by a closed or half-closed door. The number of sculptured pictures is seventy-four. The workmanship is attributed to Jakanachari, the famous sculptor and architect of the Hoysala Ballala kings, under whom Hindu art in Mysore reached its highest point of excellence. The temple stands in a square cloistered court of great beauty, with entrance porches, and some fine stambhas or lamp pillars.

BANGALORE.—This delightful city is one of the pleasantest and most attractive in India. It stands in the centre of the Mysore plateau, 3,113 feet above the sea, its climate being noted for its healthiness and suitability to European constitutions. The mean temperature is seventy-six degrees, and the average rainfall thirty-six inches. The death-rate of the native city is only seventeen per 1,000, and of the cantonment fifteen.

The plain is level, broken only by a few slight elevations, and

TIPU SULTAN'S TOMB, SERINGAPATAM.

interspersed with several beautiful tanks. The old native city, or *pet*, covers an area of two and one-third square miles, with a population of 65,000. The bazars are narrow and irregular, with many handsome houses of prosperous merchants. There is much stir and bustle, with plenty of lively trade.

The cantonments are scattered over a wide area of about twelve square miles, with a population of nearly 100,000. Within this area is the British Residency, a splendid range of public offices. The central jail, one of the finest in India, the central college, the magnificent new palace of the maharaja, the barracks, the racecourse, parade-ground and public park, the handsome Trinity church, the museum, the Roman Catholic cathedral, the Wesleyan chapel, the handsome bungalows of officers and European residents, the beautiful botanical gardens of Lal Bagh, the bandstand, St. John's Hill, dotted with the cottages of a large number of pensioned European soldiers, and all the other concomitants of a first-class British cantonment. The principal hotels are the "Bowring" and the "Cubbon," and there is a first-class Dak bungalow. The fort, rebuilt in stone in the first year of Haidar Ali's reign, has played a conspicuous part in British Indian history. The prison cell of Sir David Baird, during his captivity after Baillie's defeat in 1780, is still shown, a room twelve feet square, so low that a man cannot stand upright in it.

Most of the leading handicrafts of a large Indian city are to be seen in the Bangalore bazars. Silks of durable texture and brilliant patterns are sold by weight. Cotton cloth, printed, or with silk borders, gold and silver lace, jewellery, electroplating and leather tanning, are special industries, and their sale carried on in all the crowded streets, but specially at open stalls in the picturesque *Dodda pet*. The jail is noted for its manufacture of carpets, mostly of Persian or Turkish designs.

In the museum are some of the most perfect of the sculptures of the famous temples of Halebid, the ancient capital of the Mysore kings in the 13th century. Halebid, the old capital of the Rajput Ballalas of Mysore, is 110 miles north of Mysore city, and very seldom visited by travellers. Its temples rank with the greatest masterpieces of Indian architecture.

The great temple of Halebid is the noblest example of the Chalukyan style. It was never finished, having been stopped by the Musalman conquest, A.D. 1310. It is a double temple. It stands on a terrace six feet high. Round this runs a wonderful frieze of 2,000 elephants, following all the windings of the ground plan. Above it is a frieze of lions, then a band of scroll-work of infinite beauty and variety of design, over which is a frieze of horsemen, then another scroll, and a frieze representing mythological subjects. Above all these are two more friezes of beasts and birds, then a scroll-work cornice, bearing a rail divided into panels, each containing two figures, over which are windows of pierced slabs of stone, divided at regular intervals by sculptured columns. The abutments are richly ornamented by carved figures of gods five and a half feet in height. Above all would have risen pyramidal towers, had the temple been finished.

Tumkur and Harihar are both very ancient places in a picturesque

FALLS OF THE KAVERI, SIVASAMUDRAM.

country on the Mysore State Railway, 43 and 210 miles respectively from Bangalore. There is, however, nothing of sufficient importance to attract any traveller not specially interested in Hindu archæology.

There are six episcopal churches of England in Bangalore, under the supervision of the Bishop of Madras—St. Mark's, in St. Mark's Square, in connection with which is a boarding-school for European boys and girls and the cantonment orphanage; Trinity, in Trinity Road; St. John's, in St. John's Hill; All Saints, in Shoolay; St. Paul's, in New Market Road, and one in the fort. Of these St. Paul's is occupied by a Tamil congregation, and is under the charge of the Society for the Propagation of the Gospel. Bishop Cottom's schools and college provide good education for English boys and girls, based on the principles of the Church of England.

There is a church of the Scottish Establishment in Cubbon Road, on the north side of the Parade. Morning and evening services are held, and a Sunday-school is carried on. There is a good boys' and girls' school, both day and boarding, under the management of this church. The Wesleyan Mission carries on work in English and Tamil in the civil and military station, and in Kanarese in the city.

In the English circuit there are two chapels, one in East Parade, and one in Cleveland Town, St. John's Hill. The ministers' residences adjoin the chapels. Services are also conducted in the infantry and cavalry barracks, at the city railway station, in the fort, and at the Kolar gold mines. A girls' school for European and Eurasian children is attached to each chapel, and a free school is maintained in Shoolay. A home for poor children has recently been opened in the compound of East Parade Chapel. Adjoining the chapel premises there is a soldiers' home. Immediately behind the chapel on St. John's Hill is a young men's Christian institute, and at a little distance in Haines' Road a reading-room for pensioners. There are also in connection with the chapels, Sunday-schools, temperance associations, and mothers' meetings.

The *Tamil* work is under the superintendence of a European missionary, who resides in Promenade Road, Cleveland Town, St. John's Hill. The principal chapel is in Haines' Road. Another is in course of erection in Shoolay. A girls' boarding-school adjoins the missionary's house in Cleveland Town. There is an English middle-school for boys in the bazar. There are Anglo-vernacular schools in

THE DODDA PET, BANGALORE.

Mutucheri and Shoolay, and five Tamil schools. For girls there are five day-schools.

The missionary is assisted by a native minister, catechists, Zenana visitors, and Bible-women.

In the *Kanarese* circuit there are two European missionaries and a native minister. The senior missionary, who is also general superintendent of all the Wesleyan Missions in the Mysore Province and on the Nilgiri Hills, resides at No. 6, Fort Road. The Kanarese chapel is in Nagartara Pettah in the city. The senior missionary has charge of a theological class. The high school is on the mission premises in Fort Road. A girls' boarding-school adjoins the mission houses. In the city and suburbs there are four Kanarese schools for boys and three for girls.

The London Mission conducts its operations in the civil and military station and in the city.

The Tamil chapel is situated in the Infantry Road, and is under the care of a native pastor. Two schools teaching up to the lower fourth standard are sustained in this part of Bangalore. Three native female agents are employed in visiting the homes of Hindu families. Evangelist work is carried on by an ordained native evangelist with the aid of other members of the church. The Tamil work generally is under the supervision of a European missionary, who lives in St. Mark's Square.

One of the European missionaries labours among the English-speaking portion of the Hindu community by private intercourse, Bible-classes, lectures and in other ways. His work is not confined to Bangalore, but extends to many other important stations.

In former years English services were conducted in the chapel in the Infantry Road; but when the Scotch church was opened these were discontinued, the English congregation joining that of the Presbyterians.

In the city the work is carried on in the Kanarese language. The congregation, which is under the care of a native pastor, worships in a chapel near the Yellahunka Gate of the city. Without this gate is a high school under the charge of a European missionary, who resides at No. 4, St. Mark's Square.

Two missionaries are engaged in Kanarese work, one of them having special charge of the work in the adjacent country.

On the mission premises there is a theological seminary conducted by two of the missionaries, the two vernacular languages and English being used in the course of instruction. On the same premises there is also a boarding-school for girls. In the city there are four girls' day-schools and a reading-room. Evangelistic work is carried on in another building by the native pastor with the help of other Christians. A lady missionary is employed in superintending female education. Two Bible-women also are employed; there are two Sunday-schools.

The English work of the Methodist Episcopal Mission is under the charge of an American missionary. The chapel is situated in Myrtle Street, Richmond Town. Regular preaching services are held on Sunday and during the week. There is also a Sunday-school. Regular services and Sunday-school are also held in the native chapel, Memorial Street, St. John's Hill.

The English minister resides in Kingston Cross Street, Richmond Town. Their English educational work is at Baldwin High Schools, Nos. 5 & 6, Hosúr Road. The principal is helped by a staff of twelve teachers. Both boarders and day-scholars are admitted. The instruction is carried to the matriculation standard of the Madras University. Among the subjects taught a prominent place is given to systematic Bible study.

The native work is under the superintendence of an American missionary, with the aid of an assistant and seven native helpers. The chapel and mission-house are in Memorial Street, St. John's Hill. Regular services are held every week in the chapel. The Sunday-schools, twenty in number, are held in various parts of Bangalore.

The ladies attached to the Church of England Zenana Mission, in the Old Museum Road, have established three schools for Muhammadan girls, and visit Muhammadan families for the purpose of instructing the female members of those households.

The Baptist Church is supported from local resources. The chapel is situated in the Commissariat Road. The services and work of the church are carried on in the English language. There is a Sunday-school connected with the congregation. The church is under the care of an English minister, who resides at No. 22, Richmond Road.

There is an auxiliary of the Bible and Religious Tract Societies, under the direction of committees. In connection with them colporteurs are employed in Bangalore and various other stations. Besides Scriptures and other books received from London, vernacular translations of the Bible and other vernacular publications prepared by these two societies are sold at the depository in Cubbon Road.

The Roman Catholic churches of Bangalore are under the jurisdiction of the Bishop of Mysore. The principal churches are St. Patrick's Cathedral, in Shoolay; St. Francis Xavier's, in St. John's Hill; St. Mary's, in Blackpully, and St. Joseph's, near the fort. There are usually three or four services every Sunday in each church, as well as Sunday-schools in the English, Tamil, and Kanarese languages. The work of this church engages the services of a large number of priests and several nuns, who belong to the order of the Good Shepherd.

St. Joseph's College give a university training to European and Eurasian youths, and there are excellent girls' schools under the direction of the nuns of the Good Shepherd.

THE NILGIRI HILLS.—The traveller who has been faithfully following the routes laid down in this book, will have had about enough of the hot plains and cities of the Madras Presidency, and will long for the coolness and greenery of the world-renowned Nilgiri Hills, the sanatarium and holiday place of the European population of all Southern India. Two trains each day arrive at Mettupalaiyam, the insignificant village which is the present terminus of the Nilgiri branch of the Madras Railway. The time-table is—

		Ordinary.	*Mail.*
Madras .	depart	7. 0 a.m.	5.45 p.m.
Jalarpet . .	„	2.38 p.m.	12.47 a.m.
Salem . .	„	8.35 „	4.26 „
Erode . . .	„	11.10 „	6.22 „
Podanur . .	„	3.26 a.m.	9.29 „
Coimbatore . .	„	3.47 „	9.43 „
Mettupalaiyam	„	5.15 „	11. 0 „

There are good refreshment rooms at Jalarpet, Salem, Erode, and Podanur. I advise those who are coming from stations south of Jalarpet, to take the ordinary train, so as to arrive at Mettupalaiyam at 5.15 A.M., and get the hot and dusty drive to the foot of the ghat done in the early dawn.

The three important stations of the Nilgiri Hills, Coonoor, Wellington, and Utakamand, are all reached from Mettupalaiyam. There is an hotel near the station from which tongas may be had, or they may be ordered from the hotels at Utakamand. The whole distance is thirty-two and a half miles, of very good well-metalled road—viz.:

Mettupalaiyam to Foot of Ghat . . .	6 miles.
Foot of Ghat to Coonoor	15 „
Coonoor to Wellington	$2\frac{1}{2}$ „
Wellington to Utakamand	9 „

COONOOR.

Good horses make the journey in about six hours.

Coonoor is 6,000 feet above sea level, with a population of 5,000, of whom 2,000 are Europeans. It is proposed to construct a Righi Railway to Coonoor from Mettupalaiyam. The town presents all the usual features of a popular Indian Hill station—churches, chapels, schools, library, gymkhana, shops and hotels. It is picturesquely scattered on the sides of the beautiful basin formed by the expansion of the Jakatalla Valley, at the mouth of a gorge, surrounded by wooded hills. The climate of Coonoor is cool and equable, the mean annual temperature being sixty-two degrees. In the colder months it ranges about forty-five to fifty degrees. There are about twenty miles of excellent and beautiful pleasure drives, the hedges of which are bright with roses, fuchsias, dahlias, heliotropes, lantanas, sunflowers, passion flowers, and many others.

It is a lovely spot, every turn of the roads opening some fresh view of noble mountains, steep precipices, sweeps of forest, and the rich fertile plains beyond.

Wellington is on Jakatalla Hill, two or three miles distant from Coonoor, 6,100 feet above the sea. This is the principal military sanitarium of Madras, and is very salubrious and invigorating. The handsome range of barracks was built in 1857. In sheltered spots and nooks of the hills all round Coonoor and Wellington, it is possible to grow all sorts of European vegetables, and the soil is so fertile that three or four crops are often raised in the year. New potatoes, cauliflowers, tomatoes, green peas, lettuce, beets, carrots, and red or white raspberries, may be looked for at the various meals of the excellent hotels on the Nilgiris.

Utakamand is always spoken of by Europeans with fond affection as "*Ooty.*" It has a population of 15,000, of which 3,000 are Christians, and about 600 Europeans. It lies 7,228 feet above the sea level; the mean temperature is fifty-eight degrees. The town is cradled in an amphitheatre of lovely hills, on which the bungalows are scattered. In the hollow centre, an artificial lake has been formed, surrounded by a beautiful drive. The vegetation is luxuriant and abundant. Utakamand is the administrative headquarters of the Nilgiri Hills' district, and the permanent society of the place consists of the civil service, well-to-do coffee-planters, and others who have made this delightful spot their Indian home.

There are at least six mountains with an elevation exceeding 8,000 feet within easy reach of Utakamand. The loftiest is Dodabetta, 8,760 feet. The finest view is from Elk Hill. The scenery of the best portion of the Nilgiris lies immediately round the station, and can be explored with ease and comfort in carriages. By the time the traveller has visited the Botanical Gardens, the Kalhatti and Barhyar Gardens, the Dodabetta cinchona plantation—all under Government supervision, the Hobart Park, Orange Valley, the

THE LAKE, UTAKAMAND.

M M

Mysore Ditch, the Basle Mission at Keti and the Lawrence Asylum, full particulars of which are given in the excellent local handbook, he will have seen most of the grandest views in the district, and the many beautiful gorges and cascades which everywhere abound. A delightful day excursion may be made to Mur Kurti Peak, a distance of fourteen miles. One side of this mountain is a sheer precipice of nearly 7,000 feet, and the view from the summit is superb.

Nilgiri means "the Blue Mountains." The district consists of a mountain plateau, with an average elevation of 6,500 feet, and covering an area of 725 square miles. The mountains rise like abrupt walls from the plains for about 4,000 to 6,000 feet.

The plateau consists chiefly of undulating grassy hills, breaking into lofty ridges and abrupt rocky cliffs on the outer edge. The narrow valleys contain pretty streams and cascades, and in the hollow of the hill-side nestle beautiful little evergreen woods or copses, called *sholas*, giving a distinctive feature of great interest to this lovely mountain scenery. In the summer, these *sholas* are often a mass of white, yellow and red blossom, and the neighbouring ravines are sweet with the long white flowers of the scented Nilgiri lily, or the pale blue lobelia. The grassy slopes are covered with strobilanthes, whose masses of blue flowers are said to have given the name of "Nilgiri" to the range. There are few districts in India which present such an endless variety of trees, shrubs, and flowering plants and herbs. The Michelia nilagirica flourishes everywhere, covered with large white blossom from July to October, and at other times gay with scarlet seeds. The eugenias are dense masses of thick, leathery, aromatic, dark-green foliage. There are many varieties of beautiful ilexes, and several kinds of elæocarpus, with bright red leaves and long branches of white or pink flowers. A small variety of mahua; the tree from whose blossom most of the native spirit of India is distilled, is very abundant, the fruit of which is made into pickles and is much esteemed; and besides these, are teak, blackwood, sandalwood trees, cedars, eucalyptus, litsæas, gordonias, cinnamon trees, rhododendrons, red myrtles, and an endless variety of the most beautiful orchids, ferns and brambles.

Animal life is fairly abundant for a district so much resorted to by Europeans, but tiger, bear, sambhar deer and ibex, are only found in the remotest gorges. There are plenty of leopards, wild boars, hyænas, jungle sheep, porcupines, woodcock, snipe, spur fowl, jungle and pea fowl, and for the last ten years game has been preserved by a close season. There are eighteen peaks in the Nilgiris ranging from 6,000 to nearly 9,000 feet above sea level, and six practicable passes or ghats leading up from the surrounding plains.

The principal crops of the district are coffee, tea, and cinchona.

TRAVELLING IN THE NILGIRI HILLS.

The planting of coffee has been very successful. In 1875, there were only 126 plantations, but in 1889 the number had reached over 600, the total crop of which is from 4,000 to 5,000 tons annually. They employ 12,000 labourers, and there are about 200 European planters or superintendents.

The first tea garden was planted in 1851, and there are now nearly 100, producing about a million pounds of marketable tea.

The Madras Government commenced the experimental growth of cinchona in 1860, and have now got four estates, covering nearly 3,000 acres; there are also half a dozen private ventures.

The hill tribes of the Nilgiris are among the most primitive and interesting races in India. There are five different tribes, the Todas, Badajas, Kotas, Kurumbas, and Irulas. The most attractive of them are the Todas; tall, well-proportioned, and athletic, with bold independent carriage, and finely-moulded, sinewy limbs which show they are sprung from no effeminate race. Their aquiline nose, receding forehead, and rounded profile, with their black bushy beards and eyebrows, give them a decidedly Jewish appearance. Their dress consists of a single cloth, worn in a manner which sets off their muscular forms, something in the fashion in which the Highlander wears his plaid. The costume of the women is much the same as the men, the toga being wrapped round them to cover the entire person from shoulder to ankle. The men average five feet eight inches, and the women five feet one inch. They are copper coloured, and the men are very hairy. They are lazy and dirty, and practise polyandry, a woman marrying all the brothers in one family. Their sole occupation is cattle-herding and dairy work. They live in huts, twelve or fifteen feet square, built of bamboo closely laid together, fastened with rattans and thatched. They sleep on a raised clay platform covered with the skins of deer or buffalo. The dairy is also their temple, for they worship the cow. Their religion is extremely primitive, with a good deal of demonolatry introduced. Their religious customs are all woven in with their pastoral pursuits, and when anyone dies, they kill a cow, to supply the deceased with milk in the next world. They number less than a thousand all told, and are slowly dying out. They are the aristocratic tribe of the Nilgiri Hills, and receive tribute from the others. Their children are very pretty.

The Badagas are Hindu in religion, and their chief temple is on the top of Rangaswami Peak, 5,937 feet. They wear quaint ornaments, rings, bracelets, armlets, necklaces, and nose rings of brass, iron, or silver. They number 25,000.

The Kotas, or "cowkillers," live in villages of thirty to sixty huts, with mud walls and thatched roofs. They are not idolaters, but worship ideal gods, of whom they have no images. There are about 1,000 of them.

The Kurumbas, or "shepherds," are the most uncivilised; very

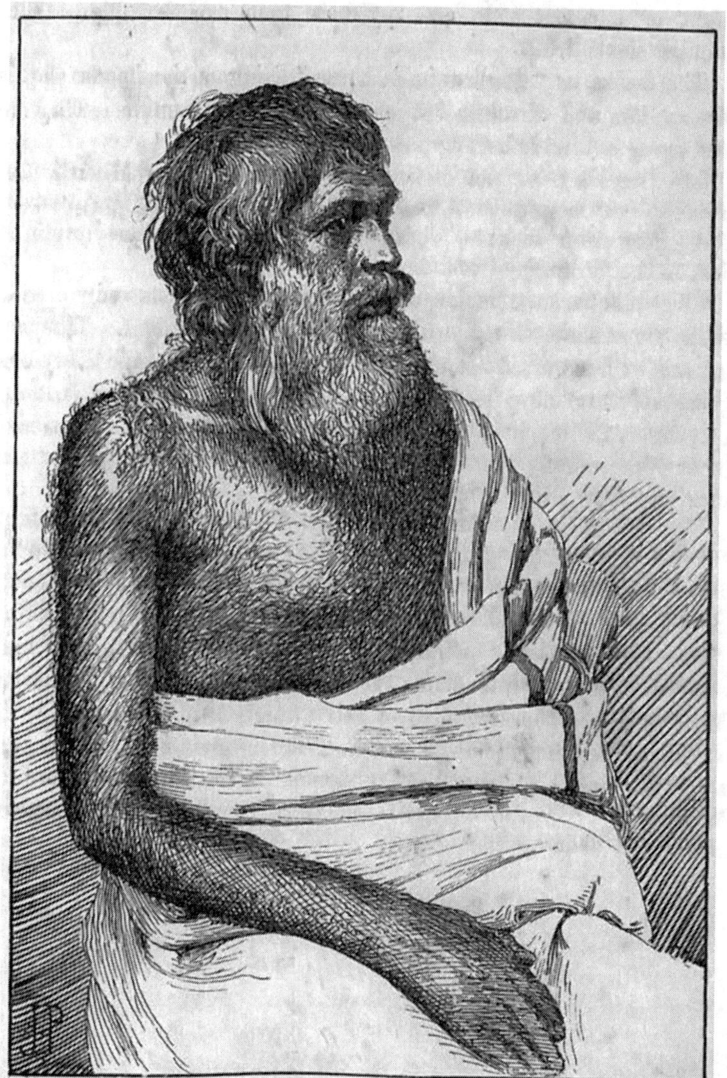

A TODA.

ugly, with matted unkempt locks, and almost naked bodies, wearing only a waist cloth. They worship natural objects, and greatly reverence the Todas. They live in long huts, forty or fifty feet long, eight or ten feet wide, and not more than five feet high. They number about 3,000.

The Irulas, or "dwellers in darkness," living on the lowest slopes, are an idle and dissolute lot, but are very good hunters. They are fast dying out, and there are less than 1,000 left.

Mr. Breek's pamphlet on these tribes, published by Allen & Co., London, may be purchased in the shops at Utakamand; it gives very full information about all these interesting people, whose origin is lost in the darkness of past ages.

The antiquarian remains of the Nilgiri Hills consist only of rude stone monuments placed on the summits of hills or ridges. They are agrams, or funeral circles, cairns, barrows, cromlechs, and kistvaens. Some of these have been opened, and explored; weapons, pottery, clay figures, flint and bronze tools or weapons, being discovered. They are generally supposed to be Scythian, or the work of the time of the Pandyan Kingdom of Madura, 400 B.C.

The American Reformed Church missionary is the Rev. John Scudder of Coonoor, who is also a medical man. The membership is 120, and there are schools for boys and girls. The Church Missionary Society have a church at Utakamand which, with the surrounding village stations, has a membership of about 400 converts, and nine schools with an attendance of 500 scholars. The Wesleyan Methodists are represented by a native minister at Utakamand, with a church of seventy members, and an English missionary, who has the spiritual charge of the Wesleyan soldiers at the sanatarium of Wellington. The Basle Society has agents at Kaiti and Kotagiri, among the Badaga tribes.

CHAPTER XXXVI.

MADRAS TO TANJORE.

PONDICHERRI.—There is no interest attaching to Pondicherri, beyond that of historical associations. It is the chief French settlement in the East Indies, with a steadily diminishing population, now about 140,000, possessing a fertile area of about 115 square miles.

It was settled by the French in 1674, captured from them by the Dutch in 1693, and restored in 1699. It was taken by the English in 1761, but restored again to the French in 1763; once more captured in 1778, and given back in 1785; and yet again in 1793, when it was retained by the English until 1816. It is a pleasant town, facing the sea, with excellent public buildings. The revenues are under £60,000 a-year. The funny little carriages, like perambulators, pushed by one or two coolies, which are the principal means of transit in the streets, are called "pousse-pousse."

CUDDALORE is the administrative headquarters of South Arcot District, situated on a backwater formed by the confluent estuaries of two rivers. It is a Hindu city, with a population of about 45,000; a pleasant sea-breezy place, with a good harbour for native coasting vessels; the imports and exports reach a total value of about £130,000, mainly rice, sugar, coal, and grain. There is a native and European town, the latter being scattered on a slightly elevated plain, traversed by good roads lined with avenues of trees. Cuddalore was one of the early stations of the East India Company, who erected a factory in 1683, and built Fort St. David during the following ten years. There is nothing left of it but a few ruined walls and a choked ditch.

PORTO NOVO is a small seaport town of 8,000 inhabitants. The Danes and Portuguese had factories here in the 17th century and here, in 1781, Sir Eyre Coote defeated Haidar Ali, and practically saved the Madras Presidency. Very pretty mats are made here from the leaves of the wild pineapple.

CHILAMBARAM (the atmosphere of wisdom), is a town of some importance, with a considerable trade in the weaving of silk and cotton cloth, giving employment to a large portion of its population of 20,000. There is a good Dak bungalow here. It was a place of much strategic importance during the wars of the Karnatic.

During December, a great religious mela or fair is held, its celebrated temples being reverenced throughout all Southern India, and even in Ceylon. The great pagoda of Kanak Sabha, or Golden Shrine, sacred to Siva and his wife Parvati, is very ancient. Fergusson says that some portions date as far back as the 10th and 11th centuries; the temple of Parvati and the Great Gopuras to the 14th or 15th; and the Hall of One Thousand Columns to the beginning of the 16th.

Tradition asserts that the earliest portions of this vast structure were built by Hiranya Varna Chakrasti, the golden-coloured king, who was here cured of leprosy. Some writers say that they are the work of a Kashmir prince of the 5th century, who brought with him 3,000 Brahmans from the north. To this day the temple belongs to about 250 families of a peculiar sect of Brahmans, twenty of whom are always on duty at a time, for a period of twenty days, which it takes to make the complete ceremonial tour at the different shrines of the temple, where daily offerings are made. These Dikshatar Brahmans only marry among themselves, and it is said there are no members of their sect anywhere but at Chilambaram. They collect alms all over South India, when not on duty in the temples.

This splendid group of buildings measures 600 yards by 500 yards, covering thirty-nine acres. Two walls, each thirty feet high, surround it; and at each of the four corners stands a solid gopura or pyramid 122 feet high, faced with granite blocks forty feet long,

MAHAMOHAN TANK, COMBACONUM.—ANNUAL FESTIVAL.

and five feet thick, covered with copper. The Hall of One Thousand Pillars is magnificent, looking like a forest of granite columns, all monoliths, twenty-five feet high. In the centre is the shrine of Parvati, a very beautiful building, containing a golden canopy, with superb bullion fringes. The sanctuary is an ugly copper-roofed enclosure, with an image of Siva dancing, in the interior. The Miratha Sabha is a perfect gem. The Pillyar temple contains a huge idol, the largest belly god in India. The Sivaganga, or Golden Tank, 150 feet square, is very handsome, surrounded on all sides with spacious flights of steps. There is also a curious well, built of granite rings placed one on the other, each ring cut from a single block. Fergusson gives a description, with plans of this extraordinary temple, pp. 350—55. In the town are a large number of native rest-houses, seventy in all, which are crowded with pilgrims at the time of the mela.

MAYAVARAM is a town of 24,000 inhabitants, on the banks of the Kaveri. It is a great place of pilgrimage, and there are two pagodas of some importance. The gopura of the Shiva temple is 162 feet high.

COMBACONUM is one of the most important cities in the Madras Presidency, with a population of more than 50,000. It is situated in the richest tract of the Kaveri delta. Formerly the capital of the Chola kingdom, it is one of the most ancient and sacred towns in Southern India, and is so celebrated for its learning as to be spoken of as the Indian Oxford. It is much resorted to by learned Indians, and great numbers of pilgrims.

The older buildings have disappeared, though fragments of them are plentiful enough in the walls of those of more recent date. There is a very beautiful gopura, not one of the largest, but rich in detail and decoration. The largest pagoda is in twelve stories, and is fully 160 feet high. The temple of Siva is approached by a curious arched passage, 330 feet long, lined with shops on either side.

The Mahamohan tank is one of the handsomest in India, its banks being studded with fine temples, flights of steps, and a very large and ancient pagoda of red brick. There are a number of huge idol cars, like that of Jagganath, which at the annual festival are dragged by thousands of people.

The Beauchamp College at Combaconum is one of the best in India.

TANJORE.—This important city of 60,000 inhabitants is situated in what has been justly termed the garden of South India. It is on the vast Delta of the Kaveri, a highly cultivated and populous district, irrigated by a network of canals, and dotted with magnificent groves of cocoanut trees. There are more than 8,000 Hindu temples in this wealthy district, that in Tanjore city being the finest in India. The grand anicut on the Kaveri, which feeds the irrigation canals, is said to have been made by a Chola king in the 3rd century. It was originally a solid mass of rough stone, 1,080 feet in length, sixty feet wide, and eighteen feet deep, stretching across the whole width of one of the outlets of the Kaveri River. The irrigation works of Tanjore are unusually interesting to those who care to see such feats of engineering.

Tanjore was the capital of the Chola dynasty, one of the greatest of the ancient Hindu monarchies from the 10th to the 14th century. It has been a place of great consequence as a political capital, a seat of learning, and a religious centre for the last 1,200 years.

The travellers' bungalow is situated near the little fort. The fort, palace, and temple of Tanjore present a group of buildings unrivalled in Southern India.

The fort surrounds the entire city, and was built by the Nayakar kings of Tanjore; afterwards enlarged by the kings of the Maratha dynasty. The citadel contains a tank of very fine pure water, the great temple, and a small Christian church built by Schwartz, the well-known missionary, whose beautiful tomb, by Flaxman, is a notable specimen of the work of this famous sculptor.

On one of the ramparts is a monster gun, called Raja Gopala, made of rings of iron welded together, and bound with hoops of brass. This gun is twenty-four feet five inches long, with an outside circumference of ten feet three inches, and a bore of two feet two inches. It was made by one of the Vaishnava Nayakar kings. It has only been fired once, when the inhabitants were warned by beat of drum to clear out of the town. It was fired by a train of powder two miles long, which took forty minutes to reach the gun. All went well! It is the palladium of the fort, and was worshipped in hours of peril.

The palace covers a large area. Its main features are the seven-storied tower, the hall of the Nayakar kings (recently excavated after a burial of 150 years), the arsenal, and the Nayakar Durbar Hall.

MOAT AND RAMPARTS, TANJORE.

The seven-storied tower has a very imposing appearance from a distance, but a closer view disillusionizes. It is a barbaric mixture of Saracenic and European architecture, and was built by Serfoji I., occupying thirty-five years in the erection.

The Nayakar Durbar Hall is a fine quadrangle. It is the most pure and perfect specimen of Nayakar architecture in existence, and, differing from Madura, is purely Indian. Within this hall is the noble statue by Chantrey of Raja Sivaji, the greatest of the Maratha kings. It is placed upon the ancient stone on which the Nayakar kings sat to administer justice. This is a huge monolith of granite, twenty-four feet long, eighteen feet broad, and three feet thick, round the edge of which run sculptures representing the wars of demons. The stately south façade of the Durbar Hall should be carefully examined. The foliated arches between the pillars, now filled up with stucco, were formerly open, giving free access to the hall. Here councils of war were held.

The great pagoda of Tanjore differs from almost every other Dravidian temple, in having been conceived as a whole on a well-defined plan, persevered in to its completion. It consists of two courtyards, the outer, about 250 feet square, and the inner, about 500 feet by 250 feet, in which the temple itself stands. The buildings date from the beginning of the 14th century, onwards.

The central tower of the great pagoda is the finest in India of its kind. Its base is a square of ninety-six feet, and the height 208 feet. It covers the holy of holies, in which the chief idol of the temple is placed. The shadow at noon does not project beyond the base. The huge circular dome at the top is a granite monolith, and tradition says that an inclined plane of five miles in length was built, up which this enormous stone was rolled to the top of the tower, by forced labour. Round the basement is an inscription in ancient Tamil characters, giving an account of the various contributions of the pious to the erection of the building. The porch and main entrance is singularly fine.

The gateway tower is one of the oldest portions of the temple; it is dedicated to Vrihatisvaran, one of the names of Siva. It was built about A.D. 1330, by one of the kings of Conjeveram, who is said to have built altogether 108 similar temples in Southern India, of which this is the largest. The large sculptured figure at the entrance is the familiar door-keeper of Dravidian temples: he has four hands, with two of which he invites the worshippers to enter, while the other two are held up in warning against presumption.

Half-way between the entrance-gate and the great pagoda, is the famous Nandi, or sacred bull of Siva. It is crouching down under a superb pillared shrine elaborately decorated with sculpture, and surrounded by trees. The dimensions of the bull are sixteen feet from muzzle to rump, seven feet wide across the back, twelve feet two inches

THE MAIN GATEWAY, TANJORE TEMPLE.

high to the top of the head, ten feet four inches to the top of the hump, and seven feet five inches to the top of the back. It is sculptured from a solid block of syenite, and its daily anointing with oil has produced an effect equal to the finest bronze. The block of stone is said to have been brought a distance of 400 miles.

On the north side of the great tower is a small temple dedicated to Pawati, and a singularly beautiful shrine sacred to Soubramanya, the younger son of Siva, the Hindu god of war. It is of a much later period than the great pagoda itself, probably about the middle of the

15th century. It is remarkable for the wonderful skill and minuteness with which the details of its sculptured decorations have been worked out. The figures in the recesses are various representations of Soubramanya.

Against one of the outer walls of Soubramanya's temple is placed a sacred cistern and sculptured water-spout, that ought not to be passed by unobserved. The water which flows out of the spout has been poured over the idol inside, and is drunk by the Hindu worshippers as a meritorious and purifying act.

The inner side of the courtyard is arcaded, and is probably the oldest portion of the entire temple fabric. The 216 compartments are occupied by lingams of black stone.

Many of the idols in this great temple are very ancient, centuries older than any of its buildings. There are a great number of smaller temples and shrines within the boundaries of the Temple, but they do not call for any detailed description.

The finest brass and metal work in India is made at Tanjore and Madura. Sir Geo. Birdwood says that in its bold forms and elaborately inwrought ornamentation it recalls the descriptions by Homer of the work of the artists of Sidon in bowls of antique fame. Some are simply etched, others deeply cut in mythological designs, and others diapered all over with *crustae* of the leaf pattern, seen in Assyrian sculptures, copper on brass, or silver on copper, producing an effect often of quite regal grandeur.

The gold and silver jewellery and *repoussé* work of Tanjore is superb, and purely Indian, generally of mythological designs. Pretty paintings on Talc are sold in the bazars.

The calicoes made here are of very excellent quality, and are woven in coloured threads into striped, checked, or tartan cloth. Striped silk materials are very beautiful, and costly silk pile carpets are also turned out of the Tanjore looms.

Curious figures of pith and wax, as well as idols and temple furnishing in brass and other metals, are a special manufacture of this city.

Tanjore is a great missionary centre; there are no less than twenty-five stations within the district, the principal societies represented being the Leipsic Lutheran, the Society for the Propagation of the Gospel, and the Wesleyan Methodist. The Wesleyan chief, Mr. W. H. Findlay, M.A., lives at Negapatam, where there is an excellent college and High school. The Society for the Propagation of the Gospel headquarters are also at Negapatam, the clergyman in charge being the Rev. T. H. Dodson, B.A.

Negapatam was one of the earliest settlements of the Portuguese on the Coromandel coast. It is an important seaport town of 55,000 inhabitants, carrying on a brisk trade with Ceylon, Burma, and the Straits Settlements.

Its imports and exports are nearly a million sterling. The trade is largely carried on by Labbais, Musalmans who are half Arab and half Hindu in origin, a bold, active, thrifty race, who develop a great capacity for commerce. There is a fine Jesuit college of St. Joseph, with 400 or 500 students and eighteen professors, and the Wesleyans have a thriving mission.

Three miles from Negapatam, at the little seaport of Nagar, is a celebrated mosque with five minarets of from six to ten stories, the highest of which is 150 feet, and can be seen at sea twenty miles off. It was erected by a Maratha Raja of Tanjore nearly 200 years ago. At its annual festival it is resorted to by Musalman pilgrims from all over India.

Twenty-five miles north of Negapatam is Tranquebar, settled by the Danes in 1616, and purchased from them by the English in 1845 for £20,000. It is interesting as the first mission station occupied in India by Protestants, founded by two Lutheran missionaries, Ziegenbalg and Plütschan, in 1706. It is now the headquarters of the Leipsic Evangelical Lutheran Mission. The quaint old Danish fort still stands on the shore, separated from cultivated land by a wide strip of sand.

CHAPTER XXXVII.

TRICHINOPOLI AND MADURA.

TRICHINOPOLI.—Trichinopoli is, after Madras, the largest city in the Presidency, and in point of population, the twenty-fifth in magnitude and importance in all India. In the census of 1881 its population was 84,449, occupying 13,630 houses. Hindus numbered 61,000, Musalmans 12,000, and Christians 11,000. It is the administrative headquarters of the district, a garrison town, a municipality, and an important railway centre. There is a good Dak bungalow. It is situated on the right bank of the Kaveri, fifty-six miles from the sea, which is here a wide and deep river.

Trichinopoli is a place of much historic interest. It figures in the traditions of the South Indian dynasties for five centuries B.C., and was an important centre, and sometimes capital, during the whole of the dynasties of the Pandyan kings. Towards the close of the 16th century, it fell under the dominion of the Nayakan kings of Madura. The greater portion of the fort, and most of the city itself, was built during the reign of the first king, Viswanatha. Choka Nayakan about 100 years afterwards removed his seat of government from Madura to Trichinopoli, erecting the building now known as the Nawab's palace.

Trichinopoli played a conspicuous part in the wars of the Karnatic. It was besieged by the French in 1751, who were drawn off from its walls by the brilliant capture of Arcot by Clive; but it was the centre round which the war raged, and was the subject of successive sieges and blockades for many months, culminating in the memorable struggle of 1754 between Major Laurence and M. Lally under General Dupleix, ended at last by the completion of a provisional treaty between the French and English. Every popular history of India gives an account of the famous siege of Trichinopoli, the best of which, perhaps, will be found in the pages of "Orme's History of the Military Transactions of the British Nation in Indostan from the year 1745," of which a reprint was published in Madras in 1861, and can be got at Messrs. Higinbotham's or any good bookseller in that city.

The great rock of Trichinopoli is a mass of gneiss, rising abruptly out of the plain, like a huge boulder, to a height of 273 feet above the street at its foot. This fortress-crowned rock is conspicuous all over the town, especially when viewed from the river, and forms one of the most striking and picturesque objects in India. The refraction of the sun's rays on this huge bare mass makes Trichinopoli likewise one of the hottest places in India. The fort should, therefore, be visited in the early morning, the view across the country at sunrise, with the noble Kaveri River winding its way through the plain, being singularly beautiful. Trichinopoli stands in a vast expanse of flat country broken only by French Rocks, a chain of low hills about forty feet high, the pretty Golden Rock, 100 feet high, and the Pagodas of Seringham, until the eye reaches the long blue line of the Tale Malai range in the far north.

The old fortifications surrounding the rock, the scenes of many a fight described by Orme, were all demolished thirty years ago, and nothing is now left except the citadel and the small temple which crowns the summit. This is approached by a pillared passage cut in the rock, with elaborate sculptures on the capitals of the columns and the frieze above. Emerging from this covered way, a further flight of steps is cut in the rock on the open. In 1849 a crowd of pilgrims were descending this passage after visiting the temple, when, owing to a panic, 250 persons were crushed to death. The Siva temple on the top is dedicated to Ganapate. There is a large Nandi bull covered with silver, and some images of Siva, Parvati, Skanda, and Ganapate. The old moat of the fort has been filled up, and laid out as a boulevard.

A little distance to the south of the rock is the restored Nawab's

THE ROCK OF TRICHINOPOLI.

palace, now used for public offices. Between the rock and the main gate of the fort is a very handsome *teppakulam*, or raft-tank, with flights of stone steps, and a very picturesque shrine in the middle. At the south-east corner of the tank is a house which is said to have been the residence of Clive. It may be identified by stone elephants kneeling on each side of the doorway.

Trichinopoli is famous for the peculiar and beautiful workmanship displayed in its gold and gemmed jewellery. The designs, like those of Delhi, have suffered from Anglo-Indian custom, and have departed from native purity, but nothing can exceed their technical excellence. The rose chains, and heart-pattern necklaces and bracelets are the best specimens.

Muslins of great beauty are woven and printed here, and stuffs of mixed silk and cotton, of pretty striped and chequered patterns. Some pretty ornaments, such as inkstands, paper-weights and table-tops, are made from a curious shell marble found in the district.

The most important local industry is the manufacture of cigars, in which a large portion of the population is employed. The tobacco used is chiefly imported from Dindigal in the Madura district, that of local growth being very inferior and coarse.

The Leipsic Lutherans, the Wesleyan Methodists, and the Society for the Propagation of the Gospel have missions established in and round Trichinopoli.

SERINGHAM.—Seringham (or, to be very accurate, *Srirangam*) is a town of 20,000 inhabitants two miles north of Trichinopoli, almost in the centre of the island of the same name, formed by a prolonged bifurcation of the Kaveri. The northern branch of this fork is called the Coleroon, the southern retaining the original name. The town is famous for its magnificent temple dedicated to Vishnu, whose vast walls embrace not only the sacred buildings, but the greater part of the town itself.

The island is reached by a long brick and stone bridge of thirty-two arches, each of sixty feet span. The temple is a mile distant, along a road overshadowed with noble trees. The double walls enclose an area 960 yards long by 825 yards wide. It is undoubtedly the largest temple in India. Fergusson says that the Great Northern Gopura, leading to Trichinopoli, is one of the most imposing masses in Southern India, and, probably because it was never finished, is in severe and good taste. Its present height is under 200 feet: if it had been finished it would have risen to a height of 300 feet.

At its base it measures 130 feet wide by 100 feet in depth. The passage through is twenty-one feet six inches wide, and forty-three feet high. The jambs or gateposts are splendid granite monoliths, and the roofing slabs throughout are twenty-four feet long. The general effect of the fifteen great gate-towers and connecting walls of this stupendous temple, with the porticoed enclosures filled with foliage between, which may be viewed from any coign of 'vantage, is at once an unequalled, impressive, and intensely picturesque sight.

The details of the temple are full of interest. The Hall of One Thousand Columns, all of which are granite monoliths, stands in a

THE GREAT TEMPLE OF SERINGHAM.

magnificent courtyard, a mass of elaborate sculptured decoration. The outer enclosure is a bazar filled with shops for the supply of the hosts of pilgrims. Other enclosures contain the residences of

HALL OF A THOUSAND COLUMNS, SERINGHAM.

attendant Brahmans. There are several very beautiful tanks and gardens. The whole of the buildings belong to the 17th and 18th centuries, many of them being unfinished.

The workmanship and carving of this temple is distinctly inferior, with the exception of the sculptured horsemen in front of the pillars in the Hall of One Thousand Columns.

INNER GATEWAY, SERINGHAM.

The figures on the gopuras are not carved in stone, but are moulded in stucco. In fact the interest of this pagoda rests in its vastness as a whole, and the picturesqueness of its details.

The temple possesses an interesting treasury, which should be inspected. The jewels of the idols are quaint in design and perfect in workmanship, and include many unusually fine specimens of the unrivalled skill of the goldsmiths of the district.

AN ASCETIC, SERINGHAM TEMPLE.

The best time to visit Seringham is during the great annual mela, or religious fair, a moveable feast, which, however, always comes in during the month of December or January. At this time one of the great enclosures is roofed in and handsomely decorated. Round the sides are booths in which are placed curious groups of figures illustrating the stories of the gods. The interest of any temple is of course doubled when its courts are thronged with groups of pilgrim worshippers.

Seringham and its temples were used by the French as a fortress and arsenal during the wars of the Karnatic.

JAMBUKESHWAR. — About a mile from Seringham is the Sivaite temple of Jambukeshwar, smaller, but much finer in detail, than its stupendous neighbour. It is built on a uniform and well-arranged plan, with fine effect. It is probably 100 years older than Seringham, belonging to a better period of architecture; portions of it are older still, as far back as the 12th century. Between the two gateways of

FORTRESS OF DINDIGAL.

the second enclosure is a very beautiful portico of cruciform shape, leading to the door of the sanctuary. The fine tank, with a pretty pavilion in the centre, is fed by a perpetual spring. The temple consists of four quadrangles, one inside the other, measuring respectively 810 yards by 500, 215 by 65, 102 by 65, and 42 by 41 yards. The outer quadrangle is again surrounded by four streets of houses and shops. The largest gopura is only 100 feet high.

DINDIGAL is a town of 15,000 inhabitants half way between Trichinopoli and Madura, in the midst of a fertile country in which much tobacco, croton, sarsaparilla, coffee, cardamoms, senna and other valuable crops are grown. There are a large number of Christians here, more than 2,000 in all, who formerly lived in a separate quarter, their houses having a cross on the roof. This place is famous for the manufacture of muslin turbans embroidered with gold.

A fine old fortress, in very good preservation, crowns a remarkable wedge-shaped rock, 1,220 feet above the sea, which, as a place of great strategical importance, commanding the passes between Coimbatore and Madura, has been the scene of many battles and sieges. It was the centre of operations from which Haidar Ali conducted his scheme of rebellion, that ended in his becoming the founder of a brief but eventful dynasty.

AMMAYANAYAKANUR is the station for the Palnai Hills, the loftiest peak of which is 7,000 feet above sea level, where beautiful scenery and excellent sport may be obtained; but no accommodation or supplies are available for the ordinary traveller.

MADURA is the chief town of the district, situated on the bank of the Vaigai River, with a population of 74,000, mostly Hindus. From time immemorial it has been the political and religious capital of the extreme South of India. Its traditional line of Pandyan kings goes back far beyond the Christian era, and in later times it played a leading part in Indian history under Viswanath, who founded the Nayakan dynasty in 1559, and his sixth successor, the powerful monarch Tirumala Nayak, to whom its noblest architecture is due, and who reigned 1623—59. Tirumala was the greatest of his line, and his magnificence and military exploits are duly recorded in the letters of Jesuit missionaries stationed in his country during his reign. His kingdom extended over the whole district south of a line roughly drawn from Calicut to Cuddalore, but fell to pieces after his death, his line being finally extinguished by Chanda Sahib in 1740.

The Dak bungalow is close to the station.

The great temple of Madura is rendered doubly holy by being one of the chosen residences of Siva. It forms a parallelogram 282 yards by 248, surrounded by nine gopuras, one of which is 152 feet high. It presents all the usual characteristics of a fine Dravidian temple. The thousand pillared hall was built by Arya Nayak about 1550. The tank is surrounded by arcades, and is singularly beautiful. The sanctuary was built by Viswanath about 1560. The whole interior of this marvellous temple is one mass of superb carving, the sculptures of Madura being undoubtedly the finest in Southern India. There are some curious frescoes in the arcades round the tank, some of which are very objectionable.

GREAT TEMPLE, MADURA.

The PUDU MANDAPAM, known as Tirumala's Choultrie, is a marvellous building. It is a pillared hall 111 yards long by thirty-five wide, with four ranges of columns, 120 in all, each of which differs from the other, and all most elaborately sculptured. A full account of it, with plan and illustration, is to be found in Fergusson's "Indian Architecture," pp. 359—365. It is said that this choultrie cost over a million sterling, and the temple four millions; not an excessive estimate, considering the elaborateness and quantity of the sculpture, and that it is executed in the hardest granite.

TANK, MADURA TEMPLE.

The façade of the choultrie is adorned with yalis, monsters of the lion type, trampling on elephants, and with groups of warriors on rearing horses, slaying men or tigers. The whole building is in complete preservation, and was built by Tirumala as a guest-house for Siva, who consented to pay the king an annual visit of ten days on condition that a hall worthy of his dignity was built for his reception. Immediately opposite the entrance to the choultrie is a huge unfinished pagoda, destined by Tirumala to be the finest edifice of the kind in all India. It measures fifty-eight yards by thirty-six. The entrance through it is twenty-one feet nine inches wide, and the lofty granite door-posts are monoliths sixty feet high, carved with exquisite scroll patterns of foliage and other fine carvings.

The celebrated palace of Tirumala is the most perfect relic of secular architecture in the Madras presidency. It covers a vast area of ground, and its buildings have been mostly utilised for public purposes. The central palace is now the Collectorate, and has been restored by Government at considerable expenditure. The main structure consists of an open court and lofty hall. The courtyard is 100 yards square, surrounded by galleries crowned with domes. The hall occupies the whole of one side of the quadrangle, its lofty dome, seventy-three feet high and sixty-one in diameter, being supported by rough-hewn granite columns covered with *chunam*.

The central area of the yard was used for gladiatorial or wild beast fights, and other pageants. The whole edifice forms one of the finest public buildings in India.

The Tam Kam, on the opposite bank of the river to Madura, was built by Tirumala for wild beast fights and other shows, but has no architectural interest.

The Teppa Kulam, or great tank, is a mile and a half outside the city, also built by Tirumala. The banks are faced with hewn granite, surmounted with a handsome parapet, beneath which runs a continuous paved gallery. In the centre is a square island with a lofty domed temple in the middle, and dainty little shrines at the four corners. Once a year, at festival time, the banks are lighted up with 10,000 lamps, while the idols from the pagoda are drawn round in a *teppam* or raft. The neighbourhood of this tank is the favourite evening drive for European residents.

Madura is well laid out with wide handsome streets and market-places. A ruined gateway is all that remains of the old fort built by Viswanath.

Christianity is making rapid progress in the district of Madura. In the census of 1881 there were 85,000 in the Madura district, and they will probably exceed 100,000 in that of 1891.

There was a Jesuit Church in Madura in the beginning of the 17th century, where a Portuguese priest ministered to a small congregation of fishermen converted by Francis Xavier. In 1606 Robert de Nobilis came to Madura, adopted the life, diet and dress of a religious devotee. He founded the flourishing mission which now numbers 70,000 converts, ministered to by 14 European and a number of native priests, who perform service in 350 chapels throughout the district. The whole cost of the mission is said not to exceed £2,500 a year.

The mission stations of the Madura district are mainly in the hands of the American Board, who have thirteen American and thirteen native missionaries employed, with about 5,000 communicants and as many scholars in their various district churches and schools.

The brass work of Madura is, like that of Tanjore, the very finest in India. The gold- and silver-smith's work is also famous. One of the most beautiful presents brought home from India by the Prince of Wales was a silver throne of great beauty made at Madura, and given him by the priests of the various temples. Madura is also celebrated for the manufacture of stained cloths, known as Madura cloths. They are very coarse, printed very effectively in two colours only, red and black, with mythological subjects taken from the Ramayana and Mahabharata; sometimes they are touched up in yellow by hand-painting. They are made chiefly for the service of the temples, and are hard to get, except by favour of the priests. Madura is also noted for its handsome turbans, embroidered with gold lace or thread. The pierced and glazed pottery of Madura is very artistic and of the highest quality. It is best in the form of water-bottles, with a globular bowl and long upright neck, the bowl being pierced so as to circulate air round an inner porous bowl; the outer bowl and neck are rudely fretted over by notches in the clay, and are glazed dark green, or a rich golden brown.

If the traveller wishes to visit the sacred island of RAMESHWARAM, he must undertake a weary cross-country journey of 105 miles through Ramnad in bullock-carts or palkis. Fergusson is of opinion that if it were proposed to select one temple which should exhibit all the beauties of the Dravidian style in their greatest perfection and at the same time exemplify all its characteristic defects of design, the choice would inevitably fall on that of Rameshwaram. He gives some account of it, with plans and illustrations, pp. 355—359.

It was built by the Ramnad rajas during the 17th century, on a low sandy island in the Gulf of Manaar. It stands on rising ground, in a quadrangular enclosure 340 yards by 220; with its majestic towers and gateways, its vast colonnades, its walls encrusted with carved work and statuary, it fully justifies Mr. Fergusson's criticism. The most striking features of the temple are the massiveness of workmanship, slabs of forty feet long being used in doorways and ceilings, and the marvellous pillared hall surrounding the inner shrine.

RAMNAD, sixty-seven miles on the way, is an ancient town of 10,000 or 12,000 inhabitants, with a ruined fort and royal palace, now in the hands of a zemindar, the descendant of the old rajas.

Any of the English civilians resident at Madura will give information about the journey, which I expect involves carrying supplies and sleeping in a bullock-cart all the way there and back.

A COUNTRY BULLOCK-CART.

CHAPTER XXXVIII.

TINNEVELLI.

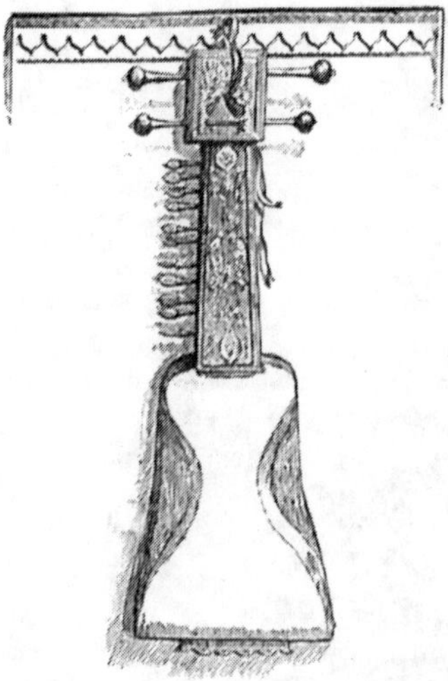

TINNEVELLI is the largest town of the district to which it gives the name, but the administrative head-quarters are located at Palamkotta, two and a half miles distant, across the river Tambraparni. The population of the two towns is 42,000. There is a fine Siva temple here, which Fergusson (page 366) cites as giving a good general idea of the arrangement of large Dravidian temples, having been built on one plan and finished out of hand without subsequent alteration or change. It is a double temple, and the whole area measures 284 yards by 193. Its details call for no special remark.

There is some pretty scenery and two or three fine waterfalls in ghats above Tinnevelli district, especially at Papanasham and Courtallum, twenty-nine and thirty-eight miles distant respectively from Tinnevelli. At Papanasham there is a very holy temple, and the fish in the river are quite tame, coming up to be fed by the Brahmans. There are several good bungalows at Courtallum, which is the sanitarium and holiday place for the Tinnevelli district.

The great attraction of Tinnevelli for many travellers will be to visit the mission stations of the Jesuits, the Church Missionary Society, and the Society for the Propagation of the Gospel, the most successful in all British India. There are 160,000 Christians in the Tinnevelli district, of whom about 100,000 belong to these two Church missions, and 60,000 to the Roman Catholic Church.

The history of the Roman Catholic Church in Tinnevelli practically dates from the 16th century. It was here that Francis Xavier began his work as the apostle to the Indies. The fishermen of the coast, protected by the Portuguese against Musalman oppression, had become Christians, and Xavier formed them into churches. They still speak of themselves as the children of St. Francis, and at Tuticorin they

COURTALLUM.

form a third of the population. Robert de Nobilis took up and extended Xavier's work, and the district is hallowed by the martyrdoms of Criminale and De Britto. The church suffered severely from the suppression of the Society of Jesus in 1773, the French revolution, and the local troubles of the close of the last century, and their numbers declined, their people being left to the perfunctory care of Goanese priests. In 1837, however, Tinnevelli was taken in hand by French Jesuits, and since then the mission has made steady progress. In 1851 there were 23,000 Roman Catholics in the Tinnevelli district; in 1871, 53,000; in 1881, 57,000. I have not been able to get the returns of the present year, but there must be at least 60,000. They had, in 1881, fifty-nine churches, ninety-six chapels, forty-eight boys' schools, and six girls' schools, with 2,500 scholars in all. They have also three native convents and three orphanages.

The work of Protestant missions in Tinnevelli dates back more than a 100 years. The first trace of it is found in the journals of Schwartz, whose name is memorable in the annals of Christian missionary work, and occurs in the year 1771. The first convert was a Brahman widow, Clorinda by name, whose zeal for her new-found faith led to the erection, in Palamkotta, of a little church, the remains of which are still extant. From that time the work grew and expanded little by little under the auspices of the Society for Promoting Christian Knowledge, till at the beginning of the present century the number of native Protestant Christians in Tinnevelli had reached the total of 4,000. But it is from the year 1820 that we must date that larger development of missionary operations, which has resulted in the formation and organisation of the now existing native Church. It was in that year that the Church Missionary Society, at the invitation of a zealous chaplain, Mr. Hough, entered the field. Rhenius was the first and chief missionary; he was followed by many others, of whom Pettitt, Tucker, Ragland, Fenn, Sargent, and Thomas rank conspicuously. In 1826 the Society for the Propagation of the Gospel took up the work transferred to their hands by the Society for Promoting Christian Knowledge, and added their contingent of labourers, among whom are the honoured names of Bower, Brotherton, Pope, Caldwell, Kearns, and Kennet.

The following table of statistics will afford a bird's-eye view of the visible results of missionary work in Tinnevelli.

STATISTICS OF THE TINNEVELLI MISSIONS FOR THE YEAR 1888–89.

Number of Villages occupied.	Number of Native Clergy.	Baptized.	Catechumens.	Total Number of Adherents.	Communicants.	Scholars.
C. M. S. 1018	67	46,525	9,328	55,853	12,112	13,219
S. P. G. 618	46	30,646	9,068	39,714	7,912	10,305
Total 1636	113	77,171	18,396	95,567	20,024	23,524

The steady growth of these missions is shown by the fact that the number of adherents was in 1851, 36,000; 1871, 50,000; 1881, 82,000; and in 1889, 96,000.

In 1877 the two veteran missionaries, Dr. Caldwell of the Society for the Propagation of the Gospel, and Dr. Sargent, of the Church Missionary Society, were raised to the episcopate, and, as coadjutors of the Bishop of Madras, continued to direct the operations of the societies with which they were respectively connected. Last year (1889) Bishop Sargent was removed by death, after a vigorous missionary career extending over a period of fifty-four years.

The territory occupied in Tinnevelli as the sphere of the Church

MISSION CHURCH, TINNEVELLI.

Missionary Society operations, stretches southward from the limits of the Madura district to a boundary within about twelve miles of Cape Comorin. It is bounded on the west by the mountain chain of the Southern Ghats, while on its eastern side it has a broken boundary line, now receding inwards, and now coinciding with the coast-line of the eastern sea.

The native Church in connection with this mission has assumed very considerable proportions, and has reached a somewhat advanced stage of organisation. Sixty-seven ordained native pastors, and about a hundred catechists, with the partial assistance of the local Christian schoolmasters, are engaged in ministering to the spiritual needs of 46,525 souls. This large community is scattered over 1,018 towns and villages, sometines in large, but often in small congregations. Such congregations are collected into "pastorates," which pastorates are, in their turn, grouped into "districts." There are ten such "districts" in the Church Missionary Society at Tinnevelli, each one represented by its own "church council," which transacts all business connected with the pastorates and congregations comprised within its jurisdiction. The native pastors of a district are *ex officio* members of their district church council, and with them are associated a number of lay-members elected to the post. The present "districts" are the outcome of a former system, under which a number of European missionaries divided up the field of labour into workable areas, and each took sole charge of the area allotted as his portion. These European "stationed missionaries" have been withdrawn, but the districts which they ruled, and the bungalows which they built as their headquarters, with boarding-schools and premises attached thereto, still remain as convenient divisions and centres of the work. Missionaries' bungalows, each one the natural centre and head-quarters of a "district," are found at Palamkotta, Dohnavur, Mengnanapuram, Suireseshapuram, Panneivilei, Pannikulam, Nallur, Suranḍei, Vageikulam, and Sachiapuram. Of these the last two are best reached from the Satur and Koilpatti stations of the South Indian Railway, while the remainder must be approached from Palamkotta, the headquarters of the mission. The work is unified by means of a provincial or central council, which is a representative assembly, deliberative and executive. This central council meets annually in Palamkotta, and is the natural medium for dealing with all general questions affecting the welfare of the native Church.

The theological class of native Church agents is conducted by the Rev. T. Kember in Palamkotta, with the assistance of competent native helpers. The students, during their course of study, are expected also to engage in the practical work of preaching. Mr. Kember also superintends an ordination class for the special training of candidates for the ministry. A few men of superior culture and status are sent for a more advanced course of divinity to Madras.

The north Tinnevelli district is worthy of more than a passing mention. It was the scene in former years of the itinerancy of missionaries Raglan, Fenn and Meadows, and has always been worked more or less independently of the South Tinnevelli districts.

It is the only district which now has a European missionary in pastoral charge; all the others being associated and combined under one superintending head, and worked from Palamkotta as centre.

The direct missionary or evangelistic work is well sustained. More than eighty native evangelists are engaged in preaching all over the district. Some of the congregations have organised bands of workers who preach in the adjacent non-Christian villages. The Tinnevelli Church has also sent evangelists to the Kols, Mauritius and Ceylon, besides furnishing agents for other outlying Tamil missions. In North Tinnevelli, a superior native evangelist, Rev. Samuel Paul, is engaged in fostering this zeal for evangelistic work. But direct missionary labours, in the aggressive aspect, are not left merely to the discretion of the native Christian community. A quartette of Cambridge men, Messrs. Walker, Carr, Douglas and Storrs, has been specially assigned to this branch of missionary work. They are free to work on purely spiritual lines, as associated itinerants. It is their province to preach the gospel to the non-Christians of Tinnevelli, with special attention to the Brahmans and higher caste Hindus. By special services of an evangelistic type they seek to deepen the spiritual life and increase the missionary zeal of native Christians. It is proposed, too, by the association with these European evangelists of educated natives of superior culture, to raise up a higher order of native pastors and evangelists. The headquarters of this Tamil Itinerancy are placed in Palamkotta, as being the key and centre of the province.

The district is covered with village elementary schools, worked by the various church councils, in which the children of Christian parents receive primary education. For boys, who seek a higher education, there are boarding-schools at Palamkotta, Dohnavur, Mengnanapuram, Sieviseshapurum, Panneivilei, Pannikulam, Nallur, Surandei and Sachiapuram. The standard up to which instruction is afforded in most of these boarding-schools is that of the middle-school examination, which qualifies for certain posts under Government employment, and is the stepping stone to higher education. The Mengnanapuram boarding-school has, in addition, a matriculation class, and passes boys through the entrance examination of the Madras University. But the most important school for the education of Christian boys is the high school of Palamkotta, of which E. Keyworth is principal, ably assisted by native Christian graduates and others. The school is very efficient and successful as an educational establishment. The grade of education in this school is that of the matriculation standard. Christian boys who wish to proceed to a still higher grade are passed on in due course to the Tinnevelli college, of which Rev. H. Schaffter, B.A., is principal, and which, along with its larger work among non-Christians, includes also a hostel for Christian youths. In this manner means are afforded for Christian lads of Tinnevelli to pursue their studies as far as the F.A. of the Madras University. Those who wish to proceed to their degree are then recommended to continue their studies in the Madras Christian College. The normal work is under the superintendence of Rev. T. Kember, who thus provides the mission with its schoolmasters and teachers.

As in the case of boys, the ordinary elementary instruction of Christian girls is conducted in the local village schools. A higher grade of education is furnished in the girls' boarding-schools of Palamkotta, Panneurlei, Mengnanapuram, Nallur, Sachiapuram and Surandei. Of these, the Mengnanapuram [Elliot Tuxford] school is under the able management of Mrs. Thomas and her daughter, who are now to be further assisted by Miss Vines, a lady newly come from England; while that of Sachiapuram is under the direction of Mrs. Finnimore. The rest are affiliated to the Palamkotta Sarah Tucker institution, the great central home of Christian female education in Tinnevelli, which every traveller should visit. Here are trained all the Christian schoolmistresses of the mission, and hence proceed influences which are doing more than words can express to raise the position and status of women in South India. This institution has a large number of branches scattered through the district, in which hundreds of non-Chiristian girls, including many Brahman children, are being instructed in the first principles of the Christian faith. Great stress is laid both in boys' and girls' schools on religious instruction, as the one basis of true knowledge. Many of the leading Christians are converts from the mission schools, while others who had never had the courage of their convictions, and are Hindus still, have been influenced and permeated by the truth of Christianity. The Tinnevelli Mission College, under the management of the Rev. H. Schaffter, B.A., has more than 400 students, and is doing good work in a large Hindu town. Mr. Schaffter is ably seconded in his work by Mr. F. Ardell, a well-trained schoolmaster. As noticed before, the education in this college is carried up to the F.A. grade of the Madras

University. Bible instruction is faithfully given each day. In Strivikuntan, a town to the east, an existing Anglo-Vernacular school has just been affiliated to the Tinnevelli College; and Mr. Schaffter is now proposing to open similar schools in other large towns in the district. In the North Tinnevelli district, Anglo-Vernacular mission schools are at work in the towns of Strevilliputur and Sankeraninar Koil, under the superintendence of Rev. A. K. Finnimore. These schools are characterised by faithful Bible instruction, and a zealous concern for the spiritual welfare of the students. Mr. Schaffter is always ready to make opportunities for evangelists to address his students.

The Church of England Zenana Missionary Society is represented in Tinnevelli by three European lady missionaries: Misses Gehrich, Blyth, and Hodge, who have their headquarters in Palamkotta. Their special work is that of evangelising the heathen women of the district, and, with this object in view, they instruct pupils privately in the houses, teaching them to read the Bible. They are assisted in this useful work by thirty-four Bible-women, engaged in instructing 655 pupils in twenty-four towns and villages. This important work is being gradually extended, and seems capable of almost unlimited expansion. The Zenana ladies also superintend some schools for heathen girls, of which that in the large town of Viradapatti, is worthy of special mention. The work of this society in North Tinnevelli has, through local difficulties, been temporarily abandoned, except in two towns situated by the railway, but it is to be resumed and established on a firmer basis. A "Convert's Home" has recently been opened in Palamkotta, and two inmates, women won from heathenism, already testify to the usefulness and importance of this branch of missionary enterprise.

TUTICORIN is not an attractive place, and travellers who are desirous of reaching Ceylon from this port had better make whatever waiting for the steamer may be necessary at Tinnivelli or Madura. If it rains, the mud is terrible; if the sun shines, the dust is a perfect scourge. The soil is shallow, and very little of it, the region being one of heavy sand, quite bare of herbage. It is, however, a very thriving seaport town, with a population of 16,000. It is sixth in volume of foreign trade of all the ports in India, the annual value of its imports and exports reaching close upon two millions sterling. Shipping has to anchor two to three miles from shore, cargo being conveyed in boats of about twenty tons, for which there is a well-sheltered shallow harbour. The British India coast steamers call once a week each way. The chief exports are rice, cotton, coffee, sugar, chillies, cattle, horses, sheep, and poultry, mainly to Ceylon, with which there is a large stream of passenger traffic.

The pearl fisheries of Tuticorin are very ancient, and were known to the Greeks and Romans. They are mentioned by Pliny. The pearl and conch shell fisheries are a Government monopoly. The pearls now yield no revenue, and the conch shells only some £3,000 annually. The divers are paid £2 10*s*. per 1,000, and the Government get about £11 or £12 for the same number. The pearl and shell fishers and divers are all Roman Catholics, as are most of the fishermen on the Ceylon coast.

The British India steamers leave for Colombo weekly. The distance is 150 miles, and the time occupied on the voyage about sixteen hours. They are excellent boats. If the traveller is returning direct to Bombay, he will find the eight days' voyage from Tuticorin a pleasant change from the long railway journey, and the calls at the various ports on the way afford a charming variety.. The distance is 886 miles; about five whole days are spent in port, and three at sea.

CHAPTER XXXIX.

CEYLON.

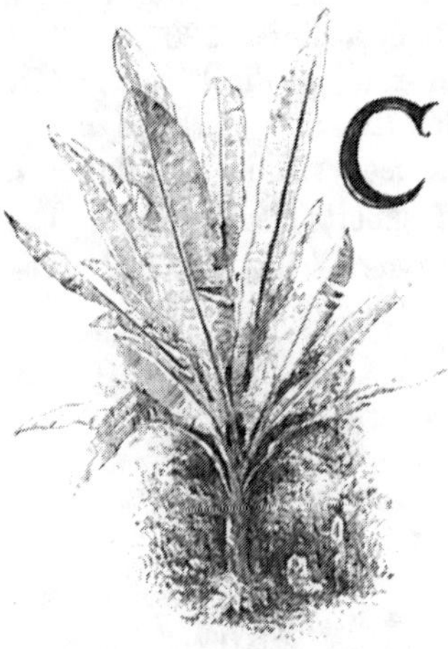

CEYLON is not part of our Indian Empire, but few tourists in India will leave this important Crown Colony out of their route; and this volume would be incomplete without a chapter giving some brief information about it.

We have been in possession of the Island of Ceylon since 1815, when we finally subjugated the King of Kandy. Mr. John Ferguson, one of the most accomplished men in Ceylon, has kindly furnished me with some particulars which he had carefully compiled, showing the condition of the island at that time, and which, compared with the statistics of the Blue Book for 1888, give striking evidence of the material prosperity which sixty years of British rule brings to such a country as Ceylon, and such a people as the Cingalese and Tamils, which form its population.

I give a few of these facts in comparison one with the other.

	In 1815.	In 1888.
Population	750,000	2,800,000.
Number of houses	20,000	500,000.
Military force required	6,000 troops	1,000.
Revenue	£226,000	£1,540,000.
Imports and exports	£546,000	£9,800,000.
Roads	Sand and gravel tracks only	2,250 miles of good roads.
Railways	None	180 miles.
Tonnage of shipping	75,000 tons	4,500,000 tons.
Expenditure on Education by Government	£3,000	£46,000.

	In 1815.	In 1888.
Health expenditure	£1,000	£60,000.
Post-offices	4	130.
Area under cultivation	400,000 acres	3,100,000 acres.
Live stock	250,000 head	1,500,000 head.
Carts and carriages	50	20,000.

But besides, there are in the island 1,100 miles of telegraph, a Government savings-bank with 10,000 depositors, 120 excellent hospitals and dispensaries, with a first-rate medical college for natives. If Ceylon had remained under the rule of the Kandyan kings, none of this progress would have been visible. Ceylon is a purely agricultural country, as its lists of exports clearly show. The following is a short list of the exports of some of the principal crops of Ceylon for 1886:—

	£
Cardamoms	22,000
Areca nuts	100,000
Quinine	300,000
Cinnamon and cinnamon oil	115,000
Cocoa nuts and fibre	70,000
Cacao	40,000
Coffee	600,000
Cotton	20,000
Cocoa-nut oil	24,000
Tea	370,000
Tobacco	80,000

Fifteen years ago the great staple crop of Ceylon was coffee, which, in the years 1868, 1869, and 1870, reached an average export of £4,000,000. This industry is, unhappily, being slowly destroyed by a minute fungus which has attacked the leaf, working deadly mischief all over Ceylon, and especially in the young plantations which, at a capital outlay of nearly £3,000,000, were brought under coffee cultivation in the years 1870—74. The slow but sure destruction of this valuable industry is shown by the list of exports from 1877 to 1888, which are as follows, in cwts.:—

Year.	Cwt.	Year.	Cwt.
1877	620,000	1883	323,000
1878	825,000	1884	315,000
1879	670,000	1885	224,000
1880	454,000	1886	180,000
1881	564,000	1888	140,000
1882	260,000		

Many of the coffee planters of Ceylon have been hopelessly ruined, and if it had not been possible for the valuable cleared lands to be brought under other profitable crops, it would have gone hard with the colony. The planters of Ceylon are shrewd, industrious men, with a large Scottish element among them, and they seem to be finding their salvation in tea and quinine.

In 1872 there were not 500 acres of cinchona (quinine-tree) in all Ceylon, with an export of bark not reaching 12,000 lb.; while to-day there are at least 30,000 acres under cultivation, with an export of 14,000,000 lb. of bark.

In 1876 the exports of tea were just 23 lb., in 1887 they were 14,000,000 lb., and in 1888 24,000,000 lb., and Ceylon bids fair to rival the most important districts in Northern India in its tea-growing capacity. The teas are of a high character, fine flavour, and perfectly pure, and I see no reason why India and Ceylon should not in course of time supplant China teas to a very large extent. I visited several of the finest tea-plantations in Ceylon, and in many cases found the young tea-plants growing up in a forest of stumps, all that was left of what was once a valuable coffee estate, destroyed by the fell fungus. Tea will prove of greater value to the colony than coffee growing, as it employs rather more than twice the number of hands per acre.

Other coffee planters are turning their attention to the cacao-tree, on which the bean grows which gives us our cocoa and chocolate. The export of this product has grown from 10 cwt. in 1878 to 12,000 cwt. in 1888, and is likely, in a very few years, to reach ten times this amount. Cardamoms have risen in the same space of time from 14,000 lb. to 280,000 lb. It will be readily seen from these figures that although the destruction of the coffee-tree has been disastrous to a large number of planters, the colony is recovering itself with great buoyancy, and is probably more solidly prosperous to-day than at any previous period of its history.

The only industry in Ceylon which is not agrarian is plumbago mining. This is entirely in the hands of the Cingalese, who work mines up to 300 feet in depth in a very primitive fashion, obtaining some £350,000 worth annually of the finest plumbago in the world.

It appeared to me, in the short visit I was able to pay to this interesting tropical colony, that its main dependence in future must be on tea; and the best authorities tell me that the export will in a very few years reach thirty or forty million pounds, worth some two millions sterling. I was also told by coffee planters that the ravages of the disease are abating, and that the colony will be able to produce in future an average export of coffee of about one million sterling, or one-fourth of what was produced at the highest period of its prosperity. It is quite evident, however, from the figures I have given, that the deficit of three millions on coffee is fast being overtaken, and that the general prospects of Ceylon agriculture are bright enough.

There is no doubt that the change of culture in Ceylon from coffee to tea will be of great benefit to the masses of the population, from the largely increased employment which it will afford. Almost all the plantation labour is carried on by Tamils, from Southern India, the Cingalese refusing to do coolie work, devoting themselves entirely to trading, small farming, carting produce (a large industry), and to handicrafts. To these Tamils Ceylon is a heaven upon earth. In their own country their average earnings per family of five reaches about £6 in the year, or less than a 1*d.* per head per day, a condition of things that appears almost incredible to English minds, and in which recurrent famines, terrible in their results, are certain. The Tamils employed on a Ceylon tea estate have the wealth of Crœsus compared with their relatives at home. They have good huts, cheap food, small gardens, medical attendance, and can earn from 6*d.* to 9*d.* per day. I doubt if, considering the climate and cost of living, there are any labouring classes in the world better off than the Tamil families settled on the plantations of Ceylon.

The revenues of the colony steadily increase. In 1887 they were £1,340,000, in 1888 they increased to £1,540,000. The public debt is two and a quarter millions, and has been incurred for Colombo Harbour, railway extension, water-works, &c.

The trade of Ceylon, as everywhere else in the East, is overwhelmingly in the hands of the English. Of 6,733 vessels entered and cleared in 1888 at Ceylon ports, British shipping formed six-sevenths of the whole; and the same proportion applies to merchandise.

Ceylon gets on without a poor-law. A very few old persons get a charitable allowance from the Government, varying from 2*s.* to 25*s.* each per month; but it amounts to very little on the whole.

Employment is plentiful, the people are thrifty, the cost of living is extremely small, and the young and strong are glad to care for the aged and weak.

The Local Government of Ceylon consists of the following Boards:—

1st. *The Executive and Legislative Councils*, which are of the same composition and exercise the same functions as I have already described with regard to Hong Kong or Singapore. None of the members are elective, but there is always a Cingalese and a Tamil member on the Legislative Council.

2nd. *Municipal Councils*, of which the majority are elected by occupiers rented at £7 a year, the rest being nominated by the Governor. In Colombo there are five official and nine elective members. The other two boroughs in the island are Kandy and Galle.

3rd. *Local Boards*, in populous districts, composed in the same manner as the municipalities. There are ten of these local boards in Ceylon. The qualification is an occupancy of not less than £3 10*s*.

4th. *The Village Council.*—This is a council elected by a constituency composed of every male inhabitant of the village, or groups of villages, who is twenty-one years of age. There are forty-eight of these village councils.

Anything approaching party politics is quite unknown in Ceylon. There is a tendency to jobbery, which, however, is kept in check by the official members. On the whole, the system of local government appears admirably suited for the budding intelligence and education of the people, and will, no doubt, be extended as the social conditions improve and justify.

I have already spoken of wages paid on tea, coffee, cinchona, and other plantations, as ranging from 6*d*. to 9*d*. per day. The general rate of wages for labour in Colombo and other towns, for such work as stablemen, messengers, porters, gardeners, &c., is about the same, twelve to fifteen rupees a month, the rupee being worth 1*s*. 5*d*. Men in more responsible positions, such as warehousemen, foremen of gangs of coolies, &c., are paid 35*s*. to 40*s*. per month. Skilled workmen, bookbinders, machinists, compositors, cabinet-makers, and carpenters get 45*s*. to 50*s*. per month. Good clerks and bookkeepers, £40 to £50 a year. These wages will appear very meagre to an English workman, but I expect the Cingalese is better off with these wages than the English workman with his. The Cingalese wants no fire, no meat, no woollen clothes, no beer; his house costs a tenth of the English workman's; he dresses in a shilling's-worth of cotton cloth, and only wears a pennyworth of it when he is working. He is content with two meals a day of rice, at 5*s.* per bushel, and vegetables flavoured with curry, and has half-a-farthing's worth of dried fish on

CINGALESE WORKMAN.

Sunday. He has never felt cold in his life, and the climate he lives in enables him to thrive as well on his simple vegetarian diet as an Englishman at home can on beef and mutton. Everywhere they give the constant impression of being a joyous, contented, sober, well-nourished people.

The Government of Ceylon, like that of every Crown colony, is virtually a despotism, tempered by the Colonial Office, and "question time" in the House of Commons. The governor selects such men, in addition to his leading permanent officials, as he believes can best advise him, and the decisions of this council become the will of the Government. The influence of a really able, energetic, independent governor, thoroughly just and impartial, is practically paramount, and every successive governor strives to leave behind him, as the record of his term of office, some public work of utility—an education scheme, a college, a hospital. A bronze statue of Sir Edward Barnes stands opposite the Queen's House in Colombo, but his real monuments are the great macadamized road to Kandy, the bridge of boats on the Kelani River at Colombo, and the superb satin-wood bridge at Peradenia. The railway to Kandy keeps green the memory of Sir Henry Ward; Sir Hercules Robinson has left his record in every province of the island, especially in irrigation works, and Sir William Gregory's massive stone monument is a mile long—the famous Colombo breakwater. Sir Arthur Gordon is set upon restoring to their ancient usefulness the great tanks at Kalaweava, which, when completed, will be seven miles square, twenty feet deep, and will send water down a canal fifty-four miles long, irrigating a vast area through the dry season; an area now almost unpeopled, but which 2,000 years ago, watered by these ancient tanks, had a population of at least a quarter of a million, whose ancient cities and temples, smothered in jungle, are still among the wonders of the East.

Colombo owes its existence as a seaport to the genius of Sir John Coode, the great engineer. Before the existence of the breakwater, Galle was the chief port of Ceylon, the coaling station of the Peninsular and Oriental Company and other lines of steamers trading with Calcutta and the East. Poor Galle is now quite extinguished by its powerful rival, whose harbour, easily accessible by day or night, provides safe and easy anchorage for the entire passing trade of the East, as well as for the bulk of the export and import trade of Ceylon. The harbour is over 500 acres in extent, more than half of which has a depth of from twenty-six to forty feet at low water spring tides. In this deep water twenty-four sets of double-screw moorings, suited for vessels of the largest class, drawing twenty-five feet and over, have been laid down, furnishing accommodation far in excess of the present requirements of the trade, which, however, will in good time require it all and more.

The first block of the magnificent breakwater was laid by the Prince of Wales on December 8th, 1875, and the lamps of the lighthouse shone out over the Indian Ocean on the night of January 27th, 1885.

The breakwater thus took nearly ten years to complete. The shore portion, or "root-work," extends over four and a half acres, reclaimed from the sea, having a solid wall of concrete blocks to the sea front, and a fine wharf about 1,000 feet long on the harbour side, with a depth at low water of fourteen feet, accommodating a considerable

THE COLOMBO BREAKWATER.

number of good-sized vessels engaged in the coasting trade. From this wharf the breakwater starts, in sixteen feet of water at low tide, extending northwards for over 3,000 feet, then curving inwards for another 1,000 feet or more, which, with the shore portion, makes a total length of 4,877 feet, or close upon a mile in length. The breakwater ends in about forty feet of water at lowest tides with a circular head sixty-two feet in diameter, on which there is a fine lighthouse, visible for ten miles. This circular head is formed of concrete in mass, in a wrought-iron caisson under low water, and of concrete blocks above the level. The breakwater itself is composed of a mound of granite rubble stone, raised by convict labour from quarries about twelve miles distant. The rubble mound, after being allowed twelve months to consolidate, was levelled off by means of divers to depths varying from thirteen feet below water at the land end to twenty-four feet below water at the breakwater head. Upon the mound, thus levelled, huge concrete blocks from sixteen to thirty-two tons in weight are founded, extending up to eight feet above low water, the whole being finished off with a capping of concrete in mass, four feet thick, throughout the whole length of the breakwater.

During the south-west monsoon the sea breaks over the whole length in columns of spray fifty feet high, a marvellous sight which I was not privileged to see, the north-east monsoon blowing while I was at Colombo. But I have since seen a fine photograph of it in Sir John Coode's office at Westminster, which was more like Niagara Falls turned upside down than anything else.

The total cost of this wonderful feat of engineering skill was a little over £700,000, but its value to the colony is far beyond price. Before its construction vessels were often delayed days, and even weeks during the south-west monsoon, owing to the impossibility of loading and unloading shore-boats in the tremendous swell which rolled across the open roadstead, while even during the lulls of the monsoon the damage to cargo and the loss overboard, as well as the extra cost of operation was very great indeed. The value of this great undertaking to the port of Colombo is best shown by the fact that since 1882, when the breakwater first began to afford material protection to shipping, the tonnage of the port has increased from 1,700,000 to very nearly 5,000,000 tons, inward and outward. The revenue in 1888 was £67,000.

It is proposed some day to meet the breakwater with a northern arm from the opposite shore which would make the harbour smooth water in every wind that blows. The mercantile interests press this further development of the harbour upon the Government with some vigour, but the present Government prefer, and as I think rightly, to push on other public works, viz., railway extension, irrigation tanks, and the further fortification of Colombo. But if the trade of the port continues to increase in anything like the proportion of the last few years, some extension of the harbour and the building of a good dry-dock will become imperative.

The breakwater makes a very fine promenade when the wind is off shore, but is very little resorted to by the inhabitants. I walked to the end and back one fine evening, but it was deserted except by three or four natives lazily fishing, and by small processions of crabs making short cuts over the breakwater from the open sea to the more succulent feeding grounds of the harbour.

The Grand Oriental Hotel at Colombo is one of the sights of the East. It is a caravanserai with 100 bedrooms, and when two or three Peninsular and Oriental steamers are in port these rooms are all filled, and couches are laid out in the verandahs and passages for the surplus. Its dining-room will seat 300 people, and its huge verandah facing the sea is crowded with pedlars and vendors of the precious stones for which Ceylon is famous, a trade largely supplemented by Birmingham enterprise. These brigands are mostly Moormen, descendants of a colony of Arabians who have waxed mighty in the retail trade of Ceylon. They address their customers with bland confidence, introducing themselves in various guises. One informed me that he was "Streeter's confidential buyer," another introduced himself as "the personal friend of Lord Rothschild," and a third as the "favourite jewel-broker of the Prince of Wales." They vary their list of distinguished patrons for Americans, substituting Tiffany, General Grant, and Vanderbilt, while they dazzle Australians by enormous prices. I was told over and over again, "If you was an Australian my price would be 1,000 rupees, but for Englishman I take 200," finally coming down to twenty. No one escapes in the long run. Scornful sceptics begin by treating every stone as "Brummagem Glass," and threatening the pedlars with a stick, but they always end by being taken into a dark corner to see a sapphire gleam in the light of a wax match, and come on board with a dozen bits of coloured glass wrapped up in cotton wool, for which they have given £2 or £3 each. If glass, these so-called precious stones are only worth a few pence; if genuine, they would be worth £50 each. One may, however, go to respectable shops, known to bankers and merchants, and buy very pretty things made of third-class sapphires and cat's-eyes cheaply enough, after two or three days patient chaffering; there is one jeweller who has a small stock of really good things, but every fine stone that is found finds a ready market at its full value in Calcutta, London, or Paris, and the splendid stones purchased by transient passengers are either flawed or otherwise inferior in colour or quality, or are other stones than represented.

A SHOP ON THE KANDY ROAD, COLOMBO.

The finding and cutting of gems is an important trade in Ceylon. At Kandy the cutters are seen in their little shops working a cast-iron cylinder with a bow, like a drill, on which they grind the uncut sapphire or ruby, which are the gems most frequently discovered. The zircon, a smoky-coloured diamond, the amethyst, the chrysoberyl, or cat's-eye, a gem which has lately come into fashion, and for which great prices are demanded, garnets, spinel rubies, tourmalines, and the pretty moonstone which was so popular a purchase at the Colonial Exhibition in London a year or two back, are all found in various parts of Ceylon, mostly about Ratnapura [the city of gems].

Ceylon is also celebrated for fine pearls, gathered from oyster or mussel banks on the north-west coast.

The Pettah, or native market-place, is, as is always the case in the East, a scene of busy life, full of varieties of costume, race, and colour. The traders in Ceylon are Moormen and Cingalese; the labourers are mostly Tamils from Southern India. The Moormen wear cotton trousers and jacket, with a curious beehive-shaped hat of plaited grass, dyed in various colours. The Cingalese wear a sheet of brightly coloured calico twisted round the hips, and reaching to the feet like a petticoat, with a white jacket. They delight in long hair, which they twist up into a chignon, combing it back all round the forehead. Their only "hat" is a round tortoise-shell comb, which every Cingalese wears as a sacred duty. The Tamils wear as little as possible, and the children of all sorts nothing at all except a bit of string round the waist or neck, from which is suspended a charm to ward off the attacks of their favourite devil. The Cingalese women and men dress very much alike, and it is often difficult to tell which is which until you realise that the men wear a comb and the women hair-pins. Besides the Pettah, or central market, there are others clustered round the suburbs, to which the villagers on their own side of the town resort. One of these is on each side of a curious bridge of boats, about 500 feet long, two miles out of the town on the Kandy road, composed of twenty-one boats anchored at each end, from which two are slipped every day for two hours to let the traffic through. The Cingalese are a rice-eating people; rice and some curried vegetable, such as cocoa-nut, jack-fruit, or plantain, with a little dried fish, forming their diet all the year round. Fish, fruit, and vegetables, therefore, are the chief stocks of all the markets. The vehicular traffic of the country, except a few carriages in Colombo and Kandy, is drawn by bullocks. These animals are often very beautiful, being all of the Zebu breed of India, which are generally to be seen attached to Wombwell's menageries under the name of "Brahman Bull." There is a pretty little variety, about the size of a small pony, that are used in gigs and other carriages, and can travel thirty miles a day at a trot of about five miles an hour. The bit is a piece of rope passed through a hole in the nostrils. The Buddhist religion, though forbidding the killing of any animal does not seem to forbid their torture, and these poor brutes are most cruelly treated by their drivers. The Government has been obliged to enact severe penalties for this offence.

The streets of Colombo are broad and well-made, with a gravel of rich, dark red colour, which contrasts pleasantly with the profuse foliage of the endless gardens and trees which line the footpath, the poorest hut having a bit of garden about it. The town is placed on a neck of land between a magnificent sheet of fresh water and the sea, so that every street has its vista ending in bright and sparkling water, giving a special charm to the town that I have never seen anywhere else. There are no fine buildings in Colombo. The Governor's residence, called Queen's House, the Government buildings, the Cathedral, Clock Tower, and other public institutions call for no comment on the score of architectural merit. The Museum is the finest building in the town, well situated in the midst of the Cinnamon Gardens, now a public park.

The Barracks are a series of buildings capable of accommodating 5,000 soldiers. We are able, however, to "hold down" our Cingalese subjects with a single regiment.

THE KANDY RAILWAY.—The Ceylon railways are a Government monopoly, and there are 185 miles open for traffic. The carriages are horribly uncomfortable, the first-class being no better than the third-class on an English trunk line. Heavy excess is charged on luggage. The journey to Kandy lasts five hours, an average speed of fifteen miles an hour. For some miles out of Colombo the train runs through a flat country, chiefly under rice cultivation or in grass for cattle. The whole area is one vast swamp, every crop being profusely irrigated, the cattle, mostly black buffaloes, feeding knee-deep in water. Wherever there is a knoll or a bit of rising ground a beautiful tropical picture forms itself: a clump of quaint cottages and barns, surrounded by palms, jack-fruit trees, bananas, and vegetable gardens, the dark red tiles of the buildings, the bright-yellow and crimson dresses of the peasants, and the brown skins of the native children relieving the

THE DEKANDA VALLEY.

intense and somewhat monotonous tropical green. Presently the Kelani-Ganga river, the greatest stream of water in the island, is crossed by a very fine iron bridge, and on the other side a branch line turns off to the quarries, from which were got the stones for building the breakwater at Colombo. Fifty miles from Colombo the railway commences its great climb of 6,000 feet to Nuwera Eliya. It creeps up the flank of a magnificent mountain, Allagalla, 'whose high peak,

SENSATION ROCK.

crowning a sheer precipice, dominates the whole valley. From the summit of Allagalla the old Kandyan kings used to hurl those whom they suspected of treason. On the opposite side of the great green valley of Dekanda are the Camel Mountain, so called from its resemblance to that animal, and the Bible Mountain, with a chain of connecting peaks 4,000 to 5,000 feet above the sea. In the valley are seen terraced fields of pale green rice, the flower-like branches of the Kekuna trees, magnificent forest trees covered with purple and pink blossoms, palms of all kinds, and here and there noble specimens of the great talipot palm and patches of luxuriant tropical jungle, bright with a score of different brilliant flowers or creepers which throw themselves from one tree-top to the other, as they tower above the tangled undergrowth. Beautiful waterfalls are revealed up the glens as the train climbs slowly by, while others rush under the railway bridges, to leap into mid-air and lose themselves in clouds of mist and spray, on which the sun dances in all the colours of the rainbow. Every now and then a glimpse beneath is obtained of the fine road constructed long since by the English Government to enable them to take and keep possession of the ancient capital, which had been wrested from the Portuguese and Dutch by the valiant old Kandyan kings; this road is now superseded by the railway. A few miles from Kandy the train, after passing through several tunnels, runs over what is called "Sensation Rock," skirting the edge of the cliff so closely that the sight drops a thousand feet before it rests on anything on which a blade of grass or a tropical creeper can lay hold. Just beyond this exciting scene the dividing ridge of two water-sheds is crossed, and in a very short time the train reaches the lovely valley of Kandy, runs into the station, and by seven o'clock the traveller finds himself comfortably settled at the Queen's Hotel.

Ceylon is an island of villages, and Kandy, though the ancient capital, is not much more than a group of two or three villages, containing in all a population of 22,000. It has little of general interest, the only buildings of any importance being the gaol, the barracks, three or four churches and chapels, the Government office, and the world-renowned Temple of the Sacred Tooth of Buddha; this latter being an insignificant little shrine of no great antiquity or architectural beauty, its only interest lying in its peculiarly sacred character, rendering it the heart from which all Buddhist sentiment in Ceylon ebbs and flows.

The temple is a small building, with a good-sized courtyard surrounding it, the outer walls of which are decorated with hideous ill-executed frescoes of the various punishments in the Buddhist Hell, differing very little in character from those one so often sees depicted in Roman Catholic churches in Italy. The deepest and hottest hell, with the most gruesome fiends to poke the fire, is reserved for those who rob a Buddhist priest or plunder a Buddhist temple. The great relic, which is two inches long and one inch thick, is preserved in a gold and jewelled shrine, covered by a large silver bell in the centre of an octagonal tower with pointed roof. It is only exposed to view once a year, but I understand that five rupees will open the door.

In the porch of the temple are groups of horrible beggars, who display their various wounds and defects of nature with much liberality. The most popular appears to be a monster with a huge tooth growing through his under lip. I suppose his popularity is due to the fact that his horrible tooth is nearer to the genuine article in the shrine than could be found outside the mouth of a hippopotamus.

The kings and priests of Burma, Siam, and Cambodia send regular yearly tribute to the Temple of the Sacred Tooth, and more or less reverence is paid to it in India, China, and Japan.

The real charm of Kandy lies in its beautiful situation. The town itself is lost to view in green tropical foliage. It is built on the banks of a large artificial tank or lake, about three miles in circumference, surrounded by beautiful hills five or six hundred feet above its surface, on which are dotted here and there the pretty bungalows of tea-planters, and other well-to-do inhabitants. A pleasant morning may be spent wandering about the lovely lanes of these hills, in any of which may be gathered from the hedgerows bunches of "hot-house" flowers, which would fetch a guinea at Covent Garden Market. From their heights magnificent views of the high mountain ranges of Ceylon are obtained, all richly timbered to the summits.

I have found growing wild on these charming hills sunflowers, roses, dracænas, poinsettas, mimosas, lantanas, balsams, iconias, petreas, passion-flowers, and a dozen other varieties of beautiful blooms familiar to me in English hot-houses.

The afternoon is the best time to visit the Government Botanical Gardens at Peradenia, whose distinguished director, Dr. Triman, has done so much to develop the agricultural resources of the colony. The entrance to the garden is through a fine avenue of tall india-rubber trees, towering into the air 100 feet, spreading out into enormous leafy crowns fifty or sixty feet in diameter, their huge roots, longer than the tree is high, creeping over the surface of the ground like great snakes, sometimes growing straight up in the air till they attach themselves to the lower branches, thus forming stout props to support the weight of heavy foliage, and enable it to resist storm and tempest.

There is no need in this garden for the familiar notice, "Keep off the grass." If you venture on the lawns without high boots, nasty

INDIA-RUBBER TREE, PERADENIA.

little leeches the thickness of a hair wriggle through your trousers and stockings, and suck your blood until they swell out to the thickness of a lead pencil. Instances are known in which men have gone to sleep on the grass in Ceylon, and have been found dead, sucked to death by hundreds of these horrible creatures. It is also necessary to beware of "snakes in the grass." The day I visited these gardens one of the gardeners was bitten by a snake, and was lying dangerously ill in the hands of a native doctor, who possessed secret remedies handed down to him from his forefathers by word of mouth only. While I was enjoying a cup of tea at Dr. Triman's bungalow another gardener brought a fine lively cobra which he had just caught, tied by a string to a stick, striking its fangs vigorously into every object that was thrust towards its head. On the whole, therefore, it is well to keep to the paths and beaten tracks as much as possible to avoid these gentry, as well as centipedes and black scorpions, which are equally plentiful. Immediately inside the garden-gate is a wondrously beautiful group of all the palms indigenous to the island. Here is the cocoa-nut, with its cylindrical trunk two feet thick, soaring up into the air 150 feet, crowned with a huge tuft of feathery leaves eighteen or twenty feet long, with great bunches of fruit clustering in their shade, the Palmyra palm, which, according to a famous Tamil poem, can be put to 801 different uses. Its leaves are circular, with seventy or eighty ribs, opening like a great fan. These leaves are used by the natives to thatch their cottages, to make matting for floor and ceiling, bags and baskets, hats and caps, fans, umbrellas and paper. The fruits, as well as the young seedlings, are cooked and eaten as a nutritious vegetable, and from the flower-spikes, alas! the native obtains palm wine or toddy, which can be distilled into stronger arrack. The Sago palm and its relative, the Kitul palm, yield not only the nutritious pith which makes the familiar pudding of our childhood, but also produce excellent sugar and splendid fibre for rope-making and other purposes. The Areca-nut palm produces the well-known betel nut, which rolled up in leaves of the betel pepper, with a little lime and tobacco, makes the favourite "chaw" of the natives of Ceylon and India, a harmless though nasty practice, for which they will sacrifice meat, drink, washing, and lodging. More beautiful than these is the queen of all palms, the Talipot, which for thirty years from its birth pushes up its straight white shining trunk, with its crown of dark-green leaves, till it reaches a height of 100 feet or more. Then it blooms—and such a bloom!—a tall pyramidal spike of white blossoms forty feet above its crown of huge green fans, perhaps the noblest flower the world produces. Each bloom forms a nut, and the tree, having scattered its seeds to become palms in their turn, dies of the supreme effort. I was fortunate enough to see a magnificent talipot in full bloom, and to obtain a good photograph of its marvellous beauty. The travellers' palm is one that contains quantities of perfectly pure water in the thick ends of its leaves. The cabbage palm has a capital edible imitation of that homely vegetable as its fruit, and the oil palm, with a dozen other varieties, are all to be found in flourishing growth in the remarkable clump of palms I am trying to describe so feebly.

The next point of interest is a plantation of nutmeg and clove trees, further on are jack-fruit trees, with their huge fruit growing from the

GIANT BAMBOOS, PERADENIA.

trunk and weighing fifty or sixty pounds each ; bread-fruit, pomelces, the candle tree, the magnificent *Anthurium Regale*, with its vari-coloured leaves, three feet long by two feet wide, are all passed and will be examined with interest and curiosity. The path leads on into a dense piece of jungle, in which giant creepers, with stems six or eight inches thick, climb to the tops of the highest trees with profuse blossoms, of all sizes and colours, while the ground is covered with all kinds of tropical ferns, including the lovely *Adiantum Farleyense*, the gold and silver ferns, great tree-ferns, *Adiantum Peruvianum*, and a hundred other varieties of ferns, lycopodiums, and ground plants. But the great sight is the giant bamboo, which grows in mighty clumps by the bank of the fine river that flows round the gardens. These form enormous green thickets more than 100 feet high, and the same in thickness, consisting of eighty or 100 tall cylindrical stems, each from one to two feet thick. They grow so closely crowded together that a cat would find it difficult to find her way through. They shoot seventy or eighty feet into the air without a break, and then spread out into immense branches of slender little leaves that give the appearance of gigantic green ostrich feathers. As everyone knows, the bamboo is one of the most useful plants that grow in the tropics, and I might fill my book with a description of all the uses to which it may be put.

The garden swarms with pretty striped squirrels and with bright-plumaged tropical birds, while hanging from the branches of the trees are swarms of great flying foxes, which live upon the different kinds of fruit, and very often get drunk on the sweet palm sap, being found lying helplessly incapable by the vessels which the natives leave out all night to catch the juice. But there is no end to the botanical wonders of this unrivalled and fascinating garden of Peradenia.

NUWERA ELIYA is the great health resort of Ceylon, and lies in a beautiful valley 6,200 feet above the level. In the advertisements of its hotels the inducement is held out to Europeans who are baking in the oven of Colombo, that "Nuwera Eliya is so cold as to make it possible to burn open fires all the year round."

There are several excellent hotels, which during the winter months are almost deserted. These, with the pretty cottages of private residents, are picturesquely scattered on the green hills, surrounding a fine lake about two miles long, stocked with English trout. The highest peak in the island, Peduru Galla, rises from Nuwera Eliya, which, with the neighbouring mountains, forest-clad to the summit, are the home of the wild elephant, which still exists in Ceylon in considerable numbers. There are also leopards, cheetahs, tiger-cats, jackals, elk, wild-boar, monkeys, and crested eagles to be found in these ancient and sombre forests. The ascent of Peduru Galla is easy and may be made the greater part of the way on horseback.

Six miles from Nuwera Eliya, at Hakgala, is the beautiful hill garden attached to Dr. Triman's department, as a supplement to Peradenia. This garden is under the charge of Mr. Nock, who is always glad to welcome travellers who wish to see it.

From Nuwera Eliya, a very interesting expedition may be made to Adam's Peak, the sacred mountain of Ceylon, through beautiful

ADAM'S PEAK.

scenery, the particulars of which may be obtained in the excellent local guide-book published in Colombo. I was not able to take this excursion myself, so can give no information based upon experience. There are, however, good government rest-houses placed at intervals of about fifteen miles along all the roads of Ceylon, clean and comfortable, containing a good guest-room, and half a dozen simply furnished bed-rooms. Plain meals are provided at reasonable fixed charges.

Travellers returning to Kandy from Nuwera Eliya will find a pleasant alternative route by driving through Ramboda and a fine mountain pass to Gampola, a station on the Kandy Railway. This is a distance of forty miles, and with a halt of two hours at Ramboda rest-house, can be accomplished with the same pair of horses in time to catch the last train to Kandy. The scenery the whole way is superb, and at Ramboda there are two or three very fine waterfalls close to the rest-house. The road is a good one, descending nearly 5,000 feet, giving the greatest possible variety of vegetation in the gradual change from the cool temperature of Nuwera Eliya, to the tropical heat of Kandy.

The most interesting and important antiquity in Ceylon is the ancient Buddhist city of ANURADHAPURA, to the north of Kandy, which was the capital of Ceylon from B.C. 400 to A.D. 770. It is totally deserted, in the midst of an almost uninhabited jungle, and involves a journey of some hardship, with a night and a day in a bullock-cart. The landlord of the Queen's Hotel at Kandy will arrange the details of the journey for any traveller anxious to go. Full particulars of these extraordinary ruins, with many illustrations, will be found in Chapter VIII. of Fergusson's "Indian Architecture," in which twenty pages are devoted to the Buddhist antiquities of Ceylon.

The total population of Ceylon is 2,800,000, of whom 1,850,000 are native Cingalese, 700,000 are Tamils from Southern India, 200,000 Moormen and Malays, and 22,000 Europeans and Eurasians. The religious census shows that 1,700,000 of the population are Buddhist, 600,000 Hindu, 200,000 Muhammadan, and 270,000 Christians.

The Roman Catholics are in overwhelming majority among Christian denominations (220,000 of the whole), their missionary enterprise having been as successful in Ceylon as everywhere else throughout the East.

The Buddhist priests are very ignorant, and exercise little or no moral restraint over their people, who are more attached to their ancient superstition of devil-worship than they appear to be to Buddhism, which they only respect so far as the outside of the cup and platter is concerned. The devil-dancer and his curate, the tom-tom beater, have a good time in Ceylon, and there are 2,735 of these scoundrels distributed throughout the island. They are simply professional exorcists, and as everything untoward—bad weather, sickness, and what not—is the direct result of devils, they are in continual request. It speaks ill for Buddhism that 2,000 years of influence over the Cingalese has not destroyed this base and grovelling superstition, which has rooted itself so deeply that even native Christians will resort to it secretly in great emergencies.

DEVIL DANCER, CEYLON.

The Roman Catholic Church has been at work longer than the Protestants, having entered the mission field with the Portuguese conquerors 350 years ago, who brought with them the usual army of ecclesiastics. Their methods of conversion were bound to succeed more or less. The Inquisition played its part, "conversion" was the only gate to employment open to the natives, and the priests didn't object to these converts "bowing in the house" of Buddha, if they were reasonably often at mass. But whatever the methods pursued by the Roman Catholic missionary, they manage to get and keep disciples.

The Dutch cleared out the Portuguese in 1656, and although they had no inquisition, they refused employment to any native who refused to make profession of the Protestant religion. In 1796 the English cleared out the Dutch, and in 1815 were in possession of the whole island. There was not much missionary spirit in English churches during the dawn of this century, but as early as 1812 the Baptist Missionary Society commenced operation in Ceylon, followed in 1818 by the Church Mission Society, and a little later by the Wesleyans, who are now the most active of all in the island.

Seventy years of Protestant missionary enterprise has produced 22,000 Episcopalians, 20,000 Wesleyans, 13,000 Presbyterians (a large proportion of whom, however, are descendants of the Dutch), and 5,000 Baptists, in all 60,000 Protestants, old and young, of all sorts, as contrasted with 220,000 Romanists. A pamphlet, containing full particulars of the missions established in different parts of Ceylon, may be obtained at the bookseller's in Colombo.

CHAPTER XL.

THE NORTH-WEST FRONTIER OF INDIA.

BY THE HON. GEORGE N. CURZON, M.P.

In the *Nineteenth Century* for July, 1888, appeared an article under my name, entitled "The Scientific Frontier an Accomplished Fact," in which I endeavoured, from the experience of a recent visit to the regions concerned, to give a brief account of the existing north-west boundary of India, its passes, fortifications, and road and railway communications; arguing from the information there collected, that some approximation to a scientific frontier, *i.e.*, a frontier fixed by conditions—physical, ethnographical, political, or geographical, or a combination of these—qualified to give it precision, and likely to give it permanence, had recently been acquired by the joint action of the statesmen and generals who are responsible for the defence of our Indian Empire. Mr. Caine has asked me to supply him with an abridged version of this article for his work, in order to assist visitors to India either in a tour to the frontier regions, or in a preliminary study of the frontier problem; and I very gladly accede to his request. Two and a half years, however, of unremittent activity on the part of the Indian Government and its officers having resulted in considerable additions both to the extent and strength of the border therein described, and my former account having consequently become obsolete, I have entirely rewritten it for this work, and now present it in a shape which will, I hope, be fairly suited to the general purposes which Mr. Caine has in view.

The north-west frontier of India is that extreme border-line which runs in a general direction from north-east to south-west, from the mighty barrier of the Karakoram and Hindu Kush ranges (continuations of the same mountain system) to the waters of the Indian Ocean. Its supreme interest lies in the physical fact that it is the only side upon which India ever has been, or ever can be, invaded by land, and in the political fact that it confronts a series of territories, inhabited by wild and turbulent, by independent or semi-dependent tribes, behind whom looms the grim figure of Russia, daily advancing into clearer outline from the opposite or north-west quarter. It is to protect the Indian Empire, its peoples, its trades, its laboriously established government, and its accumulated wealth, from the insecurity and possible danger arising from a further Russian advance across the intervening space, that the frontier which I am about to describe has been traced and fortified. Politicians of all parties have agreed that, while the territorial aggrandisement of Russia is permissible over regions where she replaces barbarism even by a crude civilisation, there can be no excuse for allowing her to take up a position in territories acknowledging our sway, where she can directly menace British interests in India, or indirectly impose an excessive strain upon the resources and the armed strength of our Eastern dominions. The guardianship of the frontier is, therefore, an act of defence, not of defiance, and is an elementary and essential obligation of Imperial statesmanship.

Broadly speaking, the most distinctive physical characteristic of the north-west frontier through the greater part of its extent is a range of mountains rising from the west side of the Indus valley, and pierced by a large number of defiles, passes, or valleys conducting to the higher plateaux of Afghanistan and Baluchistan. This mountain range, known for a considerable portion of its length as the Sulaiman Range, extends from the upper waters of the Indus almost to the Indian Ocean, diminishing in altitude as it proceeds from north to south. Originally it was supposed that there were but three or four passes or cracks by which this mountain barrier was perforated, and that if British soldiers only stood sentinel at their exits an invader would have no other alternative but to come down and be annihilated. Modern surveys, however, have shown that the number of available passes is nearer 300 than three; a discovery which has suggested the policy of establishing friendly relations with the tribes who hold them, and thus acquiring an indirect control over their western mouths. For just as the main physical feature of the frontier is this mountain wall with its narrow lateral slits, so the main political feature is the existence in the tracts of country thus characterised of a succession of wild and warlike tribes, owning allegiance to no foreign potentate, but cherishing an immemorial love for freedom and their native hills.

The frontier is often spoken of at home as though it were a thin streak directly dividing India from Afghanistan, which upon that hypothesis would be conterminous powers. With the exception of the extreme north, it is not in reality till we come in the south to the outskirts of Pishin that British territory ever touches Afghan soil. Through the whole remaining distance an intervening belt of mountains, sometimes over 100 miles in width, is held by these native tribes, whose general attitude has in recent years become more friendly towards England than towards Afghanistan, and who are gradually being transformed into an irregular frontier guard of the Indian Empire. It is the forward move from the old Indus valley line across this middle belt, the relations entered into with its occupants, and the opportunity thus acquired for swift movement, should the necessity arise, to the support or defence of valuable positions beyond, that has during the last five years gradually transformed the unscientific frontier of Sir John Lawrence into the scientific frontier of Lords Dufferin and Lansdowne. I will now proceed to a delineation of the new border.

The north-west frontier may be divided into four sections, presenting different geographical and strategical features, although parts of the same system. The first of these is the extreme northern line starting from the snows of the Central Asian plateau, and defining the borders, (1), of a number of small native states dependent upon the larger feudatory state of Kashmir; (2), of Kashmir itself; and (3), of British territory in the upper parts of the Indus valley. The second is the important section commanding the northern gateways into Afghanistan, and approached by the northern branches of the main system of Indian railways. This section may be defined as extending from the Kabul River, north of Peshawar, to Dera Ismail Khan on the right bank of the Indus, a distance of some 200 miles. It has a twofold objective in Afghanistan, viz., Kabul and Ghazni; and it contains a group of positions and interests connected therewith which constitute a distinct department of the problem of frontier defence. The third section is that which contains the southern approaches to Afghanistan and its corresponding system of railways and roads, also with a double Afghan objective, viz., Kelat-i-Ghilzai and Kandahar. Formerly this section was identical with the west boundary of the Indus valley, from Dera Ismail Khan to the old frontier post of Jacobabad, a distance of about 350 miles. The labours of the last five years, however, consequent upon the Russian war scare of 1885, have resulted in a wide and invaluable extension of this border, the outposts of which have been pushed forward far into Pishin and British Baluchistan, and which, instead of being severed from Afghanistan by unknown and perilous mountain tracts, inhabited by savage and hostile tribes, now touch the southern confines of the Amir at the Kwajah Amran Range, within sixty miles of Kandahar. The principal positions of this section, which advances a wedge-shaped projection towards South Afghanistan, are the Gomul and Zhob valleys, the Khojak Pass and Chaman, Quetta and the Bolan Pass The fourth section of the frontier starts from the point where the old Indus valley is resumed, and is identical with the line separating the Indian province of Sind from the territories of native Baluchistan. This concluding section touches the sea a little to the west of Karachi, which is both its main outlet and the maritime base of supply for the entire frontier line from Peshawar to the Indian Ocean. Such are the four sub-divisions under which the frontier may be considered. I will now proceed to describe each of them in turn.

I.—It is only within the last few years that the extreme north sections of the Indian frontier, stretching beyond the furthest limits of Kashmir to the borders of the Central Asian Pamirs, has been thought worthy of serious notice by British strategists. The despatch of a Russian lightly equipped mountain column from Turkestan in this direction in 1878, and the discussion of this line of advance in every Russian plan of campaign against India, have suggested the advisability of safeguarding it against possible attack; although the general result of the explorations of Colonels Lockhart and Woodthorpe in 1885—6, and of Captain Younghusband in 1889, has been to show that the Pamir passes, which are of great altitude and severity, are not available for serious purposes of invasion. To guard, however, against any evil in this quarter, a political resident has recently been established at the important post of Gilgit, the northern capital of Kashmir, with a garrison from the quota of Kashmir troops selected for Imperial service. This officer exercises control over the dependent principalities of Chitral, Mastuj, Yasin, and Hunza, the first of which are vassals of Kashmir, whilst the last named is within the sphere of British political influence. The actual boundary may be considered as extending to the Baroghil Pass, the principal Central Asian avenue of descent into India, leading from the

Afghan territories of Wakhan on the Ab-i-Panja, or lower source of the Oxus. Gilgit is itself connected by a good cart-road, 190 miles long, with the military station of Rawal Pindi on the main line of the North West Railway; and surveys have already been made for a railroad which in the not distant future may deposit travellers almost at the threshold of the famous "Roof of the World."

South of Wakhan the frontier on the west touches the little-known and unexplored country of Kafiristan, inhabited by a peculiar race of people, who have resisted contact alike with Afghans and English, and are now one of the few remaining mysteries of the East. Then occurs a mountainous tract inhabitated by independent, and sometimes hostile, sometimes semi-allied tribes, inhabiting the upper basin of the Indus, and occasionally necessitating punitive expeditions, though seldom anything more serious: and we are thus brought to the point where the Kabul River flows into the Indus, at which my second section may be said to begin.

II.—We now approach that part of the frontier which contains the eastern approaches to the Afghan capital, Kabul, and to the scarcely less important Afghan military post, Ghazni, commanding the main road between Kabul and Kandahar. Peshawar is at present the northern terminus of the system of railway communications with this section from the heart of India. Here the main line of the North-West or Punjab Railway from Delhi and Lahore comes to an end, having passed *en route* the large military cantonments of Rawal Pindi, and having crossed the Indus at Attock, forty-four miles before reaching Peshawar, by a fine, fortified iron girder bridge at a point where the river is compressed between the barriers of a dark and sullen gorge. There was formerly a bridge of boats below the fort a little higher up the stream, near the spot where, according to one account, Alexander is said to have crossed the Indus; but this has now disappeared. Attock is regarded by the military authorities as a most important position; and it has been in contemplation to erect here very powerful fortifications, and to convert the place into an unassailable stronghold of defence, where an army retiring from the advanced posts on the frontiers might retard an invader for an indefinite length of time.

The interesting and romantic city of Peshawar—which is almost more worthy of a visit than any in India, so varied are its sights, so strange and fierce-looking its peoples, so picturesque its bazars—is situated on a tongue of land projecting wedgewise into the amphitheatre of mountains which close India on this side from the outer world. At a distance, however, of ten miles from the town, they are pierced by the celebrated defile known as the Khaibar Pass, which is the shortest and most direct route to Kabul, distant 180 miles. Peshawar, though it has large contonments, and is an imposing military station, is almost unfortified. The issues either of defence or attack would be decided before the arrival of an invading force, in the windings of that eventful pass. Peshawar, however, is not actually upon the frontier; the ultimate outpost of British arms being nine miles further on at Jamrud, on the extremity of the plain, and at the doorway of the Khaibar. Jamrud consists of a mud fort, rather like a big turret-ship of the most improved and hideous modern type, plastered over with clay and moored on the plain. Till lately it was in contemplation to fortify Jamrud and to continue the railway from Peshawar to this point, with a view of perhaps ultimately ascending the Khaibar, the surveys having long ago been made and the construction as far as Jamrud authorised. Recently, however, there has been a revulsion of feeling in favour of an easier railroad, extending towards Afghanistan in a more northerly direction by following the course of the Kabul River up the Michni Pass. Surveys for this line have now been made, and it is likely that it will before long be carried out.

Immediately beyond Jamrud the hills open by a narrow portal upon the plains, and the Khaibar Pass begins. Here, too, begins the strip of border highland before indicated, peopled by semi-independent tribes, of whom the Afridis, estimated at 20,000 strong, are the most powerful and independent. They have often fought against us in the past, and the last time Shere Ali went through the Khaibar, with unceremonious impartiality they plundered and appropriated his baggage. Our policy has for some years been wisely devoted to conciliating these tribes, many of whose best warriors now pass through the ranks of our native army, and whom we subsidise to guard and keep open the Khaibar. The Khaibar Corps of Rifles is the name of the local regiment raised from them, and commanded by native officers; and it is as smart and workmanlike a body of men as can be conceived. It was with an Afridi cavalry escort that I rode up the Pass, and the castles or fortified posts, the principal of which is Ali Masjid, that line its course, are held by their levies or Chowkidars. On two days in the week,-Tuesday and Friday, the Khaibar is open by arrangement with them for the passage of convoys coming down from Kabul and Central Asia, an armed escort being provided by the Afridis, who also align the heights with sentinels. I met one of these caravans coming down, a long string of well-loaded camels, oxen, asses, and mules, attended by bearded warriors with marked Israelitish features and the stature of a Saul. These arrangements work so well, that the Khaibar is not only absolutely safe as now in times of peace, but that in case of the outbreak of war, we might rely with certainty upon our subsidised allies to co-operate with us, either for the purpose of guarding our own advance, or of resisting the descent of a hostile force. Many of them volunteered for service in the late Black Mountain Expedition; and their loyalty may be considered assured. An Afridi garrison occupies the important fortified position of Lundi Kotal at the further end of the Pass, which may consequently be taken as the furthest limit of British jurisdiction, and as in reality marking the point upon the main road to Kabul where Afghan territory begins. An excellent road runs up the Pass to Lundi Kotal, which is in telegraphic communication with India. In fact the British frontier might very legitimately be coloured upon maps, not to Jamrud but to Lundi Kotal, and the entire Khaibar Pass may be considered to have been brought by the effective dispositions of Colonel Warburton under British control.

If we now retrace our steps and follow the Indus Valley down from Attock, we find that a railway has been completed from the large military station of Rawal Pindi, sixty miles further south on the main line to Kushalgarh, eighty miles distant on the left bank of the river. Kushalgarh is the starting-point for Kohat, thirty miles; and from there a good road leads to the frontier post of Thal, sixty miles. Near here is the mouth of the Kuram Valley, the second great avenue of approach from Afghanistan into India or *vice versâ*, up which Sir F. Roberts marched in 1879 to the Peiwar Kotal, where he fought a great battle, and to the precipitous crux of the Shutargardan Pass. The Kuram Valley is wide, open, and well-watered, and a good road, made by our troops in 1879, leads up to Kuram Fort at its upper end, and on over the mountains to Kabul. This entire district, which may be compared to a second tongue of land, protruded in the direction of the Afghan frontier, was one of the assigned territories, made over to Great Britain by the Treaty of Gandamak with Yakub Khan in 1879. At the close of the war, in order to escape the cost of direct administration, it was handed over to the local tribe of the Turis, in reward for their loyalty and assistance. For all practical purposes, however, it may be regarded as British territory; and the idea has been entertained of placing a garrison outpost at its further extremity. The only drawback to the pass is the snow on the Shutargardan, by which it is sometimes blocked for months in winter.

The next important post on the Indus is Kalabagh. There is a talk of bridging the river here, at a point where, with current still confined, it emerges from the hills and enters upon its shifting and straggling passage through the plains of the Derajat. Opposite to Kalabagh, upon the frontier, is situated the very important military post of Bunnu upon the Kuram River. Surveys have been made for a railway from Kalabagh to Bunnu; and a railway has also been proposed from Kalabagh to Kushalgarh, where the communication with the main line already exists, and on to Attock.

Bunnu is now considered, and is likely to remain, one of the most important points along the entire frontier. Already it is the centre of an excellent system of frontier roads, one of which runs hither due north from Dera Ismail Khan (ninety miles), and another, also from Dera Ismail Khan, describing a circuitous route by the frontier post of Tank (110 miles). From Bunnu the road is continued to Thal; and there, as before stated, the more northerly road from Kohat comes in, and the two continue an amalgamated course up the Kuram Valley. Bunnu therefore commands the southern approach to the latter avenue of ingress into Afghanistan and Kabul. But it also commands the entry to the at present little known and unexplored Tochi Valley, which is beginning to be recognised as a strategical line of the first importance, inasmuch as it is the shortest and most direct route to Ghazni. The Tochi Valley is certain, before long, to be brought under British influence; and when it has been thoroughly reconnoitred, and a road constructed along it to Ghazni, the second great place of arms in Eastern Afghanistan will be within easy access of British troops, and can be occupied without delay for purposes either of defence or advance.

Bunnu possesses the further advantage of being in communication, though not in direct connection, with a second lateral railway branch, pushed forward in a westerly direction from the main north-west line. This is in reality a continuation of the old Salt Line (which ran from Lala Musa, twenty miles south of Jhelam, to the mines at Kheura, near the river Jhelam), westwards for 150 miles to Khund, near the Indus, where a branch line runs north to Mianwali (twenty miles), above which the river is crossed by a ferry at Isa Khel. This northern branch will probably be continued to Kalabagh or to whatever point is selected for the talked-of bridge. From Khund, the main continuation turns to the south, and, skirting the left bank of the Indus, arrives at Bhakkar (sixty miles), whence a road leads to a bridge of boats across the river, communicating with the important transriparian post of Dera Ismail Khan, the southern terminus of Section II.

Between the Kabul River and this place I have shown that there exist three main outlets from Afghanistan, the Khaibar Pass, Kuram Valley, and Tochi Pass, leading respectively to or from Kabul and Ghazni. I have also shown that the posts commanding the eastern entrance to these passes are connected by excellent roads with the Indus River, and that the river is approached also at three points by the Indian railway system, viz., at Attock, at Kushalgarh, and at Mianwali. Such are the existing strategical communications in this section of the north-west frontier.

But before passing on, there may also be classified under Section II. a fourth avenue of ingress into Afghanistan, piercing the mountains immediately opposite Dera Ismail Khan, on the dividing line, so to speak, between Section II. and III. This is the Gumal Pass, which provides an alternative road to Ghazni, and has long been the principal caravan route from the Afghan interior in this central portion of the frontier. Strange to say, although the inland connections of the Gumal are in the main from the north, it is from the west or south that it has, a few months only before I write, been approached for the first time by a British force, and has been tranquilly absorbed within the extending radius of British sway. This notable achievement, which a few years ago would have been regarded as impossible, has, in January of the present year (1890), been successfully accomplished by Sir Robert Sandeman, the able Chief Commissioner of British Baluchistan, who, starting from Pishin in 1889, traversed the Zhob country and accepted offers of allegiance from its tribal occupants; till he presently struck the Gumal River, and explored and descended the pass as far as its embouchure on to the Derajat. The Gumal tribes have hitherto been set down as hostile and impracticable; but the Waziris, who are the most important of their number, came in to Sir R. Sandeman, and volunteered submission. This singularly felicitous expedition has, therefore, resulted in the peaceful acquisition of control over yet another of the main doorways into India, and has enabled us to guard against what might have been a troublesome flanking movement on the part of an enemy advancing from the direction of Kandahar. A road is now being constructed from Pishin through the Khob Valley, and will open into the Gumal. Apozai has been selected as the headquarters of a British political agent; and the Gumal, like the Khaibar and Kuram on the north and the Bolan on the south, may henceforward be regarded as effectively under British control.

III.—Before proceeding to an examination of the recent changes in the third section, we will follow the railway from Bhakkur, where we left it, down the east bank of the Indus, 100 miles, to Mahmud Kot. There a short branch line of ten miles leads to Kuraichi, a point opposite to the station of Dera Ghazi Khan, where also is a bridge of boats; while the main prolongation soon after joins the trunk line from Lahore at Multan, its entire length since it left Lalla Musa having been 350 miles. This is the fourth line of communication with the central railway system of India.

From Multan the combined railways now move on a single line south and south-west for 280 miles to Sukkur, where the river, here separating into two channels, has been spanned, for the first time since leaving Attock, by a colossal iron cantilever bridge, the main span of which, 820 feet in length, is at once an æsthetic monstrosity and a mechanical marvel. Its principle of construction is not unlike that of the Forth Bridge in Scotland; and the Lansdowne Bridge, as it is now called, has the honour of being the greatest prodigy of engineering effort, and the ugliest object east of the Levant.

Just beyond Sukkur the railway diverges, at Ruk junction, northwards to the military station of Jacobabad, till recently our frontier outpost in these parts. The old line of frontier between Dera Ismail Khan and Jacobabad was regulated by the formidable range of the Sulaiman Mountains, which here abut on the hot and sandy plain of the Derajat that stretches to the waters of the Indus. Jacobabad, though the southern limit of this section (and as such involving an inversion of the order in which I have so far proceeded), affords the best starting-point for a description of the new frontier, which practically starts from here, and has been determined by considerations connected with the southern rather than with the northern extremity of the intervening region.

From Jacobabad the Sind-Pishin Railway runs in a northerly direction for a hundred miles to the junction of Sibi, traversing a plain of appalling and absolute sterility, almost without water, and in summer a perfect furnace, most desolate among the funereal deserts of Baluchistan. As we approach Sibi, however, the welcome outline of hills on the horizon, though bleak and colourless, gives a fresh zest to the depressed imagination; and we find ourselves contemplating the Great Wall of India at one of the most interesting and historic points of its whole extent. For here we are in the neighbourhood of the Bolan Pass, and the famous Quetta Railway, so long the despair of engineers, and the bugbear and bone of contention between politicians, which might long ago have shared the abortive fate of its luckless analogue the Suakin-Berber Railway in Egypt, had not the troops of the Czar, in a happy moment for the Indian tactician and the alarmist about frontier defence, swooped down upon Penjdeh in the month of March, 1885.

The railway from Ruk to Sibi was first begun upon the renewal of war with Afghanistan after the murder of Sir Louis Cavagnari in 1879, the object being to facilitate the advance of a British column by the Bolan and Quetta route from the south upon Kandahar. When Sibi was reached it became necessary to decide by what opening the mountain barrier should be pierced and the rails conducted to Quetta. Broadly speaking, there were two alternatives—the Bolan Pass, debouching into the plain at Rindli, sixteen miles to the north-west; and a more circuitous route through the ranges to the north-east by the impressive defile known as the Chuppar Rift and the Nari Gorge. The difficulties and costliness of the Bolan route were felt to constitute so grave an obstacle that the other, or, as it is called, the Harnai line, was chosen, and work was commenced in the same year. This is the line that was foolishly suspended by the Liberal Government in 1881, in the first flush of their unreasoning desire to reverse *ab initiò* the policy of their predecessors, but that was tentatively recommenced by them in December 1883. Definite sanction was given to its complete construction in July 1884; and the line was opened to passenger traffic right through to Quetta, a distance of 155 miles, early in 1887.

When I travelled along this line in the month of January there had been a deep fall of snow, and the surrounding scenery, wild and imposing at any time, was rendered additionally grand. The change in temperature between the lower and higher levels is very sensibly felt, though the ascent, being circuitous, is less steep than by the Bolan, the gradient being nowhere more than one in forty. It has been a costly railway to build, a great deal of tunnelling and cutting and bridging being required. The journey, though slow and laborious (fourteen hours, or eleven miles an hour), and frequently impeded or delayed, is worth making, if only to see the natural surroundings, and particularly the Chuppar Rift, a spot 5,500 feet above the sea, where a vast sloping mountain wall is cleft right in twain by a tremendous perpendicular fissure disclosing the windings of a singularly contracted and gloomy gorge. At Bostan, 134 miles from Sibi, the railway emerges upon the upland plain of Pishin, and the remaining twenty-one miles by the Quetta loop line to Quetta are speedily accomplished.

This is the original and first Quetta railroad. The second and later line, shorter, steeper, and more direct, runs straight up the Bolan Pass, and enters the plain of Quetta from the other or south-west side. I travelled by the one line on my outward, by the other on my return journey.

The Bolan route, rejected, as I have pointed out, in 1879, was suddenly determined upon in the pressure exercised by the Russian scare in the spring of 1885. Pushed forward with the haste that is born of panic, amid the greatest engineering difficulties, and under a climate that in the summer months wrought fearful havoc among the beasts of burden, and more especially the camels employed, the rails reached Quetta in August, 1886, and the entire line, 100 miles long from Sibi, was opened to passenger traffic on the first of April, 1887.

Leaving Sibi we swiftly cross the plain to Rindli, at the foot of the mountains, and enter the famous Bolan Pass, through which our armies have now several times marched to the invasion of Afghanistan, by the Kundalani Gorge. The Bolan is a pass in the most precise and orthodox sense of the term; for throughout the sixty miles of its length it takes the form of a defile, in the narrowest places only some twenty yards wide, though in others expanding to more than a mile, confined by mountain walls of uniform ruggedness though of varying height. The material of which these are composed is a gravelly amalgam, readily yielding to climatic or aqueous disintegration, so that the heights are fretted into strange and distorted shapes. The floor of the pass is also the bed of the river from which it takes its name, in the dry season a rough and stony channel, along which the rails are laid, often in pools of water, but after the rains of July and August filled by a gross and powerful torrent that sweeps down the gorge, tearing up the sleepers and twisting the rails into extraordinary contortions. Hence the great costliness of keeping up the present line, a large portion of which has to be relaid every autumn. The sullenness and sterility of the pass can scarcely be conceived. Till lately there were but five trees throughout its entire length, which were proudly pointed out to the traveller.

From Rindli to Hirokh, a distance of fifty miles, the railroad follows the track of the river through scenery of the above description. Then comes the finest ten miles of the pass, from Hirokh to Kotal. The mountain walls converge, the angle of cleavage increases in abruptness, and the gorge twists in and out in sharp zigzags. The difficulty arising both from the steepness of the gradient—in many places as much as one in twenty-three—and from the sharpness of the curves, induced the authorities, who, as has been pointed out, were building in headlong haste, to construct a temporary metre-gauge line through this section of the pass; and accordingly a change of trains was formerly necessitated both at Hirokh and at Kotal. A realignment of the track with the broader gauge has since been carried out between these two points, while the Abt system of ascending steep inclines, the main feature of which is the use of a cogwheel catching in the teeth of a double central rail, has been adopted. Since the completion of this work the broad gauge runs continuously from Sibi to Quetta.*

Emerging from the northern gates of the pass at Kotal Darwaza, 5,800 feet, the present railroad traverses the level upland plain known as the Dasht-i-be-daulat, or "waste of without-wealth" (such is the change in its fertility that has been effected since the British occupation, that it is jokingly proposed to substitute *ba* for *be*, which would make it the "plain of with-wealth"), and after a run of twenty-five miles enters Quetta from the south-west, joining there the Bostan loop line which approaches from the opposite direction.

Quetta occupies what military critics describe as a very strong, if not a theoretically impregnable position. Situated in the middle of the Quetta Niabat or district, a tract some forty miles long by three broad, and 5,600 feet above the sea, it absolutely commands the approach to the Bolan Pass, and is itself protected on its flanks by the

* So disastrous, however, have again been the floods of the past rainy season, and such the damage wrought to the Bolan railway, that the possibility of its abandonment has been seriously discussed, and may ultimately be realised, as soon as a railway through the Gumal and Zhob valleys to Pishin is ready to supply its place.

VIEW FROM THE QUETTA PLAIN.

lofty peaks of the Chehiltan range, 12,000 feet, on the south-west, and by the Zarghun plateau on the north-east, separated by the Sarakula Pass from the snowy crags of Takatu, 11,390 feet. The town contains nothing of interest; but its cantonments accommodated at the time of my visit two regiments of native infantry and one of native cavalry, two British regiments, two British batteries of artillery, and a corps of native sappers, no mean force.

Quetta, which originally belonged to the Khan of Kelat, was first occupied by British troops after the signature of the Treaty of Jacobabad in 1876, between the Khan, the Sirdars, and the British Government. In the succeeding years proposals emanated from the Khan himself to hand over to us the Quetta district for administration, resulting in the year 1882 in an arrangement by which we took over that territory upon payment of an annual quit rent; the culminating step followed in 1883, when the Khan made it over to the British Government in perpetuity with full sovereign rights. Quetta has therefore for some time been an acknowledged British possession. From the Quetta Niabat we now extract a revenue more than double that which it ever produced before. The Bolan Pass, the jurisdiction of which, along with the right to levy tolls, we also purchased from the Khan, has been prudently freed by the Government from all imposts, with the result of an enormously increased traffic, and greater security and ease of communication. The entire history of British interference in Kelat may be quoted as a triumphant answer to those who decry British interference anywhere, and extol the odious theory of sedentary and culpable inaction.

Quetta, however, is not the limit of the British frontier. North and north-east of the Quetta plain stretches the great region of Pishin, which, with that of Sibi, was assigned to the British by the Treaty of Gandamak in 1879. Though nominally Afghan, they had never been permanently occupied or held by the Amir; and the change was one from a precarious and ill-sustained authority to a recognised and stable government. For some time there appears to have been a doubt at headquarters as to whether these concessions should be retained; but the home Government having eventually decided in the affirmative, they have since been acknowledged as part of British territory, and were in 1887 incorporated in what is now known as British Baluchistan, administered by a Chief Commissioner resident at Quetta. The region embraced by the somewhat vague geographical titles of

Sibi and Pishin, which has been determined by the most careful and exhaustive investigation with the chiefs of the local tribes, may be said, roughly speaking, to extend from Sibi, including the districts of Thal Chotiali and Harnai, to the Toba plateau on the north. Pishin itself, an area of some 3,000 square miles, commencing in the neighbourhood of Bostan, may be said to extend west to the Kwajah Amran range, or southern boundary of Afghanistan, and north-east to the Zhob Valley, which I have before mentioned.

This is the great expanse of territory, till lately desolated by marauding tribes and owning no central authority, that has almost involuntarily and by accident passed into British hands, and has since been industriously surveyed, explored, and pacified by British agents. A great military road has been constructed from Dera Ghazi Khan through the Bori Valley by Loralai to Pishin, opening up the middle portions of this region. On the south a second military road runs up the Bolan Pass. To the west a third has been coustructed from Bostan to the frontier fort of Chaman, on the west or Afghan side of the Amran range. The railroad advances in the same direction, and the site of the frontier upon that side are the interesting subjects to which I now turn.

Quetta, as has been said, commands the approach to the Bolan Pass. But the approach to Quetta is itself commanded by the Khojak Pass through the lofty Amran range to the north-west. This long and striking range, the highest point of which is 8,864 feet, is the southern border of Afghanistan, and must be crossed by any army marching to or from Kandahar. It is pierced by three main passes, the Khojak, the Rhogani, and the Gwajah; the first-named being the most important, inasmuch as it is the direct route to Kandahar. If the Bolan Pass is the key to India on the side of Baluchistan, the Khojak Pass is the key to Baluchistan on the side of Afghanistan. How prodigiously strong must be the position which embraces the occupation of both can easily be imagined.

The strategical operations of the last five years have been principally devoted to strengthening this advanced segment of the frontier. The railroad has been extended from Quetta to the foot of the Khojak Pass, and a tunnel, 4,000 yards in length, has just been driven through the mountains beneath the pass, emerging at the frontier fort of Chaman, sixty miles from Kandahar. A sufficient supply of rails for the extension to the latter place, when required, is stored in Pishin. At the same time, an impregnable defensive position has been fortified at Baleli, a few miles beyond Quetta, which it is the opinion of the military experts that no army in the world could force.

The railroad from Quetta to the Khojak first traverses the loop to Bostan, twenty-one miles, and then diverges westwards across a level plain. The Lora River is crossed by a high-level bridge, and, in thirty-three miles, the junction of Gulistan Karez is reached, whence a line of eight miles proceeds to Kila Abdulla, the starting-point of the line for the tunnel, another eight miles further on. Before the tunnel was finished the range could be easily surmounted by the Khojak Pass, along whose gradients has also been constructed an excellent military road. If we mount to its summit, 7,500 feet, and take the last step on to the crest of the ridge, there suddenly bursts upon our view one of those unique and startling spectacles which remain imprinted on the memory for ever. For miles and miles below us lies out-stretched the great Kadani plain, an ocean of yellow sand, broken only by island rocks and ridges, and rolling evenly to the horizon, where on the west the tumbled billows of the Rijistan desert, a howling wilderness, seem under a light wind to smoke against the sky; while in the northern distance a range of mountains sixty miles distant hides from our eyes the site of Kandahar. It is a historic and a wonderful landscape. Descending the steeper gradients of the pass on the north side we arrive shortly at the fort of Chaman, situated about a quarter of a mile from the base of the range. At present Chaman is only a mud fort, occupied by a company of a native regiment, though capable of being greatly strengthened by outworks and fortifications. The actual frontier may be described as an imaginary line drawn a few miles beyond Chaman. Thenceforward all is Afghanistan. Standing there upon the *ultima Thule* of British territory in the heart of Central Asia, his must be a sluggish heart that does not feel a thrill of excitement at the memories of the past, of confidence in the destinies of the future. Behind is India with all its majestic associations, its wealth, its millions of peoples, its armies, its amazing strategical strength. In front stretch the 500 miles of Afghanistan; and beyond in the remote distance is the formidable rival, to save India from whom all these precautions have been taken, and who, if he ever starts forth upon that 500 miles march, will probably be advancing to a ruinous destruction.

The line of the Amran range is therefore the new frontier of India in these parts. Its direction north and south from the two extremities of this range are more difficult to trace, because of the uncertain boundaries of the assigned districts, and because of the absence of precise delimitation. Roughly speaking, however, we shall not be far wrong if we prolong the line on the south to Nushki, a point about 100 miles from the Khojak Pass; while Sir R. Sandeman's recent expedition enables us to continue it north-east over the Toba plateau and by way of the Zhob valley to the Gumal Pass, where the dividing line from Section II. is touched. Throughout the mountainous region thus enclosed, our recent policy has had the effect of conciliating the wild native clans, and of introducing tranquillity where lawlessness before prevailed. The Brahuis, Bugtis, Marris, and Boris, whose history has been one of perpetual feud and petty rapine, and who were a scourge to the entire region, are now fairly reconciled both to each other and to the British Government, by whom they are in many cases employed and paid to guard the roads, to detect crime, and to enforce order. Conciliation has been the keynote of British policy in these parts. *Parcere subjectis pacisque imponere morem*, even more than *debellare superbos*, has been the motto which we have wisely borrowed from Imperial Rome.

Such then is the new Indian frontier along this third section. Its advantages are obvious. For the old line from Dera Ismail Khan to Jacobabad, running along a river valley, never healthy, and in summer time almost deadly, commanded by the Sulaiman Mountains, the numerous passes through which were not in our own hands but were at the mercy of an invader, has been substituted a greatly advanced line, in an elevated and salubrious region, requiring much fewer fortified posts and a smaller body of men to defend, with the mountain ranges behind instead of in front, and their passes in our own instead of an alien possession. The security which this new frontier gives to our Indian Empire can scarcely be over estimated. A Russian advance from Herat upon Kandahar, and from Kandahar upon Quetta, is henceforward beset by so many dangers that it is scarcely likely to be attempted, and if attempted, is certain to be repelled. As soon as the steps which are now being taken, and which I have described, to place the more northern sections of the frontier in a similar state of defence are completed, then for the first time may something like invulnerability be predicated of the entire frontier, and the 20th century will be unlikely to witness any horrifying resurrection of an Alexander or a Nadir Shah.

IV. Upon the fourth and concluding section of the frontier, from Jacobabad to the Indian Ocean, it is unnecessary here to dwell. The physical conditions render it improbable that India can ever be invaded from this quarter. Indeed, the old frontier line, traced along the Indian Valley at the base of the mountain border of Baluchistan, may here also be considered for all practical purposes to have been pushed forward several degrees to the west; for the native chieftains of Baluchistan have now so thoroughly accepted British suzerainty, that it can be no exaggeration to include their country within the political borders of the Indian Empire. In this quarter Persia is the neighbouring state; and the ascendancy of Great Britain in South Persia and on the Indian Ocean is so well established that a northern invader is in the last degree unlikely to go so far and foolishly out of his path in order to attack. Karachi, as I have pointed out, is the southern terminus, and the port of debarcation of the frontier region. Strongly fortified, possessing an excellent harbour, and well provided with facilities for rapid railway communication with the interior, it is admirably adapted to be the maritime base of the great system of military and civil enterprise which I have described; and he who first lands upon its quays, or there leaves Indian shores, will in the spacious and solid character of its public works observe what to the newcomer is a fair type of much that remains to be seen later on, and to the departing guest is a memory of many a heart-stirring experience along the north-west frontier of the Indian Empire.

HOMEWARD BOUND.

INDEX.

REFERENCES TO THE MAPS FOR EACH PLACE MENTIONED IN "PICTURESQUE INDIA."

NOTE.—*The spelling in the Maps occasionally differs slightly from that in the Book.*

Place	Map
ABBOTTABAD	C b
Abu, M.	C g
Adam's Peak	G q
Adoni	E m
Agra	E f
Ahmadabad	C h
Ahmadnagar	C h
Ajmir	D f
Ajodhya	H f
Ajunta	D i
Akyab	L m
Aligarh	F f
Ali Masjid Ft.	B c
Alipur	C d
Allahabad	B e
Alwar	E f
Amballa	E d
Amber	D f
Amrawati	E i
Amritsar	D d
Amu Daria (Oxus)	A a
Animalle	E o
Ankai Tonkai	D i
Anuradhapura	G p
Aravalli Hills	C g
Arconum	F n
Arcot	F n
Assye	D i
Attock	C c
Aurangabad	D k
Ava	L m
Azimgarh	H f
BACKERGUNGE	M h
Badami	D m
Bagh	D h
Baijnath	E d
Bairamghat	G f
Baizwada	G b
Bakkur	B d
Balsar	C i
Benares	H g
Banda	C m
Bandelkhand	F g
Bandikui	E f
Bangalore	E n
Bara Banki	G f
Bardhwan	K h
Bareilly	F e
Baroda	C h
Barrackpur	L h
Bassein	L n
Belaspur	E d
Belgaum	H r
Bellary	E m
Beypore	D o
Bhamo	M l
Bhartpur	E f
Bhawalpur	B e
Bhilsa	E h
Bhopal	E k
Bhor Ghat	C k
Bhotan	L f
Bhusawal	D i
Bidar	E l
Bijapur	C h
Bijnour	F e
Bikanir	C e
Bindrabun	E f
Birsingpur	G g
Bolan Pass	A e
Bombay	C k
Bowanipur	I f
Brahmaputra R.	M g
Broach	C i
Buxar	H g
CALCUTTA	L h
Calicut	D o
Cambay	C h
Cauveri	E o
Cawnpore	G f
Ceylon	G p
Chamba	E c
Champanir	D f
Chaundergerry	D n
Chelambram	F o
Chilianwala	C c
Chitor	D g
Chota Nagpur	H h
Chumbi	L f
Closepet	E n
Cochin	E o
Coconada	H l
Colaba	C k
Coleroon	F o
Colombo	F q
Conjeveram	F n
Coromandel	G n
Cuddalore	F o
Cuddapah	F m
Cuttack	I i

THE END.